"수능과 내신 1등급을 위한 자기주도 학습서"

올림포스
분석·변형문제

독해의 기본 1

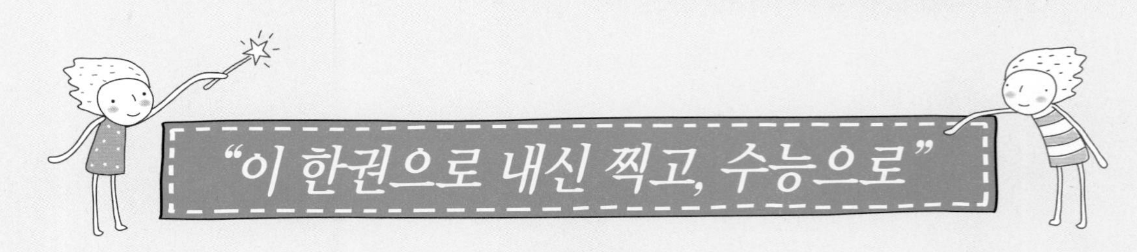

"수험생 여러분 안녕하세요~!
본서를 공부에 도움이 될 만한 큰 그림을 아래와 같이 안내해드리니 꼭 읽어보시기 바랍니다."

1. 완벽한 문장 구조 분석

전체 문장을 철저하게 분석하여 문장 마다 지니게 되는 문장의 형식을 완벽하게 정리하여 정확한 해석을 원하는 학생들의 이해를 도왔다.

- 문장의 성분 중 주성분(S/V/O/V) 표시 : 문장 안에 있는 주성분에 밑줄을 그어 바로 그 아래에 표시했다. 주어(S), 동사(V)는 물론이고, 특히 3형식과 5형식에서 필요한 목적어(O) 표시뿐만 아니라 4형식에서 간접목적어(I.O)와 직접목적어(D.O)를 모두 표시했고, 2형식에서 필요한 주격보어(S.C)와 5형식에서 필요한 목적격보어(O.C) 역시 모두 밝혔다.
- 문장의 성분 중 수식어구 표시 : 문장이 길어지는 이유 중 절대적인 이유를 차지하는 수식어구를 모두 괄호(소괄호, 중괄호, 대괄호)로 묶어 끊어 읽기가 어떻게 되는지를 밝혔다.

2. 직독직해와 의역을 동시에

구조 분석된 문장의 의미 덩어리로 끊어 읽기가 가능하게 된 직독직해와 직독직해가 다소 불편한 학생들을 위한 의역 역시 모두 망라했다.

3. 문법 & 구문 NOTE 정리

평소 문법을 어렵게 느끼는 학생들을 위해 각각의 문장 안에 들어 있는 중요 문법과 구문을 모두 정리함으로써 학교 내신과 수능을 준비하도록 자세하게 정리했다.

4. 논리적 사고 방식에 더 논리를 더하다

문장 해석을 하고 난 후 단락의 내용 정리가 되지 않는 학생들을 위한 지침서이자 잘 정리된 비문학 도서가 될 만한 논리 필독서라 하기에 지나침이 부족하지 않는 필독서가 되리라 자부한다. 특히 본서에 나오는 74지문에 대한 소재, 주제, 논리적 사고 과정, 무엇보다 10+@(글의 논리 전개방식을 뜻하는 숫자 10)에 대한 명쾌한 정리로 학생들의 논리는 'THE 논리'가 완성됨에 환희를 느껴보자.

5. 어법 선택 & 연결어

본서의 자랑이자 누구도 따라 올 수 없는 치명적 매력과 학생들의 HELPER임에 틀림없는 어법 선택!! 본 교재에 나오는 74개의 단락에서 수능과 내신에 나올 만한 어법 문제는 REAL 100% 모두 출제했으니 문법에서 이제 탈출하여 자유롭게 비상하길 바란다!!

6. 어휘 및 구동사/콜로케이션 등 숙어 정리

본서에서 자랑할 만한 내용 중 하나가 모든 지문에 나오는 구동사(Phrasal verb), 콜로케이션(Collocation) 등 숙어(관용구, Idiom) 정리이겠다. 현장에서 수업을 해보면, 수험생들은 문장 속에 들어 있는 모르는 단어가 있다면 사전을 찾아서라도 알 수 있다고 하지만, 2단어 이상으로 구성되어 있는 단어·문구나 표현 즉 구동사/콜로케이션/숙어를 찾기는 어렵다고들 한다. 이러한 점을 본서에서는 모두 찾아 정리했으니 안심하길 바란다.

7. 자세한 문제 해설

학생들에게 필요한 문제 해결 능력을 늘리기 위해 본 교재에 나오는 문제에 대한 해설을 자세히 설명했다. 특히 문제에서 요구하는 정답에 대한 해설뿐만 아니라 오답에 대한 해설 역시 친절하게 작성함으로써 독해 문제 해결 능력을 끌어 올렸다.

8. 변형문제, 특히 서술형평가 문제

전국에 소재하는 고등학교 기출문제를 분석하여 엄선된 객관식 변형문제를 다뤘다. 특히 본서에 저술한 서술형평가 문제를 접하고 문제를 푸는 순간 학생들의 감탄이 절로 나오리라 믿어 의심치 않는다.

9. 우선순위 영단어 수록

수능/모의고사/EBS/교과서 등에 나오는 수능 관련 어휘를 Big Data를 적용해 우선순위로 재정리한 어휘를 수록했으니 어휘량이 부족한 수험생에게는 하나의 교재 안에 단어장을 추가적으로 들고 다니는 스마트한 교재일 것이다.

10. 이제는 고3이다!!

EBS 올림포스(1), (2)에 이은 EBS 수능특강 역시 여러분들이 넘어야 할 산임에 틀림없다. 고3을 먼저 경험하고 싶거나 특히 영어 실력을 키우고 싶다면 가까운 서점이나 인터넷에서 본 저자가 집필한 수능특강 교재를 찾아보기를 바란다.

"뿌리 깊은 나무는 바람에 흔들리지 않습니다.
힘들고 고된 여정이라고 생각되는 학생이 있다면, 더 달콤한 열매가 기다리고 있다는 희망을 잊지 말고
본서를 통해 여러분의 꿈을 이루기 위한 디딤돌로 여기고 밟고 넘어가도록 노력합시다!"
From 정윤호 영어 연구소

"수능과 내신 1등급을 위한 자기주도 학습서"

올림포스
분석·변형문제

CONTENTS

독해의 기본 1

주제 · 제목

글의 논리	Enumeration (열거)
제목	인간과 동물, 식물들의 유전자 공유
주제	지구상의 모든 종들이 조상을 공유한다는 것은 명백한 사실이다.

수능 ANALYSIS

001 어법 선택 & 연결어

[What / That] is a fact beyond all doubt **[is / are]** **[what / that]** we share an ancestor with every other species of animal and plant on the planet. We know this **[because / because of]** some genes are recognizably the same genes in all living creatures, **[including / included]** animals, plants and bacteria. And, (　　　　　　), the genetic code itself — the dictionary **[which / by which]** all genes **[translate / are translated]** — **[is / are]** the same across all **[alive / living]** creatures **[what / that]** **[have ever looked at / have ever been looked at]**. We are all cousins. Your family tree includes not just obvious cousins **[alike / like]** chimpanzees and monkeys but also **[mice / mouse]**, buffaloes, iguanas, snails, dandelions, **[gold / golden]** eagles, mushrooms, whales, and **[bacteria / bacterium]**. All **[is / are]** our cousins. Every last one of them. Isn't **[what / that]** a **[far / very]** more wonderful thought than any myth? And the **[almost / most]** wonderful thing of all **[is / are]** **[what / that]** we know for certain it is **[literal / literally]** true.

주제문 지구상의 모든 종들이 조상을 공유한다는 것은 명백한 사실이다.

{What is a fact (beyond all doubt)} / is / {that we share an ancestor / (with every other species of animal and plant) (on the planet)}.

- What: 〈주·관〉, is: V, a fact: S.C → 전체 S: 전혀 의심할 여지없는 하나의 사실인 것은
- is: V — 이다
- that: 〈종·접〉, we: S, share: V — 우리는 조상을
- an ancestor: O — 공유하고 있다
- S.C: 지구상의 다른 모든 종의 동 · 식물들과

전혀 의심할 여지없는 하나의 사실인 것은 우리가 지구상의 다른 모든 종의 동 · 식물들과 조상을 공유하고 있다는 것이다.

노트
- beyond all doubt : 아무런 의심 없이
- share A with B : A와 B를 공유하다
- 〈관계대명사 what〉 : 관계대명사 that / which 사용 불가

〈명사절 : 주어〉			
~~선행사~~	what	~~주어~~	is
	선행사를 포함한 관계대명사 (=the thing(s) which/that ~) : ~하는 것(들)은/이		동사

is	동사
동사	is : 관계대명사 what절이 주어로 사용되면 동사는 주로 단수동사 사용함

- 〈what vs. that〉

	관계대명사(불완전한 문장)	접속사(완전한 문장)
what	○ 선행사를 포함하고 있기 때문에 what 앞에 선행사 불필요	×
that	○ that 앞에 선행사 필요	○

근거1 어떤 유전자들은 모든 생명체에게 똑같이 있다.

We / know this / {because some genes are (recognizably) the same genes / (in all living creatures), / (including animals, plants and bacteria)}.

- We: S, know: V, this: O — 우리는 이 사실을 알 수 있다
- because: 〈종·접〉, some genes: S, are: V — 어떤 유전자들은 존재하는 유전자와 쉽게 알 수 있을 정도로
- the same genes: S.C — 똑같기 때문에
- living: 〈현재분사〉 — 모든 살아 있는 생물에게
- 동물, 식물, 그리고 박테리아를 포함한

어떤 유전자들은 동물, 식물, 그리고 박테리아를 포함한 모든 살아 있는 생물에게 존재하는 유전자와 쉽게 알 수 있을 정도로 똑같기 때문에 우리는 이 사실을 알 수 있다.

노트 ■ 〈원인/이유〉 : ~ 때문에

전치사	because of	+(동)명사 / 명사 상당어구
	due to	
	for	
	on account of	
	owing to	
	thanks to	
종속접속사	as	+주어+동사 ~
	because	
	now(that)	
	since	

■ 〈including 용법〉

현재분사(형용사)	~을 포함하는	명사를 뒤에서 후치 수식함
분사구문(부사)	~을 포함하여	부대상황
전치사		형용사구, 부사구
		유사 표현 : regarding, concerning, considering

근거2 유전자 암호는 모든 살아 있는 생물에게 동일하게 존재한다.

(And), / (above all), / the genetic code itself / — the dictionary / (by which all genes are translated) / — is the same / (across all living creatures) / {that have (ever) been looked at}.

그리고 / 무엇보다도 / 유전자 암호가(S) / 사전 / 〈전치사+관·대〉 모든 유전자들이(S) 해석되는(V〈수동태〉) / 동일하다(V, S.C) / 〈전치사〉 모든 살아 있는 〈현재분사〉 생물에 〈선행사〉 걸쳐 / 〈주·관〉 / 이제까지 관찰된(V〈현재완료 수동〉)

그리고 무엇보다도 유전자 암호 — 모든 유전자들이 해석되는 사전 — 가 이제까지 관찰된 모든 살아 있는 생물에 걸쳐 동일하다.

노트

■ above all : 무엇보다도

■ 〈재귀대명사 vs. 대명사〉 : 재귀대명사의 강조적 용법

주어	~	주어와 다름 대명사	주어와 동일 재귀대명사
the genetic code		it	itself

■ 〈전치사+관계대명사 vs. 관계대명사〉 : 관계부사와 같기 때문에 뒤 문장이 완전한 문장이 나온다. 전치사는 맨 뒤로 보낼 수 있는데 이때 전치사의 목적어가 없기 때문에 관계대명사절은 불완전하다.

선행사	전치사+관계대명사 =관계부사	주어	동사			완전한 문장
선행사	관계대명사	주어	동사	전치사	~~목적어~~	불완전한 문장

■ 〈주격관계대명사절의 수의 일치〉 : 선행사를 포함하고 있는 관계대명사 what 사용 불가

선행사	주격관계대명사절		
	주격관계대명사	~~주어~~	동사
all living creatures	that		have ever been looked at

■ 〈look at / over / in / out / for〉

look	at	~을 쳐다보다
	over	~을 대충 훑어보다[살펴보다](=watch)
	in	~을 들여다보다, 조사/검토하다
	out	~을 내다보다, 조심하다
	for	~을 찾다, 구하다, 바라다

주제문(재진술) 모든 생명체는 모두 사촌(같은 조상을 공유)이다.

We / are all cousins.

우리는(S) / (V) 모두 사촌이다(S.C)

우리는 모두 사촌이다.

주제문(재진술) 당신은 침팬지, 원숭이 뿐만 아니라 다른 생명체들과도 사촌(같은 조상을 공유)이다.

Your family tree / includes / not just obvious cousins / (like chimpanzees and monkeys) / but also mice, buffaloes, iguanas, snails, dandelions, golden eagles, mushrooms, whales, and bacteria.

여러분의 가계도는(S) / 포함한다(V) / 명백한 사촌들을(O₁) 포함할 뿐 아니라 / 〈전치사〉 침팬지와 원숭이 같은 / 생쥐, 버팔로, 이구아나, 달팽이, 민들레, 검독수리, 버섯, 고래, 그리고 박테리아도 또한(O₂)

여러분의 가계도는 침팬지와 원숭이 같은 명백한 사촌들을 포함할 뿐 아니라 생쥐, 버팔로, 이구아나, 달팽이, 민들레, 검독수리, 버섯, 고래, 그리고 박테리아도 포함한다.

노트

■ family tree : 가계도, 족보

■ mouse : 쥐(복수형 : mice)

■ bacterium : 박테리아(복수형 : bacteria)

■ 〈상관접속사 not only A but also B〉 : A뿐만 아니라 B도(병렬구조) / as well=too

not only =just =simply =merely =alone	A	but 주어 also 동사	B	–
		but 주어+동사		(as well)
		;(세미콜론) 주어+동사		as well
		,(콤마) 주어+동사		
		.(마침표) 주어+동사		
B as well as A(주어는 B)				

■ 〈혼동하기 쉬운 어휘〉

likely	형용사	~일 것 같은 (be to 동사원형 : ~일 것 같다)
	부사	아마(probably)
alike	서술적 형용사 (보어로만 사용, 명사 수식 불가)	동일한
	부사	똑같이
like	전치사	~처럼
	동사	좋아하다

주제문(재진술) 모든 생명체는 모두 사촌(같은 조상을 공유)이다.

All / are our cousins. / Every last one of them.

모두가(S) / (V) 우리의 사촌이다(S.C) / 그것들 모두가

모두가 다 우리의 사촌인 것이다. 그것들 모두가.

주제문(강조) 지구상의 모든 종들이 조상을 공유한다는 것은 명백한 사실이다.

Isn't / that / (a far) more wonderful thought / than any myth?

아닌가?(V) / 그것은(S) / 훨씬 더 멋진 생각이(S.C) / 어떠한 근거 없는 믿음보다도

그것은 어떠한 근거 없는 믿음보다도 훨씬 더 멋진 생각이 아닌가?

노트 ■ 〈비교급 vs. 원급 강조〉

비교급 강조 표현	원급 강조 표현
much, even, still, by far, far, a lot, lots, a great deal	very, so, quite, really, extremely, too

(And) / the most wonderful thing (of all) / is / [that we know (for certain) / {it is (literally) true}].

S: the most wonderful thing / V: is / (종·접) that / S: we / V: know / (that) / S: it / V: is / S.C: true / O / S.C

그리고 / 모든 것 중 가장 멋진 것은 / 이다 / 우리가 / 확실히 알고 있다는 점이다 / 그것이 정말로 진실이라는 것을

그리고 모든 것 중 가장 멋진 것은 우리가 그것이 정말로 진실이라는 것을 확실히 알고 있다는 점이다.

노트

■ for certain : 확실히(=certainly)

■ 〈most / almost / mostly〉

	대명사	형용사	부사
most	대부분의 것들(사람들)	대부분의	가장
almost	–	–	거의
mostly	–	–	주로, 일반적으로

■ 〈목적격종속접속사 that 생략〉 : 완전타동사의 목적어로 사용된 경우 / 관계대명사 what 사용 불가

	종속절(명사절 : 목적어) (완전한 절)		
완전타동사	that	주어	동사
know	목적격종속접속사 – 생략 가능(~하는 것을)	it	is

▶ 다음 글의 주제로 가장 적절한 것은?

① myths and facts about the genetic code
② the evidence of evolution revealed by ancient fossils
③ the importance of family trees in identifying species
④ the connection between the genetic code and diseases
⑤ the relatedness of everything through the genetic code

정답 | ⑤

해석 | ① 유전자 암호에 대한 통념과 사실
② 고대 화석에 의해 드러난 진화의 증거
③ 종을 식별하는데 있어서 가계도의 중요성
④ 유전자 암호와 질병 사이의 관련성
⑤ 유전자 암호를 통한 모든 것의 관련성

해설 | ⑤ 이 글의 주제는 지구상의 모든 종들이 조상을 공유한다는 것이다. 그리고 이 근거로 유전자 암호에 관한 이야기를 한다. 따라서 이 글의 주제로 ⑤ '유전자 암호를 통한 모든 것(모든 종)의 관련성'이 가장 적절하다.

오답 | ① 유전자 암호에 대한 사실적인 이야기는 약간 나오지만 통념적인 말은 나오지 않는다.
② 이러한 내용은 본문에 전혀 언급되어 있지 않다.
③ 종을 식별하는 것이 아니라 모든 종들이 조상을 공유한다는 것이 주제이다.
④ 이 글에는 질병에 관련된 내용이 없다.

Words

☐ recognizably
☐ ancestor
☐ creature
☐ genetic code
☐ translate
☐ obvious
☐ reveal
☐ fossil
☐ literally
☐ identify
☐ relatedness

Phrases

☐ beyond all doubt
☐ above all
☐ share A with B
☐ for certain

우선순위 영단어 역대 수능 기출 + 전국 모의고사 기출 + EBS 기출 + 교과서 기출 빈출 어휘

단어	뜻	단어	뜻	단어	뜻
identify	v. 확인하다	potential	n. 잠재력	perception	n. 지각
feature	v. 특집기사로 다루다	in terms of	~의 면에서	perspective	n. 원근화법
subject	v. ~에게 (…을) 당하게 하다	argument	n. 주장	demonstrate	v. 증명하다
emerge	v. 나타나다	encounter	v. 마주치다	strategy	n. 전략
capacity	n. 능력	appreciate	v. 문학	assumption	n. 가정
authority	n. 당국	illusion	n. 착각	impact	n. 영향
organism	n. 유기체	recall	v. 생각나게 하다	relatively	ad. 상대적으로
assume	v. 추측하다	available	a. 이용 가능한	contemporary	n. 동시대 사람
eliminate	v. 제거하다	establish	v. 설립하다	regardless of	~을 개의치 않고
account for	~을 설명하다(=explain)	commitment	n. 헌신	confine	v. 국한시키다
critical	a. 중대한	decline	n. 쇠퇴	priority	n. 우선

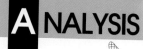

01 다음 글을 읽고, |조건|에 맞게 주어진 주제문을 완성하시오.

| 조건 |

* (A)는 3단어, (B)는 2단어로 쓸 것
* 본문에 있는 단어만을 사용할 것
* 필요한 경우, 문맥과 어법에 맞게 변형할 것

What is a fact beyond all doubt is that we share an ancestor with every other species of animal and plant on the planet. We know this because some genes are recognizably the same genes in all living creatures, including animals, plants and bacteria. And, above all, the genetic code itself — the dictionary by which all genes are translated — is the same across all living creatures that have ever been looked at. We are all cousins. Your family tree includes not just obvious cousins like chimpanzees and monkeys but also mice, buffaloes, iguanas, snails, dandelions, golden eagles, mushrooms, whales, and bacteria. All are our cousins. Every last one of them. Isn't that a far more wonderful thought than any myth? And the most wonderful thing of all is that we know for certain it is literally true.

⬇

With species of all animals and plants on Earth, we have (A) ____________ ____________ ____________ due to the fact that (B) ____________ ____________ in living creatures we share are identical.

02 다음 빈칸에 들어갈 말로 가장 적절한 것은?

What is a fact beyond all doubt is that ________________________. We know this because some genes are recognizably the same genes in all living creatures, including animals, plants and bacteria. And, above all, the genetic code itself — the dictionary by which all genes are translated — is the same across all living creatures that have ever been looked at. We are all cousins. Your family tree includes not just obvious cousins like chimpanzees and monkeys but also mice, buffaloes, iguanas, snails, dandelions, golden eagles, mushrooms, whales, and bacteria. All are our cousins. Every last one of them. Isn't that a far more wonderful thought than any myth? And the most wonderful thing of all is that we know for certain it is literally true.

① we share an ancestor with all living creatures
② we are distinguished from other species
③ humans were all born in the same ancestor
④ all living creatures have genes
⑤ humans and animals live in harmony

03 다음 글의 순서로 가장 적절한 것은?

What is a fact beyond all doubt is that we share an ancestor with every other species of animal and plant on the planet.

(A) We are all cousins. Your family tree includes not just obvious cousins like chimpanzees and monkeys but also mice, buffaloes, iguanas, snails, dandelions, golden eagles, mushrooms, whales, and bacteria.

(B) We know this because some genes are recognizably the same genes in all living creatures, including animals, plants and bacteria. And, above all, the genetic code itself — the dictionary by which all genes are translated — is the same across all living creatures that have ever been looked at.

(C) All are our cousins. Every last one of them. Isn't that a far more wonderful thought than any myth? And the most wonderful thing of all is that we know for certain it is literally true.

① (A) - (B) - (C)　② (B) - (A) - (C)　③ (B) - (C) - (A)
④ (C) - (A) - (B)　⑤ (C) - (B) - (A)

04 밑줄 친 부분 중 문맥상 옳지 않은 것은?

What is a fact beyond all doubt is that we ① share an ancestor with every other species of animal and plant on the planet. We know this because some genes are ② recognizably the same genes in all living creatures, including animals, plants and bacteria. And, above all, the genetic code itself — the dictionary by which all genes are ③ translated — is the same across all living creatures that have ever been looked at. We are all cousins. Your family tree ④ excludes not just obvious cousins like chimpanzees and monkeys but also mice, buffaloes, iguanas, snails, dandelions, golden eagles, mushrooms, whales, and bacteria. All are our cousins. Every last one of them. Isn't that a far more wonderful thought than any myth? And the most wonderful thing of all is that we know for certain it is literally ⑤ true.

주제 · 제목

글의 논리	Cause & Effect (원인 & 결과)
제목	소비자에 대한 마케팅 담당자들의 이해의 필요성
주제	마케팅 담당자들은 제품에 대한 사람들의 흥미와 필요성을 파악하고 적절한 때에 행동을 해야 한다.

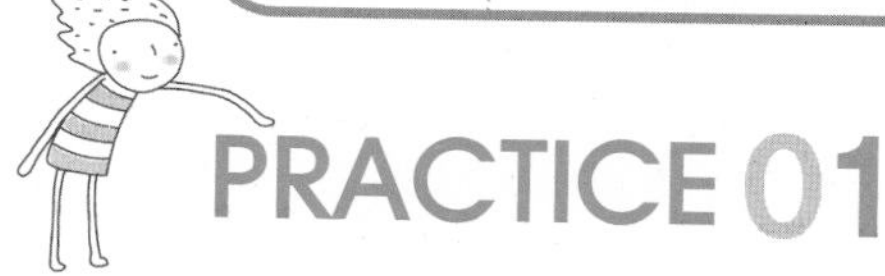

002 어법 선택 & 연결어

Some people may be on the verge of buying the product, **[where / whereas]** others may never have heard of **[it / them]**. (   ) others may have an interest in the product but **[do / does]** not have any money, while others might be aware **[of / that]** the product but **[is / are]** not yet **[interested / interesting]**; others might be **[interested / interesting]** but do not at present have a need for the product, and so forth. Marketers need to be aware of these stages and **[be / are]** prepared to act at the appropriate time. (   ), a couple who **[has / have]** just bought their first house will not currently be in the market to buy **[another / the other]** larger house, but very well might be in five to seven years' time, when perhaps they have started a family or are **[earning / earned]** more money.

원인1 사람들에 따라 제품에 대한 필요도가 다르다.

Some people / may be (on the verge of buying the product), / (whereas others may never have heard of it).

- Some people (S): 어떤 사람들은
- may be (V)
- (on the verge of buying the product): 제품을 막 사려고 할 수도 있는데
- whereas 〈종·접〉 / others (S) / may never have heard of (V) / it (O): 반면에 다른 사람들은 그것에 대해 들어본 적도 없을 수 있다

어떤 사람들은 제품을 막 사려고 할 수도 있는데, 반면에 다른 사람들은 그것에 대해 들어본 적도 없을 수 있다.

노트
- on the verge of : 막 ~하려는
- heard of : ~에 대해 듣다
- 〈양보/대조〉

전치사	in spite of	+명사/명사 상당어구	비록 ~이지만
	despite		
종속접속사	though	+주어+동사	
	although		
	even though		
	even if		
	as		
	while		반면에
	whereas		

원인2 사람들에 따라 제품에 대한 흥미도가 다르다.

(Still) / others / may have an interest (in the product) / but do not have any money, / (while others might be aware of the product / but are not yet interested); / others / might be interested / but do not (at present) have a need / (for the product), / (and so forth).

- (Still): 그럼에도 불구하고
- others (S): 또 다른 사람들은
- may have (V_1) an interest (O) (in the product): 그 제품에 관심을 가지고 있을지도 모른다
- but do not have (V_2) any money (O): 하지만 돈이 전혀 없다
- while 〈종·접〉 others (S) might be (V_1): 반면에 다른 사람들은
- aware of the product (S.C): 그 제품을 알고 있을 수 있다
- but are not yet (V_2) interested (S.C): 하지만 아직 흥미가 없다
- others (S): 다른 사람들은
- might be (V_1) interested (S.C): 흥미는 있을 수 있다
- but do not (at present) have (V_2) a need (O): 하지만 현재는 필요성을 가지고 있지 않다
- (for the product): 그 제품에 대해
- (and so forth): 기타 등등

또 다른 사람들은 그 제품에 관심을 가지고 있을지도 모르지만 돈이 전혀 없으며, 반면에 다른 사람들은 그 제품을 알고 있을 수 있지만 아직 흥미가 없다. 다른 사람들은 흥미는 있을 수 있지만 현재는 그 제품에 대한 필요성을 가지고 있지 않은 것 등등의 경우가 있을 수 있다.

노트
- have[take] an interest in : ~와 이해관계가 있다, ~에 흥미[관심]를 갖다
- be aware of : ~을 알다
- not yet : 아직도 (~ 않다)
- at present : 현재는, 지금은
- have a need for : ~의 필요성을 가지다
- and so forth : 기타 등등(=and so on, and the like, etc.(=et cetera), the others, the rest, and others, and what not)
- 〈while 용법〉

부사절을 이끄는 종속접속사	
시간	~ 동안에
양보/대조	비록 ~일지라도

- 〈감정과 관련된 완전타동사〉 : 분사화가 되어 주격보어/목적격보어 자리에 나올 때 구별법
- 2형식

주어	동사	주격보어(S.C)
사람		과거분사(p.p.) – 수동(되어진, ~ 당한)
사물		현재분사(Ring) – 능동(~하고 있는, 하는)
others	are	interested
	might be	

주제문(결과) 마케팅 담당자들은 제품에 대한 사람들의 흥미와 필요성을 파악하고 적절한 때에 행동을 해야 한다.

Marketers / need to be aware of these stages / and (to) be prepared to act / (at the appropriate time).

- Marketers (S): 마케팅 담당자들은
- need (V) to be aware of these stages (O_1): 이러한 단계에 대해 알 필요가 있다
- and (to) be: 그리고 행동할
- prepared to act (O_2): 준비를 할 필요가 있다
- (at the appropriate time): 적절한 때에

마케팅 담당자들은 이러한 단계를 알고 적절한 때에 행동할 준비를 할 필요가 있다.

노트
- be prepared to R : ~할 준비가 되어 있다
- 〈need 용법〉

목적어(to R)		3형식	〈~할〉 필요가 있다, 〈~〉 해야 하다
목적어	목적격보어(to R)	5형식	〈남이〉 〈~해 줄〉 필요가 있다
동명사(Ring)		3형식	〈사람 · 물건이〉 〈~되어야 할〉 필요가 있다
목적어	목적격보어(p.p.)	5형식	〈~이〉 〈…될〉 필요가 있다, 〈~을〉 〈…되도록 할〉 필요가 있다

주제에 대한 근거 예시

(For example), / a couple / {who have (just) bought their first house} / will not (currently) be (in the market) / (to buy another larger house), / but (very well) might be (in five to seven years' time), / {when (perhaps) they have started a family / or are earning more money}.

(a couple: S(선행사), who: 〈주·관〉, have bought: V 〈현재완료〉, their first house: O, will not be: V_1, might be: V_2, when: 〈종·접〉, they: S, have started: V_1, a family: O, are earning: V_2, more money: O)

예를 들어 / 한 커플은 / 자신들의 첫 집을 막 구입한 / 현재로서는 시장에 들어오지 않을 것이다 / 또 다른 더 큰 집을 구매하기 위해 / 하지만 / 5년에서 7년의 시간 후에는 아마도 시장에 들어오게 될 가능성이 많은데 / 그때는 / 아마도 그들이 자녀를 가졌거나 / 혹은 더 많은 돈을 벌고 있을 때일 것이다

예를 들어, 자신들의 첫 집을 막 구입한 한 커플은 현재로서는 또 다른 더 큰 집을 구매하기 위해 시장에 들어오지 않겠지만, 5년에서 7년의 시간 후에는 아마도 시장에 들어오게 될 가능성이 많은데, 그때는 아마도 그들이 자녀를 가졌거나 혹은 더 많은 돈을 벌고 있을 때일 것이다.

노트
- start a family : 첫 아이를 보다
- earn money : 돈을 벌다
- 〈주격관계대명사절의 수의 일치〉 : 선행사를 포함하고 있는 관계대명사 what 사용 불가

	주격관계대명사절			
선행사(주어)	주격관계대명사	~~주어~~	동사	동사(본동사)
a couple	who		have bought	will not be

- 〈the other vs. another〉

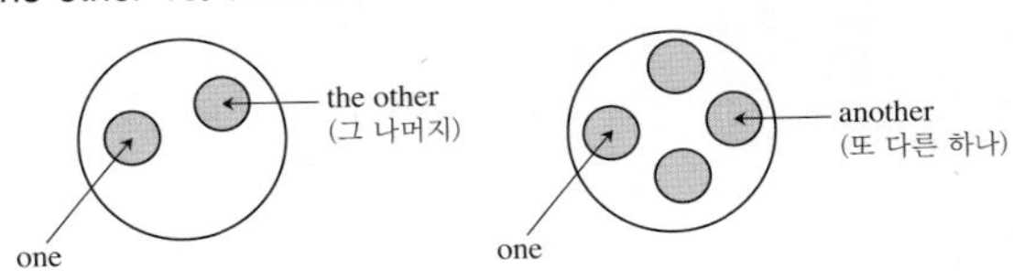

▶ **다음 글의 제목으로 가장 적절한 것은?**

① Buying Power Depends on the Product's Quality
② Contact Customers When They Are Ready to Buy
③ Is Advertising the Only Way to Promote Products?
④ Consumers Are Always Ready to Change Their Minds
⑤ Marketing: A Battle Between Consumers and Marketers

정답 | ②

해석 | ① 구매력은 제품의 질에 의존한다
② 소비자들이 살 준비가 됐을 때 접촉해라
③ 상품을 홍보하기 위한 유일한 방법은 광고를 하는 것인가?
④ 소비자들은 항상 마음을 바꿀 준비가 되어 있다
⑤ 마케팅: 소비자들과 마케팅 담당자들 간의 전투

해설 | ② 이 글의 전체적인 주제는 마케팅 담당자들은 제품에 대한 사람들(소비자들)의 흥미와 필요성을 파악하고 적절한 때에 행동을 해야 한다는 것이다. 이러한 주제문은 3번째 문장에 나타나 있는데, 주제를 통해서 생각해 봤을 때, ② '소비자들(제품에 흥미와 필요성을 갖는 사람들)이 살 준비가 됐을 때(적절한 때) 접촉하라(행동을 해야 한다)'가 가장 적절하다.

오답 | ① 제품의 질에 의존한다는 내용은 나오지 않는다.
③ 상품을 홍보하기 위한 방법이 광고를 하는 것이라는 내용은 나오지 않는다.
④ 소비자들이 마음을 바꿀 수 있는 이야기가 나오지만 이 글의 소재인 마케팅 담당자가 적절한 행동을 취해야 한다는 말은 없다.
⑤ 마케팅이란 소재는 나오지만 소비자들과 마케팅 담당자들 간의 전투에 관련된 내용은 나오지 않는다.

노트
- depend on : ~에 의지하다
- be ready to : ~할 준비가 되어 있다
- between A and B : A와 B 사이에

Words

- ☐ whereas
- ☐ appropriate
- ☐ interest
- ☐ currently
- ☐ present
- ☐ perhaps
- ☐ marketer
- ☐ stage
- ☐ quality
- ☐ advertising
- ☐ promote
- ☐ consumer
- ☐ battle

Phrases

- ☐ on the verge of
- ☐ heard of

- ☐ have[take] an interest in
- ☐ not yet
- ☐ have a need for
- ☐ be prepared to R
- ☐ earn money
- ☐ be aware of
- ☐ at present
- ☐ and so forth
- ☐ start a family

우선순위 영단어

역대 수능 기출 + 전국 모의고사 기출 + EBS 기출 + 교과서 기출 빈출 어휘

단어	뜻	단어	뜻	단어	뜻
proportion	n. 비율	significant	a. 의미심장한	species	n. 종
virtually	ad. 사실상	acknowledge	v. 인정하다	advocate	n. 옹호자
appropriate	a. 적절한	content	n. 만족	engage in	~에 참여하다
eventually	ad. 결국	phenomenon	n. 현상	term	n. 학기
asset	n. 재산	consumption	n. 소비	convince	v. ~에게 납득시키다
emission	n. 배출	executive	n. 행정상의	figure	n. 형상
generate	v. 발생시키다	measure	n. 조치	objective	n. 목적
predator	n. 포식동물	reveal	v. 드러내다	application	n. 적용
confront	v. ~에 직면하다	contribute	v. 기여하다	determine	v. 측정하다
enhance	v. 향상시키다	indicate	v. 나타내다	insight	n. 통찰력
notion	n. 개념	observe	v. 진술하다	portion	n. 비율
productivity	n. 생산성	security	n. 안전	shift	n. (교대) 근무시간
statement	n. 언급	sustain	v. 유지하다	tendency	n. 경향
access	v. ~에 접근하다	address	v. 다루다	adopt	v. 받아들이다
agriculture	n. 농업	claim	v. (목숨) 빼앗다	colleague	n. 동료
complicated	a. 복잡한	conduct	n. 행위	consistent	a. 일치하는
conventional	a. 전통적인	detail	n. 세부사항	evolution	n. 진화
fit	v. ~에 맞다	function	v. 기능하다	illustrate	v. (예를 들어) 설명하다
institution	n. 제도	interaction	n. 상호 작용	obtain	v. (노력 후에) 얻다
practice	v. 실행하다	primary	a. 주된	properly	ad. 똑바로
pursue	v. 추구하다	recognize	v. 인정(인식)하다	retain	v. 보유[유지]하다; 보류하다
scale	n. 눈금	separate	a. 분리된	sophisticated	a. 정교한
specific	a. 구체적인	substance	n. 물질	trigger	v. 촉발시키다; 촉발제
approach	v. 가까이 가다	aspect	n. (사물의) 면	contribution	n. 공헌
discipline	n. 규율	diverse	a. 다양한	emphasize	v. 강조하다
encourage	v. 용기를 돋우다	estimate	n. 평가	evolutionary	a. 진화의
evolve	v. 진화하다	exhibit	n. 전시	facilitate	v. 촉진하다
inspire	v. (사상, 감정을) 불어넣다	material	n. 물질	performance	n. 수행
plot	n. 줄거리	preference	n. 선호	prominent	a. 저명한
property	n. 속성	refer to	가리키다	reputation	n. 명성
thrive	v. 번창하다	adjust	v. 조절하다	alternative	n. 대안
analyze	v. 분석하다	association	n. 연상	awareness	n. 의식[관심]
bias	n. 성향	boost	v. 밀어올리다	characteristic	n. 특징
community	n. [생물] 군락	crack	n. 날카로운 소리	delicate	a. 우아한
equivalent	a. 동등한	evaluate	v. 평가하다	habitat	n. 서식지
impression	n. 인상	install	v. 설치하다	literally	ad. 아주
perceive	v. 인식하다	rate	v. ~의 등급을 가지다	register	v. 등록[기록]하다
release	v. 방출하다	requirement	n. 요구	secure	v. 확보하다
ultimately	ad. 궁극적으로	underlying	a. 숨은	vague	a. 모호한
accelerate	v. 가속화되다; 가속화하다	accompany	v. 동반하다	alter	v. 바꾸다

변형문제

01 다음 글을 읽고, |조건|에 맞게 빈칸 (A), (B)를 채우시오.

| 조건 |
* (A)는 3단어, (B)는 2단어로 쓸 것
* [보기]에서 선택한 단어를 한 번씩만 쓸 것
(단, (A)의 경우, 주어진 단어 외의 2단어를 추가할 것, (B)의 경우, [보기] 외의 1단어를 추가할 것)
* 필요한 경우, 문맥과 어법에 맞게 변형할 것

[보기] stage / seek / hurry / prepare / responsible / teach / prompt / verge / search / think

Some people may be (A) ____________ ____________ ____________ of buying the product, whereas others may never have heard of it. Still others may have an interest in the product but do not have any money, while others might be aware of the product but are not yet interested; others might be interested but do not at present have a need for the product, and so forth. Marketers need to be aware of these stages and (B) ____________ ____________ to act at the appropriate time. For example, a couple who have just bought their first house will not currently be in the market to buy another larger house, but very well might be in five to seven years' time, when perhaps they have started a family or are earning more money.

02 다음 글을 읽고, |조건|에 맞게 주어진 요약문을 완성하시오.

| 조건 |
* (A)는 3단어, (B), (C)는 각각 1단어로 쓸 것
* 본문에 있는 단어만을 그대로 쓸 것

Some people may be on the verge of buying the product, whereas others may never have heard of it. Still others may have an interest in the product but do not have any money, while others might be aware of the product but are not yet interested; others might be interested but do not at present have a need for the product, and so forth. Marketers need to be aware of these stages and be prepared to act at the appropriate time. For example, a couple who have just bought their first house will not currently be in the market to buy another larger house, but very well might be in five to seven years' time, when perhaps they have started a family or are earning more money.

⬇

Successful marketers are required to recognize (A) ____________ ____________ ____________ for customers to purchase the product because a level of customers' (B) ____________ in the product and the amount of (C) ____________ they have are different.

03 다음 글을 읽고, |조건|에 맞게 주어진 요약문을 완성하시오.

| 조건 |
* (A)는 1단어, (B)는 2단어로 쓸 것
* [보기]에서 선택한 단어를 한 번씩만 쓸 것(단, (B)의 경우, [보기] 외의 1단어를 추가할 것)
* 필요한 경우, 문맥과 어법에 맞게 변형할 것

[보기] identical / alike / diverse / unexpected / prepare / learn / teach / prepare / spend / aware / provide / sustain

Some people may be on the verge of buying the product, whereas others may never have heard of it. Still others may have an interest in the product but do not have any money, while others might be aware of the product but are not yet interested; others might be interested but do not at present have a need for the product, and so forth. Marketers need to be aware of these stages and be prepared to act at the appropriate time. For example, a couple who have just bought their first house will not currently be in the market to buy another larger house, but very well might be in five to seven years' time, when perhaps they have started a family or are earning more money.

⬇

Since individual perceptions on products are (A) ____________, marketers should (B) ____________ ____________ to grasp their perceptions of products and act at the right time.

04 다음 글의 순서로 가장 적절한 것은?

Some people may be on the verge of buying the product, whereas others may never have heard of it.

(A) Marketers need to be aware of these stages and be prepared to act at the appropriate time.

(B) Still others may have an interest in the product but do not have any money, while others might be aware of the product but are not yet interested; others might be interested but do not at present have a need for the product, and so forth.

(C) For example, a couple who have just bought their first house will not currently be in the market to buy another larger house, but very well might be in five to seven years' time, when perhaps they have started a family or are earning more money.

① (A) - (B) - (C)
② (B) - (A) - (C)
③ (B) - (C) - (A)
④ (C) - (A) - (B)
⑤ (C) - (B) - (A)

UNIT 01

주제 · 제목

글의 논리	Enumeration (열거)
제목	인간의 특성: 온고지신
주제	인간들은 과거의 것을 물려받아 점진적으로 발전시킨다.

PRACTICE 02

003 어법 선택 & 연결어

[Little / Few] philosophers would deny **[what / that]** human beings are, to a great extent, historical — **[what / that]** we inherit things from the past, change **[it / them]**, and then **[pass them on / pass on them]** to future generations. Language, (   ), is something **[what / that]** we learn and change as we use **[it / them]**, and the same is true of science — scientists start with a body of theory, and then go on **[either / both]** to confirm or to disconfirm **[it / them]**. The same is (   ) true of social institutions, such as the family, the state, banks, churches, and so on — most of **[which / them]** **[is / are]** **[modifying / modified]** forms of earlier practices or institutions. Human beings, (   ), never begin their existence from scratch, but always within some kind of context — a context that **[changes / change]**, sometimes **[radical / radically]** within a single generation.

주제문 인간은 과거의 것을 물려받아 변형하여 다음 세대로 물려준다.

Few philosophers(S, 거의 어느 철학자도) / would deny(V, 부정하지 않을 것이다) / {that(〈종·접〉) human beings(S, 인간들이) are(V, 이다), / (to a great extent)(대부분), / historical(S.C, 역사적이라는 것)} / — {that(〈종·접〉) we(S, 즉 우리가) inherit(V₁) things(O) (from the past)(과거로부터 무엇인가를 물려받아), / change(V₂) them(O)(그것을 변형하고), / and (then)(그런 다음) pass(V₃) them(O)(그것을 물려준다) / (on to future generations)(다음 세대로)}. (O)

인간들이 대부분 역사적이라는 것, 즉 우리가 과거로부터 무엇인가를 물려받아 그것을 변형하고 그런 다음 그것을 다음 세대로 물려준다는 것을 거의 어느 철학자도 부정하지 않을 것이다.

노트
- to a great extent : 크게, 대부분
- inherit A from B : B로부터 A를 물려받다
- pass A on to B : A를 B에게 넘겨주다
- 〈few / a few / a little / little〉

수	few	거의 없는(부정)	+복수N+복수V
	a few	약간(긍정)	
양	a little	약간(긍정)	+단수N+단수V
	little	거의 없는(부정)	

- 〈what vs. that〉

	관계대명사(불완전한 문장)	접속사(완전한 문장)
what	○ 선행사를 포함하고 있기 때문에 what 앞에 선행사 불필요	×
that	○ that 앞에 선행사 필요	○

예시1 이 예시로 언어와 과학이 있다.

Language(S, 언어는), / (for example)(예를 들어), / is(V) something(S.C〈선행사〉, 어떤 것이다) / (that(〈목·관〉) we(S, 우리가) learn(V₁) and change(V₂)(배우고 변형한다)) / (as(〈종·접〉) we(S) use(V) it(O)(우리가 사용할 때)), / and the same(S, 그리고 같은 것이) is(V) true(S.C) of science(과학에도 적용되는데) / — scientists(S) start(V₁)(과학자들은 시작한다) / (with a body of theory)(많은 이론으로부터), / and (then) go(V₂) on(그런 다음 나아가) / either to confirm or to disconfirm it(그것을 확인하거나 부당성을 증명한다).

예를 들어, 언어는 우리가 배우고 사용할 때 변형하는 것이고, 같은 것이 과학에도 적용되는데 과학자들은 많은 이론으로부터 시작하고 그런 다음 나아가 그것을 확인하거나 부당성을 증명한다.

노트
- be true of : ~에 적용되다
- start with : ~와 함께 출발하다
- body : 떼, 무리, 일단; 다수, 대부분(a body of+단수/복수명사 : 많은 ~)
- go on to : 이어서 ~을 하기 시작하다
- 〈목적격관계대명사 that〉 : 타동사의 목적어가 없는 경우 / 선행사를 포함하고 있는 관계대명사 what 사용 불가

	〈목적격관계대명사절〉			
선행사	목적격관계대명사	주어	동사	~~목적어~~
something	생략 가능 : (that)	we	learn and change	

- 〈go on vs. go on to〉

	뜻	의미
go on+(동)명사	~을 계속하다	쉬지 않고 계속하다
go on to R	(하나의 동작이 끝나고) 계속해서 ~을 이어가다	(쉬었다가) 계속 이어가다 / 앞에 먼저 한 행동이 있고, 그에 연이은 행동을 말할 때 사용

■ 〈상관접속사〉 : 병렬구조

종류				뜻
not	A	but	B	A가 아니라 B (=B, not A)
not only		but also		A뿐만 아니라 B도 (=B as well as A)
either		or		A와 B 둘 중 하나
neither		nor		A와 B 둘 다 아닌
both		and		A와 B 둘 다

예시2 이 예시로 사회제도가 있다.

The same / is (also) true of social institutions, / {such as the family, the state, banks, churches, (and so on)} / — {most of which are modified forms / (of earlier practices or institutions)}.

(The same: S 같은 것이 / is: V / true: S.C 또한 사회제도에서도 적용된다 / 가족, 국가, 은행, 교회 등과 같은 / most of which: 〈수량형용사+관·대〉 / are: V / modified: 〈과거분사〉 / forms: S.C / 그것들 대부분은 수정된 형태이다 / 이전의 / 관행이나 제도의)

같은 것이 또한 가족, 국가, 은행, 교회 등과 같은 사회제도에서도 적용되는데 그것들 대부분은 이전의 관행이나 제도의 수정된 형태들이다.

노트
■ social institution : 사회제도
■ A such as B : B와 같은 A
■ and so on : 기타 등등(=and so forth, and the like, etc.(=et cetera), the others, the rest, and others, and what not)
■ 〈혼동 어휘〉 : 철자가 비슷해서 혼동

stat	e	주, 말하다
	ue	동상
	ure	키, 신장, 위상
	us	지위, 상태

■ 〈수량형용사+관계대명사〉 : 수량형용사 다음에 나오는 관계대명사 자리에 대명사 사용 불가

수량형용사		관계대명사
none of, neither of, any of, either of, some of, many of, most of, much of, few of, both of, half of, each of, one of, two of, all of, several of, a number of, both of	+	whom(사람) which(사물) whose(소유)

주제문(재진술) 인간은 항상 특정 상황에서 변화하고 있다.

Human beings, / (therefore), / never begin their existence / (from scratch), / but (always) (within some kind of context) / — a context {that changes, / (sometimes) (radically) / (within a single generation)}.

(Human beings: S 인간은 / 그러므로 / never begin: V / their existence: O / 그들(인간)의 존재를 시작하지 않는다 / 아무런 사전 준비 없이 / 하지만 항상 어떤 종류의 상황 속에서 / a context: 〈선행사〉 / that: 〈주·관〉 / changes: V / 즉 변화하는 상황 / 가끔은 / 근본적으로 / 한 세대 안에서도)

그러므로 인간은 절대 아무런 사전 준비 없이 존재를 시작하지 않고 항상 어떤 종류의 상황, 즉 변화하는 상황, 가끔은 한 세대 안에서도 근본적으로 변화하는 그런 상황 속에서 시작한다.

노트
■ from scratch : 아무런 사전 준비 없이
■ never(not) A but B : A가 아니라 B
■ 〈동격〉 : A 즉 B(A=B)

A	or (즉, 말하자면)	B
	namely (즉)	
	that is (to say) (즉, 다시 말해서)	
	대쉬(—) (즉)	
	in other words (바꾸어 말하면)	

■ 〈주격관계대명사절의 수의 일치〉 : 선행사를 포함하고 있는 관계대명사 what 사용 불가

	주격관계대명사절		
선행사	주격관계대명사	~~주어~~	동사
a context	that		changes

▶ 다음 글의 주제로 가장 적절한 것은?

① the reasons generation gaps occur over time
② the gradual process of learning in early humans
③ the conservative tendency of national institutions
④ the roles of past experiences in predicting the future
⑤ the successive nature of human knowledge and institutions

정답 | ⑤

해석 | ① 시간이 지나면서 세대 차이가 발생하는 이유
② 초기 인간들의 점진적인 학습 과정
③ 국가 제도의 보수적인 경향
④ 미래를 예측하는 것에서 과거의 경험들의 역할
⑤ 인간의 지식과 제도의 연속적인 특징

해설 | ⑤ 이 글의 주제는 인간들은 과거의 것을 물려받아 점진적으로 발전시킨다는 것이다. 그리고 그 근거로 첫째, 언어와 과학을 들고, 둘째, 사회제도를 든다. 따라서 이 글의 흐름을 봤을 때, ⑤ '인간의 지식(언어와 과학)과 제도(사회제도)의 연속적인 특징(과거의 것을 물려받아 점진적으로 발전)'이 적절하다.

오답 | ① 세대 차이가 발생하는 이유에 관한 말이 나오지 않는다.
② 점진적인 학습 과정에 관한 소재는 나오지만 초기 인간들에 관한 내용은 나오지 않는다.
③ 국가 제도는 이 글에서 하나의 예시일 뿐, 보수적인 경향에 관한 내용은 아니다.
④ 미래를 예측하는 내용은 나오지 않는다.

노트
■ succeed : (동사) 성공하다
■ success : (명사) 성공
■ successive : (형용사) 연속적인
■ successful : (형용사) 성공적인

Words

☐ philosopher	☐ theory	☐ existence
☐ deny	☐ confirm	☐ context
☐ human beings	☐ disconfirm	☐ radically
☐ historical	☐ social institution	☐ occur
☐ inherit	☐ state	☐ conservative
☐ generation	☐ modify	☐ successive

Phrases

☐ to a great extent	☐ inherit A from B
☐ pass A on to B	☐ be true of
☐ start with	☐ go on to
☐ A such as B	☐ from scratch
☐ never(not) A but B	

우선순위 영단어 역대 수능 기출 + 전국 모의고사 기출 + EBS 기출 + 교과서 기출 빈출 어휘

단어	뜻	단어	뜻	단어	뜻
approximately	ad. 대략	arrangement	n. 배치	benefit	v. ~에게 이롭다
complete	v. 완성하다	conservation	n. 보존	constitute	v. 구성하다
context	n. 환경	convey	v. 나르다	crash	v. 깨지다
crucial	a. 결정적인	current	a. 현재의	dismiss	v. 해고하다
equipment	n. 장치	expand	v. 팽창하다	extinction	n. 소멸
extreme	a. 극한의	guarantee	n. 보증	implication	n. 함축
incentive	n. 장려책	ingredient	n. 재료	innovation	n. 개혁
intensely	ad. 몹시	interpret	v. 해석하다	match	n. 시합
proceed	v. 나아가다	psychologist	n. 심리학자	rational	a. 합리적인
recommend	v. 추천하다	recruit	v. 고용하다	region	n. 지방
reward	n. 보상	self-esteem	n. 자존감	subsequent	a. 차후의
superior	a. 우수한	suppress	v. 누르다	track	v. 추적하다
transform	v. 변화하다	tremendous	a. 엄청난	vulnerable	a. 취약한
abandon	v. 버리다	acquire	v. 취득하다	adolescent	n. 청소년
anthropologist	n. 인류학자	anticipate	v. 예상하다	apparently	ad. 분명히
associate	v. 연상하다	assure	v. 확신시키다	budget	n. 예산
charge	v. (대금을) 청구하다	circumstance	n. 상황	classify	v. 구분하다
collapse	v. 무너지다	component	n. 구성 성분	compound	v. 악화시키다
condition	v. 조건을 붙이다	conflict	n. 전투	construction	n. 구상
contract	v. 수축하다	contribute to	~의 한 원인이 되다	distinct	a. 뚜렷한
distribution	n. 배분	document	v. 기록하다	enterprise	n. 기업
exceed	v. 능가하다	extensive	a. 광범위한	extraordinary	a. 대단한
identical	a. 동일한	indicator	n. 척도	inevitable	a. 불가피한
infant	n. 유아	infected	n. 감염	innate	a. 내재적인
intense	a. 강렬한	interval	n. 기간	manufacture	n. 제조
note	n. 음조	obstacle	n. 장애(물)	participant	n. 참여자
patent	v. 특허를 얻다	persist	v. 지속하다	precisely	ad. 정확하게
project	v. 투사하다	purchase	v. 구매하다	recognition	n. 인식

변형문제

01 다음 글을 읽고, |조건|에 맞게 주어진 요약문을 완성하시오.

| 조건 |
* (A), (B)는 각각 1단어, (C)는 2단어로 쓸 것
* 본문에 있는 표현을 찾아 그대로 쓸 것

Few philosophers would deny that human beings are, to a great extent, historical — that we inherit things from the past, change them, and then pass them on to future generations. Language, for example, is something that we learn and change as we use it, and the same is true of science — scientists start with a body of theory, and then go on either to confirm or to disconfirm it. The same is also true of social institutions, such as the family, the state, banks, churches, and so on — most of which are modified forms of earlier practices or institutions. Human beings, therefore, never begin their existence from scratch, but always within some kind of context — a context that changes, sometimes radically within a single generation.

⬇

According to the article, three things that we inherit from the past are (A) ____________ (B) ____________, and (C) ____________ ____________.

02 다음 글을 읽고, |조건|에 맞게 빈칸 (A), (B), (C)를 채우시오.

| 조건 |
* (A), (B), (C)는 각각 1단어로 쓸 것
* [보기]에서 선택한 단어를 한 번씩만 쓸 것
* 필요한 경우, 문맥과 어법에 맞게 변형할 것

[보기] alternate / modify / simplify / benefit / reject / intensify / need / scratch / maturity / assistance / disconfirm

Few philosophers would deny that human beings are, to a great extent, historical — that we inherit things from the past, change them, and then pass them on to future generations. Language, for example, is something that we learn and change as we use it, and the same is true of science — scientists start with a body of theory, and then go on either to confirm or to (A) ____________ it. The same is also true of social institutions, such as the family, the state, banks, churches, and so on — most of which are (B) ____________ forms of earlier practices or institutions. Human beings, therefore, never begin their existence from (C) ____________, but always within some kind of context — a context that changes, sometimes radically within a single generation.

03 다음 글을 읽고, |조건|에 맞게 주어진 주제문을 완성하시오.

| 조건 |
* (A), (B)는 각각 1단어로 쓸 것
* [보기]에서 선택한 단어를 한 번씩만 쓸 것
* [보기]를 변형 없이 그대로 쓸 것

[보기] preparation / responsibility / history / language / fundamental / motivational / institutional / social / science / confirmation

Few philosophers would deny that human beings are, to a great extent, historical — that we inherit things from the past, change them, and then pass them on to future generations. Language, for example, is something that we learn and change as we use it, and the same is true of science — scientists start with a body of theory, and then go on either to confirm or to disconfirm it. The same is also true of social institutions, such as the family, the state, banks, churches, and so on — most of which are modified forms of earlier practices or institutions. Human beings, therefore, never begin their existence from scratch, but always within some kind of context — a context that changes, sometimes radically within a single generation.

⬇

Without any (A) ____________, humans never begin their existence and always begin with a certain kind of changing situation. Also, they sometimes begin in a situation where there is a (B) ____________ change in a generation.

04 다음 글을 읽고, |조건|에 맞게 요약문을 완성하시오.

| 조건 |
* (A), (B)는 각각 1단어로 쓸 것
* [보기]에서 선택한 단어를 한 번씩만 쓸 것
* [보기]를 변형 없이 그대로 쓸 것

[보기] share / act / enlarge / offer / achieve / broaden / pass / move / increase / generate / cut

Few philosophers would deny that human beings are, to a great extent, historical — that we inherit things from the past, change them, and then pass them on to future generations. Language, for example, is something that we learn and change as we use it, and the same is true of science — scientists start with a body of theory, and then go on either to confirm or to disconfirm it. The same is also true of social institutions, such as the family, the state, banks, churches, and so on — most of which are modified forms of earlier practices or institutions. Human beings, therefore, never begin their existence from scratch, but always within some kind of context — a context that changes, sometimes radically within a single generation.

⬇

Humans are likely to (A) ____________ and alter things on the basis of what they have inherited from the past so that they can (B) ____________ things down to the future generation.

주제 · 제목

글의 논리	Examples (예시)
제목	인간의 기억: 환경을 추론할 수 있는 힘
주제	우리는 기억을 활용하여 우리가 지냈던 환경을 추론할 수 있다.

PRACTICE 03

004 어법 선택 & 연결어

[Metaphorical / Metaphorically] speaking, human memory is **[alike / like]** a public library **[what / that]** **[organize / organizes]** **[its / their]** books according **[to / as]** their **[predicting / predicted]** popularity. **[Frequent / Frequently]** **[checking / checked]** out books, (   ), popular books (e.g., the Dan Brown blockbusters), **[will make / will be made]** **[available / availably]** in special spaces **[near / nearly]** the entrance of the library to make **[it / this]** easy **[of / for]** members to find **[it / them]**. (   ), **[less / more]** popular books (e.g., the books by Herta Müller, recipient of the 2009 Nobel Prize in Literature), the ones rarely **[checked / checking]** out in the past, **[will place / will be placed]** in the back of the library. **[Because / Because of]** the environment being (   ) **[reflected / reflecting]** in our memory, we can use our memory to make inferences about the environment. We can infer, (   ), **[what / that]** the more **[fluently / fluent]** we retrieve an item from memory, the more often we **[should have encountered / must have encountered]** **[it / them]** in the past.

예시 인간의 기억은 공공도서관과 유사하다.

(Metaphorically speaking), / human memory / is like a public library / (that organizes its books) / (according to their predicted popularity).

- Metaphorically speaking: 비유적으로 말하여
- human memory: S, 인간의 기억은
- is like: V, 공공
- a public library: O(선행사), 도서관과 유사하다
- that: (주·관)
- organizes: V, 책을 정리하는
- its books: O
- according to: (구전치사)
- their predicted popularity: 예측되는 인기도에 따라

비유적으로 말하여, 인간의 기억은 예측되는 인기도에 따라 책을 정리하는 공공도서관과 유사하다.

노트

- metaphorically speaking : 비유를 하자면, 은유적으로 말해 보자면
- be like : ~와 같다
- 〈혼동하기 쉬운 어휘〉

likely	형용사	~일 것 같은 (be to 동사원형 : ~일 것 같다)
	부사	아마(probably)
alike	서술적 형용사 (보어로만 사용, 명사 수식 불가)	동일한
	부사	똑같이
like	전치사	~처럼
	동사	좋아하다

- 〈주격관계대명사절의 수의 일치〉 : 선행사를 포함하고 있는 관계대명사 what 사용 불가

선행사	주격관계대명사절		
	주격관계대명사	~~주어~~	동사
a public library	that		organizes

- 〈according to / according as〉 : ~에 따르면

구전치사	according to	(동)명사
종속접속사	according as	주어+동사

예시 인기 있는 책들은 찾기 쉬운 곳에 있다.

Frequently checked out books, / (that is), / popular books (e.g., the Dan Brown blockbusters), / will be made available / (in special spaces) / (near the entrance of the library) / (to make it easy / for members to find them).

- Frequently: 〈부사〉
- checked: 〈p.p〉
- books: S, 빈번하게 대출되는 책들
- that is: 즉 (=〈동격〉)
- popular books: 인기 있는 책들은
- (e.g., the Dan Brown blockbusters): (예를 들어 Dan Brown의 크게 성공한 소설)
- will be made: V〈미래 수동〉, 이용할 수 있을
- available: S.C, 것이다
- in special spaces: 특별한 공간에서
- near: 〈전치사〉, 도서관의 입구 근처의
- it: 〈가O〉
- easy: O.C
- for members: 〈의·S〉
- to find them: 〈진O〉, 도서관 회원들이 쉽게 찾을 수 있도록

빈번하게 대출되는 책들, 즉 인기 있는 책들(예를 들어 Dan Brown의 크게 성공한 소설)은 도서관 회원들이 쉽게 찾을 수 있도록 도서관의 입구 근처의 특별한 공간에서 이용할 수 있을 것이다.

노트

- check A out : A를 대출받다(수동태 시, be checked out)
- that is : 즉
- e.g. : 예를 들어(라틴어 exempli gratia를 줄인 것. for example로 읽음)
- 〈동격〉 : A 즉 B(A=B)

A	or (즉, 말하자면)	B
	namely (즉)	
	that is (to say) (즉, 다시 말해서)	
	대쉬(—) (즉)	
	in other words (바꾸어 말하면)	

- 〈make 상태동사〉 : 수동태 시, be made+주격보어(형용사/명사)

make	목적어	목적격보어	해석
〈상태동사〉	명사/ 명사 상당어구	형용사	~가 …한 상태로 만들다
		명사	

• make가 '~을 …한 상태로 만들다'라는 의미로 사용될 경우, make를 상태동사라 칭한다. 이때 주의사항은 목적격보어 자리에 사용하는 형용사 대신 부사를 사용할 수 없다는 점이다.

■ 〈near / nearby / nearly〉

	부사	형용사	전치사	동사
near	(거리/시간상으로) 가까이, 거의	(거리/시간상으로) 가까운	(거리상으로) ~에서 가까이 (숫자 앞에 쓰여) 거의[약]	(시간/거리상으로) 가까워지다 [다가오다], ~에 접근하다
nearby	인근에, 가까운 곳에, 거의, 대략; 간신히, 가까스로, 밀접하게, 면밀하게	[주로 명사 앞에 씀] 인근의, 가까운 곳의	–	–
nearly	거의	–	–	–

■ 〈가목적어 it / 진목적어 to R〉

동사	가목적어	목적격보어	의미상 주어	진목적어
consider feel find make think	it (this, that, there 사용 불가)	형용사 명사	for+목적격 (주어와 진목적어의 주체가 다를 경우 사용)	to 동사원형
make	it	easy	for members	to find them.

예시 덜 인기 있는 책들은 찾기 힘든 곳에 있다.

(In contrast), / less popular books / {(e.g., the books) (by Herta Müller, recipient of the 2009 Nobel Prize in Literature)}, / the ones / (rarely) (checked out in the past), / will be placed / (in the back of the library).

반대로 / 덜 인기 있는 책들 (S) / =〈동격〉 (예를 들어 2009년 노벨 문학상 수상자인 Herta Müller의 책들) =〈동격〉 / 즉 (that/which were) 과거에 거의 대출되지 않았던 책들은 (p.p) / 놓여 있을 것이다 (V〈미래 수동〉) / 도서관 뒤편에

반대로 덜 인기 있는 책들(예를 들어 2009년 노벨 문학상 수상자인 Herta Müller의 책들), 즉 과거에 거의 대출되지 않았던 책들은 도서관 뒤편에 놓여 있을 것이다.

노트
■ in contrast : 대조적으로
■ place A in the back of : A를 ~ 뒤에 두다(수동태 시, be placed in the back of)
■ 〈동격〉 : A(명사), B(명사) (A가 주어, B라는 A)

동격(B라는 A)		
명사(A)	,(콤마)	명사(B)
Herta Müller		recipient

■ 〈준부정어〉

부사	hardly (거의 ~ 아니다)
	scarcely (거의 ~ 않다)
	barely (거의 ~ 아니게)
	seldom (좀처럼 ~ 않는)
	rarely (좀처럼 ~하지 않는)
형용사/부사	little (거의 ~ 없는)
	few (거의 ~ 없는)

■ 〈주격관계대명사+be동사 생략〉

–	생략할 수 있음	
명사 (선행사)	(주격관계대명사 +be동사)	현재분사(Ring) – 능동(~하고 있는)
		과거분사(p.p.) – 수동(~되어진, 당한)
		명사
		형용사(구) (~하는, ~할)
		부사
		전치사구
the ones	(that/which were)	checked out

주제문 우리의 기억을 활용하여 환경에 관해 추론할 수 있다.

{Because of the environment / being (thus) reflected in our memory}, / we can use our memory / (to make inferences) / (about the environment).

환경 때문에 (which/that is) / 이와 같이 우리의 기억 속에 반영되는 〈진행 수동〉 / 우리는 자신의 기억을 활용할 수 있다 (S V O) / 추론하기 위해서 (O) / 환경에 관해

이와 같이 우리의 기억 속에 반영되고 있는 환경 때문에, 우리는 자신의 기억을 활용하여 환경에 관해 추론할 수 있다.

노트 ■ make[draw] an inference : 추론을 내리다
■ 〈원인/이유〉 : ~ 때문에

전치사	because of	+(동)명사 / 명사 상당어구
	due to	
	for	
	on account of	
	owing to	
	thanks to	
종속접속사	as	+주어+동사 ~
	because	
	now(that)	
	since	

■ 〈분사의 태/시제/의미상의 주어/부정〉

분사의 종류	조합	해석	태: 능동	태: 수동	시제: 단순	시제: 완료	의미상의 주어	부정
현재분사 (능동)	동사 + 형용사	~하는	Ring	(being) p.p	Ring	having p.p	주격 +분사	not/ never +분사
과거분사 (수동)		~되는						

예시 우리가 쉽게 기억하는 것은 과거에 빈번히 접했던 것이라 추론할 수 있다.

We can infer, / (for example), / {that the more (fluently) / we retrieve an item (from memory), / the more (often)

우리는 추론할 수 있다 (S V) / 예를 들어 / 〈종·접〉 더 쉽게 〈부사〉 / 우리가 기억에서 어떤 항목을 생각해 낼수록 (S V O) (O) / 더욱 빈번하게

/ we must have encountered it / (in the past)}.
S V O

우리는 그것을 접했었음이 틀림없다 과거에

예를 들어, 우리가 기억에서 어떤 항목을 더 쉽게 생각해 낼수록, 우리는 과거에 그것을 더욱 빈번하게 접했었음이 틀림없다고 추론할 수 있다.

노트 ■ 〈what vs. that〉

	관계대명사(불완전한 문장)	접속사(완전한 문장)
what	○ 선행사를 포함하고 있기 때문에 what 앞에 선행사 불필요	×
that	○ that 앞에 선행사 필요	○

■ 〈the 비교급 ~, the 비교급〉 : ~하면 할수록, 더 …하다

the	비교급	~,	the	비교급	~
	more			more	
	-er			-er	

■ 〈조동사+have+p.p.〉

• 과거 사실에 대한 추측

종류	뜻(의미)
may(might have p.p)	~이었을지도 모른다 (과거 사실에 대한 약한 추측)
must have p.p.	~이었음에 틀림이 없다 (과거 사실에 대한 강한 추측)
can not have p.p.	~이었을 리가 없다 (과거 사실에 대한 부정적인 추측)
could have p.p.	~할 수도 있었다 (과거 사실에 대한 아쉬움이나 가능성)
would have p.p.	~했을 것이다 (과거 사실에 대한 유감)

• 과거 사실에 대한 후회

종류	뜻
should (ought to) have p.p.	~했었어야 했는데 (하지 못했다)
need not have p.p.	~할 필요가 없었는데 (했다)
shouldn't have p.p.	~하지 말았어야 했는데 (했다)

▶ 다음 글의 제목으로 가장 적절한 것은?

① Sources of the Popularity of Books
② Ways to Use Monthly Book Reviews
③ How Is Human Memory Organized?
④ What Is the Nature of the Human Emotion System?
⑤ Frequently Checked Out Books: The Best Books?

정답 | ③

해석 | ① 책의 인기의 원천
② 월간 서평을 이용하는 방법
③ 인간의 기억은 어떻게 조직되어 있는가?
④ 인간의 감정 체계의 특성은 무엇인가?
⑤ 빈번하게 대출되는 책이 가장 좋은가?

해설 | ③ 이 글의 주제는 인간은 기억을 활용하여 우리가 지냈던 환경을 추론할 수 있다는 것이다. 그리고 그 근거로 공공도서관에 비유를 한다. 공공도서관에서 인기 있는 책들은 찾기 쉬운 곳에 있고 덜 인기 있는 책들은 찾기 힘든 곳에 있는 것처럼 인간의 뇌도 많이 접했던 것은 쉽게 기억하고 덜 접했던 것은 잘 기억하지 못한다고 설명한다. 이러한 비유와 주제를 봤을 때, ③ '인간의 기억은 어떻게 조직되어(많이 접했던 것은 쉽게 기억하고 덜 접했던 것은 잘 기억하지 못하는 것) 있는가?'가 적절하다.

오답 | ① 이 글의 소재는 인간의 기억이고 책의 인기의 원천에 관한 내용은 존재하지 않는다.
② 월간 서평을 이용하는 방법은 내용에 없다.
④ 인간의 감정 체계의 특성에 관한 내용은 존재하지 않는다.
⑤ 빈번하게 대출되는 책이 가장 좋은 것인지에 대한 내용은 존재하지 않는다.

Words

☐ metaphorically ______
☐ organize ______
☐ predict ______
☐ blockbuster ______
☐ available ______
☐ entrance ______
☐ in contrast ______
☐ recipient ______
☐ literature ______
☐ rarely ______
☐ environment ______
☐ reflect ______
☐ infer ______
☐ fluently ______
☐ memory ______
☐ popularity ______
☐ emotion ______
☐ frequently ______

Phrases

☐ metaphorically speaking ______
☐ check A out ______
☐ e.g. ______
☐ place A in the back of ______
☐ be like ______
☐ that is ______
☐ in contrast ______
☐ make[draw] an inference ______

변형문제

01 다음 글을 읽고, |조건|에 맞게 빈칸 (A), (B), (C)를 채우시오.

| 조건 |
* (A), (B), (C)는 각각 1단어로 쓸 것
* [보기]에서 선택한 단어를 한 번씩만 쓸 것
* 필요한 경우, 문맥과 어법에 맞게 변형할 것

[보기] outcome / profit / popularity / usefulness / conservation / inference / return / retrievable / refer / use

Metaphorically speaking, human memory is like a public library that organizes its books according to their predicted (A) ____________. Frequently checked out books, that is, popular books (e.g., the Dan Brown blockbusters), will be made available in special spaces near the entrance of the library to make it easy for members to find them. In contrast, less popular books (e.g., the books by Herta Müller, recipient of the 2009 Nobel Prize in Literature), the ones rarely checked out in the past, will be placed in the back of the library. Because of the environment being thus reflected in our memory, we can use our memory to make (B) ____________ about the environment. We can infer, for example, that the more fluently we (C) ____________ an item from memory, the more often we must have encountered it in the past.

02 다음 글을 읽고, |조건|에 맞게 주어진 요약문을 완성하시오.

| 조건 |
* (A), (B)는 각각 1단어로 쓸 것
* [보기]에서 선택한 단어를 한 번씩만 쓸 것
* 필요한 경우, 문맥과 어법에 맞게 변형할 것

[보기] more / failure / necessary / expose / offer / disadvantage / easy / memorize / affect / differ

Metaphorically speaking, human memory is like a public library that organizes its books according to their predicted popularity. Frequently checked out books, that is, popular books (e.g., the Dan Brown blockbusters), will be made available in special spaces near the entrance of the library to make it easy for members to find them. In contrast, less popular books (e.g., the books by Herta Müller, recipient of the 2009 Nobel Prize in Literature), the ones rarely checked out in the past, will be placed in the back of the library. Because of the environment being thus reflected in our memory, we can use our memory to make inferences about the environment. We can infer, for example, that the more fluently we retrieve an item from memory, the more often we must have encountered it in the past.

⬇

The use of our own memory helps us infer environment in the past. For instance, we can infer that the (A) ____________ it is for us to think of an item in memory, the more frequently we must have been (B) ____________ to it in the past.

03 다음 글을 읽고, |조건|에 맞게 빈칸 (A), (B)를 채우시오.

| 조건 |
* (A), (B)는 각각 1단어로 쓸 것
* 본문에 있는 단어를 찾아 쓸 것
* 필요한 경우, 문맥과 어법에 맞게 변형할 것

Metaphorically speaking, human memory is like a public library that organizes its books according to their predicted popularity. Frequently checked out books, that is, popular books (e.g., the Dan Brown blockbusters), will be made available in special spaces near the entrance of the library to make it easy for members to find them. In contrast, less popular books (e.g., the books by Herta Müller, recipient of the 2009 Nobel Prize in Literature), the ones rarely checked out in the past, will be placed in the back of the library. Because of the environment being thus reflected in our memory, we can use our memory to make inferences about the environment. We can infer, for example, that the more fluently we retrieve an item from memory, the more often we must have encountered it in the past.

⬇

Individual memory can be compared with a public library where books are arranged in accordance with their (A) ____________, and an item from our memory is fluently recollected depending on its (B) ____________.

04 다음 글을 읽고, |조건|에 맞게 본문에 밑줄 친 빈칸을 완성하시오.

| 조건 |
* 「The+비교급+부사+주어+동사」 구문을 활용하여 9단어로 쓸 것
* [보기]에서 선택한 단어를 한 번씩만 쓸 것
* 필요한 경우, 문맥과 어법에 맞게 변형할 것

[보기] fluent / memory / by / an / the / we / item / retrieve / from / more / restore / environment

Metaphorically speaking, human memory is like a public library that organizes its books according to their predicted popularity. Frequently checked out books, that is, popular books (e.g., the Dan Brown blockbusters), will be made available in special spaces near the entrance of the library to make it easy for members to find them. In contrast, less popular books (e.g., the books by Herta Müller, recipient of the 2009 Nobel Prize in Literature), the ones rarely checked out in the past, will be placed in the back of the library. Because of the environment being thus reflected in our memory, we can use our memory to make inferences about the environment. We can infer, for example, that ____________ ____________ ____________ ____________ ____________ ____________ ____________ ____________ ____________, the more often we must have encountered it in the past.

요지 · 주장

글의 논리	Examples (예시)
제목	변화가 주는 불편함
주제	사람들은 변화하는 것이 불편하기 때문에 꺼린다.

수능 ANALYSIS

005 어법 선택 & 연결어

We are always reluctant to make long-term changes **[because / because of]** they can be uncomfortable. We are **[essential / essentially]** creatures of habit. We do things a certain way, and our habits become **[integrating / integrated]** into our behavior. If you have any question about this, just **[transfer / transferring]** your wristwatch to **[another / the other] hand**. **[As though / Even though]** it should not make the slightest difference **[which / on which]** hand it **[wears / is worn]**, you will soon **[find / found]** **[what / that]** you are very aware of the change, and it may even feel cumbersome or **[awkward / awkwardly]**. **[Return / Returning]** the watch to **[its / their]** usual place **[bring / brings]** back a feeling of comfort. If feelings of discomfort accompany **[so / such]** minor an alteration, how **[very / much]** more so with significant behavior changes? **[It / This]** is easy to imagine **[why some people consider / why do some people consider]** change **[virtual / virtually]** **[intolerable / intolerably]**.

주제문 우리는 변화를 하는 것이 불편하기 때문에 변화를 꺼린다.

We / are (always) reluctant / (to make long-term changes) / (because they can be uncomfortable).

We(S, 우리는) / are(V) (always) reluctant(S.C) — 항상 꺼린다 / (to make long-term changes)(O) — 장기간의 변화를 만들기 위해서 / (because(〈종·접〉) they(S) can be(V) uncomfortable(S.C)) — 그들이 불편할 수 있기 때문에

우리는 장기간의 변화를 만들기를 항상 꺼리는데 그것이 불편할 수 있기 때문이다.

노트
- be reluctant to R : ~을 주저하다, 망설이다
- make a change : ~을 변경하다
- 〈빈도부사의 위치〉

		빈도부사		
be동사 / 조동사	+	always(100%)	+	일반동사
		usually(60% ~ 80%)		
		often(50% ~ 60%)		
		sometimes(40%)		
		seldom / hardly / rarely(20%)		
		never(0%)		

- 〈원인/이유〉 : ~ 때문에

전치사	because of	+(동)명사 / 명사 상당어구
	due to	
	for	
	on account of	
	owing to	
	thanks to	
종속접속사	as	+주어+동사 ~
	because	
	now(that)	
	since	

근거1 우리는 습관의 동물이다.

We / are (essentially) creatures (of habit).

We(S, 우리는) / are(V) (essentially) creatures (of habit)(S.C) — 본질적으로 습관의 동물이다

우리는 본질적으로 습관의 동물이다.

근거2 우리의 습관은 우리의 행동으로 나타난다.

We / do things (a certain way), / and our habits / become integrated (into our behavior).

We(S, 우리는) / do(V) things(O) (a certain way) — 특정한 방식으로 일을 한다 / and our habits(S) — 그리고 우리의 습관은 / become(V) integrated(S.C) (into our behavior) — 우리의 행동으로 통합된다

우리는 특정한 방식으로 일을 하며 우리의 습관은 우리의 행동으로 통합된다.

노트
- be integrated into : ~로 융화/통합되다
- 〈be / get / become 구별〉

동사	용법
be	주어가 어떤 상태인지 표현
get	주어가 겪고 있는 상태의 변화를 표현
become	주어가 변화를 겪고 어떻게 되었는지 변화의 결과 표현

예시 손목시계를 평소와 다른 손으로 옮겨보라.

{If you / have any question / (about this)}, / (just) transfer your wristwatch / (to the other hand).

{If(〈종·접〉) you(S) — 만약 여러분이 / have(V) any question(O) — 어떠한 의구심을 가진다 / (about this)} — 이 점에 대해서, / (just) transfer(V) your wristwatch(O) — 여러분의 손목시계를 옮겨보아라 / (to the other hand) — 다른 손으로

여러분이 이 점에 대해 어떠한 의구심이라도 갖고 있다면 여러분의 손목시계를 다른 손으로 옮겨보기만 해보아라.

노트
- transfer A to B : A를 B로 옮기다

■ 〈직접명령문〉

긍정문	동사원형(R)	~해라
부정문	Don't+R	~하지 마라
	Never+R	

■ 〈the other vs. another〉

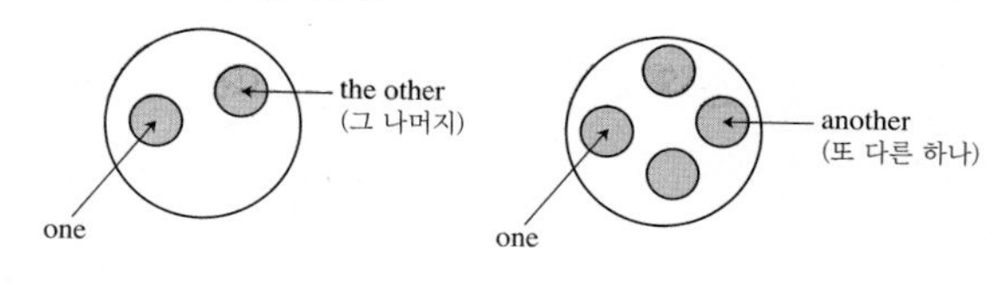

예시 이 조그만 변화도 불편하다고 느낄 것이다.

{Even though it / should not make the slightest difference
〈종·접〉 S(이것이) V O(가장 사소한 차이도 만들지 않아야 하지만)

/ (on which hand it is worn)}, / you / will (soon) find /
〈의문형용사〉 S V(손목시계를 어느 손에 찼는지) S(여러분은) V(곧 찾을 것이다)

(that you are very aware of the change), / and it / may
〈종·접〉 S V S.C O(그 변화를 정말 인식하고 있다는 것을) S(그리고 그것은)

(even) feel cumbersome or awkward.
V $S.C_1$ $S.C_2$ (심지어 성가시거나 어색하다고 느껴질 수도 있다)

손목시계를 어느 손에 찼는지는 (너무 사소해서) 가장 사소한 차이도 만들지 않아야 하지만 여러분은 그 변화를 정말 인식하고 있다는 것을 곧 알게 될 것이며, 그것은 심지어 성가시거나 어색하다고 느껴질 수도 있을 것이다.

노트 ■ make a difference : 차이를 만들다

■ be aware of : ~을 알다

■ 〈양보/대조〉

전치사	in spite of	+명사/명사 상당어구	비록 ~이지만
	despite		
종속접속사	though	+주어+동사	
	although		
	even though		
	even if		
	as		
	while		반면에
	whereas		

■ 〈간접의문문 – 전치사의 목적어 자리에 사용되는 경우〉

전치사	목적어			
on	〈간접의문문〉 : 명사절			
	의문형용사	명사	주어	동사
	which	hand	it	is down

■ 〈what vs. that〉

	관계대명사(불완전한 문장)	접속사(완전한 문장)
what	○ 선행사를 포함하고 있기 때문에 what 앞에 선행사 불필요	×
that	○ that 앞에 선행사 필요	○

■ 〈find / found〉

원형	과거	과거분사	현재분사	뜻
find	found	found	finding	v. 발견하다, 알다
found	founded	founded	founding	v. 설립하다

■ 〈감각동사〉

감각동사	주격보어(S.C)	
feel, look, seem, sound, taste, appear, smell	형용사(분사 : 현재분사/과거분사)	
	명사	
	like(전치사)	(that)+주어+동사
		(동)명사
	~~alike~~	
	~~likely~~	

예시 평상시에 차는 곳으로 되돌리면 편안한 느낌을 받는다.

{Returning the watch / (to its usual place)} / brings back
〈동명사〉 O S(그 시계를 되돌리는 것이 / 평상시 차는 곳으로) V(편안한 느낌을)

a feeling of comfort.
O(되돌려준다)

그 시계를 평상시 차는 곳으로 되돌리는 것이 편안한 느낌을 되돌려준다.

노트 ■ return A to B : A를 B로 되돌리다

■ bring A back : A를 돌려주다, A를 다시 가져다[데려다] 주다

■ 〈동명사구가 주어 자리에 사용된 경우〉 : 단수 취급으로 동사는 단수동사를 사용함

주어 : 동명사구	동사
Returning the watch to its usual place	brings back

■ 〈이어동사〉

타동사	명사	부사	(○)
타동사	부사	명사	(○)
타동사	대명사	부사	(○)
타동사	부사	대명사	(×)
brings	back	it(=a feeling of comfort)	(×)

주제문(강조) 이렇게 작은 변화도 불편한 느낌이 들기에 더욱 더 큰 변화일 경우에는 엄청난 불편한 느낌이 든다.

{If feelings (of discomfort) / accompany so minor an
〈종·접〉 S(만약 불편한 느낌이) V O(그렇게 작은 변화에 수반한다면)

alteration}, / how much more so / (with significant
(얼마나 훨씬 더 많은 것들이 있겠는가) (중요한 행동 변화와)

behavior changes)?
(관련해서)

불편한 느낌이 그렇게 작은 변화에 수반한다면 중요한 행동 변화와 관련해서는 얼마나 훨씬 더 많은 불편한 느낌을 수반하겠는가?

노트 ■ 〈관사의 위치〉

so / how / too / as	형용사	a/an	명사
such / what / many / quite / rather / half	a/an	형용사	명사

■ 〈생략〉

If	feelings of discomfort	accompany	~	how much more	feelings of discomfort	accompany	~
	주어	동사			주어	동사	
					(생략 가능)		

■ 〈비교급 vs. 원급 강조〉

비교급 강조 표현	원급 강조 표현
much, even, still, by far, far, a lot, lots, a great deal	very, so, quite, really, extremely, too

주제문(재진술) 사람들이 변화를 꺼려하는지는 명백하다.

It is easy / [to imagine / {why some people / consider change (virtually) intolerable}].

(가S) V S.C / 〈의문사〉 S V / 〈간접의문문〉 / 〈진S〉 / O 〈부사〉 O.C

쉬운 일이다 상상하는 것은 왜 일부 사람들이 변화를 거의 참을 수 없는 것으로 생각하는지

일부 사람들이 왜 변화를 거의 참을 수 없는 것으로 생각하는지를 상상하는 것은 쉬운 일이다.

노트 ■ 〈가주어, 진주어 구문〉

가주어	동사	진주어
It (This/That/There 사용 불가)	–	that+주어+동사(완전한 절)
		to 동사원형
		동명사
		의문사+주어+동사(간접의문문)
		if/whether+주어+동사
It	is	to imagine

■ 〈간접의문문 – 의문사가 있는 경우〉

	〈간접의문문〉 : 완전타동사의 목적어(완전한 문장)		
완전타동사	의문사	주어	동사
imagine	why	some people	consider

■ 〈consider 동사의 쓰임〉 : 5형식인 경우

consider	목적어	목적격보어
		as+보어
		(to be) 보어

▶ 다음 글의 요지로 가장 적절한 것은?

① 신체와 관련이 있는 행동은 한 번 습관화되면 고치기가 쉽지 않다.
② 장기간의 변화는 단기간의 변화보다 더 많은 스트레스를 야기한다.
③ 행동에 작은 변화를 주는 것이 좋은 습관을 형성하는 데 도움이 된다.
④ 사람들은 습관화된 행동을 바꿀 때 느끼는 불편함 때문에 변화를 꺼린다.
⑤ 형성된 좋은 습관은 불편함을 유발했던 일들을 쉽게 처리할 수 있게 해준다.

정답 | ④

해설 | ④ 이 글의 주제는 사람들이 변화하는 것이 불편하기 때문에 꺼린다는 것이다. 따라서 글의 요지로 가장 적절한 것은 주제와 일맥상통하는 ④이다.

오답 | ① 신체와 관련이 있는 행동은 본문에 언급되어 있지 않다.
② 변화라는 소재는 나오지만 이 글은 장기간의 변화와 단기간의 변화를 구별하는 글이 아니다.
③ 이 글에 작은 변화를 주는 것이 좋은 습관을 형성한다는 내용은 나오지 않는다.
⑤ 이 글은 좋은 습관이 불편함을 유발하는 일들을 쉽게 처리한다는 내용이 아니라 평소 습관에 맞지 않는 변화를 하면 불편함을 유발하여 꺼린다는 것이다.

Words

- ☐ reluctant
- ☐ wristwatch
- ☐ awkward
- ☐ accompany
- ☐ alteration
- ☐ intolerable

Phrases

- ☐ be reluctant to R
- ☐ be integrated into
- ☐ make a difference
- ☐ return A to B
- ☐ make a change
- ☐ transfer A to B
- ☐ be aware of
- ☐ bring A back

변형문제

01 다음 글을 읽고, |조건|에 맞게 주어진 요지를 완성하시오.

| 조건 |

* (A), (B)는 각각 1단어로 쓸 것
* 본문에 있는 단어만을 변형 없이 사용할 것

We are always reluctant to make long-term changes because they can be uncomfortable. We are essentially creatures of habit. We do things a certain way, and our habits become integrated into our behavior. If you have any question about this, just transfer your wristwatch to the other hand. Even though it should not make the slightest difference on which hand it is worn, you will soon find that you are very aware of the change, and it may even feel cumbersome or awkward. Returning the watch to its usual place brings back a feeling of comfort. If feelings of discomfort accompany so minor an alteration, how much more so with significant behavior changes? It's easy to imagine why some people consider change virtually intolerable.

⬇

Individuals are (A) ____________ to make a change because of the (B) ____________ they feel when altering long habitual behavior.

02 다음 글을 읽고, |조건|에 맞게 빈칸 (A), (B)를 채우시오.

| 조건 |

* (A), (B)는 각각 1단어로 쓸 것
* [보기]에서 선택한 단어를 한 번씩만 쓸 것
* 필요한 경우, 문맥과 어법에 맞게 변형할 것

[보기] combine / infuse / evolve / integrate / intolerance / cumbersome / convenience / tolerable / accompany / changeable / immerse

We are always reluctant to make long-term changes because they can be uncomfortable. We are essentially creatures of habit. We do things a certain way, and our habits become integrated into our behavior. If you have any question about this, just transfer your wristwatch to the other hand. Even though it should not make the slightest difference on which hand it is worn, you will soon find that you are very aware of the change, and it may even feel (A) ____________ or awkward. Returning the watch to its usual place brings back a feeling of comfort. If feelings of discomfort accompany so minor an alteration, how much more so with significant behavior changes? It's easy to imagine why some people consider change virtually (B) ____________.

03 다음 글을 읽고, |조건|에 맞게 주어진 주제문을 완성하시오.

| 조건 |
* 동명사로 시작하는 주어를 만들되 4단어로 쓸 것
* 본문에 있는 단어만을 사용할 것
* 필요한 경우, 문맥과 어법에 맞게 변형할 것

We are always reluctant to make long-term changes because they can be uncomfortable. We are essentially creatures of habit. We do things a certain way, and our habits become integrated into our behavior. If you have any question about this, just transfer your wristwatch to the other hand. Even though it should not make the slightest difference on which hand it is worn, you will soon find that you are very aware of the change, and it may even feel cumbersome or awkward. Returning the watch to its usual place brings back a feeling of comfort. If feelings of discomfort accompany so minor an alteration, how much more so with significant behavior changes? It's easy to imagine why some people consider change virtually intolerable.

⬇

______ ______ ______ ______ is not preferred due to its discomfort when changes occur.

04 다음 문장이 들어갈 부분으로 가장 적절한 곳을 고르시오.

Even though it should not make the slightest difference on which hand it is worn, you will soon find that you are very aware of the change, and it may even feel cumbersome or awkward.

We are always reluctant to make long-term changes because they can be uncomfortable. We are essentially creatures of habit. (①) We do things a certain way, and our habits become integrated into our behavior. (②) If you have any question about this, just transfer your wristwatch to the other hand. (③) Returning the watch to its usual place brings back a feeling of comfort. (④) If feelings of discomfort accompany so minor an alteration, how much more so with significant behavior changes? (⑤) It's easy to imagine why some people consider change virtually intolerable.

요지 · 주장

글의 논리	Examples (예시)
제목	다른 사람들에 대한 인식을 통해 자신의 내면을 보는 힘
주제	다른 사람들의 부정적인 특징을 보고 자신도 그런 점을 가지고 있는지 확인할 수 있다.

PRACTICE 01

006 어법 선택 & 연결어

One day **[during / while] [driven / driving]** my car, I kept **[noticing / from noticing]** things **[what / that] [was / were]** wrong with all **[another / the other]** cars on the road. One had a taillight out, one was **[spewing / spewed]** dark smoke out of **[its / their]** tailpipe, and **[another / the other]** had a bad tire. **[When / Then]** I realized **[what / that]** if any of these things **[was / were]** wrong with my car, I wouldn't know **[it / them] [because / because of]** I was busy **[to drive / driving]**. I, too, could have a taillight out and not even know about **[it / them]**. We don't have eyes in the back of our heads; we don't "see" **[us / ourselves] [complete / completely]**. ( ) we can develop awareness and use anything **[what / that] [happen / happens]** to us and others as great learning experiences. Instead of **[projection / projecting]** negative traits onto others, **[look / looking]** first inside to see **[if / that]** you have a trace of **[which / what]** you **[found / find]** so **[awful / awfully]** in others.

예시 운전 중에 다른 자동차들의 잘못된 점들을 발견한다.

(One day) / (while (I was) driving my car), / I kept noticing things / {that were wrong / (with all the other cars) / (on the road)}.

- One day: 어느 날
- while: 〈종·접〉, driving: 〈현·분〉, my car: O — 내 자동차를 운전하는 동안
- I: S, kept: V, noticing: S.C — 나는 어떤 것을 계속해서
- things: 〈선행사〉 — 발견했다
- that: 〈주·관〉, were: V, wrong: S.C — 잘못된
- with all the other cars: 모든 다른 자동차의
- on the road: 길 위에 있는

어느 날 나는 내 자동차를 운전하는 동안 길 위에 있는 모든 다른 자동차의 잘못된 것들을 계속해서 발견했다.

노트
- one day : 어느 날, 언젠가
- 시간 : ~ 동안

전치사	during	+ 명사 / 명사 상당어구
종속접속사	while	+ 주어 + 동사

- 〈분사구문 – 문두〉 : 주절과 종속절의 위치는 서로 바뀔 수 있음

종속절(→ 분사구문)				주절	
종속접속사	주어	동사 : 상황에 맞게 아래처럼 바뀜			
〈그대로 사용하면 의미 강조〉	(주절의 주어와 같으면 생략하고, 다르면 주격으로 사용함)	(being) (having been) 생략 가능	Ring(현재분사)	주어	동사
			p.p.(과거분사)		
			형용사		
			명사		
while	(I was) 생략		driving	I	kept

- 〈주격관계대명사절의 수의 일치〉 : 선행사를 포함하고 있는 관계대명사 what 사용 불가

	주격관계대명사절		
선행사	주격관계대명사	~~주어~~	동사
things	that		were

- 〈keep 동사의 쓰임〉

(목적어)	현재분사 (Ring)	(~가) …하는 것을 유지하다
	from 동명사 (Ring)	(~가) …하는 것을 막다

One had a taillight out, / one was spewing dark smoke / (out of its tailpipe), / and another had a bad tire.

- One: S, had: V, a taillight out: O — 어떤 자동차는 미등에 불이 들어오지 않았고
- one: S, was spewing: V〈과거진행〉, dark smoke: O — 어떤 자동차는 검은 연기를 뿜어내고 있었고
- out of its tailpipe: 배기관으로
- another: S, had: V, a bad tire: O — 그리고 또 다른 자동차는 타이어의 상태가 나빴다

어떤 자동차는 미등에 불이 들어오지 않았고, 어떤 자동차는 배기관으로 검은 연기를 뿜어내고 있었고, 또 다른 자동차는 타이어의 상태가 나빴다.

노트
- out of : ~로부터
- 〈the other vs. another〉

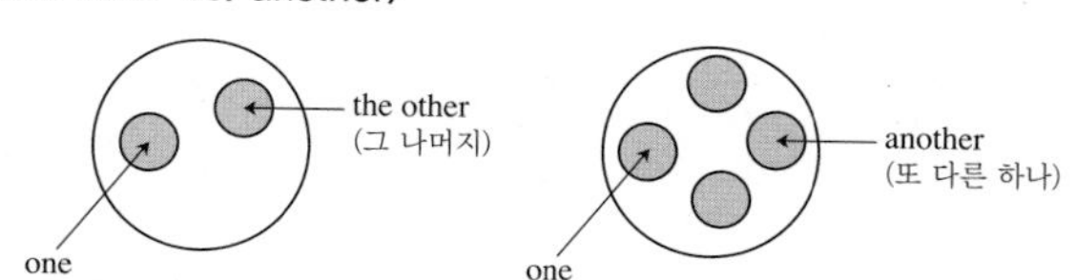

예시 내 자동차도 잘못이 있다면 나는 바쁘기 때문에 그것들을 알지 못했다.

(Then) I realized / {that (if any of these things were wrong with my car), / I wouldn't know it / (because I was busy (in) driving)}.

- Then I realized: I: S, realized: V — 그러고 나서 나는 깨달았다
- that: 〈종·접〉 (O), if: 〈종·접〉, any of these things: S, were: V — 만약 이러한 것들 중 어떤 것이
- wrong with my car: S.C — 내 자동차에 문제가 있다면
- I: S, wouldn't know: V, it: O — 나는 그것들을 알지 못할 것이라는 것을
- because: 〈종·접〉, I: S — 운전하기
- was: V, busy: S.C, driving: 〈동명사〉 — 바쁘기 때문에

그러고 나서 내 자동차가 이러한 것들 중 어떤 것에 잘못이 있다면 나는 운전하느라 바쁘기 때문에 그것들을 알지 못할 것이라는 것을 깨달았다.

노트
- be busy (in) 동명사 : ~하느라 바쁘다

■ 〈부사 vs. 접속부사〉

시간	Then	주어	동사		
	When	주어	동사,	주어	동사 ~
장소	There	주어	동사		
	Where	주어	동사,	주어	동사 ~

■ 〈what vs. that〉

	관계대명사(불완전한 문장)	접속사(완전한 문장)
what	○ 선행사를 포함하고 있기 때문에 what 앞에 선행사 불필요	×
that	○ that 앞에 선행사 필요	○

■ 〈가정법 과거〉 : 현재 사실에 대한 반대를 가정할 때 사용한다.

• 만약 ~한다면, …할 텐데. : 종속절과 주절은 서로 자리가 바뀌어도 무관

종속절			주절	
If	주어	동사	주어	동사
		과거형 동사		조동사과거형
		were		(would/should/could/
		were to 동사원형		might)+동사원형
if	any of these things	were	I	wouldn't know

■ 〈주어와 동사의 수의 일치〉

• A of B : 일반적인 경우에 A가 주어

• A of B : A가 부분/부분인 경우에 B가 주어

	A	B	
분수	two – thirds 등	주어	동사 (B에 수의 일치)
부분	a group of, all of, a lot of, any of, a number of, both of, each of, either of, few of, half of, many of, most of, much of, neither of, none of, one of, part of, percent of, several of, some of, the rest, two of 등		
	any of	these things	~~was~~ were

■ 〈원인/이유〉 : ~ 때문에

전치사	because of	+(동)명사 / 명사 상당어구
	due to	
	for	
	on account of	
	owing to	
	thanks to	
종속접속사	as	+주어+동사 ~
	because	
	now(that)	
	since	

■ 〈전치사 in이 생략된 경우〉

	목적어			
spend	시간/노력/돈/에너지 등	(in) 생략 가능	동명사	~하는 데 …을 소비하다
waste	돈/시간/재능 등			~하는 데 …을 낭비하다
have	a hard time			~하는 데 어려움을 가지다
	trouble			
	difficulty			
be	busy			~하는 데 바쁘다
There	is no use			~해봐도 소용없다

I, (too), could have a taillight out / and not (even) know (about it).

S / V_1 / O / V_2

나는 또한 자동차 미등에 불이 들어오지 않을 수 있고 / 심지어 알지 못할 수 있다 / 그것에 대하여

내 자동차 또한 미등에 불이 들어오지 않을 수 있고 나는 그것에 대하여 심지어 알지 못할 수 있다.

노트 ■ know about : ~에 대하여 알고[듣고] 있다

주제문(강조) 우리는 우리 자신을 완전히 보지 못한다.

We don't have eyes / (in the back of our heads); / we don't "see" ourselves / (completely).

S V O / S V O〈재·대〉 〈부사〉

우리는 눈을 가지고 있지 않다 / 머리 뒤에 / 우리 자신을 '보지'는 못한다 / 완전히

우리는 머리 뒤에 눈을 가지고 있지 않아서 우리 자신을 완전히 '보지'는 못한다.

노트 ■ have eyes in the back of your head : 뒤통수에도 눈이 있다, 모든지 꿰뚫어 보고 있다

■ 〈재귀대명사 vs. 대명사〉

		주어와 다름	주어와 동일
주어	~	대명사	재귀대명사
we		us	ourselves

■ 〈혼동 어휘〉

	동사	형용사	명사	부사
complete	완수하다	완전한, 완벽한	–	–
completion	–	–	완성, 완수	–
competition	–	–	경쟁, 대회	–
competitor	–	–	경쟁자	
competence	–	–	능력, 자격	–
incompetence	–	–	무능력	–
complement	보완하다	–	보완, 보충	–
compliment	칭찬하다	–	칭찬	
complimentary	–	칭찬하는, 무료의	–	–
complimentarily	–	–	–	찬사로, 무료로
competitive	–	경쟁적인	–	–
competent	–	유능한, 적임의, 자격이 있는	–	–
completely	–	–	–	완전히, 전적으로
competitively	–	–	–	경쟁적으로
competently	–	–	–	유능하게

주제문(강조) 우리는 다른 사람들을 통해 학습을 할 수 있다.

(But) we can develop awareness / and use anything / {that happens (to us and others)} / (as great learning experiences).

S V_1 O / V_2 O〈선행사〉 / 〈주·관〉 V / 〈전치사〉 〈현재분사〉

하지만 우리는 인식을 발달시킬 수 있으며 / 어떤 것을 사용할 수 있다 / 우리와 다른 사람들에게 일어나는 / 큰 학습 경험으로 사용할 수

하지만 우리는 인식을 발달시킬 수 있으며 우리와 다른 사람들에게 일어나는 일들을 큰 학습 경험으로 사용할 수 있다.

노트 ■ happen to : ~에게 일어나다
■ **〈주격관계대명사절의 수의 일치〉** : 선행사를 포함하고 있는 관계대명사 what 사용 불가

선행사	주격관계대명사절		
	주격관계대명사	~~주어~~	동사
anything	that		happens

주제문 다른 사람들의 부정적인 특징을 보고 자신도 그런 점을 가지고 있는지 확인할 수 있다.

(Instead of [〈전치사〉] projecting [〈동명사〉] negative traits onto others), /
다른 사람에게 부정적인 특징을 보여 주는 대신에

look [V] first inside / [to see / {if [〈종·접〉] you [S] have [V] a trace [O] / (of [〈전치사〉]
O〈간접의문문〉
먼저 내면을 들여다보아라 보기 위해서 여러분이 흔적을 가지고 있지는 않은지를

what [〈목·관〉] you [S] find [V] so awful [O.C] in others)}].
O
여러분이 다른 사람에게서 발견한 매우 끔찍한 것의

다른 사람에게 부정적인 특징을 보여 주는 대신에 여러분이 다른 사람에게서 발견한 매우 끔찍한 것의 흔적을 여러분이 가지고 있지는 않은지 먼저 (여러분의) 내면을 들여다보아라.

노트 ■ instead of : 대신에
■ project A onto B : A를 B에 투영하다
■ look inside : 속을 살펴보다
■ **〈의문사가 없는 간접의문문〉** : if/whether+주어+동사
• 〈if / wether / that 구별법〉 : that 사용 불가

			if	whether	that
명사절	주어 자리		×	○	○
명사절	목적어 자리	타동사의 목적어	○	○	○
명사절	목적어 자리	전치사의 목적어	×	○	○
명사절	보어 자리		×	○	○
명사절	진주어 자리		○	○	○
부사절	동사 수식		○	○	○
형용사절	명사 수식		×	×	○
간접의문문	S/O/C		○	○	×
–	–	–	if ~ or not(○) if or not(×)	whether or not(○) whether ~ or not(○)	×

■ **〈직접명령문〉**

긍정문	동사원형(R)	~해라
부정문	Don't+R	~하지 마라
부정문	Never+R	~하지 마라

■ **〈전치사의 목적어로 사용된 목적격관계대명사 what〉**

전치사	목적격관계대명사절(명사절 : 전치사의 목적어)					
	~~선행사~~	what	주어	불완전타동사	~~목적어~~	목적격보어
of		선행사를 포함한 관계대명사 (=the thing(s) which/that ~) : ~하는 것은/이	you	find		awful

■ **〈5형식 구조에서 find 동사의 쓰임〉**

find	목적어	목적격보어
(경험하여) 알다, 깨닫다, 인지(認知)하다, (시험해 보고) 알다		현재분사(Ring) – 능동(~하고 있는)
		과거분사(p.p.) – 수동(~되어진, 당한)
		(to be) 형용사, 명사
		형용사
		to do
		R

▶ **다음 글에서 필자가 주장하는 바로 가장 적절한 것은?**
① 한 번 내린 결정을 되돌리지 마라.
② 타인의 잘못을 보고 자신을 돌아보아라.
③ 과거의 경험이 판단을 흐리지 않도록 하라.
④ 자신보다 타인에게 너그러운 태도를 보여라.
⑤ 주위의 조언을 참고하되 자신의 판단을 믿어라.

정답 | ②
해설 | ② 이 글의 주제는 다른 사람들의 부정적인 특징을 보고 자신도 그런 점을 가지고 있는지 확인할 수 있다는 것이다. 필자의 주장은 마지막 문장에 나타난다. 마지막 문장에서 필자는 '다른 사람에게 부정적인 특징을 보여 주는 대신에 여러분이 다른 사람에게서 발견한 매우 끔찍한 것의 흔적을 여러분이 가지고 있지는 않은지 먼저 (여러분의) 내면을 들여다보아라.'라고 말을 한다. 따라서 가장 적절한 것은 ②이다.
오답 | ① '한 번 내린 결정을 되돌리지 마라.'는 내용은 존재하지 않는다.
③ '과거의 경험이 판단을 흐리지 않도록 하라.'는 내용은 존재하지 않는다.
④ 이 글의 소재는 '자신과 타인'이 관련되어 있지만 '타인에게 너그러운 태도를 보여라.'라는 내용은 존재하지 않는다.
⑤ '주위의 조언을 참고하되 자신의 판단을 믿어라.'라는 내용은 존재하지 않는다.

Words

☐ one day
☐ notice
☐ tailight
☐ spew
☐ smoke
☐ tailpipe
☐ tire
☐ realize
☐ wrong
☐ back
☐ completely
☐ develop
☐ awareness
☐ happen
☐ project

☐ negative
☐ trait
☐ trace
☐ awful

Phrases

☐ one day
☐ be busy (in) 동명사
☐ have eyes in the back of your head
☐ project A onto B
☐ out of
☐ know about
☐ happen to
☐ instead of
☐ look inside

우선순위 영단어 역대 수능 기출 + 전국 모의고사 기출 + EBS 기출 + 교과서 기출 빈출 어휘

단어	뜻	단어	뜻	단어	뜻
regular	n. 단골손님	reinforce	v. 증진시키다	relative	n. 친척
reliable	a. 신뢰성 있는	replace	v. 대신하다	restore	v. 복원하다
sensitive	a. 민감한	simultaneously	ad. 동시에	struggle	v. 애쓰다
substantial	a. 내용이 풍부한	symptom	n. 증상	take over	(~보다) 더 커지다
territory	n. 영토	urge	v. 주장하다	yield	n. 생산
adapt	v. 각색[개작]하다	appeal	n. 호소	assess	v. 평가하다
category	n. 범주	clue	n. 실마리	competition	n. (집합) 경쟁자
complex	a. 복잡한	composition	n. 구성	consciousness	n. 의식
deal with	처리하다	debase	v. 저하시키다	derive	v. (즐거움 등을) 얻다
diminish	v. 감소하다	finance	v. 자금을 대다	financial	a. 금융의
flexible	a. 적응성이 있는	foundation	n. 토대	frequency	n. 빈번함
harsh	a. 거친	hold	n. 지배력	imply	v. 포함하다
influential	a. 영향력 있는	inhabit	v. ~에 살다	intend	v. ~할 작정이다
interpretation	n. 해석	investment	n. 투자	label	v. ~에 명칭을 붙이다
landscape	n. 지물	means	n. 돈	occupy	v. 차지하다
overall	a. 종합적인	permanent	a. 영구적인	present	v. 나타내다
promote	v. 촉진하다	reflect	v. 되새겨보다	represent	v. 대표하다
resistance	n. 저항	scarcity	n. 부족	significantly	ad. 유의미하게
submit	v. 제출하다	surface	v. 표면화하다	transmit	v. 전하다
variation	n. 변화	accurate	a. 정확한	adequate	a. 적절한
aggressive	a. 호전적인	archaeologist	n. 고고학자	arise	v. 발생하다
arrange	v. 가지런히 하다	assign	v. (가치, 기능 등을) 부여하다	attribute	v. 탓으로 돌리다
autonomy	n. 자치권	average	v. 평균을 내다	capture	v. 점유하다
client	n. 의뢰인	cognitive	a. 인지의[인식의]	come up with	~을 생각해내다
confirm	v. 확인하다	consequently	ad. 따라서	considerable	a. 적지 않은
constantly	ad. 끊임없이	contain	v. 포함하다	convert	v. 개종시키다
cultivate	v. 구축하다	define	v. 규정하다	deliver	v. 분만하다
desperation	n. 절망	dissolve	v. 용해시키다	diversity	n. 다양성
dominant	a. 우세한	draft	v. 징집하다	ecological	a. 생태적인
efficiency	n. 효율(성)	end up -ing	결국 ~하게 되다	enormous	a. 막대한
expertise	n. 전문가적 의견	extent	n. 크기	fiber	n. 섬유
given	~을 고려해 볼 때	harbor	v. ~에게 거처를 주다	household	a. 가족의
hypothesis	n. 가설	impose	v. 부과하다	incredible	a. 믿을 수 없는
issue	v. 발행하다	likelihood	n. 가능성	literature	n. 문헌
maintain	v. 유지하다	majority	n. 대다수	make sense	v. 이치에 맞다

변형문제

01 다음 글을 읽고, 필자가 주장하는 것을 |조건|에 맞게 빈칸 (A), (B)를 채우시오.

| 조건 |
* (A)는 3단어, (B)는 4단어로 쓸 것
* 본문에 있는 단어를 찾아 그대로 쓸 것

One day while driving my car, I kept noticing things that were wrong with all the other cars on the road. One had a taillight out, one was spewing dark smoke out of its tailpipe, and another had a bad tire. Then I realized that if any of these things were wrong with my car, I wouldn't know it because I was busy driving. I, too, could have a taillight out and not even know about it. We don't have eyes in the back of our heads; we don't "see" ourselves completely. But we can develop awareness and use anything that happens to us and others as great learning experiences. Instead of projecting negative traits onto others, look first inside to see if you have a trace of what you find so awful in others.

⬇

Look (A) ____________ ____________ ____________ by watching (B) ____________ ____________ ____________ ____________ and see if you have them

02 다음 글을 읽고, |조건|에 맞게 주어진 요약문을 완성하시오.

| 조건 |
* (A), (B)는 각각 1단어로 쓸 것
* 본문에 있는 단어만을 그대로 사용할 것

One day while driving my car, I kept noticing things that were wrong with all the other cars on the road. One had a taillight out, one was spewing dark smoke out of its tailpipe, and another had a bad tire. Then I realized that if any of these things were wrong with my car, I wouldn't know it because I was busy driving. I, too, could have a taillight out and not even know about it. We don't have eyes in the back of our heads; we don't "see" ourselves completely. But we can develop awareness and use anything that happens to us and others as great learning experiences. Instead of projecting negative traits onto others, look first inside to see if you have a trace of what you find so awful in others.

⬇

Although it is impossible to explore ourselves completely, a level of (A) ____________ can be raised and experiences learnt from others and of us become in (B) ____________.

03 다음 문장이 들어갈 부분으로 가장 적절한 곳을 고르시오.

> Then I realized that if any of these things were wrong with my car, I wouldn't know it because I was busy driving.

One day while driving my car, I kept noticing things that were wrong with all the other cars on the road. (①) One had a taillight out, one was spewing dark smoke out of its tailpipe, and another had a bad tire. (②) I, too, could have a taillight out and not even know about it. (③) We don't have eyes in the back of our heads; we don't "see" ourselves completely. (④) But we can develop awareness and use anything that happens to us and others as great learning experiences. (⑤) Instead of projecting negative traits onto others, look first inside to see if you have a trace of what you find so awful in others.

04 다음 글의 순서로 적절한 것은?

> One day while driving my car, I kept noticing things that were wrong with all the other cars on the road.

(A) But we can develop awareness and use anything that happens to us and others as great learning experiences. Instead of projecting negative traits onto others, look first inside to see if you have a trace of what you find so awful in others.

(B) I, too, could have a taillight out and not even know about it. We don't have eyes in the back of our heads; we don't "see" ourselves completely.

(C) One had a taillight out, one was spewing dark smoke out of its tailpipe, and another had a bad tire. Then I realized that if any of these things were wrong with my car, I wouldn't know it because I was busy driving.

① (A) - (B) - (C)　② (B) - (A) - (C)　③ (B) - (C) - (A)
④ (C) - (A) - (B)　⑤ (C) - (B) - (A)

UNIT 02

요지 · 주장

글의 논리	Comparison & Contrast (비교 & 대조)
제목	영화의 중요한 특성
주제	영화에서 중요한 부분은 기술적인 부분이 아니라 이야기 부분이다.

PRACTICE 02

007 어법 선택 & 연결어

Everybody **[has / have]** a story **[what / that]** they have always wanted to tell, and **[make / making]** a movie **[is / are]** a good way to tell **[it / them]**. The word *magic* has always been **[associating / associated]** with the film industry, and while some people consider the technical achievements of filmmakers to be the magic part of films, I am of the belief **[which / that]** the *story* part of a movie is the *real* magic. *ET: The Extraterrestrial* did not capture our hearts with **[its / their]** technologically **[advancing / advanced]** gadgets; it was the story **[what / that]** **[drew in us / drew us in]**. While that movie did have a pretty big budget, my point is **[what / that]** it did not need to have one in order to succeed. You should not be afraid to have great expectations for your film if you *really* believe in the story. Who knows, maybe your story is **[a lot / very]** more **[interesting / interested]** than you think, and if people at a film festival agree with this notion, then your story could take off.

일반적인 사실 영화를 만드는 것은 자신의 이야기를 말하는 좋은 방법이다.

Everybody / has a story / {that they have (always) wanted to tell}, / and (making a movie) / is a good way (to tell it).

(Everybody: S 모든 사람은 / has: V / a story: O(선행사) 이야기를 가지고 있다 / that: 〈목·관〉 / they: S / have (always) wanted: V 언제나 자신이 말하길 원했던 / to tell: O / making a movie: 〈동명사〉 S 그리고 영화를 만드는 것은 / is: V / a good way: S.C 그것을 말하는 하나의 좋은 방법이다)

모든 사람은 언제나 자신이 말하길 원했던 이야기를 가지고 있으며, 영화를 만드는 것은 그것을 말하는 하나의 좋은 방법이다.

노트
- tell a story : 이야기를 말하다
- make a movie : 영화를 제작하다
- 〈주어와 동사의 수의 일치〉
  - each / every / any + 단수동사
- 〈목적격관계대명사 that〉 : to부정사의 목적어가 없는 경우 / 선행사를 포함하고 있는 관계대명사 what 사용 불가

	〈목적격관계대명사절〉 : to tell의 목적어가 없는 경우				
선행사	목적격관계대명사	주어	타동사	목적어	
a story	that : 〈생략 가능〉	they	have wanted	to tell	~~목적어~~

- 〈동명사구가 주어 자리에 사용된 경우〉 : 단수 취급으로 동사는 단수동사를 사용함

주어 : 동명사구	동사
making a movie	is ~

주제문(주장) 영화에서 중요한 부분은 기술적인 부분이 아니라 이야기 부분이다.

The word *magic* / has (always) been associated / (with the film industry), / and / {while some people consider / the technical achievements (of filmmakers) / to be the magic part of films}, / I am of the belief / {that the *story* part (of a movie) / is the *real* magic}.

(The word *magic*: S '마법'이라는 단어는 / has (always) been associated: V 〈현재완료 수동〉 항상 연관되어 왔다 / with the film industry: 영화 산업과 함께 / and: 그리고 / while: 〈종·접〉 / some people: S / consider: V 반면에 어떤 사람들은 고려한다 / the technical achievements (of filmmakers): O 영화 제작자들의 기술적인 업적을 / to be the magic part of films: O.C 영화의 마법과 같은 부분으로 / I: S / am: V / of the belief 나는 믿음을 가지고 있다 / that: 〈종·접〉 =〈동격〉 / the *story* part (of a movie): S 영화의 '이야기' 부분이 / is: V / the *real* magic: S.C '진짜' 마법이라는)

'마법'이라는 단어는 항상 영화 산업과 연관되어 왔는데, 어떤 사람들은 영화 제작자들의 기술적인 업적을 영화의 마법과 같은 부분으로 생각하지만, 나는 영화의 '이야기' 부분이 '진짜' 마법이라는 믿음을 가지고 있다.

노트
- be associated with : ~와 관련되다
- 〈while 용법〉

부사절을 이끄는 종속접속사	
시간	~ 동안에
양보/대조	비록 ~일지라도

- 〈동격의 that〉 : ~라는 A(관계대명사 which/what 사용 불가)

추상명사 (A)	종속절(명사절 – 완전한 문장)		
	that	주어	동사 ~
answer / belief / chance / claim / conclusion / dream / evidence / extent / fact / faith / hope / idea / likelihood / news / notion / pledge / possibility / promise / proposal / question / recognition / reply / request / result / sense / statement / suggestion / testament / theory / view / wickedness 등	종속 접속사	–	–

■ 〈consider 동사의 쓰임〉 : 5형식인 경우(~을 …라고 생각하다)

consider	목적어	목적격보어
		as+보어
		(to be) 보어

근거1 'ET'에서 우리의 마음을 사로잡은 것은 기술적인 부분이 아니라 이야기이다.

ET: The Extraterrestrial / did not capture our hearts / (with its technologically advanced gadgets); / it / was the story / (that drew us in).

ET: The Extraterrestrial (S) 'ET: The Extraterrestrial'은 / did not capture (V) our hearts (O) 우리의 마음을 사로잡은 것이 아니다 / technologically 〈부사〉 advanced 〈과거분사〉 그것의 기술적으로 진보한 장치들로 / it (S) 그것은 / was (V) / the story S.C〈선행사〉 이야기였다 / that 〈주·관〉 drew (V) us (O) 우리를 빠져들게 한

'ET: The Extraterrestrial'은 그것의 기술적으로 진보한 장치들로 우리의 마음을 사로잡은 것이 아니었다. 우리를 빠져들게 한 것은 바로 그 이야기였다.

노트 ■ draw A in : A를 빠져들게 하다
■ capture A with B : A를 B로 사로잡다
■ 〈It be A that B 강조구문〉 : B한 것은 바로 A이다

It	be동사	강조하고 싶은 말	that (경우에 따라 아래처럼 바꿔 사용 가능)	
~~This~~ ~~That~~ ~~There~~	시제에 따라 달라짐	주어	관계대명사	who
		목적어		whom
		보어		which
		부사(구, 절)	관계부사	when
		〈동사는 사용 불가〉		where
It	was	the story	that ~	

■ 〈이어동사〉

타동사	명사	부사	(○)
타동사	부사	명사	(○)
타동사	대명사	부사	(○)
타동사	부사	대명사	(×)
drew	in	us	(×)

근거2 이 영화가 성공하기 위해 많은 비용을 들일 필요는 없다.

(While that movie did have / a pretty big budget), / my point / is {that it did not need / to have one / (in order to succeed)}.

While 〈종·접〉 that movie (S) did have (V) 그 영화가 들이긴 했지만 / a pretty big budget (O) 꽤 많은 비용을 / my point (S) 내 요점은 / is (V) / that 〈종·접〉 it (S) did not need (V) 많은 비용을 들일 필요가 없었다 / to have one (S.C) / one (O) 그것이 = a pretty big budget / in order to succeed 성공하기 위해서

그 영화가 꽤 많은 비용을 정말로 들이긴 했지만, 내 요점은 그것이 성공하기 위해 많은 비용을 들일 필요가 없었다는 것이다.

노트 ■ 〈동사 강조 표현〉

do / does / did	+동사원형(R)
=정말로(really, certainly)	

■ 〈what vs. that〉

	관계대명사(불완전한 문장)	접속사(완전한 문장)
what	○ 선행사를 포함하고 있기 때문에 what 앞에 선행사 불필요	×
that	○ that 앞에 선행사 필요	○

■ 〈need 용법〉

목적어(to R)		3형식	〈~할〉 필요가 있다, 〈~〉 해야 하다
목적어	목적격보어(to R)	5형식	〈남이〉 〈~해 줄〉 필요가 있다
동명사(Ring)		3형식	〈사람 · 물건이〉 〈~되어야 할〉 필요가 있다
목적어	목적격보어(p.p.)	5형식	〈~이〉 〈…될〉 필요가 있다, 〈~을〉 〈…되도록 할〉 필요가 있다

■ ~하기 위해서(긍정문)

주어	동사	목적		
		so that	주어	may(can, will) R
		in order that		
		in order to R		
		so as to R		
		to R		

주제문(재진술) 이야기가 좋으면 영화에 대해 큰 기대를 가질 수 있다.

You / should not be afraid / (to have great expectations) / (for your film) / {if you (*really*) believe in the story}.

You (S) 여러분은 / should not be (V) afraid (S.C) 두려워하지 않아야 한다 / 큰 기대를 갖는 것을 / 여러분의 영화에 대해 / if 〈종·접〉 you (S) believe in (V) the story (O) 만약 여러분이 '정말로' 이야기가 좋다고 생각한다면

여러분이 '정말로' 이야기가 좋다고 생각한다면 여러분의 영화에 대해 큰 기대를 갖기를 두려워하지 않아야 한다.

노트 ■ be afraid to R : ~하는 게 두렵다
■ have great expectations : 굉장한 유산이 굴러 들어올 것 같다
■ believe in : ~을 믿다

주제문(재진술) 영화 관련된 일을 하는 사람들이 당신의 이야기가 재밌다고 하면 급격한 인기를 얻을 수 있다.

Who knows, / (maybe) your story / is (a lot) more interesting / than you think, / and / {if people (at a film festival) / agree with this notion}, / (then) your story / could take off.

누가 아는가 / 어쩌면 여러분의 이야기가 your story (S) / is (V) 훨씬 더 재미있을지 / more interesting (S.C) / you (S) think (V) 여러분이 생각하는 것보다 / 그리고 / if 〈종·접〉 people (S) 만약 영화 축제에 있는 사람들이 / agree (V) 이러한 생각에 동의한다면 / your story (S) 여러분의 이야기는 / could take off (V) 급격히 인기를 얻을 수 있다

누가 아는가, 어쩌면 여러분의 이야기가 여러분이 생각하는 것보다 훨씬 더 재미있을지, 그리고 만약 영화 축제에 있는 사람들이 이러한 생각에 동의한다면 여러분의 이야기는 급격히 인기를 얻을 수 있다.

노트 ■ who know? : 아무도 몰라, 누가 알겠냐?
■ agree with : ~에 동의하다

■ take off : 급격히 인기를 얻다[유행하다]
■ 〈비교급 vs. 원급 강조〉 : 훨씬 더

비교급 강조 표현	원급 강조 표현
much, even, still, by far, far, a lot, lots, a great deal	very, so, quite, really, extremely, too

■ 〈감정과 관련된 완전타동사〉 : 분사화가 되어 주격보어/목적격보어 자리에 나올 때 구별법
• 2형식

주어	동사	주격보어(S.C)
사람		과거분사(p.p.) – 수동(되어진, ~ 당한)
사물		현재분사(Ring) – 능동(~하고 있는, 하는)
your story	is	interesting

▶ 다음 글의 요지로 가장 적절한 것은?
① 자전적 이야기는 영화의 좋은 소재가 된다.
② 영화의 성공에 가장 중요한 것은 이야기이다.
③ 공상과학 영화가 영화 산업의 발전을 이끌었다.
④ 사람들은 영화를 통해 다른 이의 삶을 경험한다.
⑤ 첨단 기술이 영화 속 내용을 현실로 만들고 있다.

정답 | ②
해설 | ② 이 글의 주제는 '영화에서 중요한 부분은 기술적인 부분이 아니라 이야기 부분이다'라는 것이다. 따라서 주제를 봤을 때, 이 글의 요지로 가장 적절한 것은 ②이다.
오답 | ① 이 글에서 자서전 이야기에 관한 내용은 존재하지 않는다.
③ 공상과학 영화인 'ET'가 영화 산업의 발전을 이끈 것은 사실이지만 이 글에서는 주제를 위한 하나의 근거일 뿐이다.
④ 사람들이 영화를 통해 다른 이의 삶을 경험한다는 내용은 존재하지 않는다.
⑤ 첨단 기술이 영화 속 내용을 현실로 만든다는 내용은 존재하지 않는다.

Words

☐ magic
☐ consider
☐ technical
☐ achievement
☐ filmmaker
☐ extraterrestrial
☐ capture
☐ gadget
☐ budget

Phrases

☐ tell a story
☐ be associated with
☐ capture A with B
☐ have great expectations
☐ who know?
☐ take off
☐ make a movie
☐ draw A in
☐ be afraid to R
☐ believe in
☐ agree with

우선순위 영단어

역대 수능 기출 + 전국 모의고사 기출 + EBS 기출 + 교과서 기출 빈출 어휘

단어	뜻	단어	뜻	단어	뜻
modify	v. 수정하다	molecule	n. 분자	monitor	v. 감시하다
motivation	n. 동기부여	mutual	a. 공유하고 있는	narrative	n. 이야기
nutrient	n. 영양소	object	n. 대상	observation	n. 관찰
obviously	ad. 분명히	opponent	n. 상대	preserve	v. 보존하다
prevent	v. 막다	professional	n. 전문가	prompt	a. 즉각적인
prospect	n. 기대	range	n. 영역	reaction	n. 반응
readily	ad. 쉽사리	recipient	n. 수혜자	reduce	v. 줄이다
regulate	v. 규제하다	reluctant	a. 싫어하는	remains	n. 유물
render	v. ~을 …하게 하다	sibling	n. 형제	state	v. 말하다
strain	n. 긴장하다	string	v. 끈	stroke	n. 뇌졸중
suggest	v. 암시하다	surgery	n. 외과 수술	victim	n. 희생양
accessible	a. 접근할 수 있는	adjustment	n. 적응	agenda	n. 안건
alternative	n. 대체	analogy	n. 유추	announce	v. 알리다

PRACTICE 02

변형문제

01 다음 글을 읽고, |조건|에 맞게 주어진 요지를 완성하시오.

| 조건 |
* (A), (B)는 각각 1단어로 쓸 것
* 본문에 있는 단어만을 사용할 것
* 필요한 경우, 문맥과 어법에 맞게 변형할 것

Everybody has a story that they have always wanted to tell, and making a movie is a good way to tell it. The word *magic* has always been associated with the film industry, and while some people consider the technical achievements of filmmakers to be the magic part of films, I am of the belief that the *story* part of a movie is the *real* magic. *ET: The Extraterrestrial* did not capture our hearts with its technologically advanced gadgets; it was the story that drew us in. While that movie did have a pretty big budget, my point is that it did not need to have one in order to succeed. You should not be afraid to have great expectations for your film if you *really* believe in the story. Who knows, maybe your story is a lot more interesting than you think, and if people at a film festival agree with this notion, then your story could take off.

⬇

The most essential factor to the (A) ____________ of the movie is the (B) ____________.

02 다음 글을 읽고, |조건|에 맞게 주어진 요약문을 완성하시오.

| 조건 |
* (A), (B), (C)는 각각 1단어로 쓸 것
* [보기]에서 선택한 단어를 한 번씩만 쓸 것
* 필요한 경우, 문맥과 어법에 맞게 변형할 것

[보기] programs / support / estimation / funds / devices / image / appeal / relevance / reality / encouragement

Everybody has a story that they have always wanted to tell, and making a movie is a good way to tell it. The word *magic* has always been associated with the film industry, and while some people consider the technical achievements of filmmakers to be the magic part of films, I am of the belief that the *story* part of a movie is the *real* magic. *ET: The Extraterrestrial* did not capture our hearts with its technologically advanced gadgets; it was the story that drew us in. While that movie did have a pretty big budget, my point is that it did not need to have one in order to succeed. You should not be afraid to have great expectations for your film if you *really* believe in the story. Who knows, maybe your story is a lot more interesting than you think, and if people at a film festival agree with this notion, then your story could take off.

⬇

Without massive (A) ____________, the movie named ET was successful not because of its high-tech (B) ____________, but because of its (C) ____________ story.

03 다음 글을 읽고, |조건|에 맞게 주어진 주제문을 완성하시오.

| 조건 |
* (A)는 1단어, (B), (C)는 2단어로 쓸 것
* [보기]에서 선택한 단어를 한 번씩만 쓸 것
* [보기]를 변형 없이 그대로 쓸 것

[보기] technologies / intriguing / emotional / financial / cutting-edge / sums / donation / resources / satisfactory / motivational

Everybody has a story that they have always wanted to tell, and making a movie is a good way to tell it. The word *magic* has always been associated with the film industry, and while some people consider the technical achievements of filmmakers to be the magic part of films, I am of the belief that the *story* part of a movie is the *real* magic. *ET: The Extraterrestrial* did not capture our hearts with its technologically advanced gadgets; it was the story that drew us in. While that movie did have a pretty big budget, my point is that it did not need to have one in order to succeed. You should not be afraid to have great expectations for your film if you *really* believe in the story. Who knows, maybe your story is a lot more interesting than you think, and if people at a film festival agree with this notion, then your story could take off.

⬇

As long as the story in a movie is (A) ____________, the success of that movie can be expected without massive (B) ____________ ____________ and (C) ____________ ____________.

04 다음 문장이 들어갈 부분으로 가장 적절한 곳을 고르시오.

While that movie did have a pretty big budget, my point is that it did not need to have one in order to succeed.

Everybody has a story that they have always wanted to tell, and making a movie is a good way to tell it. (①) The word *magic* has always been associated with the film industry, and while some people consider the technical achievements of filmmakers to be the magic part of films, (②) I am of the belief that the *story* part of a movie is the *real* magic. (③) *ET: The Extraterrestrial* did not capture our hearts with its technologically advanced gadgets; it was the story that drew us in. (④) You should not be afraid to have great expectations for your film if you *really* believe in the story. (⑤) Who knows, maybe your story is a lot more interesting than you think, and if people at a film festival agree with this notion, then your story could take off.

요지 · 주장

글의 논리	Spotlight
제목	인도의 소음공해의 법 제정의 필요성
주제	인도는 소음공해의 통제와 방지를 위한 적절한 법을 다양한 분야의 법률을 참조하여 재빠르게 만들어야 한다.

PRACTICE 03

008 어법 선택 & 연결어

In India, in the absence of a specific legislation for control and prevention of the noise pollution, one has to seek provisions in various branches of law and regulations. There **[has / have]** been no doubt **[what / that]** the available provisions in various branches of law **[is / are]** inadequate, unscientific and crude. In **[almost / most]** of the **[developing / developed]** countries specific legislation **[has made / has been made]** and scientific methods for investigation of noise pollution **[have invented / have been invented]**. (   ), there **[is / are]** no specific and **[detailing / detailed]** legislation to control the noise pollution. (   ), there **[is / are]** an urgent need **[what / that]** the Central Government of India **[should have managed / should manage]** to get a legislation **[passing / passed]** for the control of noise pollution. Some legislation **[regarding / regarded]** water and air pollution **[has made / has been made]** in India.

주제문 인도에는 소음공해의 통제와 방지를 위한 적절한 법이 없기 때문에 다양한 분야의 조항을 참고해야 한다.

(In India), / (in the absence of a specific legislation / (for control and prevention of the noise pollution), / one(S) has to seek(V) provisions(O) / (in various branches of law and regulations).

인도에서는 / 특별한 법이 없는 상황이므로 / 소음공해의 통제와 방지를 위한 / 우리는 조항을 찾아야만 한다 / 다양한 분야의 법률과 규정에서

인도에서는 소음공해의 통제와 방지를 위한 특별한 법이 없는 상황이므로 다양한 분야의 법률과 규정에서 (적절한) 조항을 찾아야만 한다.

노트
- in the absence of : ~ 없을 때에, 부재 시에
- legislation for : ~에 찬성하는 입법[법안]
- a branch of : ~의 분야

상황 그러나 다양한 분야에서의 법률과 규정은 부적절하고, 비과학적이며 미숙하다.

There has been(V〈현재완료〉) no doubt(S) / {that(〈종·접〉) the available provisions(S) / (in various branches of law) / are(V) inadequate(S.C₁), unscientific(S.C₂) and crude(S.C₃)}.

=〈동격〉: no doubt = that절

의심의 여지가 없다 / 활용 가능한 조항들이 / 다양한 분야의 법률과 규정에 있는 / 부적절하고, 비과학적이며, 미숙하다는

(그러나) 다양한 분야의 법률과 규정에 있는 활용 가능한 법 조항들이 부적절하고, 비과학적이며, 미숙하다는 것에는 의심의 여지가 없다.

노트
- no doubt : 분명 ~할 거다, ~라는 것에는 의심의 여지가 없다
- 〈There is 도치구문〉

긍정문	There	is	단수 주어	~이 있다
		are	복수 주어	

부정문	There	is no	단수 주어	~이 없다
		are no	복수 주어	

• 유도부사 **there**와 함께 도치구문을 이루는 be동사(is/are/was/were) 대신에 완전자동사 **appear**, **come**, **exist**, **follow**, **live**, **stand** 등을 사용할 수 있다.

■ 〈동격의 that〉 : ~라는 A(관계대명사 which/what 사용 불가)

추상명사 (A)	종속절(명사절 – 완전한 문장)		
	that	주어	동사 ~
answer / belief / chance / claim / conclusion / dream / evidence / extent / fact / faith / hope / idea / likelihood / news / notion / pledge / possibility / promise / proposal / question / recognition / reply / request / result / sense / statement / suggestion / testament / theory / view / wickedness 등	종속 접속사	–	–

대조 선진국에서는 소음공해에 대한 과학적인 방법들이 고안된다.

(In most of the developed(〈과거분사〉) countries) / specific(S) legislation / has been made(V〈현재완료 수동〉) / and scientific methods(S) / (for investigation) (of noise pollution) / have been invented(V〈현재완료 수동〉).

대부분의 선진국에서는 / 특별한 법 제정이 / 이루어졌고 / 과학적인 방법들이 / 소음공해의 조사를 위한 / 고안되었다

대부분의 선진국에서는 (소음공해를 다루는) 특별한 법 제정이 이루어졌고, 소음공해의 조사를 위한 과학적인 방법들이 고안되었다.

노트
- developed country : 선진국

■ 〈most / almost / mostly〉

	대명사	형용사	부사
most	대부분의 것들(사람들)	대부분의	가장
almost	–	–	거의
mostly	–	–	주로, 일반적으로

■ 〈수동태 시제〉

과거 수동	현재 수동	미래 수동
was/were p.p	am/is/are p.p	will be p.p
과거진행 수동	현재진행 수동	미래진행 수동
was/were being p.p	am/is/are being p.p	×
과거완료 수동	현재완료 수동	미래완료 수동
had been p.p	have/has been p.p	will have been p.p
과거완료진행 수동	현재완료진행 수동	미래완료진행 수동
×	×	×

주제문(설명) 인도에서는 소음공해를 위한 특별하고 상세한 법이 이루어지지 않았다.

(At present), there is no specific and detailed legislation
현재 / is: V / no specific and detailed legislation: S 특별하고 상세한 법률제정이 없다

/ (to control the noise pollution).
O 소음공해를 통제하기 위한

현재, (인도에는) 소음공해를 통제하기 위한 특별하고 상세한 법률제정이 이루어지지 않은 상태이다.

노트 ■ at present : 현재

주제문(강조) 인도 정부는 소음공해 통제를 위한 법률을 재빠르게 제정하고 통과시켜야 한다.

(However), / there is / an urgent need / {that the Central
그러나 / 있다 (V) / 긴박한 필요성이 (S) / =〈동격〉 that: 〈종·접〉 / the Central Government: S 인도 중앙정부가

Government (of India) / should manage to get a legislation
should manage: V / to get a legislation: O 법률을 제정해 통과시켜야 할

passed / (for the control of noise pollution)}.
소음공해의 통제를 위해

그러나 인도 중앙정부가 소음공해의 통제를 위해 법률을 제정해 통과시켜야 할 긴박한 필요성이 있다.

노트 ■ 〈목적어 자리에 to부정사를 취하는 완전타동사〉

주어	완전타동사	목적어
–	afford / agree / ask / attempt / care / choose / claim / dare / decide / demand / desire / determine / elect / expect / fail / guarantee / hope / intend / learn / manage / need / offer / plan / pretend / promise / refuse / resolve / seek / threaten / volunteer / want / wish 등	to 동사원형

■ 〈get 동사의 쓰임〉

get	목적어	〈목적격 보어〉	〈5형식〉	목적어와 목적격 보어의 관계
		과거분사	[물건을] ~하게 하다	수동
		형용사 / 현재분사	~을 (…의 상태가) 되게 하다	능동
		to R	[남에게] ~시키다	능동

상황 수질오염과 대기오염에 관한 일부 법률제정은 인도에서 이루어졌다.

Some legislation / (regarding water and air pollution)
S 일부 법률제정은 / 수질오염과 대기오염에 관한

/ has been made / (in India).
V〈현재완료 수동〉 이미 이루어졌다 / 인도에서

수질오염과 대기오염에 관한 일부 법률제정은 이미 인도에서 이루어졌다.

노트 ■ 〈~에 관해서는, ~의 점에서는〉

〈전치사〉		〈목적어 자리〉
regarding about concerning pertaining to as to as for in regard to(of) as regards with regard to	+	대명사 명사 동명사 관계대명사 what절 간접의문문(의문사+주어+동사)

■ 〈주격관계대명사+be동사 생략〉

명사	(주격관계대명사 +be동사)	
		Ring(현재분사) – 능동
		p.p.(과거분사) – 수동
		형용사
		부사
		명사
		전치사구
Some legislation	(which/that is)	regarding

▶ 다음 글에서 필자가 주장하는 바로 가장 적절한 것은?

① 인도 국민들에게 소음공해의 심각성을 알려야 한다.
② 인도에서의 소음공해를 규제할 법규 마련이 시급하다.
③ 개발도상국의 공해문제를 해결할 국제기구 창설이 필요하다.
④ 공해문제의 해결은 정부와 국민 간의 긴밀한 협조가 요구된다.
⑤ 각종 오염문제의 해결을 위해 과학적 조사가 이루어져야 한다.

정답 | ②

해설 | ② 이 글의 주제는 '인도에는 소음공해의 통제와 방지를 위한 적절한 법을 다양한 분야의 법률을 참조하여 재빠르게 만들어야 한다.'이다. 그리고 5번째 문장을 보면, 필자는 '인도 중앙정부가 소음공해의 통제를 위해 법률을 제정해 통과시켜야 할 긴박한 필요성이 있다.'고 말한다. 따라서 인도에서 소음공해를 규제할(소음공해의 통제를 위해) 법규 마련이 시급하다(법률을 제정해 통과시켜야 할 긴박한 필요성이 있다)는 ②가 적절하다.

오답 | ① 소음공해라는 소재는 맞지만 심각성을 알려야 한다는 관점이 다르다.
③ 국제기구 창설에 관련된 내용은 존재하지 않는다.
④ 공해문제의 해결이라는 소재는 맞지만 이를 위해 정부와 국민 간의 긴밀한 협조가 요구된다는 내용은 존재하지 않는다.
⑤ 오염문제의 해결이라는 소재는 맞지만 과학적 조사가 이루어져야 한다는 관점이 나오지 않는다.

Words

- ☐ absence
- ☐ developed country
- ☐ specific
- ☐ legislation
- ☐ control
- ☐ prevention
- ☐ pollution
- ☐ provision
- ☐ branch
- ☐ regulation
- ☐ doubt
- ☐ inadequate
- ☐ unscientific
- ☐ crude
- ☐ investigation
- ☐ invent
- ☐ detailed
- ☐ urgent
- ☐ need
- ☐ regarding

Phrases

- ☐ in the absence of
- ☐ a branch of
- ☐ at present
- ☐ legislation for
- ☐ no doubt

우선순위 영단어

역대 수능 기출 + 전국 모의고사 기출 + EBS 기출 + 교과서 기출 빈출 어휘

단어	뜻	단어	뜻	단어	뜻
apply	v. 응용하다	assessment	n. 평가	attempt	v. 시도하다
auditory	a. 청각의	combine	v. 결합하다	commercial	a. 상업적인
competitive	a. 경쟁력을 갖춘	complementary	a. 상호 보완적인	compromise	n. 타협
concentrate	v. 집중하다	confidence	n. 신임	conservative	a. 보수적인
consideration	n. 고려사항	consistently	ad. 일관하여	constant	변함없는
consume	v. 소비하다	crop	n. 농작물	disaster	n. 재앙
disperse	v. 흩어지다	display	v. 보여 주다	distinction	n. 차별
distinguish	v. 두드러지게 하다	district	n. 구역	ecosystem	n. 생태계
enclose	v. 동봉하다	enforce	v. 강요하다	entail	v. 수반하다
exert	v. (힘, 지식 등을) 쓰다	extract	v. 추출하다	float	v. 뜨다
foster	v. 기르다	genetic	a. 유전의	graze	v. (목초를) 먹다
hollow	a. 속이 빈	implement	v. 이행하다	inappropriate	a. 부적합한
independence	n. 독립	instruction	n. 지시	integrate	v. 통합시키다
integrity	n. 성실	investigate	v. 조사하다	involve	v. 연루시키다
irrelevant	a. 무관한	launch	v. 발사하다	manipulable	a. 다룰 수 있는
mass	n. 덩어리	matter	v. 중요하다	mold	n. 틀
motivate	v. 자극하다	navigate	v. 길을 찾다[방향을 읽다]	norm	n. 규범
nutrition	n. 영양소	operation	n. 사업	outcome	n. 결과
outlet	n. 배출	overcome	v. 극복하다	peer	v. 주의해서 보다
portrait	n. 초상화	precise	a. 정확한	predict	v. 예상하다
previously	ad. 이전에	principal	a. 주요한	qualify	v. 자격을 얻다
reasonable	a. 온당한	reference	n. ~에 대해 말하기	relevant	a. 관련된
rely on	v. 의존하다	reproduction	n. 번식	resolve	v. 결심하다
rewarding	a. (활동 등이) 보람 있는	sensory	a. 감각의	shrink	v. 줄어들다
slightly	ad. 약간	soar	v. 높이 날다	solution	n. 해결책

변형문제

01 다음 글을 읽고, |조건|에 맞게 필자의 주장을 완성하시오.

| 조건 |
* 10단어로 쓸 것
* [보기]에서 선택한 단어를 한 번씩만 쓸 것
* 필요한 경우, 문맥과 어법에 맞게 변형할 것

[보기] scientific / need / make / a / for / to / noise / regulate / legislation / urgent / pollution / research / detailed / investigation / developed

In India, in the absence of a specific legislation for control and prevention of the noise pollution, one has to seek provisions in various branches of law and regulations. There has been no doubt that the available provisions in various branches of law are inadequate, unscientific and crude. In most of the developed countries specific legislation has been made and scientific methods for investigation of noise pollution have been invented. At present, there is no specific and detailed legislation to control the noise pollution. However, there is an urgent need that the Central Government of India should manage to get a legislation passed for the control of noise pollution. Some legislation regarding water and air pollution has been made in India.

⬇

India ________ ________ ________ ________ ________ ________ ________ ________ ________ ________.

02 다음 글의 내용과 일치하지 않는 것은?

In India, in the absence of a specific legislation for control and prevention of the noise pollution, one has to seek provisions in various branches of law and regulations. There has been no doubt that the available provisions in various branches of law are inadequate, unscientific and crude. In most of the developed countries specific legislation has been made and scientific methods for investigation of noise pollution have been invented. At present, there is no specific and detailed legislation to control the noise pollution. However, there is an urgent need that the Central Government of India should manage to get a legislation passed for the control of noise pollution. Some legislation regarding water and air pollution has been made in India.

① 인도에는 소음공해의 통제와 방지를 위한 특별한 법이 없다.
② 인도의 다양한 분야의 법률과 규정에 있는 법 조항들은 비과학적이다.
③ 대부분의 선진국에서는 소음공해를 다루는 법 제정이 이루어졌다.
④ 선진국에서는 소음공해의 조사를 위한 과학적인 방법이 고안되었다.
⑤ 인도에서 수질오염과 대기오염에 관한 모든 법률 개정은 이루어졌다.

03 다음 글을 읽고, |조건|에 맞게 빈칸 (A), (B)를 채우시오.

| 조건 |

* (A), (B)는 1단어로 쓸 것
* [보기]에서 선택한 단어를 한 번씩만 쓸 것
* 필요한 경우, 문맥과 어법에 맞게 변형할 것

[보기] instead / regard / crude / unprofessional / with / absent / present / insufficient / unnecessary / terms / insignificant

In India, in the (A) ____________ of a specific legislation for control and prevention of the noise pollution, one has to seek provisions in various branches of law and regulations. There has been no doubt that the available provisions in various branches of law are inadequate, unscientific and (B) ____________. In most of the developed countries specific legislation has been made and scientific methods for investigation of noise pollution have been invented. At present, there is no specific and detailed legislation to control the noise pollution. However, there is an urgent need that the Central Government of India should manage to get a legislation passed for the control of noise pollution. Some legislation regarding water and air pollution has been made in India.

04 다음 글을 읽고, |조건|에 맞게 주어진 요약문을 완성하시오.

| 조건 |

* (A)는 1단어, (B)는 2단어, (C)는 1단어로 쓸 것
* 본문에 있는 단어만을 사용하되 그대로 쓸 것

In India, in the absence of a specific legislation for control and prevention of the noise pollution, one has to seek provisions in various branches of law and regulations. There has been no doubt that the available provisions in various branches of law are inadequate, unscientific and crude. In most of the developed countries specific legislation has been made and scientific methods for investigation of noise pollution have been invented. At present, there is no specific and detailed legislation to control the noise pollution. However, there is an urgent need that the Central Government of India should manage to get a legislation passed for the control of noise pollution. Some legislation regarding water and air pollution has been made in India.

⬇

A majority of developed nations enact a (A) ____________ associated with noise pollution and devise (B) ____________ ____________ for examining noise pollution, whereas India has not yet an efficient and effective (C) ____________ to regulate noise pollution.

목적

글의 논리	Cause & Effect (원인 & 결과)
제목	건물을 새로 증축한 것을 기념하기 위한 초대장
주제	노인 복지관의 새 증축의 완공에 대한 감사를 표한다.

수능 ANALYSIS

009 어법 선택 & 연결어

Dear Resident of Smalltown:

After ten long months of work, the **[beautiful new / new beautiful]** addition to the Smalltown Senior Center **[has been completed / has completed]**. This wonderful new space will serve as a library, conference room, and entertainment venue for our residents and the community. We think this lovely space — with skylights and **[oversizing / oversized]** windows — will also make a beautiful spot for functions such as weddings and parties. We have had tremendous support from the community in **[raising / rising]** funds for this project. To show our appreciation, we will have an open house on Sunday, January 21, from 1 to 4 P.M. We hope you **[join / will join]** us for cake and punch.

Sincerely,
Monica Diamond
Honorary Chairperson, Smalltown Senior Center

설명(원인) 10개월의 긴 공사 후에 노인 복지관의 새 증축이 완공되었다.

Dear Resident of Smalltown:
Smalltown 주민 여러분

(After ten long months of work), / the beautiful new addition (S) / (to the Smalltown Senior Center) / has been completed (V(현재완료 수동)).
10개월의 긴 공사 후에 / 아름다운 새 증축이 / Smalltown 노인 복지관의 / 완공되었습니다

10개월의 긴 공사 후에 Smalltown 노인 복지관의 아름다운 새 증축이 완공되었습니다.

노트
- an addition to : ~에 부가된 물건(사람)
- 〈혼동 어휘〉

	동사	형용사	명사	부사
complete	완수하다	완전한, 완벽한	–	–
completion	–	–	완성, 완수	–
competition	–	–	경쟁, 대회	–
competitor	–	–	경쟁자	
competence	–	–	능력, 자격	–
incompetence	–	–	무능력	–
complement	보완하다	–	보완, 보충	–
compliment	칭찬하다	–	칭찬	
complimentary	–	칭찬하는, 무료의	–	–
complimentarily	–	–	–	찬사로, 무료로
competitive	–	경쟁적인	–	–
competent	–	유능한, 적임의, 자격이 있는	–	–
completely	–	–	–	완전히, 전적으로
competitively	–	–	–	경쟁적으로
competently	–	–	–	유능하게

This wonderful new space (S) / will serve (V) / (as a library, conference room, and entertainment venue) / (for our residents and the community).
이 아름다운 새 공간은 / 역할을 할 것입니다 / 도서관, 회의실, 그리고 오락 장소로서의 / 우리 주민과 지역 사회를 위해

이 아름다운 새 공간은 우리 주민과 지역 사회를 위한 도서관, 회의실, 그리고 오락 장소로서의 역할을 할 것입니다.

노트
- serve as : ~의 역할을 하다
- 〈형용사의 어순〉

관사/지시사	수량	주관적	사실(객관적 형용사)							+ 명사
관사	수량	의견 (opinion)	크기 (size)	성질/모양 (shape)	상태	연령	색깔(색상) (color)	원천 (origin)	재료 (material)	소속/목적/종류 (purpose)	
this		wonderful			new						space

(that 종·접)

We (S) / think (V) / {this lovely space (S) / — (with (전치사) skylights (O₁) and oversized (p.p) windows (O₂)) / — will (also) make (V) / a beautiful (O) ...} (O)
우리는 생각합니다 / 이 아름다운 공간은 / 채광창과 큰 규모의 창문을 가진 / 또한 될 것이다 / 기능을 위한

spot (for functions) / (such as weddings and parties)}.

아름다운 장소가 결혼식이나 파티와 같은

채광창과 큰 규모의 창문을 가진 이 아름다운 공간은 또한 결혼과 파티와 같은 행사를 수행하기 위한 아름다운 장소가 될 것이라고 생각합니다.

노트 ■ A such as B : B와 같은 A
■ **〈목적격종속접속사 that 생략〉** : 완전타동사의 목적어로 사용된 경우 / 관계대명사 what 사용 불가

	종속절(명사절 : 목적어) (완전한 절)			
완전타동사	that	주어	동사	목적어
think	목적격종속접속사 – 생략 가능(~하는 것을)	this lovely space	will make	a beautiful spot ~

We / have had tremendous support / (from the community) / (in raising funds) / (for this project).
S V〈현재완료〉 O

우리는 엄청난 지원을 받았습니다 지역 사회로부터 기금 마련에 이 프로젝트를 위한

우리는 이 프로젝트를 위한 기금 마련에 지역 사회로부터 엄청난 지원을 받았습니다.

노트 ■ raise[collect] fund : 기금을 모집하다
■ 〈rise / raise / arise / arouse / rouse〉

원형	과거	과거분사	현재분사	뜻
rise	rose	risen	rising	vi. 오르다, 일어나다
raise	raised	raised	raising	vt. 올리다, 기르다
arise	arose	arisen	arising	vi. 발생하다, 기인하다
arouse	aroused	aroused	arousing	vt. (감정) 불러 일으키다, 자극하다
rouse	roused	roused	rousing	vt. 깨우다, 일으키다

주제문(결과) 완공을 기념으로 감사를 표하고자 공개를 한다.

(To show our appreciation), / we / will have an open house / (on Sunday, January 21), / (from 1 to 4 P.M.)
S V O

우리의 감사를 표하고자 우리는 공개일을 가질 것입니다 1월 21일 일요일 오후 1시에서 4시까지

우리의 감사를 표하고자 1월 21일 일요일 오후 1시에서 4시까지 공개일을 가질 것입니다.

노트 ■ from A to B : A에서 B까지

We / hope / (종·접 that) {you will join us / (for cake and punch)}.
S V S V O
O

우리는 바랍니다 여러분이 오셔서 즐기시기를 케이크와 펀치 음료를

오셔서 케이크와 펀치 음료를 즐기시기를 바랍니다.

노트 ■ **〈목적격종속접속사 that 생략〉** : 완전타동사의 목적어로 사용된 경우 / 관계대명사 what 사용 불가

	종속절(명사절 : 목적어) (완전한 절)			
완전타동사	that	주어	동사	목적어
hope	목적격종속접속사 – 생략 가능(~하는 것을)	you	will join	us

Sincerely,
Monica Diamond
Honorary Chairperson, Smalltown Senior Center

Monica Diamond 드림
Smalltown 노인 복지관 명예 의장

▶ **다음 글의 목적으로 가장 적절한 것은?**

① 노인 복지관의 시설 개선을 촉구하려고
② 노인 복지관 증축 공간 공개일에 초대하려고
③ 노인 복지관에 필요한 물품 기부를 요청하려고
④ 노인 복지관 보수 공사 사업 참여를 안내하려고
⑤ 새로 개장한 노인 복지관 프로그램을 소개하려고

정답 | ②

해설 | ② 이 글의 주제는 노인 복지관의 새 증축의 완공에 대한 감사를 표하는 것인데, 감사를 표하고자 노인 복지관을 공개를 한다고 하며 오셔서 케이크와 음료수를 즐기기를 바란다고 나온다. 따라서 이 글의 목적은 노인 복지관 증축 공간 공개일에 초대하는 것이다.

오답 | ① 노인 복지관은 시설 개선이 이미 완료되었기 때문에 목적으로 적절하지 않다.
③ 이 글에 물품 기부를 요청하는 말은 나오지 않는다.
④ 이 글에 노인 복지관 공사 사업 참여에 대한 안내말은 나오지 않는다.
⑤ 이 글에 노인 복지관 프로그램에 대한 말은 나오지 않는다.

Words

- ☐ resident
- ☐ addition
- ☐ complete
- ☐ serve
- ☐ conference
- ☐ entertainment
- ☐ venue
- ☐ community
- ☐ skylight
- ☐ function
- ☐ wedding
- ☐ tremendous
- ☐ support
- ☐ raise
- ☐ fund
- ☐ appreciation
- ☐ January
- ☐ punch
- ☐ honorary
- ☐ chairperson

Phrases

- ☐ an addition to
- ☐ A such as B
- ☐ from A to B
- ☐ serve as
- ☐ raise[collect] fund

우선순위 영단어

역대 수능 기출 + 전국 모의고사 기출 + EBS 기출 + 교과서 기출 빈출 어휘

단어	뜻	단어	뜻	단어	뜻
stock	n. 가게	subtle	a. 미묘한	succession	n. 연속
sufficient	a. 충분한	take advantage of	v. ~을 이용하다	toxic	a. 유독한
trait	n. 특성	valid	a. 유효한	variable	a. 가변적인
vital	a. 중요한	accommodate	v. 수용하다	account	n. 이야기
accuracy	n. 정확도	adolescence	n. 청년기	affect	v. 영향을 미치다
archaeological	a. 고고학적인	barrier	n. 울타리	biodiversity	n. 생물의 다양성
burst	v. 불쑥 움직이다	catastrophe	n. 참사	character	n. 인격
colony	n. (동물의) 집단	comment	n. 견해	committee	n. 위원회
companion	n. 동반자	compelling	a. 거부할 수 없는	concept	n. 개념
concern	v. ~에 관계하다	considerate	a. 배려하는	contact	n. 연락
cooperative	a. 협동의	corporate	a. 기업의	crush	v. 부수다
cue	n. 신호	descendant	n. 자손	description	n. 묘사
device	n. 장치	dilemma	n. 궁지	dimension	n. 차원
distraction	n. 정신이 흐트러짐	distress	n. 고통	due	a. 응당 치러져야 할
effective	a. 효과적인	emit	v. 내뿜다	employ	v. (사람을) 쓰다
engage	v. 고용하다	era	n. 시대	ethical	a. 윤리의
ethnic	a. 민족의	exceedingly	ad. 대단히	expectation	n. 기대
expert	n. 전문가	fine	a. 가느다란	gauge	v. 판단하다
go through	v. 경험하다	grasp	v. 움켜쥐다	ignore	v. 무시하다
illustration	n. 실례	immediate	a. 인접한	immense	a. 거대한
immersion	n. 몰입	indication	n. 지표	instantly	ad. 즉시
instructor	n. 교사	intellectual	n. 지식인	interruption	n. 방해
liquid	n. 액체	logical	a. 논리적인	master	n. 정통한 사람
modest	a. 평범한	multiply	v. 증가하다	notice	v. 알아채다
novel	n. 새로운	occasion	n. 경우	official	n. 공무원
offspring	n. 후예	overlook	v. 간과하다	passage	n. (문장, 연설의) 한 절
physical	n. 물리적	poison	n. 독살하다	presence	n. 존재
primarily	ad. 주로	primitive	a. 원시적인	procedure	n. 절차
random	a. 무작위의	reality	n. 현실	recovery	n. 복귀
reduction	n. 감소	regarding	~에 대하여	relieve	v. 경감하다
representation	n. 재현	representative	n. 대표자	reproduce	v. 번식하다
restriction	n. 제한	retirement	n. 은퇴	revenue	n. 소득
reverse	v. 반대로 하다	review	v. 재검토하다	routine	n. 일상적인
routinely	ad. 일상적으로	score	v. 점수를 매기다	shoot	v. 쏜살같이 통과하다
sign up for	등록하다	split	v. 쪼개다	spot	v. 목격하다
stability	n. 안정성	stack	v. 쌓아올리다	status	n. 지위
subjective	a. 주관적인	swap	v. 교체하다	take action	조치를 취하다
take on	덤벼들다	take up	v. 차지하다	temporary	a. 일시적인
temptation	n. 유혹	theme	n. 주제	thereby	ad. 그것에 의하여
urban	a. 도시의	verify	v. (진실인지) 확인하다	virtue	n. 덕목

변형문제

01 다음 글의 내용과 일치하지 않는 것은?

Dear Resident of Smalltown:

After ten long months of work, the beautiful new addition to the Smalltown Senior Center has been completed. This wonderful new space will serve as a library, conference room, and entertainment venue for our residents and the community. We think this lovely space — with skylights and oversized windows — will also make a beautiful spot for functions such as weddings and parties. We have had tremendous support from the community in raising funds for this project. To show our appreciation, we will have an open house on Sunday, January 21, from 1 to 4 P.M. We hope you'll join us for cake and punch.

Sincerely,
Monica Diamond
Honorary Chairperson, Smalltown Senior Center

① 노인 복지관의 새 증축이 완공되었다.
② 노인 복지관은 여러 가지 역할로 사용될 것이다.
③ 노인 복지관은 결혼과 파티와 같은 행사를 수행할 수도 있다.
④ 노인 복지관 증축을 위해 지역 사회로부터 지원을 받았다.
⑤ 노인 복지관은 감사를 표하고자 2월 21일에 공개를 할 것이다.

02 밑줄 친 부분 중 문맥상 옳지 않은 것은?

Dear Resident of Smalltown:

After ten long months of work, the beautiful new addition to the Smalltown Senior Center has been ① completed. This wonderful new space will ② serve as a library, conference room, and entertainment venue for our residents and the community. We think this lovely space — with skylights and oversized windows — will also make a beautiful spot for ③ functions such as weddings and parties. We have had ④ tiny support from the community in raising funds for this project. To show our appreciation, we will have an ⑤ open house on Sunday, January 21, from 1 to 4 P.M. We hope you'll join us for cake and punch.

Sincerely,
Monica Diamond
Honorary Chairperson, Smalltown Senior Center

03 다음 글의 요약문을 보고 빈칸 (A), (B)에 들어갈 말로 가장 적절한 것은?

Dear Resident of Smalltown:

After ten long months of work, the beautiful new addition to the Smalltown Senior Center has been completed. This wonderful new space will serve as a library, conference room, and entertainment venue for our residents and the community. We think this lovely space — with skylights and oversized windows — will also make a beautiful spot for functions such as weddings and parties. We have had tremendous support from the community in raising funds for this project. To show our appreciation, we will have an open house on Sunday, January 21, from 1 to 4 P.M. We hope you'll join us for cake and punch.

Sincerely,
Monica Diamond
Honorary Chairperson, Smalltown Senior Center

⬇

A Smalltown Senior Centor has been (A) ____________ and will be made public to thank those who have provided (B) ____________ support for it.

	(A)	(B)
①	finished	enormous
②	finished	tiny
③	completed	trivial
④	changed	enormous
⑤	changed	tiny

04 다음 글의 문장 중 무관한 문장을 고르시오.

Dear Resident of Smalltown:

After ten long months of work, the beautiful new addition to the Smalltown Senior Center has been completed. ① This wonderful new space will serve as a library, conference room, and entertainment venue for our residents and the community. ② This beautiful space will be charged for rent. ③ We think this lovely space — with skylights and oversized windows — will also make a beautiful spot for functions such as weddings and parties. ④ We have had tremendous support from the community in raising funds for this project. ⑤ To show our appreciation, we will have an open house on Sunday, January 21, from 1 to 4 P.M. We hope you'll join us for cake and punch.

Sincerely,
Monica Diamond
Honorary Chairperson, Smalltown Senior Center

목적

글의 논리	Cause & Effect (원인 & 결과)
제목	주문 건에 대한 발송 실수
주제	주문 건과 다르게 발송한 것에 대한 사과를 표하고 앞으로의 방안 대책을 설명한다.

PRACTICE 01

010 어법 선택 & 연결어

I understand how upset you **[must have been / must be]** when you discovered **[what / that]** our shipping office sent you the wrong order **[a little / a few]** days ago. Please **[accepting / accept]** my sincere apologies for that error. After investigating **[that / what]** caused the mistake, I **[found / founded]** **[what / that]** we have two H. Browns in our customer files; hence, the shipping office **[mistake / mistakenly]** sent you **[the other / another]** Mr. H. Brown's order. To ensure **[what / that]** we do not repeat this error, we will always include full first names on all paperwork and double-check the account numbers. Again, I apologize for the inconvenience we caused you. We will give a 15% discount on your next order.

설명(원인) 발송부서에서 잘못된 주문 건을 발송한 것에 대한 사과

I / understand / (how upset you must have been) /
S V 〈의문사〉 S.C S V — O
저는 이해합니다 당신이 얼마나 화가 나셨을지

[when you discovered / {that our shipping office / sent
〈종·접〉 S V 〈목·종〉 S V — O
당신이 발견했을 때 저희 발송부서가 당신께

you the wrong order / (a few days ago)}].
I.O D.O
잘못된 주문 건을 발송한 것을 며칠 전에

며칠 전에 저희 발송부서에서 잘못된 주문 건을 발송한 것을 알고 얼마나 화가 나셨을지 이해가 됩니다.

노트 ■ a few days ago : 수일 전에
■ 〈조동사+have+p.p.〉
• 과거 사실에 대한 추측

종류	뜻(의미)
may(might have p.p)	~이었을지도 모른다 (과거 사실에 대한 약한 추측)
must have p.p.	~이었음에 틀림이 없다 (과거 사실에 대한 강한 추측)
can not have p.p.	~이었을 리가 없다 (과거 사실에 대한 부정적인 추측)
could have p.p.	~할 수도 있었다 (과거 사실에 대한 아쉬움이나 가능성)
would have p.p.	~했을 것이다 (과거 사실에 대한 유감)

• 과거 사실에 대한 후회

종류	뜻
should (ought to) have p.p.	~했었어야 했는데 (하지 못했다)
need not have p.p.	~할 필요가 없었는데 (했다)
shouldn't have p.p.	~하지 말았어야 했는데 (했다)

■ 〈must have p.p. vs. should have p.p.〉

용법				뜻
당위성	should / must	R	–	~해야만 한다
과거 사실에 대한 후회	should	have	p.p.	~했었어야 했는데 (하지 못했다)
과거 사실에 대한 강한 추측	must	have	p.p.	~이었음에 틀림이 없다

■ 〈간접의문문 – 전치사의 목적어 자리에 사용되는 경우〉

타동사	목적어			
understand	〈간접의문문〉: 명사절			
	의문부사	주격보어	주어	동사
	how	upset	you	must have been

■ 〈what vs. that〉

	관계대명사(불완전한 문장)	접속사(완전한 문장)
what	○ 선행사를 포함하고 있기 때문에 what 앞에 선행사 불필요	×
that	○ that 앞에 선행사 필요	○

■ 〈few / a few / a little / little〉

수	few	거의 없는(부정)	+복수N+복수V
	a few	약간(긍정)	
양	a little	약간(긍정)	+단수N+단수V
	little	거의 없는(부정)	

(Please) accept / my sincere apologies / (for that error).
V O
받아주시기를 바랍니다 저의 진심 어린 사과를 이 잘못에 대한

이 잘못에 대한 저의 진심 어린 사과를 받아주시기를 바랍니다.

노트 ■ accept an apology : 사죄를 받아들이다
■ 〈직접명령문〉

긍정문	R	~해라
	Please+R	~해 주세요

부정문	Don't+R	~하지 마라
	Never+R	

설명(원인에 대한 이유) 잘못된 주문 건을 발송한 이유

{After investigating / (what caused the mistake)}, / I / found / {that we have two H. Browns / (in our customer files)}; / (hence), / the shipping office / (mistakenly) sent / you the other Mr. H. Brown's order.

조사한 후 / 실수를 야기한 것을 / 저는 / 알게 되었습니다 / 두 분의 H. Brown 씨가 계시다는 것을 / 저희의 고객 명단에 / 따라서 / 저희 발송부서는 / 잘못 발송했습니다 / 당신에게 다른 H. Brown 씨의 주문 건을

실수의 원인을 조사한 후, 저는 저희의 고객 명단에 두 분의 H. Brown 씨가 계시다는 것을 알게 되었습니다. 따라서, 저희 발송부서는 귀하께 다른 H. Brown 씨의 주문 건을 잘못 발송한 것입니다.

노트 ■ 〈동명사의 목적어로 사용된 주격관계대명사 what〉 : 선행사가 필요한 주격 관계대명사 that 사용 불가

		주격관계대명사절(명사절 : 동명사의 목적어)				
전치사	동명사	~~선행사~~	what	~~주어~~	타동사	목적어
After	investigating		선행사를 포함한 관계대명사 (=the thing(s) which/that ~) : ~하는 것은/이		caused	the mistake

■ 〈find / found〉

원형	과거	과거분사	현재분사	뜻
find	found	found	finding	v. 발견하다, 알다
found	founded	founded	founding	v. 설립하다

■ 〈what vs. that〉

	관계대명사(불완전한 문장)	접속사(완전한 문장)
what	○ 선행사를 포함하고 있기 때문에 what 앞에 선행사 불필요	×
that	○ that 앞에 선행사 필요	○

■ 〈the other vs. another〉

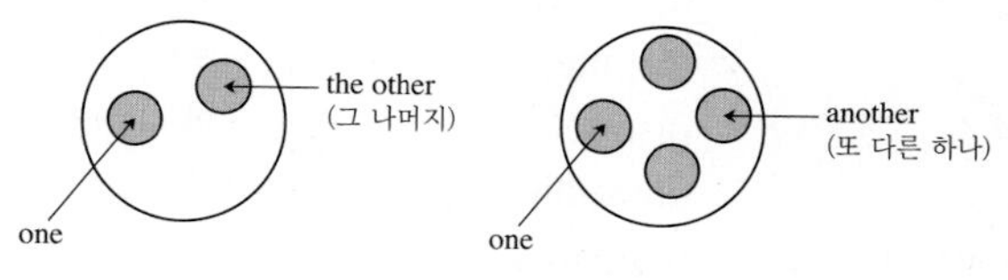

주제문(결과) 모든 서류에 완전한 이름을 포함시키고 계정 번호를 두 번 확인할 것이다.

{To ensure / (that we do not repeat this error)}, / we / will (always) include / full first names / (on all paperwork) / and double-check the account numbers.

확실히 하기 위해 / 이러한 잘못이 반복되지 않도록 / 저희는 / 항상 포함시키고 / 완전한 이름을 / 모든 서류에 / 계정 번호를 두 번 확인하겠습니다

이러한 잘못이 반복되지 않도록 확실히 하기 위해, 저희는 모든 서류에 항상 완전한 이름을 포함시키고 계정 번호를 두 번 확인할 것입니다.

노트 ■ 〈빈도부사의 위치〉

be동사 / 조동사	+	빈도부사	+	일반동사
		always(100%)		
		usually(60% ~ 80%)		
		often(50% ~ 60%)		
		sometimes(40%)		
		seldom / hardly / rarely(20%)		
		never(0%)		

설명(결과) 발송부서에서 잘못된 주문 건을 발송한 것에 대한 사과

(Again), / I apologize / (for the inconvenience) / (we caused you).

다시 한 번 / 사과드립니다 / 불편에 대해 / 저희가 끼친

다시 한 번 저희가 끼친 불편에 대해 사과드립니다.

노트 ■ apologize for : ~에 대해 사과하다
■ 〈목적격관계대명사 that 생략〉 : 수여동사의 간접목적어가 없는 경우 / 선행사를 포함하고 있는 관계대명사 what 사용 불가

	〈목적격관계대명사절〉				
선행사	목적격관계대명사	주어	수여동사	간접목적어	~~직접목적어~~
the inconvenience	생략 가능 : (that)	we	caused	you	

We / will give a 15% discount / (on your next order).

우리는 / 15퍼센트를 할인해드리겠습니다 / 다음번 구매 시

다음번 구매 시 15퍼센트를 할인해드리도록 하겠습니다.

▶ 다음 글의 목적으로 가장 적절한 것은?

① 물품 구매 시 할인 정보를 홍보하려고
② 제품에 결함이 발생한 이유를 해명하려고
③ 회사의 물품 배송 실수에 대해 사과하려고
④ 회사의 고객 개인 정보 보호 방침을 알리려고
⑤ 구매자의 성과 이름을 모두 기입할 것을 당부하려고

정답 | ③

해설 | ③ 이 글의 첫 두 문장을 보면 잘못 발송한 이야기를 하며 그에 대한 사과를 하고 있으므로 ③이 적절하다.

오답 | ① 물품 구매 시 할인 정보를 홍보하는 것이 아니라 사과의 목적으로 할인을 제공하는 것이다.
② 제품의 결함이 아닌 배송 실수에 대해 사과하고 있다.
④ 고객 정보 보호 방침에 관한 내용은 나오지 않는다.
⑤ 구매자의 성과 이름을 모두 기입할 것을 당부하는 것이 아니라 사과를 하며 다음부터는 실수를 하지 않기 위해 기입할 것이라고 설명하는 것이다.

Words

- ☐ upset
- ☐ discover
- ☐ shipping office
- ☐ order
- ☐ accept
- ☐ sincere
- ☐ apology
- ☐ error
- ☐ investigate
- ☐ mistake
- ☐ customer
- ☐ hence
- ☐ ensure
- ☐ repeat
- ☐ include
- ☐ paperwork
- ☐ double-check
- ☐ account
- ☐ inconvenience
- ☐ discount

Phrases

- ☐ a few days ago
- ☐ apologize for
- ☐ accept an apology

우선순위 영단어 역대 수능 기출 + 전국 모의고사 기출 + EBS 기출 + 교과서 기출 빈출 어휘

단어	뜻	단어	뜻	단어	뜻
voyage	v. 여행하다	weigh	v. 무게[체중]가 ~이다	witness	n. 증인
absorb	v. 흡수하다	accommodation	n. 숙박 설비	accumulate	v. 쌓이다
additional	a. 추가의	after all	어쨌든	ambiguous	a. 불명확한
apparent	a. ~인 것처럼 보이는	appliance	n. 기구	appreciation	n. 이해
article	n. 글	atmosphere	n. 분위기	attach	v. 붙이다
attain	v. 이루다	audience	n. 관객	be aware of	~을 알다
beneficial	a. 유익한	biological	a. 생물학의	breakthrough	n. 돌파구
calculate	v. 계산하다	capital	n. 자본	cause	n. 대의명분
cease	v. 그만두다	celebrate	v. 공표하다	celebrity	n. 유명인
circulation	n. 순환	come about	일어나다	commission	n. 의회
concentration	n. 집중	concerning	a. ~에 관한	confrontation	n. 대립
considerably	ad. 상당히	consist of	~로 구성되다	construct	v. 건설하다
convenient	a. 편리한	cope with	~에 잘 대처하다	critic	n. 비평가
currency	n. 널리 통용되는 것	decay	n. 부식	defeat	v. ~를 이기다
deliberately	ad. 고의로	dense	a. 밀도가 높은	department	n. 부서
deposit	v. 축적하다	depression	n. 불경기	descend	v. 내려가다
desperately	ad. 필사적으로	detect	v. 감지하다	deteriorate	v. 악화되다
diagnose	v. 진단하다	direction	n. 방향	dispute	v. 논쟁하다
disruption	n. 파괴	distort	v. 왜곡하다	distract	v. 주의를 딴데로 돌리다
disturbance	n. 장애	domain	n. 영역	domestic	a. 가정의
donation	n. 기부금	drain	v. 고갈시키다	dramatically	ad. 극적으로
elaborate	a. 공들인	elicit	v. 이끌어내다	empower	v. 권한을 부여하다
evaporate	v. 증발하다	evoke	v. (감정, 기억을) 불러내다	excess	n. 과잉
exhausted	a. 기진맥진한	expenditure	n. 지출 비용	exploit	v. 이용하다
explore	v. 탐험하다	exposure	n. 노출	exterior	a. 외부의
external	a. 외부의	extremely	ad. 지나치게	faculty	n. 교수단
fairly	ad. 상당히	fascinating	a. 황홀하게 하는	federal	a. 연방의

변형문제

01 다음 글의 내용과 일치하지 않는 것은?

I understand how upset you must have been when you discovered that our shipping office sent you the wrong order a few days ago. Please accept my sincere apologies for that error. After investigating what caused the mistake, I found that we have two H. Browns in our customer files; hence, the shipping office mistakenly sent you the other Mr. H. Brown's order. To ensure that we do not repeat this error, we will always include full first names on all paperwork and double-check the account numbers. Again, I apologize for the inconvenience we caused you. We will give a 15% discount on your next order.

① 발송부서에서 물건을 잘못 발송했다.
② 실수의 원인은 명단에 같은 이름의 사람이 있었던 것이다.
③ 실수가 발생하지 않도록, 모든 서류에 완전한 이름을 포함시키려 한다.
④ 실수가 발생하지 않도록, 계정 번호를 한 번에 확실히 확인할 것이다.
⑤ 다음번 구매 시 15%를 할인해 줄 것이다.

02 밑줄 친 부분 중 문맥상 옳지 않은 것은?

I understand how ① happy you must have been when you discovered that our shipping office sent you the wrong order a few days ago. Please ② accept my sincere apologies for that error. After investigating what caused the ③ mistakes, I found that we have two H. Browns in our customer files; hence, the shipping office mistakenly sent you the other Mr. H. Brown's order. To ensure that we do not repeat this ④ error, we will always include full first names on all paperwork and double-check the account numbers. Again, I ⑤ apologize for the inconvenience we caused you. We will give a 15% discount on your next order.

03 다음 문장이 들어갈 부분으로 가장 적절한 곳을 고르시오.

> To ensure that we do not repeat this error, we will always include full first names on all paperwork and double-check the account numbers.

(①) I understand how upset you must have been when you discovered that our shipping office sent you the wrong order a few days ago. (②) Please accept my sincere apologies for that error. (③) After investigating what caused the mistake, I found that we have two H. Browns in our customer files; hence, the shipping office mistakenly sent you the other Mr. H. Brown's order. (④) Again, I apologize for the inconvenience we caused you. (⑤) We will give a 15% discount on your next order.

04 다음 글의 문장 중 무관한 문장을 고르시오.

I understand how upset you must have been when you discovered that our shipping office sent you the wrong order a few days ago. ① Please accept my sincere apologies for that error. ② After investigating what caused the mistake, I found that we have two H. Browns in our customer files; hence, the shipping office mistakenly sent you the other Mr. H. Brown's order. ③ It is not our responsibility to be mislaid. ④ To ensure that we do not repeat this error, we will always include full first names on all paperwork and double-check the account numbers. ⑤ Again, I apologize for the inconvenience we caused you. We will give a 15% discount on your next order.

목적

글의 논리	Cause & Effect (원인 & 결과)
제목	만족스럽지 못한 식사에 대한 불만
주제	식당에서 만족스럽지 못한 식사를 하여 불만을 제기한다.

PRACTICE 02

011 어법 선택 & 연결어

Dear Ma and Pa:

I recently dined at your restaurant, and I had an **[interested / interesting]** experience. I **[had heard / heard]** only good things about your establishment, so I decided **[trying / to try] [out it / it out]** for myself. **[Little I know / Little did I know]** my meal would turn out to be so bad. I ordered the *hungry man's special*. The special included a large helping of **[mashing / mashed]** potatoes. I began eating and after only one large bite of the potatoes, I **[found / founded]** huge lumps in my food. The gravy was cold, and the chicken was greasy. Your restaurant has a good reputation, and I wish only good things for you in the future, but I **[did want / did to want]** you to know about **[my / I] [dinning / dine]** experience. I left your restaurant **[felt / feeling] [hungry / hungrily]** and upset. That's not the way I thought a customer should feel after dining at Ma and Pa's Kettle.

Sincerely,
Gail James

원인 만족스럽지 못한 식사를 한 이유

Dear Ma and Pa:

Ma and Pa 식당 측에게

I(S: 저는) / (recently) dined(V: 최근에 식사를 했습니다) / (at your restaurant)(당신들이 운영하는 식당에서), / and(그리고) / I(S: 저는) / had(V) an interesting〈현재분사〉 experience(O: 재미있는 경험을 했습니다).

저는 최근에 당신들이 운영하는 식당에서 식사를 했는데, 재미있는 경험을 했습니다.

노트 ■ 〈분사의 역할 및 종류〉

분사의 역할	형용사	명사 수식	전치 수식
			후치 수식
		보어 사용	주격보어
			목적격보어
분사의 종류	현재분사(Ring)	능동	~하는, ~하고 있는
	과거분사(p.p.)	수동	~되는, ~ 당하는, 이미 된

I(S: 저는) / had heard(V〈과거완료〉) only good things(O: 좋은 점만을 들었습니다) / (about your establishment)(당신들의 시설에 대해), / so(그래서) / I(S: 저는) / decided(V: 결정했습니다) / to try it out(O: 그것을 시험 삼아 이용해 보기로) / (for myself〈재귀대명사〉)(직접).

당신들의 시설에 대해 좋은 점만을 들어서 시험 삼아 직접 그곳을 이용해 보기로 했습니다.

노트 ■ try A out : A를 테스트 해 보다
■ for oneself : 스스로

■ 〈목적어 자리에 to부정사를 취하는 완전타동사〉

주어	완전타동사	목적어
–	afford / agree / ask / attempt / care / choose / claim / dare / decide / demand / desire / determine / elect / expect / fail / guarantee / hope / intend / learn / manage / need / offer / plan / pretend / promise / refuse / resolve / seek / threaten / volunteer / want / wish 등	to 동사원형

■ 〈이어동사〉

타동사	명사	부사	(○)
타동사	부사	명사	(○)
타동사	대명사	부사	(○)
타동사	부사	대명사	(×)
try	out	it	(×)

■ 〈재귀대명사 vs. 대명사〉

주어	~	주어와 다름	주어와 동일
		대명사	재귀대명사
I		me	myself

Little〈부정어〉 did〈조동사〉 I(S) know(V: 저는 거의 알지 못했습니다) / (종·접 that) (my meal(S: 제 식사가) / would turn out(V) to be so bad(S.C)(O: 아주 형편없는 것으로 밝혀지리라는 것을)).

저는 제 식사가 아주 형편없는 것으로 밝혀지리라는 것을 전혀 알지 못했습니다.

노트 ■ turn out to be : ~임이 밝혀지다

■ 〈부정어구 문두 도치〉

부정어(구)	〈도치〉		
Never / Seldom / Rarely / Scarcely / Hardly / No / Only / Little / Few / Nor 등	조동사	주어	동사원형
	have / has / had	주어	p.p.
	do(does/did)	주어	동사원형
	be동사	주어	−
Little	did	I	know

■ 〈목적격종속접속사 that 생략〉 : 완전타동사의 목적어로 사용된 경우 / 관계대명사 what 사용 불가

	종속절(명사절 : 목적어) (완전한 절)		
완전타동사	that	주어	동사
know	목적격종속접속사 – 생략 가능(~하는 것을)	my meal	would turn out

I / ordered / the *hungry man's special*.
S V O
저는 주문했습니다 'hungry man's special'을

저는 'hungry man's special'을 주문했습니다.

The special / included / a large helping / (of mashed potatoes).
S V O 〈과거분사〉
그 특별 메뉴에는 포함했습니다 아주 많은 양의 으깬 감자 한 그릇을

그 특별 메뉴에는 아주 많은 양의 으깬 감자 한 그릇이 포함되어 있었습니다.

노트 ■ helping : (식사 때 한 사람 몫으로 덜어 주는 음식의) 양[그릇] (=serving)
■ mashed potato : 으깬 감자

I / began eating / and / (after only one large bite of the potatoes), / I / found huge lumps / (in my food).
S V O
저는 먹기 시작했습니다 그리고 감자를 단 한 입 크게 물고 난 후에 저는 매우 커다란 덩어리가 있음을 알게 되었습니다 제 음식에서
S V O

저는 먹기 시작했는데, 감자를 단 한 입 크게 물고 난 후에 제 음식에 매우 커다란 덩어리가 있음을 알게 되었습니다.

노트 ■ a bite of : ~의 한 입
■ 〈3형식에서 목적어 자리에 to R/Ring 둘 다 사용 가능〉

	완전타동사		목적어
주어	begin	~을 시작하다	to R/Ring (의미 차이 없음)
	cease	~을 중단하다	
	continue	~을 계속하다	
	deserve	~할 가치/자격/권리가 있다	
	dislike	~을 싫어하다	
	hate		
	like	~을 좋아하다	
	love	~을 사랑하다	
	neglect	~하는 것을 소홀히 하다	
	prefer	~쪽을 좋아하다	
	require	~을 요구하다	
	start	~을 시작하다	

■ 〈find / found〉

원형	과거	과거분사	현재분사	뜻
find	found	found	finding	v. 발견하다, 알다
found	founded	founded	founding	v. 설립하다

The gravy / was cold, / and / the chicken / was greasy.
S V S.C S V S.C
그레이비는 차가웠습니다 그리고 닭고기는 기름투성이였습니다

그레이비는 차가웠으며 닭고기는 기름투성이였습니다.

주제문(결과) 그 식사로 인해 기분이 언짢아서 불만을 제기

Your restaurant / has a good reputation, / and / I / wish only good things / (for you) / (in the future), / but / I did want / you to know / (about my dining experience).
S V O S V O
당신들의 식당은 좋은 평판을 얻고 있습니다 그리고 저는 좋은 일들만이 일어나기를 바랍니다 당신들에게 미래에 하지만 저는
S V O O.C 〈전치사〉 〈의·주〉 〈동명사〉
원했습니다 당신들이 알아주기시기를 제가 식사를 하면서 했던 경험에 대해

당신들의 식당은 좋은 평판을 얻고 있으며 당신들에게 장래에 좋은 일들만이 일어나기를 바라지만, 저는 당신들이 제가 식사를 하면서 했던 경험에 대해 알아주시기를 정말로 원했습니다.

노트 ■ know about : ~에 대하여 알고[듣고] 있다
■ 〈want의 용법〉

주어	want	목적어(to R)		주어가 ~하는 것을 원하다	3형식
		목적어	목적격보어 (to R)	주어는 목적어가 ~하는 것을 원하다	5형식

I / left your restaurant / (feeling hungry and upset).
S V O S.C1 S.C2 〈분사구문〉
저는 당신들의 식당을 떠났습니다 배고프고 기분이 언짢은 채

저는 배고프고 기분이 언짢은 채 당신들의 식당을 떠났습니다.

노트 ■ 〈부대상황 – 연속동작〉

주어	동사	대등접속사	주어	동사
I	left	and	I	feel
		(and I) 생략 → feeling ~ (부대상황 : 연속동작)		

■ 〈감각동사〉

감각동사	주격보어(S.C)	
feel, look, seem, sound, taste, appear, smell	형용사(분사 : 현재분사/과거분사)	
	명사	
	like(전치사)	(that)+주어+동사
		(동)명사
	~~alike~~	
	~~likely~~	

That / is not the way / [(I thought) / a customer / should
S V S.C S V S V
그것은 모습이 아닙니다 제가 생각하기에 고객이 느껴야만
〈삽입절〉
(~~how~~)

feel / {after dining / (at Ma and Pa's Kettle)}].

하는 / 식사 후에 〈동명사〉 / Ma and Pa's Kettle에서

제가 생각하기에 그것이 Ma and Pa's Kettle에서 고객이 식사 후에 느껴야 하는 모습은 아닙니다.

노트 ■ 〈관계부사〉 : how 대신에 사용되는 that은 관계부사 대용어라고 함

용도	선행사	관계부사	전치사+관계대명사
시간	the time	when	in/at/on+which
장소	the place	where	in/at/on+which
이유	the reason	why	for which
방법	(the way)	how	in which
	the way how는 같이 사용 못함, the way, the way in which, the way that은 사용 가능		

■ 〈관계부사 how절 안에서의 삽입절〉

	〈관계부사 how절〉				
the way	~~how~~	I	thought	a customer	should feel
		〈삽입절〉		주어	동사

Sincerely,
Gail James

Sincerely,
Gail James 드림

▶ 다음 글의 목적으로 가장 적절한 것은?

① 식당 종업원의 불친절에 항의하려고
② 식당의 성공 비결을 알려 줄 것을 부탁하려고
③ 고객의 취향에 맞는 메뉴 개발을 식당에 제안하려고
④ 재료의 신선도가 음식의 질을 결정함을 강조하려고
⑤ 주문한 음식이 형편없었다는 것을 식당 측에 알리려고

정답 | ⑤

해설 | ⑤ 이 글의 주제는 식당에 만족스럽지 못한 식사를 하여 불만을 제기하는 것이다. 전체적인 흐름을 보면 그 원인을 설명하고 불만을 제기하는 식으로 나타나 있다. 그 원인으로 주문한 음식의 질이 상당히 좋지 않았다. 따라서 목적으로 가장 적절한 것은 ⑤이다.

오답 | ① 식당에 항의하는 관점은 맞지만 이 글의 소재는 식당 종업원의 불친절이 아니라 형편없는 음식이다.
② 식당의 성공 비결을 알려 줄 것을 부탁하는 내용은 나오지 않는다.
③ 고객의 취향에 맞는 메뉴 개발을 식당에 제안하는 내용은 나오지 않는다.
④ 음식의 질이라는 소재는 나오지만 재료의 신선도가 결정한다는 내용은 나오지 않는다.

Words

☐ recently ______
☐ restaurant ______
☐ establishment ______
☐ decide ______
☐ meal ______
☐ include ______
☐ mashed potato ______
☐ bite ______
☐ lump ______
☐ gravy ______
☐ greasy ______
☐ reputation ______

Phrases

☐ try A out ______
☐ turn out to be ______
☐ know about ______
☐ for oneself ______
☐ a bite of ______

우선순위 영단어 역대 수능 기출+전국 모의고사 기출+EBS 기출+교과서 기출 빈출 어휘

단어	뜻	단어	뜻	단어	뜻
former	a. 이전의	frequent	a. 빈번한	frustration	n. 좌절
gain	n. 증가	garment	n. 옷	grab	v. 쥐다
handle	v. 다루다	hinder	v. 방해하다	improve	v. 발전하다
in charge of	~을 관리[지배]하고 있는	in favor of	~을 선호하여	inadequate	a. 불충분한
individual	a. 개개의	induce	v. 권유하다	inevitably	ad. 불가피하게
inferior	a. (품질이) 열등한	inherent	a. 타고난	initially	ad. 처음에는
insignificant	a. 하찮은	insulation	n. 단열	integral	a. 필수의
intimacy	n. 친분	invariably	ad. 항상	investigation	n. 조사
isolate	v. 격리시키다	lower	v. 낮추다	management	n. 취급
manufacturer	n. 제조업자	medieval	a. 중세의	merely	ad. 한낱

PRACTICE 02

변형문제

01 다음 글의 필자가 드러낸 분위기로 가장 적절한 것은?

Dear Ma and Pa:

I recently dined at your restaurant, and I had an interesting experience. I had heard only good things about your establishment, so I decided to try it out for myself. Little did I know my meal would turn out to be so bad. I ordered the *hungry man's special*. The special included a large helping of mashed potatoes. I began eating and after only one large bite of the potatoes, I found huge lumps in my food. The gravy was cold, and the chicken was greasy. Your restaurant has a good reputation, and I wish only good things for you in the future, but I did want you to know about my dining experience. I left your restaurant feeling hungry and upset. That's not the way I thought a customer should feel after dining at Ma and Pa's Kettle.

Sincerely,
Gail James

① happy ② sleepy ③ fascinated
④ displeased ⑤ scary

02 다음 글의 문장 중 무관한 문장을 고르시오.

Dear Ma and Pa:

I recently dined at your restaurant, and I had an interesting experience. I had heard only good things about your establishment, so I decided to try it out for myself. Little did I know my meal would turn out to be so bad. I ordered the *hungry man's special*. The special included a large helping of mashed potatoes. ① I began eating and after only one large bite of the potatoes, ② I found huge lumps in my food. ③ The gravy was cold, and the chicken was greasy. ④ The food in the restaurant was fantastic. ⑤ Your restaurant has a good reputation, and I wish only good things for you in the future, but I did want you to know about my dining experience. I left your restaurant feeling hungry and upset. That's not the way I thought a customer should feel after dining at Ma and Pa's Kettle.

Sincerely,
Gail James

03 다음 글의 순서로 가장 적절한 것은?

Dear Ma and Pa:

I recently dined at your restaurant, and I had an interesting experience. I had heard only good things about your establishment, so I decided to try it out for myself. Little did I know my meal would turn out to be so bad.

(A) I ordered the *hungry man's special*. The special included a large helping of mashed potatoes. I began eating and after only one large bite of the potatoes, I found huge lumps in my food.

(B) The gravy was cold, and the chicken was greasy. Your restaurant has a good reputation, and I wish only good things for you in the future, but I did want you to know about my dining experience.

(C) I left your restaurant feeling hungry and upset. That's not the way I thought a customer should feel after dining at Ma and Pa's Kettle.

Sincerely,
Gail James

① (A) - (B) - (C)　② (A) - (C) - (B)　③ (B) - (C) - (A)
④ (C) - (A) - (B)　⑤ (C) - (B) - (A)

04 다음 문장이 들어갈 부분으로 가장 적절한 곳을 고르시오.

Your restaurant has a good reputation, and I wish only good things for you in the future, but I did want you to know about my dining experience.

Dear Ma and Pa:

I recently dined at your restaurant, and I had an interesting experience. I had heard only good things about your establishment, so I decided to try it out for myself. Little did I know my meal would turn out to be so bad. I ordered the *hungry man's special*. (①) The special included a large helping of mashed potatoes. (②) I began eating and after only one large bite of the potatoes, I found huge lumps in my food. (③) The gravy was cold, and the chicken was greasy. (④) I left your restaurant feeling hungry and upset. (⑤) That's not the way I thought a customer should feel after dining at Ma and Pa's Kettle.

Sincerely,
Gail James

목적

글의 논리	Cause & Effect (원인 & 결과)
제목	Alice Jenkins를 위한 추천서
주제	Alice Jenkins를 수석 손해 사정사 자리에 고려하도록 추천한다.

012 어법 선택 & 연결어

Dear Alan Smith:

I'm happy to be **[written / writing]** this letter for Ms. Jenkins. Alice Jenkins would make an **[outstanded / outstanding]** senior claims adjuster at Insurance Partners, and I would encourage you **[considering / to consider]** her for the position. I first met Alice when she came to Protect-All Insurance as a new claims adjuster. She reported **[direct / directly]** to me for the three years of her tenure with that company until 2015, when I retired. In the first three years I followed Alice's career, I watched her **[to become / become]** one of the **[almost / most]** knowledgeable problem-solvers in the company. **[While / During]** these three years, she handled fire, earthquake, and flood insurance **[most / almost]** **[exclusive / excusively]**. In my professional opinion, Alice is ready for more responsibility and challenge in her profession and I feel **[confidently / confident]** she will be an asset to your company.

Yours truly,
Della Johnson

주제문(결과) Alice Jenkins를 수석 손해 사정사 자리에 고려하는 것에 대한 추천

Dear Alan Smith:
Alan Smith에게

I (S, 저는) / am (V) happy (S.C, 기쁩니다) / (to be writing this letter (O) 이 편지를 쓰게 되어) / (for Ms. Jenkins) Jenkins 양에 대한).

안녕하세요. Jenkins 양에 관한 이야기를 하기 위해 오늘 이 편지를 쓰게 되어 기쁩니다.

노트 ■ 〈감정형용사〉

주어(사람)	be동사	형용사(감정)	that / 주어 / 동사 ~
			(for + 목적격) to R
		happy, angry, glad, sorry, worry 등	

■ 〈4형식을 3형식으로 바꿀 때 사용하는 전치사 for〉

주어	+	동사	+	간접목적어	+	직접목적어	(4)
		buy, build, find, choose, leave, make, order, prepare, write 등					
수동태 시 → 주어 + 직접목적어 + for + 간접목적어 (3)							

Alice Jenkins (S, Alice Jenkins는) / would make (V) an outstanding (〈현재분사〉) senior (O) claims adjuster / (at Insurance Partners), / and / I (S) / would (V) encourage you (O) / to consider (O.C) / her (for the position).

Insurance Partners에 뛰어난 수석 손해 사정사가 될 것입니다 그리고 저는 당신에게 권해드립니다 고려할 것을 그녀를 그 자리에

Alice Jenkins는 Insurance Partners에 뛰어난 수석 손해 사정사가 될 것이며, 저는 귀하께서 그녀를 그 자리에 고려할 것을 권해드립니다.

노트 ■ a claims adjuster : 보험 청구 사정인
■ 〈5형식 불완전타동사의 목적격보어〉 : 수동태 전환 시, 2형식 문장(be p.p. + to R)

주어	불완전타동사	목적어	목적격보어
–	advise / allow / ask / assume / beg / cause / command / compel / condition / decide / design / drive / enable / encourage / expect / forbid / force / instruct / intend / invite / lead / like / motivate / order / permit / persuade / predispose / pressure / program / push / require / teach / tell / train / trust / urge / want / warn / wish 등	–	to 동사원형

원인 그녀와 같이 업무를 봤을 때의 일

I (S, 저는) / (first) met (V, 처음 만났습니다) / Alice (O, Alice를) / {when (〈종·접〉) she (S) came (V) to Protect-All Insurance 그녀가 Protect-All Insurance에 왔을 때 / (as a new claims adjuster)} 새로운 손해 사정사로.

Alice가 새로운 손해 사정사로 Protect-All Insurance에 왔을 때 저는 그녀를 처음 만났습니다.

노트 ■ come to : ~에 오다

She / reported (directly) (to me) / (for the three years of her tenure) (with that company) (until 2015), / (when I retired).

She(S) 그녀는 / reported(V) 저에게 직접 업무 보고를 했습니다 / for the three years 3년의 / of her tenure 재직기간 동안 / with that company 그 회사에서 / until 2015 2015년까지 / when(〈종·접〉) I(S) retired(V) 제가 은퇴했을 때

2015년에 제가 은퇴할 때까지 그 회사에서 3년의 재직기간 동안 그녀는 저에게 직접 업무 보고를 했습니다.

노트 ■ report to : ~에게 보고하다

(In the first three years) / (I followed Alice's career), / I / watched her become one of the most knowledgeable problem-solvers / (in the company).

In the first three years 처음 3년 동안 / (when) I(S) followed(V) Alice's career(O) 제가 Alice의 경력을 지켜보았던 / I(S) 저는 / watched(V) her(O) become one of the most knowledgeable problem-solvers(O.C; one of the most knowledgeable problem-solvers: S.C) 그녀가 되는 것을 보았습니다 / 가장 해박한 문제 해결사 중 한 명이 되는 것을 보았습니다 / in the company 회사에서

제가 Alice의 경력을 지켜보았던 처음 3년 동안, 그녀가 회사에서 가장 해박한 문제 해결사 중 한 명이 되는 것을 보았습니다.

노트 ■ 〈관계부사〉 : 선행사와 관계부사는 서로 같이 사용할 수도 있고 둘 중 하나는 생략할 수도 있다.

용도	선행사	관계부사	전치사+관계대명사
시간	the time	when	in/at/on+which
장소	the place	where	in/at/on+which
이유	the reason	why	for which
방법	(the way)	how	in which
	the way how는 같이 사용 못함, the way, the way in which, the way that은 사용 가능 (how 대신에 사용되는 that은 관계부사 대용어라고 함)		

■ 〈지각동사〉

지각동사		목적어	목적격보어
see	보다	–	〈목적어와 목적격보어의 관계가 능동일 때〉 동사원형(R) – 완료 현재진행(Ring) – 진행, 순간, 찰나, 계속
watch	보다		
look at	보다		
behold	보다		
hear	듣다		〈목적어와 목적격보어의 관계가 수동일 때〉 과거분사(p.p.)
listen to	듣다		
feel	느끼다		
observe	관찰하다		
perceive	인식하다		〈to부정사는 불가〉 : 수동태 문장 전환 시 가능
notice	인식하다		

■ 〈be / get / become 구별〉

동사	용법
be	주어가 어떤 상태인지 표현
get	주어가 겪고 있는 상태의 변화를 표현
become	주어가 변화를 겪고 어떻게 되었는지 변화의 결과 표현

■ 〈one of+복수명사〉 : ~ 중의 하나

one (주어 : 단수)	of	복수명사
one		problem-solvers

■ 〈most / almost / mostly〉

	대명사	형용사	부사
most	대부분의 것들(사람들)	대부분의	가장
almost	–	–	거의
mostly	–	–	주로, 일반적으로

(During these three years), / she handled / fire, earthquake, and flood insurance / (almost) (exclusively).

During(〈전치사〉) these three years 이 3년 동안 / she(S) handled(V) 그녀는 처리했습니다 / fire(O_1) 화재, earthquake(O_2), and flood insurance(O_3) 지진, 그리고 홍수에 관한 보험을 / almost exclusively 거의 독점적으로

이 3년 동안, 그녀는 화재, 지진, 그리고 홍수에 관한 보험을 거의 독점적으로 처리했습니다.

노트 ■ 〈while 용법〉

부사절을 이끄는 종속접속사	
시간	~ 동안에
양보/대조	비록 ~일지라도

주제문(결과) Alice Jenkins를 수석 손해 사정사 자리에 고려하는 것에 대한 추천

(In my professional opinion), / Alice is ready (for more responsibility and challenge) (in her profession) and I / feel confident / {she will be an asset (to your company)}.

In my professional opinion 저의 전문가적인 견해로 / Alice(S) is(V) ready(S.C) Alice는 준비가 되어 있습니다 / for more responsibility and challenge 더 많은 책임과 도전을 위한 / in her profession 그녀의 직업에 대해 / I(S) 저는 / feel(V) confident(S.C) 확신합니다 / (that) she(S) will be(V) an asset(S.C) to your company 그녀가 귀하의 회사에 인재가 될 것을

저의 전문가적인 견해로 Alice는 그녀의 직업에 더 많은 책임과 도전을 위한 준비가 되어 있으며 그녀가 귀하의 회사에 인재가 될 것을 확신합니다.

노트 ■ be ready for : ~할 준비가 되다
■ I feel confident that+주어+동사 : 나는 ~을 확신하고 있다
■ an asset to : ~에게 귀중한 것, ~의 자산
■ 〈인지/확신 형용사〉 : 이러한 형용사는 뒤에 명사절로 that절이나 간접의문문 등을 취할 수 있다.

주어 (사람)	be동사	형용사 (인지/확신)	that (생략 가능)	주어	동사 ~
			of+동명사		
		aware, certain, conscious, proud, sure, confident, convinced, fearful, ignorant			

■ 〈감각동사〉

감각동사	주격보어(S.C)	
feel, look, seem, sound, taste, appear, smell	형용사(분사 : 현재분사/과거분사)	
	명사	
	like(전치사)	(that)+주어+동사
		(동)명사
	~~alike~~	
	~~likely~~	

Yours truly,
Della Johnson

Della Johnson 올림

▶ 다음 글의 목적으로 가장 적절한 것은?

① 직원 추천을 부탁하려고
② 담당 업무를 설명하려고
③ 업무 조정을 요청하려고
④ 경력 직원을 추천하려고
⑤ 입사 제안을 거절하려고

정답 | ④

해설 | ④ 이 글의 주제는 'Alice Jenkins를 수석 손해 사정사 자리에 고려하도록 추천하는 것'이다. 따라서 직원 추천을 부탁한다는 ④가 적절하다.

오답 | ① 직원 추천이라는 소재는 맞지만 부탁하는 것이 아니라 추천하는 관점이다.
② 담당 업무를 설명하는 것은 추천하는 이유의 한 가지일 뿐이다.
③ 업무 조정을 요청하는 내용은 나오지 않는다.
⑤ 입사 제안을 거절하는 내용은 나오지 않는다.

Words

- ☐ outstanding
- ☐ senior
- ☐ insurance
- ☐ encourage
- ☐ consider
- ☐ position
- ☐ tenure
- ☐ company
- ☐ retire
- ☐ career
- ☐ knowledgeable
- ☐ handle
- ☐ earthquake
- ☐ flood
- ☐ exclusively
- ☐ professional
- ☐ opinion
- ☐ responsibility
- ☐ confident

Phrases

- ☐ come to
- ☐ be ready for
- ☐ report to
- ☐ an asset to

우선순위 영단어 역대 수능 기출+전국 모의고사 기출+EBS 기출+교과서 기출 빈출 어휘

단어	뜻	단어	뜻	단어	뜻
mobility	n. 이동(성)	myth	n. 신화	numerous	a. 매우 많은
obligation	n. 의무	obvious	a. 명료한	operate	v. 운영하다
opportunity	n. 기회	organization	n. 단체	outstanding	a. 아직 처리되지 않은
overlap	v. 겹치다	ownership	n. 소유	package	n. 소포
paradox	n. 역설	parallel	v. 유사하다	pass on	v. ~을 넘겨주다
pay off	v. 지불하다	periodically	ad. 정기적으로	persuasion	n. 설득
phase	n. 단계	physician	n. 내과 의사	physiological	a. 생리적인
pile	v. 쌓다	pollutant	n. 오염물질	practical	a. 실용적인
presentation	n. 제시	presumably	ad. 아마	prey	n. 먹이
privilege	v. ~에게 특권을 주다	productive	a. 생산적인	progress	n. 전진
propel	v. 추진하다	prosperous	a. 번창하고 있는	protein	n. 단백질
provoke	v. 유발하다	pupil	n. 학생	radical	a. 급진적인
reasoning	n. 추론	regional	a. 지역적인	relevance	n. 타당성
remind	v. 상기시키다	replacement	n. 교체[대체]물	replicate	v. 복제하다

01 다음 글의 밑줄 친 부분 중 가리키는 대상이 다른 것은?

Dear ① Alan Smith:

I'm happy to be writing this letter for Ms. Jenkins. Alice Jenkins would make an outstanding senior claims adjuster at Insurance Partners, and I would encourage you to consider ② her for the position. I first met Alice when she came to Protect-All Insurance as a new claims adjuster. ③ She reported directly to me for the three years of her tenure with that company until 2015, when I retired. In the first three years I followed ④ Alice's career, I watched her become one of the most knowledgeable problem-solvers in the company. During these three years, ⑤ she handled fire, earthquake, and flood insurance almost exclusively. In my professional opinion, Alice is ready for more responsibility and challenge in her profession and I feel confident she will be an asset to your company.

Yours truly,
Della Johnson

02 다음 문장이 들어갈 부분으로 가장 적절한 곳을 고르시오.

> During these three years, she handled fire, earthquake, and flood insurance almost exclusively.

Dear Alan Smith:

I'm happy to be writing this letter for Ms. Jenkins. Alice Jenkins would make an outstanding senior claims adjuster at Insurance Partners, and I would encourage you to consider her for the position. (①) I first met Alice when she came to Protect-All Insurance as a new claims adjuster. (②) She reported directly to me for the three years of her tenure with that company until 2015, when I retired. (③) In the first three years I followed Alice's career, (④) I watched her become one of the most knowledgeable problem-solvers in the company. (⑤) In my professional opinion, Alice is ready for more responsibility and challenge in her profession and I feel confident she will be an asset to your company.

Yours truly,
Della Johnson

03 다음 글의 순서로 가장 적절한 것은?

Dear Alan Smith:

(A) During these three years, she handled fire, earthquake, and flood insurance almost exclusively. In my professional opinion, Alice is ready for more responsibility and challenge in her profession and I feel confident she will be an asset to your company.

(B) I first met Alice when she came to Protect-All Insurance as a new claims adjuster. She reported directly to me for the three years of her tenure with that company until 2015, when I retired. In the first three years I followed Alice's career, I watched her become one of the most knowledgeable problem-solvers in the company.

(C) I'm happy to be writing this letter for Ms. Jenkins. Alice Jenkins would make an outstanding senior claims adjuster at Insurance Partners, and I would encourage you to consider her for the position.

Yours truly,
Della Johnson

① (A) - (B) - (C) ② (B) - (A) - (C) ③ (B) - (C) - (A)
④ (C) - (A) - (B) ⑤ (C) - (B) - (A)

04 Alice Jenkins에 관한 내용으로 적절하지 <u>않은</u> 것은?

Dear Alan Smith:

I'm happy to be writing this letter for Ms. Jenkins. Alice Jenkins would make an outstanding senior claims adjuster at Insurance Partners, and I would encourage you to consider her for the position. I first met Alice when she came to Protect-All Insurance as a new claims adjuster. She reported directly to me for the three years of her tenure with that company until 2015, when I retired. In the first three years I followed Alice's career, I watched her become one of the most knowledgeable problem-solvers in the company. During these three years, she handled fire, earthquake, and flood insurance almost exclusively. In my professional opinion, Alice is ready for more responsibility and challenge in her profession and I feel confident she will be an asset to your company.

Yours truly,
Della Johnson

① 그녀는 Alan과 Protect-All Insurance에서 처음 만났다.
② 그 회사에서 3년 동안 그녀는 Johnson에게 업무 보고를 했다.
③ 그녀는 회사에서 가장 해박한 문제 해결사 중 한 명이었다.
④ 그녀는 화재, 지진, 홍수에 관한 보험을 거의 독점적으로 처리했다.
⑤ 그녀는 그녀의 직업에 대한 책임과 도전을 위한 준비가 되어 있다.

UNIT 04

심경 · 분위기

글의 논리	Story
제목	Charlie가 길을 잃은 이야기
주제	Charlie가 길을 잃고 절망감에 빠졌다.

수능 ANALYSIS

013 어법 선택 & 연결어

There **[was / were]** a ravine in the forest and Charlie **[made / had made]** his way into **[it / them]** through an early morning fog. All the ravine looked the same in the daylight, the **[high / highly]** walls, the masses of weeds and wild berry bushes, the trees. He had **[wandered / wondered]** around for a while, **[following / followed]** the little paths **[made / making]** by dirt **[washed / washing]** down from the hillside, but finally he sat down on a log and stared straight ahead without **[seeing / see]**. There **[was / were]** a dullness about him now. He **[had / had had]** so **[many / much]** scares, heard so many **[terrified / terrifying]** noises, got **[startling / startled]** by so **[many / much]** shadows, **[hurt / been hurt]** so often **[that / what]** all his senses **[wore / were worn]** to a flat hopelessness. He would just **[sit / seat]** here forever. It was not the first time Charlie **[had lost / had been lost]**, but never before **[had there been / there had been]** this finality.

이야기 Charlie가 길을 잃은 이야기

There was(V: 골짜기가 있었다) a ravine(S) / (in the forest: 숲에) / and(그리고) / Charlie(S: Charlie는) / had made(V〈과거완료〉) his way(O) into it(그곳으로 걸어 들어갔다) / (through an early morning fog: 이른 아침 안개를 뚫고).

숲에 골짜기가 있었고, Charlie는 이른 아침 안개를 뚫고 그곳으로 걸어 들어갔다.

노트
- make one's way into : ~ 안으로 나아가다(들어가다)
- 〈There is 도치구문〉

긍정문	There	is	단수 주어	~이 있다
		are	복수 주어	
부정문	There	is no	단수 주어	~이 없다
		are no	복수 주어	

• 유도부사 **there**와 함께 도치구문을 이루는 be동사(is/are/was/were) 대신에 완전자동사 **appear**, **come**, **exist**, **follow**, **live**, **stand** 등을 사용할 수 있다.

All the ravine(S: 모든 골짜기는) / looked(V) the same(S.C: 똑같아 보였다) / (in the daylight, the high walls, the masses of weeds and wild berry bushes, the trees: 햇빛이 드리워진, 높은 절벽, 우거진 잡초, 산딸기 덤불 그리고 나무들 속에서).

햇빛이 드리워진, 높은 절벽, 우거진 잡초, 산딸기 덤불 그리고 나무들 속에서 골짜기는 모두 똑같아 보였다.

노트
- look the same : 똑같이 보이다
- 〈high / highly〉

high	형용사	높은
	부사	높게
	명사	높은 곳
highly	부사	매우(=very)

He(S: 그는) / had wandered around(V〈과거완료〉: 주변을 헤매다가) / (for a while: 잠시), / {following(〈분사구문〉 작은 길을 따라) the little paths(걷다가) / (made by dirt: 〈과거분사〉 진흙으로 만들어진) / (washed down from the hillside: 〈과거분사〉 산 중턱에서 씻겨져 내려오면서), / but(하지만) / (finally: 마침내) / he(S) sat down(V₁: 그는 주저앉았다) / (on a log: 통나무에) / and(그리고) / stared straight ahead(V₂: 앞을 곧장 응시했다) / (without(〈전치사〉) seeing(〈동명사〉): 아무것도 눈에 들어오는 것 없이)}.

그는 주변을 잠시 헤매다가 산 중턱에서 진흙에 씻겨져 내려오면서 만들어진 작은 길을 따라 걷다가, 마침내 통나무에 주저앉고 앞을 곧장 응시했으나 아무것도 눈에 들어오지 않았다.

노트
- wander around : 이리저리 돌아다니다
- for a while : 잠시 동안
- follow a path : 길을 따라가다
- wash A down : A를 씻다
- sit down : 앉다
- stare straight ahead : 똑바로 앞을 노려보다
- 〈wonder / wander〉

원형	과거	과거분사	현재분사	뜻
wonder	wondered	wondered	wondering	v. 이상하게 여기다
wander	wandered	wandered	wandering	v. 돌아다니다

- 〈분사구문 – 문미〉 : 주절과 분사구문의 위치가 서로 바뀌어도 무관

주절		종속절(→ 분사구문)			
주어	동사	종속 접속사	주어	동사 : 상황에 맞게 아래처럼 바뀜	
		〈그대로 사용하면 의미 강조〉	(주절의 주어와 같으면 생략하고, 다르면 주격으로 사용함)	(being)	Ring(현재분사)
				(having been) 생략 가능	p.p.(과거분사)
					형용사
					명사
He	had wandered around	–	–	–	following ~

■ 〈주격관계대명사+be동사 생략〉

명사	(주격관계대명사 +be동사)	Ring(현재분사) – 능동
		p.p.(과거분사) – 수동
		형용사
		부사
		명사
		전치사구
the little paths	(which/that were)	made ~
dirt	(which/that was)	washed down ~

There was a dullness / (about him) / (now).

V 흐릿함이 있을 뿐이었다 / S / 그에 대한 / 지금은

지금은 그에게 흐릿함이 있을 뿐이었다.

주제문(이야기) Charlie는 길을 잃고 부상을 입으면서 절망감에 빠졌다.

He / had had so many scares, / heard so many terrifying noises, / got startled / (by so many shadows), / been hurt so often / {that all his senses were worn / (to a flat hopelessness)}.

S 그는 / V_1〈과거완료〉 / O 너무나 많은 무서운 것을 겪었고 / V_2 〈현재분사〉 너무나 많은 소음을 들었고 / O / V_3 S.C 놀랐고 / 너무나 많은 그림자에 의해 / V_4 너무 자주 다쳐서 / 〈종·접〉 / S 그의 모든 감각은 / V〈수동태〉 닳아서 / 완전한 절망감에

그는 너무나 많은 무서운 것을 겪었고, 너무나 많은 무서운 소음을 들었고, 너무나 많은 그림자에 놀랐고, 너무 자주 다쳐서 그의 모든 감각은 닳아서 완전한 절망감뿐이었다.

노트 ■ wear : 닳게[해지게] 하다, 써서 낡게 하다
(wear – wore – worn – wearing)

■ 〈공통관계〉 : A가 공통

A	(X+Y)	=	AX+AY
A	(X+Y+Z+α)	=	AX+AY+AZ+Aα
(X+Y)	A	=	XA+YA
A	(X+Y+Z)	=	AX+AY+AZ
had	(had+heard +got+been)	=	had had+had heard +had got+had been

■ 〈부정수량형용사〉 : 막연한 수나 양의 정도를 표시하는 형용사

수(數)	few(a few), some(any), a lot of(lots of), a good(or great), plenty of, enough, all, no, many	복수명사+복수동사
양(量)	little(a little), some(any), a lot of, a good(or great), deal of, plenty of, enough, all, no, much	단수명사+단수동사

■ 〈get 동사의 쓰임〉

get	〈주격보어〉	〈2형식〉
	과거분사	~ 당하다, ~의 상태로 되다
	현재분사	~하기 시작하다
	형용사	~의 상태가 되다, ~하기에 이르다
	to do	서서히 ~하게 되다

■ 〈원인과 결과를 동시에 나타내는 표현〉 : '너무 ~해서 그 결과 …하다' (종속접속사 that 생략 가능)

원인(너무 ~해서)				결과(그 결과 ~하다)		
so	형용사	a(n)+명사		(that)	주어	동사 ~
such	a(n)	형용사	명사	that	주어	동사 ~

결과	so	(that)	원인
원인	, so	(that)	결과

이야기 Charlie가 길을 잃은 이야기

He / would (just) sit / (here) / (forever).

S 그는 / V 앉아 있을 것이었다 / 여기에 / 영원토록

그는 영원토록 여기에 앉아 있을 것이었다.

노트 ■ 〈sit / seat / set〉

원형	과거	과거분사	현재분사	뜻
sit	sat	sat	sitting	vi. 앉다, ~에 놓여 있다
seat	seated	seated	seating	vt. 앉히다
set	set	set	setting	vt. 두다, ~을 놓다

It / was not the first time / (when) (Charlie had been lost), / but / (never before) / had there been this finality.

S 이것은 / V / S.C〈선행사〉 처음이 아니었다 / S / V〈과거완료 수동〉 Charlie가 길을 잃은 것은 / 하지만 / 전에는 / V〈과거완료〉 / S.C 결코 이러한 결말을 맞아 본 적은 없었다

Charlie가 길을 잃은 것은 처음이 아니었지만 전에는 결코 이러한 결말을 맞아 본 적은 없었다.

노트 ■ never before : ~ 한 적이 없다

■ 〈관계부사〉 : 선행사와 관계부사는 서로 같이 사용할 수도 있고 둘 중 하나는 생략할 수도 있다.

용도	선행사	관계부사	전치사+관계대명사
시간	the time	when	in/at/on+which
장소	the place	where	in/at/on+which
이유	the reason	why	for which
방법	(the way)	how	in which
	the way how는 같이 사용 못함, the way, the way in which, the way that은 사용 가능 (how 대신에 사용되는 that은 관계부사 대용어라고 함)		

■ 〈부정어구 문두 도치〉 : never before had there been this finality을 정치시키면 there had never been this finality before이다. 여기에서 there는 유도부사이고 동사는 had been이고 주어는 this finality이다.

부정어(구)	〈도치〉		
Never / Seldom / Rarely / Scarcely / Hardly / No / Only / Little / Few / Nor 등	조동사	주어	동사원형
	have / has / had	주어	p.p.
	do(does/did)	주어	동사원형
	be동사	주어	–
never before	had	there	been

▶ 다음 글에 드러난 Charlie의 심경으로 가장 적절한 것은?

① excited and hopeful
② frightened and desperate
③ bored and indifferent
④ relieved and sympathetic
⑤ ashamed and embarrassed

정답 | ②

해석 | ① 신나고 희망찬
② 무섭고 절망적인
③ 지루하고 무관심한
④ 다행이고 연민을 느끼는
⑤ 부끄럽고 당황한

해설 | ② 이 글에서 'scares'라는 단어와 'terrifying', 'hopelessness'라는 단어를 사용하며 현재 Charlie가 희망이 없고 무서운 상황임을 알 수 있기 때문에 ② '무섭고 절망적인'이 적절하다.

오답 | ① 이 글의 내용과 반대되는 말이다.
③ 지루하고 무관심한 것보다는 무섭고 절망적인 상황이다.
④ 다행스러워 하고 연민을 느끼는 상황이 아니다.
⑤ 'embarrassed'는 맞지만 'ashamed(부끄러운)'는 현재 상황과 맞지 않는다.

Words

- ☐ fog
- ☐ weed
- ☐ wild berry
- ☐ bush
- ☐ wander
- ☐ dirt
- ☐ hillside
- ☐ log
- ☐ stare
- ☐ dullness
- ☐ scare
- ☐ terrifying
- ☐ startled
- ☐ flat
- ☐ hopelessness
- ☐ finality
- ☐ desperate
- ☐ indifferent
- ☐ embarrassed

Phrases

- ☐ make one's way into
- ☐ wander around
- ☐ follow a path
- ☐ sit down
- ☐ never before
- ☐ look the same
- ☐ for a while
- ☐ wash A down
- ☐ stare straight ahead

우선순위 영단어

역대 수능 기출 + 전국 모의고사 기출 + EBS 기출 + 교과서 기출 빈출 어휘

단어	뜻	단어	뜻	단어	뜻
reserve	v. 유보하다	resident	n. 주민	respond	v. 반응하다
revolution	n. 혁명	ritual	n. 의식	seal	v. 다물다
section	n. (책 등에서) 절	seize	v. 붙잡다	share	n. 몫
solid	a. 고체의	stabilize	v. 고정시키다	statistics	n. 통계 수치
stem from	~에서 기인[유래]하다	stimulate	v. 자극하다	stimulus	n. 자극
strive	v. 노력하다	supplement	n. 보충	surpass	v. (양, 정도가) ~를 능가하다
temperature	n. 체온	tolerant	a. 잘 견디는	tolerate	v. 참다
trace	n. 자취	typically	ad. 전형적으로	underscore	v. 뒷받침하다
undertake	v. 일을 맡다	unique	a. 독특한	upcoming	a. 다가오는
upset	v. (계획 따위를) 망쳐 놓다	utter	a. 전적인	validity	n. 타당성
valuable	a. 귀중한	verbal	a. 말의	visualize	v. 생생하게 마음에 그리다
volume	n. 정도	well-intended	a. 선의의	absence	n. 부재
absolutely	ad. 절대적으로	accomplishment	n. 업적	achievement	n. 성취
aesthetic	a. 미(美)의	agricultural	a. 농업의	alert	a. 기민한
alteration	n. 개조	analysis	n. 분석	arbitrary	a. 임의의

01 밑줄 친 부분 중 문맥상 옳지 않은 것은?

There was a ravine in the forest and Charlie had made his way into it through an early morning fog. All the ravine looked the ① different in the daylight, the high walls, the masses of weeds and wild berry bushes, the trees. He had ② wandered around for a while, following the little paths made by dirt washed down from the hillside, but finally he sat down on a log and stared straight ahead without seeing. There was a dullness about him now. He had had so many ③ scares, heard so many terrifying noises, got startled by so many shadows, been hurt so often that all his senses were worn to a flat hopelessness. He would just sit here ④ forever. It was not the first time Charlie had been ⑤ lost, but never before had there been this finality.

02 다음 문장이 들어갈 부분으로 가장 적절한 곳을 고르시오.

> All the ravine looked the same in the daylight, the high walls, the masses of weeds and wild berry bushes, the trees.

There was a ravine in the forest and Charlie had made his way into it through an early morning fog. (①) He had wandered around for a while, following the little paths made by dirt washed down from the hillside, but finally he sat down on a log and stared straight ahead without seeing. (②) There was a dullness about him now. (③) He had had so many scares, heard so many terrifying noises, got startled by so many shadows, been hurt so often that all his senses were worn to a flat hopelessness. (④) He would just sit here forever. (⑤) It was not the first time Charlie had been lost, but never before had there been this finality.

03 다음 글의 순서로 가장 적절한 것은?

There was a ravine in the forest and Charlie had made his way into it through an early morning fog.

(A) There was a dullness about him now. He had had so many scares, heard so many terrifying noises, got startled by so many shadows, been hurt so often that all his senses were worn to a flat hopelessness.

(B) All the ravine looked the same in the daylight, the high walls, the masses of weeds and wild berry bushes, the trees. He had wandered around for a while, following the little paths made by dirt washed down from the hillside, but finally he sat down on a log and stared straight ahead without seeing.

(C) He would just sit here forever. It was not the first time Charlie had been lost, but never before had there been this finality.

① (A) - (B) - (C)
② (A) - (C) - (B)
③ (B) - (A) - (C)
④ (B) - (C) - (A)
⑤ (C) - (A) - (B)

04 다음 글의 문장 중 무관한 문장을 고르시오.

There was a ravine in the forest and Charlie had made his way into it through an early morning fog. All the ravine looked the same in the daylight, the high walls, the masses of weeds and wild berry bushes, the trees. ① He had wandered around for a while, following the little paths made by dirt washed down from the hillside, but finally he sat down on a log and stared straight ahead without seeing. ② There was a dullness about him now. ③ He had had so many scares, heard so many terrifying noises, got startled by so many shadows, been hurt so often that all his senses were worn to a flat hopelessness. He would just sit here forever. ④ Fortunately, he got out of the woods. ⑤ It was not the first time Charlie had been lost, but never before had there been this finality.

UNIT 04

심경 · 분위기

글의 논리	Story
제목	범죄 현장이 된 집
주제	Anne과 Marco의 집이 범죄 현장이 되었다.

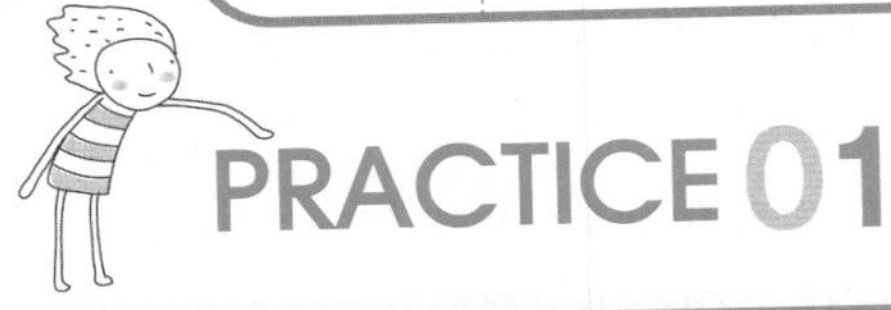

PRACTICE 01

014 어법 선택 & 연결어

Anne and Marco's comfortable home **[immediate / immediately]** **[become / becomes]** a crime scene. Anne is **[sitting / seating]** on the sofa in the living room. Someone **[has placed / placed]** a blanket around her shoulders, but she's still **[trembled / trembling]**. Police cars **[park / are parked]** on the street outside the house, **[their / its]** red lights **[flashed / flashing]**, **[pulsed / pulsing]** through the front window and **[circle / circling]** the pale walls. Anne **[seats / sits]** immobile on the sofa and **[stare / stares]** ahead **[even if / as if]** **[hypnotized / hypnotizing]** by **[them / it]**. Marco, his voice **[breaken / breaking]**, **[have given / has given]** the police a quick description of the baby — six months old, blond, blue eyes, about sixteen pounds, **[wearing / worn]** a disposable diaper and a plain, pale pink onesie. The house is **[swarmed / swarming]** with **[uniforming / uniformed]** police officers. They fan out and methodically begin to search the house, but the baby **[is gone / goes]**.

주제(이야기) Anne과 Marco의 집이 범죄 현장이 되었다.

Anne and Marco's comfortable home / (immediately) becomes a crime scene.

S: Anne과 Marco의 편안한 집은 / 즉시 / V S.C: 범죄 현장이 된다

Anne과 Marco의 편안한 집은 즉각 범죄 현장이 된다.

노트 ■ 〈주어와 동사의 수의 일치〉

명사	and	명사's	명사	동사
〈소유격〉			주어	

(〈수의 일치〉: 명사 – 동사)

■ 〈be / get / become 구별〉

동사	용법
be	주어가 어떤 상태인지 표현
get	주어가 겪고 있는 상태의 변화를 표현
become	주어가 변화를 겪고 어떻게 되었는지 변화의 결과 표현

이야기 범죄 현장이 된 Anne과 Marco의 집에 대한 이야기

Anne / is sitting / (on the sofa) / (in the living room).

S: Anne은 / V〈현재진행〉: 앉아 있다 / 소파에 / 거실에 있는

Anne은 거실의 소파에 앉아 있다.

노트 ■ sit on : ~의 위에 앉아 있다

■ 〈sit / seat / set〉

원형	과거	과거분사	현재분사	뜻
sit	sat	sat	sitting	vi. 앉다, ~에 놓여 있다
seat	seated	seated	seating	vt. 앉히다
set	set	set	setting	vt. 두다, ~을 놓다

Someone / has placed a blanket / (around her shoulders), / but / she is (still) trembling.

S: 누군가 / V〈현재완료〉 O: 담요를 둘러 주었다 / 그녀의 어깨에 / 하지만 / S V〈현재진행〉: 그녀는 여전히 몸을 떨고 있다

누군가 그녀의 어깨에 담요를 둘러 주었지만 그녀는 여전히 몸을 떨고 있다.

Police cars / are parked / (on the street) / (outside the house), / {their red lights flashing, pulsing / (through the front window) / and / circling the pale walls}.

S: 경찰차가 / V〈수동태〉: 주차되어 있고 / 거리에 / 집 밖에 / 〈의·S〉 〈독립분사구문〉: 그 차들의 빨간 불빛이 번쩍이고, 깜빡거리며 / 앞쪽 창을 통해 / 그리고 / 색이 옅은 벽에 둥근 원을 그리면서

경찰차가 집 밖의 거리에 주차되어 있고, 그 차들의 빨간 불빛이 번쩍이고 앞쪽 창을 통해 깜빡거리며 색이 옅은 벽에 둥근 원을 그린다.

노트 ■ pulse through : 고동쳐 ~을 흐르다

■ 〈독립분사구문 – 문미〉 : 주절의 주어와 다를 경우 분사 앞에 분사의 행위자(주체)를 주격으로 사용함

주절		종속절(→ 독립분사구문)			
주어	동사	종속 접속사	주어	동사 : 상황에 맞게 아래처럼 바뀜	
		〈그대로 사용하면 의미 강조〉	(주절의 주어와 같으면 생략하고, 다르면 주격으로 사용함)	(being) (having been) 생략 가능	Ring(현재분사) / p.p.(과거분사) / 형용사 / 명사
Police cars	are parked	–	their red lights	–	flashing, pulsing ~ and circling ~

Anne / sits immobile / (on the sofa) / and / stares (ahead) / (as if hypnotized by them).

S: Anne은 / V_1: 움직이지 않고 / S.C: 앉아 있고 / 소파에 / 그리고 / V_2: 앞을 응시한다 / 〈종·접〉 (she is) 〈과거분사〉 마치 그 불빛들에 의해 최면술에 걸리듯

Anne은 소파에 움직이지 않고 앉아 있고 마치 그 불빛들에 의해 최면술에 걸린 듯 앞을 응시한다.

노트

■ stare ahead : 앞을 노려보다

■ 〈유사보어＝준보어〉 : 두 문장을 한 문장으로 합치면서 불필요한 부분을 삭제하여 그 한 문장의 의미를 빠르게 전달하려는 의도에서 사용한다.

My cat	was	happy	when	it	died.
주어	불완전자동사	형용사(보어)	종속접속사	주어	완전자동사

My cat	died	happy
주어	불완전자동사	형용사(보어)

• 1번째 문장에서 died는 완전자동사로 명백하게 1형식 동사지만 2번째 문장에서 died는 뒤에 보어를 가질 수 있는 마치 불완전자동사로 사용되었다. 이렇듯 1형식 완전자동사가 뒤에 보어를 가져서 마치 2형식 불완전자동사로 사용될 때 사용되는 형용사보어를 유사보어 또는 준보어라고 한다. 여기에서 유사하다는 말고 준하다는 말은 동일하게 똑같다는 말이 아니라 비슷하다는 의미이기 때문에 보어와 동일한 것이 아니라 마치 보어처럼 사용되었다는 의미로 이해하면 된다.

주어	완전자동사	주격보어	~한 상태로 …하다
	die	형용사 명사 현재분사 과거분사	
	break		
	go		
	lay		
	marry		
	live		
	run		
	return		
	sit		
	stand		
	be (born)		
	meet		
	part		

■ 〈even vs. as〉

종속 접속사	even though	＋주어＋동사	비록 ~이지만	양보/대조
	even if			
	as though		마치 ~처럼	가정법
	as if			

■ 〈분사구문 – 문미〉 : 주절과 분사구문의 위치가 서로 바뀌어도 무관

주절		종속절(→ 분사구문)			
주어	동사	종속 접속사	주어	동사 : 상황에 맞게 아래처럼 바뀜	
		〈그대로 사용하면 의미 강조〉	(주절의 주어와 같으면 생략하고, 다르면 주격으로 사용함)	(being) (having been) 생략 가능	Ring(현재분사)
					p.p.(과거분사)
					형용사
					명사
Anne	sits, stares	as if	(she is) 생략		hypnotized

Marco, / (his voice breaking), / has given the police a quick description of the baby / — {six months old, blond, blue eyes, about sixteen pounds, / (wearing a disposable diaper and a plain, pale pink onesie)}.

S: Marco는 / 〈의·S〉 〈독립분사구문〉 갈라지는 목소리로 / V〈현재완료〉 / I.O: 경찰에게 아기에 대해 / D.O: 간단한 묘사를 해주었다 / 생후 6개월에, 금발 머리이고, 눈이 파란색이며, 약 16파운드의 체중이고 / 〈분사구문〉 일회용 기저귀와 무늬가 없는 옅은 분홍색의 한 조각짜리 아기 옷을 입고 있다고

Marco는 갈라지는 목소리로 아기가 생후 6개월에, 금발 머리이고, 눈이 파란색이며, 약 16파운드의 체중이고, 일회용 기저귀와 무늬가 없는 옅은 분홍색의 한 조각짜리 아기 옷을 입고 있다고 경찰에게 아기에 대해 간단한 묘사를 해주었다.

노트

■ 〈독립분사구문 – 문중〉 : 주절의 주어와 다를 경우 분사 앞에 분사의 행위자(주체)를 주격으로 사용함

주어	종속절(→ 독립분사구문)				동사
	종속접속사	주어	동사 : 상황에 맞게 아래처럼 바뀜		
	〈그대로 사용하면 의미 강조〉	(주절의 주어와 같으면 생략하고, 다르면 주격으로 사용함)	(being) (having been) 생략 가능	Ring(현재분사)	
				p.p.(과거분사)	
				형용사	
				명사	
Marco	–	his voice	–	breaking	has given

■ 〈분사구문 – 문미〉 : 주절과 분사구문의 위치가 서로 바뀌어도 무관

주절		종속절(→ 분사구문)			
주어	동사	종속 접속사	주어	동사 : 상황에 맞게 아래처럼 바뀜	
		〈그대로 사용하면 의미 강조〉	wearing의 주체	(being) (having been) 생략 가능	Ring(현재분사)
					p.p.(과거분사)
					형용사
					명사
Marco	has given	–	the baby	–	wearing

The house / is swarming / (with uniformed police officers).

S: 집 안에는 / V〈현재진행〉: 무리 지어 다닌다 / 〈과거분사〉 제복을 입은 경찰관이

집 안에는 제복을 입은 경찰관이 무리 지어 다닌다.

노트

■ be swarming with : 북적이다[＝be overrun(crowded, thronging, bustling, jammed) with]

■ 〈분사의 역할 및 종류〉

분사의 역할	형용사	명사 수식	전치 수식
			후치 수식
		보어 사용	주격보어
			목적격보어
분사의 종류	현재분사(Ring)	능동	~하는, ~하고 있는
	과거분사(p.p.)	수동	~되는, ~ 당하는, 이미 된

They / fan out / and / (methodically) / begin to search
S 그들은 / V_1 흩어진다 / 그리고 / 체계적으로 / V_2 O 집을 뒤지기 시작한다

the house, / but / the baby is gone.
하지만 / S 아기는 V(수동태) 사라졌다

그들은 흩어져서 체계적으로 집을 뒤지기 시작하지만 아기는 사라졌다.

노트 ■ fan out : 펼쳐지다[퍼지다], ~을 펼치다
■ 〈3형식에서 목적어 자리에 to R / Ring 둘 다 사용 가능〉

	완전타동사		목적어
주어	begin	~을 시작하다	to R/Ring (의미 차이 없음)
	cease	~을 중단하다	
	continue	~을 계속하다	
	deserve	~할 가치/자격/권리가 있다	
	dislike	~을 싫어하다	
	hate		
	like	~을 좋아하다	
	love	~을 사랑하다	
	neglect	~하는 것을 소홀히 하다	
	prefer	~쪽을 좋아하다	
	require	~을 요구하다	
	start	~을 시작하다	

▶ 다음 글의 상황에 나타난 분위기로 가장 적절한 것은?

① lively and festive
② cozy and peaceful
③ serious and urgent
④ calm and lonely
⑤ monotonous and relaxing

정답 | ③

해석 | ① 활기차고 축제 분위기의
② 아늑하고 평화로운
③ 심각하고 긴박한
④ 조용하고 외로운
⑤ 단조롭고 마음을 편안하게 해 주는

해설 | ③ 이 글의 내용은 범죄 현장이 된 집이다. 이 글에서 Anne과 Marco의 아기는 사라졌고 경찰관들은 집 안에서 무리 지어 다니며 아기를 찾고 있다. 그리고 Anne은 몸을 떨고 있고(trembling), Marco의 목소리는 갈라져 있다. 이러한 내용들을 봤을 때, 글의 상황에 나타난 분위기로 가장 적절한 것은 ③ '심각하고 긴박한' 이다.

오답 | ① 아기를 잃어버린 상황이고 열심히 찾고 있는 상황이라 '활기차고 축제 분위기' 라는 말은 적절하지 않다.
② 아기를 잃어버리고 집이 범죄 현장이 됐으므로 '아늑하고 평화로운' 은 적절하지 않다.
④ 아기를 잃어버렸기 때문에 'lonely' 라고 생각할 수도 있지만 현재 경찰관들이 무리 지어 다니면서 아기를 수색하고 있으므로 'calm(조용하고)' 은 적절하지 않다.
⑤ 아기를 잃어버리고 경찰관들이 찾고 있는 상황을 봤을 때, '단조롭고 마음을 편안하게 해 주는' 이란 단어는 적절하지 않다.

Words

☐ comfortable
☐ immediately
☐ crime scene
☐ blanket
☐ tremble
☐ flash
☐ pulse
☐ front window
☐ pale wall
☐ immobile
☐ hypnotize
☐ description
☐ blond
☐ disposable diaper
☐ plain
☐ swarm
☐ methodically
☐ lively
☐ monotonous

Phrases

☐ sit on
☐ stare ahead
☐ fan out
☐ pulse through
☐ be swarming with

우선순위 영단어 역대 수능 기출 + 전국 모의고사 기출 + EBS 기출 + 교과서 기출 빈출 어휘

단어	뜻	단어	뜻	단어	뜻
arc	n. 호	architect	n. 건축가	artificial	a. 인조의
assignment	n. 임무	attachment	n. 애착	attribute A to B	A를 B의 탓으로 돌리다
babble	v. 옹알이하다	bargain	n. 흥정	bark	n. 나무껍질

변형문제

01 다음 글의 밑줄 친 부분 중 가리키는 대상이 다른 것은?

Anne and Marco's comfortable home immediately becomes a crime scene. ① Anne is sitting on the sofa in the living room. Someone has placed a blanket around ② her shoulders, but ③ she's still trembling. Police cars are parked on the street outside the house, their red lights flashing, pulsing through the front window and circling the pale walls. ④ Anne sits immobile on the sofa and stares ahead as if hypnotized by them. Marco, his voice breaking, has given the police a quick description of the baby — six months old, blond, blue eyes, about sixteen pounds, wearing a disposable diaper and a plain, pale pink onesie. The house is swarming with uniformed police officers. They fan out and methodically begin to search the house, but ⑤ the baby is gone.

02 밑줄 친 부분 중 문맥상 옳지 않은 것은?

Anne and Marco's comfortable home immediately becomes a crime scene. Anne is sitting on the sofa in the living room. Someone has placed a blanket around her shoulders, but she's still ① trembling. Police cars are parked on the street outside the house, their red lights flashing, pulsing through the front window and circling the pale walls. Anne sits ② mobile on the sofa and stares ahead as if ③ hypnotized by them. Marco, his voice breaking, has given the police a quick description of the baby — six months old, blond, blue eyes, about sixteen pounds, wearing a ④ disposable diaper and a plain, pale pink onesie. The house is swarming with ⑤ uniformed police officers. They fan out and methodically begin to search the house, but the baby is gone.

03 다음 문장이 들어갈 부분으로 가장 적절한 곳을 고르시오.

They fan out and methodically begin to search the house, but the baby is gone.

Anne and Marco's comfortable home immediately becomes a crime scene. Anne is sitting on the sofa in the living room. Someone has placed a blanket around her shoulders, but she's still trembling. (①) Police cars are parked on the street outside the house, their red lights flashing, pulsing through the front window and circling the pale walls. (②) Anne sits immobile on the sofa and stares ahead as if hypnotized by them. (③) Marco, his voice breaking, has given the police a quick description of the baby — six months old, blond, blue eyes, about sixteen pounds, wearing a disposable diaper and a plain, pale pink onesie. (④) The house is swarming with uniformed police officers. (⑤)

04 다음 글의 문장 중 무관한 문장을 고르시오.

Anne and Marco's comfortable home immediately becomes a crime scene. Anne is sitting on the sofa in the living room. ① Someone has placed a blanket around her shoulders, but she's still trembling. ② She fell asleep happily. ③ Police cars are parked on the street outside the house, their red lights flashing, pulsing through the front window and circling the pale walls. ④ Anne sits immobile on the sofa and stares ahead as if hypnotized by them. ⑤ Marco, his voice breaking, has given the police a quick description of the baby — six months old, blond, blue eyes, about sixteen pounds, wearing a disposable diaper and a plain, pale pink onesie. The house is swarming with uniformed police officers. They fan out and methodically begin to search the house, but the baby is gone.

UNIT 04

심경 · 분위기

글의 논리	Story
제목	Sondra의 친구 Emma와 관련된 일화
주제	Emma와 자신의 딸 Sondra의 관계에 대한 엄마의 고민

PRACTICE 02

015 어법 선택 & 연결어

My daughter Sondra had a friend in sixth grade **[what / that]** would never look **[direct / directly]** at me (we'll call her "Emma"). Emma wasn't shy, but she gave me the feeling she **[was hiding / was hiden]** something. When I served an after-school snack in the kitchen, she wanted to eat upstairs. If I suggested the girls **[play / played]** outside **[where / which]** I could see **[them / it]**, she encouraged Sondra **[to stay / staying]** in the rec room. She seldom smiled or said please or thank you. One day, I **[found / founded]** a purse in the street by our house. **[Opened / Opening]** **[them / it]** up to **[find / found]** the owner's identification, I saw **[that / what]** it belonged to Emma's mom. The purse also contained $600 cash! (   ), I called Emma's mom — who picked up the purse without even **[to say / saying]** thank you. It confirmed my feelings **[that / what]** Sondra's relationship with Emma needed **[to monitor / to be monitored]**.

이야기 Sondra의 친구 Emma와 관련된 일화

My daughter Sondra (S, 내 딸 Sondra에게는) / had (V) a friend (O, 친구가 있다) 〈선행사〉 / (in sixth grade) (6학년인) /

{that (〈주·관〉) would never look (directly) at (V) me (O) (결코 나를 똑바로 쳐다보려 하지 않는) / (we (S) will call (V) her (O) "Emma" (O.C)) (우리는 그녀를 Emma라고 부른다)}.

내 딸 Sondra에게는 결코 나를 똑바로 쳐다보려 하지 않는 6학년인 친구 한 명(우리는 그녀를 Emma라고 부르려 한다)이 있었다.

노트
- look at : ~을 (자세히) 살피다
- 〈주격관계대명사 that절〉 : 선행사를 포함하고 있는 관계대명사 what 사용 불가

선행사	주격관계대명사절		
	주격관계대명사	~~주어~~	동사
a friend	that		would never look at

- 〈look at / over / in / out / for〉

look	at	~을 쳐다보다
	over	~을 대충 훑어보다[살펴보다](=watch)
	in	~을 들여다보다, 조사/검토하다
	out	~을 내다보다, 조심하다
	for	~을 찾다, 구하다, 바라다

- 〈call 불완전타동사의 쓰임〉 : ~을 …라고 부르다(수동태 시, be called+주격보어)

주어	불완전타동사	목적어	목적격보어
	call		명사
			형용사

Emma (S, Emma는) / wasn't (V) shy (S.C, 부끄러워하지 않았다), / but (하지만) / she (S, 그녀는) / gave (V) me (I.O) the feeling (D.O, 나에게 느낌을 주었다) / =〈동격〉 (that) (she (S) was hiding (V) something (O)) (무언가를 숨기고 있다는).

Emma는 부끄러워하지 않았지만 그녀는 무언가를 숨기고 있다는 느낌을 나에게 주었다.

노트
- 〈동격의 that〉 : ~라는 A(관계대명사 which/what 사용 불가)

추상명사 (A)	종속절(명사절 – 완전한 문장)		
	(that)	주어	동사 ~
answer / belief / chance / claim / conclusion / dream / evidence / extent / fact / faith / hope / idea / likelihood / news / notion / pledge / possibility / promise / proposal / question / recognition / reply / request / result / sense / statement / suggestion / testament / theory / view / wickedness 등	종속 접속사 (생략 가능)	–	–

{When (〈종·접〉) I (S, 내가) / served (V) an after-school snack (O, 방과 후에 먹는 간식을 주었을 때) / (in the kitchen) (부엌에서)}, / she (S, 그녀는) / wanted (V) to eat upstairs (O, 위층에서 먹기를 원했다).

내가 방과 후에 먹는 간식을 부엌에서 주었을 때 그녀는 위층에서 먹기를 원했다.

노트
- 〈목적어 자리에 to부정사를 취하는 완전타동사〉

주어	완전타동사	목적어
–	afford / agree / ask / attempt / care / choose / claim / dare / decide / demand / desire / determine / elect / expect / fail / guarantee / hope / intend / learn / manage / need / offer /	to 동사원형

	plan / pretend / promise / refuse / resolve / seek / threaten / volunteer / want / wish 등	

{If I suggested (that) / (the girls play outside) / (where I could see them)}, / she / encouraged Sondra / to stay in the rec room.

(종·접) S V / S V (O) / 〈관·부〉 S / V O / S / V O / O.C

만약 내가 제안하면 / 여자아이들이 바깥에서 놀기를 / 내가 아이들을 볼 수 있는 / 그녀는 / Sondra에게 부추겼다 / 집에 있는 / 오락실에 머물도록

내가 아이들을 볼 수 있는 바깥에서 놀기를 제안하면 그녀는 Sondra가 집에 있는 오락실에 머물도록 부추겼다.

노트
- play outside : 야외에서 놀다
- stay in : (밖으로) 나가지 않다[집에 있다]
- 〈목적격종속접속사 that 생략〉 : 완전타동사의 목적어로 사용된 경우 / 관계대명사 what 사용 불가

	종속절(명사절 : 목적어) (완전한 절)		
완전타동사	(that)	주어	동사
suggested	목적격종속접속사 – 생략 가능(~하는 것을)	the girls	play

- 〈관계부사〉 : 선행사와 관계부사는 서로 같이 사용할 수도 있고 둘 중 하나는 생략할 수도 있다.

용도	선행사	관계부사	전치사+관계대명사
시간	the time	when	in/at/on+which
장소	the place	where	in/at/on+which
이유	the reason	why	for which
방법	(the way)	how	in which
	the way how는 같이 사용 못함, the way, the way in which, the way that은 사용 가능 (how 대신에 사용되는 that은 관계부사 대용어라고 함)		

- 〈조동사 should의 용법〉 : 주장/명령/요구/제안 동사

〈주절〉			〈종속절〉 : 명사절(타동사의 목적어)			
주어	타동사		종속접속사 (that)	주어	동사	
	주장	insist, argue			당위성일 경우	(should) 동사원형
	요구(청)/부탁	require, demand, ask, desire, request, stipulate, move, beg, mandate				
	명령	command, order				
	충고	advise, urge			일반적 사실인 경우	주절의 동사와 시제 일치
	결정	agree, decide, decree, determine				
	소망	wish, pray, prefer				
	제안/권장	suggest, propose, recommend				

- 〈5형식 불완전타동사의 목적격보어〉 : 수동태 전환 시, 2형식 문장(be p.p.+to R)

주어	불완전타동사	목적어	목적격보어
–	advise / allow / ask / assume / beg / bring / cause / command / compel / condition / decide / design / drive / enable / encourage / expect / forbid / force / inspire / instruct / intend / invite / lead / like / motivate / order / permit / persuade / predispose / pressure / proclaim / prod / program / provoke / push / require / teach / tell / train / trust / urge / want / warn / wish 등	–	to 동사원형

She / (seldom) smiled / or / said please or thank you.

S / V_1 / V_2 O

그녀는 / 거의 미소를 짓지 않았다 / 또는 / '제발' 이나 '감사합니다' 라는 말을 거의 하지 않았다

그녀는 거의 미소를 짓지도 않았으며 혹은 '제발' 이나 '감사합니다' 라는 말을 거의 하지 않았다.

노트
- 〈부정어의 종류〉

완전부정어	부사	not (~ 아닌)
		never (결코 ~ 아닌)
	형용사	no (~도 아닌)
	대명사/부사/형용사	neither (~도 아니다)
	대명사/부사/형용사	none (아무도 ~ 아니다)
	대명사/부사/명사	nothing (조금도[결코] ~ 않다)
준부정어	부사	hardly (거의 ~ 아니다)
		scarcely (거의 ~ 않다)
		barely (거의 ~ 아니게)
		seldom (좀처럼 ~ 않는)
		rarely (좀처럼 ~하지 않는)
	형용사/부사	little (거의 ~ 없는)
		few (거의 ~ 없는)

(One day), / I / found a purse / (in the street) / (by our house).

S V O

어느 날 / 나는 / 지갑 하나를 발견했다 / 거리에서 / 우리 집 옆에 있는

어느 날 나는 우리 집 옆에 있는 거리에서 지갑 하나를 발견했다.

노트
- one day : 언젠가[어느 날] (미래의 어느 시기나 과거의 특정한 날을 가리킴)
- 〈find / found〉

원형	과거	과거분사	현재분사	뜻
find	found	found	finding	v. 발견하다, 알다
found	founded	founded	founding	v. 설립하다

{Opening it up / (to find the owner's identification)}, / I / saw / (that it belonged to Emma's mom).

O 〈분사구문〉 / S V / (종·접) S V / O

그것을 열었을 때 / 주인의 신분증명서를 찾기 위해 / 나는 / 보았다 / 그것이 Emma의 엄마 것이라는 것을

주인의 신분증명서를 찾기 위해 그것을 열었을 때 그것이 Emma의 엄마 것이라는 것을 알았다.

노트
- open A up : A를 열다
- belong to : ~ 소유[것]이다, ~에 속하다

■ 〈분사구문 – 문두〉: 주절과 종속절의 위치는 서로 바뀔 수 있음

종속절(→ 분사구문)				주절	
종속접속사	주어	동사 : 상황에 맞게 아래처럼 바뀜		주어	동사
〈그대로 사용하면 의미 강조〉	(주절의 주어와 같으면 생략하고, 다르면 주격으로 사용함)	(being) (having been) 생략 가능	Ring(현재분사) / p.p.(과거분사) / 형용사 / 명사		
–	–	–	Opening	I	saw

■ 〈이어동사〉

타동사	명사	부사	(○)
타동사	부사	명사	(○)
타동사	대명사	부사	(○)
타동사	부사	대명사	(×)
Opening	up	it	(×)

■ 〈what vs. that〉

	관계대명사(불완전한 문장)	접속사(완전한 문장)
what	○ 선행사를 포함하고 있기 때문에 what 앞에 선행사 불필요	×
that	○ that 앞에 선행사 필요	○

The purse / (also) contained $600 cash!
(S: 그 지갑은 / V / O: 또한 현금 600달러가 들어 있었다!)

그 지갑에는 또한 현금 600달러가 들어 있었다!

(Naturally), / I / called Emma's mom — {who picked up the purse / (without even saying thank you)}.
(당연히 / S: 나는 / V / O〈선행사〉: Emma의 엄마에게 전화했는데 / 〈주·관〉 V: 그녀는 그 지갑을 / O: 가져갔다 / 〈전치사〉 동명사 O: 감사하다는 말도 없이)

당연히 나는 Emma의 엄마에게 전화했는데, 그녀는 감사하다는 말도 없이 그 지갑을 가져갔다.

노트 ■ pick up A : A를 집다(들어 올리다)

It / confirmed my feelings / {that Sondra's relationship / (with Emma) / needed to be monitored}.
(S: 이것은 / V / O: 내 느낌을 더 분명하게 해주었다 / =〈동격〉 〈종·접〉 / S: Sondra의 관계는 / Emma와의 / V / O〈to R 수동〉: 관찰될 필요가 있다는)

그 일은 Sondra의 Emma와의 관계를 관찰할 필요가 있다는 내 느낌을 더 분명히 해주었다.

노트 ■ a relationship with : ~와의 관계

■ 〈need 용법〉

목적어(to R)		3형식	〈~할〉 필요가 있다, 〈~〉 해야 하다
목적어	목적격보어(to R)	5형식	〈남이〉 〈~해 줄〉 필요가 있다
동명사(Ring)		3형식	〈사람 · 물건이〉 〈~되어야 할〉 필요가 있다
목적어	목적격보어(p.p.)	5형식	〈~이〉 〈…될〉 필요가 있다, 〈~을〉 〈…되도록 할〉 필요가 있다

■ 〈to R의 태와 시제〉

태	능동태	to R
	수동태	to be p.p.
시제	단순시제 : 본동사 시제와 동일	to R
	완료시제 : 본동사 시제보다 한 시제 앞선 시제	to have p.p.
	완료 수동	to have been p.p.

▶ 다음 글에 드러난 'I'의 심경으로 가장 적절한 것은?

① joyful and satisfied
② curious and excited
③ relaxed and relieved
④ sorrowful and scared
⑤ uncomfortable and displeased

정답 | ⑤

해석 | ① 기뻐하고 만족스러워하는
② 궁금해 하고 들뜬
③ 편안하고 안도해하는
④ 슬프고 무서워하는
⑤ 불편하고 불쾌한

해설 | ⑤ 이 글의 내용은 Sondra의 엄마가 Sondra와 Emma의 관계에 대한 고민을 하는 글이다. Emma와의 일화를 이야기하며 Sondra에게 친구들을 볼 수 있는 바깥에서 놀기를 제안하면 Emma는 그녀가 밖에 못 나가도록 부추겼고, Emma 엄마와의 일화도 있는데, Emma의 엄마에게 지갑을 찾아 주었을 때, 그녀는 감사하다는 말도 없이 그냥 지갑을 가져갔을 뿐이었다. 이러한 일화들을 봤을 때, 가장 적절한 것은 그녀가 불편하고 불쾌한 감정을 느끼고 있다는 ⑤이다.

오답 | ① 'I'는 현재 Emma와 Sondra의 관계에 대해 고민하고 걱정을 하고 있으므로 기뻐하고 만족스러워한다는 것은 적절하지 않다.
② 'I'는 궁금해 하고 들떠있지 않고 관계에 대해 걱정하고 불편해하고 불쾌해하고 있다.
③ 'I'는 잘못된 친구를 사겼을까봐 불편해하고 있으므로 편안하고 안도해한다는 말은 적절하지 않다.
④ 'I'의 감정이 슬프다는 내용은 없고 무서워하지도 않고 있다.

Words

☐ grade
☐ directly
☐ hide
☐ serve
☐ after-school snack
☐ upstairs
☐ encourage
☐ rec room
☐ seldom
☐ purse
☐ contain
☐ naturally

☐ confirm		☐ curious		☐ uncomfortable	
☐ relationship		☐ relaxed		☐ displeased	
☐ monitor		☐ scared			

Phrases

☐ look at		☐ play outside	
☐ stay in		☐ one day	
☐ open A up		☐ belong to	
☐ pick up A		☐ a relationship with	

우선순위 영단어

역대 수능 기출 + 전국 모의고사 기출 + EBS 기출 + 교과서 기출 빈출 어휘

단어	뜻	단어	뜻	단어	뜻
bill	n. 청구서	bold	a. 과감한	bond	n. 유대
by product	n. 부산물	cancel	v. 취소하다	career	v. (제멋대로) 달리다
carve	v. 조각하다	cast	v. 던지다	cell	n. 세포
challenge	v. 도전하다	chemical	n. 화학물질	claw	n. (고양이, 매 따위의) 발톱
clear	v. 맑게 하다	collectively	ad. 집합적으로	combination	n. 결합
command	v. 명령하다	committed	a. 전념하는	compensation	n. 보상
competent	a. 유능한	complication	n. 문제	conclude	v. 결론짓다
configuration	n. 외형	conscious	a. 의식하는	constraint	n. 제약
contamination	n. 감염	core	a. 핵심적인	counterpart	n. 상대방
craft	v. 정교하게 다듬다	crude	a. 조야한	decade	n. 10년
declare	v. 선언하다	definition	n. 정의	demand	n. 요구
demonstration	n. 실연	depiction	n. 묘사	describe	v. 묘사하다
desperate	a. 자포자기의	devastating	a. 파괴하는	diagnosis	n. 진단
dictate	n. 명령	dietary	a. 음식의	digest	v. 소화하다
discount	v. 고려하지 않다	dispense	v. 분배하다	disrupt	v. 혼란에 빠뜨리다
dissatisfaction	n. 불만족	distribute	v. 배포하다	divine	a. 성스러운
dose	n. (약 등의) 투여량	drive	v. ~을 몰다	driving force	n. 추진력
dynamic	a. 역동적인	ecology	n. 생태	edge	n. 변두리
element	n. 요소	emotion	n. 감정	encouragement	n. 격려
escape	v. 피하다	establishment	n. 확립	evidence	n. 증거
evident	a. 명백한	exclude	v. 배제하다	exercise	n. 연습
exhibition	n. 전시회	experienced	a. 노련한	expose	v. 노출시키다
extinct	a. 멸종된	fabric	n. 직물	faint	a. 희미한
fashion	n. 방식	faulty	a. 결함이 있는	fertilizer	n. 비료
fierce	a. 사나운	frame	n. (사람, 동물의) 신체	fundamental	a. 근본적인
gap	n. 단절	generation	n. 생성	govern	v. 지배하다
gradually	ad. 서서히	guild	n. 조합	harvest	v. 수확하다
height	n. 절정	homogeneous	a. 동질의	illuminate	v. 비추다
imitate	v. 모방하다	immensely	ad. 엄청나게	implicit	a. 잠재하는
in advance	미리	in time	마침내	inborn	a. 타고난
income	n. 소득	independent	a. 독립적인	individuality	n. 개성
industrial	a. 산업의	influence	v. 영향을 주다	infrastructure	n. 하부조직
initial	a. 처음의	inspiration	n. 기발한 생각	instruct	v. 지시하다
intact	a. 손상되지 않은	interpersonal	a. 사람과 사람 사이의	interrupt	v. 방해하다
intervention	n. 개입	intrinsic	a. 본질적인	introduction	n. 도입

변형문제

01 다음 글의 밑줄 친 부분 중 가리키는 대상이 다른 것은?

My daughter Sondra had a friend in sixth grade that would never look directly at me (we'll call her "Emma"). Emma wasn't shy, but ① she gave me the feeling she was hiding something. When I served an after-school snack in the kitchen, ② she wanted to eat upstairs. If I suggested the girls play outside where I could see them, ③ she encouraged Sondra to stay in the rec room. She ④ She smiled or said please or thank you. One day, I found a purse in the street by our house. Opening it up to find the owner's identification, I saw that it belonged to Emma's mom. The purse also contained $600 cash! Naturally, I called Emma's mom — ⑤ she picked up the purse without even saying thank you. It confirmed my feelings that Sondra's relationship with Emma needed to be monitored.

02 Emma에 관한 설명으로 적절한 것은?

My daughter Sondra had a friend in sixth grade that would never look directly at me (we'll call her "Emma"). Emma wasn't shy, but she gave me the feeling she was hiding something. When I served an after-school snack in the kitchen, she wanted to eat upstairs. If I suggested the girls play outside where I could see them, she encouraged Sondra to stay in the rec room. She seldom smiled or said please or thank you. One day, I found a purse in the street by our house. Opening it up to find the owner's identification, I saw that it belonged to Emma's mom. The purse also contained $600 cash! Naturally, I called Emma's mom — who picked up the purse without even saying thank you. It confirmed my feelings that Sondra's relationship with Emma needed to be monitored.

① 그녀는 부끄러움이 많다.
② 그녀는 항상 솔직했다.
③ 그녀는 Sondra가 집에만 있도록 부추겼다.
④ 그녀는 지갑을 잃어버렸었다.
⑤ Sondra가 그녀의 지갑을 찾아주었다.

03 다음 문장이 들어갈 부분으로 가장 적절한 곳을 고르시오.

> Naturally, I called Emma's mom — who picked up the purse without even saying thank you.

My daughter Sondra had a friend in sixth grade that would never look directly at me (we'll call her "Emma"). Emma wasn't shy, but she gave me the feeling she was hiding something. When I served an after-school snack in the kitchen, she wanted to eat upstairs. (①) If I suggested the girls play outside where I could see them, she encouraged Sondra to stay in the rec room. (②) She seldom smiled or said please or thank you. (③) One day, I found a purse in the street by our house. Opening it up to find the owner's identification, (④) I saw that it belonged to Emma's mom. The purse also contained $600 cash! (⑤) It confirmed my feelings that Sondra's relationship with Emma needed to be monitored.

04 다음 괄호 안에서 문맥상 적절한 것을 고르시오.

> My daughter Sondra had a friend in sixth grade that would never look directly at me (we'll call her "Emma"). Emma wasn't shy, but she gave me the feeling she was hiding something. When I (A) **[reserved / served]** an after-school snack in the kitchen, she wanted to eat upstairs. If I suggested the girls play (B) **[inside / outside]** where I could see them, she encouraged Sondra to stay in the rec room. She seldom smiled or said please or thank you. One day, I found a purse in the street by our house. (C) **[Opening / Closing]** it up to find the owner's identification, I saw that it belonged to Emma's mom. The purse also contained $600 cash! Naturally, I called Emma's mom — who picked up the purse without even saying thank you. It confirmed my feelings that Sondra's relationship with Emma needed to be monitored.

	(A)	(B)	(C)
①	reserved	inside	Opening
②	reserved	inside	Closing
③	reserved	outside	Opening
④	served	outside	Opening
⑤	served	inside	Closing

심경 · 분위기

글의 논리	Story
제목	할아버지와 배를 타고 나갔다 만난 파도에 대한 이야기
주제	할아버지와 배를 타고 나갔다 인생에서 본 것 중 가장 큰 파도를 만났을 때의 이야기

PRACTICE 03

016 어법 선택 & 연결어

"No. This is only the eye of the storm. It is the calm part of the storm, and it could start getting bad again any minute." Just as Grandpa said that, the wind picked up and I looked out at the ocean. The biggest wave I had ever **[been seeing / seen]** in my life **[headed / was headed]** toward our ship. I was **[frightened / frightening]**! I didn't make a move toward the stairway, but just stood there **[looking / looked]** at the wave. I watched the big, dark wave as if it **[is / were]** in slow motion until lightning **[flashing / flashed]** and woke me from my daze. The wave hit the boat with an **[amazing / amazed]** force, **[knocked / knocking]** me off my feet. I reached for something to grab but there **[was / were]** nothing. I soon realized **[that / what]** I was in the ocean, and the waves were all around me. I saw something **[to float / floating]** in the water next to me and **[grabbing / grabbed]** **[it / them]** and **[held / holding]** on for my life.

이야기 할아버지와 배를 타고 나갔다 만난 파도에 대한 이야기

"No. / This(S 이것은) / is(V) / only the eye of the storm(S.C 단지 폭풍우의 눈이야). / It(S 이것은) / is(V) / the calm part of the storm(S.C 폭풍우의 조용한 부분이지), / and(그리고) / it(S 그것은) could start(V) getting bad(O 나빠지기 시작할 수 있어) / (again)(다시) / (any minute)(당장에라도)."

아니야

"아니야. 이것은 단지 폭풍우의 눈이야. 폭풍우의 조용한 부분이지. 그리고 그것은 당장에라도 다시 나빠지기 시작할 수 있어."

노트
- get bad : 나빠지다
- (at) any minute (now) : 지금 당장에라도[금방이라도]
- 〈3형식에서 목적어 자리에 to R / Ring 둘 다 사용 가능〉

	완전타동사		목적어
주어	begin	~을 시작하다	to R/Ring (의미 차이 없음)
	cease	~을 중단하다	
	continue	~을 계속하다	
	deserve	~할 가치/자격/권리가 있다	
	dislike	~을 싫어하다	
	hate		
	like	~을 좋아하다	
	love	~을 사랑하다	
	neglect	~하는 것을 소홀히 하다	
	prefer	~쪽을 좋아하다	
	require	~을 요구하다	
	start	~을 시작하다	

(Just as(〈종·접〉) Grandpa(S 할아버지가) / said(V) that(O)(그렇게 말씀하신 바로 그대로)), / the wind(S 바람은) / picked up(V 더욱 강해졌다) / and / I(S 그리고 나는) / looked out at(V) the ocean(O)(대양을 내다보았다).

할아버지가 그렇게 말씀하신 바로 그대로 바람은 더 강해졌고 나는 대양을 내다보았다.

노트
- just as : 꼭 ~처럼
- pick up : 더 강해지다
- look out at : ~을 바라보다
- 〈Just as〉 : 마치 ~처럼

〈종속절〉			〈주절〉	
Just as	주어	동사 ~,	주어	동사 ~.
〈종속접속사〉 : 마치 ~처럼				

The biggest wave(S 가장 큰 파도가) / {(목·관 that) I(S) had ever seen(V〈과거완료〉) / (in my life)}(내가 인생에서 본 것 중) / was headed(V〈수동태〉) (toward our ship)(우리의 배를 향했다).

내 인생에서 본 것 중 가장 큰 파도가 우리의 배를 향했다.

노트
- head A toward B : A를 B로 향하다(수동태 시, A be headed toward B)
- 〈목적격관계대명사 that〉 : 타동사의 목적어가 없는 경우 / 선행사를 포함하고 있는 관계대명사 what 사용 불가

	〈목적격관계대명사절〉				
선행사 : 주어	목적격관계대명사	주어	타동사	~~목적어~~	동사
The biggest wave	that : 〈생략 가능〉	I	had seen		was headed

I(S 나는) / was(V) frightened(S.C 무서웠다)!

나는 무서웠다!

I / didn't make a move / (toward the stairway), / but

S 나는 / V_1 움직이지 않고 / 계단을 향해

just stood there / (looking at the wave).

V_2 그저 거기 서 있었다 / 〈분사구문〉 파도를 바라보면서

나는 계단을 향해 움직이지 않고 그저 거기에서 파도를 바라보며 서 있었다.

노트

■ make a move : (여정을) 떠나다

■ look at : ~을 (자세히) 살피다[검토/진찰하다]

■ **〈감정과 관련된 완전타동사〉** : 분사화가 되어 주격보어/목적격보어 자리에 나올 때 구별법

• 2형식

주어	동사	주격보어(S.C)
사람		과거분사(p.p.) – 수동(되어진, ~ 당한)
사물		현재분사(Ring) – 능동(~하고 있는, 하는)
I	was	frightened

■ **〈분사구문 – 문미〉** : 주절과 분사구문의 위치가 서로 바뀌어도 무관

주절		종속절(→ 분사구문)			
주어	동사	종속 접속사	주어	동사 : 상황에 맞게 아래처럼 바뀜	
		〈그대로 사용하면 의미 강조〉	(주절의 주어와 같으면 생략하고, 다르면 주격으로 사용함)	(being) (having been) 생략 가능	Ring(현재분사) / p.p.(과거분사) / 형용사 / 명사
I	stood	–	–	–	looking

I / watched the big, dark wave / (as if it were in slow

S 나는 / V 크고 어두운 파도를 보았다 O / 〈종·접〉 S V 마치 그것이 슬로 모션처럼

motion) / {until lightning flashed and / woke me / (from

움직이는 / 〈종·접〉 S V_1 번개가 번쩍여 / V_2 O 나를 깨울 때까지 / 나의

my daze)}.

멍한 상태로부터

번개의 번쩍임이 나를 멍한 상태로부터 깨울 때까지 나는 마치 슬로 모션처럼 움직이는 크고 어두운 파도를 보았다.

노트

■ wake A from one's daze : A를 멍에서 깨우다

■ 〈as if 가정법〉

주절		종속절				
주어	동사	as if (as though)	주어	동사		
	현재 시제			과거시제 (were, 과거동사, 조동사R)	주절 동사와 같은 시제 사실의 반대	현실(재) 반대 : (현재) 그렇지 않는 데 마치 ~인 것처럼 (현재) 하다
	과거 동사					과거 반대 : (과거에) 그렇지 않는 데 마치 ~인 것처럼 (과거에) 했다
	현재 시제			과거완료(had p.p.) 시제 (had p.p., 조동사 과거형 have p.p.)	주절의 동사보다 이전 사실의 반대	과거 반대 : (과거에) 그렇지 않는 데 마치 ~였던 것처럼 (현재) 한다
	과거 동사					대과거 반대 : (과거에 이전에) 그렇지 않는 데 마치 ~였던 것처럼 (과거에) 했다

The wave / hit the boat / (with an amazing force), /

S 그 파도는 / V O 보트를 강타했던 / 〈전치사〉 〈현재분사〉 O 놀라운 힘으로

(knocking me off my feet).

〈분사구문〉 그리고 나를 넘어뜨려 움직이지 못하게 했다

그 파도는 놀라운 힘으로 보트를 강타해 나를 넘어뜨려 움직이지 못하게 했다.

노트

■ hit A with B : A를 B로 치다

■ off one's feet : 움직이지 못해서, 기동할 수 없을 정도로

■ **〈분사구문 – 문미〉** : 주절과 분사구문의 위치가 서로 바뀌어도 무관

주절		종속절(→ 분사구문)			
주어	동사	종속 접속사	주어	동사 : 상황에 맞게 아래처럼 바뀜	
		〈그대로 사용하면 의미 강조〉	(주절의 주어와 같으면 생략하고, 다르면 주격으로 사용함)	(being) (having been) 생략 가능	Ring(현재분사) / p.p.(과거분사) / 형용사 / 명사
The wave	hit	–	–	–	knocking

I / reached for something / (to grab) / but / there was

S 나는 / V 손을 뻗었다 / 잡기 위해서 / 하지만 / V 아무것도

nothing.

S 없었다

나는 뭐라도 붙잡기 위해 손을 뻗었지만 아무것도 없었다.

노트

■ reach for : ~을 잡으려고 손을 뻗다

■ 〈There is 도치구문〉

긍정문	There	is	단수 주어	~이 있다
		are	복수 주어	
부정문	There	is no	단수 주어	~이 없다
		are no	복수 주어	

• 유도부사 **there**와 함께 도치구문을 이루는 be동사(is/are/was/were) 대신에 완전자동사 **appear**, **come**, **exist**, **follow**, **live**, **stand** 등을 사용할 수 있다.

I / (soon) realized / (that I was in the ocean), / and /

S 나는 / V 곧 깨달았다 / 〈종·접〉 S V O 내가 대양 안에 있음을 / 그리고

the waves / were (all) (around me).

S 파도가 / V 내 주변에 있었다

나는 곧 내가 대양 안에 있음을 깨달았다. 그리고 내 주변에는 온통 파도였다.

노트

■ 〈what vs. that〉

	관계대명사(불완전한 문장)	접속사(완전한 문장)
what	○ 선행사를 포함하고 있기 때문에 what 앞에 선행사 불필요	×
that	○ that 앞에 선행사 필요	○

I (S, 나는) / saw (V1) something (O) floating (O.C) (무언가가 떠 있는 것을 보았다) / (in the water) (물 위에) / (next to me) (내 옆에서) / and (그리고) / grabbed (V2) it (O) and held on (V3) (그것을 붙잡고 매달렸다) / (for my life) (살기 위해서).

나는 옆에 물 위에 떠 있는 뭔가를 보았고 그것을 붙잡고 살기 위해 매달렸다.

노트
- next to : ~ 바로 옆에
- hold on : (놓치지 않게) 붙잡다
- 〈지각동사〉

지각동사		목적어	목적격보어
see	보다	–	〈목적어와 목적격보어의 관계가 능동일 때〉 동사원형(R) – 완료 현재진행(Ring) – 진행, 순간, 찰나, 계속 〈목적어와 목적격보어의 관계가 수동일 때〉 과거분사(p.p.) 〈to부정사는 불가〉 : 수동태 문장 전환 시 가능
watch			
look at			
behold			
(over) hear	듣다		
listen to			
feel	느끼다		
observe	관찰하다		
perceive	인식하다		
notice			
saw		something	floating

▶ 다음 글의 상황에 나타난 분위기로 가장 적절한 것은?

① peaceful and lively
② mysterious and strange
③ hopeless and desperate
④ festive and adventurous
⑤ boring and monotonous

정답 | ③

해석 | ① 평화롭고 활기찬
② 불가사의하고 이상한
③ 희망이 없고 절망적인
④ 축제 분위기이고 모험으로 가득한
⑤ 지루하고 단조로운

해설 | ③ 이 글은 할아버지와 배를 타고 나갔을 때, 큰 파도를 만난 이야기이다. 이 글에서 'frightened'라는 단어를 사용하여 무서운 상황임을 알 수 있고, 'I'는 뭐라도 붙잡기 위해 손을 뻗었지만 주위엔 아무것도 없었고 살기 위해 발버둥 치고 있는 상황이다. 따라서 이 상황에 나타난 분위기로 가장 적절한 것은 ③ '희망이 없고 절망적인' 분위기이다.

오답 | ① 이 글은 큰 파도가 강타하며 생명의 위협을 느끼고 있는 상황이기 때문에 평화롭고 활기차다는 분위기는 적절하지 않다.
② 이 글에 파도가 치는 행동이 불가사의하고 이상하다고 나오지 않는다.
④ 이 글에서 현재 생명의 위협을 느끼고 있기 때문에 축제 분위기라는 것은 적절하지 않다.
⑤ 이 글에서 현재 상황은 굉장히 급박하기 때문에 지루하고 단조롭다는 표현은 적절하지 않다.

Words

- ☐ calm part
- ☐ wave
- ☐ frightened
- ☐ stairway
- ☐ knock
- ☐ grab
- ☐ float
- ☐ hopeless
- ☐ festive

Phrases

- ☐ get bad
- ☐ just as
- ☐ look out at
- ☐ make a move
- ☐ wake A from one's daze
- ☐ off one's feet
- ☐ next to
- ☐ (at) any minute (now)
- ☐ pick up
- ☐ head A toward B
- ☐ look at
- ☐ hit A with B
- ☐ reach for
- ☐ hold on

우선순위 영단어 역대 수능 기출 + 전국 모의고사 기출 + EBS 기출 + 교과서 기출 빈출 어휘

단어	뜻	단어	뜻	단어	뜻
involved	a. 관여하는	irritate	v. 노하게 하다	isolated	a. 단 하나의
lack	n. 부족	latter	n. 후자(나중에 언급된 것)	leap	v. 껑충 뛰다
let alone	~은 말할 것도 없이	let go of	(손에 쥔 것을) 놓다	literacy	n. 읽고 쓸 줄 아는 능력

PRACTICE 03

01 밑줄 친 부분 중 문맥상 옳지 않은 것은?

"No. This is only the eye of the storm. It is the calm part of the storm, and it could start getting ① bad again any minute." Just as Grandpa said that, the wind picked up and I looked out at the ocean. The biggest wave I had ever seen in my life was headed toward our ship. I was ② frightened! I didn't make a move toward the stairway, but just stood there looking at the wave. I watched the big, dark wave as if it were in ③ slow motion until lightning flashed and woke me from my daze. The wave hit the boat with an amazing force, knocking me off my feet. I reached for something to grab but there was ④ something. I soon realized that I was in the ocean, and the waves were all around me. I saw something ⑤ floating in the water next to me and grabbed it and held on for my life.

02 다음 상황에서 'I'에게 할 수 있는 조언으로 가장 적절한 것은?

"No. This is only the eye of the storm. It is the calm part of the storm, and it could start getting bad again any minute." Just as Grandpa said that, the wind picked up and I looked out at the ocean. The biggest wave I had ever seen in my life was headed toward our ship. I was frightened! I didn't make a move toward the stairway, but just stood there looking at the wave. I watched the big, dark wave as if it were in slow motion until lightning flashed and woke me from my daze. The wave hit the boat with an amazing force, knocking me off my feet. I reached for something to grab but there was nothing. I soon realized that I was in the ocean, and the waves were all around me. I saw something floating in the water next to me and grabbed it and held on for my life.

① Every cloud has a sliver lining.
② Life is voyage.
③ Let bygones be bygones.
④ Big fish are caught in a big river.
⑤ A friend in need is a friend indeed.

03 다음 글의 순서로 가장 적절한 것은?

> "No. This is only the eye of the storm. It is the calm part of the storm, and it could start getting bad again any minute."

(A) Just as Grandpa said that, the wind picked up and I looked out at the ocean. The biggest wave I had ever seen in my life was headed toward our ship. I was frightened! I didn't make a move toward the stairway, but just stood there looking at the wave.

(B) I watched the big, dark wave as if it were in slow motion until lightning flashed and woke me from my daze. The wave hit the boat with an amazing force, knocking me off my feet.

(C) I reached for something to grab but there was nothing. I soon realized that I was in the ocean, and the waves were all around me. I saw something floating in the water next to me and grabbed it and held on for my life.

① (A) - (B) - (C)　② (B) - (A) - (C)　③ (B) - (C) - (A)
④ (C) - (A) - (B)　⑤ (C) - (B) - (A)

04 다음 문장이 들어갈 부분으로 가장 적절한 곳을 고르시오.

> The wave hit the boat with an amazing force, knocking me off my feet.

"No. This is only the eye of the storm. It is the calm part of the storm, and it could start getting bad again any minute." Just as Grandpa said that, the wind picked up and I looked out at the ocean. The biggest wave I had ever seen in my life was headed toward our ship. (①) I was frightened! (②) I didn't make a move toward the stairway, but just stood there looking at the wave. (③) I watched the big, dark wave as if it were in slow motion until lightning flashed and woke me from my daze. (④) I reached for something to grab but there was nothing. I soon realized that I was in the ocean, and the waves were all around me. (⑤) I saw something floating in the water next to me and grabbed it and held on for my life.

내용 일치/불일치

글의 논리	Story
제목	인기 있는 작곡가 중 한 사람인 Paul Creston에 대한 설명
주제	미국의 음악가 Paul Creston의 일생

수능 ANALYSIS

017 어법 선택 & 연결어

[Most / Mostly] self-**[teaching / taught]**, Paul Creston became one of the **[almost / most]** popular composers of the mid-20th century. A conservative musician, Creston claimed his greatest influences to be long-**[dead / deadly]** composers. The hallmark of his style was rhythmic originality. (   ), he might **[call / be called]** an American impressionist. Creston achieved renown when his Symphony No. 1 **[won / had won]** the New York Music Critics' Circle Award in 1941. He had already received a Guggenheim Fellowship in 1938. His work **[performed / was performed]** **[wide / widely]** in the aftermath of World War II, but it faded from the concert repertoire with the rise of academic music in the 1960s. Several of his works **[inspired / were inspired]** by the **[poem / poetry]** of Walt Whitman. He died in Poway, California, a suburb of San Diego.

이야기 인기 있는 작곡가 중 한 사람인 Paul Creston에 대한 설명

(Mostly self-taught), / Paul Creston / became / one (of the most popular composers) / (of the mid-20th century).

- (Mostly: 〈부사〉, self-taught: 〈분사구문〉) 주로 독학으로 공부한
- Paul Creston: S, Paul Creston은
- became: V, 되었다
- one (of the most popular composers): S.C, 가장 인기 있는 작곡가 중 한 사람이
- (of the mid-20th century): 20세기 중반에

주로 독학으로 공부한 Paul Creston은 20세기 중반에 가장 인기 있는 작곡가 중 한 사람이 되었다.

노트 ■ 〈분사구문 – 문두〉 : 주절과 종속절의 위치는 서로 바뀔 수 있음

<table>
<tr><th colspan="4">종속절(→ 분사구문)</th><th colspan="2">주절</th></tr>
<tr><td>종속 접속사</td><td>주어</td><td colspan="2">동사 : 상황에 맞게 아래처럼 바뀜</td><td rowspan="5">주어</td><td rowspan="5">동사</td></tr>
<tr><td rowspan="4">〈그대로 사용하면 의미 강조〉</td><td rowspan="4">(주절의 주어와 같으면 생략하고, 다르면 주격으로 사용함)</td><td rowspan="4">(being) (having been) 생략 가능</td><td>Ring(현재분사)</td></tr>
<tr><td>p.p.(과거분사)</td></tr>
<tr><td>형용사</td></tr>
<tr><td>명사</td></tr>
<tr><td>–</td><td>–</td><td>–</td><td>self-taught</td><td>Paul Creston</td><td>became</td></tr>
</table>

■ 〈be / get / become 구별〉

동사	용법
be	주어가 어떤 상태인지 표현
get	주어가 겪고 있는 상태의 변화를 표현
become	주어가 변화를 겪고 어떻게 되었는지 변화의 결과 표현

■ 〈one of＋복수명사〉 : ~ 중의 하나

one (주어 : 단수)	of	복수명사
one		composers

■ 〈most / almost / mostly〉

	대명사	형용사	부사
most	대부분의 것들(사람들)	대부분의	가장
almost	–	–	거의
mostly	–	–	주로, 일반적으로

A conservative musician, / Creston / claimed / his greatest influences / to be long-dead composers.

- A conservative musician, = 〈동격〉 Creston
- A conservative musician: S, 보수적인 음악가였던
- Creston: Creston은
- claimed: V, 주장했다
- his greatest influences: O, 자신에게 가장 큰 영향을 미친 사람들은
- to be long-dead composers: O.C, 오래전 죽은 작곡가라고

보수적인 음악가였던 Creston은 자신에게 가장 큰 영향을 미친 사람들은 오래전 죽은 작곡가라고 주장했다.

노트 ■ 〈동격〉 : A(명사), B(명사) (A가 주어, B라는 A)

동격(B라는 A)		
명사(A)	,(콤마)	명사(B)
A conservative musician		Creston

■ 〈claim 동사의 쓰임〉

• 3형식일 경우 : (사실이라고) ~을 주장[단언]하다

claim	목적어
	명사
	to R
	that＋주어＋동사

• 5형식일 경우 : ~을 …라고 주장하다

claim	목적어	목적격보어
		to be＋보어

The hallmark (of his style) / was rhythmic originality.

- The hallmark (of his style): S, 그의 스타일의 특징은
- was: V
- rhythmic originality: S.C, 리드미컬한 독창성이었다

그의 스타일의 특징은 리드미컬한 독창성이었다.

(Harmonically), / he / might be called / an American impressionist.

- (Harmonically): 화성 면에서
- he: S, 그는
- might be called: V(수동태), 아마도 불릴 것이다
- an American impressionist: S.C, 미국 인상주의자라고

화성 면에서 그는 아마도 미국 인상주의자라고 불릴 것이다.

노트 ■ 〈call 동사의 쓰임〉: ~을 …라고 부르다(수동태 시, be called+주격보어)

주어	불완전타동사	목적어	목적격보어
	call		명사
			형용사

Creston / achieved renown / {when his Symphony No. 1 won the New York Music Critics' Circle Award / (in 1941)}.

S Creston은 / V O 유명세를 얻었다 / 〈종·접〉 / S 그의 1번 교향곡이 / V O 뉴욕 음악 비평가 협회상을 수상했을 때 / 1941년에

Creston은 그의 1번 교향곡이 1941년에 뉴욕 음악 비평가 협회상을 수상하였을 때 유명세를 얻었다.

He / had (already) received / a Guggenheim Fellowship / (in 1938).

S 그는 / V〈과거완료〉 이미 받았다 / O 구겐하임 연구비를 / 1938년에

그는 이미 1938년에 구겐하임 연구비를 받았다.

His work / was performed (widely) / (in the aftermath of World War II), / but / it faded / (from the concert repertoire) (with the rise of academic music) (in the 1960s).

S 그의 작품은 / V〈수동태〉 널리 공연되었다 / 부사 / 2차 세계대전의 직후에 / 하지만 / S V 그것은 서서히 사라졌다 / 음악회 연주곡목에서 / O 〈with 부대상황〉 학구적인 음악이 떠오르면서 / O.C 1960년대에

그의 작품은 2차 세계대전의 직후에 널리 공연되었지만 그것은 1960년대에 학구적인 음악이 떠오르면서 음악회 연주곡목에서 서서히 사라졌다.

노트 ■ fade from : ~에서 희미해지다
■ 〈with 부대상황〉

<table>
<tr><th>with</th><th>목적어</th><th colspan="3">목적격보어</th></tr>
<tr><td rowspan="5">~하면서,
~한채로</td><td rowspan="5"></td><td colspan="3">형용사(구)</td></tr>
<tr><td colspan="3">부사(구)</td></tr>
<tr><td colspan="3">전치사구</td></tr>
<tr><td rowspan="2">분사</td><td>현재분사
(Ring)</td><td>능동
(목적어가 목적격보어를 ~하고 있는)</td></tr>
<tr><td>과거분사
(p.p.)</td><td>수동
(목적어가 목적격보어에게 당하는, 되어진)</td></tr>
<tr><td>with</td><td>the rise of academic music</td><td colspan="3">in the 1960s</td></tr>
</table>

Several of his works / were inspired / (by the poetry of Walt Whitman).

S 그의 작품 중 몇몇은 / V〈수동태〉 영감을 받았다 / Walt Whitman의 시에 의해서

그의 작품 중 몇몇은 Walt Whitman의 시에서 영감을 받았다.

노트 ■ be inspired by : ~에 의해 영감을 받다
■ 〈주어와 동사의 수의 일치〉
• A of B : 일반적인 경우에 A가 주어
• A of B : A가 부분/부분인 경우에 B가 주어

<table>
<tr><th colspan="2">A</th><th>B</th><th rowspan="3">동사
(B에 수의 일치)</th></tr>
<tr><td>분수</td><td>two – thirds 등</td><td rowspan="2">주어</td></tr>
<tr><td>부분</td><td>a group of, all of, a lot of, any of, a number of, both of, each of, either of, few of, half of, many of, most of, much of, neither of, none of, one of, part of, percent of, several of, some of, the rest, two of 등</td></tr>
<tr><td></td><td>Several of</td><td>his works</td><td><s>was inspired</s>
were inspired</td></tr>
</table>

■ 〈poem / poetry / poet〉

poem	(한 편의) 시	복수형 : poems
poetry	(집합적) 시집	단/복수 동일
poet	시인	복수형 : poets

He / died / (in Poway, California, a suburb of San Diego).

S 그는 / V 사망했다 / 샌디에이고 근교의 캘리포니아주 포웨이에서

그는 샌디에이고 근교의 캘리포니아주 포웨이에서 사망했다.

▶ Paul Creston에 관한 다음 글의 내용과 일치하지 <u>않는</u> 것은?

① 오래전에 죽은 작곡가들이 자신에게 영향을 주었다고 주장했다.
② 리드미컬한 독창성을 스타일의 특징으로 한다.
③ 1938년에 구겐하임 연구비를 받았다.
④ Walt Whitman의 시에 영감을 주었다.
⑤ 캘리포니아주의 포웨이에서 사망했다.

정답 | ④

해설 | ④ Walt Whitman의 시에서 영감을 받은 작품들이 있다는 내용이 있으므로 ④는 글의 내용과 일치하지 않는다.

오답 | ① 2번째 문장에 나타나 있다.
② 3번째 문장에 나타나 있다.
③ 6번째 문장에 나타나 있다.
⑤ 9번째 문장에 나타나 있다.

Words

- ☐ popular
- ☐ composer
- ☐ century
- ☐ musician
- ☐ claim
- ☐ long-dead
- ☐ hallmark
- ☐ style
- ☐ harmonically
- ☐ impressionist
- ☐ achieve
- ☐ renown
- ☐ symphony
- ☐ critic
- ☐ award
- ☐ receive
- ☐ fellowship
- ☐ inspire
- ☐ suburb

Phrases

- ☐ fade from
- ☐ be inspired by

우선순위 영단어 역대 수능 기출 + 전국 모의고사 기출 + EBS 기출 + 교과서 기출 빈출 어휘

단어	뜻	단어	뜻	단어	뜻
magnificent	a. 훌륭한	maintenance	n. 정비사	make up	v. 구성하다
margin	n. 차이	massive	a. 거대한	mature	a. 심사숙고한
microorganism	n. 미생물	millennium	n. 천 년간	minimal	a. 최소의
misconception	n. 오해	moderate	a. 적절한	monotonous	a. 단조로운
morale	n. 근로 의욕	mount	v. (점진적으로) 증가하다	must have p.p.	~했음에 틀림없다
neglect	v. 무시하다	negotiation	n. 협상	nonverbal	a. 비언어적인
now that	~이니(까)	obscure	v. 흐리게 하다	occasional	a. 이따금의
odd	a. 이상한	odds	n. 승산	oppose	v. ~에 반대하다
orbit	n. 궤도	order	v. 주문하다	organize	v. (경매 등을) 개최하다
out of order	고장 난	overwhelm	v. 압도하다	owe ~ to ...	v. ~는 … 때문이다
participate	v. 참여하다	patron	n. 후원자	peasant	n. 농민
pebble	n. 조약돌	personality	n. 성격	pesticide	n. 살충제
point out	v. 지적하다	predictable	a. 예측 가능한	preservation	n. 보존
prestigious	a. 명망 있는	priest	n. 사제	principle	n. 원리
probability	n. 가망	procedural	n. 절차상의	proficient	a. 능숙한
profit	n. 수익	prone	a. ~하기 쉬운	publish	v. 발표하다
punishment	n. 처벌	qualification	n. 자격 부여; 필요 조건	quality	n. 질
quantity	n. 양	quest	n. 탐구	radiation	n. 방사
raise	v. (자식을) 기르다	rank	v. 자리 잡다	reason	v. 판단하다
reasonably	ad. 합리적으로	receipt	n. 수입[수령]액	reflection	n. 성찰
regularly	ad. 정기적으로	rejection	n. 거부	relate	v. 보고하다
remarkable	a. 주목할 만한	reminder	n. 생각나게 하는 것	reproductive	a. 번식의
require	v. 요구하다	researcher	n. 연구원	residential	a. 거주하는
respondent	n. 응답자	responsibility	n. 책임	restraint	n. 규제
restrict	v. 제한하다	result in	(결과를) 초래하다	resume	v. 회복하다
retire	v. 은퇴하다	roam	v. 돌아다니다	sense	n. 어의
shelter	n. 은신처	shiver	v. 떨다	significance	n. 의미
slip	v. 풀다	slope	n. 경사면	solitary	a. 무리짓지 않는
somewhat	ad. 다소	spin	v. (실 등을) 짜다	spontaneous	a. 자연스러운
spouse	n. 배우자	spread	v. 펴다	sprout	v. 갑자기 자라다
stand	n. 태도	stereotype	n. 고정관념	stick	v. 들러 붙다

변형문제

01 다음 글을 읽고, |조건|에 맞게 빈칸을 채우시오.

| 조건 |
* (A), (B), (D)는 2단어, (C)는 숫자로 쓸 것
* 본문에 있는 표현을 찾아 그대로 쓸 것

Mostly self-taught, Paul Creston became one of the most popular composers of the mid-20th century. A conservative musician, Creston claimed his greatest influences to be long-dead composers. The hallmark of his style was rhythmic originality. Harmonically, he might be called an American impressionist. Creston achieved renown when his Symphony No. 1 won the New York Music Critics' Circle Award in 1941. He had already received a Guggenheim Fellowship in 1938. His work was performed widely in the aftermath of World War II, but it faded from the concert repertoire with the rise of academic music in the 1960s. Several of his works were inspired by the poetry of Walt Whitman. He died in Poway, California, a suburb of San Diego.

Paul Creston:

1. insisted that he was affected by (A) ____________ ____________.
2. featured (B) ____________ ____________ in his work.
3. obtained a research fee in (C) ____________.
4. due to the emergence of (D) ____________ ____________, the selection and performance of his work vanished gradually.

02 다음 글을 읽고, Creston에 대해 답할 수 없는 것은?

Mostly self-taught, Paul Creston became one of the most popular composers of the mid-20th century. A conservative musician, Creston claimed his greatest influences to be long-dead composers. The hallmark of his style was rhythmic originality. Harmonically, he might be called an American impressionist. Creston achieved renown when his Symphony No. 1 won the New York Music Critics' Circle Award in 1941. He had already received a Guggenheim Fellowship in 1938. His work was performed widely in the aftermath of World War II, but it faded from the concert repertoire with the rise of academic music in the 1960s. Several of his works were inspired by the poetry of Walt Whitman. He died in Poway, California, a suburb of San Diego.

① What song did he win the New York Music Critics' Association Award?
② When did he get the money for Guggenheim Fellowship?
③ Was he married?
④ What inspired some of his works?
⑤ Where did he die?

03 Paul Creston에 대한 설명으로 일치하는 것은?

Mostly self-taught, Paul Creston became one of the most popular composers of the mid-20th century. A conservative musician, Creston claimed his greatest influences to be long-dead composers. The hallmark of his style was rhythmic originality. Harmonically, he might be called an American impressionist. Creston achieved renown when his Symphony No. 1 won the New York Music Critics' Circle Award in 1941. He had already received a Guggenheim Fellowship in 1938. His work was performed widely in the aftermath of World War II, but it faded from the concert repertoire with the rise of academic music in the 1960s. Several of his works were inspired by the poetry of Walt Whitman. He died in Poway, California, a suburb of San Diego.

① 그는 주로 좋은 스승을 만나 공부한 작곡가이다.
② 그에게 가장 큰 영향을 미친 사람들은 현재 활동하고 있는 작곡가라고 생각했다.
③ 그의 스타일의 특징은 리드미컬한 독창성이었다.
④ 그는 1938년에 유명세를 얻었다.
⑤ 그의 작품 중 몇몇은 Walt Whitman의 노래에서 영감을 받았다.

04 다음 글을 읽고, |조건|에 맞게 빈칸 (A), (B)를 채우시오.

| 조건 |

* (A), (B)는 각각 1단어로 쓸 것
* 본문에 있는 단어만을 사용할 것
* 필요한 경우, 문맥과 어법에 맞게 변형할 것

Mostly self-taught, Paul Creston became one of the most popular composers of the mid-20th century. A conservative musician, Creston claimed his greatest influences to be long-dead composers. The hallmark of his style was rhythmic originality. Harmonically, he might be called an American impressionist. Creston achieved renown when his Symphony No. 1 won the New York Music Critics' Circle Award in 1941. He had already received a Guggenheim Fellowship in 1938. His work was performed widely in the aftermath of World War II, but it faded from the concert repertoire with the rise of academic music in the 1960s. Several of his works were inspired by the poetry of Walt Whitman. He died in Poway, California, a suburb of San Diego.

⬇

Creston thought the people who (A) _____________ him were long dead composers, and he was one of the most (B) _____________ composers of the 20th century.

내용 일치/불일치

글의 논리	Story
제목	Al-Jazari에 대한 설명
주제	Al-Jazari는 인간의 편리를 위한 실용적인 목적으로 기계를 창조하는 첫 번째 발명가이다.

PRACTICE 01

018 어법 선택 & 연결어

Al-Jazari (1136-1206) was a Muslim scholar, inventor, mechanical engineer, artisan, artist and mathematician. He is best **[knowing / known]** for writing '*The Book of Knowledge of Ingenious Mechanical Devices*' in 1206. He **[remembers / is remembered]** for his automaton designs, **[including / included]** water-operated **[one / ones]**. Most of them **[is / are]** decorative fanciful objects, **[despite / though]** some also serve a function. Al-Jazari constructed a hand washing automaton first **[employing / employed]** the flush mechanism now **[using / used]** in modern toilets. It features an automaton **[stood / standing]** by a basin **[what / that]** is filled **[of / with]** water. When the user pulls the lever, the water **[releases / is released]** and the automaton refills the basin. Leonardo da Vinci **[says / is said]** **[to have influenced / to have been influenced]** by the classic automatons of Al-Jazari. Al-Jazari appears **[to be / to have been]** the first inventor to display an interest in **[creation / creating]** human-like machines for practical purposes such as **[use / using]** the environment for human comfort.

이야기 Al-Jazari에 대한 설명

Al-Jazari (1136-1206) / was / a Muslim scholar, inventor, mechanical engineer, artisan, artist and mathematician.

(S: Al-Jazari(1136-1206)는 / V: 였다 / S.C₁ S.C₂: 이슬람의 학자이자, 발명가, / S.C₃ S.C₄ S.C₅ S.C₆: 기계 설계자, 장인, 예술가 및 수학자)

Al-Jazari(1136-1206)는 이슬람의 학자이자 발명가, 기계 설계자, 장인, 예술가 및 수학자였다.

He / is (best) known / (for writing / '*The Book of Knowledge of Ingenious Mechanical Devices*') / (in 1206).

(S: 그는 / V(수동태): 가장 잘 알려져 있다 / 쓴 것으로 / '독창적인 기계 장치 지식에 관한 책'을 / 1206년에)

그는 1206년에 '독창적인 기계 장치 지식에 관한 책'을 쓴 것으로 가장 잘 알려져 있다.

노트 ■ 〈상태 수동태〉: 수동의 전치사 by 이외 다른 전치사를 사용하는 경우
• be known by/to/for/as

	과거분사	전치사	뜻
be동사	known	by+수단, 판단	~에 의해서 알려지다
		to+동사원형	~한 것으로 알려져 있다
		to+대상	~에게 알려지다
		for+이유, 근거	~로 알려지다, ~ 때문에 알려지다
		as+자격, 신분	~로서 알려지다

He / is remembered / (for his automaton designs), / (including water-operated ones).

(S: 그는 / V(수동태): 기억된다 / 그의 자동 장치 설계에 대해서 / 물로 작동되는 것을 포함한)

그는 물로 작동되는 것을 포함한 자동 장치를 설계한 사람으로 기억된다.

노트 ■ be remembered for : ~으로 기억되다[유명하다]
■ 〈including 용법〉

현재분사(형용사)	~을 포함하는	명사를 뒤에서 후치 수식함
분사구문(부사)	~을 포함하여	부대상황
전치사		형용사구, 부사구
		유사 표현 : regarding, concerning, considering

Most of them / are decorative fanciful objects, / (though some / (also) serve a function).

(S: 그러한 자동 장치들의 대부분은 / V / S.C: 장식용으로 만든 별난 물건이다 / 〈종·접〉 비록 / S: 몇몇은 / V O: 또한 실제로 기능을 수행하지만)

그러한 자동 장치들의 대부분은 장식용으로 만든 별난 물건이지만, 몇몇은 또한 실제로 기능을 수행할 수 있다.

노트 ■ serve [fulfill, perform] a function : 역할을 수행하다
■ 〈주어와 동사의 수의 일치〉
• A of B : 일반적인 경우에 A가 주어
• A of B : A가 부분/부분인 경우에 B가 주어

	A	B	
분수	two - thirds 등	주어	동사 (B에 수의 일치)
부분	a group of, all of, a lot of, any of, a number of, both of, each of, either of, few of, half of, many of, most of, much of, neither of, none of, one of, part of, percent of, several of, some of, the rest, two of 등		
	Most of	them	~~is~~ are

■ 〈양보/대조〉

전치사	in spite of	+명사/명사 상당어구	비록 ~이지만
	despite		
종속접속사	though	+주어+동사	
	although		
	even though		
	even if		
	as		
	while		반면에
	whereas		

Al-Jazari / constructed / a hand washing automaton / (which was) (first) (employing the flush mechanism) / (which was) (now used in modern toilets).

S: Al-Jazari는 / V: 개발하였다 / O: 손 씻기 자동 장치를 / 〈현재분사〉 처음으로 수세식 기계 구조를 사용한 / 〈과거분사〉 지금도 현대적인 화장실에 사용되는

Al-Jazari는 지금도 현대적인 화장실에 사용되는 수세식 기계 구조를 처음으로 사용한 손 씻기 자동 장치를 개발하였다.

노트 ■ 〈주격관계대명사+be동사 생략〉

명사	(주격관계대명사+be동사)	
		Ring(현재분사) – 능동
		p.p.(과거분사) – 수동
		형용사
		부사
		명사
		전치사구
a hand washing automaton	(which/that was)	employing ~
the flush mechanism		used ~

It / features an automaton / (which is) (standing by a basin) / (that is filled with water).

S / V: 이것은 자동 장치로 구성된 특징을 지니고 있다 / O / 〈현재분사〉 〈선행사〉 세면대 옆에서 서 있는 / 〈주·관〉 V〈수동태〉 물로 채워진

그것은 물로 채워진 세면대 옆에서 서 있는 자동 장치로 구성된 특징을 지니고 있다.

노트 ■ be filled with : ~로 가득 차다(=be full of)
■ stand by : 가만히[그냥] 있다, ~ 옆에 서 있다
■ 〈주격관계대명사절의 수의 일치〉 : 선행사를 포함하고 있는 관계대명사 what 사용 불가

선행사	주격관계대명사절		
	주격관계대명사	~~주어~~	동사
a basin	that		is filled

■ 〈주격관계대명사+be동사 생략〉

명사	(주격관계대명사+be동사)	
		Ring(현재분사) – 능동
		p.p.(과거분사) – 수동
		형용사
		부사
		명사
		전치사구
an automaton	(which/that is)	standing ~

(When the user pulls the lever), / the water / is released / and / the automaton / refills the basin.

〈종·접〉 S V O: 사용자가 레버를 당기면 / S: 물이 / V〈수동태〉: 나온다 / 그리고 / S: 자동 장치가 / V O: 세면대의 물을 다시 채운다

사용자가 레버를 당기면 물이 나오고 옆에 서 있던 자동 장치가 세면대의 물을 다시 채운다.

Leonardo da Vinci / is said / {to have been influenced / (by the classic automatons of Al-Jazari)}.

S: Leonardo da Vinci가 / V〈수동태〉: 말한다 / 〈to R의 완료 수동〉 영향을 받았다고 / Al-Jazari의 고전적 자동 장치에 의해

Leonardo da Vinci가 Al-Jazari의 고전적 자동 장치에 영향을 받았다고 한다.

노트 ■ be influenced by : ~에 영향을 받다
■ 〈to R의 태와 시제〉

태	능동태	to R
	수동태	to be p.p.
시제	단순시제 : 본동사 시제와 동일	to R
	완료시제 : 본동사 시제보다 한 시제 앞선 시제	to have p.p.
	완료 수동	to have been p.p.

Al-Jazari / appears / to have been the first inventor / {to display an interest / (in creating human-like machines) / (for practical purposes) / (such as using the environment / for human comfort)}.

S: Al-Jazari는 / V: 보인다 / 〈to R의 완료 시제〉 S.C: 첫 번째 발명가였던 것처럼 / O: 흥미를 보인 / 〈동명사〉 인간과 유사한 기계를 창조하는데 / 실용적인 목적으로 / 〈동명사〉 환경을 이용하는 / 인간의 편리를 위하여

Al-Jazari는 인간의 편리를 위하여 환경을 이용하는 것과 같은 실용적인 목적으로 인간과 유사한 기계를 창조하는 데 흥미를 보인 첫 번째 발명가였던 것처럼 보인다.

노트 ■ display[show] an interest : 관심을 표시하다
■ A such as B : B와 같은 A
■ 〈appear 동사의 쓰임〉 : ~처럼 보이다

appear	주격보어
	that절
	to R
	분사
	to be 보어
	as+보어

▶ Al-Jazari에 관한 다음 글의 내용과 일치하는 것은?

① 그의 업적을 기록한 책이 1206년에 후손들에 의해 간행되었다.
② 설계한 대부분의 기계 장치들은 실제로 작동 가능하다.
③ 수세식 기계 구조를 채택한 손 씻기 자동 장치를 발명했다.
④ 레오나르도 다빈치에게 과학적인 영향을 받았다.
⑤ 인간의 편리성보다는 환경 보호에 더 관심이 있었다.

정답 | ③

해설 | ③ 5번째 문장에 수세식 기계 구조를 처음으로 사용한 손 씻기 자동 장치를 개발했다고 나타나 있다.

오답 | ① 1206년에 간행된 책이 후손들에 의해 발행되었다는 내용은 없다.
② 4번째 문장을 보았을 때, 자동 장치들의 대부분은 장식용인 것을 알 수 있다.
④ 8번째 문장을 보았을 때, 레오나르드 다빈치가 그에게 과학적인 영향을 받았다는 것을 알 수 있다.
⑤ 9번째 문장을 보았을 때, 인간의 편리성을 위해 환경을 이용한다는 것을 알 수 있다.

Words

- ☐ Muslim
- ☐ scholar
- ☐ inventor
- ☐ mechanical
- ☐ engineer
- ☐ mathematician
- ☐ device
- ☐ water-operated
- ☐ object
- ☐ mechanism
- ☐ toilet
- ☐ feature
- ☐ refill
- ☐ classic
- ☐ display
- ☐ interest
- ☐ human-like
- ☐ practical
- ☐ environment

Phrases

- ☐ be known for
- ☐ serve [fulfill, perform] a function
- ☐ be influenced by
- ☐ A such as B
- ☐ be remembered for
- ☐ be filled with
- ☐ stand by
- ☐ display[show] an interest

우선순위 영단어

역대 수능 기출 + 전국 모의고사 기출 + EBS 기출 + 교과서 기출 빈출 어휘

단어	뜻	단어	뜻	단어	뜻
stir	v. (감정을) 일으키다	straightforward	a. 간단한	stride	v. 성큼성큼 걷다
sue	v. 고소하다	supplier	n. 공급자	surrounding	a. 환경
survey	n. (설문) 조사	sustainable	a. 계속할 수 있는	swell	v. 팽창시키다
switch	v. 바꾸다	systematic	a. 체계적인	tension	n. 긴장
theory	n. 이론	threaten	v. 위협하다	timid	a. 겁 많은
tout	v. 장점을 내세우다	transfer	v. 옮기다	translate	v. 바꾸다
transparent	a. 투명한	trap	n. 함정	trend	n. 경향
ultimate	a. 궁극적인	undergo	v. 경험하다	validate	v. ~의 정당성을 인정하다
vanish	v. 사라지다	wage	n. 임금	wheat	n. 밀
when it comes to	~에 관한 한	widespread	a. 널리 보급되어 있는	withdraw	v. 철회하다
withdrawal	n. (심리적인) 위축	withhold	v. 보류하다	work out	v. ~을 산출하다
settlement	n. 해결	absurd	a. 불합리한	abundant	a. 풍부한
acclaim	n. 갈채	accounting	n. 계산	act on	v. ~에 따라 행동하다
adapt to	~에 적응하다	adaptation	n. 적응	administer	v. 관리하다
administrative	a. 관리의	admission	n. 시인	admit	v. 입학을 허락하다
affirm	v. 확언하다	agency	n. 원동력	air	v. (의견을) 발표하다
allocate	v. 할당하다	ally	n. 우군	amount to	(총액, 금액) ~에 달하다
ankle	n. 발목	anthropology	n. 인류학	antibiotic	n. 항생의
anxiety	n. 불안	appealing	a. 매력적인	apply to	~에 지원하다
appoint	v. 지정[임명]하다	argue	v. 논쟁하다	array	n. 배열
artifact	n. 문화 유물	aspiration	n. 열의	assemble	v. 조립하다

01 다음 글을 읽고, |조건|에 맞게 주어진 요약문을 완성하시오.

| 조건 |
* (A), (B), (C)는 각각 1단어로 쓸 것
* [보기]에서 선택한 단어를 한 번씩만 쓸 것
* 필요한 경우, 문맥과 어법에 맞게 변형할 것

[보기] early / prevent / clean / last / similar / equal / pragmatic / radical / late / functional / rational

Al-Jazari (1136-1206) was a Muslim scholar, inventor, mechanical engineer, artisan, artist and mathematician. He is best known for writing '*The Book of Knowledge of Ingenious Mechanical Devices*' in 1206. He is remembered for his automaton designs, including water-operated ones. Most of them are decorative fanciful objects, though some also serve a function. Al-Jazari constructed a hand washing automaton first employing the flush mechanism now used in modern toilets. It features an automaton standing by a basin that is filled with water. When the user pulls the lever, the water is released and the automaton refills the basin. Leonardo da Vinci is said to have been influenced by the classic automatons of Al-Jazari. Al-Jazari appears to have been the first inventor to display an interest in creating human-like machines for practical purposes such as using the environment for human comfort.

⬇

Al-Jazari is considered as the (A) ____________ inventor who presents an interest in producing devices that are (B) ____________ to humans and have (C) ____________ aims like employing the environment for the comfort of humans.

02 다음 문장이 들어갈 부분으로 가장 적절한 곳을 고르시오.

It features an automaton standing by a basin that is filled with water.

Al-Jazari (1136-1206) was a Muslim scholar, inventor, mechanical engineer, artisan, artist and mathematician. He is best known for writing '*The Book of Knowledge of Ingenious Mechanical Devices*' in 1206. He is remembered for his automaton designs, including water-operated ones. (①) Most of them are decorative fanciful objects, though some also serve a function. (②) Al-Jazari constructed a hand washing automaton first employing the flush mechanism now used in modern toilets. (③) When the user pulls the lever, the water is released and the automaton refills the basin. (④) Leonardo da Vinci is said to have been influenced by the classic automatons of Al-Jazari. (⑤) Al-Jazari appears to have been the first inventor to display an interest in creating human-like machines for practical purposes such as using the environment for human comfort.

03 다음 중 지칭하는 대상이 다른 하나는?

Al-Jazari (1136-1206) was ① a Muslim scholar, inventor, mechanical engineer, artisan, artist and mathematician. ② He is best known for writing '*The Book of Knowledge of Ingenious Mechanical Devices*' in 1206. ③ He is remembered for his automaton designs, including water-operated ones. Most of them are decorative fanciful objects, though some also serve a function. Al-Jazari constructed a hand washing automaton first employing the flush mechanism now used in modern toilets. It features an automaton standing by a basin that is filled with water. When the user pulls the lever, the water is released and the automaton refills the basin. ④ A person is said to have been influenced by the classic automatons of Al-Jazari. Al-Jazari appears to have been ⑤ the first inventor to display an interest in creating human-like machines for practical purposes such as using the environment for human comfort.

04 Al-Jazari에 대한 설명으로 적절하지 않은 것은?

Al-Jazari (1136-1206) was a Muslim scholar, inventor, mechanical engineer, artisan, artist and mathematician. He is best known for writing '*The Book of Knowledge of Ingenious Mechanical Devices*' in 1206. He is remembered for his automaton designs, including water-operated ones. Most of them are decorative fanciful objects, though some also serve a function. Al-Jazari constructed a hand washing automaton first employing the flush mechanism now used in modern toilets. It features an automaton standing by a basin that is filled with water. When the user pulls the lever, the water is released and the automaton refills the basin. Leonardo da Vinci is said to have been influenced by the classic automatons of Al-Jazari. Al-Jazari appears to have been the first inventor to display an interest in creating human-like machines for practical purposes such as using the environment for human comfort.

① 그는 이슬람의 학자였다.
② 그는 1206년에 기계에 관한 책을 썼다.
③ 그는 자동 장치를 설계했다.
④ 그가 만든 자동 장치들은 모두 장식용이다.
⑤ 그는 레오나르드 다빈치에게 영향을 주었다.

UNIT 05 내용 일치/불일치

글의 논리	Story
제목	Anthony에 대한 설명
주제	여성 인권 운동가 Anthony의 생애

PRACTICE 02

019 어법 선택 & 연결어

American social reformer and leader of the movement for women's suffrage (the right to vote), Susan B. Anthony was a **[determined / determining]** pioneer of women's equality and other social causes. With Elizabeth Cady Stanton, **[whom / what]** she met in 1851, Anthony was the principal organizer and ideological voice of the National Woman Suffrage Association **[what / that]** they **[formed / had formed]** in 1869. Anthony led a group of women to the polls in Rochester, New York, in 1872 to test women's suffrage under the Fourteenth Amendment. Her arrest, trial, and sentence of a fine **[what / that]** she refused **[to pay / paying]** **[to become / became]** a model for other suffrage protests. **[Despite / Although]** she did not live to see women **[gain / to gain]** the vote, Anthony's single-minded advocacy of equal justice for women **[has credited / has been credited]** with helping **[to win / winning]** social and political gains for women and **[launches / launching]** the women's movement in the twentieth century.

이야기 Anthony에 대한 설명

American social reformer and leader / (of the movement for women's suffrage (the right to vote)), / Susan B. Anthony / was a determined pioneer / (of women's equality and other social causes).

(S: 미국의 사회 개혁가이며 지도자인 =〈동격〉 여성 투표권 운동의 / Susan B. / Anthony는 (V) 〈과거분사〉 결연한 개척자였다 (S.C) / 여성 평등과 다른 사회적 대의의)

미국의 사회 개혁가이며 여성 투표권 운동의 지도자인 Susan B. Anthony는 여성 평등과 다른 사회적 대의의 결연한 개척자였다.

노트 ■ 〈동격〉: A(명사), B(명사) (A가 주어, B라는 A)

동격(B라는 A)			
명사(A)	,(콤마)	명사(구/절)(B)	동사
American social reformer and leader of the movement for women's suffrage (the right to vote)	,	Susan B. Anthony	was

(With Elizabeth Cady Stanton), / (whom she met / in 1851), Anthony / was the principal organizer and ideological voice / (of the National Woman Suffrage Association) / (that they formed / in 1869).

(〈선행사〉 Elizabeth Cady Stanton과 함께 / 〈목·관〉 S V 그녀(Anthony)가 만났던 / 1851년에 / Anthony는 (S) (V) / 주요 설립자이며 (S.C₁) 이념적 대변자였다 (S.C₂) / 〈선행사〉 미국 여성 투표권 협회의 / 〈목·관〉 S V 그들이 조직한 / 1869년에)

1851년에 Anthony가 만난 Elizabeth Cady Stanton과 함께 그녀는 그들이 1869년에 조직한 미국 여성 투표권 협회의 주요 설립자이며 이념적 대변자였다.

노트 ■ 〈목적격관계대명사 that〉: 타동사의 목적어가 없는 경우 / 선행사를 포함하고 있는 관계대명사 what 사용 불가

선행사	목적격관계대명사	주어	타동사	~~목적어~~
Elizabeth Cady Stanton	whom : (생략 가능)	she	met	
the National Woman Suffrage Association	that : (생략 가능)	they	formed	

■ 〈what vs. that〉

	관계대명사(불완전한 문장)	접속사(완전한 문장)
what	○ 선행사를 포함하고 있기 때문에 what 앞에 선행사 불필요	×
that	○ that 앞에 선행사 필요	○

Anthony / led a group of women / (to the polls) (in Rochester, New York), / (in 1872) / (to test women's suffrage) (under the Fourteenth Amendment).

(Anthony는 (S) / 한 무리의 여성들을 이끌고 갔다 (V, O) / 투표소로 / 뉴욕의 로체스터에 있는 / 1872년에 / 여성의 투표권을 (O) 시험하기 위해 / 미국 연방 헌법 수정 제14조 하에서)

Anthony는 미국 연방 헌법 수정 제14조 하에서 여성의 투표권을 시험하기 위해 1872년에 뉴욕의 로체스터에 있는 투표소로 한 무리의 여성들을 이끌고 갔다.

노트 ■ lead A to B : A를 B로 이끌다

Her arrest, trial, and sentence (of a fine) / (that she refused to pay) / became a model / (for other suffrage protests).

(S_1 그녀의 체포, S_2 재판, 그리고 S_3 벌금의 선고는 〈선행사〉 〈목·관〉 S 그녀가 V 내기를 O 거부한 / V 본보기가 S.C 되었다 / 다른 투표권 시위들에)

그녀의 체포, 재판, 그리고 그녀가 내기를 거부한 벌금의 선고는 다른 투표권 시위들에 본보기가 되었다.

노트
- pay a fine : 벌금을 내다
- 〈목적격관계대명사 that 생략〉

	〈목적격관계대명사절〉				
선행사	목적격관계대명사	주어	타동사	목적어	
a fine	that : 생략 가능	she	refused	to pay	~~목적어~~

- 〈목적어 자리에 to부정사를 취하는 완전타동사〉

주어	완전타동사	목적어
–	afford / agree / ask / attempt / care / choose / claim / dare / decide / demand / desire / determine / elect / expect / fail / guarantee / hope / intend / learn / manage / need / offer / plan / pretend / promise / refuse / resolve / seek / threaten / volunteer / want / wish 등	to 동사원형

- 〈be / get / become 구별〉

동사	용법
be	주어가 어떤 상태인지 표현
get	주어가 겪고 있는 상태의 변화를 표현
become	주어가 변화를 겪고 어떻게 되었는지 변화의 결과 표현

{Although she did not live / (to see women gain the vote)}, / Anthony's single-minded advocacy / (of equal justice) (for women) / has been credited {with helping to win social and political gains / (for women) / and / launching the women's movement / (in the twentieth century)}.

(〈종·접〉 S 비록 그녀는 V 죽었지만 / 〈지각동사〉 O O.C 여성이 투표권을 얻는 것을 보지 못하고 / Anthony의 한결같은 지지는 S / 평등한 정의에 대한 / 여성에 대한 / V〈현재완료 수동〉 공이 있다고 여겨져 왔다 / 〈동명사1〉 O 사회·정치적 이득을 얻는 것을 도운 것 / 여성을 위한 / 그리고 / 〈동명사2〉 O 여성 운동을 시작한 것에 대해 / 20세기에)

비록 그녀는 여성이 투표권을 얻는 것을 보지 못하고 죽었지만, 여성에 대한 평등한 정의에 대한 Anthony의 한결같은 지지는 여성을 위한 사회·정치적 이득을 얻는 것을 도운 것과 20세기의 여성 운동을 시작한 것에 공이 있다고 여겨져 왔다.

노트
- be credited with : ~로 명성을 얻다

- 〈양보/대조〉

전치사	in spite of	+명사/명사 상당어구	비록 ~이지만
	despite		
종속접속사	though	+주어+동사	
	although		
	even though		
	even if		
	as		
	while		반면에
	whereas		

- 〈지각동사〉

지각동사		목적어	목적격보어
see	보다	–	〈목적어와 목적격보어의 관계가 능동일 때〉 동사원형(R) – 완료 현재진행(Ring) – 진행, 순간, 찰나, 계속 〈목적어와 목적격보어의 관계가 수동일 때〉 과거분사(p.p.) 〈to부정사는 불가〉 : 수동태 문장 전환 시 가능
watch			
look at			
behold			
hear	듣다		
listen to			
feel	느끼다		
observe	관찰하다		
perceive	인식하다		
notice			
see		women	gain

- 〈help 동사의 쓰임〉

help	목적어		3형식
	(to) R		
help (준사역동사)	목적어	목적격보어	5형식
		(to) R	

▶ Susan B. Anthony에 관한 다음 글의 내용과 일치하지 않는 것은?

① 미국의 사회 개혁가였다.
② 미국 여성 투표권 협회를 조직했다.
③ 1872년에 여성들을 투표소로 이끌고 갔다.
④ 자신에게 선고된 벌금을 내기를 거부했다.
⑤ 여성이 투표권을 얻는 것을 본 후 생을 마감했다.

정답 | ⑤

해설 | ⑤ 5번째 문장에서 그녀는 여성이 투표권을 얻는 것을 보지 못하고 죽었다고 나오기 때문에 글의 내용과 일치하지 않는다.

오답 | ① 1번째 문장에 나타나 있다.
② 2번째 문장에 나타나 있다.
③ 3번째 문장에 나타나 있다.
④ 4번째 문장에 나타나 있다.

Words

☐ movement ____ ☐ determined ____ ☐ equality ____
☐ right ____ ☐ pioneer ____ ☐ social ____

☐ cause		☐ poll		☐ vote	
☐ organizer		☐ arrest		☐ advocacy	
☐ ideological		☐ trial		☐ justice	
☐ association		☐ refuse		☐ political	
☐ form		☐ protest			

Phrases

☐ lead A to B		☐ pay a fine	
☐ be credited with			

우선순위 영단어 역대 수능 기출 + 전국 모의고사 기출 + EBS 기출 + 교과서 기출 빈출 어휘

단어	뜻	단어	뜻	단어	뜻
assert	v. 확언하다	associated with	~와 관련된	astonishing	a. 놀라운
astronomer	n. 천문학자	astronomy	n. 천문학	at the expense of	~을 희생하며
attend to	~에 귀를 기울이다	attractive	a. 매력적인	authentic	a. 진본[진품]인
ban	v. 금지하다	be accustomed to	~에 익숙해지다	be associated with	~과 관련되다
be engaged in	~에 종사하다	be expected to	~하도록 기대되다	be supposed to do	~하기로 되어 있다
bear	v. 견디다	behavior	n. 행동	billion	n. 10억
blade	n. 칼날	bother	v. 괴롭히다	boundary	n. 경계
breed	v. (새끼를) 낳다	broad	a. 폭이 넓은	bundle	n. 꾸러미
burden	n. 부담	burrow	n. 굴	call for	v. ~을 요구하다
capitalism	n. 자본주의	case	n. 실정	challenging	a. 도전적인
charity	n. 자선[구호]단체	chronic	a. 만성적인	clarify	v. 명확하게 하다
classic	a. 고전적인	closet	n. 작은 방	cognition	n. 인지
collaboration	n. 협력	collective	a. 종합적인	comparison	n. 설정
compete	v. 경쟁하다	compile	v. 편집하다	composer	n. 작곡가
comprehend	v. 이해하다	conceive	v. (아이를) 배다, 임신하다	concrete	a. 명확한
confident	a. 자신 있는	constituent	n. 유권자	contaminate	v. 오염시키다
contend	v. 주장하다	contradiction	n. 모순	contradictory	a. 논쟁이 되고 있는
controversial	a. 물의를 일으키는	conversely	ad. 반대로	conviction	n. 확신
cooperation	n. 협력	correct	a. 옳은	correlation	n. 상호 관계
corridor	n. 복도	corruption	n. 부패	costly	ad. 희생이 큰
crawl	v. 기다	credibility	n. 신뢰성	credit	n. 수료 증명
creep	v. 기다	criminal	a. 범죄자	crystal	n. 결정체
cultivation	n. 경작	curb	n. (차도와 보도 사이의) 연석	density	n. 농도
descent	n. 하강	deserve	v. ~할 만하다	destruction	n. 파괴
deterioration	n. 퇴보	devastate	v. 파괴하다	diabetes	n. 당뇨병
dilute	v. 묽게 하다	disastrous	a. 비참한	disguise	n. 변장
disregard	v. 무시[묵살]하다	distinctive	a. 독특한	distressed	a. 괴로워하는
dye	n. 염료	embody	v. 포함하다	empathy	n. 공감
emperor	n. 황제	emphasis	n. 강조	empire	n. 제국
endangered	a. 멸종 위기에 있는	endeavor	n. 노력	endure	v. 견디다
enrich	v. ~을 질적으로 향상시키다	entertain	v. 즐겁게 하다	enthusiastic	a. 열렬한
enthusiastically	ad. 열정적으로	entrepreneur	n. 기업가	environment	n. 환경
envision	v. 마음속에 그리다	erosion	n. 침식	essential	a. 필수적인
evaluation	n. 평가	exclaim	v. 외치다	expense	n. 비용
explicit	a. 명시적인	exploitation	n. 착취	extend	v. 뻗다

변형문제

01 다음 글을 읽고, |조건|에 맞게 빈칸 (A), (B), (C)를 채우시오.

| 조건 |

* (A), (B), (C)는 각각 1단어로 쓸 것
* [보기]에서 선택한 단어를 1번씩만 쓸 것
* 필요한 경우, 문맥과 어법에 맞게 변형할 것

[보기] protest / gain / justice / voice / position / prepare / compare / struggle / engage / remember / credit / autonomy

American social reformer and leader of the movement for women's suffrage (the right to vote), Susan B. Anthony was a determined pioneer of women's equality and other social causes. With Elizabeth Cady Stanton, whom she met in 1851, Anthony was the principal organizer and ideological voice of the National Woman Suffrage Association that they formed in 1869. Anthony led a group of women to the polls in Rochester, New York, in 1872 to test women's suffrage under the Fourteenth Amendment. Her arrest, trial, and sentence of a fine that she refused to pay became a model for other suffrage protests. Although she did not live to see women (A) ____________ the vote, Anthony's single-minded advocacy of equal (B) ____________ for women has been (C) ____________ with helping to win social and political gains for women and launching the women's movement in the twentieth century.

02 다음 글을 읽고, |조건|에 맞게 주어진 요약문을 완성하시오.

| 조건 |

* (A)는 2단어, (B)는 1단어로 쓸 것
* 본문에 있는 단어만을 사용할 것
* 필요한 경우, 문맥과 어법에 맞게 변형할 것

American social reformer and leader of the movement for women's suffrage (the right to vote), Susan B. Anthony was a determined pioneer of women's equality and other social causes. With Elizabeth Cady Stanton, whom she met in 1851, Anthony was the principal organizer and ideological voice of the National Woman Suffrage Association that they formed in 1869. Anthony led a group of women to the polls in Rochester, New York, in 1872 to test women's suffrage under the Fourteenth Amendment. Her arrest, trial, and sentence of a fine that she refused to pay became a model for other suffrage protests. Although she did not live to see women gain the vote, Anthony's single-minded advocacy of equal justice for women has been credited with helping to win social and political gains for women and launching the women's movement in the twentieth century.

⬇

Susan B. Anthony who is known as a (A) ____________ ____________ in America established the National Woman Suffrage Association. In 1872, she took women to the polls, although she was dead before women was eligible for the (B) ____________.

03 다음 글을 읽고, |조건|에 맞게 주어진 요지를 완성하시오.

| 조건 |

* (A)는 4단어, (B) 1단어로 쓸 것
* 본문에 있는 단어만을 사용할 것
* 필요한 경우, 문맥과 어법에 맞게 변형할 것

American social reformer and leader of the movement for women's suffrage (the right to vote), Susan B. Anthony was a determined pioneer of women's equality and other social causes. With Elizabeth Cady Stanton, whom she met in 1851, Anthony was the principal organizer and ideological voice of the National Woman Suffrage Association that they formed in 1869. Anthony led a group of women to the polls in Rochester, New York, in 1872 to test women's suffrage under the Fourteenth Amendment. Her arrest, trial, and sentence of a fine that she refused to pay became a model for other suffrage protests. Although she did not live to see women gain the vote, Anthony's single-minded advocacy of equal justice for women has been credited with helping to win social and political gains for women and launching the women's movement in the twentieth century.

⬇

In the 20th century, Anthony's support for and devotion to women's equality has been publicly recognized and appreciated because she put her entire efforts into (A) ____________ ____________ ____________ ____________ for women and initiated the women's (B) ____________.

04 다음 문장이 들어갈 부분으로 가장 적절한 곳을 고르시오.

Anthony led a group of women to the polls in Rochester, New York, in 1872 to test women's suffrage under the Fourteenth Amendment.

(①) American social reformer and leader of the movement for women's suffrage (the right to vote), Susan B. Anthony was a determined pioneer of women's equality and other social causes. (②) With Elizabeth Cady Stanton, whom she met in 1851, Anthony was the principal organizer and ideological voice of the National Woman Suffrage Association that they formed in 1869. (③) Her arrest, trial, and sentence of a fine that she refused to pay became a model for other suffrage protests. (④) Although she did not live to see women gain the vote, Anthony's single-minded advocacy of equal justice for women has been credited with helping to win social and political gains for women and launching the women's movement in the twentieth century. (⑤)

내용 일치/불일치

글의 논리	Story
제목	The Springbok에 대한 설명
주제	The Springbok 문양은 백인 남아공 국민들에게 자부심과 국가적 스포츠 권력이 상징이다.

PRACTICE 03

020 어법 선택 & 연결어

The Springbok emblem **[wore / was worn]** by South African national sporting teams throughout **[almost / most]** of the 20th century. It continues **[to wear / to be worn]** by the South African national rugby team today, **[knowing / known] [universal / universally]** as the Springboks. The designation began on South Africa's first rugby tour to the British Isles in 1906. Team captain Paul Roos coined the term to prevent the British press **[inventing / from inventing]** one for **[them / it]**. The 1906 Springboks were **[high / highly] [successive / successful]**, **[win / winning] [near / nearly]** all their matches **[including / included]** Wales, the top British Isles nation at the time. (   ), South Africa's national sporting teams wore the emblem until the 1990s. The Springbok emblem proved to be **[high / highly]** divisive as national sporting teams **[limited / were limited]** to the white minority population until the 1980s. For white South Africans, the emblem was a symbol of pride and national sporting power.

이야기 The Springbok에 대한 설명

The Springbok emblem / was worn / (by South African national sporting teams) / (throughout most of the 20th century).

(S: 스프링복 문양은 / V〈수동태〉: 패용되었다 / 남아공 국가대표팀들에 의해 / 거의 20세기 내내)

스프링복 문양은 남아공 국가대표팀들에 의해 거의 20세기 내내 패용되었다.

노트 ■ 〈혼동 어휘〉

through	전치사	~을 통하여
throughout	전치사	[장소] ~의 도처에, [시간] ~ 동안, ~ 내내
	부사	도처에, 완전히, 철저하게
though	접속사	~에도 불구하고
thorough	형용사	철저한, 완전한

■ 〈most / almost / mostly〉

	대명사	형용사	부사
most	대부분의 것들(사람들)	대부분의	가장
almost	–	–	거의
mostly	–	–	주로, 일반적으로

It / continues to be worn / {by the South African national rugby team (today)}, / (which is) {known (universally) as the Springboks}.

(S: 이것은 / V, O〈to R 수동〉: 오늘날에도 계속 패용되고 있다 / 남아공 국가대표 럭비팀에 의해 / 〈과거분사〉 세계적으로 스프링복스라고 알려져 있는)

이것은 세계적으로 스프링복스라고 알려져 있는 남아공 국가대표 럭비팀에 의해 오늘날에도 계속 패용되고 있다.

노트 ■ 〈3형식에서 목적어 자리에 to R / Ring 둘 다 사용 가능〉

	완전타동사		목적어
주어	begin	~을 시작하다	to R/Ring (의미 차이 없음)
	cease	~을 중단하다	
	continue	~을 계속하다	
	deserve	~할 가치/자격/권리가 있다	
	dislike	~을 싫어하다	
	hate		
	like	~을 좋아하다	
	love	~을 사랑하다	
	neglect	~하는 것을 소홀히 하다	
	prefer	~쪽을 좋아하다	
	require	~을 요구하다	
	start	~을 시작하다	

■ 〈to R의 태와 시제〉

태	능동태	to R
	수동태	to be p.p.
시제	단순시제 : 본동사 시제와 동일	to R
	완료시제 : 본동사 시제보다 한 시제 앞선 시제	to have p.p.
	완료 수동	to have been p.p.

■ 〈주격관계대명사＋be동사 생략〉

명사	(주격관계대명사 ＋be동사)	Ring(현재분사) – 능동
		p.p.(과거분사) – 수동
		형용사
		부사
		명사
		전치사구
the South African national rugby team	(which is)	known ~

■ 〈상태 수동태〉: 수동의 전치사 by 이외 다른 전치사를 사용하는 경우

• be known by/to/for/as

	과거분사	전치사	뜻
be동사	known	by+수단, 판단	~에 의해서 알려지다
		to+동사원형	~한 것으로 알려져 있다
		to+대상	~에게 알려지다
		for+이유, 근거	~로 알려지다, ~ 때문에 알려지다
		as+자격, 신분	~로서 알려지다

The designation / began / (on South Africa's first rugby tour) / (to the British Isles) / (in 1906).

(The designation: S 이 명칭은 / began: V 시작했다 / 남아공 럭비팀이 최초로 원정경기를 떠나면서 / 영국제도로 / 1906년에)

이 명칭은 1906년 남아공 럭비팀이 최초로 영국제도로 원정경기를 떠나면서 (사용되기) 시작했다.

노트 ■ begin on [with, at, by]: ~부터 시작하다

Team captain Paul Roos / coined the term / (to prevent / the British press / from inventing one for them).

(Team captain Paul Roos: S 팀의 주장인 Paul Roos는 / coined: V / the term: O 그 명칭을 고안해냈다 / 만들어내지 못하게 / the British press: O 영국 언론이 / 자기네들을 부르는 말을)

팀의 주장인 Paul Roos는 영국 언론이 자기네들을 (임의로) 부르는 말을 만들어 내지 못하도록 하기 위해 그 명칭을 고안해냈다.

노트 ■ 〈방해/금지〉

주어	완전타동사	목적어	전치사	목적어
	keep prohibit deter bar hinder prevent protect discourage stop		from	

The 1906 Springboks / were (highly) successful, / (winning nearly all their matches) / {including Wales, the top British Isles nation / (at the time)}.

(The 1906 Springboks: S 1906년의 스프링복스들은 / were: V / successful: S.C 매우 성공적이었다 / winning: 〈분사구문〉 / all their matches: O 거의 모든 경기를 이기면서 / 영국제도의 최강팀인 / 웨일즈와의 경기를 포함하여 / 그 당시)

1906년의 스프링복스들은 매우 성공적이어서 그 당시 영국제도의 최강팀인 웨일즈와의 경기를 포함하여 거의 모든 경기를 이겼다.

노트 ■ at the time: 그 당시, 그 시기, 그 때

■ 〈high / highly〉

high	형용사	높은
	부사	높게
	명사	높은 곳
highly	부사	매우(=very)

■ 〈succeed 어휘 변화〉

	동사	명사	형용사	부사
succeed	성공하다	–	–	–
success	–	성공	–	–
successor	–	후임자, 상속자	–	–
successful	–	–	성공적인	–
successive	–	–	연속적인	–
successfully	–	–	–	성공적으로
successively	–	–	–	연속하여, 잇따라서

■ 〈분사구문 – 문미〉: 주절과 분사구문의 위치가 서로 바뀌어도 무관

주절		종속절(→ 분사구문)			
주어	동사	종속 접속사	주어	동사 : 상황에 맞게 아래처럼 바뀜	
		〈그대로 사용하면 의미 강조〉	(주절의 주어와 같으면 생략하고, 다르면 주격으로 사용함)	(being) (having been) 생략 가능	Ring(현재분사) p.p.(과거분사) 형용사 명사
The 1906 Springboks	were	–	–	–	winning

■ 〈near / nearby / nearly〉

	부사	형용사	전치사	동사
near	(거리/시간상으로) 가까이, 거의	(거리/시간상으로) 가까운	(거리상으로) ~에서 가까이 (숫자 앞에 쓰여) 거의[약]	(시간/거리상으로) 가까워지다 [다가오다], ~에 접근하다
nearby	인근에, 가까운 곳에, 거의, 대략; 간신히, 가까스로, 밀접하게, 면밀하게	[주로 명사 앞에 씀] 인근의, 가까운 곳의	–	–
nearly	거의	–	–	–

■ 〈including 용법〉

현재분사(형용사)	~을 포함하는	명사를 뒤에서 후치 수식함
분사구문(부사)	~을 포함하여	부대상황
전치사		형용사구, 부사구
		유사 표현 : regarding, concerning, considering

■ 〈동격〉: A(명사), B(명사) (A가 주어, B라는 A)

동격(B라는 A)		
명사(A)	,(콤마)	명사(B)
Wales		the top British Isles nation at the time

(Thereafter), / South Africa's national sporting teams / wore / the emblem / (until the 1990s).

(Thereafter: 그 이후로 / South Africa's national sporting teams: S 남아공 국가대표팀들은 / wore: V 패용하였다 / the emblem: O 그 문양을 / 1990년대까지)

그 이후로 남아공 국가대표팀들은 그 문양을 1990년대까지 패용하였다.

The Springbok emblem / proved to be (highly) divisive
S 스프링복 문양은 / V / S.C 큰 불화의 상징임이 증명되었다

/ {as national sporting teams / were limited / (to the
(종·접) / S 국가 대표팀(국가 대표팀에 들어가는 것)은 / V(수동태) 국한되었기 때문이다

white minority population) / (until the 1980s)}.
소수의 백인 국민들에게만 / 1980년대까지

스프링복 문양은 대표팀들의 문호가 1980년대까지 소수의 백인 국민들에게만 국한되었기 때문에 큰 불화의 상징임이 확인되었다.

노트
■ be limited to : ~에 제한되다
■ 〈prove 동사의 쓰임〉

prove	주격보어	–	〈2형식〉
	(to be) 보어	–	~임이 알려지다, ~으로 판명되다
prove	목적어		〈3형식〉
	that	주어+동사	~을 입증하다
prove	목적어	목적격보어	〈5형식〉
		(to be) 보어	~이 (~임을) 증명하다

■ 〈원인/이유〉 : ~ 때문에

전치사	because of	+(동)명사 / 명사 상당어구
	due to	
	for	
	on account of	
	owing to	
	thanks to	
종속접속사	as	+주어+동사 ~
	because	
	now(that)	
	since	

(For white South Africans), / the emblem / was a symbol
백인 남아공 국민들에게는 / S 그 문양이 / V / S.C 상징이었다

/ (of pride and national sporting power).
자부심과 국가적 스포츠 권력의

백인 남아공 국민들에게는 그 문양이 자부심과 국가적 스포츠 권력의 상징이었다.

▶ Springbok emblem에 관한 다음 글의 내용과 일치하는 것은?

① 남아공 국가대표팀들이 20세기에 걸쳐 가끔 패용하였다.
② 오늘날 남아공 국가대표 럭비팀은 더 이상 패용하지 않는다.
③ 1906년 이래로 1990년대까지 남아공 국가대표팀들이 패용하였다.
④ 1980년대까지 화합의 상징으로 인식되었다.
⑤ 남아공 흑인 국민들에게는 자부심의 상징이었다.

정답 | ③

해설 | ③ 3번째 문장에서 1906년에 사용하기 시작한 것을 알 수 있고, 6번째 문장에서 1990년대까지 패용하였던 것을 알 수 있기 때문에 ③이 글의 내용과 일치한다.

오답 | ① 1번째 문장에서 거의 20세기 내내 패용한 것을 알 수 있기 때문에 일치하지 않는다.
② 2번째 문장에서 오늘날에도 계속 패용되고 있다는 것을 알 수 있기 때문에 일치하지 않는다.
④ 7번째 문장에서 1980년대까지 불화의 상징임을 알 수 있기 때문에 일치하지 않는다.
⑤ 8번째 문장에서 흑인 국민들이 아니라 백인 국민들에게 자부심의 상징이었음을 알 수 있기 때문에 일치하지 않는다.

Words

- ☐ wear
- ☐ sporting team
- ☐ throughout
- ☐ continue
- ☐ rugby
- ☐ British
- ☐ isle
- ☐ coin
- ☐ term
- ☐ press
- ☐ highly
- ☐ successful
- ☐ nearly
- ☐ match
- ☐ including
- ☐ prove
- ☐ limit
- ☐ symbol
- ☐ pride

Phrases

- ☐ be known as
- ☐ at the time
- ☐ begin on [with, at, by]
- ☐ be limited to

변형문제

01 다음 질문에 대한 답을 위 글에서 모두 찾아 영어로 된 완전한 한 개의 문장으로 쓰시오.

The Springbok emblem was worn by South African national sporting teams throughout most of the 20th century. It continues to be worn by the South African national rugby team today, known universally as the Springboks. The designation began on South Africa's first rugby tour to the British Isles in 1906. Team captain Paul Roos coined the term to prevent the British press from inventing one for them. The 1906 Springboks were highly successful, winning nearly all their matches including Wales, the top British Isles nation at the time. Thereafter, South Africa's national sporting teams wore the emblem until the 1990s. The Springbok emblem proved to be highly divisive as national sporting teams were limited to the white minority population until the 1980s. For white South Africans, the emblem was a symbol of pride and national sporting power.

Q: According to the above article, why did the Springbok emblem bring up a major conflict?

A: Because ______________________________.

02 다음 글을 읽고, |조건|에 맞게 빈칸 (A), (B)를 채우시오.

| 조건 |

* (A), (B)는 1단어로 쓸 것
* [보기]에서 선택한 단어를 한 번씩만 쓸 것
* 필요한 경우, 문맥과 어법에 맞게 변형할 것

[보기] trust / faith / pride / loyalty / visible / outstanding / distinguishable / divide / memorize / nationality

The Springbok emblem was worn by South African national sporting teams throughout most of the 20th century. It continues to be worn by the South African national rugby team today, known universally as the Springboks. The designation began on South Africa's first rugby tour to the British Isles in 1906. Team captain Paul Roos coined the term to prevent the British press from inventing one for them. The 1906 Springboks were highly successful, winning nearly all their matches including Wales, the top British Isles nation at the time. Thereafter, South Africa's national sporting teams wore the emblem until the 1990s. The Springbok emblem proved to be highly (A) ______________ as national sporting teams were limited to the white minority population until the 1980s. For white South Africans, the emblem was a symbol of (B) ______________ and national sporting power.

03 다음 글의 순서로 가장 적절한 것은?

The Springbok emblem was worn by South African national sporting teams throughout most of the 20th century. It continues to be worn by the South African national rugby team today, known universally as the Springboks.

(A) The designation began on South Africa's first rugby tour to the British Isles in 1906. Team captain Paul Roos coined the term to prevent the British press from inventing one for them.

(B) The 1906 Springboks were highly successful, winning nearly all their matches including Wales, the top British Isles nation at the time. Thereafter, South Africa's national sporting teams wore the emblem until the 1990s.

(C) The Springbok emblem proved to be highly divisive as national sporting teams were limited to the white minority population until the 1980s. For white South Africans, the emblem was a symbol of pride and national sporting power.

① (A) - (B) - (C)
② (B) - (A) - (C)
③ (B) - (C) - (A)
④ (C) - (A) - (B)
⑤ (C) - (B) - (A)

04 밑줄 친 부분 중 문맥상 옳지 않은 것은?

The Springbok emblem was ① worn by South African national sporting teams throughout most of the 20th century. It ② continues to be worn by the South African national rugby team today, known universally as the Springboks. The designation began on South Africa's first rugby tour to the British Isles in 1906. Team captain Paul Roos ③ coined the term to prevent the British press from inventing one for them. The 1906 Springboks were highly successful, winning nearly all their matches including Wales, the top British Isles nation at the time. Thereafter, South Africa's national sporting teams wore the emblem until the 1990s. The Springbok emblem proved to be highly ④ divisive as national sporting teams were limited to the white minority population until the 1980s. For ⑤ black South Africans, the emblem was a symbol of pride and national sporting power.

도표 · 실용문

글의 논리	Spotlight
제목	남성과 여성의 같이 운동하는 대상
주제	남성과 여성의 함께 운동하는 사람에 대한 조사

수능 ANALYSIS

021 어법 선택 & 연결어

With Whom Do You Most Often Exercise?

Exercise Companionship for Men and Women from 2003 to 2006

The graph above shows the percentage of men and women responses on exercise companionship from a survey **[conducting / conducted]** from 2003 to 2006. More than half of both men and women reported **[that / what]** they exercised **[lonely / alone]**, **[which / what]** represented the largest category of companionship for the two groups. The second highest response category for the two groups, **[what / which]** had the largest percentage point gap between men **[and / or]** women, was **[exercised / exercising]** with family members. More male respondents reported exercising with friends or neighbors **[to / than]** female respondents. No other exercise companion group for men and women, **[respective / respectively]**, **[were / was]** **[more / less]** **[favored / favoring]** than co-workers. For female respondents, the percentage of exercising with family members **[were / was]** more than twice **[those / that]** of exercising with friends or neighbors.

주제문 누구와 함께 가장 자주 운동하는가?

With Whom / Do You / Most Often Exercise?
누구와 함께 / 당신은 하는가 / 가장 자주 운동을

당신은 누구와 함께 가장 자주 운동하는가?

설명 함께 운동하는 사람들에 대한 조사 내용

Exercise Companionship / for Men and Women / from 2003 to 2006.
운동 상대 / 남성과 여성의 / 2003년부터 2006년까지

2003년부터 2006년까지 남성과 여성의 운동 상대

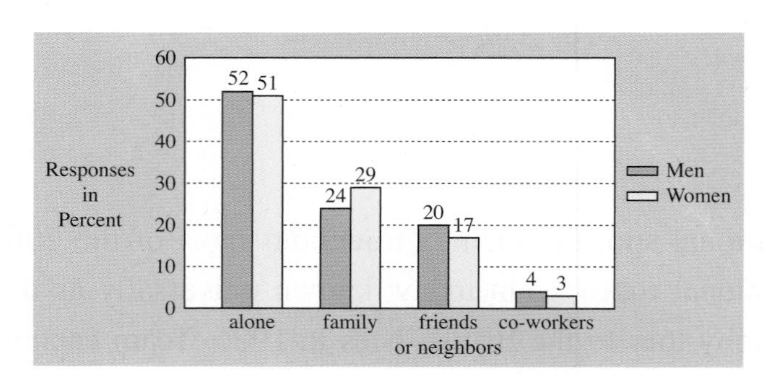

The graph (S) / above shows (V) / the percentage (O) / (of men and women responses) / (on exercise companionship)
위 그래프는 / 보여 주고 있다 / 퍼센트 값을 / 남성과 여성의 반응의 / 함께 운동하는 사람에 관한

/ (from a survey) (conducted from 2003 to 2006).
(which is) 〈과거분사〉
설문조사에서 나온 / 2003년부터 2006년까지 실시된

위 그래프는 2003년에서 2006년까지 실시된 설문조사에서 함께 운동하는 사람에 관한 남성과 여성의 반응을 퍼센트 값으로 보여 주고 있다.

노트
■ from A to B : A에서 B까지
■ 〈주격관계대명사＋be동사 생략〉

명사	(주격관계대명사＋be동사)	Ring(현재분사) – 능동
		p.p.(과거분사) – 수동
		형용사
		부사
		명사
		전치사구
a survey	(which/that is)	conducted

① More than half of both men and women (S) / reported (V) / {that (종·접) they (S) exercised (V) (alone)}, / {which (주·관) represented (V) / the largest category (O) (of companionship) / (for the two groups)}.
절반 이상의 남성과 여성은 / 응답했다 / 그들이 혼자 운동한다고 〈선행사〉 / 이는 대표했다 / 가장 큰 비율을 / 두 그룹에서

절반 이상의 남성과 여성은 그들이 혼자 운동한다고 응답했는데, 이는 두 그룹에서 가장 큰 비율을 차지했다.

노트
■ 〈주어와 동사의 수의 일치〉
• A of B : 일반적인 경우에 A가 주어
• A of B : A가 부분/부분인 경우에 B가 주어

	A	B	
분수	two – thirds 등	주어	동사 (B에 수의 일치)
부분	a group of, all of, a lot of, any of, a number of, both of, each of, either of, few of, half of, many of, most of, much of, neither of, none of, one of, part of, percent of, several of, some of, the rest, two of 등		
	half of	both men and women	reported

■ 〈상관접속사〉 : 병렬구조

종류				뜻
not	A	but	B	A가 아니라 B (=B, not A)
not only		but also		A뿐만 아니라 B도 (=B as well as A)
either		or		A와 B 둘 중 하나
neither		nor		A와 B 둘 다 아닌
both		and		A와 B 둘 다

■ 〈what vs. that〉

	관계대명사(불완전한 문장)	접속사(완전한 문장)
what	○ 선행사를 포함하고 있기 때문에 what 앞에 선행사 불필요	×
that	○ that 앞에 선행사 필요	○

■ 〈alone vs. lonely〉

	형용사	서술적 형용사	부사
alone	(명사/대명사 바로 뒤에서 수식하여) ~뿐(only)	혼자의, 고독한	혼자, 홀로
lonely	고독한, 고립된, 외로운	–	–

■ 〈주격관계대명사절〉 : 계속적 용법으로는 that 사용 불가

		주격관계대명사절		
선행사	,(콤마)	주격관계대명사	~~주어~~	동사
앞 문장 전체	〈계속적 용법〉	which		represented

② The second highest response category / (for the two groups), {which had the largest percentage point gap / (between men and women)}, / was exercising (with family members).

(The second highest response category: S, 두 번째로 큰 응답 범주는 / for the two groups: 두 집단에서 / which: 〈주·관〉 / had: V / the largest percentage point gap: O, 이건 가장 큰 비율 값의 차이가 있었는데 / between men and women: 남성과 여성 사이에서 / was exercising: V, 가족과 함께 운동하는 것이었다)

두 집단에서 두 번째로 큰 응답 범주는 가족과 함께 운동하는 것이었는데, 이 경우 남성과 여성 사이에서 가장 큰 비율 값의 차이가 발생하였다.

노트 ■ between A and B : A와 B 사이에

③ More male respondents / reported / exercising (with friends or neighbors) / (than female respondents).

(More male respondents: S, 더 많은 남성 응답자들이 / reported: V, 응답했다 / exercising: O, 친구나 이웃과 함께 운동한다고 / than female respondents: 여성 응답자들에 비해)

남성 응답자들이 여성 응답자들에 비해 더 많이 친구나 이웃과 함께 운동한다고 응답했다.

노트 ■ 〈목적어 자리에 동명사를 취하는 완전타동사〉

주어	완전타동사	목적어
–	admit / avoid / consider / delay / deny / enjoy / escape / experience / finish / give up / include / mind / mute / Practice / put off / recommend / replace / report 등	Ring (동명사)

④ No other exercise companion group / (for men and women), / (respectively), / was less favored / than co-workers.

(No other exercise companion group: S, 운동 동반자는 없었다 / for men and women: 어떤 다른 남성과 여성 두 그룹도 / respectively: 각각 / was: V / less favored: 〈수동태〉 덜 선호되는 / than co-workers: 직장 동료보다)

남성과 여성 두 그룹에서, 각각 직장 동료보다 덜 선호되는 운동 동반자는 없었다.

노트 ■ less A than B : B보다 덜 A한

■ 〈respect 품사별 변화에 따른 의미〉

	명사	동사	형용사	부사
respect	존경, 존중	존경하다, 존중하다	–	–
respectful	–	–	경의를 표하는, 존중하는	–
respectable	–	–	존경할만한, 〈질 · 수량 · 크기 등이〉 상당한, 꽤 많은	–
respective	존경할 만한 사람, 훌륭한 사람	–	–	–
respectively	–	–	–	[보통 문장 끝에 둠] 각각, 저마다, 제각기, 각자

■ 〈비교급으로 최상급을 의미하는 표현〉 : 표면적으로는 비교 구문이지만 의미는 최상급인 경우를 말한다.

부정주어 ~ as[so]+원급+as (~만큼 …한 것은 아니다)
=부정주어 ~ 비교급+than (~보다 더 …한 것은 아니다)
=주어 ~ 비교급+than any other+단수명사 (~보다 더 …하다)
=주어 ~ 비교급+than all (the) other+복수명사 (~보다 더 …하다)

⑤ (For female respondents), / the percentage (of exercising with family members) / was more than

(For female respondents: 여성 응답자들의 경우 / the percentage: S, 사람들의 비율은 / of exercising with family members: 가족과 함께 운동하는 / was: V / more than: 두 배 이상이었다)

twice / that of exercising (with friends or neighbors).
친구나 이웃과 함께 운동하는 비율의

여성 응답자들의 경우 가족과 함께 운동하는 사람들의 비율은 친구나 이웃과 함께 운동하는 비율의 두 배 이상이었다.

노트 ■ 〈percent vs. percentage〉: 수의 일치

a	percent	of	A	동사
			주어	

a	percent	of	A	동사
주어				

▶ 다음 도표의 내용과 일치하지 않는 것은?

정답 | ⑤

해설 | ⑤ 이 문장에서는 여성 응답자들의 경우 가족과 함께 운동하는 사람들의 비율이 친구나 이웃과 함께 운동하는 비율의 두 배 이상이라고 하는데, 도표에서는 가족과 함께 운동하는 사람들의 비율은 친구나 이웃과 함께 운동하는 비율의 두 배 이하이다. 따라서 ⑤가 도표의 내용과 일치하지 않는다.

Words

☐ exercise
☐ response
☐ survey
☐ conduct
☐ report
☐ represent
☐ category
☐ gap
☐ male
☐ respondent
☐ neighbor
☐ female
☐ companion
☐ respectively
☐ favor
☐ co-worker

Phrases

☐ from A to B
☐ less A than B
☐ between A and B

우선순위 영단어 역대 수능 기출 + 전국 모의고사 기출 + EBS 기출 + 교과서 기출 빈출 어휘

단어	뜻	단어	뜻	단어	뜻
fade away	v. 서서히 사라지다	fall apart	다 망가지다	famine	n. 기근
fascination	n. 매력	fatigue	n. 싫증	fault	n. 결점
fee	n. 요금	fertility	n. 비옥함	figure out	알아내다
fitness	n. 체력	flap	v. 퍼덕거리다	flat	n. (영국의) 아파트
flee	v. 도피하다	flexibility	n. 유연성	flick	v. 홱 흔들다
formation	n. (지층의) 계통	formulate	v. 표현하다; 형성하다	fragile	a. 연약한
fragment	n. 조각	friction	n. 마찰	gender	n. 성(性)
generous	a. 후한	genuine	a. 진심에서 우러난	genuinely	ad. 진정으로
gifted	a. 타고난 재능이 있는	glow	v. 빛나다	grant	v. 허가하다
grateful	a. 감사하는	gravity	n. 중력	greed	n. 탐욕
grocery store	n. 식료품점	habitual	a. 특유의	herb	n. 약초
hierarchy	n. 계급[계층]제도	hire	v. 고용하다	hostility	n. 적대감
hypothesize	v. 가정하다	ignorance	a. 무지	immoral	a. 부도덕한
impress	v. 깊은 인상을 주다	impressive	a. 감동적인	improvement	n. 개선
impulse	n. 추진력	in person	직접	in the first place	애당초
in the meantime	반면	in tune	조화로운	incorporate	v. 포함하다
infirm	a. 병약한	informed	a. 정보에 근거한	initiate	v. 시작하다
inject	v. 주입하다	instead of	~ 대신에	instill	v. 스며들게 하다
instinct	n. 본능	instrument	n. 가구	insufficient	a. 불충분한
intentional	a. 의도적인	interconnect	v. 서로 연결하다	interference	n. 간섭
intimate	n. 막역한 벗	intricate	a. 복잡한	introduce	v. 도입하다

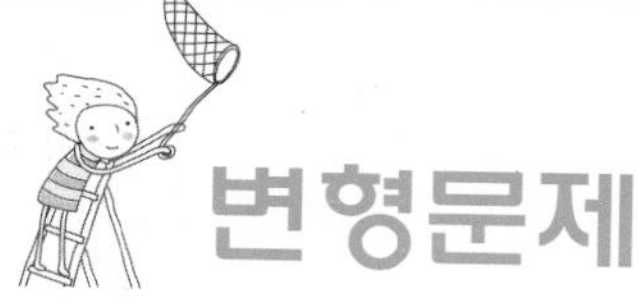

변형문제

01 다음 표를 보고 문장의 빈칸을 채우시오. ([보기]에 있는 단어를 사용하시오.)

[보기] first / second / highest / lowest / largest / shortest

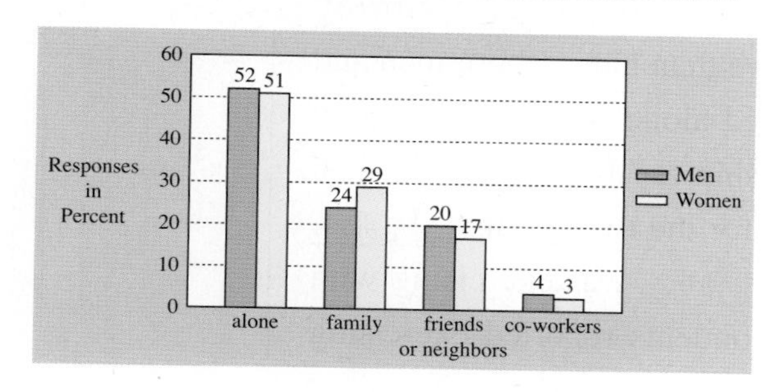

The (A) ___________ (B) ___________ response category for the two groups, which had the (C) ___________ percentage point gap between men and women, was exercising with family members.

02 밑줄 친 ⓐ ~ ⓔ의 문맥상의 의미로 어색한 것은?

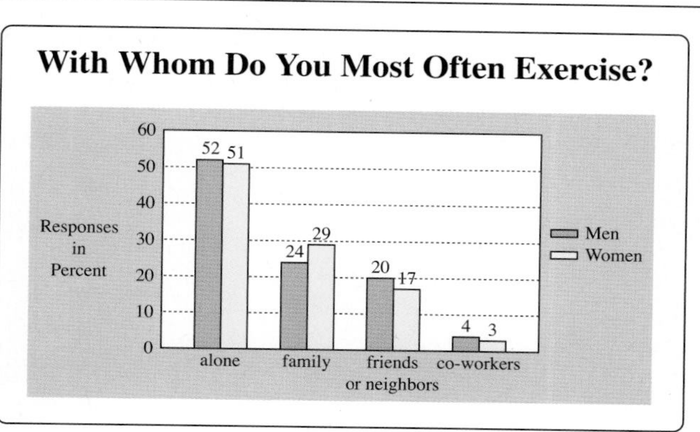

The graph above shows the percentage of men and women responses on ⓐ exercise companionship from a survey conducted from 2003 to 2006. More than half of both men and women reported that they exercised ⓑ alone, which represented the largest category of companionship for the two groups. The second highest ⓒ response category for the two groups, which had the largest percentage point gap between men and women, was exercising with family members. More male respondents reported exercising with friends or neighbors than female respondents. No other exercise companion group for men and women, respectively, was less ⓓ favored than co-workers. For female respondents, the percentage of exercising with family members was more than ⓔ twice that of exercising with friends or neighbors.

① ⓐ : physical or mental activity that you do to stay healthy or become stronger
② ⓑ : without any other people
③ ⓒ : a spoken or written answer
④ ⓓ : a thing that you do to help somebody
⑤ ⓔ : two times; on two occasions

03 다음 밑줄 친 한글 문장을 주어진 |조건|에 맞춰서 표를 보고 영작하시오.

| 조건 |

* 관계대명사 which를 이용할 것
* 11단어로 된 문장을 만들 것
* had / between을 사용할 것

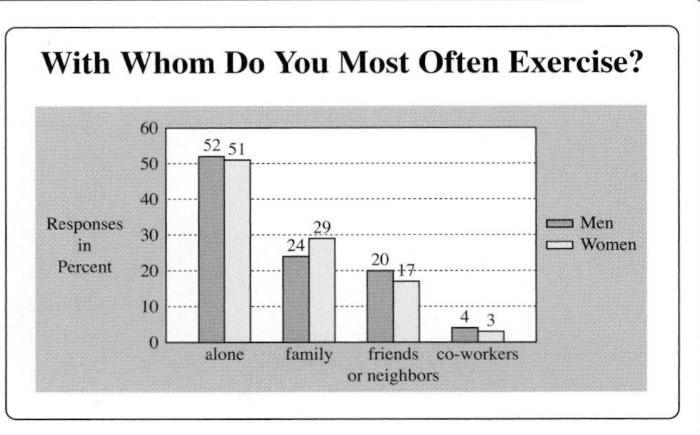

The graph above shows the percentage of men and women responses on exercise companionship from a survey conducted from 2003 to 2006. More than half of both men and women reported that they exercised alone, which represented the largest category of companionship for the two groups. The second highest response category for the two groups, 남성과 여성 사이에서 가장 큰 비율 값의 차이가 발생하는, was exercising with family members. More male respondents reported exercising with friends or neighbors than female respondents. No other exercise companion group for men and women, respectively, was less favored than co-workers. For female respondents, the percentage of exercising with family members was more than twice that of exercising with friends or neighbors.

04 밑줄 친 부분 중 문맥상 옳지 않은 것은?

With Whom Do You Most Often Exercise?

Exercise Companionship for Men and Women from 2003 to 2006

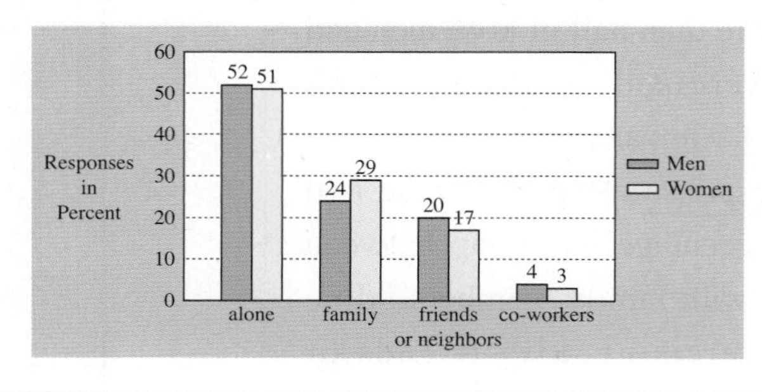

The graph above shows the percentage of men and women responses on exercise companionship from a survey conducted from 2003 to 2006. ① More than half of both men and women reported that they exercised alone, which represented the largest category of companionship for the two groups. The ② third highest response category for the two groups, which had the largest percentage point gap between men and women, was exercising with family members. ③ More male respondents reported exercising with friends or neighbors than female respondents. ④ No other exercise companion group for men and women, respectively, was less favored than co-workers. For female respondents, the percentage of exercising with family members was ⑤ less than twice that of exercising with friends or neighbors.

도표 · 실용문

글의 논리	Question & Answer (질문 & 대답)
제목	Taylor Community 요가수업
주제	Taylor Community 요가수업에 대한 광고

022 어법 선택 & 연결어

Taylor Community Yoga
Free in February!

[Are / Is] one of your New Year's resolutions to get in shape? Then **[taking / take]** the first step by **[join / joining]** us for a free yoga class **[presented / presenting]** by the Taylor District on Thursday, February 1st.

We encourage you **[inviting / to invite]** your friends, family, and any fitness enthusiast you know **[taking / to take]** advantage of this free opportunity to take care of your body and mind with Taylor Community yoga!

* Ages 10+ are welcome to attend.
* If you currently have a Yoga Punch Pass, **[save / saving]** the punch for **[the other / another]** day!

Taylor Community Hall
Thursday, February 1st 2018
6:45 PM - 7:45 PM

대답 몸매를 가꾸기 위한 방법인 Taylor Community 요가수업에 대한 광고

Taylor Community Yoga
Taylor Community의 무료 요가수업
Free in February!
2월에

Taylor Community의 2월 무료 요가수업!

질문 새해 다짐들 중에서 하나는 몸매를 바꾸는 것인가?

Is / one (of your New Year's resolutions) / to get in shape?
(Is: V, 것인가요? / one: S / of your New Year's resolutions: 새해 다짐들 중에 하나는 / to get in shape: S.C, 몸매를 가꾸는)

새해 다짐들 중에서 하나는 몸매를 가꾸는 것인가요?

노트
■ get in shape : 좋은 몸 상태(몸매)를 유지하다
■ 〈one of＋복수명사＋단수동사〉 : ~ 중의 하나

one (주어 : 단수)	of	복수명사	단수동사
one		your New Year's resolutions	is

대답 몸매를 가꾸기 위한 방법인 Taylor Community 요가수업에 대한 광고

(Then) take the first step / (by joining us) / (for a free yoga class) / (which/that is) presented by the Taylor District / on Thursday, February 1st).
(take: V / the first step: O, 첫발을 내디뎌 보아요 / by: 〈전치사〉 joining: 〈동명사〉 us: O, 참여함으로써 / for a free yoga class: 무료 요가수업에 / presented: 〈과거분사〉, Taylor 지구에서 제공하는 / on Thursday, February 1st: 2월 1일 목요일에)

2월 1일 목요일 Taylor 지구에서 제공하는 무료 요가수업에 참여함으로써 첫발을 내디뎌 보아요.

노트
■ take[make] the first step : 첫발을 내디디다
■ join A for B : B에 A를 참여시키다
■ 〈직접명령문〉

긍정문	R	~해라
	Please＋R	~해 주세요
부정문	Don't＋R	~하지 마라
	Never＋R	

■ 〈부사 vs. 접속부사〉

시간	Then	주어	동사		
	When	주어	동사,	주어	동사 ~
장소	There	주어	동사		
	Where	주어	동사,	주어	동사 ~

■ 〈주격관계대명사＋be동사 생략〉

명사	(주격관계대명사＋be동사)	Ring(현재분사) – 능동
		p.p.(과거분사) – 수동
		형용사
		부사
		명사
		전치사구
a free yoga class	(which/that is)	presented

We / encourage / you to invite your friends, family, and any fitness enthusiast (that) / (you know) / (to take advantage of this free opportunity) / (to take care of your body and mind) / (with Taylor Community yoga)!

S: We — 저희는 / V: encourage — 권장합니다 / O: you / O.C: to invite ... — 여러분의 친구, 가족, 어떤 건강 애호가인지 간에 ... 초대해서 / (you know): S you, V know — 여러분이 알고 있는 / this free opportunity (O) — 이번 무료 기회를 / 이용하도록 / your body (O₁) and mind (O₂) — 몸과 마음을 돌볼 / with Taylor Community yoga — Taylor Community 요가수업을 통해

친구, 가족, 그리고 여러분이 알고 있는 어떤 건강 애호가인지 간에 초대해서 Taylor Community 요가수업을 통해 몸과 마음을 돌볼 이번 무료 기회를 이용하도록 권해보세요!

노트
- take advantage of : 이용하다, ~을 이용하여 …하다; 편승하다 (=make use of ~ for gain, impose upon)
- take care of : ~을 돌보다, 뒷바라지하다
- 〈5형식 불완전타동사의 목적격보어〉 : 수동태 전환 시, 2형식 문장(be p.p. +to R)

주어	불완전타동사	목적어	목적격보어
–	advise / allow / ask / assume / beg / cause / command / compel / condition / decide / design / drive / enable / encourage / expect / forbid / force / instruct / intend / invite / lead / like / motivate / order / permit / persuade / predispose / pressure / program / push / require / teach / tell / train / trust / urge / want / warn / wish 등	–	to 동사원형

- 〈목적격관계대명사 that〉 : 타동사의 목적어가 없는 경우 / 선행사를 포함하고 있는 관계대명사 what 사용 불가

선행사	〈목적격관계대명사절〉 목적격관계대명사	주어	타동사	~~목적어~~
your friends, family, and any fitness enthusiast	생략 가능 : (that)	you	know	

* Ages 10+ / are welcome / to attend.

S: Ages 10+ — 10세 이상은 / V: are — 환영합니다 / S.C: welcome / to attend — 참여하기를

* {If you / (currently) have a Yoga Punch Pass}, / save the punch / (for another day)!

(종·접) If — 만약 / S: you — 여러분이 / V: have / O: a Yoga Punch Pass — 현재 Yoga Punch Pass를 갖고 계시다면 / V: save / O: the punch — 그 펀치 패스권을 아껴두세요! / for another day — 다른 날을 위해

* 10세 이상의 참여를 환영합니다.
* 현재 Yoga Punch Pass를 갖고 계시다면, 그 펀치 패스권을 다른 날을 위해 아껴두세요!

노트
- be welcome to+R : 얼마든지 ~해도 좋다
- save A for B : A를 B를 위해 아끼다

Taylor Community Hall
Taylor Community Hall

Thursday, February 1st 2018
2018년 2월 1일 목요일

6:45 PM - 7:45 PM
오후 6:45 – 오후 7:45

Taylor Community Hall
2018년 2월 1일 목요일
오후 6:45 – 오후 7:45

▶ Taylor Community Yoga Free in February에 관한 다음 안내문의 내용과 일치하는 것은?

① 1달 간 무료로 요가수업을 수강할 수 있다.
② 초대한 친구 또는 가족과 함께 참여해야 한다.
③ 10세 이하의 어린이를 대상으로 한다.
④ Yoga Punch Pass가 있어야 이용할 수 있다.
⑤ Taylor Community Hall에서 1시간 동안 진행된다.

정답 | ⑤

해설 | ⑤ 오후 6:45 ~ 오후 7:45분까지 Taylor Community Hall에서 진행된다고 했으므로 ⑤가 일치한다.

오답 | ① 3번째 문장을 보면 1달간 무료로 수강하는 것이 아니라 2월 1일 하루 무료로 수강할 수 있는 것이기 때문에 일치하지 않는다.
② 친구, 가족과 함께 참여해야 하는 것이 아니라 가족, 친구에게 권장하라 하기 때문에 일치하지 않는다.
③ 10세 이상의 참여를 환영으로 한다고 했으므로 ③은 일치하지 않는다.
④ Yoga Punch Pass가 있으면 다른 날을 위해 아껴두라고 했기 때문에 ④는 일치하지 않는다.

Words

- ☐ community
- ☐ resolution
- ☐ join
- ☐ present
- ☐ district
- ☐ encourage
- ☐ invite
- ☐ fitness
- ☐ enthusiast
- ☐ opportunity
- ☐ mind
- ☐ attend
- ☐ currently
- ☐ save

Phrases

- ☐ get in shape
- ☐ join A for B
- ☐ take care of
- ☐ take[make] the first step
- ☐ take advantage of
- ☐ be welcome to+R

우선순위 영단어

역대 수능 기출 + 전국 모의고사 기출 + EBS 기출 + 교과서 기출 빈출 어휘

단어	뜻	단어	뜻	단어	뜻
intuitively	ad. 직관적으로	invention	n. 발명	involvement	n. 관여
keep up with	~에 뒤지지 않다	labor	n. 고생	landmark	n. 획기적인 발견
layer	n. 층	lethal	a. 치명적인	level	n. 단계
life span	n. 수명	linger	v. 오래 머무르다	literary	a. 문학의
litter	n. 쓰레기	livelihood	n. 생계	logic	n. 논리
long-term	a. 장기적인	look after	v. 돌보다	mammal	n. 포유동물
maneuver	v. 교묘히 다루다	manuscript	n. 원고	marine	a. 바다의
masterpiece	n. 걸작	meanwhile	ad. 그 사이에	medication	n. 약물
meet	v. 만나다	merchant	n. 상인	mighty	a. 강한
migrate	v. 이주하다	mine	v. 캐다	minimize	v. 최소화하다
misfortune	n. 불행	naive	a. 순수한	nearby	a. 가까이에
nervous	a. 초조해 하는	noble	a. 귀족의	normal	a. 정상의
not to mention	~은 말할 필요도 없이	notorious	a. 악명 높은	nutritional	a. 영양상의
objectively	ad. 객관적으로	occupational	a. 직업의	offend	v. 기분을 상하게 하다
offer	n. 제안	on the spot	현장에서	ongoing	a. 진행 중의
opposite	n. 반대(편)	optimize	v. 최대한으로 활용하다	option	n. 선택 사항
organic	a. 유기체의	orientation	n. 방침	outlook	n. 전망
outperform	v. 더 나은 결과를 내다	outright	a. 공공연한	overtake	v. 앞지르다
panic	v. 당황하게 하다	particle	n. 입자	particular	a. 특정한
particularly	ad. 특히	passion	n. 열정	paw	n. (동물의) 발
peak	n. 산꼭대기	persuasive	a. 설득력 있는	phrase	n. 구
pick up	익히게 되다	piece	n. 작품	pitch	n. 음의 고저
place an order	주문하다	portray	v. 말로 묘사하다	pose	v. 제기하다
possession	n. 소유	posture	n. 자세	precision	n. 정확성
prescribe	v. 처방하다	prescription	n. 처방	presume	v. 감히 ~하다
primate	n. 영장류	prime	a. 주요한	prior to	~에 앞서
profile	n. 옆모습	profound	a. 엄청난	promotion	n. 판촉
promptly	ad. 즉시	proposition	n. 제안	prospective	a. 장래의
purpose	n. 목적	pursuit	n. 추구	rage	n. 격노
reassure	v. 안심시키다	recurrent	a. 되풀이되는	refer to A as B	A를 B로 언급하다
regulation	n. 규제	relief	n. 위안	relieved	a. 안도하는
removal	n. 제거	resentful	a. 분개한	resist	v. 잘 견디다
resource	n. 자원	respectful	a. 공손한	respectively	ad. 각각의
respiratory	a. 호흡의	restoration	n. 복원	revolve	v. 회전하다
ridiculous	a. 웃기는	rigid	a. 단단한	roar	n. (맹수 등이) 포효하는 소리
rodent	n. 설치류	rotary	a. 회전하는	roughly	ad. 대략
rude	a. 무례한	scarce	a. 부족한	scary	a. 겁 많은
screen	v. 가려내다	sculpture	n. 조각품	sector	n. 분야
seemingly	ad. 표면적으로	selection	n. 선택	sensation	n. 느낌
shade	n. 차양	similarly	ad. 비슷하게	slavery	n. 노예제도

PRACTICE 01

01 다음 글의 내용과 일치하지 않는 것은?

Taylor Community Yoga
Free in February!

Is one of your New Year's resolutions to get in shape? Then take the first step by joining us for a free yoga class presented by the Taylor District on Thursday, February 1st.

We encourage you to invite your friends, family, and any fitness enthusiast you know to take advantage of this free opportunity to take care of your body and mind with Taylor Community yoga!

* Ages 10+ are welcome to attend.
* If you currently have a Yoga Punch Pass, save the punch for another day!

Taylor Community Hall
Thursday, February 1st 2018
6:45 PM - 7:45 PM

① 2월 1일 목요일에 무료 요가수업을 한다.
② 10세 이상의 참여를 권장한다.
③ Yoga punch pass를 써야 한다.
④ Taylor Community Hall에서 진행된다.
⑤ 시간은 1시간이다.

02 다음 글의 목적으로 가장 적절한 것은?

Taylor Community Yoga
Free in February!

Is one of your New Year's resolutions to get in shape? Then take the first step by joining us for a free yoga class presented by the Taylor District on Thursday, February 1st.

We encourage you to invite your friends, family, and any fitness enthusiast you know to take advantage of this free opportunity to take care of your body and mind with Taylor Community yoga!

* Ages 10+ are welcome to attend.
* If you currently have a Yoga Punch Pass, save the punch for another day!

Taylor Community Hall
Thursday, February 1st 2018
6:45 PM - 7:45 PM

① To promote the free yoga class.
② To inform merits of yoga
③ To learn yoga
④ To apologize for skipping yoga class
⑤ To explain the fun of yoga

03 다음 글을 읽고, 답할 수 없는 것은?

Taylor Community Yoga
Free in February!

Is one of your New Year's resolutions to get in shape? Then take the first step by joining us for a free yoga class presented by the Taylor District on Thursday, February 1st.

We encourage you to invite your friends, family, and any fitness enthusiast you know to take advantage of this free opportunity to take care of your body and mind with Taylor Community yoga!
* Ages 10+ are welcome to attend.
* If you currently have a Yoga Punch Pass, save the punch for another day!

Taylor Community Hall
Thursday, February 1st 2018
6:45 PM - 7:45 PM

① When does the yoga class begin?
② Is the yoga class free?
③ Where is the yoga class held?
④ What time does the yoga class start?
⑤ What is the preparation for the yoga class?

04 다음 빈칸에 들어갈 말을 글에서 찾아 적으시오.

Taylor Community Yoga
Free in February!

Is one of your New Year's resolutions to get in shape? Then take the first step by joining us for a (A) ___________ yoga class presented by the Taylor District on Thursday, February 1st.

We encourage you to invite your friends, family, and any fitness enthusiast you know to take advantage of this free opportunity to take care of your body and mind with Taylor Community yoga!
* Ages 10+ are welcome to attend.
* If you currently have a Yoga Punch Pass, save the punch for another day!

Where : (B) ___________ ___________ ___________
When : (C) ___________, ___________ ___________.

도표 · 실용문

글의 논리	Comparison & Contrast (비교 & 대조)
제목	온라인 쇼핑과 점포 쇼핑에 대한 비교
주제	미국 십 대들의 성별에 따른 온라인 쇼핑과 점포 쇼핑에 대한 선호도

PRACTICE 02

023 어법 선택 & 연결어

U.S. Teens Are Increasingly [Dividing / Divided] in Their Shopping Preferences

% of teens in the United States who **[prefers / prefer] [to shop / shopping]** online / in stores, by gender

The graph above shows shopping preferences of U.S. teens by gender for three periods: the spring of 2013, the fall of 2013, and the spring of 2014. For all the periods, more males and females purchased things in stores than online. ( ), online shopping purchases increased over time for both males **[or / and]** females. The percentages of male online shopping preference **[were / was]** higher than **[that / those]** of female online shopping preference for all the periods. In the spring of 2013, more than 75% of both males **[and / or]** females made purchases in stores.

주제문 미국 십 대들의 성별에 따른 온라인 쇼핑과 점포 쇼핑에 대한 선호도

U.S. Teens / Are (Increasingly) Divided / (in Their Shopping Preferences)
(U.S. Teens: S 미국 십 대들이 / Are ... Divided: V(수동태) 점점 더 나뉜다 / 쇼핑 선호도 면에서)

미국 십 대들이 쇼핑 선호도 면에서 점점 더 나뉜다

% of teens / (in the United States) / (who prefer shopping online / in stores), / (by gender)
(teens: (선행사) 십 대들의 비율 / 미국에서 / who: (주·관) / prefer: V 온라인 혹은 / shopping online: O 점포 쇼핑을 선호하는 / 성별로)

온라인 혹은 점포 쇼핑을 선호하는 미국 십 대들의 성별 비율

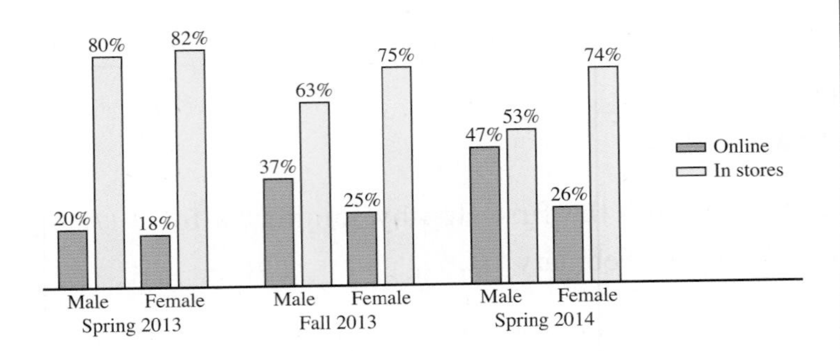

비교 십 대 남성과 여성의 선호도에 대한 비교

The graph above / shows / shopping preferences (of U.S. teens) / (by gender) / (for three periods): / the spring of 2013, the fall of 2013, and the spring of 2014.
(The graph above: S 위의 그래프는 / shows: V 보여 준다 / shopping preferences: O 미국 십 대들의 쇼핑 선호도를 / 성별로 / 세 개의 기간인 / 2013년 봄, 2013년 가을과 2014년 봄)

위의 그래프는 세 개의 기간인, 2013년 봄, 2013년 가을과 2014년 봄의 미국 십 대들의 쇼핑 선호도를 성별로 보여 준다.

노트 ■ by gender : 성별로

① (For all the periods), / more males and females / purchased / things / (in stores) / (than online).
(모든 기간 동안 / more males and females: S 더 많은 남성과 여성이 / purchased: V 구매했다 / things: O 물건을 / 점포에서 / 온라인보다)

모든 기간 동안 더 많은 남성과 여성이 온라인에서보다 점포에서 물건을 구매했다.

② (However), / online shopping purchases / increased / (over time) / (for both males and females).
(그러나 / online shopping purchases: S 온라인 쇼핑 구매가 / increased: V 증가했다 / 시간이 흐르면서 / 남성과 여성 모두에게 있어)

하지만 시간이 흐르면서 남성과 여성 모두에게 있어 온라인 쇼핑 구매가 증가했다.

노트 ■ over time : 오랜 시간에 걸쳐, 시간이 지나면서, 시간이 흐르는 동안
■ 〈상관접속사〉 : 병렬구조

종류				뜻
not	A	but	B	A가 아니라 B (=B, not A)
not only	A	but also	B	A뿐만 아니라 B도 (=B as well as A)
either	A	or	B	A와 B 둘 중 하나
neither	A	nor	B	A와 B 둘 다 아닌
both	A	and	B	A와 B 둘 다

③ The percentages / (of male online shopping preference) / were higher / than those (of female
(The percentages: S 비율은 / 남성의 온라인 쇼핑 선호도 / were: V / higher: S.C 더 높았다 / 여성의 온라인 쇼핑)

online shopping preference) / (for all the periods).
선호도 비율보다 / 모든 기간 동안

모든 기간 동안 남성의 온라인 쇼핑 선호도의 비율은 여성의 온라인 쇼핑 선호도의 비율보다 높았다.

노트 ■ 〈percent vs. percentage〉: 수의 일치

a	percent	of	A	동사
			주어	

a	percent	of	A	동사
주어				

■ 〈병렬구조〉: 우등비교급 higher than 뒤에 있는 those는 주어를 지시하는 지시대명사이다.

The percentages	of ~	were	higher than	those	of ~
주어		동사	〈우등비교급〉	〈지시대명사〉 =주어	

④ (In the spring of 2013), / more than 75% of / both males and females / made purchases / (in stores).
2013년 봄에 / 75퍼센트보다 많은 비율이 / 남성과 여성 모두(S) / 구매했다(V, O) / 점포에서

2013년 봄에 남성과 여성 모두 75퍼센트보다 많은 비율이 점포에서 구매를 했다.

노트 ■ make a purchase: 물건을 사다

⑤ (In the spring of 2014), / the gap / {between the female preference (for online) and (in store shopping)} / was just 10 percentage points, / {while it was slightly more / (in the case of males)}.
2014년 봄에 / 차이는(S) / 여성의 온라인 쇼핑과 점포 쇼핑에 대한 선호도 / (V) 겨우 10퍼센트 포인트였지만(S.C) / 〈종·접〉 S V 그 차이는 약간 더 컸다 / 남성의 경우에는

2014년 봄에 여성의 온라인 쇼핑과 점포 쇼핑에 대한 선호도의 차이는 겨우 10퍼센트였지만, 그 차이는 남성의 경우에는 약간 더 컸다.

노트 ■ between A and B: A와 B 사이에
■ in the case of: ~에 관하여는, ~에 관하여 말하면(=as regards)
■ 〈while 용법〉

부사절을 이끄는 종속접속사	
시간	~ 동안에
양보/대조	비록 ~일지라도

▶ 다음 도표의 내용과 일치하지 않는 것은?

정답 | ⑤

해설 | ⑤ 도표에서는 2014년 봄에 여성의 온라인 쇼핑과 점포 쇼핑의 차이가 48퍼센트 포인트이고 남성의 경우보다 훨씬 크다. 그러나 이 글에서는 차이가 10퍼센트 포인트라고 하고 남성의 경우가 더 크다고 설명하므로 ⑤는 도표의 내용과 일치하지 않는다.

Words

☐ teens
☐ increasingly
☐ divide
☐ preference
☐ online
☐ store
☐ gender
☐ spring
☐ fall
☐ graph
☐ above
☐ period
☐ purchase
☐ over time
☐ gap

Phrases

☐ by gender
☐ make a purchase
☐ in the case of
☐ over time
☐ between A and B

우선순위 영단어 역대 수능 기출 + 전국 모의고사 기출 + EBS 기출 + 교과서 기출 빈출 어휘

단어	뜻	단어	뜻	단어	뜻
slide	v. 미끄럼틀	snap	v. 부러지다	soak	v. 흡수하다
source	n. 근원	souvenir	n. 기념품	span	v. 뼘으로 재다
specifically	ad. 구체적으로 말하면	specimen	n. 표본	speculate	v. 사색하다
spine	n. 척추	splendid	a. 훌륭한	sponsor	n. 후원자
square	n. 정사각형(의)	stage	v. 연출하다	standard	a. 일반적인
starve	v. 굶주리다	steady	a. 꾸준한	strength	n. 강도

변형문제

01 다음 표를 보고 물음에 답하시오.

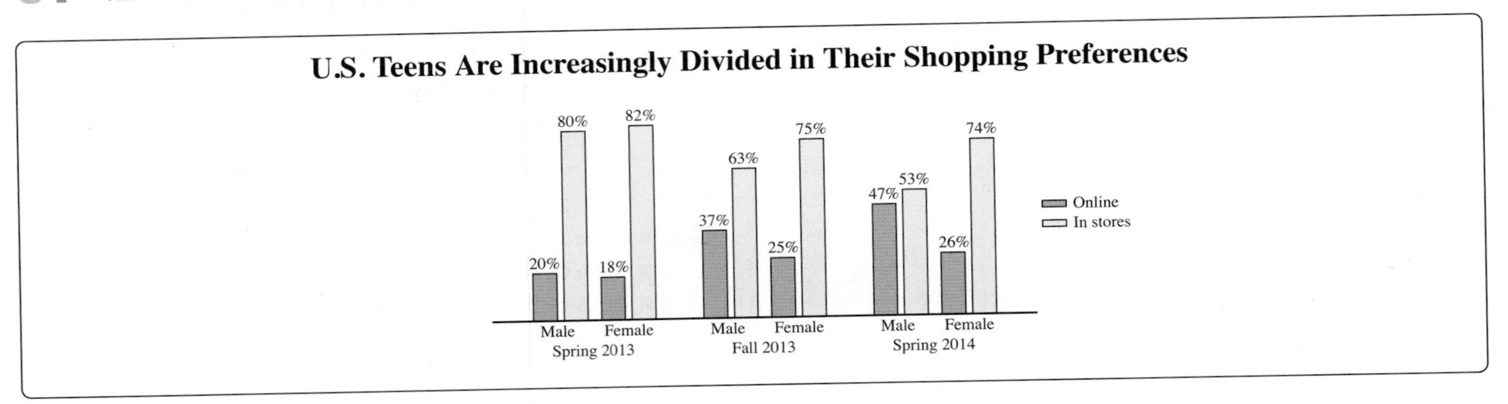

Q: When is the biggest difference in online shopping mall usage between men and women?

A: ____.

02 다음 표를 보고 밑줄 친 부분 중 적절하지 않은 것은?

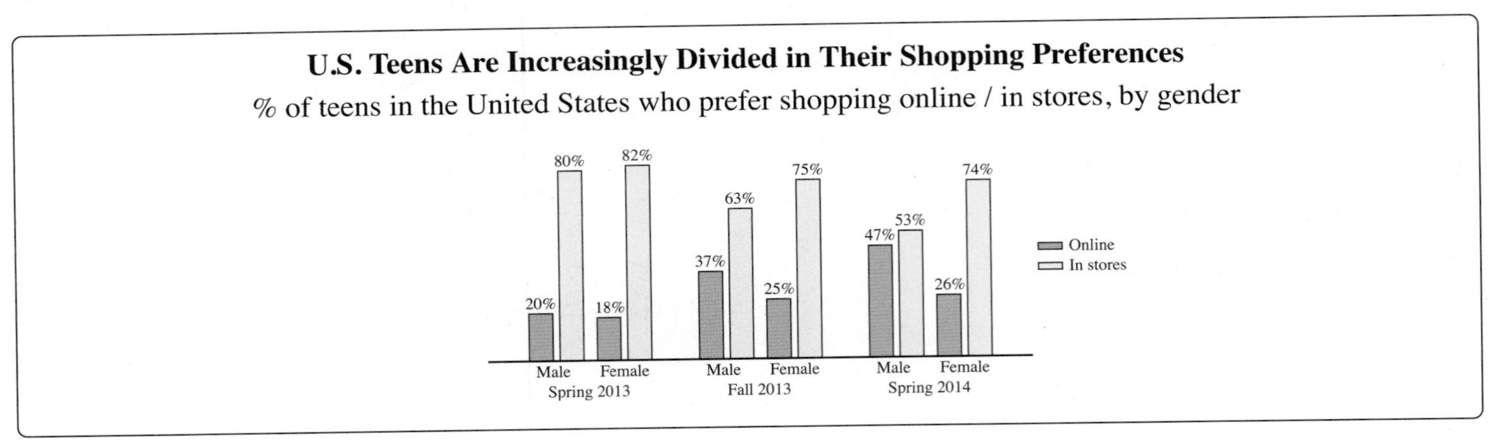

The graph above shows shopping preferences of U.S. teens by gender for three periods: the spring of 2013, the fall of 2013, and the spring of 2014. For all the periods, ① more males and females purchased things in stores than online. The percentages of male online shopping preference were ② lower than those of female online shopping preference for all the periods. In the spring of 2013, ③ more than 75% of both males and females made purchases in stores. In the spring of 2014, the gap between the female preference for online and in store shopping was just ④ 10 percentage points, while it was slightly ⑤ more in the case of males.

03 다음 표를 보고 다음 문장에서 틀린 부분을 찾아 고치시오.

U.S. Teens Are Increasingly Divided in Their Shopping Preferences

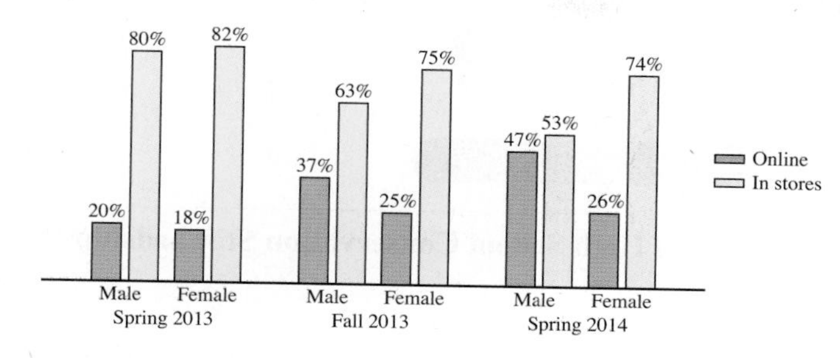

The percentages of males online shopping preference were higher than those of female online shopping preference for all the periods. In the spring of 2013, less than 75% of both males and females made purchases in stores.

04 다음 글의 내용과 일치하는 것은?

U.S. Teens Are Increasingly Divided in Their Shopping Preferences

% of teens in the United States who prefer shopping online / in stores, by gender

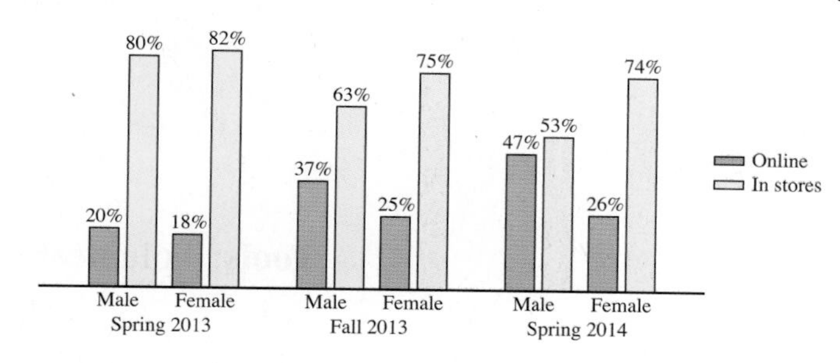

The graph above shows shopping preferences of U.S. teens by gender for three periods: the spring of 2013, the fall of 2013, and the spring of 2014. For all the periods, more males and females purchased things in stores than online. The percentages of male online shopping preference were higher than those of female online shopping preference for all the periods. In the spring of 2013, more than 75% of both males and females made purchases in stores. In the spring of 2014, the gap between the female preference for online and in store shopping was just 10 percentage points, while it was slightly more in the case of males.

① 위의 그래프는 두 개의 시간에서 미국 십 대의 쇼핑 선호도를 나타낸다.
② 모든 기간에서 남성과 여성은 온라인으로 구매를 많이 했다.
③ 모든 기간 동안 남성의 온라인 쇼핑 선호도의 비율은 여성보다 낮다.
④ 2013년 봄에는 남성과 여성 모두 75퍼센트보다 많이 구매했다.
⑤ 2014년 봄에는 여성의 온라인 쇼핑과 점포 쇼핑에 대한 선호도의 차이는 남성보다 컸다.

도표 · 실용문

글의 논리	Enumeration (열거)
제목	Redwood 고등학교 보호 관리 프로그램
주제	Redwood 고등학교 보호 관리 프로그램에 대한 광고

PRACTICE 03

024 어법 선택 & 연결어

Redwood High School Conservation Stewardship Program

Where : Daisy Meadows
When : May 12 and 26: 9 a.m. to 1 p.m. (Rain Dates: May 13 and 27)
Activities : **[Dig / Dig up]** invasive plants, **[burnt / burning]** bush
[To cleast / Clear] trails of branches
Tools : Volunteers should bring their own tools such as shovels and scissors.
Clothing : A hat, work gloves, long pants, work shoes, socks
No sandals or bare feet, **[because / due to]** the presence of poison ivy
Food and drinks : Soft drinks and water **[will provide / will be provided]**. **[Bringing / Bring]** snacks if you'd like.
Other information : Please feel free **[inviting / to invite]** friends.
Parents are welcome to come along to work or help supervise.
Contact : To sign up, please **[to contact / contact]** Paula Willson at 718-987-2345.

주제문 Redwood 고등학교 보호 관리 프로그램

Redwood High School Conservation Stewardship Program

Redwood 고등학교 (자연) 보호 관리 프로그램

열거 Redwood 고등학교 보호 관리 프로그램에 대한 광고

Where: Daisy Meadows
장소 Daisy Meadows

장소: Daisy Meadows

When: May 12 and 26: / 9 a.m. to 1 p.m. / (Rain Dates: / May 13 and 27)
시간 5월 12일과 26일 오전 9시에서 오후 1시까지 (우천시: / 5월 13일과 27일)

시간: 5월 12일과 26일, 오전 9시에서 오후 1시까지(우천시: 5월 13일과 27일)

노트 ■ (from) A to B : A에서 B까지

Activities: Dig up(V) invasive plants(O), / burning bush
활동 생태계 교란 식물을 파내기 덤불 불태우기
Clear(V) trails of branches(O)
길에서 나뭇가지 치우기

활동: 생태계 교란 식물 파내기, 덤불 불태우기
길에서 나뭇가지 치우기

노트 ■ dig A up : A를 땅에서 파내다
■ 〈직접명령문〉

긍정문	R	~해라
	Please+R	~해 주세요
부정문	Don't+R	~하지 마라
	Never+R	

Tools: Volunteers(S) / should bring(V) their own tools(O) / (such as shovels and scissors).
도구 자원봉사자는 자신들의 도구를 가져와야 합니다 삽과 가위 같은

도구: 자원봉사자는 삽과 가위 같은 자신들의 도구를 가지고 와야 합니다.

노트 ■ A such as B : B와 같은 A

Clothing: A hat, work gloves, long pants, work shoes, socks
복장 모자, 작업용 장갑, 긴 바지, 작업용 신발, 양말
No sandals or bare feet, / (due to〈전치사〉 the presence of poison ivy)
샌들이나 맨발은 허용되지 않습니다 옻나무가 있으므로

복장: 모자, 작업용 장갑, 긴 바지, 작업용 신발, 양말
옻나무가 있으므로 샌들이나 맨발은 허용되지 않습니다.

노트 ■ 〈원인/이유〉 : ~ 때문에

전치사	because of	+(동)명사 / 명사 상당어구
	due to	
	for	
	on account of	
	owing to	
	thanks to	
종속접속사	as	+주어+동사 ~
	because	
	now(that)	
	since	

Food and drinks: Soft drinks and water / will be provided. / Bring snacks / (if you'd like).

음식, 음료 / 청량음료와 물이(S) / 제공될 것입니다(V〈미래 수동〉) / 간식을(O) 가져오세요(V) / (종·접) 원하면(S V)

음식, 음료: 청량음료와 물이 제공될 것입니다. 원하면 간식을 가져오세요.

Other information: Please feel free to invite / friends. Parents / are welcome / (to come along to work / or help supervise).

다른 정보 / 자유롭게 초대하세요(V) / 친구를(O) / 부모님들이(S) / 환영합니다(V S.C) / 같이 오셔서 일하시거나 / 감독을 도우시는 것을

다른 정보: 친구를 자유롭게 초대하세요.
부모님들이 같이 오셔서 일하시거나 혹은 감독을 도우시는 것을 환영합니다.

노트
■ feel free to R : 마음대로[거리낌없이] ~하다
■ be welcome to R : 얼마든지 ~해도 좋다
■ come along : 함께 가다[오다]

Contact: (To sign up), / (please) contact / Paula Willson / at 718-987-2345.

연락처 / 등록하시려면 / 연락하세요(V) / Paula Willson에게(O) / 718-987-2345로

연락처: 등록하시려면 Paula Willson에게 718-987-2345로 연락하세요.

노트 ■ sign up : 참가하다, 가입하다, ~에 등록하다(=enlist, register, join up; sign a contract; employ)

▶ Redwood High School Conservation Stewardship Program에 관한 다음 안내문의 내용과 일치하지 않는 것은?

① 비가 오면 바로 다음 날 시행된다.
② 덤불을 태우는 일도 한다.
③ 작업 도구들은 현장에서 제공된다.
④ 맨발이나 샌들 착용은 허용되지 않는다.
⑤ 부모가 함께 일하거나 감독을 도우러 올 수 있다.

정답 | ③

해설 | ③ 자원봉사자는 삽과 가위 같은 자신들의 도구를 가지고 와야 한다고 했기 때문에 일치하지 않는다.

오답 | ① 5월 12일과 26일에 진행되고 우천시 5월 13일과 27일에 진행된다고 설명하기 때문에 일치한다.
② 활동으로 생태계 교란 식물 파내기, 덤불 불태우기, 길에서 나뭇가지 치우기를 한다고 설명하기 때문에 일치한다.
④ 옻나무가 있기 때문에 샌들이나 맨발은 허용되지 않는다고 했기 때문에 일치한다.
⑤ 부모님들이 같이 오셔서 일하거나 혹은 감독을 도우는 것을 환영한다고 했으므로 일치한다.

Words

☐ conservation
☐ stewardship
☐ meadow
☐ bush
☐ clear
☐ trail
☐ branch
☐ volunteer
☐ tool
☐ shovel
☐ bare
☐ presence
☐ provide
☐ supervise

Phrases

☐ dig A up
☐ feel free to R
☐ come along
☐ A such as B
☐ be welcome to R
☐ sign up

01 다음 안내문의 내용과 일치하는 것은?

Redwood High School Conservation Stewardship Program

Where	Daisy Meadows
When	May 12 and 26: 9 a.m. to 1 p.m. (Rain Dates: May 13 and 27)
Activities	Dig up invasive plants, burning bush Clear trails of branches
Tools	Volunteers should bring their own tools such as shovels and scissors.
Clothing	A hat, work gloves, long pants, work shoes, socks No sandals or bare feet, due to the presence of poison ivy
Food and drinks	Soft drinks and water will be provided. Bring snacks if you'd like.
Other information	Please feel free to invite friends. Parents are welcome to come along to work or help supervise.
Contact	To sign up, please contact Paula Willson at 718-987-2345.

① 시간은 5월 12일과 26일, 오전에만 진행된다.
② 덤불을 키우는 활동을 한다.
③ 삽과 가위 같은 도구들은 제공된다.
④ 복장은 샌들을 신고 오면 된다.
⑤ 청량음료와 물은 제공될 예정이다.

02 다음 글을 읽고, 물음에 답하시오.

Redwood High School Conservation Stewardship Program

Where	Daisy Meadows
When	May 12 and 26: 9 a.m. to 1 p.m. (Rain Dates: May 13 and 27)
Activities	Dig up invasive plants, burning bush Clear trails of branches
Tools	Volunteers should bring their own tools such as shovels and scissors.
Clothing	A hat, work gloves, long pants, work shoes, socks No sandals or bare feet, due to the presence of poison ivy
Food and drinks	Soft drinks and water will be provided. Bring snacks if you'd like.
Other information	Please feel free to invite friends. Parents are welcome to come along to work or help supervise.
Contact	To sign up, please contact Paula Willson at 718-987-2345.

Q: What activities do you do to protect nature?

A: We ______________________________.

03 다음 글을 읽고, 문장에 빈칸을 채우시오.

Redwood High School Conservation Stewardship Program

Where	Daisy Meadows
When	May 12 and 26: 9 a.m. to 1 p.m. (Rain Dates: May 13 and 27)
Activities	Dig up invasive plants, burning bush Clear trails of branches
Tools	Volunteers should bring their own tools such as shovels and scissors.
Clothing	A hat, work gloves, long pants, work shoes, socks No sandals or bare feet, due to the presence of poison ivy
Food and drinks	Soft drinks and water will be provided. Bring snacks if you'd like.
Other information	Please feel free to invite friends. Parents are welcome to come along to work or help supervise.
Contact	To sign up, please contact Paula Willson at 718-987-2345.

Our program goes on at Daisy Meadow, volunteers have to bring tools like (A) ________ ________ ________, and (B) ________ ________ ________ ________ are not allowed.

04 다음 밑줄 친 단어의 의미로 적절하지 않은 것은?

Redwood High School Conservation Stewardship Program

Where	Daisy Meadows
When	May 12 and 26: 9 a.m. to 1 p.m. (Rain Dates: May 13 and 27)
Activities	Dig up invasive plants, burning bush Clear trails of branches
ⓐ Tools	Volunteers should ⓑ bring their own tools such as shovels and scissors.
Clothing	A hat, work gloves, long pants, work shoes, socks No sandals or bare feet, due to the ⓒ presence of poison ivy
Food and drinks	Soft drinks and water will be provided. Bring snacks if you'd like.
Other ⓓ information	Please feel free to ⓔ invite friends. Parents are welcome to come along to work or help supervise.
Contact	To sign up, please contact Paula Willson at 718-987-2345.

① ⓐ : an instrument
② ⓑ : to cause something
③ ⓒ : the fact of being in a particular place
④ ⓓ : facts or details about somebody/something
⑤ ⓔ : to ask somebody to come to a social event

지칭 추론

글의 논리	Story
제목	손자인 Brandon과 춤을 추고 있는 아버지의 사진
주제	아버지의 사진에 대한 감상

수능 ANALYSIS

025 어법 선택 & 연결어

On my desk is a picture of my father, age seventy-two or so, in his pale blue pajamas and **[danced / dancing]** with his great-grandson, Brandon. My father is really dancing, a wide grin on his face, **[holding / held]** on to the little boy's hand. Brandon is my niece's son, probably six or seven years old when this picture **[took / was taken]**. He's **[doing / done]** the best he can for a little guy, but **[mostly / almost]** he's just standing there, **[watched / watching]** my father. At least it doesn't appear **[that /what]** the boy is dancing. My father is in bare feet, one foot **[highly / high]** in the air, as he kicks to the music. I know, without **[being / having been]** there, **[what / which]** song he **[is / are]** dancing to. It is "One O'Clock Jump," by Benny Goodman. Everyone in the picture **[are / is]** smiling or **[laughing / laughs]**.

이야기 아버지의 사진에 대한 감상

(On my desk) / is / a picture (of my father), / (age seventy-two or so), / (in his pale blue pajamas) and (dancing with ① his great-grandson, Brandon).

(On my desk): 내 책상 위에는 / is: V 있다 / a picture (of my father): S 내 아버지의 사진이 / (age seventy-two or so): 72살 즈음의 / (in his pale blue pajamas): 연한 푸른색 잠옷을 입고 / great-grandson, Brandon: =〈동격〉 / (dancing with ① his great-grandson, Brandon): 〈분사구문〉 그의 증손자인 Brandon과 춤을 추고 있는

내 책상 위에는 72살 즈음의, 연한 푸른색 잠옷을 입고 그의 증손자인 Brandon과 춤을 추고 있는 내 아버지의 사진이 있다.

노트

■ in : [착용을 나타내어] ~을 입고[끼고, 신고], 착용하여

■ 〈부사구 문두 도치〉 : 전치사구가 문두로 가는 경우

전치사구 : 〈부사구〉			
〈전치사〉	목적어	동사	주어
On	my desk	is	a picture of my father

■ 〈주격관계대명사＋be동사 생략〉

명사	(주격관계대명사 ＋be동사)	Ring(현재분사) – 능동
		p.p.(과거분사) – 수동
		형용사
		부사
		명사
		전치사구
my father	(who/that is)	in his pale blue pajamas
		dancing ~.

■ 〈동격〉 : A(명사), B(명사) (B라는 A)

동격(B라는 A)		
명사(A)	,(콤마)	명사(B)
great-grandson		Brandon

My father / is / really dancing, / (with) {a wide grin (on ② his face)}, / (holding on to the little boy's hand).

My father: 내 아버지는 / is ... dancing: V〈현재진행〉 있다 / really dancing: 정말로 춤을 추고 / {a wide grin (on ② his face)}: 〈부대상황〉 그의 얼굴에 함박 웃음을 짓고 / (holding on to the little boy's hand): 〈부대상황〉 작은 사내아이의 손을 꼭 잡고

내 아버지는 그의 얼굴에 함박웃음을 짓고 작은 사내아이의 손을 꼭 잡고 정말로 춤을 추고 있다.

노트

■ hold on to : ~을 잡고 버티다, ~을 유지해내다

■ 〈with 부대상황〉

with	목적어	목적격보어		
~하면서, ~한채로		형용사(구)		
		부사(구)		
		전치사구		
		분사	현재분사 (Ring)	능동 (목적어가 목적격보어를 ~하고 있는)
			과거분사 (p.p.)	수동 (목적어가 목적격보어에게 당하는, 되어진)
(with)	a wide grin	on his face		

■ 〈부대상황〉 : 연속동작

주어	동사	대등접속사	주어	동사
My father	is dancing	and	he	holds
		(and he) 생략 → , holding ~ (부대상황 : 연속동작)		

Brandon / is my niece's son, / (probably) (six or seven years old) / (when this picture was taken).

Brandon: S Brandon은 / is: V / my niece's son: S.C 내 조카딸의 아들이다 / (probably) (six or seven years old): 아마도 예닐곱 살이었을 것이다 / when: 〈종·접〉 / this picture: S / was taken: V〈수동태〉 이 사진이 찍혔을 때

Brandon은 내 조카딸의 아들인데, 이 사진이 찍혔을 때 아마도 예닐곱 살이었을 것이다.

He's doing the best / (he can) / (for a little guy), / but
S V〈현재진행〉 S V
그는 최선을 다하고 있다 그가 할 수 있는 작은 아이로서는 하지만

(mostly) / ③ he's just standing there, / (watching my father).
S V〈현재진행〉 〈분사구문〉 O
주로 그는 단지 거기에 서 있다 내 아버지를 바라보며

그는 작은 아이로서는 할 수 있는 최선을 다하고 있으나, 주로 그(Brandon)는 내 아버지를 바라보며 단지 거기에 서 있다.

노트
- do the best one can : 최선을 다하다(=do one's best, do all one can)
- 〈most / almost / mostly〉

	대명사	형용사	부사
most	대부분의 것들(사람들)	대부분의	가장
almost	–	–	거의
mostly	–	–	주로, 일반적으로

- 〈분사구문 – 문미〉 : 주절과 분사구문의 위치가 서로 바뀌어도 무관

주절		종속절(→ 분사구문)			
주어	동사	종속접속사	주어	동사 : 상황에 맞게 아래처럼 바뀜	
		〈그대로 사용하면 의미 강조〉	(주절의 주어와 같으면 생략하고, 다르면 주격으로 사용함)	(being) (having been) 생략 가능	Ring(현재분사) / p.p.(과거분사) / 형용사 / 명사
he	is standing	–	–	–	watching

(At least) / it doesn't appear / (that the boy is dancing).
〈가S〉 V 〈종·접〉 S V〈현재진행〉 〈진S〉
적어도 보이진 않는다 그 아이가 춤을 추고 있는 것으로

적어도 그 아이가 춤을 추고 있는 것으로 보이진 않는다.

노트
- at least : 적어도[최소한]
- 〈appear 동사의 쓰임〉 : ~처럼 보이다

appear	주격보어
	that절
	to R
	분사
	to be 보어
	as+보어

- 〈what vs. that〉

	관계대명사(불완전한 문장)	접속사(완전한 문장)
what	○ 선행사를 포함하고 있기 때문에 what 앞에 선행사 불필요	×
that	○ that 앞에 선행사 필요	○

My father / is in bare feet, / (being) {one foot high (in the air)},
S V 〈분사구문〉
내 아버지는 맨발인데 발 하나가 공중에 높이 떠 있다

/ (as ④ he kicks / to the music).
〈종·접〉 S V
마치 그가 발을 차듯이 음악에 맞추어

내 아버지는 맨발인데, 마치 그가 음악에 맞추어 발을 차듯이 발 하나가 공중에 높이 떠 있다.

노트
- 〈분사구문 – 문미〉 : 주절과 분사구문의 위치가 서로 바뀌어도 무관

주절		종속절(→ 분사구문)			
주어	동사	종속접속사	주어	동사 : 상황에 맞게 아래처럼 바뀜	
		〈그대로 사용하면 의미 강조〉	(주절의 주어와 같으면 생략하고, 다르면 주격으로 사용함)	(being) (having been) 생략 가능	Ring(현재분사) / p.p.(과거분사) / 형용사 / 명사
My father	is	–	–	(being)	one foot

- 〈high / highly〉

high	형용사	높은
	부사	높게
	명사	높은 곳
highly	부사	매우(=very)

- 〈부사절을 이끄는 종속접속사〉 : as 용법

	쓰임	해석
as+주어+동사	시간	~하고 있을 때, ~하자마자, ~하면서
	원인/이유	~ 때문에
	조건	~한다면
	양보	~일지라도
	비교	~보다/만큼
	방법/상태	~대로/~하듯이

I know, / (without having been there), / (what song / ⑤ he is dancing to).
S V 〈전치사〉 〈완료동명사〉 〈의문사〉 S V〈현재진행〉
나는 알고 있다 거기에 있지 않았지만 무슨 노래에 맞추어 그가 춤을 추고 있는지

나는 거기에 있지 않았지만 그가 무슨 노래에 맞추어 춤을 추고 있는지 안다.

노트
- dance to : ~에 맞추어 춤추다
- 〈동명사의 태 / 시제 / 부정〉

태	능동	to R
	수동	to be p.p.
시제	단순시제 : 본동사 시제와 동일	to R
	완료시제 : 본동사 시제보다 한 시제 앞선 시제	to have p.p.
	완료 수동	to have been p.p.
부정	not	Ring
	never	

- 〈간접의문문 – 의문형용사 what으로 시작되는 간접의문문〉

타동사	목적어				
know	〈간접의문문〉 : 명사절				
	what	song	he	is dancing	to
	의문형용사(어떤) : 뒤에 나오는 명사를 수식함	명사	주어	동사	전치사

■ 〈what 쓰임〉

쓰임	용법	뜻
의문대명사	주어, 목적어, 보어 사용	무엇
의문형용사	명사 수식	무슨(선택 불가능) (which는 선택 가능)
관계대명사	주어, 목적어, 보어 사용	~것 (선행사 포함, the thing(s) that/which ~)

It / is "One O'Clock Jump," / (by Benny Goodman).
S: 그것은 / V / S.C: "One O'Clock Jump"이다 / Benny Goodman의

그것은 Benny Goodman의 "One O'Clock Jump"이다.

Everyone (in the picture) / is smiling or (is) laughing.
S: 사진 속의 모두는 / V_1(현재진행) / V_2(현재진행): 미소 짓거나 웃고 있다

사진 속의 모두가 미소 짓거나 웃고 있다.

노트 ■ 〈주어와 동사의 수의 일치〉
• each / every / any + 단수동사

▶ 밑줄 친 he[his]가 가리키는 대상이 나머지 넷과 다른 것은?

정답 | ③
해설 | ③ 'He'는 앞 문장의 Brandon을 가리킨다.
오답 | ① 'his'는 앞에 있는 a picture of my father를 가리킨다.
②, ④ 'he'는 앞에 있는 My father를 가리킨다.
⑤ 'he'는 앞 문장의 My father를 가리킨다.

Words

☐ pale
☐ pajamas
☐ great-grandson
☐ wide
☐ niece
☐ probably
☐ mostly
☐ bare
☐ kick
☐ laugh

Phrases

☐ hold on to
☐ at least
☐ do the best one can
☐ dance to

우선순위 영단어 역대 수능 기출 + 전국 모의고사 기출 + EBS 기출 + 교과서 기출 빈출 어휘

단어	뜻	단어	뜻	단어	뜻
strengthen	v. 강화하다	stripe	n. 줄무늬	subsidy	n. 보조금
suffering	n. 고통	summarize	v. 요약하다	supply	v. 공급하다
support	n. 도움	surge	n. 급증	survival	v. 생존
suspect	n. 주범	sympathy	n. 동정	tactic	n. 전략
talent	n. 재능	tap	v. 두드려 만들다	tap into	활용하다
task	n. 임무	texture	n. 질감	therapeutic	a. 치료의
therapist	n. 치료사	threat	a. 위협하는	timber	n. 목재
toss	v. 흔들리다	tragedy	n. 비극	trail	n. 오솔길
transaction	n. 상거래	treat	n. 한턱	treatment	n. 치료
trial	n. 재판	triumph	n. 승리	trivial	a. 사소한
turn down	v. 거절하다	turn out	판명되다	tyrant	n. 폭군
unconscious	a. 무의식적인	unstable	a. 불안정한	utterance	n. (말로) 표현함
utterly	ad. 완전히	vacuum	n. 진공 상태	variety	n. 품종
vast	a. 방대한	vendor	n. 파는 사람	versus	~에 대하여
viewpoint	n. 관점	violation	n. (법률, 약속 등의) 위반	visual	a. 시각적인
wander	v. 헤매다	warfare	n. 교전 상태	weird	a. 이상한
well-being	n. 행복	wither	v. (식물이) 시들다	exotic	a. 외국의
abound	v. 많이 있다	abruptly	ad. 갑작스럽게	abstract	a. 추상적인
abundance	n. 풍부	accept	v. 받아들이다	acceptance	n. 받아들임

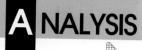

변형문제

01 다음 문장이 들어갈 부분으로 가장 적절한 곳을 고르시오.

> It is “One O’Clock Jump,” by Benny Goodman.

On my desk is a picture of my father, age seventy-two or so, in his pale blue pajamas and dancing with his great-grandson, Brandon. My father is really dancing, a wide grin on his face, holding on to the little boy’s hand. Brandon is my niece’s son, probably six or seven years old when this picture was taken. (①) He’s doing the best he can for a little guy, but mostly he’s just standing there, watching my father. (②) At least it doesn’t appear that the boy is dancing. (③) My father is in bare feet, one foot high in the air, as he kicks to the music. (④) I know, without having been there, what song he is dancing to. (⑤) Everyone in the picture is smiling or laughing.

02 다음 중 사진에 관한 내용으로 적절하지 않은 것은?

> On my desk is a picture of my father, age seventy-two or so, in his pale blue pajamas and dancing with his great-grandson, Brandon. My father is really dancing, a wide grin on his face, holding on to the little boy’s hand. Brandon is my niece’s son, probably six or seven years old when this picture was taken. He’s doing the best he can for a little guy, but mostly he’s just standing there, watching my father. At least it doesn’t appear that the boy is dancing. My father is in bare feet, one foot high in the air, as he kicks to the music. I know, without having been there, what song he is dancing to. It is “One O’Clock Jump,” by Benny Goodman. Everyone in the picture is smiling or laughing.

① Brandon과 그의 아버지가 찍혀 있다.
② 필자의 아버지는 작은 사내아이와 손을 잡고 있다.
③ 작은 아이는 춤을 추고 있는 것처럼 보이지 않는다.
④ 필자의 아버지는 맨발이다.
⑤ 사진 속의 모두는 웃고 있다.

03 다음 문장 중에서 글의 흐름에 적절하지 않은 것은?

On my desk is a picture of my father, age seventy-two or so, in his pale blue pajamas and dancing with his great-grandson, Brandon. My father is really dancing, a wide grin on his face, holding on to the little boy's hand. ① Brandon is my niece's son, probably six or seven years old when this picture was taken. ② He's doing the best he can for a little guy, but mostly he's just standing there, watching my father. ③ I'm hugging my child. ④ At least it doesn't appear that the boy is dancing. ⑤ My father is in bare feet, one foot high in the air, as he kicks to the music. I know, without having been there, what song he is dancing to. It is "One O'Clock Jump," by Benny Goodman. Everyone in the picture is smiling or laughing.

04 다음 사진 속에서 Brandon과 필자의 아버지의 분위기로 가장 적절한 것은?

On my desk is a picture of my father, age seventy-two or so, in his pale blue pajamas and dancing with his great-grandson, Brandon. My father is really dancing, a wide grin on his face, holding on to the little boy's hand. Brandon is my niece's son, probably six or seven years old when this picture was taken. He's doing the best he can for a little guy, but mostly he's just standing there, watching my father. At least it doesn't appear that the boy is dancing. My father is in bare feet, one foot high in the air, as he kicks to the music. I know, without having been there, what song he is dancing to. It is "One O'Clock Jump," by Benny Goodman. Everyone in the picture is smiling or laughing.

① sad and angry
② happy and lively
③ dangerous and urgent
④ tired and slowly
⑤ tired and emaciated

UNIT 07

지칭 추론

글의 논리	Question & Answer (질문 & 대답)
제목	Diane과 동료교사의 의사소통의 문제점
주제	의사소통을 할 때, 부정적인 태도는 자신의 권위를 약화시키고, 주변 사람의 의욕을 꺾는다.

PRACTICE 01

026 어법 선택 & 연결어

Diane made a communication mistake **[what / that] [instantly / instant]** persuaded her fellow teacher Martha **[to resent / receting]** her. What was Diane's mistake? Diane disagreed with Martha and didn't even give her a chance to explain her idea before **[rejetion / rejecting] [them / it]**. Diane wasn't interested in looking **[at / for]** the newspaper article and she did not ask Martha **[to explain / explaining]** her reasons for **[advocation / advocating]** a new science program. By **[rejetion / rejecting]** Martha's opinion without giving **[it / them]** any consideration, Diane sent Martha the message **[which / that]** she didn't respect her or **[value / valued]** her ideas. Diane's instant negativity discouraged her from sharing ideas in the future **[that / what]** could benefit the students, the science department and the school. Diane's habit of **[quick / quickly]** dismissing **[opposing / opposed]** views weakened her authority and **[limiting / limited]** progress in the science department.

결과 Diane은 그녀의 동료교사가 그녀에게 화를 내도록 만들었다.

Diane / made a communication mistake / {that (instantly) persuaded her fellow teacher Martha / to resent her}.

(Diane: S, Diane은 / made: V / a communication mistake: O〈선행사〉, 의사소통 상의 실수를 했다 / that: 〈주·관〉 / instantly: 즉시 / persuaded: V / her fellow teacher Martha: O, 그녀의 동료교사 Martha가 / to resent her: O.C, 그녀에게 화를 내도록 만든)

Diane은 그녀의 동료교사 Martha가 그녀에게 즉시 화를 내도록 만든 의사소통 상의 실수를 했다.

노트
- make a mistake : 실수하다, 잘못 생각하다
- 〈주격관계대명사절의 수의 일치〉 : 선행사를 포함하고 있는 관계대명사 what 사용 불가

	주격관계대명사절		
선행사	주격관계대명사	주어	동사
a communication mistake	that		persuaded

- 〈5형식 불완전타동사의 목적격보어〉 : 수동태 전환 시, 2형식 문장(be p.p. +to R)

주어	불완전타동사	목적어	목적격보어
–	advise / allow / ask / assume / beg / cause / command / compel / condition / decide / design / drive / enable / encourage / expect / forbid / force / instruct / intend / invite / lead / like / motivate / order / permit / persuade / predispose / pressure / program / push / require / teach / tell / train / trust / urge / want / warn / wish 등	–	to 동사원형

질문 그녀의 실수는 무엇인가?

What was / Diane's mistake?

(was: V, 무엇이었을까 / Diane's mistake: S, Diane의 실수는)

Diane의 실수는 무엇이었을까?

대답1 Diane은 동료교사의 생각에 동의하지 않고 그녀에게 설명할 기회도 주지 않았다.

Diane / disagreed (with Martha) / and / didn't (even) give / ① her a chance / (to explain her idea) / (before rejecting it).

(Diane: S, Diane은 / disagreed: V_1, Martha의 생각에 동의하지 않았다 / and: 그리고 / didn't give: V_2, 주지 않았다 / her: I.O, a chance: D.O, 그녀에게 기회를 / her idea: O, 그녀의 아이디어를 설명하기 위한 / before: 〈전치사〉, 그것을 / rejecting: 〈동명사〉, 거부하기 전에 / it: O)

Diane은 Martha의 생각에 동의하지 않았고 그것을 거부하기 전에 그녀에게 아이디어를 설명할 기회조차 주지 않았다.

노트
- disagree with : ~에 동의하지 않다
- give+IO(사람/동물)+DO(사물) : ~에게 …을 주다

대답2 Diane은 동료교사가 새로운 과학 프로그램을 옹호하는 이유에 대해 들으려고 하지 않았다.

Diane / wasn't interested / (in looking at the newspaper article) / and she did not ask / Martha to explain ② her reasons / (for advocating a new science program).

(Diane: S, Diane은 / wasn't interested: V〈수동태〉, 흥미가 없었다 / looking: 〈동명사〉, 신문 기사를 보는 데 / she: S, ask: V, 그리고 그녀는 요청도 하지 않았다 / Martha: O / to explain her reasons: O.C, Martha에게 그녀의 이유를 설명해달라는 / advocating: 〈동명사〉 / a new science program: O, 새로운 과학 프로그램을 옹호하는)

Diane은 신문 기사를 보는 데 흥미가 없었고, 그녀는 Martha에게 새로운 과학 프로그램을 옹호하는 그녀의 이유를 설명해달라는 요청도 하지 않았다.

노트
- be interested in : ~에 관심[흥미]이 있다
- ask+O+OC (to R) : ~에게 …하기를 요청하다
- 〈look at / over / in / out / for〉

look	at	~을 쳐다보다
	over	~을 대충 훑어보다[살펴보다](=watch)

	in	~을 들여다보다, 조사/검토하다
	out	~을 내다보다, 조심하다
	for	~을 찾다, 구하다, 바라다

대답3 Diane은 그녀의 동료교사를 존중하지 않는다는 메시지를 전달했다.

(By rejecting Martha's opinion) / (without giving it any consideration), / Diane / sent Martha the message / (that she didn't respect ③ her or value her ideas).

〈전치사〉 By, 〈동명사〉 rejecting, O Martha's opinion: Martha의 의견을 거부함으로써 / 〈전치사〉 without, 〈동명사〉 giving, I.O it, D.O any consideration: 전혀 고려하지 않고 / S Diane: Diane은 / V sent, I.O Martha, D.O the message: Martha에게 메시지를 전달했다 = 〈동격〉 / 〈종·접〉 that, S she, V_1 didn't respect, O her, V_2 value, O her ideas: 그녀가 그녀를 존중하지 않고 그녀의 아이디어를 가치 있게 여기지도 않는다는

전혀 고려하지 않고 Martha의 의견을 거부함으로써, Diane은 Martha에게 그녀가 그녀를 존중하지 않고 그녀의 아이디어를 가치 있게 여기지도 않는다는 메시지를 전달했다.

노트
- by + 동명사 : ~함으로써
- send + IO(사람/동물) + DO(사물) : ~에게 …을 보내다
- 〈동격의 that〉 : ~라는 A(관계대명사 which/what 사용 불가)

추상명사 (A)	종속절(명사절 – 완전한 문장)		
	(that)	주어	동사 ~
answer / belief / chance / claim / conclusion / dream / evidence / extent / fact / faith / hope / idea / likelihood / news / notion / pledge / possibility / promise / proposal / question / recognition / reply / request / result / sense / statement / suggestion / testament / theory / view / wickedness 등	종속 접속사 (생략 가능)	–	–

- 〈what vs. that〉

	관계대명사(불완전한 문장)	접속사(완전한 문장)
what	○ 선행사를 포함하고 있기 때문에 what 앞에 선행사 불필요	×
that	○ that 앞에 선행사 필요	○

대답4 Diane의 즉각적인 부정적 태도는 아이디어를 공유하려는 동료교사의 의욕을 꺾었다.

Diane's instant negativity / discouraged ④ her / (from sharing ideas) / (in the future) / {that could benefit the students, the science department and the school}.

S Diane's instant negativity: Diane의 즉각적인 부정적 태도는 / V discouraged, O her: 그녀의 의욕을 꺾었다 / 〈동명사〉 sharing, O(선행사) ideas: 아이디어를 공유하려는 / 미래에 / 〈주·관〉 that, V could benefit, O_1 the students, O_2 the science department, O_3 the school: 학생, 과학과, 그리고 학교에 도움이 될 수 있는

Diane의 즉각적인 부정적 태도는 장차 학생, 과학과, 그리고 학교에 도움이 될 수 있는 아이디어를 공유하려는 그녀의 의욕을 꺾었다.

노트
- 〈방해/금지〉

주어	완전타동사	목적어	전치사	목적어
	keep		from	
	prohibit			
	deter			
	bar			
	hinder			
	prevent			
	protect			
	discourage			
	stop			

- 〈주격관계대명사절 that〉 : 선행사를 포함하고 있는 관계대명사 what 사용 불가

선행사	전치사구	주격관계대명사절		
		주격관계대명사	~~주어~~	동사
ideas	in the future	that		could benefit

주제문(결과) Diane의 습관은 그녀의 권위를 약화시키고, 과학과의 발전을 제한했다.

Diane's habit / (of quickly dismissing opposing views) / weakened ⑤ her authority / and / limited progress / (in the science department).

S Diane's habit: Diane의 습관은 / 〈부사〉 quickly, 〈동명사〉 dismissing, 〈현재분사〉 opposing, O views: 반대 의견을 빠르게 묵살해버리는 / V_1 weakened, O her authority: 그녀의 권위를 약화시켰다 / 그리고 / V_2 limited, O progress: 발전을 제한했다 / 과학과의

반대 의견을 빠르게 묵살해버리는 Diane의 습관은 그녀의 권위를 약화시켰고 과학과의 발전을 제한했다.

노트

	전치사구				
Diane's habit	of	quickly	dismissing	opposing	views
주어	전치사	부사	동명사	현재분사	명사
		형용사 quick 불가 : 동명사 수식 불가			

- 〈부사의 역할〉 : 동사 / 형용사 / 다른 부사 / 문장 전체 / 준동사(to부정사, 동명사, 분사) 등을 수식함
- 〈분사의 역할 및 종류〉

분사의 역할	형용사	명사 수식	전치 수식
			후치 수식
		보어 사용	주격보어
			목적격보어
분사의 종류	현재분사(Ring)	능동	~하는, ~하고 있는
	과거분사(p.p.)	수동	~되는, ~ 당하는, 이미 된

▶ 밑줄 친 her가 가리키는 대상이 나머지 넷과 다른 것은?

정답 | ⑤
해설 | ⑤ 'her'는 앞에 Diane를 가리킨다.
오답 | ①, ②, ③ 'her'는 앞에 Martha를 가리킨다.
④ 'her'는 앞 문장의 Martha를 가리킨다.

Words

- ☐ instantly
- ☐ persuade
- ☐ fellow
- ☐ resent
- ☐ reject
- ☐ article
- ☐ advocate
- ☐ consideration
- ☐ respect
- ☐ value
- ☐ negativity
- ☐ department
- ☐ dismiss
- ☐ opposing
- ☐ view
- ☐ weaken
- ☐ authority
- ☐ progress

Phrases

- ☐ make a mistake
- ☐ be interested in
- ☐ disagree with
- ☐ by+동명사

우선순위 영단어

역대 수능 기출+전국 모의고사 기출+EBS 기출+교과서 기출 빈출 어휘

단어	뜻	단어	뜻	단어	뜻
accidental	a. 우연한	accomplish	v. 이룩하다	acquisition	n. 인수
act upon	~에 따라 행동하다	activate	v. 작동시키다	acute	a. 심각한
adjacent	a. 인접한	advance	v. 개선하다	advanced	a. 선진의
agent	n. 대리인	aging	n. 노화	aim	v. 목표하다
alike	a. 서로 같은	altitude	n. 고도	ambiguity	n. 모호함
ambition	n. 포부	analytical	a. 분석적인	ancestor	n. 선조
annual	a. 해마다의	annually	ad. 해마다	antioxidant	n. 산화 방지제
antique	n. 골동품	apology	n. 사과	approval	n. 승인
architecture	n. 건축	arrest	v. 억제하다	arrogant	a. 거만한
articulate	v. 분명히 말하다	artisan	n. 장인	as a whole	전체로서
as long as	~하는 한	as opposed to	~와 대조적으로	associate A with B	A와 B를 관련짓다
associated	a. 관련된	at large	전체로서	at least	적어도
athlete	n. 운동선수	attendance	n. 출석	auditorium	n. 강당
automatically	ad. 무의식적으로	awakening	n. 각성	awful	a. 끔찍한
awkward	a. 어색한	band	n. 악단	barbarian	n. 야만인
barren	a. 메마른	basis	n. 기본	be held	개최되다
be willing to	기꺼이 ~하다	beat	n. 박자	bend	n. 굽음
bizarre	a. 기괴한	blame	v. 탓하다	blend	v. 섞다
blind	a. 눈 먼	block	n. (도시의) 한 구획	boast	v. 자랑하다
break out	발발하다	brilliant	a. 총명한	brood	v. 곰곰히 생각하다
bug	v. 해충을 잡다	build up	확립하다	bulk	a. 대부분
bureaucratic	a. 관료주의적인	burglar	n. 도둑	burn	n. 화상
buzzing	a. 윙윙거리는	by and large	전반적으로	candidate	n. 후보자
capability	n. 능력	carry	v. ~을 가지고 다니다	carry out	v. 수행하다
causal	a. 원인이 되는	chamber	n. 회의실	channel	v. ~와 소통하다
chat	v. 잡담하다	clash	n. 충돌	cling to	v. 고수하다
clumsy	a. 손재주가 없는	coarse	a. 거친	coincidence	n. 우연의 일치
collect	v. 모이다	colonial	a. 식민지의	come down with	(질병 등)에 걸리다
comfort	n. 위안	commander	n. 지휘관	commercially	ad. 상업적으로
commit	v. 저지르다[범하다]	companionship	n. 동반자 관계	company	n. 회사
compass	n. 나침반	competence	n. 능력	competitor	n. 경쟁자

변형문제

01 밑줄 친 부분 중 문맥상 옳지 않은 것은?

Diane made a communication mistake that instantly persuaded her fellow teacher Martha to resent her. What was Diane's mistake? Diane ① disagreed with Martha and didn't even give her a chance to explain her idea before rejecting it. Diane wasn't ② interested in looking at the newspaper article and she did not ask Martha to explain her reasons for advocating a new science program. By ③ rejecting Martha's opinion without giving it any consideration, Diane sent Martha the message that she didn't respect her or value her ideas. Diane's instant ④ positivity discouraged her from sharing ideas in the future that could benefit the students, the science department and the school. Diane's habit of quickly ⑤ dismissing opposing views weakened her authority and limited progress in the science department.

02 다음 글의 주제로 가장 적절한 것은?

Diane made a communication mistake that instantly persuaded her fellow teacher Martha to resent her. What was Diane's mistake? Diane disagreed with Martha and didn't even give her a chance to explain her idea before rejecting it. Diane wasn't interested in looking at the newspaper article and she did not ask Martha to explain her reasons for advocating a new science program. By rejecting Martha's opinion without giving it any consideration, Diane sent Martha the message that she didn't respect her or value her ideas. Diane's instant negativity discouraged her from sharing ideas in the future that could benefit the students, the science department and the school. Diane's habit of quickly dismissing opposing views weakened her authority and limited progress in the science department.

① Ignoring the other person's thoughts results in poor results.
② When communicating, you must make your point strong.
③ Opposing opinions should be ignored.
④ When communicating, you should follow the other person's opinion.
⑤ Good ideas bring good results.

03 다음 문장이 들어갈 부분으로 가장 적절한 곳을 고르시오.

What was Diane's mistake?

Diane made a communication mistake that instantly persuaded her fellow teacher Martha to resent her. (①) Diane disagreed with Martha and didn't even give her a chance to explain her idea before rejecting it. (②) Diane wasn't interested in looking at the newspaper article and she did not ask Martha to explain her reasons for advocating a new science program. (③) By rejecting Martha's opinion without giving it any consideration, Diane sent Martha the message that she didn't respect her or value her ideas. (④) Diane's instant negativity discouraged her from sharing ideas in the future that could benefit the students, the science department and the school. (⑤) Diane's habit of quickly dismissing opposing views weakened her authority and limited progress in the science department.

04 다음 글을 읽고, Diane에게 할 수 있는 조언으로 가장 적절한 것은?

Diane made a communication mistake that instantly persuaded her fellow teacher Martha to resent her. What was Diane's mistake? Diane disagreed with Martha and didn't even give her a chance to explain her idea before rejecting it. Diane wasn't interested in looking at the newspaper article and she did not ask Martha to explain her reasons for advocating a new science program. By rejecting Martha's opinion without giving it any consideration, Diane sent Martha the message that she didn't respect her or value her ideas. Diane's instant negativity discouraged her from sharing ideas in the future that could benefit the students, the science department and the school. Diane's habit of quickly dismissing opposing views weakened her authority and limited progress in the science department.

① You should push your point a little more.
② You need to listen to other people's opinions.
③ You have to think twice before you tell me your idea.
④ You should also present positive ideas.
⑤ You should ignore the opposition.

UNIT 07

지칭 추론

글의 논리	Story
제목	Salli의 원하는 신발 구매 이야기
주제	Salli는 광고를 보고 자신이 원하는 신발을 구매하려 했으나 허위 광고였고 구매하지 못했다.

PRACTICE 02

027 어법 선택 & 연결어

A well-known shoe manufacturer sent out a mailer **[advertising / advertised]** a sale. Salli was **[exciting / excited]**, as she has a very narrow foot and the manufacturer advertised her size in styles she liked. When she went to the store, she was very **[disappointed / disappointing] [because / because of]** not one of the styles **[was / were] [availably / available]** in her size. She **[told / was told]** by a saleswoman **[what / that]** they only stocked one of each style in each size! (   ), since she **[promised / was promised]** the shoes she wanted **[was / were] [availably / available]** from the warehouse, Salli decided **[ordering / to order]** two pairs. A week **[later / latter]**, she received a phone call **[said / saying]** one pair was actually no longer being **[making / made]**. A week after that **[came a rather poignant note / a rather poignant note came]** from the saleswoman and her manager **[saying / said] [another / the other]** pair was also **[unavailably / unavailable]**. They did **[enclosing / enclose]** a 20% off coupon for her next visit. (   ) — there won't be a next time.

이야기 Salli의 원하는 신발 구매 이야기

A well-known shoe manufacturer / sent out a mailer / (which was) (advertising a sale).

- well-known: 〈과거분사〉 / shoe manufacturer: S — 잘 알려진 신발 제조업자가
- sent out: V / a mailer: O — 선전용 전단지를 발송했다
- advertising a sale: 〈현재분사〉 판매를 광고하는

잘 알려진 신발 제조업자가 판매를 광고하는 선전용 전단지를 발송했다.

노트
- ■ send A out : A를 보내다, 발송하다
- ■ 〈주격관계대명사＋be동사 생략〉

명사	(주격관계대명사 ＋be동사)	
		Ring(현재분사) – 능동
		p.p.(과거분사) – 수동
		형용사
		부사
		명사
		전치사구
a mailer	(which/that was)	advertising

Salli / was excited, / {as she has a very narrow foot / and the manufacturer advertised her size / (in styles) / (that) (she liked)}.

- Salli: S — Salli는 / was: V / excited: S.C — 신이 났다
- as: 〈종·접〉 / she: S / has: V / a very narrow foot: O — 왜냐하면 그녀는 발의 볼이 매우 좁다
- the manufacturer: S / advertised: V / her size: O — 그리고 그 제조업자가 그녀의 치수의 신발을 광고했기 때문이다
- styles: 〈선행사〉 스타일의
- she: S / liked: V — 그녀가 좋아하는

Salli는 신이 났는데, 왜냐하면 그녀는 발의 볼이 매우 좁은데 그 제조업자가 그녀가 좋아하는 스타일의 (그녀의) 치수의 신발을 광고했기 때문이었다.

노트 ■ 〈감정과 관련된 완전타동사〉 : 분사화가 되어 주격보어/목적격보어 자리에 나올 때 구별법

• 2형식

주어	동사	주격보어(S.C)
사람		과거분사(p.p.) – 수동(되어진, ~ 당한)
사물		현재분사(Ring) – 능동(~하고 있는, 하는)
Salli	was	excited

■ 〈부사절을 이끄는 종속접속사〉 : as 용법

	쓰임	해석
as＋주어＋동사	시간	~하고 있을 때, ~하자마자, ~하면서
	원인/이유	~ 때문에
	조건	~한다면
	양보	~일지라도
	비교	~보다/만큼
	방법/상태	~대로/~하듯이

■ 〈목적격관계대명사 that〉 : 타동사의 목적어가 없는 경우 / 선행사를 포함하고 있는 관계대명사 what 사용 불가

	〈목적격관계대명사절〉			
선행사	목적격관계대명사	주어	타동사	~~목적어~~
styles	생략 가능 : (that)	she	liked	

(When ① she went / to the store), / she / was very disappointed / {because not one (of the styles) / was available (in her size)}.

- When: 〈종·접〉 / she: S / went: V — 그녀가 갔을 때 / 그 가게에
- she: S — 그녀는 / was: V / very 매우 / disappointed: S.C — 실망했다
- because: 〈종·접〉 / not one: S / was: V — 왜냐하면 그 스타일로 된 어떤 신발도 없었기 때문이었다
- available: S.C — 맞는 / 그녀의 치수에

그녀가 그 가게에 갔을 때 그녀는 매우 실망했는데, 왜냐하면 그 스타일로 된 어떤 신발도 그녀의 치수에 맞는 것이 없었기 때문이었다.

노트 ■ 〈one of＋복수명사＋단수동사〉 : ~ 중의 하나

one (주어 : 단수)	of	복수명사	단수동사
one		the styles	was

■ 〈원인/이유〉 : ~ 때문에

전치사	because of	＋(동)명사 / 명사 상당어구
	due to	
	for	
	on account of	
	owing to	
	thanks to	
종속접속사	as	＋주어＋동사 ~
	because	
	now(that)	
	since	

② She / was told / (by a saleswoman) / {that they only stocked one / (of each style) / (in each size)}!

She (S) 그녀는 / was told (V(수동태)) 들었다 / (by a saleswoman) 여성 판매원으로부터 / {that (〈종·접〉) they (S) only stocked (V) one (O) 그 가게에는 하나만 갖춰 두고 있다는 것을 (O) / (of each style) 각 스타일의 / (in each size)} 각 치수마다

그녀는 여성 판매원으로부터 그 가게에는 각 치수마다 각 스타일의 신발 하나만 갖춰두고 있다는 말을 들었다!

노트 ■ 〈직접목적어 자리에 that절을 가지는 4형식 수여동사〉 : 수동태 시, be told ＋that＋주어＋동사

주어	수여동사		간접목적어	직접목적어
	advise	조언하다		(that)＋주어＋동사
	assure	장담(확신)시키다		
	convince	확신시켜주다		
	inform	알리다		
	instruct			
	notify			
	persuade	설득하다		
	promise	약속하다		
	remind	상기시키다		
	request	요청하다		
	show	보여 주다		
	teach	가르치다		
	tell	말하다		
	warn	경고하다		

■ 〈what vs. that〉

	관계대명사(불완전한 문장)	접속사(완전한 문장)
what	○ 선행사를 포함하고 있기 때문에 what 앞에 선행사 불필요	×
that	○ that 앞에 선행사 필요	○

(Still), / [since she was promised / {the shoes / (③ she wanted) / were available / (from the warehouse)}], /

(Still) 그래도 / [since (〈종·접〉) she (S) was promised (V(수동태)) 그녀는 약속을 받았기 때문에 / (목·접 that) {the shoes (S(선행사)) 신발을 / (목·관 that) (③ she (S) 그녀가 wanted (V)) 원했던 / were (V) available (S.C) 구할 수 있다는 / (from the warehouse)} 창고에서 (O)

Salli decided to order two pairs.

Salli (S) decided (V) to order two pairs (O) Salli는 두 켤레를 주문하기로 결정했다

그래도 그녀는 자신이 원했던 신발을 창고에서 구할 수 있다는 약속을 받았기 때문에 Salli는 두 켤레를 주문하기로 결정했다.

노트 ■ 〈직접목적어 자리에 that절을 가지는 4형식 수여동사〉 : 수동태 시, be told ＋that＋주어＋동사

주어	수여동사		간접목적어	직접목적어
	advise	조언하다		(that)＋주어＋동사
	assure	장담(확신)시키다		
	convince	확신시켜주다		
	inform	알리다		
	instruct			
	notify			
	persuade	설득하다		
	promise	약속하다		
	remind	상기시키다		
	request	요청하다		
	show	보여 주다		
	teach	가르치다		
	tell	말하다		
	warn	경고하다		

■ 〈since의 용법〉

종속접속사	시간	~ 이래 (죽), ~한 때부터 내내
	이유	~이므로, ~이니까
전치사	시간	~ 이래 (죽), ~부터 (내내)
부사	시간	(그때) 이래 (죽), 그 뒤[후] 줄곧

■ 〈목적격으로 사용된 종속접속사 that과 관계대명사 that은 생략 가능〉

주어	동사	목적어						
she	was promised	(that)	the shoes	(that)	she	wanted	~~목적어~~	were ~
		목적격 종속접속사 : 생략 가능	주어	목적격 관계대명사 : 생략 가능	주어	동사		동사
				목적격관계대명사절				

■ 〈목적어 자리에 to부정사를 취하는 완전타동사〉

주어	완전타동사	목적어
–	afford / agree / ask / attempt / care / choose / claim / dare / decide / demand / desire / determine / elect / expect / fail / guarantee / hope / intend / learn / manage / need / offer / plan / pretend / promise / refuse / resolve / seek / threaten / volunteer / want / wish 등	to 동사원형

(A week later), / she / received a phone call / [saying /

(A week later) 일주일 후에 / she (S) 그녀는 / received (V) a phone call (O) 전화를 받았다 / (which was) [saying (〈현재분사〉) 말하고 있는 / (that)

{one pair / was (actually) (no longer) being made}].

S — V〈과거진행 수동〉 — O

한 켤레가 사실상 더 이상 만들어지지 않고 있다는

일주일 후에 그녀는 한 켤레가 사실상 더 이상 만들어지지 않고 있다는 전화를 받았다.

노트
- receive a call : 전화를 받다
- was being p.p. : 과거진행 수동
- 〈불규칙적으로 변화하는 중요 형용사와 부사〉

원급	비교급	뜻	최상급	뜻	의미
late	later	나중의	latest	최근의	시간
	latter	후자의	last	최후의	순서

- 〈목적격종속접속사 that 생략〉 : 완전타동사의 목적어로 사용된 경우 / 관계대명사 what 사용 불가

	종속절(명사절 : 목적어) (완전한 절)		
완전타동사	that	주어	동사
saying	목적격종속접속사 – 생략 가능(~하는 것을)	one pair	was being made

- 〈주격관계대명사+be동사 생략〉

명사	(주격관계대명사+be동사)	Ring(현재분사) – 능동
		p.p.(과거분사) – 수동
		형용사
		부사
		명사
		전치사구
a phone call	(which/that was)	saying

- 〈전체부정〉 : 모두/전부 ~ 아니다, 절대 ~하지 않는다

전체 부정		
	not any one(=none) (모두 ~이 아니다) no+명사 (어느 누구도 ~ 않다) not ~ either(=neither) (둘 다 ~이 아니다) not+anything(=nothing) (아무것도[단 하나도] (~ 아니다 · 없다)) not+ever(=never) (결코 ~이 아니다) not anywhere(=nowhere)	
	no =not any	no more=not ~ anymore nobody=not ~ anybody nothing=not ~ anything no longer=not ~ any longer

(A week after that) came a rather poignant note / (from the saleswoman and ④ her manager) / {saying (the other pair was also unavailable)}.

V — S: 그 후 일주일 후에 다소 가슴 아픈 편지가 왔다

(which was) (that) — saying 〈현재분사〉

그 여성 판매원과 그녀의 관리자로부터

S V S.C — O: 다른 한 켤레도 구할 수 없다고 말하는

그 후 일주일 후에 그 여성 판매원과 그녀의 관리자로부터 다른 한 켤레도 구할 수 없다고 적힌 다소 가슴 아픈 편지가 왔다.

노트
- 〈부사구 문두 도치〉

	〈도치〉	
A week after that	came	a rather poignant Note
〈부사〉	동사	주어

- 〈주격관계대명사+be동사 생략〉
  - 현재분사 saying이 전치사구 앞에 있는 명사를 수식하는 경우

명사	전치사구	(주격관계대명사+be동사)	Ring(현재분사) – 능동
			p.p.(과거분사) – 수동
			형용사
			부사
			명사
			전치사구
a rather poignant note	from ~	(which/that was)	saying

- 〈목적격종속접속사 that 생략〉 : 완전타동사의 목적어로 사용된 경우 / 관계대명사 what 사용 불가

	종속절(명사절 : 목적어) (완전한 절)		
완전타동사	that	주어	동사
saying	목적격종속접속사 – 생략 가능(~하는 것을)	the other pair	was

- 〈the other vs. another〉

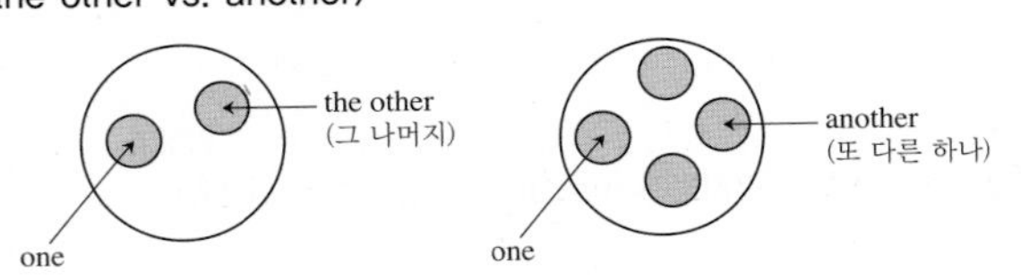

They / (did) enclose / a 20% off coupon / (for ⑤ her next visit).

S 그들은 / V 동봉하기는 했다 / O 20퍼센트 할인 쿠폰을 / 다음 방문 때에 쓸 수 있는

그들은 그녀의 다음 방문 때에 쓸 수 있는 20퍼센트 할인 쿠폰을 동봉하기는 했다.

노트
- 〈동사 강조 표현〉

do / does / did	+동사원형(R)
=정말로(really, certainly)	

Needless to say — there won't be a next time.

말할 필요도 없이 / V S: 다음 번 방문은 없을 것이다

말할 필요도 없이 다음 번 방문은 없을 것이다.

노트
- needless to say : 말할 필요도 없이, 두말하면 잔소리지만
- 〈There is 도치구문〉

긍정문	There	is	단수 주어	~이 있다
		are	복수 주어	
부정문	There	is no	단수 주어	~이 없다
		are no	복수 주어	

- 유도부사 **there**와 함께 도치구문을 이루는 be동사(is/are/was/were) 대신에 완전자동사 **appear**, **come**, **exist**, **follow**, **live**, **stand** 등을 사용할 수 있다.

▶ 밑줄 친 부분이 가리키는 대상이 나머지 넷과 다른 것은?

정답 | ④
해설 | ④ 'her'는 앞에 the saleswoman을 가리킨다.

오답 | ① 'she'는 앞 문장의 Salli를 가리킨다.
② 'she'는 앞 문장의 she와 같다.
③ 'she'는 앞의 she와 같고 이 문장에서 'she'는 Salli를 가리킨다.
⑤ 'her'는 원하는 구두를 구입하지 못한 사람인 Salli를 가리킨다.

Words

- ☐ manufacturer
- ☐ mailer
- ☐ advertise
- ☐ narrow foot
- ☐ available
- ☐ stock
- ☐ warehouse
- ☐ receive
- ☐ enclose

Phrases

- ☐ send A out
- ☐ needless to say
- ☐ receive a call

우선순위 영단어 역대 수능 기출 + 전국 모의고사 기출 + EBS 기출 + 교과서 기출 빈출 어휘

단어	뜻	단어	뜻	단어	뜻
complain	v. 불평하다	compliant	n. 유순한	comprehensible	a. 이해할 수 있는
comprise	v. 구성하다	conceal	v. 숨기다	concentrated	a. 집중된
confess	v. 자백하다	conform	v. 따르다	confusion	n. 혼란
connection	n. 연고	connotation	n. 함축	conquer	v. 쟁취하다
consistency	n. 농도	console	v. 위로하다	conspicuous	a. 눈에 띄는
consultant	n. 상담역	contradict	v. 부정하다	convinced	a. 확신하는
coral reef	n. 산호초	corporation	n. 회사	correlate	v. 상관 관계가 있다
corresponding	a. 대응하는	cottage	n. 시골의 작은 집	council	n. 심의회
counterproductive	a. 역효과의	critically	ad. 위태롭게	cupboard	n. 찬장
cure	n. 치료약	curiosity	n. 호기심	custom	n. 관습
dare	v. 감히 ~하다	definite	a. 명확한	definitely	ad. 확실히
demanding	a. 힘든	deny	v. 부정하다	depend on	~에 달려 있다
design	v. 설계하다	destiny	n. 운명	destructive	a. 파괴적인
deviation	n. 벗어남	devise	v. 고안하다	diameter	n. (원의) 지름
dig	v. (구멍 등을) 파다	dip	v. 담그다	discard	v. 버리다
discernible	a. 식별할 수 있는	disciplined	a. 훈련받은	disclose	v. 드러내다
discomfort	v. 불편하게 하다	disorder	n. 장애	dispatch	v. 전보
disposable	a. 일회용의	disprove	v. ~의 오류를 입증하다	disturb	v. 방해하다
disturbing	a. 충격적인	division of labor	n. 노동 분업	dominance	n. 지배
dominate	v. 지배하다	dramatic	a. 극적인	drought	n. 가뭄
due to	~에 기인하는	durable	a. 내구성이 있는	dust	n. 먼지
dynasty	n. 왕조	ease	n. 쉬움	edible	a. 먹을 수 있는
embrace	v. (껴)안다	emergence	n. 출현	emotional	a. 감정적인
empathic	a. 감정이입의	employee	n. 고용인	end	n. (양쪽 진영 중) 한쪽 편
engagement	n. 참여	enroll	v. 등록하다	enthusiasm	n. 열정
entitle	v. 권리	entity	n. 실재	epidemic	n. 유행병
equation	n. 방정식	escalate	v. 상승[확대, 증가]하다	essence	n. 본질
essentially	ad. 본질적으로	exact	n. 정확한	exceptionally	ad. 예외적으로
exchange	v. 교환하다	exhaust	v. 다 써버리다	expire	v. 만기가 되다
explode	v. 폭발하다	explosion	n. 폭발	explosive	a. 폭발성의

변형문제

01 다음 상황을 겪고 Salli가 느낀 심정으로 가장 적절한 것은?

A well-known shoe manufacturer sent out a mailer advertising a sale. Salli was excited, as she has a very narrow foot and the manufacturer advertised her size in styles she liked. When she went to the store, she was very disappointed because not one of the styles was available in her size. She was told by a saleswoman that they only stocked one of each style in each size! Still, since she was promised the shoes she wanted were available from the warehouse, Salli decided to order two pairs. A week later, she received a phone call saying one pair was actually no longer being made. A week after that came a rather poignant note from the saleswoman and her manager saying the other pair was also unavailable. They did enclose a 20% off coupon for her next visit. Needless to say — there won't be a next time.

① happy and excited
② tired and lazy
③ sorrowful and angry
④ urgent and dangerous
⑤ joyful and peaceful

02 밑줄 친 부분 중 문맥상 옳지 않은 것은?

A well-known shoe manufacturer sent out a mailer advertising a sale. Salli was ① excited, as she has a very narrow foot and the manufacturer advertised her size in styles she liked. When she went to the store, she was very ② happy because not one of the styles was available in her size. She was told by a saleswoman that they only stocked one of each style in each size! Still, since she was promised the shoes she wanted were ③ available from the warehouse, Salli decided to order two pairs. A week later, she received a phone call saying one pair was actually no longer being made. A week after that came a rather poignant note from the saleswoman and her manager saying the other pair was also unavailable. They did ④ enclose a 20% off coupon for her next visit. ⑤ Needless to say — there won't be a next time.

03 다음 문장이 들어갈 부분으로 가장 적절한 곳을 고르시오.

> A week after that came a rather poignant note from the saleswoman and her manager saying the other pair was also unavailable.

A well-known shoe manufacturer sent out a mailer advertising a sale. Salli was excited, as she has a very narrow foot and the manufacturer advertised her size in styles she liked. When she went to the store, she was very disappointed because not one of the styles was available in her size. (①) She was told by a saleswoman that they only stocked one of each style in each size! (②) Still, since she was promised the shoes (③) she wanted were available from the warehouse, Salli decided to order two pairs. (④) A week later, she received a phone call saying one pair was actually no longer being made. (⑤) They did enclose a 20% off coupon for her next visit. Needless to say — there won't be a next time.

04 다음 빈칸에 들어갈 문장으로 가장 적절한 것은?

> A well-known shoe manufacturer sent out a mailer advertising a sale. Salli was excited, as she has a very narrow foot and the manufacturer advertised her size in styles she liked. When she went to the store, she was very disappointed because not one of the styles was available in her size. She was told by a saleswoman that they only stocked one of each style in each size! Still, since she was promised the shoes she wanted were available from the warehouse, Salli decided to order two pairs. A week later, she received a phone call saying one pair was actually no longer being made. A week after that came a rather poignant note from the saleswoman and her manager saying the other pair was also unavailable. They did enclose a 20% off coupon for her next visit. ________________________________

① In other words, she became more fond of the store.
② Needless to say — there won't be a next time.
③ Eventually, she bought the shoes she wanted.
④ To sum up, she was satisfied with the service at the store.
⑤ Therefore, she was happy to save money.

UNIT 07

지칭 추론

글의 논리	Story
제목	소년을 구조하는 과정
주제	조난 당한 Brian을 구조하는 과정

PRACTICE 03

028 어법 선택 & 연결어

(　　　　　), a bushplane appeared. It passed directly over Brian, very low, **[touched / touching]** the water **[gentle / gently]** once, twice, and **[stopped / stopping]** with **[its / their]** floats **[gentle / gently] [bumping / bumped]** the beach in front of his shelter. The pilot cut the engine, opened the door, and got out, **[balanced / balancing]**, and **[stepping / stepped]** forward on the float to hop onto the sand without getting his feet **[wetly / wet]**. He was **[worn / wearing]** sunglasses and he **[took off them / took them off]** to stare at Brian. "I heard your emergency transmitter." He cocked his head, **[studied / studying]** Brian. "Whoa. You're him, **[aren't / are]** you? They quit **[to look / looking]**, a month, no, **[most / almost]** two months ago." Brian was standing now, but still **[silently / silent]**. His tongue seemed to be stuck to the roof of his mouth and his throat didn't work right. "My name is Brian Robeson," he said. (　　　　　) he saw **[what / that]** his stew **[did / was done]**, and he waved to **[it / them]** with his hand. "Would you like something to eat?"

이야기 소년을 구조하는 과정

(Suddenly), / a bushplane / appeared.
(S: a bushplane, V: appeared)
갑자기 / 부시플레인 한 대가 / 나타났다

갑자기, 부시플레인 한 대가 나타났다.

It / passed (directly) over Brian, / (very low), / (touching the water (gently) / once, twice), / and stopped / {with its floats (gently) bumping the beach / (in front of ① his shelter)}.
(S: It, V_1: passed, 〈분사구문〉 touching, O: the water, V_2: stopped, O: its floats, 〈부사〉 gently, O.C: bumping the beach, 〈부대상황〉)
그것은 / Brian 위쪽으로 곧장 날아왔다 / 아주 낮게 / 물에 부드럽게 닿았다 / 한 번, 두 번 / 그리고 멈추었다 / 부드럽게 모래밭에 살짝 부주를 부딪치며 / 그의 오두막 앞에 있는

그것은 Brian의 위쪽으로 아주 낮게 곧장 날아와 물에 부드럽게 한 번, 두 번 닿더니 그의 오두막 앞에 있는 모래밭에 살짝 부주를 부딪치며 멈추었다.

노트
- in front of : ~의 앞쪽에[앞에]
- 〈분사구문 – 문미〉 : 주절과 분사구문의 위치가 서로 바뀌어도 무관

주절		종속절(→ 분사구문)			
주어	동사	종속 접속사	주어	동사 : 상황에 맞게 아래처럼 바뀜	
		〈그대로 사용하면 의미 강조〉	(주절의 주어와 같으면 생략하고, 다르면 주격으로 사용함)	(being) (having been) 생략 가능	Ring(현재분사)
					p.p.(과거분사)
					형용사
					명사
It	passed	–	–	–	touching

■ 〈with 부대상황〉

with	목적어	목적격보어		
~하면서, ~한채로		형용사(구)		
		부사(구)		
		전치사구		
		분사	현재분사 (Ring)	능동 (목적어가 목적격보어를 ~하고 있는)
			과거분사 (p.p.)	수동 (목적어가 목적격보어에게 당하는, 되어진)
with	its floats	bumping		

The pilot / cut the engine, / opened the door, / and got out, / balanced, / and stepped / forward (on the float) / (to hop onto the sand) / (without getting ② his feet wet).
(S: The pilot, V_1: cut, O: the engine, V_2: opened, O: the door, V_3: got out, V_4: balanced, V_5: stepped, 〈전치사〉 without, 〈동명사〉 getting, O: his feet, O.C: wet)
조종사는 / 엔진을 끄고 / 문을 열고 / 나오고 / 균형을 잡고 / 발을 딛고는 / 부주 위에 / 모래 위로 펄쩍 뛰어 올랐다 / 그의 발을 적시지 않고

조종사는 엔진을 끄고 문을 열고 나온 다음 몸의 균형을 잡고 부주 위에 발을 딛고는 그의 발을 적시지 않고 모래 위로 펄쩍 뛰어 올랐다.

노트
- get out : 밖으로 나가다
- step forward : 내디디다
- hop onto : ~로 깡충 뛰어 오르다
- 〈get 동사의 쓰임〉

get	목적어	〈목적격 보어〉	〈5형식〉	목적어와 목적격 보어의 관계
		형용사	~을 (…의 상태가) 되게 하다	능동
		현재분사	~을 (…의 상태가) 되게 하다	능동
		to R	[남에게] ~시키다	능동
		과거분사	[물건을] ~하게 하다	수동

He / was wearing sunglasses / and he / took them off / (to stare at Brian).
S 그는 / V〈과거진행〉 선글라스를 끼고 있었다 / O / 그리고 그는 S / V O 그것을 벗었다 / Brian을 보기 위해

그는 선글라스를 끼고 있었고 Brian을 보기 위해 그것을 벗었다.

노트
- stare at : ~을 응시하다
- take A off : A를 벗다
- 〈이어동사〉

타동사	명사	부사	(○)
타동사	부사	명사	(○)
타동사	대명사	부사	(○)
타동사	부사	대명사	(×)
took	off	them	(×)

"I / heard / your emergency transmitter."
S 나는 / V 들었다 / O 네 비상 발신기에서 나는 소리를

"네 비상 발신기에서 나는 소리를 들었다."

He / cocked his head, / (studying Brian).
S 그는 / V O 고개를 갸웃하더니 / 〈분사구문〉 Brian을 유심히 보았다

그는 고개를 갸웃하더니 Brian을 유심히 보았다.

노트
- cock one's head : 고개를 옆으로 기울이다
- 〈분사구문 – 문미〉 : 주절과 분사구문의 위치가 서로 바뀌어도 무관

주절		종속절(→ 분사구문)			
주어	동사	종속 접속사	주어	동사 : 상황에 맞게 아래처럼 바뀜	
		〈그대로 사용하면 의미 강조〉	(주절의 주어와 같으면 생략하고, 다르면 주격으로 사용함)	(being) (having been) 생략 가능	Ring(현재분사)
					p.p.(과거분사)
					형용사
					명사
He	cooked	–	–	–	studying

"Whoa. / You're ③ him, / aren't you? / They / quit looking, / {a month, no, (almost) two months ago}."
이런 / S V S.C 네가 그 아이구나 / 〈부·의〉 맞지? / S 그들이 / V O 찾는 것을 / 한 달, 아니 거의 두 달 전에 그만두었어

"이런, 네가 그 아이구나, 맞지? 사람들이 찾는 걸 한 달, 아니 거의 두 달 전에 그만두었어."

노트
- 〈부가의문문〉 : be동사일 경우

주어(A)	동사(B) ~,	〈부가의문문〉 동사(B) not	〈부가의문문〉 주어(A)
You	are	aren't	you?

- 〈목적어 자리에 동명사를 취하는 완전타동사〉

주어	완전타동사	목적어
–	admit / avoid / consider / delay / deny / enjoy / escape / experience / finish / give up / include / mind / mute / Practice / put off / recommend / replace / report 등	Ring (동명사)

- 〈most / almost / mostly〉

	대명사	형용사	부사
most	대부분의 것들(사람들)	대부분의	가장
almost	–	–	거의
mostly	–	–	주로, 일반적으로

Brian / was standing / now, / but (was) still silent.
S Brian은 / V〈과거진행〉 서 있었다 / 지금 / 하지만 여전히 말이 없었다 S.C

이제 Brian은 서 있었지만 여전히 말이 없었다.

④ His tongue / seemed to be stuck / (to the roof of his mouth) / and / his throat / didn't work right.
S 그의 혀는 / V S.C 들러붙은 것처럼 보였다 / 입천장에 / 그리고 / S 목구멍이 / V 적절히 움직이지 않았다

그의 혀는 입천장에 들러붙은 것 같았고 목구멍이 적절히 움직이지 않았다.

노트
- be stuck to : ~에 들러붙다
- 〈seem 동사 쓰임〉

주어	seem	주격보어	(2형식)
		(to be) 보어	~처럼 보이다, 보기에 ~하다; ~인듯하다[것 같다], ~인 것처럼 생각되다
		to R	

"My name / is Brian Robeson," / he said.
S 제 이름은 / V / S.C Brian Robeson입니다 / S V 그는 말했다

"제 이름은 Brian Robeson입니다." 그는 말했다.

(Then) / he saw / (that his stew was done), / and ⑤ he / waved / (to it) (with his hand).
그런 다음 / S V 그는 보았다 / O 〈종·접〉 S V〈수동태〉 자신의 스튜가 다 된 것을 / 그리고 그는 S / V 흔들었다 / 그쪽을 향해 손으로

그런 다음 그는 자신의 스튜가 다 된 것을 보았고, 그는 그쪽을 향해 손을 흔들었다.

노트
- wave to : ~을 향해 손을 흔들다
- 〈부사 vs. 접속부사〉

시간	Then	주어	동사		
	When	주어	동사,	주어	동사 ~
장소	There	주어	동사		
	Where	주어	동사,	주어	동사 ~

- 〈what vs. that〉

	관계대명사(불완전한 문장)	접속사(완전한 문장)
what	○ 선행사를 포함하고 있기 때문에 what 앞에 선행사 불필요	×
that	○ that 앞에 선행사 필요	○

"Would you like something (to eat)?"
S V O

"뭘 좀 드시겠어요?"

"뭘 좀 드시겠어요?"

▶ 밑줄 친 부분이 가리키는 대상이 나머지 넷과 다른 것은?

정답 | ②

해설 | ② 'his'는 문장에서 The pilot을 가리킨다.

오답 | ① 'his'는 문장에서 Brian을 가리킨다.
③ 'him'은 문장을 보면 pilot이 Brian에게 너가 맞냐고 물어보고 있으므로 Brian을 가리킨다.
④ 'His'는 앞 문장의 Brian을 가리킨다.
⑤ 'he'는 같은 문장에서 1번째 he와 같은 인물인데, 이 인물은 앞 문장의 he와 같다. 앞 문장의 'he'는 자신이 Brian이라 말하고 있다. 따라서 'he'는 Brian을 가리킨다.

Words

- ☐ bushplane
- ☐ directly
- ☐ touch
- ☐ gently
- ☐ float
- ☐ bump
- ☐ shelter
- ☐ cut
- ☐ balance
- ☐ wet
- ☐ emergency
- ☐ transmitter
- ☐ quit
- ☐ stick
- ☐ roof
- ☐ throat
- ☐ wave

Phrases

- ☐ in front of
- ☐ step forward
- ☐ stare at
- ☐ cock one's head
- ☐ wave to
- ☐ get out
- ☐ hop onto
- ☐ take A off
- ☐ be stuck to

우선순위 영단어 역대 수능 기출 + 전국 모의고사 기출 + EBS 기출 + 교과서 기출 빈출 어휘

단어	뜻	단어	뜻	단어	뜻
export	v. 수출하다	extended	a. 길게 늘어진	extraction	n. 발굴
facility	n. 설비	fall short of	~에 미치지 못하다	falsely	ad. 거짓으로
faraway	a. 먼	fast	v. 단식시키다	favor	n. 호의
favorable	a. 우호적인	figure out	생각해내다	firm	n. 회사
flash	v. (잠깐) 비치다[번쩍이다]	flavor	n. 맛	fleet	n. 함대
flip	v. 홱 넘기다	flood	v. 물에 잠기다	flourish	v. 잘 자라다
focus on	~에 초점을 맞추다	fold	v. (옷 따위를) 개다	fortune	n. 거금
found	v. 설립하다	fountain	n. 분수	frankly	ad. 솔직하게
frantically	ad. 미친 듯이	from scratch	아무런 사전 준비[지식] 없이	frustrated	a. 실망한
fulfill	v. 이행하다	fulfillment	n. 충족함	geneticist	n. 유전학자
genuine	a. 진짜의	give out	~을 배포하다[건네주다]	glance	v. 힐끗 보다
goods	n. 상품	grain	n. 곡물	grief	n. 큰 슬픔
groan	n. 신음 소리	guidance	n. 안내	guilty	a. 유죄의
highlight	v. 두드러지게 하다	historian	n. 역사가	hold back	저지하다
honor	v. 예배하다	horizon	n. 시야	host	a. 다수의
humility	n. 겸손	identification	n. 귀속 의식	imitation	n. 흉내
immune	a. 면제된	imperative	n. 명령	in response to	~에 응하여
inaccurate	a. 부정확한	inadvertently	ad. 우연히	incidentally	ad. 우연히

01 다음 문장이 들어갈 부분으로 가장 적절한 곳을 고르시오.

Brian was standing now, but still silent.

Suddenly, a bushplane appeared. It passed directly over Brian, very low, touching the water gently once, twice, and stopped with its floats gently bumping the beach in front of his shelter. (①) The pilot cut the engine, opened the door, and got out, balanced, and stepped forward on the float to hop onto the sand without getting his feet wet. (②) He was wearing sunglasses and he took them off to stare at Brian. "I heard your emergency transmitter." (③) He cocked his head, studying Brian. (④) "Whoa. You're him, aren't you? They quit looking, a month, no, almost two months ago." (⑤) His tongue seemed to be stuck to the roof of his mouth and his throat didn't work right. "My name is Brian Robeson," he said. Then he saw that his stew was done, and he waved to it with his hand. "Would you like something to eat?"

02 다음 글의 문장 중 무관한 문장을 고르시오.

Suddenly, a bushplane appeared. It passed directly over Brian, very low, touching the water gently once, twice, and stopped with its floats gently bumping the beach in front of his shelter. ① The pilot cut the engine, opened the door, and got out, balanced, and stepped forward on the float to hop onto the sand without getting his feet wet. ② He found nothing there. ③ He was wearing sunglasses and he took them off to stare at Brian. "I heard your emergency transmitter." ④ He cocked his head, studying Brian. "Whoa. You're him, aren't you? ⑤ They quit looking, a month, no, almost two months ago." Brian was standing now, but still silent. His tongue seemed to be stuck to the roof of his mouth and his throat didn't work right. "My name is Brian Robeson," he said. Then he saw that his stew was done, and he waved to it with his hand. "Would you like something to eat?"

03 다음 글에서 Brian이 느끼고 있었을 감정을 속담으로 표현한 것으로 가장 적절한 것은?

Suddenly, a bushplane appeared. It passed directly over Brian, very low, touching the water gently once, twice, and stopped with its floats gently bumping the beach in front of his shelter. The pilot cut the engine, opened the door, and got out, balanced, and stepped forward on the float to hop onto the sand without getting his feet wet. He was wearing sunglasses and he took them off to stare at Brian. "I heard your emergency transmitter." He cocked his head, studying Brian. "Whoa. You're him, aren't you? They quit looking, a month, no, almost two months ago." Brian was standing now, but still silent. His tongue seemed to be stuck to the roof of his mouth and his throat didn't work right. "My name is Brian Robeson," he said. Then he saw that his stew was done, and he waved to it with his hand. "Would you like something to eat?"

① Dead dogs bark not.
② Big fish are caught in a big river.
③ Better a good enemy than a bad friend.
④ Patience is the art of hoping.
⑤ Your enemy makes you wise.

04 다음 글을 읽고, 문장을 주어진 |조건|에 맞게 영작하시오.

| 조건 |

* (A)는 3단어, (B)는 2단어로 쓸 것
* 본문에 있는 단어를 사용하거나 본문 내용을 활용할 것

Suddenly, a bushplane appeared. It passed directly over Brian, very low, touching the water gently once, twice, and stopped with its floats gently bumping the beach in front of his shelter. The pilot cut the engine, opened the door, and got out, balanced, and stepped forward on the float to hop onto the sand without getting his feet wet. He was wearing sunglasses and he took them off to stare at Brian. "I heard your emergency transmitter." He cocked his head, studying Brian. "Whoa. You're him, aren't you? They quit looking, a month, no, almost two months ago." Brian was standing now, but still silent. His tongue seemed to be stuck to the roof of his mouth and his throat didn't work right. "My name is Brian Robeson," he said. Then he saw that his stew was done, and he waved to it with his hand. "Would you like something to eat?"

⬇

Brian has been missing for (A) ____________ ____________ ____________, but the pilot heard the sound from the (B) ____________ ____________ and found him.

UNIT 08

단어 빈칸

글의 논리	Sequence
제목	성숙해지는 과정: 선택
주제	성숙해가는 과정은 스스로 선택하는 능력을 성장시키는 것이기 때문에 어린 나이에 선택을 하는 기회를 갖는 것은 중요하다.

수능 ANALYSIS

029 어법 선택 & 연결어

Choice is at the **[margin / core]** of human experience at any age. This **[deeply / deep]** longing to choose our own purpose, beliefs, and actions, no matter **[what / which]** age we are, **[fights / is fought]** for and **[defend / defended]** in every home, **[particular / particularly]** by children **[whose / who]** parents overlook their vital need for autonomy. Opportunities to make choices **[typical / typically]** **[increases / increase]** with age and experience. The total dependence of infants gives way, day by day and with **[increasing / decreasing]** momentum, to a desire to make choices for **[them / themselves]** — choices about **[that / what]** and **[when / which]** they want to eat, explore, and express **[them / themselves]**. The **[maturing / matured]** process is about growing the ability to make choices for **[one / oneself]**, and **[this / it]** is crucial for their development **[which / that]** kids at early ages have **[much / many]** opportunities to make choices and **[learns / to learn]** from **[it / them]**.

일반적인 사실 선택은 인간 경험의 핵심이다.

Choice / is (at the core of human experience) / (at any age).

(Choice: S 선택은 / is: V / 인간 경험의 핵심에 있다 / 어떤 나이에서든지)

선택은 어떤 나이에서든지 인간 경험의 핵심에 있다.

노트
- be at the core of : ~의 핵심이다
- at any age : 어느 나이에도

순서1 선택에 대한 깊은 갈망은 모든 가정에서 아이들에 의해 쟁취되고 보호된다.

This deep longing / (to choose our own purpose, beliefs, and actions), / (no matter what age we are), / is fought for and (is) defended / (in every home), / (particularly) / (by children) / {whose parents overlook their vital need (for autonomy)}.

(This deep longing: S 이 깊은 갈망은 / purpose: O_1, beliefs: O_2, actions: O_3 우리 자신의 목적, 신념, 그리고 행동을 선택하려는 / what age: S.C, we: S, are: V 우리가 몇 살이든지 간에 / is fought: V_1〈수동태〉 싸워 / defended: V_2〈수동태〉 쟁취되고 보호된다 / 모든 가정에서 / 특히 / children: 〈선행사〉 아이들에 의해 / whose: 〈소·관〉, parents: 〈명사〉, overlook: V, their vital need: O 부모가 아이들의 필수적인 욕구를 간과하는 / 자율성에 대한)

비록 우리가 몇 살이든지 간에, 우리 자신의 목적, 신념, 그리고 행동을 선택하려는 이 깊은 갈망은 모든 가정에서, 특히 부모가 자율성에 대한 아이들의 필수적인 욕구를 간과하는 가정의 아이들에 의해 싸워 쟁취되고 보호된다.

노트
- be fought for : ~을 위해 싸우다
- 〈복합관계대명사〉 : 복합관계대명사절은 「관계대명사+ever」 형식을 가지고, 명사와 부사적 역할을 한다.
  - 관계대명사절은 what만 명사절이고, who, which, that은 형용사절이다.

종류	명사절	부사절
whoever	anyone who	no matter who
	~하는 누구든지	누가 ~ 하더라도
whomever	anyone whom	no matter whom
	~하는 누구든지	누구를 ~ 하더라도
whichever	anything that	no matter which
	~하는 어떤 것이든	어느 것을 ~ 하더라도
whatever	anything that	no matter what
	~하는 어떤 것이든	무엇을 ~ 하더라도

- 〈소유격관계대명사 whose〉

	〈소유격관계대명사절〉			
선행사	whose	~~소유격~~	명사	동사 ~
children	〈소유격관계대명사〉		parents	overlook
	~~that~~			
	~~what~~			
	~~who~~			
	~~which~~			

순서2 선택할 기회는 나이와 경험에 따라 증가한다.

Opportunities / (to make choices) / (typically) increase / (with age and experience).

(Opportunities: S 기회는 / 선택할 / increase: V 일반적으로 증가된다 / 나이와 경험에 따라)

선택할 기회는 일반적으로 나이와 경험에 따라 증가된다.

노트
- make a choice : 선택하다
- with age : 나이가 들수록

순서3 유아기에는 부모에게 많이 의존하지만, 서서히 스스로의 선택을 하려는 욕구가 생긴다.

The total ________ (of infants) / gives way, / {(day

(S 유아기의 완전한 의존성은 / 바뀐다 / 매일)

by day) / and / (with increasing momentum)}, / to a desire (to make choices) / (for themselves) — choices / {about (what / and / when they want / to eat, explore, and express themselves)}.

그리고 점차 가속도를 내며 =〈동격〉 선택하려는 욕구로 스스로 스스로의 선택들 〈의문사〉 〈의문사〉 S V O_1 O_2 무엇을 그리고 언제 먹을지, 탐험할지, 관한 O_3 그리고 표현할지에

유아기의 완전한 의존성은, 서서히 그리고 점차 가속도를 내며, 스스로 선택 — 무엇을 그리고 언제 먹을지, 탐험할지, 그리고 표현할지에 관한 스스로의 선택들 — 하려는 욕구로 바뀐다.

노트
- give way to : (~에게) 항복하다[양보하다], (~이) 먼저 가도록 하다[양보하다]
- day by day : 내내[줄곧], 조금씩[서서히]
- with increasing momentum : 점점 더 탄력을 받아
- **〈재귀대명사의 관용적 표현〉**

help oneself to ~	~을 마음껏 먹다
enjoy oneself	즐기다
in spite of oneself	자신도 모르게
beside oneself	제정신이 아닌
by oneself	홀로
to oneself	혼자
of oneself	저절로, 제 스스로
for oneself	스스로
of itself	저절로
between ourselves	우리끼리 얘긴데
make oneself understood	~와 의사소통하다

- **〈재귀대명사 vs. 대명사〉**

		주어와 다름	주어와 동일
주어	~	대명사	재귀대명사
they		them	themselves

- **〈간접의문문 – 전치사의 목적어 2개가 대등접속사 and로 병렬구조로 되어 있는 경우〉**

의문사	간접의문문 1			대등접속사	간접의문문 2			
about	what	they	want	and	when	they	want	to eat ~
전치사	의문사	주어	동사		의문사	주어	동사	목적어
		(생략)						

주제문 성숙해가는 과정은 스스로 선택하는 능력을 성장시키는 것이다.

The maturing process / is / (about growing the ability) / {to make choices (for oneself)}, / and / it is crucial (for their development) / {that kids (at early ages) / have many opportunities / (to make choices and to learn from them)}.

〈현재분사〉 S V 〈전치사〉 〈동명사〉 O 성숙해가는 과정은 것이다 성장시키는 것에 대해 스스로 선택하는 능력을 그리고 〈가S〉 V S.C 그들의 발달에 있어서 매우 중요하다 〈종·접〉 S 어린 나이의 아이들이 V O 〈진S〉 기회를 많이 갖는 것은 선택을 하고 그것을 통해 배울 수 있는

성숙해가는 과정은 스스로 선택하는 능력을 성장시키는 것에 관한 것이며, 어린 나이의 아이들이 선택을 하고 그것을 통해 배울 수 있는 기회를 많이 갖는 것은 그들의 발달에 있어서 매우 중요하다.

노트
- be about : ~에 관하다
- crucial for : ~에 있어서 아주 중대한
- at an early age : 젊었을 때
- **〈가주어, 진주어 구문〉**

가주어	동사	진주어
It (This/That/There 사용 불가)	–	that+주어+동사(완전한 절)
		to 동사원형
		동명사
		의문사+주어+동사(간접의문문)
		if/whether+주어+동사
it	is	that ~

- **〈부정수량형용사〉** : 막연한 수나 양의 정도를 표시하는 형용사

수(數)	few(a few), some(any), a lot of(lots of), a good(or great), plenty of, enough, all, no, many	복수명사+복수동사
양(量)	little(a little), some(any), a lot of, a good(or great), deal of, plenty of, enough, all, no, much	단수명사+단수동사

▶ **다음 빈칸에 들어갈 말로 가장 적절한 것은?**

① empathy ② dependence
③ confidence ④ cooperation
⑤ responsibility

정답 | ②

해석 | ① 공감
② 의존성
③ 자신감
④ 협동심
⑤ 책임감

해설 | ② 이 글의 전체적인 내용은 선택이 인간에게 굉장히 중요하다는 것이다. 이 문장을 보면 유아기의 완전한 ________은/는 서서히 그리고 점차 가속도를 내며, 스스로 선택하려는 욕구로 바뀐다고 한다. 빈칸을 A라 하면 뒤에 스스로 선택하려는 욕구는 A와 대조된다. 따라서 선택과 대조되는 말인 'dependence (의존성)'가 가장 적절한 답이다.

오답 | ① '공감'은 글의 소재와 전혀 관련 없기 때문에 적절하지 않다.
③ '자신감'은 뒤에 나와 있는 스스로 선택하려는 욕구와 비슷한 말이기 때문에 적절하지 않다.
④ '협동심'은 글의 소재와 전혀 관련 없기 때문에 적절하지 않다.
⑤ '책임감'은 뒤에 나와 있는 스스로 선택하려는 욕구와 일맥상통하는 말이기 때문에 적절하지 않다.

노트 ■

동사	명사	형용사
depend(의존하다)	dependence(의존)	dependent(의존하는)
confide(확신하다)	confidence(확신)	confident(확신하는)
cooperate(협력하다)	cooperation(협력)	cooperative(협력하는)

Words

- ☐ core
- ☐ margin
- ☐ longing
- ☐ defend
- ☐ particularly
- ☐ overlook
- ☐ vital
- ☐ autonomy
- ☐ opportunity
- ☐ typically
- ☐ infant
- ☐ momentum
- ☐ desire
- ☐ mature
- ☐ crucial
- ☐ empathy
- ☐ confidence
- ☐ cooperation
- ☐ responsibility

Phrases

- ☐ be at the core of
- ☐ be fought for
- ☐ with age
- ☐ day by day
- ☐ be about
- ☐ crucial for
- ☐ at any age
- ☐ make a choice
- ☐ give way to
- ☐ with increasing momentum
- ☐ at an early age

우선순위 영단어

역대 수능 기출 + 전국 모의고사 기출 + EBS 기출 + 교과서 기출 빈출 어휘

단어	뜻
inclination	n. 좋아함
index	n. 지표
infer	v. 추론하다
inherently	ad. 본질적으로
initiative	n. 주도
instance	n. 경우
intelligent	a. 지적인
interact	v. 상호 작용하다
interior	n. 내부
invisible	a. 보이지 않는
irrational	a. 비합리적인
journal	n. 일기(=diary)
lap	v. (파도 등이) 찰싹거리다
leftover	a. 나머지의
lengthy	a. (시간이) 매우 긴
light	v. 비추다
load	ad. 담뿍
loyalty	n. 충성
make it	성공하다
measurement	n. 측정
indeed	ad. 사실(실은)
indulge	v. 빠지다
infestation	n. 출몰
inherit	v. 물려받다
injury	n. 부상
instant	a. 즉시의
intensify	v. 강화하다
interdependence	n. 상호 의존(성)
internal	a. 내면의
involved in	~에 연루된
jaw	n. (신체) 아래턱
jury	n. 배심원
lapse	n. 경과
legislation	n. 법률의 제정
liberal	a. 자유주의적인
likewise	ad. 게다가
logging	n. 벌목
luxury	n. 사치(품)
manipulate	v. 조작하다
mechanism	n. 기제
indefensible	a. 용납할 수 없는
inefficient	a. 비효율적인
inhabitant	n. 거주자
inhibit	v. 방해하다
inspect	v. 조사하다
intake	n. 섭취
intent	n. 목적
interfere with	~을 방해하다
intrinsically	ad. 본질적으로
irony	n. 풍자
joint	n. 이음새
laboratory	n. 실험실
lead to	~로 이어지다
legitimate	a. 합당한
license	v. 허가하다
line up	줄을 서다
look forward to -ing	~을 손꼽아 기다리다
magnify	v. 확대하다
maximize	v. 최대화하다
medicinal	a. 의약의

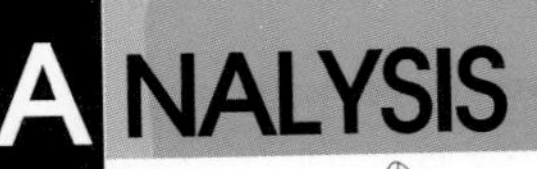

변형문제

01 다음 글을 읽고, |조건|에 맞게 주어진 요약문을 완성하시오.

| 조건 |
* (A), (B)는 각각 1단어로 쓸 것
* 본문에 있는 단어만을 사용할 것
* 필요한 경우, 문맥과 어법에 맞게 변형할 것

Choice is at the core of human experience at any age. This deep longing to choose our own purpose, beliefs, and actions, no matter what age we are, is fought for and defended in every home, particularly by children whose parents overlook their vital need for autonomy. Opportunities to make choices typically increase with age and experience. The total dependence of infants gives way, day by day and with increasing momentum, to a desire to make choices for themselves — choices about what and when they want to eat, explore, and express themselves. The maturing process is about growing the ability to make choices for oneself, and it is crucial for their development that kids at early ages have many opportunities to make choices and to learn from them.

⬇

As people get old and accumulate (A) ______________, chances for making decisions rise and the process of (B) ______________ is associated with developing the capability to choose for themselves.

02 다음 글을 읽고, |조건|에 맞게 주어진 주제문을 완성하시오.

| 조건 |
* 6단어로 쓸 것
* 본문에 있는 단어만을 사용할 것
* 필요한 경우, 문맥과 어법에 맞게 변형할 것

Choice is at the core of human experience at any age. This deep longing to choose our own purpose, beliefs, and actions, no matter what age we are, is fought for and defended in every home, particularly by children whose parents overlook their vital need for autonomy. Opportunities to make choices typically increase with age and experience. The total dependence of infants gives way, day by day and with increasing momentum, to a desire to make choices for themselves — choices about what and when they want to eat, explore, and express themselves. The maturing process is about growing the ability to make choices for oneself, and it is crucial for their development that kids at early ages have many opportunities to make choices and to learn from them.

⬇

Humans ______________ ______________ ______________ ______________ ______________ ______________.

03 다음 글을 읽고, |조건|에 맞게 빈칸 (A), (B)를 채우시오.

| 조건 |
* (A), (B)는 각각 다르게 1단어로 쓸 것
* 본문에 있는 단어를 찾아 쓸 것
* 필요한 경우, 문맥과 어법에 맞게 변형할 것

Choice is at the core of human experience at any age. This deep longing to choose our own purpose, beliefs, and actions, no matter what age we are, is fought for and defended in every home, particularly by children whose parents overlook their vital need for autonomy. Opportunities to make choices typically increase with age and experience. The total dependence of infants gives way, day by day and with increasing momentum, to a desire to make choices for themselves — choices about what and when they want to eat, explore, and express themselves. The maturing process is about growing the ability to make choices for oneself, and it is crucial for their development that kids at early ages have many opportunities to make choices and to learn from them.

⬇

With the increasing age and broadening experiences, opportunities to make a choice are on the rise. For example, infants who were fully dependent on parents become (A) ____________ along with developing the ability to choose by themselves. Therefore, having these opportunities from the (B) ____________ age is considerably significant in terms of their progress.

04 다음 글의 순서로 가장 적절한 것은?

Choice is at the core of human experience at any age.

(A) The total dependence of infants gives way, day by day and with increasing momentum, to a desire to make choices for themselves — choices about what and when they want to eat, explore, and express themselves.

(B) This deep longing to choose our own purpose, beliefs, and actions, no matter what age we are, is fought for and defended in every home, particularly by children whose parents overlook their vital need for autonomy. Opportunities to make choices typically increase with age and experience.

(C) The maturing process is about growing the ability to make choices for oneself, and it is crucial for their development that kids at early ages have many opportunities to make choices and to learn from them.

① (A) - (B) - (C)　② (B) - (A) - (C)　③ (B) - (C) - (A)
④ (C) - (A) - (B)　⑤ (C) - (B) - (A)

단어 빈칸

글의 논리	Examples
제목	익숙하지 않은 일을 할 때 사람들의 행동 방식
주제	대부분의 사람들은 반영하는 것보다 행동하기를 선호한다.

PRACTICE 01

030 어법 선택 & 연결어

A lot of us feel **[alike / like]** doing "**[something different / different something]**." Studies have shown **[what / that]** people do not like to read instructions, and **[much / many]** of **[that / what]** we do **[to read / read]** we either ignore **[and / or]** don't understand. In one test, (   ), twenty-four adults **[were asked / asked]** **[to wire / wiring]** a common household electrical plug. Only ten of the twenty-four even bothered to look at the instructions. And of those ten, seven **[consulting / consulted]** the instructions only to check the color **[coding / coded]** for the electrical wires; the rest of the information **[was ignored / ignored]**. (   ), **[almost / most]** people flunked this test. Even when the instructions are unusually important, people tend **[to pay / paying]** **[it / them]** **[few / little]** attention. As the authors of the electrical plug study noted, "Even in the case of quite unfamiliar tasks, people seem to prefer **[than act / to act]** rather than reflect."

일반적인 사실 대부분의 사람들은 다른 어떤 것을 하고 싶어 한다.

A lot of us / feel like / doing "something different."
(S / V / 〈동명사〉 / O, O)

우리 중 많은 이들은 하고 싶어 한다 "다른 어떤 것"을

우리 중 많은 이들은 "다른 어떤 것"을 하고 싶어 한다.

노트
- a lot of : 많은
- feel like+(동)명사 : ~처럼 느끼다
- 〈감각동사〉

감각동사	주격보어(S.C)	
feel, look, seem, sound, taste, appear, smell	형용사(분사 : 현재분사/과거분사)	
	명사	
	like(전치사)	(that)+주어+동사
		(동)명사
	~~alike~~	
	~~likely~~	

- 〈혼동하기 쉬운 어휘〉

likely	형용사	~일 것 같은 (be to 동사원형 : ~일 것 같다)
	부사	아마(probably)
alike	서술적 형용사 (보어로만 사용, 명사 수식 불가)	동일한
	부사	똑같이
like	전치사	~처럼
	동사	좋아하다

- 〈형용사의 후치 수식〉

〈후치 수식〉	-thing	+형용사	○
	-body		
	-one		
〈전치 수식〉	형용사+	-thing	×
		-body	
		-one	

근거1 사람들은 설명서를 읽기를 선호하지 않고, 설명서의 많은 부분을 무시하거나 이해하지 못한다.

Studies / have shown / {that people do not like / to read instructions, / and much of what we do read / we / either ignore or don't understand}.
(S / V〈현재완료〉 / 〈종·접〉 S V / O / 〈목·관〉 S V, O / S / V_1 V_2; O)

연구는 보여 주다 사람들이 좋아하지 않는다 설명서를 읽는 것을 그리고 정말로 읽는 것의 많은 부분을 우리는 무시하거나 이해하지 못한다는 것을

연구는 사람들이 설명서를 읽기를 좋아하지 않으며, 우리가 정말로 읽는 것의 많은 부분을 우리는 무시하거나 이해하지 못한다는 것을 보여 주었다.

노트
- 〈what vs. that〉

	관계대명사(불완전한 문장)	접속사(완전한 문장)
what	○ 선행사를 포함하고 있기 때문에 what 앞에 선행사 불필요	×
that	○ that 앞에 선행사 필요	○

- 〈동사 강조 표현〉

do / does / did	+동사원형(R)
=정말로(really, certainly)	

- 〈상관접속사〉 : 병렬구조

종류				뜻
not	A	but	B	A가 아니라 B (=B, not A)
not only		but also		A뿐만 아니라 B도 (=B as well as A)
either		or		A와 B 둘 중 하나
neither		nor		A와 B 둘 다 아닌
both		and		A와 B 둘 다

■ 〈3형식에서 목적어 자리에 to R / Ring 둘 다 사용 가능〉

	완전타동사		목적어
주어	begin	~을 시작하다	to R/Ring (의미 차이 없음)
	cease	~을 중단하다	
	continue	~을 계속하다	
	deserve	~할 가치/자격/권리가 있다	
	dislike	~을 싫어하다	
	hate		
	like	~을 좋아하다	
	love	~을 사랑하다	
	neglect	~하는 것을 소홀히 하다	
	prefer	~쪽을 좋아하다	
	require	~을 요구하다	
	start	~을 시작하다	

■ 〈목적어 문두 도치〉 : 목적어가 문두로 자리 이동해도 주어와 동사는 그대로 정치시킴

정치	주어	완전타동사	목적어
도치	목적어	주어	완전타동사
	much of what we do read	we	either ignore or don't understand

예시 실험에서 24명의 성인들이 가정용 전기 플러그에 전선을 연결하도록 요청받았다.

(In one test), / (for example), / twenty-four adults /
한 실험에서 / 예를 들면 / 24명의 성인들이 (S)

were asked / to wire a common household electrical plug.
V(수동태) 요청받았다 / S.C 흔한 가정용 전기 플러그에 전선을 연결하도록

예를 들면, 한 실험에서 24명의 성인들이 흔한 가정용 전기 플러그에 전선을 연결하도록 요청받았다.

노트 ■ 〈5형식 불완전타동사의 목적격보어〉 : 수동태 전환 시, 2형식 문장(be p.p. +to R)

주어	불완전타동사	목적어	목적격보어
–	advise / allow / ask / assume / beg / cause / command / compel / condition / decide / design / drive / enable / encourage / expect / forbid / force / instruct / intend / invite / lead / like / motivate / order / permit / persuade / predispose / pressure / program / push / require / teach / tell / train / trust / urge / want / warn / wish 등	–	to 동사원형

예시 24명 중 10명만이 설명서를 봤다.

Only ten (of the twenty-four) / (even) bothered (to look at the instructions).
S 24명 중 10명만이 / V 애써 보는 것까진 했다 / 설명서를

24명 중 10명만이 설명서를 애써 보는 것까진 했다.

노트 ■ 〈자동사가 뒤에 to부정사를 사용해 타동사처럼 목적어로 취하는 경우〉

	불완전자동사		목적어
주어	aim	~할 작정이다, 목표로 삼다	to R
	appear	~인 듯하다	
	arrange	미리 짜다[준비하다], 타협하다, 의논하다; 협정하다	
	bother	일부러 ~하다, ~하도록 애쓰다	
	consent	~하는 것을 동의/승낙하다	
	fight	~을 위하여 다투다	
	hesitate	주저하다, 망설이다	
	hurry	서두르다	
	long	~하기를 열망/갈망하다	
	prepare	~할 각오/마음의 준비를 하다	
	seem	~처럼 보이다, ~인 듯하다	
	serve	~의 역할을 하다	
	strive	~하려고 노력하다	
	struggle	(~하려고) 분투[고투]하다, 애쓰다	
	tend	~하는 경향이 있다	
	yearn	몹시 ~하고 싶다, 열망하다	
	wait	~하는 것을 기다리다	

■ 〈look at / over / in / out / for〉

look	at	~을 쳐다보다
	over	~을 대충 훑어보다[살펴보다](=watch)
	in	~을 들여다보다, 조사/검토하다
	out	~을 내다보다, 조심하다
	for	~을 찾다, 구하다, 바라다

예시 그 중에서 7명은 전선의 색깔 구분을 확인하기 위해서만 설명서를 보고 나머지 정보는 무시했다.

(And) / (of those ten), seven / consulted the instructions / (only to check the color coding / for the electrical wires); / the rest of the information / was ignored.
그런데 / 그 10명 중 7명은 (S) / (V) 설명서를 참조했다 (O) / 단지 색깔 구분을 확인하기 위해서만 / 그 전선들의 / 나머지 정보는 (S) / V(수동태) 무시되었다

그런데 그 10명 중 7명은 그 전선들의 색깔 구분을 확인하기 위해서만 설명서를 참조했고, 나머지 정보는 무시되었다.

노트 ■ 〈주어와 동사의 수의 일치〉
- A of B : 일반적인 경우에 A가 주어
- A of B : A가 부분/부분인 경우에 B가 주어

A		B	
분수	two – thirds 등	주어	동사 (B에 수의 일치)
부분	a group of, all of, a lot of, any of, a number of, both of, each of, either of, few of, half of, many of, most of, much of, neither of, none of, one of, part of, percent of, several of, some of, the rest, two of 등		
	the rest of	the information	~~were ignored~~ was ignored

예시 대부분의 사람들은 이 테스트에서 실패했다.

(Not surprisingly), / most people / flunked this test.

(S: most people, V: flunked, O: this test)

놀라울 것도 없이 / 대부분의 사람들은 / 이 테스트에서 실패했다

놀라울 것도 없이, 대부분의 사람들은 이 테스트에서 실패했다.

노트 ■ 〈most / almost / mostly〉

	대명사	형용사	부사
most	대부분의 것들(사람들)	대부분의	가장
almost	–	–	거의
mostly	–	–	주로, 일반적으로

근거2 설명서가 중요할 때조차도 사람들은 설명서를 잘 보지 않는다.

{Even / when the instructions / are (unusually) important},

(when: 〈종·접〉, the instructions: S, are: V, important: S.C)

심지어 / 그 설명서가 / 대단히 중요할 때도

/ people / tend / (to pay them little attention).

(people: S, tend: V, them: I.O, little attention: D.O)

사람들은 / 경향이 있다 / 거의 주의를 기울이지 않는

심지어 설명서가 대단히 중요한 때조차도 사람들은 거의 주의를 기울이지 않는 경향이 있다.

노트 ■ pay A attention : A에게 주의를 기울이다

■ tend+to R : ~하는 경향이 있다

■ 〈even when / even though / even if〉

even when	가끔씩 일어나는 일을 역접할 때 쓰이는 용법 tendency, habit 등	~일 때 조차도
even though	실제로 일어난 일을 역접, 일회성 사건	
even if	일어날지도 모르는 일	

■ 〈few / a few / a little / little〉

수	few	거의 없는(부정)	+복수N+복수V
	a few	약간(긍정)	
양	a little	약간(긍정)	+단수N+단수V
	little	거의 없는(부정)	

주제문(재진술) 대부분의 사람들은 익숙하지 않은 일을 할 때도, 반영하기보다는 행동하기를 선호한다.

{As the authors (of the electrical plug study) / noted},

(As: 〈종·접〉, the authors: S, noted: V)

전기 플러그 연구의 저자들이 / 언급했듯이

"Even / (in the case of quite unfamiliar tasks), / people

꽤 / 익숙하지 않는 과업의 경우에서조차도 / 사람들은 (people: S)

/ seem to prefer to act / rather than ________."

(seem: V, to prefer to act: S.C)

행동하기를 선호하는 것으로 보인다 / 반영하기보다

전기 플러그 연구의 저자들이 언급했듯이, "꽤 익숙하지 않은 과업의 경우에서조차도, 사람들은 반영하기보다는 행동하기를 선호하는 것으로 보인다."

노트 ■ in the case of : ~에 관하여는, ~에 관하여 말하면(=as regards)

■ A rather than B : B보다 오히려 A

■ 〈부사절을 이끄는 종속접속사〉 : as 용법

	쓰임	해석
as+주어+동사	시간	~하고 있을 때, ~하자마자, ~하면서
	원인/이유	~ 때문에
	조건	~한다면
	양보	~일지라도
	비교	~보다/만큼
	방법/상태	~대로/~하듯이

■ 〈seem 동사 쓰임〉

주어	seem	주격보어	(2형식)
		(to be) 보어	~처럼 보이다, 보기에 ~하다; ~인듯하다[것 같다], ~인 것처럼 생각되다
		to R	

■ 〈prefer 동사의 쓰임〉 : ~하는 것을 더 선호하다

prefer	〈목적어〉		(3형식)
	동명사		
	to R		
	that 주어동사		
	목적어 to(동)명사		
	목적어	〈목적격보어〉	(5형식)
		과거분사	
		to R	

▶ **다음 빈칸에 들어갈 말로 가장 적절한 것은?**

① speak ② abandon ③ create
④ reflect ⑤ compare

정답 | ④

해석 | ① 말하기 ② 포기하기 ③ 창조하기
④ 반영하기, 생각하기 ⑤ 비교하기

해설 | ④ 이 글의 주제는 사람들은 대부분 어떤 과업을 진행할 때, 생각하는 것보다는 행동하기를 선호한다는 것이다. 그리고 빈칸이 들어간 문장을 보면 사람들은 익숙하지 않은 과업에서도 ________보다는 행동하기를 선호하는 것으로 보인다고 한다. 따라서 빈칸에 들어갈 말은 행동하기와 대조되는 말이므로 'reflect(반영하다, 생각하다)'가 가장 적절하다.

오답 | ① '말하기'는 이 글의 관점과 전혀 부합하지 않는다.
② '포기하기'는 글의 내용을 보면 사람들이 거의 행동으로 옮긴다 했으므로 적절하지 않다.
③ '창조하기'는 이 글의 관점과 전혀 부합하지 않는다.
⑤ '비교하기'는 이 글에서 소재로 나오지 않는다.

Words

☐ ignore ☐ household ☐ unfamiliar
☐ wire ☐ unusually ☐ abandon

Phrases

- ☐ a lot of
- ☐ pay A attention
- ☐ A rather than B
- ☐ feel like+(동)명사
- ☐ in the case of

우선순위 영단어 역대 수능 기출+전국 모의고사 기출+EBS 기출+교과서 기출 빈출 어휘

단어	뜻	단어	뜻	단어	뜻
mention	v. 언급하다	mess	n. 혼란	mimic	a. 모방자
minister	n. 장관	miserable	n. 비참한	misery	n. 비참
misleading	a. 오도하는	mixture	n. 혼합물	moan	n. 신음
mode	n. 양식	model	v. 모형[견본]을 만들다	molecular	a. 분자의
momentous	a. 중대한	mortal	a. 치명적인	multitude	n. 다수
mutation	n. 변형	mutuality	n. 상호 의존	myriad	n. 무수
nationwide	a. 전국적으로	natural selection	n. 자연 도태	needy	a. (경제적으로) 어려운
neighborhood	n. 이웃	network	n. 망	nobility	n. 숭고
nutritious	a. 영양분이 있는	obligate	v. 의무를 지우다	occupation	n. 직업
occur	v. 발생하다	odor	n. 냄새	offset	v. 상쇄하다
on the basis of	~에 근거하여	optimal	a. 최선의	ordinary	a. 보통의
overly	ad. 과도하게	pack	v. 짐을 싸다	paralyze	v. 무력하게 만들다
parental	a. 어버이의	parking lot	n. 주차장	part	v. 갈라지다
participate in	~에 참가하다	peck	v. 쪼다	peculiar	a. 고유의
penetrate	v. 통과하다	pension	n. 연금	perceptual	a. 지각의
perish	v. 소멸하다	perpetuate	v. 영속시키다	pest	n. 해충
petty	a. 사소한	physiology	n. 생리 (현상)	pin down	속박하다
plain	a. 무늬가 없는	plant	v. 심다	plausible	a. 그럴듯한
plead	v. 탄원하다	plunge	v. 뛰어들다	pneumonia	n. 폐렴
poet	n. 시인	pore	n. 구멍	position	n. 입장
possess	v. 소유하다	pound	v. 세게 치다	prediction	n. 예측
press	n. 인쇄기	prestige	n. 명성	previous	a. 이전의
prey on	~을 잡아먹다	proclaim	v. 선언하다	produce	v. ~을 꺼내 보이다
profession	n. 직업	projected	a. 예측된	projection	n. 추정
prolong	v. 연장하다	prominently	ad. 현저하게	promising	a. 장래가 촉망되는
prone to	~하기 쉬운	prophecy	n. 예언	prose	n. 문체
psychological	a. 심리적인	put on	~을 입다	questionable	a. 의심스러운
questionnaire	n. 질문서	quota	n. 몫	racial	a. 인종의
rationalize	v. 합리화하다	react	v. 반응하다	realize	v. 실현하다
rebellion	n. 반란	receptive	a. 수용적인	recipe	n. 조리법
refund	v. 환불하다	reign	n. 치세	reinforcement	n. 보강
reinterpret	v. 재해석하다	remark	n. 말	remind A of B	A에게 B를 기억나게 하다
remove	v. 제거하다	renewable	a. 재생 가능한	repair	v. 수리하다
rescue	v. 구출하다	research	n. 연구	resemble	v. 닮다
reservation	n. 예약	reserved	a. 말이 없는	resilient	a. 원기를 회복하는
resolution	n. 방안[해결]	respect	n. 관점	response	n. 반응
restrain	v. 억제하다	restrictive	a. 제한적인	restructure	v. 재구성하다
result form	(원인)으로 초래되다	retailer	n. 소매업자	retrieve	v. 되찾다
return	n. 보답	revise	v. 개정하다	revolve around	~을 중심으로 돌아가다
risk	n. 위험을 무릅쓰고 강행하다	room	n. 여지	rough	a. 거친

PRACTICE 01

변형문제

01 다음 글을 읽고, |조건|에 맞게 주어진 주제문을 완성하시오.

| 조건 |
* (A), (B)는 각각 1단어로 쓸 것
* [보기]에서 선택한 단어를 한 번씩만 쓸 것
* 필요한 경우, 문맥과 어법에 맞게 변형할 것

[보기] listen / modify / familiarize / follow / prepare / wish / avoid / suggest / incline / commence / alternate

A lot of us feel like doing "something different." Studies have shown that people do not like to read instructions, and much of what we do read we either ignore or don't understand. In one test, for example, twenty-four adults were asked to wire a common household electrical plug. Only ten of the twenty-four even bothered to look at the instructions. And of those ten, seven consulted the instructions only to check the color coding for the electrical wires; the rest of the information was ignored. Not surprisingly, most people flunked this test. Even when the instructions are unusually important, people tend to pay them little attention. As the authors of the electrical plug study noted, "Even in the case of quite unfamiliar tasks, people seem to prefer to act rather than reflect."

⬇

Instead of (A) ____________ the instructions, a majority of people highly (B) ____________ to behave as they wish.

02 밑줄 친 부분 중 문맥상 옳지 않은 것은?

A lot of us feel like doing "something different." Studies have shown that people ① like to read instructions, and much of what we do read we either ignore or don't understand. In one test, for example, twenty-four adults were asked to wire a common household electrical plug. Only ten of the twenty-four even bothered to look at the instructions. And of those ten, seven consulted the instructions ② onlyonly to check the color coding for the electrical wires; the rest of the information was ignored. Not surprisingly, most people ③ flunkedflunked this test. Even when the instructions are ④ unusually important, people tend to pay them little attention. As the authors of the electrical plug study noted, "Even in the case of quite unfamiliar tasks, people seem to ⑤ prefer to act rather than reflect."

03 다음 글을 읽고, |조건|에 맞게 주어진 요약문을 완성하시오.

| 조건 |

* (A)는 1단어, (B)는 2단어, (C)는 1단어로 쓸 것
* [보기]에서 선택한 단어를 한 번씩만 쓸 것(단, (B)의 경우, [보기] 외의 1단어를 추가할 것)
* 필요한 경우, 문맥과 어법에 맞게 변형할 것

[보기] proper / promptly / carry / overlook / struggle / recommend / complete / comprehend / divide

A lot of us feel like doing "something different." Studies have shown that people do not like to read instructions, and much of what we do read we either ignore or don't understand. In one test, for example, twenty-four adults were asked to wire a common household electrical plug. Only ten of the twenty-four even bothered to look at the instructions. And of those ten, seven consulted the instructions only to check the color coding for the electrical wires; the rest of the information was ignored. Not surprisingly, most people flunked this test. Even when the instructions are unusually important, people tend to pay them little attention. As the authors of the electrical plug study noted, "Even in the case of quite unfamiliar tasks, people seem to prefer to act rather than reflect."

⬇

According to the experiment in the paragraph, only a small number of people (A) ____________ read the instructions and (B) ____________ ____________ the allocated tasks, which means that people would rather behave as they want than (C) ____________ tasks by following the instructions.

04 다음 문장이 들어갈 부분으로 가장 적절한 곳을 고르시오.

In one test, for example, twenty-four adults were asked to wire a common household electrical plug.

A lot of us feel like doing "something different." Studies have shown that people do not like to read instructions, and much of what we do read we either ignore or don't understand. (①) Only ten of the twenty-four even bothered to look at the instructions. (②) And of those ten, seven consulted the instructions only to check the color coding for the electrical wires; the rest of the information was ignored. (③) Not surprisingly, most people flunked this test. (④) Even when the instructions are unusually important, people tend to pay them little attention. (⑤) As the authors of the electrical plug study noted, "Even in the case of quite unfamiliar tasks, people seem to prefer to act rather than reflect."

단어 빈칸

글의 논리	Comparison & Contrast (비교 & 대조)
제목	인간과 다른 동물들의 차이점: 변화
주제	변화는 인간의 발전에 나타나는 가장 일반적인 특성이다.

031 어법 선택 & 연결어

The history of any animal species **[reveals / reveal]** a distinct sameness in behavior. A bird **[built / building] [their / its]** nest today will do **[it / them]** in **[most / almost]** exactly the same way **[that / how]** birds did **[it / them]** yesterday, a year ago, even thousands of years ago. And one can be quite **[surely / sure] [that / what]** birds will continue in this same way thousands of years from now. All animals, even the higher apes, closest to man in intelligence, **[shows / show]** this sameness over vast stretches of time. Man is different. Change is a general characteristic of human thought, human action, and human development. A house **[building / built]** today is quite different from one **[what / that] [was built / built]** thousands of years ago or even **[a little / a few]** decades ago. And we can be **[certainly / certain] [what / that]** a house **[building / built]** twenty or thirty years from now will differ greatly from **[ones / one] [building / built]** today.

비교 동물의 종들은 과거를 볼 때, 행동에 있어 뚜렷한 유사성이 나타난다.

The history (of any animal species) / reveals a distinct sameness / (in behavior).

(S: The history — 어떤 동물의 종이라도 역사를 살펴보면 / V: reveals, O: a distinct sameness — 뚜렷한 유사성이 나타난다 / (in behavior) — 행동에 있어)

어떤 동물의 종이라도 역사를 살펴보면 행동에 있어 뚜렷한 유사성이 나타난다.

비교 오늘 둥지를 짓는 새는 수천 년 전에 방식과 거의 똑같은 방식으로 둥지를 짓는다.

A bird / (which/that is) (building its nest today) / will do it / (in almost exactly the same way) / {that birds did it / yesterday, (a year ago), (even thousands of years ago)}.

(S: A bird — 새는 / 〈현재분사〉 building, O: its nest — 오늘 둥지를 짓는 / V: will do, O: it — 지을 것이다 / 거의 똑같은 방식으로 / that 〈관계부사 대용어〉, S: birds, V: did, O: it — 그렇게 했던 것과 / 어제, 1년 전, 심지어 수천 년 전에)

오늘 둥지를 짓는 새는 어제, 1년 전, 심지어 수천 년 전에 그렇게 했던 것과 거의 똑같은 방식으로 둥지를 지을 것이다.

노트 ■ 〈주격관계대명사+be동사 생략〉

명사	(주격관계대명사 +be동사)	Ring(현재분사) – 능동
		p.p.(과거분사) – 수동
		형용사
		부사
		명사
		전치사구
A bird	(which/that is)	building

■ 〈most / almost / mostly〉

	대명사	형용사	부사
most	대부분의 것들(사람들)	대부분의	가장
almost	–	–	거의
mostly	–	–	주로, 일반적으로

■ 〈관계부사〉: 선행사와 관계부사는 서로 같이 사용할 수도 있고 둘 중 하나는 생략할 수도 있다.

용도	선행사	관계부사	전치사+관계대명사
시간	the time	when	in/at/on+which
장소	the place	where	in/at/on+which
이유	the reason	why	for which
방법	(the way)	how	in which
방법	the way how는 같이 사용 못함, the way, the way in which, the way that은 사용 가능 (how 대신에 사용되는 that은 관계부사 대용어라고 함)		

비교 앞으로 수천 년 후에도 새들은 똑같은 방식을 유지할 것이다.

(And) / one / can be (quite) sure / {that birds will continue / (in this same way) / (thousands of years) / (from now)}.

(그리고 / S: one — 우리는 / V: can be, S.C: sure — 확신할 수 있다 / that 〈종·접〉, S: birds, V: will continue — 새들은 유지할 것이다 / 똑같은 방식을 / 수천 년 후에도 / 지금으로부터)

그리고 우리는 지금으로부터 수천 년 후에도 새들은 똑같은 방식을 유지할 것이라고 확신할 수 있다.

노트
■ in this same way : 이와 같은 방법으로
■ from now : 지금으로부터
■ 〈인지/확신형용사〉: 이러한 형용사는 뒤에 명사절로 that절이나 간접의문문 등을 취할 수 있다.

주어 (사람)	be동사	형용사 (인지/확신)	that (생략 가능)	주어	동사 ~
			of + 동명사		
		aware, certain, conscious, proud, sure, confident, convinced, fearful, ignorant			

■ 〈what vs. that〉

	관계대명사(불완전한 문장)	접속사(완전한 문장)
what	○ 선행사를 포함하고 있기 때문에 what 앞에 선행사 불필요	×
that	○ that 앞에 선행사 필요	○

비교 인간과 가장 유사한, 높은 지능의 유인원들조차도 오랜 기간 동안 유사성을 보여 준다.

All animals, / {(even) the higher apes}, / (who are) (closest to man in intelligence), / show this sameness / (over vast stretches of time).

All animals (S) 모든 동물들 / the higher apes 심지어 높은 지능의 유인원들조차 / closest (〈최상급〉) to 지능에 있어 man in intelligence 인간과 유사한 / show (V) this sameness (O) 유사성을 보여 준다 / over vast 엄청나게 stretches of time 오랜 기간 동안

모든 동물들, 심지어 지능에 있어 인간과 가장 유사한, 높은 지능의 유인원들조차도 엄청나게 오랜 기간 동안 이러한 유사성을 보여 주고 있다.

노트 ■ over vast stretches of time : 광대한 시간에 걸쳐서
■ 〈주격관계대명사+be동사 생략〉
• 현재분사 saying이 전치사구 앞에 있는 명사를 수식하는 경우

명사	콤마(,)	(주격관계대명사 +be동사)	Ring(현재분사) – 능동
			p.p.(과거분사) – 수동
			형용사
			부사
			명사
			전치사구
apes	,	(who are)	closest

대조 그러나 인간은 다른 동물과 다르다.

Man / is different.

Man (S) 인간은 / is (V) / different (S.C) 다르다

인간은 다르다.

주제문 변화는 인간의 발전에 나타나는 일반적인 특성이다.

_____ / is a general characteristic / (of human thought, human action, and human development).

_____ (S) 변화는 / is (V) / a general characteristic (S.C) 일반적인 특성이다 / of human 인간의 사고, thought, human action, and human development 인간의 행동, 그리고 인간에 발전에 나타나는

변화는 인간의 사고, 인간의 행동, 그리고 인간의 발전에 나타나는 일반적인 특성이다.

근거1 오늘 지어진 집은 불과 수십 년 전에 지어진 집과 매우 다르다.

A house / (which/that is) (built today) / is (quite) different / (from one) / {that was built / (thousands of years ago) / or / (even a few decades ago)}.

A house (S) 집은 / built (〈과거분사〉) today 오늘 지어진 / is (V) / (quite) different (S.C) 꽤 다르다 / from one (〈선행사〉 (=a house)) 집과 / that (〈주·관〉) was built (V〈수동태〉) 지어진 / thousands of years ago 수천 년 전에 / or 또는 / even 불과 a few decades ago 수십 년 전에 지어진

오늘 지어진 집은 수천 년 전에 지어진 또는 심지어 불과 수십 년 전에 지어진 집과 매우 다르다.

노트 ■ be different from : ~와 다르다
■ 〈주격관계대명사+be동사 생략〉

명사	(주격관계대명사 +be동사)	Ring(현재분사) – 능동
		p.p.(과거분사) – 수동
		형용사
		부사
		명사
		전치사구
A house	(which/that is)	built

■ 〈주격관계대명사절의 수의 일치〉 : 선행사를 포함하고 있는 관계대명사 what 사용 불가

	주격관계대명사절		
선행사	주격관계대명사	~~주어~~	동사
one	that		was built

■ 〈few / a few / a little / little〉

수	few	거의 없는(부정)	+복수N+복수V
	a few	약간(긍정)	
양	a little	약간(긍정)	+단수N+단수V
	little	거의 없는(부정)	

근거2 그리고 몇 십 년 후에 지어질 집도 오늘날 지어진 집과 매우 다를 것이다.

(And) / we / can be certain / [that a house / (which is) {built twenty or thirty years / (from now)} / will differ (greatly) / from one / (which is) (built today)].

(And) 그리고 / we (S) 우리는 / can be (V) certain (S.C) 확신할 수 있다 / that (〈종·접〉) a house (S) 집이 / built (〈과거분사〉) twenty 20년 or thirty years 또는 30년 후에 / from now 지금으로부터 / will differ (V) (greatly) 매우 다를 것이다 / from one ((=a house)) 집과 / built (〈과거분사〉) today 오늘날 지어진

그리고 우리는 20년 또는 30년 후에 지어질 집이 오늘날 지어진 집과 매우 다를 것이라는 것을 확신할 수 있다.

노트 ■ 〈주격관계대명사+be동사 생략〉

–	생략할 수 있음	분사(형용사 : 명사 수식)
명사 (선행사)	(주격관계대명사 +be동사)	현재분사(Ring) – 능동(~하고 있는)
		과거분사(p.p.) – 수동(~되어진, 당한)
		형용사(구) (~하는, ~할)
a house	(which/that is)	built
one		

■ be certain that＋주어＋동사 : ~을 확신하다
■ differ from : ~와 다르다

▶ 다음 빈칸에 들어갈 말로 가장 적절한 것은?

① Change ② Consistency ③ Harmony
④ Regularly ⑤ Socially

정답 | ①
해석 | ① 변화 ② 일관성 ③ 조화
④ 규칙성 ⑤ 사회성

해설 | ① 이 글의 주제는 변화가 인간의 발전에 나타나는 특성이라는 것이다. 집이 지어진 것을 볼 때 시대에 따라 다른 점을 예로 들고 있고, 인간과 다른 동물의 종을 비교하며, 다른 동물들은 시간이 지나도 뚜렷한 유사성을 띤다고 말한다. 빈칸이 들어간 문장을 보면 ______ 은/는 인간의 사고, 인간의 행동, 인간의 발전에 나타나는 일반적인 특성이라고 말한다. 따라서 인간은 계속해서 시간이 지날수록 집 같은 경우에도 변형시키고 재구성하기 때문에 가장 적절한 것은 ① 'Change' 이다.

오답 | ② '일관성' 은 인간의 특징이 아니라 다른 동물의 종의 특징이다.
③ '조화' 는 이 글의 소재와 연관되지 않는다.
④ '규칙성' 은 인간의 특징이 아니라 다른 동물 종의 특징이다.
⑤ '사회성' 은 이 글의 소재와 연관되지 않는다.

Words

☐ species
☐ reveal
☐ distinct
☐ sameness
☐ behavior
☐ nest
☐ continue
☐ ape
☐ intelligence
☐ vast
☐ stretch
☐ general
☐ characteristic
☐ development
☐ decade
☐ certain
☐ consistency
☐ harmony
☐ regularity
☐ sociality

Phrases

☐ in this same way
☐ over vast stretches of time
☐ differ from
☐ from now
☐ be different from
☐ be certain that ＋주어＋동사

우선순위 영단어 역대 수능 기출 + 전국 모의고사 기출 + EBS 기출 + 교과서 기출 빈출 어휘

단어	뜻	단어	뜻	단어	뜻
ruin	n. 파멸	runoff	n. 땅 위를 흐르는 빗물	rural	a. 시골의
sacrifice	v. 희생시키다	satellite	n. (인공)위성	satisfaction	n. 만족
scatter	v. 흩뿌리다	scent	n. 냄새	secondary	a. 부차적인
seedling	n. 묘목	seminar	n. 세미나	sentiment	n. 정서
serve	v. 도움이 되다	shallow	a. 얕은	shape	v. 모양 짓다
shelf life	n. 저장[보존]기간	shield	v. 숨기다	shrub	n. 관목
similarity	n. 유사성	simulate	v. 모의실험[훈련]을 하다	skepticism	n. 회의론
skip	v. 건너뛰다	socialization	n. 사회화	spark	v. 촉발시키다
sparse	a. 성긴	spectator	n. 관객	spill	v. 유출하다
spiral	n. 소용돌이	spirit	n. 마음	steer	v. 향하게 하다
storage	n. 저장	strand	v. 외교	stray	a. 불쑥 찾아드는
stuff	n. 재료	stunning	a. 괄목할만한	subscription	n. 구독
subsequently	ad. 이어서	suit	v. 어울리다	suitable	a. 적절한
superficial	a. 피상적인	supernatural	a. 초자연적인	superstitious	a. 미신의
supervisor	n. 감독관	surf	v. 파도 타다	swing	v. 회전하다
sympathetic	a. 동정하는	tack	v. 부가하다	take in	~을 섭취하다

변형문제

01 다음 글을 읽고, |조건|에 맞게 주어진 요약문을 완성하시오.

| 조건 |
* (A), (B)는 각각 1단어로 쓸 것
* 본문에 있는 단어만을 사용할 것
* 필요한 경우, 문맥과 어법에 맞게 변형할 것

The history of any animal species reveals a distinct sameness in behavior. A bird building its nest today will do it in almost exactly the same way that birds did it yesterday, a year ago, even thousands of years ago. And one can be quite sure that birds will continue in this same way thousands of years from now. All animals, even the higher apes, closest to man in intelligence, show this sameness over vast stretches of time. Man is different. Change is a general characteristic of human thought, human action, and human development. A house built today is quite different from one that was built thousands of years ago or even a few decades ago. And we can be certain that a house built twenty or thirty years from now will differ greatly from one built today.

⬇

Humans are shown to pursue (A) ____________ as time goes by, but no change in animals' behaviors occurs over time due to (B) ____________ which is their general characteristics.

02 다음 글을 읽고, |조건|에 맞게 주제문을 완성하시오.

| 조건 |
* (A), (B)는 각각 다르게 1단어로 쓸 것
* 본문에 있는 단어를 찾아 그대로 쓸 것
* 필요한 경우, 문맥과 어법에 맞게 변형할 것

The history of any animal species reveals a distinct sameness in behavior. A bird building its nest today will do it in almost exactly the same way that birds did it yesterday, a year ago, even thousands of years ago. And one can be quite sure that birds will continue in this same way thousands of years from now. All animals, even the higher apes, closest to man in intelligence, show this sameness over vast stretches of time. Man is different. Change is a general characteristic of human thought, human action, and human development. A house built today is quite different from one that was built thousands of years ago or even a few decades ago. And we can be certain that a house built twenty or thirty years from now will differ greatly from one built today.

⬇

Humans are different to animals because they constantly pursue changes that affect the formation of (A) ____________, how to (B) ____________, and their growth or progress.

03 다음 글을 읽고, |조건|에 맞게 빈칸 (A), (B), (C)를 채우시오.

| 조건 |
* (A)는 2단어, (B), (C)는 1단어로 쓸 것
* [보기]에서 선택한 단어를 한 번씩만 쓰되, 변형 없이 쓸 것

[보기] construction / way / strategy / change / differ / compare / design / figure / advance / advantage / strength / characteristic / altered / modify / same

The history of any animal species reveals a distinct sameness in behavior. A bird building its nest today will do it in almost exactly the same way that birds did it yesterday, a year ago, even thousands of years ago. And one can be quite sure that birds will continue in this (A) ____________ ____________ thousands of years from now. All animals, even the higher apes, closest to man in intelligence, show this sameness over vast stretches of time. Man is different. Change is a general (B) ____________ of human thought, human action, and human development. A house built today is quite different from one that was built thousands of years ago or even a few decades ago. And we can be certain that a house built twenty or thirty years from now will (C) ____________ greatly from one built today.

04 다음 글을 읽고, |조건|에 맞게 빈칸 (A), (B)를 채우시오.

| 조건 |
* (A), (B)는 각각 다르게 1단어로 쓸 것
* [보기]에서 선택한 단어를 한 번씩만 쓸 것
* 필요한 경우, 문맥과 어법에 맞게 변형할 것

[보기] feature / similarity / try / train / adopt / pursue / devote / avoid / prohibit / keep / different

The history of any animal species reveals a distinct sameness in behavior. A bird building its nest today will do it in almost exactly the same way that birds did it yesterday, a year ago, even thousands of years ago. And one can be quite sure that birds will continue in this same way thousands of years from now. All animals, even the higher apes, closest to man in intelligence, show this sameness over vast stretches of time. Man is different. Change is a general characteristic of human thought, human action, and human development. A house built today is quite different from one that was built thousands of years ago or even a few decades ago. And we can be certain that a house built twenty or thirty years from now will differ greatly from one built today.

⬇

The distinct (A) ____________ between humans and animals is said that humans do not show a sameness in behavior since (B) ____________ constant changes is a human characteristic.

단어 빈칸

글의 논리	Spotlight
제목	진열대에 있는 비싼 상품이 주는 효과
주제	앵커는 파는 용도도 있지만 대비 효과를 내는 용도로 사용한다.

PRACTICE 03

032 어법 선택 & 연결어

The one psychophysics term on the lips of Prada store managers **[are / is]** "anchor." In the luxury trade, **[what / that]** **[describe / describes]** an incredibly high-priced article displayed **[mainly / main]** **[to manipulate / manipulate]** consumers. The anchor is for sale — but it's okay if no one buys **[them / it]**. It's really there for contrast. It makes everything else **[to look / look]** **[affordable / affordably]** by comparison. "This has been a strategy **[what / that]** **[goes / go]** back to the seventeenth century," Paco Underhill, the author of the book *Why We Buy*, said recently. "You sold one thing to the king, but everyone in court had to have a **[fewer / lesser]** one. **[There're / There's]** the $500 bag in the window, and **[that / what]** you walk away with **[are / is]** the T-shirt."

일반적인 사실 프라다 매장 매니저가 자주 말하는 용어는 '앵커(고정장치)'이다.

The one psychophysics term / (on the lips of Prada store managers) / is "anchor."

The one psychophysics term(S) 한 가지 정신 물리학적 용어는 / on the lips of Prada 프라다 매장 매니저가 / store managers 자주 입에 올리는 / is(V) "anchor."(S.C) '앵커' 이다

프라다 매장 매니저가 자주 입에 올리는 한 가지 정신 물리학적 용어는 '앵커(고정장치)'이다.

노트 ■ on the lips of : ~의 입에 오르내려서

일반적인 사실 명품 거래에서 전시되어 있는 앵커는 비싼 물건을 묘사한다.

(In the luxury trade), / that / describes an incredibly high-priced article / (which is) (displayed mainly) / (to manipulate consumers).

(In the luxury trade) 명품 거래에서 / that(S) 그것은 / describes(V) / incredibly〈부사〉 믿을 수 없을 정도로 / high-priced〈과거분사〉 article(O) 비싼 물건을 묘사한다 / displayed〈과거분사〉 mainly〈부사〉 주로 전시되어 있는 / to manipulate consumers 소비자를 조종하기 위해

명품 거래에서 그것은 주로 소비자를 조종하기 위해 전시되어 있는 믿을 수 없을 정도로 비싼 물건을 묘사한다.

노트 ■ 〈주격관계대명사+be동사 생략〉

–	생략할 수 있음	분사(형용사 : 명사 수식)
명사(선행사)	(주격관계대명사+be동사)	현재분사(Ring) – 능동(~하고 있는)
		과거분사(p.p.) – 수동(~되어진, 당한)
		명사
		형용사(구) (~하는, ~할)
		부사
		전치사구
article	(which/that is)	displayed

주제문 앵커는 판매용이기도 하지만 팔지 않아도 상관없다.

The anchor / is for sale / — but / it's okay / (if no one buys it).

The anchor(S) 앵커는 / is for sale(V) 판매용이다 / but 하지만 / it(S) 's(V) okay(S.C) 상관없다 / if(종·접) no one(S) 아무도 그것을 / buys(V) it(O) 사지 않아도

앵커는 판매용이긴 하지만 아무도 그것을 사지 않아도 상관없다.

노트 ■ for sale : 팔려고 내놓은
■ no one+단수동사 : 어느 누구도 ~ 않다
■ 〈전체부정〉 : 모두/전부 ~ 아니다, 절대 ~하지 않는다

<table>
<tr><td rowspan="2">전체 부정</td><td colspan="2">not any one(=none) (모두 ~이 아니다)
no+명사 (어느 누구도 ~ 않다)
not ~ either(=neither) (둘 다 ~이 아니다)
not+anything(=nothing) (아무것도[단 하나도] (~ 아니다 · 없다))
not+ever(=never) (결코 ~이 아니다)
not anywhere(=nowhere)</td></tr>
<tr><td>no
=not any</td><td>no more=not ~ anymore
nobody=not ~ anybody
nothing=not ~ anything
no longer=not ~ any longer</td></tr>
</table>

근거 앵커는 대비 효과를 위해 있다.

It's / (really) (there) / (for contrast).

It(S) 's(V) 그것은 / really there 정말로 거기 있는 것이다 / for contrast 실제로는 대비 효과를 위해

그것은 실제로는 대비 효과를 위해 거기 있는 것이다.

근거 앵커와 다른 것을 비교해 볼 때, 다른 것이 적당한 가격으로 보이게 만든다.

It / makes everything else / look ________ / (by comparison).

It(S) 그것은 / makes(V) / everything else(O) 다른 모든 것들과 / look ____(O.C) 가격이 알맞은 것처럼 보이게 만든다 / by comparison 비교해보면

그것은 다른 모든 것을 비교해 보면 가격이 알맞은 것처럼 보이게 만든다.

노트
- by comparison : 그에 비해
- look + 형용사 : ~처럼 보이다
- 〈make 사역동사〉

make	목적어	목적격보어	해석
〈사역동사〉	명사/ 명사 상당어구	동사원형(R)	~가 …하도록 시키다
		과거분사(p.p)	~가 …하게 당하다
makes	everything else	look	-

- 〈형용사의 후치 수식〉

〈후치 수식〉	-thing	+형용사	○
	-body		
	-one		
〈전치 수식〉	형용사+	-thing	×
		-body	
		-one	

- 〈감각동사〉

감각동사	주격보어(S.C)	
feel, look, seem, sound, taste, appear, smell	형용사(분사 : 현재분사/과거분사)	
	명사	
	like(전치사)	(that)+주어+동사
		(동)명사
	~~alike~~	
	~~likely~~	

- 〈혼동하기 쉬운 어휘〉

likely	형용사	~일 것 같은 (be to 동사원형 : ~일 것 같다)
	부사	아마(probably)
alike	서술적 형용사 (보어로만 사용, 명사 수식 불가)	동일한
	부사	똑같이
like	전치사	~처럼
	동사	좋아하다

근거에 대한 이야기 앵커에 대한 이야기

"This / has been a strategy / (that goes back to the seventeenth century)," Paco Underhill, / the author (of the book *Why We Buy*), / said (recently).

This(S) 이것은 / has been(V〈현재완료〉) a strategy(S.C〈선행사〉) 전략입니다 / that(〈주·관〉) goes back(V) 17세기까지 거슬러 올라가는 / Paco Underhill(S) Paco Underhill은 =〈동격〉 the author 저자인 / (of the book *Why We Buy*) '우리는 왜 구입하는가'의 / said(V) (recently) 최근 말했다

"이것은 17세기까지 거슬러 올라가는 전략입니다." '우리는 왜 구입하는가'의 저자인 Paco Underhill은 최근 말했다.

노트
- go back to : ~로 거슬러 올라가다(=originate in, begin[start] with)
- 〈주격관계대명사절의 수의 일치〉 : 선행사를 포함하고 있는 관계대명사 what 사용 불가

	주격관계대명사절		
선행사	주격관계대명사	~~주어~~	동사
a strategy	that		goes back to

- 〈동격〉 : A(명사), B(명사) (A가 주어, B라는 A)

동격(B라는 A)			
명사(A)	,(콤마)	명사(구/절)(B)	동사
Paco Underhill	,	the author of the book *Why We Buy*	said

"You / sold one thing / (to the king), / but / everyone (in court) / had to have a lesser one. / There's the $500 bag / (in the window), / and (what you walk away with) / is the T-shirt."

You(S) 여러분이 / sold(V) one thing(O) 한 가지를 팔았다면 / (to the king) 왕에게 / but 하지만 / everyone(S) (in court) 궁정의 모든 사람들은 / had to have(V) a lesser one(O) 그보다 더 못한 것을 갖고 있어야만 합니다 / There's(V) the $500 bag(S) 500달러짜리 가방이 있다 / (in the window) 진열대에는 / what(〈목·관〉) you(S) walk away with(V) → S 여러분이 갖고 나오는 것은 / is(V) the T-shirt(S.C) 티셔츠뿐입니다

"여러분이 왕에게 한 가지를 팔았다면, 궁정의 모든 사람들은 그보다 더 못한 것을 갖고 있어야만 합니다. 진열대에는 500달러짜리 가방이 있지만, 여러분이 갖고 나오는 것은 티셔츠일 뿐입니다."

노트
- sell + IO + DO : ~에게 …을 팔다
- lesser : [little의 이중비교급] 더욱 작은[적은], 작은[적은] 편의
- 〈4형식을 3형식으로 바꿀 때 사용하는 전치사〉 : 전치사 to를 취하는 동사

주어	+	동사	+	간접목적어	+	직접목적어	(4)
		give, bring, pass, send, show, sell, hand, lend, offer, teach 등					
수동태 시 → 주어+직접목적어+to+간접목적어 (3)							

- walk away with : ~을 갖고 달아나다, 착복하다, ~을 수월하게 차지하다
- 〈There is 도치구문〉

긍정문	There	is	단수 주어	~이 있다
		are	복수 주어	
부정문	There	is no	단수 주어	~이 없다
		are no	복수 주어	

• 유도부사 **there**와 함께 도치구문을 이루는 be동사(is/are/was/were) 대신에 완전자동사 **appear**, **come**, **exist**, **follow**, **live**, **stand** 등을 사용할 수 있다.

- 〈관계대명사 what절이 주어로 사용되는 경우〉 : 관계대명사 what절이 주어로 사용되면 동사는 주로 단수동사 사용함, that/which 사용 불가

	관계대명사절(명사절 : 주어)				
~~선행사~~	what	주어	동사	~~목적어~~	동사
	선행사를 포함한 관계대명사 (=the thing(s) which/that ~) : ~하는 것(들)은/이	you	walk away with		is

▶ 다음 빈칸에 들어갈 말로 가장 적절한 것은?

① shabby ② fancy
③ affordable ④ expensive
⑤ unnoticeable

정답 | ③

해석 | ① 초라한
② 화려한
③ 가격이 알맞은
④ 값비싼
⑤ 눈에 띄지 않는

해설 | ③ 이 글의 주제는 앵커는 파는 용도도 있지만 대비 효과를 내는 용도로 사용한다는 것이다. 앵커는 굉장히 비싼 물건으로 되어 있고, 4번째 문장을 보면 이는 대비 효과를 위하여 존재한다고 설명한다. 빈칸이 있는 문장을 보면 '그것은 다른 모든 것을 비교해 보면 가격이 것처럼 보이게 만든다.' 라고 나와 있다. 앵커는 값 비싸고, 다른 모든 것은 앵커와 대비된다고 설명하기 때문에 값비싼의 반대말인 ③ 'affordable(가격이 적당하다)' 는 것이 가장 적절하다.

오답 | ① 앵커는 값비싼 물건이라고만 나오고 화려하다는 말은 나오지 않으므로 적절하지 않다.
② 다른 모든 것이 화려하다는 것은 글의 관점과 일치하지 않는다.
④ 앵커와 대비해서 다른 모든 것들은 가격이 알맞아 보이는 것이므로 반대되는 말이다.
⑤ 앵커와 비교해 다른 물건들이 눈에 띄지 않는지는 글에 내용에 나오지 않으므로 적절하지 않다.

Words

- ☐ psychophysics
- ☐ anchor
- ☐ describe
- ☐ incredibly
- ☐ manipulate
- ☐ contrast
- ☐ shabby
- ☐ fancy
- ☐ affordable

Phrases

- ☐ on the lips of
- ☐ by comparison
- ☐ walk away with
- ☐ for sale
- ☐ go back to

우선순위 영단어 역대 수능 기출 + 전국 모의고사 기출 + EBS 기출 + 교과서 기출 빈출 어휘

단어	뜻	단어	뜻	단어	뜻
take off	벗다	technique	n. 기법	temporarily	ad. 일시적으로
tempting	a. 군침이 도는	tend	v. 돌보다	terrify	v. 겁나게 하다
that is	즉	the former	n. 전자	the latter	n. 후자
thoughtful	a. 사려 깊은	thread	n. 맥락	thumb	v. 엄지손가락
tissue	n. 조직	to some extent	어느 정도	tolerance	n. 관용
translation	n. 번역	trial and error	n. 시행착오	trim	v. 잘라내다
troop	n. 무리	trunk	n. 몸통	try on	~을 신어[입어] 보다
tumble	v. 굴러 떨어지다	twist	v. 꼬다	typical	a. 전형적인
undercut	v. 약화하다	undermine	v. 몰래 손상시키다	undesirable	a. 바람직하지 않은
undisturbed	a. 건드리지 않은	undoubtedly	ad. 틀림없이	unintentionally	ad. 의도하지 않게
union	n. 결합	utilize	v. 활용하다	various	a. 다양한
vehicle	n. 탈 것	venue	a. 장소	version	n. ~판
vertically	ad. 수직으로	virtual	a. ~와 다름없는	visible	a. 눈에 보이는
welfare	n. 복지	whereas	ad. 반면에	wind up -ing	결국 ~가 되다
wipe out	지우다	withstand	v. 살아남다	worsen	v. 악화되다
wound	v. 부상	youngster	n. 어린아이	awake	a. 깨어 있는
catch	n. 책략	grieve	v. 몹시 슬퍼하다	a great deal of	많은 (양의)
a host of	수많은	a series of	일련의	absolute	a. 절대적인
absorption	n. 몰두; 흡수	abuse	v. 학대하다	academic	a. 학원의
accent	n. 말씨	accepted	a. 일반적으로 용인된	accord	v. (권위, 지위 등을) 부여하다
according to	~에 따르면	accordingly	ad. 상응하게	accumulated	a. 축적된
achieve	v. 달성하다	acoustic	a. 음향의	actual	a. 실재상의
adequately	ad. 적절히	adhere to	~에 달라붙다	adjust to	~에 적응하다
advent	n. 출현	adversity	n. 역경	advertisement	n. 광고(=ad)

변형문제

01 다음 글을 읽고, |조건|에 맞게 주어진 요약문을 완성하시오.

| 조건 |
* (A), (B), (C)는 각각 다르게 1단어로 쓸 것
* 본문에 있는 단어만을 사용할 것
* 필요한 경우, 문맥과 어법에 맞게 변형할 것

The one psychophysics term on the lips of Prada store managers is "anchor." In the luxury trade, that describes an incredibly high-priced article displayed mainly to manipulate consumers. The anchor is for sale — but it's okay if no one buys it. It's really there for contrast. It makes everything else look affordable by comparison. "This has been a strategy that goes back to the seventeenth century," Paco Underhill, the author of the book *Why We Buy*, said recently. "You sold one thing to the king, but everyone in court had to have a lesser one. There's the $500 bag in the window, and what you walk away with is the T-shirt."

⬇

In the luxury trade, the role of extremely (A) ____________ item is to make it seem affordable to other goods for (B) ____________ and (C) ____________.

02 다음 글을 읽고, |조건|에 맞게 문제를 완성하시오.

| 조건 |
* (A)는 3단어, (B)는 1단어로 쓸 것
* 본문에 있는 단어를 찾아 쓸 것
* 필요한 경우, 문맥과 어법에 맞게 변형할 것

The one psychophysics term on the lips of Prada store managers is "anchor." In the luxury trade, that describes an incredibly high-priced article displayed mainly to manipulate consumers. The anchor is for sale — but it's okay if no one buys it. It's really there for contrast. It makes everything else look affordable by comparison. "This has been a strategy that goes back to the seventeenth century," Paco Underhill, the author of the book *Why We Buy*, said recently. "You sold one thing to the king, but everyone in court had to have a lesser one. There's the $500 bag in the window, and what you walk away with is the T-shirt."

⬇

In the article above, "anchor" is indicated as a costly product (A) ____________ ____________ ____________ and is for (B) ____________.

03 밑줄 친 부분 중 문맥상 옳지 않은 것은?

The one psychophysics term on the lips of Prada store managers is "anchor." In the luxury trade, that describes an incredibly ① high-priced article displayed mainly to manipulate consumers. The anchor is for sale — but it's okay if no one ② buys it. It's really there for ③ contrast. It makes everything else look ④ unreasonable by comparison. "This has been a strategy that goes back to the seventeenth century," Paco Underhill, the author of the book *Why We Buy*, said recently. "You sold one thing to the king, but everyone in court had to have a ⑤ lesser one. There's the $500 bag in the window, and what you walk away with is the T-shirt."

04 다음 문장이 들어갈 부분으로 가장 적절한 곳을 고르시오.

The anchor is for sale — but it's okay if no one buys it.

The one psychophysics term on the lips of Prada store managers is "anchor." (①) In the luxury trade, that describes an incredibly high-priced article displayed mainly to manipulate consumers. (②) It's really there for contrast. It makes everything else look affordable by comparison. (③) "This has been a strategy that goes back to the seventeenth century," Paco Underhill, the author of the book *Why We Buy*, said recently. (④) "You sold one thing to the king, but everyone in court had to have a lesser one. (⑤) There's the $500 bag in the window, and what you walk away with is the T-shirt."

UNIT 09

짧은 어구 빈칸

글의 논리	Sequence
제목	직원들이 개인과 팀의 목적을 검토
주제	분기마다 모여서 개인과 팀의 목적을 검토하는 것은 미래에 어느 부분에 에너지를 집중시킬 필요가 있는지 확인하게 해준다.

수능 ANALYSIS

033 어법 선택 & 연결어

Every quarter, staff members at Big Brothers/Big Sisters of Santa Clara County get together to review individual and team objectives. Each person **[talk / talks]** about **[what / that]** he or she **[has been doing / has been done]** and **[identify / identifies]** how those accomplishments have helped **[to achieve / achieving]** the agency's aspirations. (   ), a staff member puts a checkmark next to each of the goals and priorities (posted on the wall) **[what / that]** each person **[have / has]** helped the agency **[come / coming]** closer to **[realize / realizing]**. This process **[is followed / follows]** by rounds of applause, whoops, and hollers. At the end of the session, **[say / says]** executive director Sheila Kriefels, "We have a visual statement about **[what / that]** we have all been able to accomplish as an agency. This also gives us the chance to notice any gaps between **[what / that]** each of one of us **[is / are]** doing **[or / and]** what we all **[had said / said]** we wanted the agency **[achieving / to achieve]**, and then **[there / where]** we might need to focus more of our energies in the future to achieve our common vision."

순서1 Big Brothers/Big Sisters의 직원들은 분기마다 모여서 개인과 팀의 목적을 검토한다.

(Every quarter), / staff members (S) / (at Big Brothers/Big Sisters) / (of Santa Clara County) / get together (V) / (to review individual and team objectives).

분기마다 / 직원들은 / Big Brothers/Big Sisters의 / Santa Clara 카운티의 / 모이다 / 개인과 팀의 목적을 검토하기 위해서

Santa Clara 카운티의 Big Brothers/Big Sisters의 직원들은 분기마다 모여서 개인과 팀의 목적을 검토한다.

노트 ■ get together : 모이다

순서2 각자 자신이 한 업적과 기관에 어떤 도움을 줬는지 확인한다.

Each person (S) / talks (V_1) / {about 〈전치사〉 (what 〈의문사〉 he or she (S) has been doing (V〈현재완료진행〉)) (O)} / and identifies (V_2) (how 〈의문사〉 those accomplishments (S) have helped (V〈현재완료〉)) (O) / to achieve the agency's aspirations (O).

각자 / 말한다 / 자신이 무엇을 해오고 있는지에 대해서 / 그리고 어떻게 그러한 업적들이 도움되었는지를 확인한다 / 그 기관의 목표를 성취하는 데

각자 자신이 무엇을 해왔는지 말하고 그러한 업적이 그 기관의 목표를 성취하는 데 어떻게 도움이 되었는지 확인한다.

노트 ■ talk about : ~에 대해 이야기하다
■ have/has been Ring : 현재완료진행
■ 〈주어와 동사의 수의 일치〉
• each / every / any + 단수동사

■ 〈help 동사의 쓰임〉 : 3형식일 경우

help	목적어
–	(to) R

■ 〈간접의문문〉
• 전치사의 목적어 자리

	〈간접의문문〉		
전치사	의문대명사	주어	동사
about	what	he or she	has been doing

• 타동사의 목적어 자리

	〈간접의문문〉		
타동사	의문사	주어	동사
identifies	how	those accomplishments	have helped

순서3 그 후, 기관의 목표를 실현하는 데 개인이 도왔던 목표와 우선 사항을 체크한다.

(Then), / a staff member (S) / puts (V) a checkmark (O) / (next to each of the goals and priorities 〈선행사〉) / (posted 〈과거분사〉 on the wall) / (that 〈목·관〉 each person (S) has helped (V〈현재완료〉) / the agency (O) come closer (O.C) to realizing).

그런 다음 / 한 직원이 / 체크 표시를 한다 / 목표와 우선 사항들 각각의 옆에 / (벽에 게시된) / 각 개인이 도왔던 / 기관이 실현하는 데 / 더 가까이 가도록

그런 다음 한 직원이 기관이 (목표를) 실현하는 데 더 가까이 가도록 각 개인이 도왔던 (벽에 게시된) 목표와 우선 사항들 각각의 옆에 체크 표시를 한다.

노트 ■ puts A next to B : A를 B 옆에 하다
■ come close to (동)명사 : 하마터면 [거의] ~할 뻔하다
■ 〈help 동사의 쓰임〉 : 5형식일 경우

help	목적어	목적격보어
〈준사역동사〉		(to) R

■ 〈관계대명사의 이중 한정〉: 2개의 관계대명사절이 동일한 선행사를 수식하는 경우

	주격관계대명사절		목적격관계대명사절					
the goals and priorities	(주격 관계 대명사 +be동사)	posted ~	that	each person	has helped	the agency	come closer to realizing	목적어 (X)
선행사	(which/that are 생략)	과거 분사	목적격 관계 대명사	주어	동사	목적어	목적격 보어	동명사 realizing의 목적어 없음

순서4 이후에 몇 차례의 박수와 함성을 지른다.

This process / is followed / (by rounds of applause, whoops, and hollers).
(This process: S, 이러한 과정 다음에는 / is followed: V〈수동태〉, 잇따른다 / rounds of applause: 몇 차례의 박수, / whoops, and hollers: 와 하는 함성과 크게 놀라는 소리가)

이러한 과정 다음에는 몇 차례의 박수, 와 하는 함성과 크게 놀라는 소리가 잇따른다.

노트
- ■ a round of : 일련의 것, 많은
- ■ A followed by B : B로 이어지는 A
- ■ A be followed by B : A 다음에 B가 이어진다, A 다음에 B가 있다

주제문 분기마다 모여서 개인과 팀의 목적을 검토하는 것은 미래에 어느 부분에 에너지를 집중시킬 필요가 있는지 확인하게 해준다.

(At the end of the session), / says / executive director Sheila Kriefels, / "We ________ / {________ (what we have (all) been able to accomplish) / (as an agency)}. / This / (also) gives us the chance / (to notice any gaps) / {between (what each of one of us is doing) / and what we (all) had said / (we wanted the agency to achieve)}, / and (then) / {where we might need to focus more of our energies) / (in the future) / (to achieve our common vision)}."

(At the end of the session: 그 시간이 끝날 때에 / says: V, 말한다 / executive director Sheila Kriefels: S, 이사인 Sheila Kriefels는 / We: S / ________: V / O (statement), 우리는 시각적인 진술서를 가지고 있습니다 / what: 〈목·관〉, we: S, have (all) been able to accomplish: V〈현재완료〉, 우리 모두가 성취할 수 있었던 것에 대한 / as an agency: 한 기관으로서 / This: S, 이것은 / gives: V, us: I.O, the chance: D.O, 또한 우리에게 기회를 줍니다 / any gaps: O_1, 어떤 차이든지 본 / what: 〈목·관〉, each of one of us: S, is doing: V〈현재진행〉, 우리 각자가 하고 있는 일 사이에 / we: S, had said: V〈과거완료〉, 그리고 우리가 말했던 일 / (that) we: S, wanted: V, the agency: O, to achieve: O.C, 우리 모두가 기관이 성취하기를 원한다고 (O_1) / and (then): 그런 다음 / where: 〈의문사〉, we: S, might need to focus: V, more of our energies: O, 우리 에너지의 더 많은 부분을 어디에 집중시킬 필요가 있는지를 (O_2) / in the future: 미래에 / to achieve our common vision: 우리의 공통적인 비전을 성취하기 위해)

그 시간이 끝날 때에 이사인 Sheila Kriefels는 "우리는 한 기관으로서 우리 모두가 성취할 수 있었던 것에 대한 시각적인 진술서를 가지고 있습니다. 이것은 또한 우리에게 우리 각자가 하고 있는 일과 우리 모두가 기관이 성취하기를 원한다고 말했던 일 사이에 생긴 어떠한 차이든지 본 다음, 우리의 공통적인 비전을 성취하기 위해 미래에 우리 에너지의 더 많은 부분을 어디에 집중시킬 필요가 있는지를 볼 수 있는 기회를 줍니다."라고 말한다.

노트
- ■ at the end of : ~의 말에
- ■ be able to R : ~할 수 있다
- ■ 〈전치사의 목적어로 사용된 목적격관계대명사 what〉: 선행사를 필요로 하는 that 사용 불가

		관계대명사절(명사절 : 전치사의 목적어)			
전치사	선행사 (X)	what	주어	동사	목적어 (X)
about		선행사를 포함한 관계대명사 (=the thing(s) which/that ~) : ~하는 것은/이	we	have been able to accomplish	

- ■ give+IO+DO : ~에게 …을 주다
- ■ between A and B : A와 B 사이에
- ■ 〈간접의문문 – 타동사의 목적어 자리에 사용된 경우〉

		between A and B					의문사	주어	동사	목적어
to notice	any gaps	between	what ~	and	what ~	, and then	where	we	might need	to focus ~
	목적어1					대등접속사	목적어2 〈간접의문문〉			

■ 〈목적격관계대명사 what〉: 선행사를 포함한 관계대명사(=the thing(s) which/that ~) (~하는 것은/이)

• 동사의 목적어가 없는 경우

		〈목적격관계대명사절〉			
between	선행사 (X)	what	each of one of us	is doing	목적어 (X)
		목적격관계대명사	주어	동사	

• 목적격보어의 목적어가 없는 경우

		〈목적격관계대명사절〉								
and	선행사 (X)	what	we all	had said	(that)	we	wanted	the agency	to achieve	목적어 (X)
		목적격 관계 대명사	주어	동사	목적격 종속 접속사	주어	동사	목적어	목적격보어	
					목적어					

■ 〈want 용법〉

주어	want	목적어(to R)		주어가 ~하는 것을 원하다	3형식
		목적어	목적격보어 (to R)	주어는 목적어가 ~하는 것을 원하다	5형식

■ 〈need 용법〉

목적어(to R)		3형식	〈~할〉 필요가 있다, 〈~〉 해야 하다
목적어	목적격보어(to R)	5형식	〈남이〉 〈~해 줄〉 필요가 있다
동명사(Ring)		3형식	〈사람 · 물건이〉 〈~되어야 할〉 필요가 있다
목적어	목적격보어(p.p.)	5형식	〈~이〉 〈…될〉 필요가 있다, 〈~을〉 〈…되도록 할〉 필요가 있다

▶ 다음 글의 빈칸에 들어갈 말로 가장 적절한 것은?

① recreate the process of
② criticize one another for
③ are forced to forget about
④ have a visual statement about
⑤ predict future performance on

정답 | ④
해석 | ① ~의 과정을 재현하다
② ~에 대해 서로를 비판하다
③ ~에 대해 어쩔 수 없이 잊다
④ ~에 대한 시각적인 진술서를 가지고 있다
⑤ ~에 대한 미래의 실적을 예측하다
해설 | ④ 이 글의 내용은 직원들이 분기마다 모여서 개인과 팀의 목적을 검토하는 것이다. 그리고 이를 검토할 때, 벽에 게시된 목표와 우선 사항을 각각 옆에 표시를 한다. 이런 점을 볼 때, 빈칸에는 목표와 우선 사항을 표시한다는 말이 나와야 하는데 이 말로 가장 적절한 것은 ④이다.
오답 | ① 과정을 재현한다는 소재는 나오지 않는다.
② 서로 비판하는 것이 아니라 서로 박수를 치며 격려하기 때문에 반대된다.
③ 잊어버리는 것이 아니라 목표와 우선 사항을 기억하는 것이기 때문에 적절하지 않다.
⑤ 미래의 실적을 예측하는 것이 아니라 미래에 어느 부분에 집중해야 하는지를 판단하는 것이기 때문에 적절하지 않다.

Words

☐ quarter
☐ review
☐ objective
☐ identify
☐ accomplishment
☐ achieve
☐ agency
☐ aspiration
☐ checkmark
☐ priority
☐ applause
☐ whoop
☐ holler
☐ session
☐ executive director

Phrases

☐ get together
☐ have/has been Ring
☐ come close to (동)명사
☐ A followed by B
☐ at the end of
☐ between A and B
☐ talk about
☐ puts A next to B
☐ a round of
☐ A be followed by B
☐ be able to R

우선순위 영단어 역대 수능 기출 + 전국 모의고사 기출 + EBS 기출 + 교과서 기출 빈출 어휘

단어	뜻	단어	뜻	단어	뜻
advertising	n. 광고	affection	n. 애정	affectionate	a. 애정 깊은
affliction	n. 고통	affluent	a. 부유한	aftermath	n. (사고 등) 직후의 시기
aggravate	v. 더욱 악화시키다	alertness	a. 기민함	alleviate	v. 경감시키다
along with	~와 함께	alternate	v. 번갈아 일어나다	alternatively	ad. 혹은
altogether	a. 완전히	altruism	n. 이타주의	amass	v. 모으다
amazing	a. 놀라운	amphibian	n. 양서류	ample	a. 풍부한
an array of	일련의 ~	analyst	n. 분석가	anatomy	n. 해부
anchor	v. 정박시키다	angle	n. 시각	anonymity	n. 익명
antenna	n. 안테나	anxious	a. 열망하는	apart from	~은 제외하고
apologize	v. 사과하다	appearance	n. 외모	applause	n. 박수갈채
applicant	n. 지원자	appointment	n. 임용	appraisal	n. 평가
apprehend	v. 파악하다	approximate	a. 대략의	arena	n. 경기장
armchair	a. 이론뿐인	arouse	v. 일으키다	arrogantly	ad. 거만하게
artificially	ad. 인위적으로	aspiring	a. 향학열에 불타는	assault	v. 습격하다
assistant manager	n. 차장	at the same time	동시에	athletic	a. 운동을 잘 하는

변형문제

01 다음 글을 읽고, |조건|에 맞게 주어진 요약문을 완성하시오.

| 조건 |
* (A)는 3단어, (B)는 1단어로 쓸 것
* 본문에 있는 단어만을 사용할 것
* 필요한 경우, 문맥과 어법에 맞게 변형할 것

Every quarter, staff members at Big Brothers/Big Sisters of Santa Clara County get together to review individual and team objectives. Each person talks about what he or she has been doing and identifies how those accomplishments have helped to achieve the agency's aspirations. Then, a staff member puts a checkmark next to each of the goals and priorities (posted on the wall) that each person has helped the agency come closer to realizing. This process is followed by rounds of applause, whoops, and hollers. At the end of the session, says executive director Sheila Kriefels, "We have a visual statement about what we have all been able to accomplish as an agency. This also gives us the chance to notice any gaps between what each of one of us is doing and what we all had said we wanted the agency to achieve, and then where we might need to focus more of our energies in the future to achieve our common vision."

⬇

Employees at Big Brothers/Big Sisters (A) ____________ ____________ ____________ to identify how much they have contributed to the (B) ____________ in order to achieve its goals.

02 다음 글을 읽고, |조건|에 맞게 빈칸 (A), (B), (C)를 채우시오.

| 조건 |
* (A), (B), (C)는 1단어로 쓸 것
* [보기]에서 선택한 단어를 한 번씩만 쓸 것
* 필요한 경우, 문맥과 어법에 맞게 변형할 것

[보기] compare / end / compensate / realize / economical / social / practical / visual / changes / losses / earnings / gaps / years / accept

Every quarter, staff members at Big Brothers/Big Sisters of Santa Clara County get together to review individual and team objectives. Each person talks about what he or she has been doing and identifies how those accomplishments have helped to achieve the agency's aspirations. Then, a staff member puts a checkmark next to each of the goals and priorities (posted on the wall) that each person has helped the agency come closer to (A) ____________. This process is followed by rounds of applause, whoops, and hollers. At the end of the session, says executive director Sheila Kriefels, "We have a (B) ____________ statement about what we have all been able to accomplish as an agency. This also gives us the chance to notice any (C) ____________ between what each of one of us is doing and what we all had said we wanted the agency to achieve, and then where we might need to focus more of our energies in the future to achieve our common vision."

03 다음 글을 읽고, |조건|에 맞게 주어진 요약문을 완성하시오.

| 조건 |

* (A), (B), (C)는 각각 다르게 1단어로 쓸 것
* [보기]에서 선택한 단어를 한 번씩만 그대로 쓸 것

[보기] present / search / gather / differentiate / narrow / modify / observe / survey / point / draw / impose / implement / mark

Every quarter, staff members at Big Brothers/Big Sisters of Santa Clara County get together to review individual and team objectives. Each person talks about what he or she has been doing and identifies how those accomplishments have helped to achieve the agency's aspirations. Then, a staff member puts a checkmark next to each of the goals and priorities (posted on the wall) that each person has helped the agency come closer to realizing. This process is followed by rounds of applause, whoops, and hollers. At the end of the session, says executive director Sheila Kriefels, "We have a visual statement about what we have all been able to accomplish as an agency. This also gives us the chance to notice any gaps between what each of one of us is doing and what we all had said we wanted the agency to achieve, and then where we might need to focus more of our energies in the future to achieve our common vision."

⬇

Workers at Big Brothers/Big Sisters:

(A) ____________ to inspect individual and team objectives → (B) ____________ next to each goal and priority → design a visual statement regarding what accomplishments have been made to (C) ____________ differences between what individuals are performing and what they all expected their agency to succeed.

04 다음 글의 순서로 가장 적절한 것은?

Every quarter, staff members at Big Brothers/Big Sisters of Santa Clara County get together to review individual and team objectives. Each person talks about what he or she has been doing and identifies how those accomplishments have helped to achieve the agency's aspirations.

(A) Then, a staff member puts a checkmark next to each of the goals and priorities (posted on the wall) that each person has helped the agency come closer to realizing. This process is followed by rounds of applause, whoops, and hollers.

(B) At the end of the session, says executive director Sheila Kriefels, "We have a visual statement about what we have all been able to accomplish as an agency.

(C) This also gives us the chance to notice any gaps between what each of one of us is doing and what we all had said we wanted the agency to achieve, and then where we might need to focus more of our energies in the future to achieve our common vision."

① (A) - (B) - (C)　② (A) - (C) - (B)　③ (B) - (A) - (C)
④ (B) - (C) - (A)　⑤ (C) - (A) - (B)

짧은 어구 빈칸

글의 논리	Examples
제목	인간의 인식 능력
주제	인간의 얼굴, 목소리, 사진 등을 인식하는 능력이 사회 활동을 하는 데 도움을 준다.

PRACTICE 01

034 어법 선택 & 연결어

Humans have an **[extraordinary / extraordinarily]** large capacity for **[recognization / recognizing]** faces, voices, and pictures. As we **[wonder / wander]** through a stream of sights, sounds, tastes, odors, and tactile impressions, some novel and some **[previous / previously]** **[experiencing / experienced]**, we have **[few / little]** trouble **[to tell / telling]** the two apart. In a remarkable experiment, participants **[were shown / showed]** 10,000 pictures for five seconds each. Two days **[latter / later]**, they correctly identified 8,300 of **[them / it]**. No computer program to date can perform face recognition as well as a human child can. Why is this? Humans are among the **[little / few]** species **[what / whose]** **[unrelated / unrelating]** members exchange favors, such as trading goods, engaging in social contracts, or **[form / forming]** organizations. If we **[had been / were]** not able to recognize faces, voices, or names, we would not be able to tell **[whom / what]** we'd encountered previously, and (   ), not recall **[who / which]** treated us **[fair / fairly]** and who **[cheating / cheated]**. (   ), social contracts of reciprocity — "I share my food with you today, and you return the favor tomorrow" — **[could not be reinforced / could not reinforce]**.

주제문 인간은 얼굴, 목소리, 사진을 인식하는 능력을 지닌다.

Humans / have an extraordinarily large capacity / (for recognizing faces, voices, and pictures).

(Humans: S 인간은 / have: V / capacity: O 엄청나게 큰 능력을 가지고 있다 / recognizing: 〈동명사〉 / faces: O_1 / voices: O_2 / pictures: O_3 / O 얼굴, 목소리, 그리고 사진을 인식하는)

인간은 얼굴, 목소리, 그리고 사진을 인식하는 엄청나게 큰 능력을 가지고 있다.

노트 ■ a capacity for : ~에 대한 재능

주제문(재진술) 인간은 새로운 것과 경험한 것을 구분할 수 있다.

{As we wander / (through a stream of sights, sounds, tastes, odors, and tactile impressions)}, / (some novel and some previously experienced), / we have little trouble / (telling the two apart).

(As: 〈종·접〉 / we: S / wander: V 우리가 거닐 때 / through: 〈전치사〉 / sights: O_1 / sounds: O_2 / tastes: O_3 / odors: O_4 / impressions: O_5 / O 연속적으로 이어지는 모습, 소리, 맛, 냄새, 그리고 촉각의 인상들 속을 / 〈독립분사구문〉 일부는 새로운 것이고 일부는 이전에 경험한 것인데 / we: S / have: V 우리는 어려움을 / trouble: O 겪지 않는다 / (in) / telling: 〈동명사〉 / the two: O / O 그 두 부류를 구별하는 데)

우리가 연속적으로 이어지는 모습, 소리, 맛, 냄새, 그리고 촉각의 인상들 속을 거닐 때 일부는 새로운 것이고 일부는 이전에 경험한 것인데, 우리는 그 두 부류를 구별하는 데 거의 어려움을 겪지 않는다.

노트
- ■ wander through : ~를 헤매다
- ■ a stream of : ~의 연속, 계속
- ■ tell[know] (the two) apart : (양자를) 구별[분간]하다
- ■ 〈wonder / wander〉

원형	과거	과거분사	현재분사	뜻
wonder	wondered	wondered	wondering	v. 이상하게 여기다
wander	wandered	wandered	wandering	v. 돌아다니다

- ■ 〈독립분사구문 – 문두〉 : 주절의 주어와 다를 경우 분사 앞에 분사의 행위자(주체)를 주격으로 사용함

종속절(→ 독립분사구문)				주절	
종속접속사	주어	동사 : 상황에 맞게 아래처럼 바뀜			
〈그대로 사용하면 의미 강조〉	(주절의 주어와 같으면 생략하고, 다르면 주격으로 사용함)	(being) (having been) 생략 가능	Ring(현재분사)	주어	동사
			p.p.(과거분사)		
			형용사		
			명사		
–	some (of them)	(being)	novel	we	have
			experienced		

- ■ 〈전치사 in이 생략된 경우〉

	목적어			
spend	시간/노력/돈/에너지 등	(in) 생략 가능	동명사	~하는 데 …을 소비하다
waste	돈/시간/재능 등			~하는 데 …을 낭비하다
have	a hard time			~하는 데 어려움을 가지다
	trouble			
	difficulty			
be	busy			~하는 데 바쁘다
There	is no use			~해봐도 소용없다

■ 〈few / a few / a little / little〉

수	few	거의 없는(부정)	+복수N+복수V
	a few	약간(긍정)	
양	a little	약간(긍정)	+단수N+단수V
	little	거의 없는(부정)	

예시 실험에서 참가자들에게 5초 동안 10,000장의 사진을 보여 주었다.

(In a remarkable experiment), / participants(S 참가자들에게) / were shown(V(수동태)) 10,000 pictures(O) / (for five seconds each).

주목할 만한 실험에서 / 10,000장의 사진을 보여 주었다 / 각각 5초 동안

주목할 만한 실험에서 참가자들에게 5초 동안 각각 10,000장의 사진을 보여 주었다.

노트 ■ show+IO+DO : ~에게 …을 보여 주다[수동태 시, S (IO)+be shown +DO]

예시 이틀 후에 확인할 때, 8,300장의 사진을 정확히 확인했다.

(Two days later), / they(S 그들은) / (correctly) identified(V) 8,300 of them(O).

이틀 후에 / 8,300장의 사진을 정확히 확인하였다

이틀 후에 그들은 8,300장의 사진을 정확히 확인하였다.

노트 ■ 〈불규칙적으로 변화하는 중요 형용사와 부사〉

원급	비교급	뜻	최상급	뜻	의미
late	later	나중의	latest	최근의	시간
	latter	후자의	last	최후의	순서

■ 〈혼동 어휘〉

	동사	형용사	명사	부사
correct	정정하다, 교정하다	옳은, 정확한	–	–
correction	–	–	정정, 수정	–
corrective	–	바로잡는, 수정의	–	–
collect	모으다, 수집하다	–	–	–
collection	–	–	수집품, 소장품	–
collective	–	집단의, 공동의	–	–
correctly	–	–	–	바르게, 정확하게
collectively	–	–	–	집합적으로, 총괄하여

주제문(재진술) 인간의 얼굴 인식 능력은 컴퓨터 프로그램보다도 뛰어나다.

No computer program(S 어떤 컴퓨터 프로그램도) (to date)(지금까지) / can perform(V 잘 수행하는 것은 없다) / face recognition(O 얼굴 인식을) / as well as a human child(S) can(V).

인간 아동이 할 수 있는 만큼

지금까지 어떤 컴퓨터 프로그램도 인간 아동만큼 얼굴 인식을 잘 수행하는 것은 없다.

노트 ■ No+명사 : 어떤 명사도 ~하지 않는다

■ to date : 지금까지

■ 〈as well as 의미〉

• 상관접속사로 쓰이는 경우 : A뿐만 아니라 B도 (병렬구조) / as well=too

not only	A	but 주어 also 동사	B	–
=just		but 주어+동사		(as well)
=simply		;(세미콜론) 주어+동사		as well
=merely		,(콤마) 주어+동사		
=alone		.(마침표) 주어+동사		
B as well as A(주어는 B)				

• 동등(원급)비교로 쓰이는 경우 : B만큼 A한

지시부사			접속사/유사관계대명사
as	형용사	원급	as
	부사		

■ 〈대동사 / 생략〉

주어	동사	목적어	〈동등비교〉	주어	대동사
~	can perform	face recognition	as well as	a human child	can.
					=can perform face recognition.

Why is this?

왜일까?

강조 인간은 호의적 행위를 할 수 있는 몇 안 되는 종이다.

Humans(S 인간은) / are(V) (among the few species(선행사)) / (whose(소·관) unrelated(과거분사 관련이 없는) members(명사) exchange(V) favors(O)), / (such as trading(동명사1) goods(O), engaging(동명사2) in social contracts, or forming(동명사3) organizations(O)).

몇 안 되는 종 중의 하나이다 / 구성원들이 호의적 행위를 주고받는 / 물건을 교환하고, 사회적 계약에 참여하고, 또는 조직을 형성하는 것과 같은

인간은 관련이 없는 구성원들 간에 물건을 교환하고, 사회적 계약에 참여하고, 또는 조직을 형성하는 것과 같은 호의적 행위를 주고받는 몇 안 되는 종 중의 하나이다.

노트 ■ A such as B : B와 같은 A

■ engage in : ~에 관여[참여]하다, ~를 ~에 관여[참여]하게 하다

■ 〈between vs. among〉

전치사	between	~ 사이에	둘 사이	혼용
	among		셋 이상	

■ 〈소유격관계대명사 whose〉

	〈소유격관계대명사절〉			
선행사	whose	~~소유격~~	명사	동사 ~
the few species	〈소유격관계대명사〉		unrelated members	exchange
	~~that~~			
	~~what~~			
	~~who~~			
	~~which~~			

강조 인간이 얼굴, 목소리, 사진 등을 인식할 수 없다면 서로 간의 호의를 베풀기 힘들었을 것이다.

(If we were not able to recognize / faces, voices, or names), / we would not be able to tell / (whom we'd encountered previously), / and (as a consequence), / not recall / (who treated us fairly) / and / (who cheated).

(종·접) If, S we, V were not able to recognize (만약 우리가 인식할 수 없다면), O_1 faces, O_2 voices (얼굴, 목소리,), O_3 names (이름을), S we, V_1 would not be able to tell (우리는 구별할 수가 없을 것이며), O: (의문사) whom, S we'd, V encountered previously (누구를 우리가 전에 만났는지를), and (그리고), as a consequence (그 결과), V_2 not recall (기억해내지 못할 것이다), O_1: (의문대명사) who, V treated, O us fairly (누가 우리를 공정하게 대하는지를), and (그리고), O_2: (의문대명사) who, V cheated (누가 우리를 속였는지를)

만일 우리가 얼굴, 목소리, 이름을 인식할 수 없다면 우리는 이전에 만났던 사람이 누구인지를 구별할 수가 없을 것이며 그 결과 누가 우리를 공정하게 대하고 누가 우리를 속였는지를 기억해내지 못할 것이다.

노트
- be able to R : ~할 수 있다
- tell : 분간하다, 구별[식별]하다(=distinguish)
- as a consequence : ~의 결과(로서)
- **〈가정법 과거〉** : 현재 사실에 대한 반대를 가정할 때 사용한다. (만약 ~한다면, …할 텐데.)
  - 종속절과 주절은 서로 자리가 바뀌어도 무관

종속절			주절	
If	주어	동사	주어	동사
		과거형 동사		조동사과거형 (would/should/could/might)+동사원형
		were		
		were to 동사원형		
if	we	were not able to recognize	we	would not be able to tell

- **〈간접의문문〉**
  - 의문대명사 whom으로 이끌리는 경우

		목적어 : 간접의문문		
we	would not be able to tell	whom	we	had encountered
주어	동사	의문대명사	주어	동사

  - 의문대명사 who로 이끌려 대등접속사 and로 병렬구조를 이루는 경우

	목적어1 : 간접의문문				목적어2 : 간접의문문	
recall	who	treated	us	and	who	cheated.
타동사	의문대명사	동사	목적어		의문대명사	동사

- **〈생략〉** : 대등접속사 and로 병렬구조로 공통관계(would not be able to)가 들어 있는 경우

				(생략)	
we	would not be able to	tell	and	(would not be able to)	recall
주어	동사1			동사2	

(Hence), / social contracts (of reciprocity) / — {"I / share my food / (with you) (today), / and you / return the favor (tomorrow)"} / — ______________.

따라서 (Hence), S social contracts (사회적 상호 관계의 계약은), S I (내가), V share, O my food (내 음식을 나누고), with you (너와), today (오늘), and you (그리고 너는), S you, V return, O the favor (그 신세를 갚는다), tomorrow (내일), V ______ (강화될 수 없을 것이다)

따라서, "오늘 내가 내 음식을 너와 나누고 너는 내일 그 신세를 갚아."와 같은 사회적 상호 관계의 계약은 강화될 수 없을 것이다.

노트
- share A with B : A를 B와 나누다

▶ 다음 빈칸에 들어갈 말로 가장 적절한 것은?

① could not be reinforced
② could unintentionally change
③ would happen all the time in society
④ would be usually informal and unwritten
⑤ would be superior to other social contracts

정답 | ①

해석 | ① 강화될 수 없을 것이다
② 의도하지 않게 변할 것이다
③ 사회 안에서 항상 발생할 것이다
④ 대개 비공식적이고 기술되지 않을 것이다
⑤ 다른 사회적 계약보다 우수할 것이다

해설 | ① 이 글의 주제는 인간의 얼굴, 목소리, 사진등을 인식하는 능력이 사회 활동을 하는 데 도움을 준다는 것이다. 그리고 만약 이 인식 능력이 없으면 서로가 서로를 알아보지 못하게 된다고 설명한다. 이 인식 능력이 없으면 서로가 서로를 알아보지 못하게 되면서 사회적 상호 관계의 계약은 에 적절한 말은 ① '강화될 수 없을 것이다'이다. 서로를 인식하지 못하면 계약을 해도 누구랑 했는지 기억하지 못하기 때문이다.

오답 | ② 의도하지 않게 변할 수는 있지만 이 글의 관점은 인식 능력을 통해 사회 활동을 하는 데 도움을 준다는 것이기 때문에 관점이 다르다.
③ 이 글의 필자는 인식 능력 덕분에 사회 활동을 한다고 설명하기 때문에 글의 관점과 반대되는 말이다.
④ 기술되지 않을 수도 있지만 비공식적이라는 말은 글의 소재와 일치하지 않는다.
⑤ 인식 능력이 없으면 사회 활동이 힘들다고 주장하기 때문에 필자의 주장과 반대되는 말이다.

노트 ③ happen
- **〈완전자동사는 수동태 불가〉** : 수동태는 능동태의 목적어가 수동태의 주어로 가는 경우를 말한다. 자동사는 뒤에 목적어를 가지지 못하기 때문에 수동태로 사용할 수 없다. 이러한 주요 완전자동사는 아래와 같다.

work(작용하다)	count(가치가 있다, 중요하다)
matter(문제가 되다, 중요하다)	tell(효력이 있다)
be(있다)	disappear(사라지다)
exist(존재하다)	graduate(졸업하다)
happen(발생하다)	occur(발생하다)
do(충분하다, 적합하다)	pay(이득이 되다)
come(오다)	die(죽다)
go(가다)	ive(살다)
miss(실종되다)	sit(앉다)
sleep(자다)	stand(서다)
stay(머무르다)	swim(수영하다)

⑤ superior to

■ 〈라틴어에서 유래한 비교급 구문〉 : 일반적인 비교급은 뒤에 than(~보다)을 사용하지만 라틴어에서 유래한 형용사의 비교급에서는 than이 아니라 to(~보다)를 사용함에 주의해야 한다.

prefer	to
senior	
junior	
superior	
inferior	
prior	

Words

☐ extraordinarily
☐ capacity
☐ wander
☐ stream
☐ odor
☐ tactile
☐ impression
☐ novel
☐ previously
☐ remarkable
☐ correctly
☐ recognition
☐ species
☐ unrelated
☐ engage in
☐ contract
☐ cheat
☐ hence

Phrases

☐ a capacity for
☐ a stream of
☐ to date
☐ engage in
☐ as a consequence
☐ wander through
☐ tell[know] (the two) apart
☐ A such as B
☐ be able to R
☐ share A with B

우선순위 영단어

역대 수능 기출 + 전국 모의고사 기출 + EBS 기출 + 교과서 기출 빈출 어휘

단어	뜻	단어	뜻	단어	뜻
attainment	n. 달성	attention	n. 돌봄	attest	v. 입증하다
attitude	n. 태도	attorney	n. 법정 대리인	attract	v. 끌다
attune	v. 조율하다	auction	n. 경매	authoritarian	n. 권위주의의
automatic	a. 자동의	autonomous	a. 자율의	availability	n. 유효성
awaken	v. 불러일으키다	bachelor	n. 학사	backbone	n. 중추
backfire	n. 역발	backpack	n. 배낭	balance	v. 균형을 잡다
balanced	균형이 잡힌	bandage	n. 붕대	banish	v. 추방하다
bank account	n. 은행 계좌	barely	ad. 가까스로	be apt to do	~하는 경향이 있다
be bound to	반드시 ~하다	be capable of	~할 능력이 있다	be composed of	~로 구성되다
be concerned with	~에 관심이 있다	be derived from	~에서 파생하다[시작하다]	be immersed in	~에 몰두[열중]하다
be inclined to do	~하는 경향이 있다	be made up of	~로 구성되다	be subject to	~의 대상이다
be true of	~에 적용되다	be up to	~에 종사하다	befriend	v. ~의 친구가 되다
bet	v. 내기를 걸다	better off	a. 유복한	beverage	n. 음료수
bind	v. 제본하다	biologist	n. 생물학자	biology	n. 생명 활동
bits and pieces	n. 이런저런 것들	bombard	v. 퍼붓다	botanical	a. 식물학의
brace	v. 떠받치다	break	n. 균열	break down	무너지다
breeding	n. 교양	bribe	n. 뇌물(을 주다)	brilliance	n. 명석함
bring about	유발[초래]하다	bring up	양육하다	bud	n. 꽃봉오리
built-in	a. 내재된	bulb	n. 구근	bunch	n. (꽃)다발
by definition	당연히	by the same token	같은 이유로	by way of	~하기 위해
bystander	n. 구경꾼	calculation	n. 계산	can afford to	~할 형편이 되다

변형문제

01 다음 글을 읽고, |조건|에 맞게 주어진 제목을 완성하시오.

| 조건 |
* 4단어로 쓸 것
* 본문에 주어진 단어만을 사용할 것
* 필요한 경우, 문맥과 어법에 맞게 변형할 것

Humans have an extraordinarily large capacity for recognizing faces, voices, and pictures. As we wander through a stream of sights, sounds, tastes, odors, and tactile impressions, some novel and some previously experienced, we have little trouble telling the two apart. In a remarkable experiment, participants were shown 10,000 pictures for five seconds each. Two days later, they correctly identified 8,300 of them. No computer program to date can perform face recognition as well as a human child can. Why is this? Humans are among the few species whose unrelated members exchange favors, such as trading goods, engaging in social contracts, or forming organizations. If we were not able to recognize faces, voices, or names, we would not be able to tell whom we'd encountered previously, and as a consequence, not recall who treated us fairly and who cheated. Hence, social contracts of reciprocity — "I share my food with you today, and you return the favor tomorrow" — could not be reinforced.

⬇

The human ____________ ____________ ____________ ____________

02 다음 글을 읽고, |조건|에 맞게 주어진 요약문을 완성하시오.

| 조건 |
* (A), (B)는 각각 다르게 1단어로 쓸 것
* 본문에 있는 단어만을 변형 없이 그대로 사용할 것

Humans have an extraordinarily large capacity for recognizing faces, voices, and pictures. As we wander through a stream of sights, sounds, tastes, odors, and tactile impressions, some novel and some previously experienced, we have little trouble telling the two apart. In a remarkable experiment, participants were shown 10,000 pictures for five seconds each. Two days later, they correctly identified 8,300 of them. No computer program to date can perform face recognition as well as a human child can. Why is this? Humans are among the few species whose unrelated members exchange favors, such as trading goods, engaging in social contracts, or forming organizations. If we were not able to recognize faces, voices, or names, we would not be able to tell whom we'd encountered previously, and as a consequence, not recall who treated us fairly and who cheated. Hence, social contracts of reciprocity — "I share my food with you today, and you return the favor tomorrow" — could not be reinforced.

⬇

The contracts for (A) ____________ interaction cannot be strengthened if humans are unable to (B) ____________ or distinguish who has treated us equitably and who has deceived us.

03 다음 글을 읽고, |조건|에 맞게 주어진 요약문을 완성하시오.

| 조건 |

* (A), (B), (C)는 각각 다르게 1단어로 쓸 것
* [보기]에서 선택한 단어를 한 번씩만 쓸 것
* 필요한 경우, 문맥과 어법에 맞게 변형할 것

[보기] weaken / prosper / strengthen / fail / continue / correct / remember / prioritize / encourage / achieve / teach / detect

Humans have an extraordinarily large capacity for recognizing faces, voices, and pictures. As we wander through a stream of sights, sounds, tastes, odors, and tactile impressions, some novel and some previously experienced, we have little trouble telling the two apart. In a remarkable experiment, participants were shown 10,000 pictures for five seconds each. Two days later, they correctly identified 8,300 of them. No computer program to date can perform face recognition as well as a human child can. Why is this? Humans are among the few species whose unrelated members exchange favors, such as trading goods, engaging in social contracts, or forming organizations. If we were not able to recognize faces, voices, or names, we would not be able to tell whom we'd encountered previously, and as a consequence, not recall who treated us fairly and who cheated. Hence, social contracts of reciprocity — "I share my food with you today, and you return the favor tomorrow" — could not be reinforced.

⬇

Although humans are able to distinguish differences before and after, social interactions cannot be (A) ____________ if recognizing faces (B) ____________ because who has treated fairly and who has deceived us cannot be (C) ____________.

04 다음 문장이 들어갈 부분으로 가장 적절한 곳을 고르시오.

Two days later, they correctly identified 8,300 of them.

Humans have an extraordinarily large capacity for recognizing faces, voices, and pictures. As we wander through a stream of sights, sounds, tastes, odors, and tactile impressions, some novel and some previously experienced, we have little trouble telling the two apart. (①) In a remarkable experiment, participants were shown 10,000 pictures for five seconds each. (②) No computer program to date can perform face recognition as well as a human child can. Why is this? (③) Humans are among the few species whose unrelated members exchange favors, such as trading goods, engaging in social contracts, or forming organizations. (④) If we were not able to recognize faces, voices, or names, we would not be able to tell whom we'd encountered previously, and as a consequence, not recall who treated us fairly and who cheated. (⑤) Hence, social contracts of reciprocity — "I share my food with you today, and you return the favor tomorrow" — could not be reinforced.

짧은 어구 빈칸

글의 논리	Story
제목	동료와 직급이 낮은 사람들과의 관계
주제	직장에서 자신보다 높은 사람 뿐만 아니라 동료와 직급이 낮은 사람들과의 관계를 좋게 형성하는 것이 중요하다.

PRACTICE 02

035 어법 선택 & 연결어

[Remembering / Remember], the dwarves were the ones who saved Snow White when she was down. And **[this / it]** wasn't her pretty face **[what / that]** won their loyalty, but it was her **[hard / hardly]** work. She didn't groan and moan about working as a housekeeper, **[even though / as though]** she was born a princess. She did her work **[cheerful / cheerfully]** and made **[herself / her]** **[indispensable / indispensably]** to the dwarves. And that is **[what / that]** you need to do at your job. Never **[making / make]** the mistake of thinking **[what / that]** only higher-ups can help you. Winning the respect of your peers — and even coworkers who **[is / are]** lower in the company hierarchy — **[is / are]** always worthwhile. If you're having difficulty with your immediate boss, a human resources manager or a senior boss will often consider **[what / that]** others say about you. Peer support can be **[importantly / important]** in **[saving / save]** your situation.

이야기 난쟁이에게 구원을 받은 백설 공주 이야기

Remember(V, 기억하라), / (that) {the dwarves(S, 난쟁이들이) / were(V) the ones(S.C(선행사)) / (who(주·관) saved(V) 백설 공주를 Snow White(O, 구한))(사람이었다는 것을, O) / (when(종·접) she(S) was down(V))(그녀가 힘들 때)}.

백설 공주가 힘들 때 그녀를 구해준 것은 바로 난쟁이들이었다는 것을 기억하라.

노트
- be down : (기분이) 다운되어 있다, (컨디션이) 저하되어 있다
- 〈직접명령문〉

긍정문	R	~해라
	Please+R	~해 주세요
부정문	Don't+R	~하지 마라
	Never+R	

- 〈주격관계대명사절의 수의 일치〉 : 선행사를 포함하고 있는 관계대명사 what 사용 불가

	주격관계대명사절		
선행사	주격관계대명사	~~주어~~	동사
the ones	who		saved

(And)(그리고) / it(S) / wasn't(V) her pretty face(S.C(선행사), 그녀의 예쁜 얼굴이 아니다) / (that(주·관) won(V) their loyalty(O), 그들의 충성심을 얻은 것이), / but it(S) was(V) her hard work(S.C, 아니라 바로 그녀가 열심히 일한 덕분이었다).

그리고 그들의 충성심을 얻은 것은 그녀의 예쁜 얼굴이 아니라 바로 그녀가 열심히 일한 덕분이었다.

노트
- 〈It be A that B 강조구문〉 : B한 것은 바로 A이다

It	be동사	강조하고 싶은 말	that (경우에 따라 아래처럼 바꿔 사용 가능)	
~~This / That / There~~	시제에 따라 달라짐	주어 목적어 보어 부사(구, 절) 〈동사는 사용 불가〉	관계대명사	who
				whom
				which
			관계부사	when
				where
It	wasn't	her pretty face	that(주격관계대명사)	

- 〈상관접속사〉 : 병렬구조

종류				뜻
not	A	but	B	A가 아니라 B (=B, not A)
not only	A	but also	B	A뿐만 아니라 B도 (=B as well as A)
either	A	or	B	A와 B 둘 중 하나
neither	A	nor	B	A와 B 둘 다 아닌
both	A	and	B	A와 B 둘 다

- 〈what vs. that〉

	관계대명사(불완전한 문장)	접속사(완전한 문장)
what	○ 선행사를 포함하고 있기 때문에 what 앞에 선행사 불필요	×
that	○ that 앞에 선행사 필요	○

- 〈hard / hardly〉

hard	형용사	어려운	hardly	부사	거의 ~하지 않는
	부사	열심히			

She(S, 그녀는) / didn't groan(V₁) and moan(V₂)(투덜거리고 불평을 하지 않았다) / (about(전치사) working(동명사) as a(O, 살림을 맡아 해 주는 사람으로)

housekeeper), / (even though she was born a princess).

〈종·접〉 S V S.C 〈유사보어〉

일하는 것에 대해 비록 그녀는 공주로 태어났지만

그녀는 공주로 태어났지만 살림을 맡아 해 주는 사람으로 일하는 것에 대해 투덜거리고 불평을 하지 않았다.

노트
- moan about : ~에 대해 불평하다
- work as : ~으로 일하다
- 〈양보/대조〉

전치사	in spite of	+명사/명사 상당어구	비록 ~이지만
	despite		
종속접속사	though	+주어+동사	
	although		
	even though		
	even if		
	as		
	while		반면에
	whereas		

- 〈even vs. as〉

종속 접속사	even though	+주어+동사	비록 ~이지만	양보/대조
	even if			
	as though		마치 ~처럼	가정법
	as if			

- 〈유사보어=준보어〉 : 두 문장을 한 문장으로 합치면서 불필요한 부분을 삭제하여 그 한 문장의 의미를 빠르게 전달하려는 의도에서 사용한다.

My cat	was	happy	when	it	died.
주어	불완전자동사	형용사(보어)	종속접속사	주어	완전자동사

My cat	died	happy
주어	불완전자동사	형용사(보어)

• 1번째 문장에서 died는 완전자동사로 명백하게 1형식 동사지만 2번째 문장에서 died는 뒤에 보어를 가질 수 있는 마치 불완전자동사로 사용되었다. 이렇듯 1형식 완전자동사가 뒤에 보어를 가져서 마치 2형식 불완전자동사로 사용될 때 사용되는 형용사보어를 유사보어 또는 준보어라고 한다. 여기에서 유사하다는 말고 준하다는 말은 동일하게 똑같다는 말이 아니라 비슷하다는 의미이기 때문에 보어와 동일한 것이 아니라 마치 보어처럼 사용되었다는 의미로 이해하면 된다.

주어	완전자동사	주격보어	~한 상태로 …하다
	die	형용사 명사 현재분사 과거분사	
	break		
	go		
	lay		
	marry		
	live		
	run		
	return		
	sit		
	stand		
	be (born)		
	meet		
	part		

She / did her work / (cheerfully) / and made herself

S V_1 O V_2 O〈재·대〉

그녀는 일했다 활기차게 그리고 자신을 없어서는

indispensable / (to the dwarves).

O.C

안 될 존재로 만들었다 난쟁이들에게

그녀는 활기차게 일했고 난쟁이들에게 없어서는 안 될 존재로 자신을 만들었다.

노트
- do one's work : 직무를 수행하다
- indispensable to : ~에 없어서는 안 되는
- 〈make 상태동사〉 : 수동태 시, be made+주격보어(형용사/명사)

make	목적어	목적격보어	해석
〈상태동사〉	명사/ 명사 상당어구	형용사	~가 …한 상태로 만들다
		명사	
made	herself	indispensable	–

• make가 '~을 …한 상태로 만들다'라는 의미로 사용될 경우, make를 상태동사라 칭한다. 이때 주의사항은 목적격보어 자리에 사용하는 형용사 대신 부사를 사용할 수 없다는 점이다.

- 〈재귀대명사 vs. 대명사〉

		주어와 다름	주어와 동일
주어	~	대명사	재귀대명사
She		you	yourself

강조 당신은 직업에서 백설 공주와 같이 행동을 해야 한다.

(And) / that / is {what you need to do / (at your job)}.

S V 〈목·관〉 S V O

S.C

그리고 그것이 여러분이 해야 할 일이다 직업에서

그리고 그것이 여러분이 직업에서 해야 할 일이다.

노트
- 〈목적격관계대명사 what〉 : 타동사 do의 목적어 없음 / that 사용 불가

	관계대명사절(명사절 : 완전자동사 is의 주격보어)					
완전자동사	~~선행사~~	what	주어	타동사	목적어	
is		목적격관계대명사 선행사를 포함한 관계대명사 (=the thing(s) which/that ~) : ~하는 것(들)은/이	you	need	to do	~~목적어~~

강조 높은 사람들만이 도울 수 있다고 생각하면 안 된다.

(Never) make the mistake / {of thinking / (that only higher-ups can help you)}.

V O 〈동명사〉 〈종·접〉 S V O

O O

절대 실수를 범하지 말라 믿는 높은 사람들만이 여러분을 도울 수 있다고

높은 사람들만이 여러분을 도울 수 있다고 믿는 실수를 범하지 말라.

노트
- Never+R : ~하지 마라
- make the mistake of+동명사 : ~하는 잘못을 저지르다

■ 〈what vs. that〉

	관계대명사(불완전한 문장)	접속사(완전한 문장)
what	○ 선행사를 포함하고 있기 때문에 what 앞에 선행사 불필요	×
that	○ that 앞에 선행사 필요	○

주제문 동료, 그리고 심지어 직급이 낮은 동료들로부터 존경을 받는 것이 좋다.

(Winning the respect of your peers) / — and / {even coworkers / (who are lower / in the company hierarchy)} / — is (always) worthwhile.

(Winning: 〈동명사〉, the respect of your peers: O, 전체: S — 여러분의 동료의 존경을 받는 것은 / and: 그리고 / even: 심지어 / coworkers: 〈선행사〉 동료들로부터 / who: 〈주·관〉 / are: V / lower: S.C 더 낮은 / in the company hierarchy: 회사의 직급에서 / is: V / worthwhile: S.C — 항상 가치 있다)

여러분의 동료, 그리고 심지어 회사의 직급에서 더 낮은 동료들로부터 존경을 받는 것은 항상 가치 있다.

노트 ■ 〈동명사구가 주어 자리에 사용된 경우〉 : 단수 취급으로 동사는 단수동사를 사용함

주어 : 동명사구	삽입구	동사
Winning the respect of your peers	– and ~ –	is

■ 〈주격관계대명사절의 수의 일치〉 : 선행사를 포함하고 있는 관계대명사 what 사용 불가

	주격관계대명사절		
선행사	주격관계대명사	~~주어~~	동사
coworkers	who		are

■ 〈worth 쓰임〉

be	worth	(동)명사		~할 가치가 있다, ~할 보람이 있다
	worthy	of	(동)명사	
	worthwhile		to R	

주제문(강조) 만약 직속 상사와 어려움을 겪으면, 더 높은 사람들은 주변의 사람들의 이야기에 귀 기울일 것이다.

{If you're having difficulty / (with your immediate boss)}, / a human resources manager or a senior boss / will (often) consider / {what others say / (about you)}.

(If: 〈종·접〉 / you: S / 're having: V〈현재진행〉 / difficulty: O — 만약 여러분이 어려움을 겪고 있다면 / with your immediate boss: 직속 상사와 / a human resources manager: S_1 / a senior boss: S_2 — 인사과 매니저나 혹은 더 높은 상사들은 / will consider: V — 자주 고려할 것이다 / what: 〈목·관〉 / others: S / say: V / 전체: O — 다른 사람들이 무엇을 말하는지를 / about you: 여러분에 대해)

여러분의 직속 상사와 어려움을 겪고 있다면, 인사과 매니저나 혹은 더 높은 상사들은 자주 다른 사람들이 여러분에 대해 어떻게 말하는지를 고려할 것이다.

노트 ■ 〈전치사의 목적어로 사용된 목적격관계대명사 what〉 : 선행사를 필요로 하는 that 사용 불가

		관계대명사절(명사절 : 타동사의 목적어)			
타동사	~~선행사~~	what	주어	타동사	~~목적어~~
will consider		목적격관계대명사 선행사를 포함한 관계대명사 (=the thing(s) which/that ~) the things일 경우 : ~하는 것(들)은/이	others	say	

주제문 당신의 상황을 개선하기 위해 동료들의 지지가 중요하다.

________ / can be important / (in saving your situation).

(빈칸: S 동료들의 지지는 / can be: V / important: S.C — 중요할 수 있다 / saving: 〈동명사〉 / your situation: O — 여러분의 상황을 / 전체: 구제함에 있어서)

여러분의 상황을 구제하는 데 동료들의 지지는 중요할 수 있다.

노트 ■ 〈전치사 뒤에 나오는 목적어의 종류〉

전치사구		
전치사	+	목적어
		대명사
		명사
		동명사
		관계대명사 what절
		간접의문문(의문사+주어+동사)

▶ 다음 빈칸에 들어갈 말로 가장 적절한 것은?

① Accurate records ② Peer support
③ Higher level mentors ④ Ambitious goals
⑤ A critical attitude

정답 | ②

해석 | ① 정확한 기록
② 동료들의 지지
③ 높은 수준의 멘토
④ 야심 찬 목표
⑤ 비판적인 태도

해설 | ② 이 글의 주제는 직장에서 자신보다 높은 사람 뿐만 아니라 동료와 직급이 낮은 사람들과의 관계를 좋게 형성하는 것이 중요하다는 것이다. 그리고 빈칸의 앞 문장을 보면 직속 상사와 어려움을 겪으면, 그 이유를 판단하기 위해 주변 사람들의 이야기에 귀 기울일 것이라고 설명한다. 그러므로 주변 사람들의 이야기와 적절한 말을 고르면 ② '동료들의 지지'가 가장 적절하다.

오답 | ① 정확한 기록이 아니라 주변 사람들의 이야기라고 하였으므로 적절하지 않다.
③ 이 글의 관점은 동료와 낮은 사람들과의 관계가 중요하다고 하였으므로 글과 관점이 다르다.
④ 야심 찬 목표는 이 글의 소재와 무관하다.
⑤ 비판적인 태도는 이 글의 소재와 무관하다.

노트 ■ 〈다의어〉

record	동사	기록하다, 녹음(녹화)하다, 표시하다
	명사	기록, 이력, 전과, 성적, 음반
	형용사	기록의, 기록적

■ 〈형용사와 부사〉

high	형용사	높은	highly	부사	매우 (=very)
	부사	높게			

■ 〈혼동 어휘〉

	명사
attitude	태도, 몸가짐, 자세
altitude	고도
aptitude	재능, 소질, 성향, 적성

Words

- ☐ dwarf
- ☐ save
- ☐ loyalty
- ☐ groan
- ☐ moan
- ☐ housekeeper
- ☐ cheerfully
- ☐ indispensable
- ☐ higher-up
- ☐ win
- ☐ respect
- ☐ peer
- ☐ coworker
- ☐ hierarchy
- ☐ worthwhile
- ☐ immediate
- ☐ boss
- ☐ human resources

Phrases

- ☐ be down
- ☐ work as
- ☐ indispensable to
- ☐ moan about
- ☐ do one's work
- ☐ make the mistake of +동명사

우선순위 영단어

역대 수능 기출 + 전국 모의고사 기출 + EBS 기출 + 교과서 기출 빈출 어휘

단어	뜻	단어	뜻	단어	뜻
cap	n. 뚜껑	captive	a. 사로잡힌	carbon dioxide	n. 이산화탄소
care for	돌보다	cargo	n. 화물	carton	n. 큰 상자
casual	a. 격식을 차리지 않는	cathedral	n. 대성당	cause and effect	n. 원인과 결과
cautiously	ad. 신중하게	ceiling	n. 천장	certificate	n. 증명서
chance	n. 기회	chaos	n. 혼돈	characterize	v. 특성을 기술하다
cheat	v. 속이다	chemist	n. 화학자	chest	n. 가슴
chin	n. 턱	choke	v. 숨이 막히다	chronically	ad. 만성적으로
circular	a. 원형의	civilization	n. 문명	clan	n. 씨족
clarity	n. 명확성	cliff	n. 절벽	clip	n. 깎기
close	a. 근소한 차이로	close-knit	a. 긴밀히 연결된	cluster	n. 무리
clutch	n. (자동차의) 클러치	coastal	a. 해안의	coherent	a. 일관성 있는
collision	n. 충돌	color	v. 왜곡하다	combined	a. 결합한
come across	~을 (뜻밖에) 만나다	come upon	~을 갑자기 습격하다	comfortable	a. 편안한
commentary	n. 논평	commodity	n. 필수품	commonly	ad. 흔히
comparatively	ad. 비교적	compensate for	보충하다	complexity	n. 복잡성
comply with	순응하다	comprehensive	a. 종합적인	compress	v. 압축하다
concentrate on	~에 집중하다	conference	n. 회의	confirmation	n. 확인
conflicting	a. 상반되는	consider	v. 고려하다	constrict	v. 수축시키다
constructive	a. 건설적인	consumer	n. 소비자	contaminant	n. 오염물질
continual	a. 계속적인	continuous	a. 끊임없는	contractor	n. 계약자
contributor	n. 원인 제공자	contrive	v. 연구하다	convention	n. 관례
converse	v. 대화하다	coordinate	v. 조화를 이루다	coral	n. 산호
correspond	v. 일치하다	correspond to	~와 일치하다	corrupt	v. 타락시키다

변형문제

01 다음 글을 읽고, |조건|에 맞게 주어진 요약문을 완성하시오.

| 조건 |
* (A)는 3단어, (B)는 2단어로 쓸 것
* 본문에 있는 단어만을 사용할 것
* 필요한 경우, 문맥과 어법에 맞게 변형할 것

Remember, the dwarves were the ones who saved Snow White when she was down. And it wasn't her pretty face that won their loyalty, but it was her hard work. She didn't groan and moan about working as a housekeeper, even though she was born a princess. She did her work cheerfully and made herself indispensable to the dwarves. And that is what you need to do at your job. Never make the mistake of thinking that only higher-ups can help you. Winning the respect of your peers — and even coworkers who are lower in the company hierarchy — is always worthwhile. If you're having difficulty with your immediate boss, a human resources manager or a senior boss will often consider what others say about you. Peer support can be important in saving your situation.

⬇

It is worthwhile (A) ____________ ____________ ____________ by people who are in lower in position and your peers. Especially, (B) ____________ ____________ may be your big help when you encounter difficulty.

02 다음 글을 읽고, |조건|에 맞게 주어진 주제를 완성하시오.

| 조건 |
* (A)는 4단어, (B)는 1단어로 쓸 것
* [보기]에서 선택한 단어를 한 번씩만 쓸 것
* [보기]에서 선택한 단어를 변형하지 말고 그대로 쓸 것

[보기] without / gain / complaints / rise / regardless / compliment / working / purpose / hard / loss / solving / situation

Remember, the dwarves were the ones who saved Snow White when she was down. And it wasn't her pretty face that won their loyalty, but it was her hard work. She didn't groan and moan about working as a housekeeper, even though she was born a princess. She did her work cheerfully and made herself indispensable to the dwarves. And that is what you need to do at your job. Never make the mistake of thinking that only higher-ups can help you. Winning the respect of your peers — and even coworkers who are lower in the company hierarchy — is always worthwhile. If you're having difficulty with your immediate boss, a human resources manager or a senior boss will often consider what others say about you. Peer support can be important in saving your situation.

⬇

(A) ____________ ____________ ____________ ____________ leads to the (B) ____________ of respect from coworkers and those who are low in position.

03 다음 글을 읽고, |조건|에 맞게 빈칸 (A), (B), (C)를 채우시오.

| 조건 |

* (A), (B), (C)는 각각 다르게 1단어로 쓸 것
* [보기]에서 선택한 단어를 한 번씩만 변형하지 말고 쓸 것

[보기] higher-ups / coworkers / organization / hierarchy / salary / worthy / loyal / dispensable / managers / indispensable / records

Remember, the dwarves were the ones who saved Snow White when she was down. And it wasn't her pretty face that won their loyalty, but it was her hard work. She didn't groan and moan about working as a housekeeper, even though she was born a princess. She did her work cheerfully and made herself (A) ____________ to the dwarves. And that is what you need to do at your job. Never make the mistake of thinking that only (B) ____________ can help you. Winning the respect of your peers — and even coworkers who are lower in the company (C) ____________ — is always worthwhile. If you're having difficulty with your immediate boss, a human resources manager or a senior boss will often consider what others say about you. Peer support can be important in saving your situation.

04 다음 문장이 들어갈 부분으로 가장 적절한 곳을 고르시오.

She did her work cheerfully and made herself indispensable to the dwarves.

Remember, the dwarves were the ones who saved Snow White when she was down. (①) And it wasn't her pretty face that won their loyalty, but it was her hard work. (②) She didn't groan and moan about working as a housekeeper, even though she was born a princess. (③) And that is what you need to do at your job. (④) Never make the mistake of thinking that only higher-ups can help you. (⑤) Winning the respect of your peers — and even coworkers who are lower in the company hierarchy — is always worthwhile. If you're having difficulty with your immediate boss, a human resources manager or a senior boss will often consider what others say about you. Peer support can be important in saving your situation.

UNIT 09

짧은 어구 빈칸

글의 논리	Problem & Solution (문제 & 해결)
제목	우선순위를 정하는 이유
주제	성공하기 위해서는 매일 일들의 우선순위를 정하고 그 순위대로 행동해야 한다.

PRACTICE 03

036 어법 선택 & 연결어

[Topple / Toppling] dominoes is pretty straightforward. You line **[it / them]** up and tip over the first one. In the real world, (   ), it's **[a bit / very]** more **[complicating / complicated]**. The challenge is **[what / that]** life doesn't line everything up for us and say, "Here's **[where you should start / where should you start]**." **[Highly / High] [successive / successful]** people know this. (   ) every day they line up their priorities anew, find the lead domino, and whack away at **[them / it]** until it falls. Why does this approach work? **[Because of / Because]** extraordinary success is sequential, not simultaneous. **[What / That]** starts out linear **[becomes / become] [geometrically / geometric]**. You do the right thing and then you do the next right thing. Over time it adds up, and the geometric potential of success **[unleashes / is unleashed]**. The domino effect applies to the big picture, **[likely / like]** your work or your business, and it applies to the smallest moment in each day **[which / when]** you're trying **[deciding / to decide] [which / what]** to do next.

일반적인 사실 도미노를 쓰러뜨리는 일은 간단하다.

(Toppling dominoes) / is (pretty) straightforward.
〈동명사〉 O / S / V / S.C
도미노를 쓰러뜨리는 일은 / 꽤나 단순하다

도미노를 쓰러뜨리는 일은 꽤나 단순하다.

노트 ■ 〈동명사구가 주어 자리에 사용된 경우〉 : 단수 취급으로 동사는 단수동사를 사용함

주어 : 동명사구	동사
Toppling dominoes	is

일반적인 사실 도미노는 줄을 맞춰 세우고 첫 번째 것을 쓰러뜨리면 된다.

You / line them up / and tip over the first one.
S / V_1 / O / V_2 / O
당신은 그것들을 줄에 맞춰 세우고 / 첫 번째 것을 쓰러뜨리면 된다

그것들을 줄에 맞춰 세우고 첫 번째 것을 쓰러뜨리면 된다.

노트
■ line A up : A를 줄에 맞춰 세우다
■ tip over : ~을 뒤집어엎다
■ 〈이어동사〉

타동사	명사	부사	(○)
타동사	부사	명사	(○)
타동사	대명사	부사	(○)
타동사	부사	대명사	(×)
line	up	them	(×)

문제 실제 세상은 도미노와 달리 복잡하다.

(In the real world), / (though), / it's / (a bit) more complicated.
S V / S.C
실제 세상에서는 / 하지만 / 그것은 / 약간 더 복잡하다

하지만 실제 세상에서는 약간 더 복잡하다.

노트 ■ 〈혼동 어휘〉

through	전치사	~을 통하여
throughout	전치사	[장소] ~의 도처에, [시간] ~ 동안, ~ 내내
	부사	도처에, 완전히, 철저하게
though	접속사	~에도 불구하고
thorough	형용사	철저한, 완전한

■ 〈비교급 vs. 원급 강조〉 : 훨씬 더

비교급 강조 표현	원급 강조 표현
much, even, still, by far, far, a lot, lots, a great deal	very, so, quite, really, extremely, too

근거 삶은 시작점을 알려주지 않는다.

The challenge / is / {that life doesn't line everything up / (for us) / and / say, / "Here's / (where you should start)}."
S / V / 〈종·접〉 S / V_1 / O / S.C / V_2 / V / 〈의문사〉 S V / S
문제는 / 이다 / 삶은 모든 것을 줄 세우고 / 우리를 위해 / 그리고 / 말하지 않는 다는 것이다 / "여기서부터 / 시작하면 돼."

문제는 삶은 우리를 위해 모든 것을 줄 세우고 "여기서부터 시작하면 돼."라고 말해 주지 않는다는 것이다.

노트 ■ 〈what vs. that〉

	관계대명사(불완전한 문장)	접속사(완전한 문장)
what	○ 선행사를 포함하고 있기 때문에 what 앞에 선행사 불필요	×
that	○ that 앞에 선행사 필요	○

■ 〈There/Here is 도치구문〉

긍정문	There	is	단수 주어	~이 있다
		are	복수 주어	
부정문	There	is no	단수 주어	~이 없다
		are no	복수 주어	

• 유도부사 **there**와 함께 도치구문을 이루는 be동사(is/are/was/were) 대신에 완전자동사 **appear**, **come**, **exist**, **follow**, **live**, **stand** 등을 사용할 수 있다.

■ 〈간접의문문 – 의문대명사 whom으로 이끌리는 경우〉

		주격보어 : 간접의문문		
유도부사	동사	의문사	주어	동사
Here	is	where	you	should start

주장 성공한 사람들은 삶이 시작점을 알려주지 않는 것을 알고 있다.

Highly successful people / know this.
S: 매우 성공한 사람들은 / V O: 이것을 알고 있다

매우 성공한 사람들은 이것을 알고 있다.

노트 ■ 〈high / highly〉

high	형용사	높은
	부사	높게
	명사	높은 곳
highly	부사	매우(=very)

■ 〈succeed 어휘 변화〉

	동사	명사	형용사	부사
succeed	성공하다	–	–	–
success	–	성공	–	–
successor	–	후임자, 상속자	–	–
successful	–	–	성공적인	–
successive	–	–	연속적인	–
successfully	–	–	–	성공적으로
successively	–	–	–	연속하여, 잇따라서

주제문(해결책) 성공한 사람들은 매일 자신의 우선순위를 세우고, 우선순위에 맞게 행동한다.

(So) / (every day) / they / line up their priorities / (anew), / find the lead domino, / and / whack away at it / (until it falls).
그래서 / 매일 / S: 그들은 / V_1 O: 우선순위를 줄 세우고 / 새롭게 / V_2 O: 선두의 도미노를 찾아라 / 그리고 / V_3: 그것을 철썩 때려 / O / 〈종·접〉 S V: 쓰러뜨린다

그래서 매일 그들은 자신의 우선순위를 새롭게 줄 세우고, 선두의 도미노를 찾고, 그것을 철썩 때려 쓰러뜨린다.

노트 ■ whack away at : ~을 찰싹 치다

■ 〈find / found〉

원형	과거	과거분사	현재분사	뜻
find	found	found	finding	v. 발견하다, 알다
found	founded	founded	founding	v. 설립하다

해결책에 대한 근거1 성공은 순차적으로 일어난다.

Why / does this approach / work?

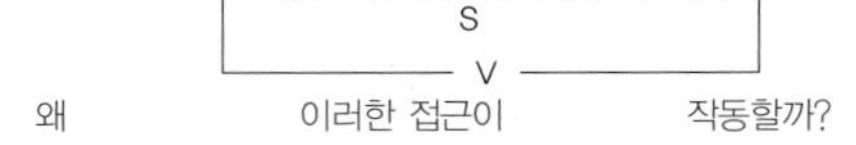

왜 / S: 이러한 접근이 / V: 작동할까?

이러한 방식이 왜 작동할까?

(Because extraordinary success / is ______________ / ______________).
〈종·접〉 S: 왜냐하면 비범한 성공은 / V / $S.C_2$: 순차적이기 때문이다 / $S.C_1$: 동시에 일어나는 것이 아니라

비범한 성공은 동시에 일어나는 것이 아니라 순차적이기 때문이다.

노트 ■ 〈원인/이유〉 : ~ 때문에

전치사	because of	+(동)명사 / 명사 상당어구
	due to	
	for	
	on account of	
	owing to	
	thanks to	
종속접속사	as	+주어+동사 ~
	because	
	now(that)	
	since	

■ 〈상관접속사〉 : 병렬구조

종류				뜻
not	A	but	B	A가 아니라 B (=B, not A)
not only		but also		A뿐만 아니라 B도 (=B as well as A)
either		or		A와 B 둘 중 하나
neither		nor		A와 B 둘 다 아닌
both		and		A와 B 둘 다

주장 성공은 기하급수적으로 증가한다.

(What starts out / linear) becomes geometric.
〈주·관〉 V / S: 선형으로 시작된 것이 / V S.C: 기하급수적이 된다

선형으로 시작된 것이 기하급수적이 된다.

노트 ■ start out : 시작하다

■ 〈관계대명사 what〉 : 관계대명사 what절이 주어로 사용되면 동사는 주로 단수동사 사용함, 관계대명사 that/which 사용 불가

주격관계대명사절 : 명사절(주어)				
~~선행사~~	what	~~주어~~	start out	동사
	선행사를 포함한 관계대명사 (=the thing(s) which/that ~) : ~하는 것은/이		동사	becomes

주장 우선순위대로 행동하면 된다.

You / do the right thing / and (then) / you / do the next
S: 여러분은 / V O: 옳은 일을 한다 / 그리고 나서 / S: 당신은 / V O: 다음의 옳은 것을

right thing.
하게 된다

여러분은 옳은 것을 하고 나면 다음의 옳은 것을 하게 된다.

노트 ■ do the right thing : 올바른[적절한] 일을 하다

주장 시간이 흐르면 기하급수적으로 성공의 잠재력이 커진다.

(Over time) / it adds up, / and / the geometric potential (of success) / is unleashed.

(Over time): 시간이 흘러 / it: S, 이것은 / adds up: V, 쌓인다 / and: 그리고 / the geometric potential: S, 기하급수적인 잠재력이 / (of success): 성공의 / is unleashed: V〈수동태〉, 펼쳐지게 된다

시간이 흘러 이것은 쌓이고 기하급수적인 성공의 잠재력이 펼쳐지게 된다.

노트 ■ over time : 오랜 시간에 걸쳐, 시간이 지나면서, 시간이 흐르는 동안
■ add up : (조금씩) 늘어나다

주장 도미노 효과는 사소한 일에도 적용된다.

The domino effect applies / (to the big picture), / (like your work or your business), / and / it applies / (to the smallest moment) / (in each day) / (when you're trying / to decide what to do next).

The domino effect: S, 도미노 효과는 / applies: V, 적용된다 / (to the big picture): 큰 그림에 / like: 〈전치사〉 / your work: O_1 / your business: O_2 / (like your work or your business): 여러분의 일이나 사업과 같은 / and: 그리고 / it: S / applies: V / it applies: 그것은 적용된다 / (to the smallest moment): 가장 작은 순간에도 / (in each day): 매일의 / when: 〈관·부〉 / you: S / 're trying: V〈현재진행〉 / when you're trying: 당신이 노력하는 순간 / to decide what to do next: O / what to do next: O〈의문사〉, 다음번에 무슨 일을 할지 결정하는

도미노 효과는 여러분의 일이나 사업과 같은 큰 그림에 적용되고, 다음번엔 무슨 일을 할지 결정하려고 노력하는 매일의 가장 작은 순간에도 적용된다.

노트 ■ apply to+(동)명사 : ~에 적용되다
■ 〈간접의문문 - to부정사의 목적어로 사용된 간접의문문〉

to부정사	목적어		
to decide	〈간접의문문〉 : 명사절		
	의문사	to	R
	what	to	do

■ 〈혼동하기 쉬운 어휘〉

likely	형용사	~일 것 같은 (be to 동사원형 : ~일 것 같다)
	부사	아마(probably)
alike	서술적 형용사 (보어로만 사용, 명사 수식 불가)	동일한
	부사	똑같이
like	전치사	~처럼
	동사	좋아하다

■ 〈try 동사 쓰임〉

try	to R	~노력/시도하다(S의 의지 있음)
	Ring	시험 삼아 한번 해보다(S의 의지 없음)

■ 〈관계부사〉 : 선행사와 관계부사는 서로 같이 사용할 수도 있고 둘 중 하나는 생략할 수도 있다.

용도	선행사	관계부사	전치사+관계대명사
시간	the time	when	in/at/on+which
장소	the place	where	in/at/on+which
이유	the reason	why	for which
방법	(the way)	how	in which
	the way how는 같이 사용 못함, the way, the way in which, the way that은 사용 가능 (how 대신에 사용되는 that은 관계부사 대용어라고 함)		

▶ 다음 빈칸에 들어갈 말로 가장 적절한 것은?

① sequential, not simultaneous
② the target you want to reach
③ motivated by not effort but luck
④ different from the domino effect
⑤ triggered by one individual's initiative

정답 | ①

해석 | ① 동시에 일어나는 것이 아니라 순차적이기
② 여러분이 도달하고자 원하는 목표이기
③ 노력이 아니라 운에 의해 조장되기
④ 도미노 효과와는 다르기
⑤ 한 개인의 솔선으로 유발되기

해설 | ① 빈칸의 문장 뒤를 보면, 옳은 것을 하고 난 후에 다음의 옳은 것을 하게 된다고 주장한다. 따라서 순차적으로 진행된다는 말인데, 이 말과 가장 적절한 것은 ① 'sequential, not simultaneous'이다.

오답 | ② 목표라는 소재는 같지만 글쓴이는 우선순위를 정하라는 관점이므로 빈칸에 적절하지 않다.
③ 운에 관한 소재는 글에서 존재하지 않으므로 적절하지 않다.
④ 글쓴이는 도미노 효과를 주장하고 있으므로 글의 내용과 반대된다.
⑤ 한 개인의 솔선으로 유발된다는 내용은 글에 존재하지 않으므로 적절하지 않다.

노트 ■ 〈상관접속사〉
• not A but B : A가 아니라 B(=B, not A)
■ 〈목적격관계대명사 생략〉

선행사	목적격관계대명사 (생략 가능)	주어	타동사	~~목적어~~

■ 〈3형식에서 목적어 자리에 to부정사를 사용하는 경우〉

주어	+	동사	+	목적어	(3)
		refuse, expect, decide, promise, wish, want, hope, manage, fail		to R	

Words

- [ ] topple
- [ ] straightforward
- [ ] complicated
- [ ] anew
- [ ] lead
- [ ] whack
- [ ] linear
- [ ] geometric
- [ ] potential
- [ ] unleash
- [ ] effect
- [ ] apply
- [ ] decide

Phrases

- [ ] line A up
- [ ] whack away at
- [ ] do the right thing
- [ ] add up
- [ ] tip over
- [ ] start out
- [ ] over time
- [ ] apply to＋(동)명사

우선순위 영단어

역대 수능 기출 + 전국 모의고사 기출 + EBS 기출 + 교과서 기출 빈출 어휘

단어	뜻	단어	뜻	단어	뜻
craftsman	n. 장인	craving	n. 갈망	creation	a. 창작
credibility	n. 신뢰성	crew	n. 제작팀	criteria	n. 기준
criterion	n. 기준	crowd	n. 관중	crowd out	~을 몰아내다(밀어내다)
cruelty	a. 잔학(잔인)함	cuisine	n. 요리(법)	customize	v. 개인의 희망에 맞추다
cut back on	~을 줄이다	daunting	a. 엄청난	day care	n. 놀이방
deadly	a. 치명적인	decent	a. 버젓한	deception	n. 속임
decompose	v. 분해시키다	decrease	v. 감소하다	dedicated	a. 헌신적인
defendant	n. 피고인	defense	n. 방어	defensive	a. 방어적인
definitive	a. 한정적인	deflect	v. 방향을 바꾸다	deforestation	n. 산림개간
degradation	n. 훼손	deliberate	a. 의도적인	delivery	n. 배송
democratize	v. ~을 민주화하다	depart	v. 떠나다	depending on	~에 따라
depict	v. 묘사하다	deplete	v. 고갈시키다	derivative	a. 파생적인
derive from	~에서 유래를 찾다	despite	v. ~임에도 불구하고	destination	n. 목적지
destroy	v. 파괴하다	detach	v. 떼어놓다	detached	a. 공정한
detailed	a. 상세한	determined	a. 결심한	deviation	n. (음의) 이탈
diagnostic	a. 진단적인	dialect	n. 방언	diaper	n. 기저귀
differentiate	v. 구분하다	disadvantage	n. 불이익	discrimination	n. 구별
disobedience	n. 불순종	disposition	n. 성향	distinguished	a. 출중한
distributor	n. 분배자	division	n. 분배	do away with	~을 제거하다
documentation	n. 서류	domination	n. 지배	doorway	n. 현관
downside	a. 불리한 면	drag	v. 끌다	drastic	a. 급격한
draw back	n. 약점	drawing	n. 제도	dull	a. 지루한
duration	n. 지속기간	earthworm	n. 지렁이	eccentric	a. 기이한
ecologically	ad. 생태학적으로	economic	a. 경제의	economics	n. 경제력
edit	v. 교정을 보다	editorial	n. 논평	effect	n. 영향
effectively	ad. 사실상	effectiveness	n. 효율성	ego	n. 자존심
electronically	ad. 전자(공학)적으로	elegant	a. 우아한	elude	v. (교묘히) 피하다
embarrassed	a. 당황한	emergency room	n. 응급실	empirical	a. 경험적인
enclosed	a. 둘러싼	encode	v. 암호로 바꾸다	endurance	n. 인내
enduring	a. 지속하는	engaged	a. 관여하는	enrichment	a. 풍부하게 함

변형문제

01 다음 글을 읽고, |조건|에 맞게 주어진 주제문을 완성하시오.

| 조건 |
* (A), (B)는 각각 다르게 1단어로 쓸 것
* 본문에 있는 단어만을 사용할 것
* 필요한 경우, 문맥과 어법에 맞게 변형할 것

Toppling dominoes is pretty straightforward. You line them up and tip over the first one. In the real world, though, it's a bit more complicated. The challenge is that life doesn't line everything up for us and say, "Here's where you should start." Highly successful people know this. So every day they line up their priorities anew, find the lead domino, and whack away at it until it falls. Why does this approach work? Because extraordinary success is sequential, not simultaneous. What starts out linear becomes geometric. You do the right thing and then you do the next right thing. Over time it adds up, and the geometric potential of success is unleashed. The domino effect applies to the big picture, like your work or your business, and it applies to the smallest moment in each day when you're trying to decide what to do next.

⬇

Like you (A) ____________ dominoes, success occurs (B) ____________ one at a time.

02 다음 글을 읽고, |조건|에 맞게 주어진 요약문을 완성하시오.

| 조건 |
* 「The＋비교급＋주어＋동사」 구문을 활용하여 8단어로 쓸 것
* 본문에서 있는 단어를 찾아 그대로 쓸 것

Toppling dominoes is pretty straightforward. You line them up and tip over the first one. In the real world, though, it's a bit more complicated. The challenge is that life doesn't line everything up for us and say, "Here's where you should start." Highly successful people know this. So every day they line up their priorities anew, find the lead domino, and whack away at it until it falls. Why does this approach work? Because extraordinary success is sequential, not simultaneous. What starts out linear becomes geometric. You do the right thing and then you do the next right thing. Over time it adds up, and the geometric potential of success is unleashed. The domino effect applies to the big picture, like your work or your business, and it applies to the smallest moment in each day when you're trying to decide what to do next.

⬇

Given that success is sequential, the more people do the right thing, ________ ________ ________ ________ ________ ________ ________ ________. Potentials of success are therefore developed over time and can be applied to business as well as plans.

03 다음 글의 순서로 가장 적절한 것은?

Toppling dominoes is pretty straightforward. You line them up and tip over the first one. In the real world, though, it's a bit more complicated. The challenge is that life doesn't line everything up for us and say, "Here's where you should start."

(A) The domino effect applies to the big picture, like your work or your business, and it applies to the smallest moment in each day when you're trying to decide what to do next.

(B) Because extraordinary success is sequential, not simultaneous. What starts out linear becomes geometric. You do the right thing and then you do the next right thing. Over time it adds up, and the geometric potential of success is unleashed.

(C) Highly successful people know this. So every day they line up their priorities anew, find the lead domino, and whack away at it until it falls. Why does this approach work?

① (A) - (B) - (C)
② (B) - (A) - (C)
③ (B) - (C) - (A)
④ (C) - (A) - (B)
⑤ (C) - (B) - (A)

04 다음 문장이 들어갈 부분으로 가장 적절한 곳을 고르시오.

Over time it adds up, and the geometric potential of success is unleashed.

Toppling dominoes is pretty straightforward. You line them up and tip over the first one. In the real world, though, it's a bit more complicated. The challenge is that life doesn't line everything up for us and say, "Here's where you should start." Highly successful people know this. (①) So every day they line up their priorities anew, find the lead domino, and whack away at it until it falls. Why does this approach work? (②) Because extraordinary success is sequential, not simultaneous. (③) What starts out linear becomes geometric. (④) You do the right thing and then you do the next right thing. (⑤) The domino effect applies to the big picture, like your work or your business, and it applies to the smallest moment in each day when you're trying to decide what to do next.

UNIT 10

긴 어구 빈칸

글의 논리	Enumeration (열거)
제목	주위의 기준에 자신의 믿음을 결정하는 경향
주제	우리의 믿음은 주변 사람들에 영향을 받는다.

수능 ANALYSIS

037 어법 선택 & 연결어

We all care **[that / what]** those around us think, and our beliefs about the world **[is / are]** strongly **[influencing / influenced]** by our peers. ( ), when it comes to the crunch, **[almost / most]** people would rather **[like / be liked]** **[to / than]** **[are / be]** right, and they tend **[adjusting / to adjust]** their beliefs to the norms of those around **[it / them]**. This is particularly **[apparently / apparent]** in the case of fashion, **[which / where]** we take our cues from other people about **[that / what]** is 'cool.' We may also think **[that / what]** various forms of questionable behaviour — such as **[illegal / illegally]** **[downloaded / downloading]** music or tax evasion — **[is / are]** acceptable on the grounds **[what / that]** 'everybody does **[them / it]**.' ( ), since we tend **[to read / reading]** things **[that / what]** **[reflects / reflect]** our prejudices and **[associates / associate]** with people who **[share / shares]** our **[altitudes / attitudes]**, we sometimes overestimate the extent **[to which / which]** other people think as we **[are / do]**. This is **[known / knowing]** **[for / as]** the *false consensus effect*.

주제문 우리의 믿음은 동료에 의해 영향을 받는다.

We all / care {what those (around us) think}, / and /
(S: We all, V: care, O: what those (around us) think — 〈목·관〉 what, S: those, V: think)
우리는 모두 / 우리 주위의 사람들이 생각하는 것을 신경 쓴다 / 그리고

our beliefs (about the world) / are (strongly) influenced / (by our peers).
(S: our beliefs, V〈수동태〉: are influenced)
세상에 대한 우리의 믿음은 / 강하게 영향받는다 / 우리의 동료에 의해

우리 모두는 우리 주위의 사람들이 생각하는 것을 신경 쓰고 세상에 대한 우리의 믿음은 우리의 동료에 의해 강하게 영향받는다.

노트
- be influenced by : ~에 영향을 받다
- 〈타동사의 목적어로 사용된 목적격관계대명사 what〉 : 선행사를 필요로 하는 that/which 사용 불가

	목적격관계대명사절(명사절 : 타동사의 목적어)			
타동사	~~선행사~~ what	주어	타동사	~~목적어~~
care	선행사를 포함한 관계대명사 (=the thing(s) which/that ~) the things일 경우 : ~하는 것(들)은/이	those	think	

주제문(재진술) 대부분의 사람들은 주위 사람들의 기준에 따라 자신의 믿음을 조정한다.

(Indeed), / (when it comes to the crunch), / most people / would rather be liked / than be right, / and / they tend {to ______ / ______ / ______}.
(〈전치사〉 to, O: the crunch; S: most people; V_2: would rather be liked (V〈수동태〉); V_1: be, S.C: right; S: they, V: tend)
사실 / 매우 어려운 상황에 관해서라면 / 대부분의 사람들은 / 환영받으려 하며 / 올바르게 되기보다는 / 그리고 / 그들은 / 자신의 믿음을 조정하는 경향이 있다 / 기준으로 / 자신의 주위에 있는 사람들의

사실, 매우 어려운 상황에 관해서라면 대부분의 사람들은 올바르게 되기보다는 환영받으려 하며 그들은 자신의 주위에 있는 사람들의 기준에 따라 자신의 믿음을 조정하는 경향이 있다.

노트
- when it comes to(전치사)+(동)명사 : ~에 관해서 말하자면
- rather A than B : B보다 오히려 A
- tend(자동사)+to R : ~하는 경향이 있다
- adjust A to B : A를 B에 맞추다
- 〈most / almost / mostly〉

	대명사	형용사	부사
most	대부분의 것들(사람들)	대부분의	가장
almost	–	–	거의
mostly	–	–	주로, 일반적으로

열거1 패션 분야에서는 다른 사람들의 반응을 보고 멋있는지 결정한다.

This / is (particularly) apparent / (in the case of fashion), / (where we take our cues / (from other people) / {about (what is 'cool.')}
(S: This, V: is, S.C: apparent; 〈관·부〉 where, S: we, V: take, O: our cues; 〈전치사〉 about, O: what is 'cool' — 〈주·관〉 what, V: is, S.C: cool)
이것은 / 특히 분명한데 / 패션의 경우에 / 그곳은 우리가 단서를 가져오는 곳이다 / 다른 사람들로부터 / '멋지다'라는 것에 대한

이것은 특히 패션의 경우에 분명한데 그곳은 '멋지다'라는 것에 대해 다른 사람들로부터 우리의 단서를 가져오는 곳이다.

노트
- in the case of : ~에 관하여는, ~에 관하여 말하면(=as regards)
- take A from B : B로부터 A를 가져오다
- 〈관계부사 where 용법〉
  - 제한적 용법 : 관계부사 앞에 콤마(,)가 없는 경우

	〈관계부사절〉 : 완전한 절		
선행사	where	주어	동사 ~
장소	~하는		

• 계속적 용법 : 관계부사 앞에 콤마(,)가 있는 경우(there는 선행사를 지칭함)

		〈관계부사절〉 : 완전한 절		
선행사(장소)	콤마(,)	where	주어	동사 ~
fashion		=and there		

■ 〈전치사의 목적어로 사용된 주격관계대명사 what〉 : 선행사가 필요한 주격관계대명사 that/which 사용 불가

전치사	목적어 : 주격관계대명사 what절				
about	~~선행사~~	what	~~주어~~	불완전자동사	주격보어
		주격관계대명사		is	'cool.'

열거2 다양한 형태의 안 좋은 행동들도 다른 사람들이 한다는 이유로 용인하기도 한다.

We (S, 우리는) / may (also) think (V, 또한 생각할지도 모른다) / [that (〈종·접〉) various forms (S, 다양한 형태는) (of questionable behaviour) (의심스러운 행동들의) / — (such as illegally (불법적으로) downloading music (〈동명사〉, O_1) or tax evasion (O_2)) (음악을 다운로드하거나 세금 회피와 같은) / — are (V) acceptable (S.C) (용인되는 것으로) / on the grounds (that (〈종·접〉) 'everybody (S) does (V) it (O).')}] (=〈동격〉, '모든 사람들이 그것을 한다' 라는 이유로)

우리는 또한 불법적으로 음악을 다운로드하거나 세금 회피와 같은 다양한 형태의 의심스러운 행동을 '모든 사람이 그것을 한다' 라는 이유로 용인되는 것으로 생각할지도 모른다.

노트
■ behaviour : (영국식) 행동(미국식 behavior)
■ A such as B : B와 같은 A
■ on the grounds that+주어+동사 : ~라는 근거[이유]로(=on the grounds of+구)
■ 〈what vs. that〉

	관계대명사(불완전한 문장)	접속사(완전한 문장)
what	○ 선행사를 포함하고 있기 때문에 what 앞에 선행사 불필요	×
that	○ that 앞에 선행사 필요	○

■ 〈동격의 that〉 : ~라는 A(관계대명사 which/what 사용 불가)

추상명사 (A)	종속절(명사절 – 완전한 문장)		
	(that)	주어	동사 ~
answer / belief / chance / claim / conclusion / dream / evidence / extent / fact / faith / hope / idea / likelihood / news / notion / pledge / possibility / promise / proposal / question / recognition / reply / request / result / sense / statement / suggestion / testament / theory / view / wickedness 등	종속 접속사 (생략 가능)	–	–

■ 〈주어와 동사의 수의 일치〉
• each / every / any+단수동사

열거3 우리는 우리의 태도와 비슷한 사람과 어울리는 경향이 있기 때문에 객관적으로 보지 못할 수 있다.

(However) (그러나), / {since (〈종·접〉, 때문에) we (S, 우리는) / tend (V) to read things (〈선행사〉) (① 읽는 경향이 있다) / (that (〈주·관〉) reflect (V) our prejudices (O)) (자신의 편견을 반영하는 것들을) / and (그리고) / associate with people (〈선행사〉) (② 사람들과 어울리는 경향이 있기) / (who (〈주·관〉) share (V) our attitudes (O)) (자신의 태도를 공유하는)}, / we (S, 우리는) / (sometimes) (때때로) overestimate (V) the extent (O〈선행사〉) (정도를 과대평가한다) / {to which (〈전치사+주·관〉) other people (S, 다른 사람들도) / think (V) (as (〈종·접〉) we (S) do (V))}. (우리가 생각하는 대로 생각하는)

그러나 우리는 자신의 편견을 반영하는 것들을 읽고 자신의 태도를 공유하는 사람들과 어울리는 경향이 있기 때문에 우리는 때때로 다른 사람들도 우리가 생각하는 대로 생각하는 정도를 과대평가한다.

노트
■ tend(자동사)+to R : ~하는 경향이 있다
■ associate with : ~와 어울리다
■ 〈since의 용법〉

종속접속사	시간	~ 이래 (죽), ~한 때부터 내내
	이유	~이므로, ~이니까
전치사	시간	~ 이래 (죽), ~부터 (내내)
부사	시간	(그때) 이래 (죽), 그 뒤[후] 줄곧

■ 〈주격관계대명사절〉 : 선행사를 포함하고 있는 관계대명사 what 사용 불가

	주격관계대명사절		
선행사	주격관계대명사	~~주어~~	동사
things	that		reflect
people	who		share

■ 〈혼동 어휘〉

	명사
attitude	태도, 몸가짐, 자세
altitude	고도
aptitude	재능, 소질, 성향, 적성

■ 〈extent 용법〉

		〈전치사〉	〈관계대명사〉			
the	extent	to	which	주어	동사 ~	~하는 정도,
	degree	to	which	주어	동사 ~	어느 정도로 ~하는지
the	point	beyond	which	주어	동사 ~	~하는 점을 넘어서
		〈완전한 절〉				

■ 〈대동사〉 : 동사(구)를 대신하는 말

〈동사〉		〈대동사〉
be	→	be
조동사		조동사
일반동사		do, does, did

주어	동사	〈종속절〉		
		종속접속사	주어	〈대동사〉 (=think)
other people	think	as	we	do.

열거4 이것은 '합의성 착각 효과'로 알려져 있다.

This / is known / (as the *false consensus effect*).
S 이것은 / V〈수동태〉 알려져 있다 / '합의성 착각 효과'로

이것은 '합의성 착각 효과'로 알려져 있다.

노트 ■ 〈상태 수동태〉 : 수동의 전치사 by 이외 다른 전치사를 사용하는 경우
• be known by/to/for/as

	과거분사	전치사	뜻
be동사	known	by+수단, 판단	~에 의해서 알려지다
		to+동사원형	~한 것으로 알려져 있다
		to+대상	~에게 알려지다
		for+이유, 근거	~로 알려지다, ~ 때문에 알려지다
		as+자격, 신분	~로서 알려지다

▶ 다음 빈칸에 들어갈 말로 가장 적절한 것은?

① follow facts that are supported by clear evidence
② trust their judgement more than their Peers' opinions
③ clearly distinguish between what they like and dislike
④ adjust their beliefs to the norms of those around them
⑤ put priority on public interests rather than personal gain

정답 | ④

해석 | ① 명백한 증거에 의해 뒷받침되는 사실을 따르는
② 동료의 의견보다 자신의 판단을 믿는
③ 자신이 좋아하는 것과 싫어하는 것을 명백히 구별하는
④ 자신의 주위에 있는 사람들의 기준에 따라 자신의 믿음을 조정하는
⑤ 개인의 이익보다 공공의 이익에 우선순위를 두는

해설 | ④ 이 글의 주제는 우리의 믿음이 주변 사람들에게 영향을 받는다는 것이다. 이러한 주제는 1번째 문장에서 나타난다. 그리고 패션 분야에서 다른 사람들의 반응을 보고 멋있는지 결정한다고 예를 든다. 이러한 내용을 봤을 때, 빈칸에 들어갈 말은 1번째 문장에서 재진술되는 표현이어야 한다. 따라서 주변 사람들에게 영향을 받는다는 표현인 ④가 가장 적절하다.

오답 | ① 글의 주제인 주변 사람들의 영향에 관한 내용과 소재가 일치하지 않으므로 적절하지 않다.
② 위 글의 주제와 논리적으로 반대되는 말이므로 적절하지 않다.
③ 자신이 선호도를 구별하는 것을 할 수 없고 주위에 영향을 받는다는 말이기 때문에 글의 관점과 반대이다.
⑤ 이익이라는 소재는 글의 내용과 적절하지 않다.

노트 ■ 〈주격관계대명사의 수의 일치〉
• follow facts〈선행사〉 that〈주·관〉 are supported ~

선행사	주격관계대명사	주어	동사 ~

• 주격관계대명사는 주어가 없는 경우를 말하고 그 없는 주어와 선행사는 같다. 따라서 선행사와 주격관계대명사절 안에 있는 동사는 '수의 일치'가 되어야 한다.

■ 〈목적격관계대명사 what〉
• clearly distinguish between what〈목·관〉 they like and dislike

선행사	what	주어	타동사	목적어

• 목적격관계대명사 what은 선행사를 포함한 관계대명사로 '~하는 것'으로 해석되고, 뒤에 목적어가 없는 경우를 말한다. 이때 what 대신에 선행사가 필요한 that을 사용할 수 없다.

■ distinguish between A and B : A와 B를 구별하다

Words

☐ care
☐ belief
☐ peer
☐ tend
☐ apparent
☐ cue
☐ questionable
☐ illegally
☐ download
☐ tax
☐ evasion
☐ acceptable
☐ reflect
☐ prejudice
☐ share
☐ attitude
☐ overestimate
☐ effect

Phrases

☐ be influenced by
☐ rather A than B
☐ adjust A to B
☐ take A from B
☐ on the grounds that +주어+동사
☐ when it comes to(전치사) +(동)명사
☐ in the case of
☐ A such as B
☐ associate with
☐ be known as

변형문제

01 다음 글을 읽고, |조건|에 맞게 주어진 주제문을 완성하시오.

| 조건 |

* 6단어로 쓸 것
* 본문에 있는 단어만을 그대로 사용할 것

We all care what those around us think, and our beliefs about the world are strongly influenced by our peers. Indeed, when it comes to the crunch, most people would rather be liked than be right, and they tend to adjust their beliefs to the norms of those around them. This is particularly apparent in the case of fashion, where we take our cues from other people about what is 'cool.' We may also think that various forms of questionable behaviour — such as illegally downloading music or tax evasion — are acceptable on the grounds that 'everybody does it.' However, since we tend to read things that reflect our prejudices and associate with people who share our attitudes, we sometimes overestimate the extent to which other people think as we do. This is known as the *false consensus effect*.

⬇

People tend to act or behave according to ____________ ____________ ____________ ____________ ____________ ____________.

02 다음 글을 읽고, |조건|에 맞게 주어진 주제문을 완성하시오.

| 조건 |

* (A), (B)는 각각 다르게 1단어로 쓸 것
* [보기]에서 선택한 단어를 한 번씩만 쓸 것
* 필요한 경우, 문맥과 어법에 맞게 변형할 것

[보기] hands / interests / bother / away / priority / support / values / surround / intimidate / assist / eyes

We all care what those around us think, and our beliefs about the world are strongly influenced by our peers. Indeed, when it comes to the crunch, most people would rather be liked than be right, and they tend to adjust their beliefs to the norms of those around them. This is particularly apparent in the case of fashion, where we take our cues from other people about what is 'cool.' We may also think that various forms of questionable behaviour — such as illegally downloading music or tax evasion — are acceptable on the grounds that 'everybody does it.' However, since we tend to read things that reflect our prejudices and associate with people who share our attitudes, we sometimes overestimate the extent to which other people think as we do. This is known as the *false consensus effect*.

⬇

We have our (A) ____________ on what people (B) ____________ us think and our beliefs are also strongly influenced by others.

03 다음 글을 읽고, |조건|에 맞게 주어진 요약문을 완성하시오.

| 조건 |
* (A), (B), (C)는 1단어로 쓸 것
* [보기]에서 선택한 단어를 한 번씩만 쓸 것
* 필요한 경우, 문맥과 어법에 맞게 변형할 것

[보기] unconscious / conscious / constant / gradual / slow / excessive / regulate / analyze / mirror / change / investigate / worry / form / revise

We all care what those around us think, and our beliefs about the world are strongly influenced by our peers. Indeed, when it comes to the crunch, most people would rather be liked than be right, and they tend to adjust their beliefs to the norms of those around them. This is particularly apparent in the case of fashion, where we take our cues from other people about what is 'cool.' We may also think that various forms of questionable behaviour — such as illegally downloading music or tax evasion — are acceptable on the grounds that 'everybody does it.' However, since we tend to read things that reflect our prejudices and associate with people who share our attitudes, we sometimes overestimate the extent to which other people think as we do. This is known as the *false consensus effect*.

⬇

We are seriously (A) ______________ about what other people think. For instance, we commonly decide what to wear by looking at the fashion of others. But most of us sometimes (B) ______________ estimate the extent to which other people think because we seem to get along with those who share our attitudes and look at things that (C) ______________ our prejudices.

04 다음 글을 읽고, |조건|에 맞게 빈칸 (A), (B)를 채우시오.

| 조건 |
* (A)는 1단어, (B)는 2단어로 쓸 것
* [보기]에서 선택한 단어를 한 번씩만 쓸 것
* 필요한 경우, 문맥과 어법에 맞게 변형할 것

[보기] crunch / evasion / to / regulation / when / grounds / it / the / penalty / reduction / come / understandings / estimation

We all care what those around us think, and our beliefs about the world are strongly influenced by our peers. Indeed, when it comes to the crunch, most people would rather be liked than be right, and they tend to adjust their beliefs to the norms of those around them. This is particularly apparent in the case of fashion, where we take our cues from other people about what is 'cool.' We may also think that various forms of questionable behaviour — such as illegally downloading music or tax (A) ______________ — are acceptable on (B) ______________ ______________ that 'everybody does it.' However, since we tend to read things that reflect our prejudices and associate with people who share our attitudes, we sometimes overestimate the extent to which other people think as we do. This is known as the *false consensus effect*.

UNIT 10

긴 어구 빈칸

글의 논리	Problem & Solution (문제 & 해결)
제목	개인보다 집단일 때의 힘
주제	각각의 능력은 집단에서 협력을 통해 더 큰 효과를 발휘한다.

PRACTICE 01

038 어법 선택 & 연결어

The source of every new idea is the same. There **[are / is]** a network of neurons in the brain, and then the network shifts. (　　　　), electricity flows in an unfamiliar pattern, a shiver of current across a circuit board of cells. (　　　　) sometimes a single network isn't enough. Sometimes a creative problem is **[such / so]** difficult **[that / what]** it requires people **[to connect / connecting]** **[its / their]** imaginations together; the answer arrives only if we collaborate. That's **[why / because]** a group is not just a **[correction / collection]** of individual talents. (　　　　), it is a chance **[for / of]** those talents to exceed **[them / themselves]**, to produce something greater than anyone thought **[possible / possibly]**. **[Then / When]** the right people come together and when they collaborate in the right way, **[that / what]** happens can often **[feel / feel like]** magic. (　　　　) it's not magic. There **[are / is]** a reason **[which / why]** some groups are more than the sum of **[its / their]** parts.

일반적인 사실 새로운 생각이 이루어지는 과정

The source (of every new idea) / is the same.
(S: 모든 새로운 생각의 원천은 / V / S.C: 동일하다)

모든 새로운 생각의 원천은 동일하다.

There is / a network (of neurons) / (in the brain), / and (then) / the network shifts.
(있다 V / S 신경 세포로 이루어진 망이 / 뇌 속에는 / 그리고 / S 그 망은 V 달라진다)

뇌 속에는 신경 세포로 이루어진 망이 있는데 게다가 그 망은 달라진다.

노트 ■ 〈There is 도치구문〉

긍정문	There	is	단수 주어	~이 있다
		are	복수 주어	
부정문	There	is no	단수 주어	~이 없다
		are no	복수 주어	

• 유도부사 **there**와 함께 도치구문을 이루는 be동사(is/are/was/were) 대신에 완전자동사 **appear**, **come**, **exist**, **follow**, **live**, **stand** 등을 사용할 수 있다.

(All of a sudden), / electricity / flows (in an unfamiliar pattern), / (a shiver of current) / (across a circuit board of cells).
(갑자기 / S 전기가 / V 낯선 패턴으로 흐르는데 / =〈동격〉 즉 이는 전류의 떨림이다 / 〈전치사〉 O 세포로 이루어진 회로판 전체에 흐르는)

갑자기 전기가 낯선 패턴으로 흐르는데, 이는 세포로 이루어진 회로판 전체에 흐르는 전류의 떨림이다.

노트 ■ (all) of a sudden : 불시에, 불쑥, 갑자기(=suddenly)
■ a shiver of : ~의 떨림
■ 〈동격〉 : A(명사), B(명사) (A가 주어, B라는 A)

동격(B라는 A)		
명사(A)	,(콤마)	명사(B)
an unfamiliar pattern		a shiver of current

문제 제기 이 과정만으로는 충분하지 않다.

(But) / (sometimes) / a single network / isn't enough.
(그러나 / 때때로 / S 단 하나의 망으로는 / V S.C 충분하지 않다)

그러나 때때로 단 하나의 망으로는 충분치 않다.

주제문 하나의 망으로는 힘들 때, 협력을 통해서 해결할 수 있다.

(Sometimes) / a creative problem / is so difficult / {(that it requires / people to connect their imaginations together; / the answer / arrives / (only if we collaborate)}.
(때때로 / S 창의적인 문제는 / V S.C 너무 어려워서 / 〈종·접〉 S 그것은 / V 필요로 한다 / O 사람들이 O.C 상상한 것을 함께 연결시키는 / S 그 답은 / V 도달한다 / 〈종·접〉 S V 우리가 협력할 때만)

때때로 창의적인 문제는 너무 어려워서 그것은 사람들이 상상한 것을 함께 연결시키는 것을 필요로 한다. 그 답은 우리가 협력할 때만 도달한다.

노트 ■ 〈원인과 결과를 동시에 나타내는 표현〉 : '너무 ~해서 그 결과 …하다' (종속접속사 that 생략 가능)

원인(너무 ~해서)				결과(그 결과 ~하다)		
so	형용사	a(n)+명사		(that)	주어	동사 ~
such	a(n)	형용사	명사	that	주어	동사 ~

결과	so	(that)	원인
원인	, so	(that)	결과

■ 〈what vs. that〉

	관계대명사(불완전한 문장)	접속사(완전한 문장)
what	○ 선행사를 포함하고 있기 때문에 what 앞에 선행사 불필요	×
that	○ that 앞에 선행사 필요	○

■ 〈5형식 불완전타동사의 목적격보어〉 : 수동태 전환 시, 2형식 문장(be p.p.+to R)

주어	불완전타동사	목적어	목적격보어
–	advise / allow / ask / assume / beg / cause / command / compel / condition / decide / design / drive / enable / encourage / expect / forbid / force / instruct / intend / invite / lead / like / motivate / order / permit / persuade / predispose / pressure / program / push / require / teach / tell / train / trust / urge / want / warn / wish 등	–	to 동사원형

■ 〈혼동 어휘〉

	명사	형용사	동사
imagine	–	–	상상하다
imagination	상상력	–	–
imaginary	–	가상의	–
imaginable	–	상상할 수 있는	–
imaginative	–	상상력이 있는	–

이유 집단이 단순히 개별적인 사람들의 모임이 아니기 때문이다.

That's (because a group / is not just a collection of individual talents).

S V 〈종·접〉 S V S.C

왜냐하면 집단은 단순히 재능이 있는 개별적인 사람들의 모임이 아니기 때문이다

그것은 집단이 단순히 재능이 있는 개별적인 사람들의 모임이 아니기 때문이다.

노트 ■ 〈This/That is because(because of) vs. This/That is why〉

This	is	because	주어	동사 ~
결과		원인		

This	is	why	주어	동사 ~
원인		결과		

■ 〈원인/이유〉 : ~ 때문에

전치사	because of	+(동)명사 / 명사 상당어구
	due to	
	for	
	on account of	
	owing to	
	thanks to	
종속접속사	as	+주어+동사 ~
	because	
	now(that)	
	since	

주제문(재진술) 집단은 각각의 사람들이 자신을 능가하게 만들어준다.

(Instead), / it / is a chance / (for those talents) / (to exceed themselves), / (to produce something greater / than anyone thought possible).

S V S.C 〈의·S〉 O〈재·대〉 O S V O.C

그 대신에 그것은 기회이다 재능이 있는 사람들이 자신들을 능가하는 즉 더 큰 일을 만들어 낼 수 있는 기회이다 어느 누가 가능하다고 생각했던 것보다

대신에 그것은 그런 재능 있는 사람들이 자신들을 능가하는, 즉 가능하다고 어느 누가 생각했던 것보다 더 큰 일을 만들어낼 수 있는 기회이다.

노트 ■ 〈가주어 it ~ 의미상의 주어 for+목적격 ~ 진주어 to R 구문〉

가주어	동사	의미상의 주어	진주어
It (This/That/There 사용 불가)		for+목적격	to 동사원형
it	is	for those talents	to exceed

■ 〈재귀대명사 vs. 대명사〉

주어	~	주어와 다름 대명사	주어와 동일 재귀대명사
those talents		them	themselves

■ 〈형용사의 후치 수식〉

〈후치 수식〉	–thing	+형용사	○
	–body		
	–one		
〈전치 수식〉	형용사+	–thing	×
		–body	
		–one	

■ 〈불완전타동사+목적어+목적격보어[to be 보어(명사/형용사)]〉 : 수동태 문장 전환 시, 'be p.p.+주격보어[(to be) 보어(명사/형용사)]' 구조로 2형식이 된다.

주어	불완전타동사	목적어	목적격보어
–	assume / announce / believe / claim / conceive / consider / declare / deem / feel / find / guess / hold / imagine / intend / presume / proclaim / prove / show / suppose / take / think / wish / discover / imagine / know	–	(to be) 보어

■ 〈유사관계대명사 than〉 : 우등비교급(–er than)일 경우

			〈유사관계대명사〉 : 목적격				
to produce	something	greater	than	anyone	thought	~~목적어~~	possible.
		〈우등비교급〉		주어	동사		목적격보어

주제문(재진술) 협력을 통해서 더 큰 일을 만들 수 있다.

(When the right people come together) / and / {when

〈종·접〉 S V 〈종·접〉

적절한 사람들이 합쳤을 때 그리고

they collaborate / (in the right way)}, / (what happens)
S V 〈주·관〉 V / S

그들이 협력할 때 적절하게 벌어지는 일은

/ can (often) feel like magic.
V O

종종 마술처럼 느껴질 수 있다

적절한 사람들이 합치고 그들이 적절하게 협력할 때 벌어지는 일은 종종 마술처럼 느껴질 수 있다.

노트
- come together : (하나로) 합치다
- in the right way : 적절한 방법으로
- feel like+(동)명사 : ~처럼 느끼다
- 〈관계대명사 what〉 : 관계대명사 what절이 주어로 사용되면 동사는 주로 단수동사 사용함, 선행사가 필요한 관계대명사 that/which 사용 불가

주격관계대명사절 : 명사절(주어)				
~~선행사~~	what	~~주어~~	동사	동사
	선행사를 포함한 관계대명사 (=the thing(s) which/that ~) : ~하는 것은/이		happens	can feel

- 〈감각동사〉

감각동사	주격보어(S.C)	
feel, look, seem, sound, taste, appear, smell	형용사(분사 : 현재분사/과거분사)	
	명사	
	like(전치사)	(that)+주어+동사
		(동)명사
	~~alike~~	
	~~likely~~	

- 〈혼동하기 쉬운 어휘〉

likely	형용사	~일 것 같은 (be to 동사원형 : ~일 것 같다)
	부사	아마(probably)
alike	서술적 형용사 (보어로만 사용, 명사 수식 불가)	동일한
	부사	똑같이
like	전치사	~처럼
	동사	좋아하다

주제문(강조) 일부 집단이 구성원들의 합을 넘어설 수 있다.

(But) / it's not magic.
S V S.C

하지만 마술이 아니다

하지만 그것은 마술이 아니다.

There is / a reason / (why ______
V S 〈관·부〉 S / V

있는 것이다 이유가 일부 집단들이 그들의 구성원의 합을 넘어서는

______).

일부 집단들이 그들의 구성원들의 합을 넘어서는 이유가 있는 것이다.

노트
- 〈관계부사〉 : 선행사와 관계부사는 서로 같이 사용할 수도 있고 둘 중 하나는 생략할 수도 있다.

용도	선행사	관계부사	전치사+관계대명사
시간	the time	when	in/at/on+which
장소	the place	where	in/at/on+which
이유	the reason	why	for which
방법	(the way)	how	in which
	the way how는 같이 사용 못함, the way, the way in which, the way that은 사용 가능 (how 대신에 사용되는 that은 관계부사 대용어라고 함)		

▶ 다음 빈칸에 들어갈 말로 가장 적절한 것은?

① imagination is considered crucial for creativity
② labor division practices aren't more resonable
③ creative ways of thinking sometimes do wonders
④ some groups are more than the sum of their parts
⑤ we must determine what talents individuals in a group have

정답 | ④

해석 | ① 상상력은 창의성에 중요한 것으로 여겨지는
② 노동 분업 관행은 더 합당하지 않은
③ 때때로 창의적인 사고방식은 기적을 행하는
④ 일부 집단들이 그들의 구성원들의 합을 넘어서는
⑤ 우리는 집단 내의 개인들이 어떠한 재능을 가지고 있는지를 결정해야 하는

해설 | ④ 이 글의 주제는 5번째 문장에서 나타난다. 이 글의 주제는 각각의 능력은 집단에서 협력을 통해 더 큰 효과를 발휘한다는 것이다. 그리고 빈칸 문장 앞의 문장을 보면 적절한 사람들이 합치고 협력할 때 벌어지는 일들이 마술처럼 느껴질 수 있다고 한다. 이 같은 글의 흐름을 보았을 때, 빈칸에 들어갈 말은 협력을 통해 큰 효과를 발휘한다는 말인 ④가 적절하다.

오답 | ① 상상력은 이 글의 소재와 전혀 일치하지 않으므로 적절하지 않다.
② 분업에 관한 내용이 아니라 협력에 관한 내용이므로 글의 소재가 반대이다.
③ 창의적인 사고방식은 이 글의 주 소재가 아니므로 적절하지 않다.
⑤ 집단 내의 개인들의 능력이 아니라 개인들이 집단에서 협력할 때에 발산되는 효과에 관한 내용이므로 글의 주제와 반대되는 말이다.

노트
- 〈5형식 문장이 2형식으로 수동태 전환〉
  - imagination is considered crucial for creativity
    S V S.C

주어	불완전타동사	목적어	목적격보어
–	consider	–	형용사(구)
	believe		
	feel		
	find		
	keep		
	leave		
	make		

- 불완전타동사 consider 동사류는 목적격보어 자리에 형용사를 가지는 5형식 문장으로 사용된다. 목적어가 주어로 자리 이동이 되면 수동태 문장이 되는데 이때 동사는 be p.p.가 되고 원래 사용된 목적격보어 자리에 있던 형용사가 그대로 주격보어(S.C)로 자리 이동을 하게 된다. 이때 주의할 점은 그 주격보어 자리에 사용된 형용사 대신에 부사를 사용할 수 없다.

■ 〈목적격관계대명사 what〉

• we must determine what〈의문형용사〉 talents individuals in a group have

선행사	what	주어	타동사	목적어

• 목적격관계대명사 what은 선행사를 포함한 관계대명사로 '~하는 것'으로 해석되고, 뒤에 목적어가 없는 경우를 말한다. 이때 what 대신에 선행사가 필요한 that을 사용할 수 없다.

■ 〈what의 용법〉

	용법	품사적 기능	명사 수식	해석
what	관계형용사	명사절 (S, O, C)	what+명사	~한 모든
	의문형용사			무슨, 어떤
	관계대명사		×	~하는 것

Words

- ☐ source
- ☐ network
- ☐ brain
- ☐ shift
- ☐ electricity
- ☐ unfamiliar
- ☐ pattern
- ☐ shiver
- ☐ current
- ☐ circuit
- ☐ cell
- ☐ require
- ☐ connect
- ☐ imagination
- ☐ collaborate
- ☐ collection
- ☐ talent
- ☐ exceed
- ☐ produce

Phrases

- ☐ (all) of a sudden
- ☐ come together
- ☐ feel like+(동)명사
- ☐ a shiver of
- ☐ in the right way

우선순위 영단어 역대 수능 기출+전국 모의고사 기출+EBS 기출+교과서 기출 빈출 어휘

단어	뜻	단어	뜻	단어	뜻
entire	a. 전체의	entrance	n. 입구	entry	n. 참가
environmentalist	n. 환경주의자	equal	n. 동등한 것	erode	v. 침식하다
erroneous	a. 잘못된	estimated	a. 추정된	evaporation	n. 증발
excavate	v. 발굴하다	excellent	a. 뛰어난	excuse	n. 이유
execute	v. 처형하다	existence	n. 존재	existential	a. 실존주의적
expansion	n. 확장	exploration	n. 탐험	face	v. ~을 향하다
facial expression	n. 얼굴 표정	factor	n. 요인	fancy	a. 멋진
far from	~와 거리가 먼	fascinate	v. 마음을 사로잡다	fat	n. 지방
fatal	a. 치명적인	feedback	n. 피드백	fellow	n. 사람
fertilize	v. (난자를) 수정시키다	fetch	v. (가서) 가져오다	fiction	n. 소설
fieldwork	n. 야외 연구	filter	n. 필터	financing	n. 재정
finding	n. 결과	fingertip	n. 손가락 끝	firsthand	a. 직접적인
fixed	a. 고정된	flame	v. (얼굴이) 확 붉어지다	flavoring	n. 향료
flaw	n. 결점	flawless	a. 흠이 없는	fleeting	a. 순식간의
flicker	v. 깜빡이다	for one thing	우선 한 가지 이유는	force	n. 힘
form	n. 문서의 양식	formerly	ad. 이전에	formula	n. 유아용 유동식
fortunately	ad. 다행히도	fossil	n. 화석	free	v. 시간을 주다
frighten	v. 겁먹게 하다	fundamentally	ad. 근본적으로	fungus	n. 균류
further	v. 발전[성공]시키다	galaxy	n. 은하	gallop	v. 전속력으로 달리다
game	n. 사냥감	gathering	n. 채집	gaze	v. 뚫어지게 보다
gene	n. 유전자	generally	ad. 일반적으로	genetically	ad. 유전적으로
geographer	n. 지리학자	geological	a. 지질학의	germ	n. 세균

변형문제

01 다음 글을 읽고, |조건|에 맞게 주어진 주제문을 완성하시오.

조건
* (A), (B)는 각각 다르게 1단어로 쓸 것 * 본문에 있는 단어를 찾아 쓸 것 * 필요한 경우, 문맥과 어법에 맞게 변형할 것

The source of every new idea is the same. There is a network of neurons in the brain, and then the network shifts. All of a sudden, electricity flows in an unfamiliar pattern, a shiver of current across a circuit board of cells. But sometimes a single network isn't enough. Sometimes a creative problem is so difficult that it requires people to connect their imaginations together; the answer arrives only if we collaborate. That's because a group is not just a collection of individual talents. Instead, it is a chance for those talents to exceed themselves, to produce something greater than anyone thought possible. When the right people come together and when they collaborate in the right way, what happens can often feel like magic. But it's not magic. There is a reason why some groups are more than the sum of their parts.

⬇

When (A) ____________ people in a group exceed themselves by close (B) ____________, the answer to a creative problem is found.

02 다음 글의 순서로 가장 적절한 것은?

The source of every new idea is the same. There is a network of neurons in the brain, and then the network shifts. All of a sudden, electricity flows in an unfamiliar pattern, a shiver of current across a circuit board of cells.

(A) But sometimes a single network isn't enough. Sometimes a creative problem is so difficult that it requires people to connect their imaginations together; the answer arrives only if we collaborate.

(B) That's because a group is not just a collection of individual talents. Instead, it is a chance for those talents to exceed themselves, to produce something greater than anyone thought possible.

(C) When the right people come together and when they collaborate in the right way, what happens can often feel like magic. But it's not magic. There is a reason why some groups are more than the sum of their parts.

① (A) - (B) - (C)　② (A) - (C) - (B)　③ (B) - (A) - (C)
④ (B) - (C) - (A)　⑤ (C) - (A) - (B)

03 다음 글을 읽고, |조건|에 맞게 주어진 요약문을 완성하시오.

| 조건 |

* (A), (B)는 각각 다르게 1단어로 쓸 것
* [보기]에서 선택한 단어를 한 번씩만 쓸 것
* 필요한 경우, 문맥과 어법에 맞게 변형할 것

[보기] unity / engage / decide / challenge / imagine / surpass / devote / overcome / assess / overvalue / struggle

The source of every new idea is the same. There is a network of neurons in the brain, and then the network shifts. All of a sudden, electricity flows in an unfamiliar pattern, a shiver of current across a circuit board of cells. But sometimes a single network isn't enough. Sometimes a creative problem is so difficult that it requires people to connect their imaginations together; the answer arrives only if we collaborate. That's because a group is not just a collection of individual talents. Instead, it is a chance for those talents to exceed themselves, to produce something greater than anyone thought possible. When the right people come together and when they collaborate in the right way, what happens can often feel like magic. But it's not magic. There is a reason why some groups are more than the sum of their parts.

⬇

A creative but difficult problem is solved not only when people cooperate each other, but also when appropriate people or talented people (A) ______________ and (B) ______________ themselves in the right manner.

04 다음 문장이 들어갈 부분으로 가장 적절한 곳을 고르시오.

That's because a group is not just a collection of individual talents.

The source of every new idea is the same. There is a network of neurons in the brain, and then the network shifts. All of a sudden, electricity flows in an unfamiliar pattern, a shiver of current across a circuit board of cells. (①) But sometimes a single network isn't enough. (②) Sometimes a creative problem is so difficult that it requires people to connect their imaginations together; the answer arrives only if we collaborate. (③) Instead, it is a chance for those talents to exceed themselves, to produce something greater than anyone thought possible. (④) When the right people come together and when they collaborate in the right way, what happens can often feel like magic. (⑤) But it's not magic. There is a reason why some groups are more than the sum of their parts.

UNIT 10

긴 어구 빈칸

글의 논리	Story
제목	강아지가 혼자 있을 때 우는 이유
주제	강아지에게 소리를 내지 않도록 훈련하는 것이 아니라 혼자 있을 때 편안하게 느끼도록 훈련시켜야 한다.

PRACTICE 02

039 어법 선택 & 연결어

A puppy will often cry, whine, whimper, or howl when he **[is left / leaves] [lonely / alone]**. This is **[basical / basically]** his way of **[call / calling]** out for attention, of calling out to make sure **[that / which]** you know he is there **[that / and that]** you have not forgotten about him. He feels **[insecurely / insecure]** when he **[is left / leaves] [lonely / alone]**; (   ), when you are out of the house and he is in his crate, or when you are in **[the other / another]** part of the house and he cannot see you. The noise he **[is making / is made]** is an expression of the anxiety he feels at being **[lonely / alone]**, so he needs **[to teach / to be taught] [what / that] [be / being] [lonely / alone] [are / is]** OK. You are not **[actual / actually] [trained / training]** the dog to stop **[to make / making]** noise; you **[are training / are trained]** him **[to feel / feeling] [comfortably / comfortable]** when he is all by **[him / himself]** and **[removing / remove]** the need to make the noise.

이야기 강아지는 혼자 놔두면 울부짖곤 한다.

A puppy / will (often) cry, whine, whimper, or howl //
(S: 강아지는 / V_1 V_2 V_3 V_4: 자주 울거나 칭얼거리거나 낑낑거리거나 울부짖곤 한다)

(when he is left alone).
(〈종·접〉 S V〈수동태〉 S.C: 혼자 놔두면)

강아지는 혼자 놔두면 자주 울거나 칭얼거리거나 낑낑거리거나 울부짖곤 한다.

노트 ■ 〈leave 동사의 쓰임〉 : 수동태 시, be left+주격보어(형용사/Ring/p.p./to R)

leave	목적어	목적격보어	〈5형식〉
		형용사	~을 (어떤 상태) 그대로 두다
		현재분사(Ring) – 능동	
		과거분사(p.p.) – 수동	
		to R	(~)하게 내버려 두다, (~)시키다

■ 〈alone vs. lonely〉

	형용사	서술적 형용사	부사
alone	(명사/대명사 바로 뒤에서 수식하여) ~뿐(only)	혼자의, 고독한	혼자, 홀로
lonely	고독한, 고립된, 외로운	–	–

이야기 강아지는 자신에게 관심을 가져달라고 운다.

This / is (basically) his way / (of calling out for attention), / (of calling out) / [to make sure / {that you know / (that) (he is there)} / and / {that you / have not forgotten / (about him)}].
(S: 이것은 / V / S.C: 기본적으로 그의 방법이다 / ①〈동명사〉: 자신에게 관심을 가져달라고 요청하는 / ②〈동명사〉: 그리고 부르는 / 확인하기 위해 / 〈종·접〉 S V: 여러분이 ... 알고 / O: (that) S V: 그가 거기 있다는 것을 / O_1 / 그리고 / 〈종·접〉 S: 여러분이 / V〈현재완료〉: 잊어버리고 있지 않다는 것을 / O_2 / 그를)

이것은 기본적으로 그가 자신에게 관심을 가져달라고 요청하는 방법이고 여러분이 그가 거기 있다는 것을 알고 여러분이 그를 잊어버리고 있지 않다는 것을 확인하기 위해 부르는 방법이다.

노트 ■ call out for : ~을 몹시 필요로 하다
■ call out : ~를 부르다[호출하다]
■ 〈make sure ~〉 : ~하는 것을 확신하다

make	sure	that	주어	동사 ~
		to R		

■ 〈what vs. that〉

	관계대명사(불완전한 문장)	접속사(완전한 문장)
what	○ 선행사를 포함하고 있기 때문에 what 앞에 선행사 불필요	×
that	○ that 앞에 선행사 필요	○

■ 〈종속접속사 that 생략 불가〉 : 대등접속사로 이어지는 뒤에 있는 종속절에서 종속접속사 that은 생략 불가

		생략 가능			대등 접속사	생략 불가		
주어	완전 타동사	(that)	주어	동사 ~	and	that	주어	동사 ~
		종속절1			but	종속절2		
					or			

이야기 강아지는 혼자 놔둘 때 불안함을 느낀다.

He / feels insecure / (when he is left alone); / (for example), / (when you are out of the house / and / he is in his crate), / or / (when you are / in another part of the house and / he cannot see you).

(He: S 그는 / feels: V / insecure: S.C 불안하게 느낀다 / when: 〈종·접〉 / he: S / is left: V〈수동태〉 / alone: S.C 혼자 놔둘 때 / for example 예를 들면 / when: 〈종·접〉 / you: S / are: V 여러분이 외출 중일 때 / and 그리고 / he: S 그가 / is: V 자기 상자에 있을 때 / or 혹은 / when: 〈종·접〉 / you: S 여러분이 / are: V / 집의 다른 곳에 있거나 / he: S / cannot see: V / you: O 그가 여러분을 보지 못할 때)

혼자 놔둘 때 그는 불안하게 느끼는데 예를 들어 여러분이 외출 중이고 그가 자기 상자에 있을 때나 혹은 여러분이 집의 다른 곳에 있고 그가 여러분을 보지 못할 때가 그런 때이다.

노트 ■ 〈감각동사〉

감각동사	주격보어(S.C)	
feel, look, seem, sound, taste, appear, smell	형용사(분사 : 현재분사/과거분사)	
	명사	
	like(전치사)	(that)＋주어＋동사
		(동)명사
	~~alike~~	
	~~likely~~	

■ 〈혼동하기 쉬운 어휘〉

likely	형용사	~일 것 같은 (be to 동사원형 : ~일 것 같다)
	부사	아마(probably)
alike	서술적 형용사 (보어로만 사용, 명사 수식 불가)	동일한
	부사	똑같이
like	전치사	~처럼
	동사	좋아하다

■ 〈the other vs. another〉

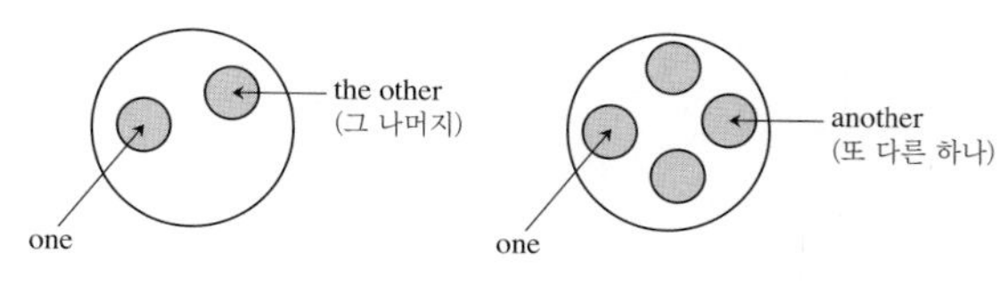

이야기 강아지는 혼자 있는 것이 괜찮다고 배울 필요가 있다.

The noise / (he is making) / is an expression / (of the anxiety) / (he feels at being alone), / so / he needs / {to be taught (that being alone is OK)}.

(The noise: S 소리는 / (목·관 that) / he: S / is making: V〈현재진행〉 그가 내는 / is: V / an expression: S.C 표현이다 / of the anxiety 불안감의 / (목·관 that) / he: S / feels: V 그가 혼자 남겨졌을 때 느끼는 / so 그래서 / he: S / needs: V 그는 배울 필요가 있다 / to be taught: 〈to R 수동〉 / that: 〈종·접〉 / being alone: 〈동명사〉 S / is: V / OK: S.C / O / O 혼자 있는 것이 괜찮다는 것을)

그가 내는 소리는 혼자 남겨졌을 때 그가 느끼는 불안감의 표현이므로 그는 혼자 있는 것이 괜찮다는 것을 배울 필요가 있다.

노트 ■ make a noise[row, scene] : 소란을 피우다

■ 〈목적격관계대명사 that〉 : 타동사의 목적어가 없는 경우 / 선행사를 포함하고 있는 관계대명사 what 사용 불가

선행사 : 주어	〈목적격관계대명사절〉 목적격관계대명사	주어	타동사	~~목적어~~	동사
The noise	that : 〈생략 가능〉	he	is making		is
the anxiety			feels		

■ 〈need 용법〉

목적어(to R)		3형식	〈~할〉 필요가 있다, 〈~〉 해야 하다
목적어	목적격보어(to R)	5형식	〈남이〉 〈~해 줄〉 필요가 있다
동명사(Ring)		3형식	〈사람 · 물건이〉 〈~되어야 할〉 필요가 있다
목적어	목적격보어(p.p.)	5형식	〈~이〉 〈…될〉 필요가 있다, 〈~을〉 〈…되도록 할〉 필요가 있다

■ 〈to R의 태와 시제〉

태	능동태	to R
	수동태	to be p.p.
시제	단순시제 : 본동사 시제와 동일	to R
	완료시제 : 본동사 시제보다 한 시제 앞선 시제	to have p.p.
	완료 수동	to have been p.p.

■ 〈동명사구가 주어 자리에 사용된 경우〉 : 단수 취급으로 동사는 단수동사를 사용함

주어	동사	목적어				
he	needs	to be taught	that	being alone	is	OK.
			종속접속사	주어 : 동명사	동사	주격보어
			to be taught의 목적어			

이야기 당신은 강아지가 혼자 있을 때, 편안함을 느끼도록 훈련을 해주어야 한다.

You / are not (actually) training the dog / to stop making noise; / you / are training him / to feel comfortable / (when he is all by himself) / and / ______________ / ______________.

(You: S 여러분은 / are not training: V〈현재진행〉 / the dog: O 그 개를 훈련하는 것이 아니다 / to stop: O.C 소리를 / making noise 내지 않도록 / you: S 여러분은 / are training: V〈현재진행〉 / him: O 그를 훈련하는 것이다 / to feel 편안하게 / comfortable: O.C 느끼도록 / when: 〈종·접〉 / he: S / is: V / by himself: 〈재·대〉 오로지 혼자 있을 때 / and 그리고 / 필요성을 제거하는 것이다 / 그 소리를 낼)

여러분은 실은 그 개가 소리를 내지 않도록 훈련하는 것이 아니다. 여러분은 그가 오로지 혼자 있을 때 편안하게 느끼도록 훈련하는 것이고 그 소리를 낼 필요성을 제거하는 것이다.

노트 ■ 〈5형식 불완전타동사의 목적격보어〉 : 수동태 전환 시, 2형식 문장(be p.p. ＋to R)

주어	불완전타동사	목적어	목적격보어
–	advise / allow / ask / assume / beg / cause / command / compel / condition / decide / design / drive / enable / encourage / expect / forbid / force / instruct / intend / invite / lead / like / motivate / order / permit / persuade / predispose / pressure / program / push / require / teach / tell / train / trust / urge / want / warn / wish 등	–	to 동사원형

■ 〈stop 동사의 쓰임〉

stop	목적어	〈3형식〉
	to R	~하기 위해서 멈추다
	Ring	~하는 것을 멈추다

■ 〈재귀대명사 vs. 대명사〉

		주어와 다름	주어와 동일
주어	~	대명사	재귀대명사
he		him	himself

■ 〈재귀대명사의 관용적 표현〉

help oneself to ~	~을 마음껏 먹다
enjoy oneself	즐기다
in spite of oneself	자신도 모르게
beside oneself	제정신이 아닌
by oneself	홀로
to oneself	혼자
of oneself	저절로, 제 스스로
for oneself	스스로
of itself	저절로
between ourselves	우리끼리 얘긴데
make oneself understood	~와 의사소통하다

■ 〈공통관계〉: A가 공통

A	(X+Y)	=	AX+AY
A	(X+Y+Z+α)	=	AX+AY+AZ+Aα
(X+Y)	A	=	XA+YA
A	(X+Y+Z)	=	AX+AY+AZ
are	(training+removing)	=	are training ~ and (are) removing ~

▶ 다음 빈칸에 들어갈 말로 가장 적절한 것은?

① giving rewards for good deeds
② raising a sociable dog companion
③ removing the need to make the noise
④ teaching him to act on simple commands
⑤ showing you are not happy with the noise

정답 | ③

해석 | ① 좋은 행동에 대해 보상을 주는
② 사교성이 있는 반려견을 키우는
③ 그 소리를 낼 필요성을 제거하는
④ 그에게 간단한 명령에 따라 행동하도록 가르치는
⑤ 여러분이 그 소리에 불만스럽다는 것을 보여 주는

해설 | ③ 이 글은 강아지가 혼자 있을 때 우는 이유에 대해 설명하는 내용이다. 강아지는 혼자 있을 때 불안함을 느껴 우는 것이기 때문에 소리를 내지 않도록 훈련하는 것보다 혼자 있을 때 편안함을 느껴 소리를 낼 필요가 없게 훈련시켜야 한다고 설명한다. 따라서 이러한 말의 재진술인 것을 찾으면 ③ '소리를 낼 필요성을 제거하는'이 적절하다.

오답 | ① 보상을 주는 것은 이 글의 소재와 알맞지 않는다.
② 같이 있을 경우에는 불안함을 느끼지 않아 울지 않을 수도 있지만 이 글의 주제는 혼자 있을 때 편안함을 느끼게 만들라는 것이므로 글의 관점과 일치하지 않는다.
④ 간단한 명령은 글의 소재인 편안함을 느끼게 만드는 것과 알맞지 않는다.
⑤ 소리를 내지 않도록 훈련하는 것이 아니라고 설명하기 때문에 글의 관점과 일치하지 않는다.

Words

☐ puppy
☐ whine
☐ whimper
☐ howl
☐ alone
☐ attention
☐ forget
☐ feel
☐ insecure
☐ noise
☐ expression
☐ anxiety
☐ train
☐ comfortable
☐ deed
☐ sociable
☐ companion
☐ remove
☐ command

Phrases

☐ call out for
☐ make a noise[row, scene]
☐ call out

우선순위 영단어 역대 수능 기출 + 전국 모의고사 기출 + EBS 기출 + 교과서 기출 빈출 어휘

단어	뜻	단어	뜻	단어	뜻
get rid of	~을 제거하다	get used to	~에 익숙해지다	give rise to	~를 생기게 하다
give way to	굴복하다	glacier	n. 빙하	glare	n. 눈부신 빛

변형문제

01 다음 글을 읽고, |조건|에 맞게 주어진 요약문을 완성하시오.

| 조건 |

* (A)는 3단어, (B)는 1단어, (C)는 2단어로 쓸 것
* 본문에 있는 단어만을 사용할 것
* 필요한 경우, 문맥과 어법에 맞게 변형할 것

A puppy will often cry, whine, whimper, or howl when he is left alone. This is basically his way of calling out for attention, of calling out to make sure that you know he is there and that you have not forgotten about him. He feels insecure when he is left alone; for example, when you are out of the house and he is in his crate, or when you are in another part of the house and he cannot see you. The noise he is making is an expression of the anxiety he feels at being alone, so he needs to be taught that being alone is OK. You are not actually training the dog to stop making noise; you are training him to feel comfortable when he is all by himself and removing the need to make the noise.

↓

The reason why a dog makes a noisy sound when left alone is because (A) ____________ ____________ ____________. To help him overcome his anxiety, make sure he experiences a sense of (B) ____________ rather than restrain him from (C) ____________ ____________.

02 다음 글을 읽고, |조건|에 맞게 주어진 주제문을 완성하시오.

| 조건 |

* (A)는 1단어, (B)는 4단어, (C)는 1단어로 쓸 것
* [보기]에서 선택한 단어를 한 번씩만 쓸 것(단, (B)의 경우, [보기] 외의 1단어를 추가할 것)
* 필요한 경우, 문맥과 어법에 맞게 변형할 것

[보기] to / learn / devise / create / their / experience / own / simplify / on / eliminate / by / avoid / develop / identify

A puppy will often cry, whine, whimper, or howl when he is left alone. This is basically his way of calling out for attention, of calling out to make sure that you know he is there and that you have not forgotten about him. He feels insecure when he is left alone; for example, when you are out of the house and he is in his crate, or when you are in another part of the house and he cannot see you. The noise he is making is an expression of the anxiety he feels at being alone, so he needs to be taught that being alone is OK. You are not actually training the dog to stop making noise; you are training him to feel comfortable when he is all by himself and removing the need to make the noise.

↓

Two solutions for dogs making noisy sound when left alone are firstly, exercising them to (A) ____________ a sense of comfort when (B) ____________ ____________ ____________ ____________ and secondly, (C) ____________ the cause or any factor related to making noise.

03 다음 글의 내용과 일치하지 않는 것은?

A puppy will often cry, whine, whimper, or howl when he is left alone. This is basically his way of calling out for attention, of calling out to make sure that you know he is there and that you have not forgotten about him. He feels insecure when he is left alone; for example, when you are out of the house and he is in his crate, or when you are in another part of the house and he cannot see you. The noise he is making is an expression of the anxiety he feels at being alone, so he needs to be taught that being alone is OK. You are not actually training the dog to stop making noise; you are training him to feel comfortable when he is all by himself and removing the need to make the noise.

① 강아지는 혼자 놔두면 울부짖곤 한다.
② 강아지가 우는 것은 자신에게 관심을 가져달라고 요청하는 것이다.
③ 강아지는 혼자 있을 때 즐겁게 논다.
④ 강아지가 내는 소리는 불안감의 표현이다.
⑤ 강아지가 소리를 내지 않기 위해 편안하게 느끼도록 해야 한다.

04 밑줄 친 부분 중 문맥상 옳지 않은 것은?

A puppy will often cry, whine, whimper, or howl when he is left ① alone. This is basically his way of calling out for attention, of calling out to make sure that you know he is there and that you have not forgotten about him. He feels ② secure when he is left alone; for example, when you are out of the house and he is in his crate, or when you are in another part of the house and he cannot see you. The noise he is making is an expression of the ③ anxiety he feels at being alone, so he needs to be taught that being alone is OK. You are not actually training the dog to ④ stop making noise; you are training him to feel ⑤ comfortable when he is all by himself and removing the need to make the noise.

UNIT 10

긴 어구 빈칸

글의 논리	Question & Answer (질문 & 대답)
제목	단방향 거울의 과학적 원리
주제	취조실에서 사용하는 단방향 거울 속에는 다양한 과학적 원리가 있다.

PRACTICE 03

040 어법 선택 & 연결어

How do one-way mirrors, the ones **[using / used]** in interrogation room, work? A one-way mirror seems to be a mirror when **[seen / seeing]** from one side, but as a window when **[seen / seeing]** from the opposite side. (   ) the window **[disguises / is disguised]** as a mirror to allow secret surveillance. (   ), there **[is / are]** no such thing **[as / that]** a one-way mirror. (   ), the amount of light **[reflecting / reflected]** from one side **[are / is]** the same as **[what / that]** **[reflecting / reflected]** from **[the other / another]**. The light **[transmitting / transmitted]** in one direction **[are / is]** the same as **[that / it]** **[transmitted / transmitting]** in the opposite direction. How then does a one-way mirror work? First, the mirror isn't totally **[reflecting / reflected]**. It transmits half the light and **[reflect / reflects]** **[another / the other]** half. The second requirement has to do with lighting. It is essential **[what / that]** the observation room **[remains / remain]** dark, **[because of / because]** if a lamp **[turned / were turned]** on, some of that light **[would pass / would have passed]** through into the interrogation room as well.

질문 취조실에서 사용되는 단방향 거울의 작동 원리는 무엇인가?

How / do one-way mirrors, / the ones / (used in interrogation room), / work?

(one-way mirrors: S 단방향 거울 / do … work: V / the ones = 〈동격〉 거울 / (which are) used: 〈과거분사〉 / in interrogation room: 취조실에서)

어떻게 / 단방향 거울 / 거울 / 취조실에서 / 사용되는 / 작동하는가?

취조실에서 사용되는 단방향 거울은 어떻게 작동하는가?

노트

■ work : (완전자동사) 작용(작동)하다

■ 〈동격〉 : A(명사), B(명사) (A가 주어, B라는 A)

동격(B라는 A)		
명사(A)	,(콤마)	명사(B)
one-way mirrors		the ones

■ 〈주격관계대명사+be동사 생략〉

명사	(주격관계대명사 +be동사)	현재분사(Ring) – 능동
		과거분사(p.p.) – 수동
		형용사
		부사
		명사
		전치사구
the ones	(which/that are)	used

대답 단방향 거울은 한쪽에서는 거울처럼 보이고, 다른 쪽에서는 창문처럼 보이는 것이다.

A one-way mirror / seems to be a mirror / (when (it is) seen from one side), / but / (as a window) // (when (it is) seen from the opposite side).

(A one-way mirror: S 단방향 거울은 / seems: V / to be a mirror: S.C 거울처럼 보이지만 / when: 〈종·접〉 / seen: 〈과거분사〉 / from one side: 한쪽에서 보면 / but: 하지만 / as a window: 창문처럼 보인다 / when (it is) seen from the opposite side: 반대 방향에서 보면)

단방향 거울은 한쪽에서 보면 거울처럼 보이지만, 반대 방향에서 보면 창문처럼 보인다.

노트

■ 〈seem 동사 쓰임〉

주어	seem	주격보어	(2형식)
		(to be) 보어	~처럼 보이다, 보기에 ~하다; ~인듯하다[것 같다], ~인 것처럼 생각되다
		to R	

■ 〈분사구문 – 문미〉 : 주절과 분사구문의 위치가 서로 바뀌어도 무관

주절		종속절(→ 분사구문)			
주어	동사	종속 접속사	주어	동사 : 상황에 맞게 아래처럼 바뀜	
		〈그대로 사용하면 의미 강조〉	(주절의 주어와 같으면 생략하고, 다르면 주격으로 사용함)	(being) (having been) 생략 가능	Ring(현재분사)
					p.p.(과거분사)
					형용사
					명사
A one-way mirror	seems	when	(it is)		seen from one side
					seen from the opposite side.

부연 설명 비밀스러운 감시 활동을 할 때 사용된다.

(Thus) / the window / is disguised / as a mirror (to allow secret surveillance).

(Thus: 그러므로 / the window: S 이 창문은 / is disguised: V(수동태) 위장된다 / as a mirror: S.C 거울로 / secret surveillance: O / to allow secret surveillance: 비밀스러운 감시활동을 허용하기 위해서)

그러므로 이 창문은 비밀스러운 감시 활동을 하기 위해 거울로 위장된다.

노트 ■ 〈5형식 불완전타동사의 목적격보어〉 : 수동태 전환 시, 2형식 문장(be p.p.+as 보어)

주어	불완전타동사	목적어	목적격보어
–	accept / achieve / announce / characterize / cite / consider / count / deem / define / describe / disguise / identify / interpret / look at / look upon / perceive / praise / present / read / reckon / refer to / recognize / regard / remember / respect / see / speak of / think of / treat / use / view / visualize 등	–	as 보어

부연 설명 물리적으로 단방향 거울은 존재하지 않는다.

(Physically), / ______ / ______.

물리적으로 / 그런 것은 존재하지 않는다 / 단방향 거울이라는

물리적으로, 단방향 거울이라는 것은 존재하지 않는다.

노트 ■ 〈There is 도치구문〉

긍정문	There	is	단수 주어	~이 있다
		are	복수 주어	
부정문	There	is no	단수 주어	~이 없다
		are no	복수 주어	

• 유도부사 **there**와 함께 도치구문을 이루는 be동사(is/are/was/were) 대신에 완전자동사 **appear**, **come**, **exist**, **follow**, **live**, **stand** 등을 사용할 수 있다.

■ 〈such A as B vs. A such as B〉

such	A	as	B	B만큼 그러한 A
A	such	as	B	B와 같은 A

부연 설명 단반향 거울의 과학적 원리

(That is), / the amount of light / (which is) (reflected from one side) / is the same / as that / (which is) (reflected from the other).

S: the amount of light, 〈과거분사〉 reflected, V: is, S.C: the same, 〈지시대명사〉 that, 〈과거분사〉 reflected

즉 / 빛의 총량은 / 한쪽에서 반사되는 / 같다 / 빛의 총량과 / 다른 쪽에서 반사되는

즉 한쪽에서 반사되는 빛의 총량은 다른 쪽에서 반사되는 빛의 총량과 같다.

노트 ■ that is (to say) : 즉[말하자면]

■ 〈유사관계대명사 as〉

the amount of light	reflected ~	the same	as	that	reflected ~
	과거분사		〈유사관계대명사〉	지시대명사(=light)	과거분사

■ 〈the same ~ as / the same ~ that〉

the	same	명사	as	주어	동사	같은 종류의 것
			that			같은 것, 바로 그것, 동일한 것
		as	단어/구/절			~와 같은

• That is the same pen as I lost.
(그것은 내가 잃어버린 펜과 같은 종류의 것이다.)

• That is the same pen that I lost.
(그것은 내가 잃어버린 바로 그 펜이다.)

■ 〈주격관계대명사+be동사 생략〉

명사	(주격관계대명사+be동사)	Ring(현재분사) – 능동
		p.p.(과거분사) – 수동
		형용사
		부사
		명사
		전치사구
the amount of light	(who/that is)	reflected
that	(which is)	

■ 〈the other vs. another〉

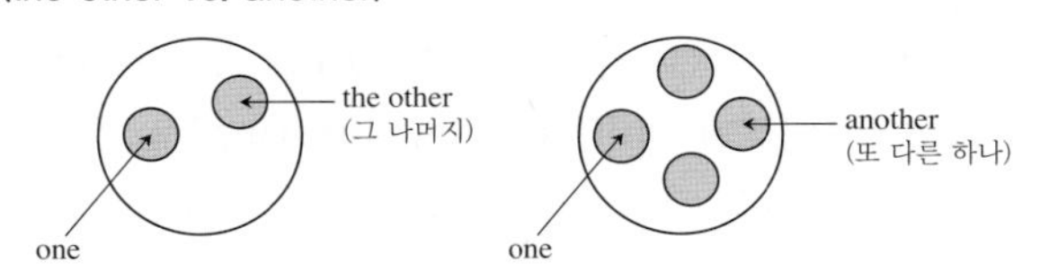

The light / (which is) (transmitted in one direction) / is the same / as that (which is) (transmitted in the opposite direction).

S: The light, 〈과거분사〉 transmitted, V: is, S.C: the same, 〈지시대명사〉 that, 〈과거분사〉 transmitted

빛의 양은 / 한쪽에서 투과되는 / 같다 / 반대쪽에서 투과되는 빛의 양과

한쪽에서 투과되는 빛의 양은 반대쪽에서 투과되는 빛의 양과 같은 것이다.

노트 ■ 〈주격관계대명사+be동사 생략〉

명사	(주격관계대명사+be동사)	Ring(현재분사) – 능동
		p.p.(과거분사) – 수동
		형용사
		부사
		명사
		전치사구
The light	(which/that is)	transmitted
that (=The light)	(which is)	

How / (then) / does a one-way mirror / work?

S: a one-way mirror, V: does ~ work

어떻게 / 그렇다면 / 단방향 거울은 / 작동하는 것일까?

그렇다면, 단방향 거울은 어떻게 작동하는 것일까?

(First), / the mirror / isn't (totally) reflecting.

S: the mirror, V〈현재진행〉: isn't reflecting

먼저 / 그 거울은 / 모든 빛을 반사시키는 것이 아니다

먼저, 그(단방향) 거울은 모든 빛을 다 반사시키는 것이 아니다.

노트 ■ 〈부분부정 vs. 전체부정〉

부분부정	not, never	+	all(모두), always(항상), necessarily(필연적으로), entirely(전적으로), altogether(완전히), exactly(정확히), totally(전체적으로), absolutely(절대적으로), completely(완전히), wholly(완전히)

전체 부정		not any one(=none) (모두 ~이 아니다) no+명사 (어느 누구도 ~ 않다) not ~ either(=neither) (둘 다 ~이 아니다) not+anything(=nothing) (아무것도[단 하나도] (~ 아니다 · 없다)) not+ever(=never) (결코 ~이 아니다) not anywhere(=nowhere)
	no =not any	no more=not ~ anymore nobody=not ~ anybody nothing=not ~ anything no longer=not ~ any longer

It / transmits half the light / and / reflects the other half.
S 단방향 거울은 / V_1 O 절반의 빛만 투과시킨다 / 그리고 / V_2 O 나머지 반은 반사시킨다

단방향 거울은 절반의 빛만 투과시키고 나머지 반은 반사시킨다.

노트 ■ 〈관사의 위치〉

so / how / too / as	형용사	a/an	명사
such / what / many / quite / rather / half	a/an	형용사	명사

The second requirement / has to do with lighting.
S 두 번째 조건은 / V 조명과 관련이 있다 O

두 번째 조건은 조명과 관련이 있다.

노트 ■ have to do with : ~와 관계가 있다, 관련되다
(=be connected [associated] with)

It / is essential / (that the observation room / remain dark), / {because / (if a lamp were turned on), / some of that light / would pass through / into the interrogation room / (as well)}.
S 이것은 / V / S.C 필수적이다 / 〈종·접〉 / S 관찰실은 / V 어두운 상태로 / S.C 유지되어야 하는 것이 / 〈종·접〉 왜냐하면 / 〈종·접〉 S V〈수동태〉〈가정법 과거〉 만약 램프가 켜지면 / 그 빛의 / S 일부가 / V 통과해 들어올 것이기 때문이다 / 취조실 안으로 / 또한

(단방향 거울이 사용될 때,) 관찰실은 어두운 상태로 유지되는 것이 필수적이다. 그 이유는 램프가 켜지면 그 빛의 일부가 취조실 안으로 통과해 들어올 것이기 때문이다.

노트 ■ turn A on : A를 켜다(수동태 시, A be turned on)
■ pass through : ~에 꿰뚫다[관통하다]
■ as well : 또한, 역시
■ 〈조동사 should의 용법〉 : 이성적/감성적 판단형용사

주절				종속절		
주어	동사	형용사		종속접속사		동사
It	be	이성적 판단	natural, right, urgent, vital, essential, necessary, important 등	(that)	주어	(should) 동사원형
		감성적 판단	a pity, strange, stupid, surprising, regrettable 등			

■ 〈what vs. that〉

	관계대명사(불완전한 문장)	접속사(완전한 문장)
what	○ 선행사를 포함하고 있기 때문에 what 앞에 선행사 불필요	×
that	○ that 앞에 선행사 필요	○

■ 〈remain 동사 쓰임〉

remain	주격보어	〈2형식〉
	형용사	[~의 상태로] 여전히 있다; 변함없이 [~의 상태]이다
	현재분사	
	과거분사	

■ 〈원인/이유〉 : ~ 때문에

전치사	because of	+(동)명사 / 명사 상당어구
	due to	
	for	
	on account of	
	owing to	
	thanks to	
종속접속사	as	+주어+동사 ~
	because	
	now(that)	
	since	

▶ **다음 빈칸에 들어갈 말로 가장 적절한 것은?**

① the brightness affects the individual's emotions
② the amount of light can be measured
③ there is no such thing as a one-way mirror
④ one-way mirrors and windows are constructed the same
⑤ reflections from the opposite side are impossible

정답 | ③

해석 | ① 빛의 밝기가 개인의 감정에 영향을 미친다
② 빛의 양은 계량 가능하다
③ 단방향 거울이란 존재하지 않는다
④ 단방향 거울과 창문은 동일하게 구성되어 있다
⑤ 반대 방향에서의 반사는 불가능하다

해설 | ③ 이 글의 주제는 취조실에서 사용하는 단방향 거울 속에는 다양한 과학적 원리가 있다는 것이다. 단방향 거울은 빛의 반사량을 조절시키고 조명을 어둡게 하여 빛이 통과하는 것을 조절한다고 한다. 이러한 내용을 봤을 때, 단방향 거울은 조명이나 빛의 반사량을 조절하지 않으면 양쪽으로 빛이 투과되어 창문같은 존재가 된다는 것이다. 따라서 빈칸에 내용에 가장 적절한 것은 ③ '단방향 거울이란 존재하지 않는다'이다.

오답 | ① 개인의 감정이라는 소재는 글의 내용에 드러나지 않는다.
② 빛의 양은 계량 가능하다는 내용은 사실이지만 이는 원리 중 하나일 뿐이고 두 원리를 통합할 수는 없다.
④ 단방향 거울과 창문은 빛의 반사량이랑 조명으로 조절되어 서로 동일하게 구성되어 있지 않다.
⑤ 반대 방향에서의 반사가 불가능한지는 글의 내용에 나와 있지 않고 글의 소재와 적절하지 않다.

노트 ■ 〈혼동하기 쉬운 동사〉

• affect / effect

affect	vt. ~에게 영향을 주다
effect	n. 결과, 효과 v. 초래하다

• find / found

원형	과거	과거분사	현재분사	뜻
find	found	found	finding	v. 발견하다, 알다
found	founded	founded	founding	v. 설립하다

• wind / wound

원형	과거	과거분사	품사/뜻
wind	wound	wound	vi. 구불거리다, 감다
wound	wounded	wounded	vt. 다치게 하다

• sit / seat / set

원형	과거	과거분사	현재분사	뜻
sit	sat	sat	sitting	vi. 앉다, ~에 놓여 있다
seat	seated	seated	seating	vt. 앉히다
set	set	set	setting	vt. 두다, ~을 놓다

Words

☐ mirror
☐ window
☐ opposite
☐ disguise
☐ allow
☐ secret
☐ physically
☐ amount
☐ reflect
☐ transmit
☐ direction
☐ totally
☐ light
☐ observation
☐ remain
☐ lamp

Phrases

☐ that is (to say)
☐ turn A on
☐ as well
☐ have to do with
☐ pass through

우선순위 영단어 역대 수능 기출 + 전국 모의고사 기출 + EBS 기출 + 교과서 기출 빈출 어휘

단어	뜻	단어	뜻	단어	뜻
glide	v. 활공하다	global	a. 총체적인	glue	n. 아교
gorgeous	a. 멋진	graduate	a. 대학원의	grind	v. 갈다
grip	n. 통제	grow out of	자라면서 ~을 그만두다	guideline	n. 지침
hand in	제출하다	handy	a. 가까이 있는	harass	v. 괴롭히다
hardship	n. 고난	hatch	v. 부화하다	have to do with	~와 관련이 있다
hazard	n. 위험	heal	v. 치유하다	hemisphere	n. 반구
hence	ad. 그러므로	herd	v. 모으다	hold on to	집착하다
hold that	~이라고 믿다[생각하다]	hook	v. 낚싯바늘로 낚다	hop	v. 올라타다
horn	n. 경적 소리	hover	v. 배회하다	humanity	n. 사람의 속성
humidity	n. 습도	humiliate	v. 굴욕감을 주다	hurdle	n. 장애물
ideal	a. 이상	illiteracy	n. 문맹	illumination	n. 조명
immigrant	n. 이민자(의)	immune system	n. 면역체계	impenetrable	a. 들어갈 수 없는
implicate	v. 연루시키다	import	n. 의미	imprint	v. (자국을) 남기다
imprison	v. 투옥하다	in a sense	어떤 점으로는	in detail	상세하게
in effect	실제로	in essence	본질적으로	in exchange for	~ 대신에
in principle	원론적으로	in relation to	~에 관하여	in retrospect	돌이켜 생각해보면
in return	보답으로	incidence	n. 발병	incident	n. 사건
incline	n. 경사면	including	~을 포함하여	incompetent	a. 무능한
inconvenience	n. 불편함	indifference	n. 무관심	indigenous	a. 토착의
indignity	n. 불명예	indispensable	a. 필수 불가결한	industrialization	n. 산업화

변형문제

01 다음 글을 읽고, |조건|에 맞게 빈칸 (A), (B), (C)를 채우시오.

| 조건 |

* 1단어로 쓸 것
* [보기]에서 선택한 단어를 한 번씩만 쓸 것
* 필요한 경우, 문맥과 어법에 맞게 변형할 것

[보기] safe / complete / reflect / cost / darkness / lighting / brightness / fix / lens / design / set / play / disguise / convex / narrow / harden

How do one-way mirrors, the ones used in interrogation room, work? A one-way mirror seems to be a mirror when seen from one side, but as a window when seen from the opposite side. Thus the window is (A) ____________ as a mirror to allow secret surveillance. Physically, there is no such thing as a one-way mirror. That is, the amount of light reflected from one side is the same as that reflected from the other. The light transmitted in one direction is the same as that transmitted in the opposite direction. How then does a one-way mirror work? First, the mirror isn't totally (B) ____________. It transmits half the light and reflects the other half. The second requirement has to do with (C) ____________. It is essential that the observation room remain dark, because if a lamp were turned on, some of that light would pass through into the interrogation room as well.

02 다음 글의 순서로 가장 적절한 것은?

How do one-way mirrors, the ones used in interrogation room, work? A one-way mirror seems to be a mirror when seen from one side, but as a window when seen from the opposite side.

(A) The second requirement has to do with lighting. It is essential that the observation room remain dark, because if a lamp were turned on, some of that light would pass through into the interrogation room as well.

(B) The light transmitted in one direction is the same as that transmitted in the opposite direction. How then does a one-way mirror work? First, the mirror isn't totally reflecting. It transmits half the light and reflects the other half.

(C) Thus the window is disgulised as a mirror to allow secret surveillance. Physically, there is no such thing as a one-way mirror. That is, the amount of light reflected from one side is the same as that reflected from the other.

① (A) - (B) - (C) ② (B) - (A) - (C) ③ (B) - (C) - (A)
④ (C) - (A) - (B) ⑤ (C) - (B) - (A)

03 다음 글을 읽고, |조건|에 맞게 요약문을 완성하시오.

| 조건 |

* (A), (B)는 각각 다르게 1단어, (C)는 2단어로 쓸 것
* [보기]에서 선택한 단어를 한 번씩만 쓸 것(단, (C)의 경우, [보기] 외의 1단어를 추가할 것)
* 필요한 경우, 문맥과 어법에 맞게 변형할 것

[보기] bright / heavy / entire / opposite / rest / last / front / side / associate / convey / measure / create / avoid

How do one-way mirrors, the ones used in interrogation room, work? A one-way mirror seems to be a mirror when seen from one side, but as a window when seen from the opposite side. Thus the window is disgulised as a mirror to allow secret surveillance. Physically, there is no such thing as a one-way mirror. That is, the amount of light reflected from one side is the same as that reflected from the other. The light transmitted in one direction is the same as that transmitted in the opposite direction. How then does a one-way mirror work? First, the mirror isn't totally reflecting. It transmits half the light and reflects the other half. The second requirement has to do with lighting. It is essential that the observation room remain dark, because if a lamp were turned on, some of that light would pass through into the interrogation room as well.

↓

The scientific principles of a one-way mirror are firstly not (A) ____________ light is reflected by the mirror. Only half of light is transmitted by the mirror and the (B) ____________ is reflected by the mirror. Therefore, in order to maintain the darkness of interrogation room, light passing through the room has to (C) ____________ ____________.

04 다음 문장이 들어갈 부분으로 가장 적절한 곳을 고르시오.

That is, the amount of light reflected from one side is the same as that reflected from the other.

How do one-way mirrors, the ones used in interrogation room, work? A one-way mirror seems to be a mirror when seen from one side, but as a window when seen from the opposite side. (①) Thus the window is disgulised as a mirror to allow secret surveillance. (②) Physically, there is no such thing as a one-way mirror. (③) The light transmitted in one direction is the same as that transmitted in the opposite direction. (④) How then does a one-way mirror work? (⑤) First, the mirror isn't totally reflecting. It transmits half the light and reflects the other half. The second requirement has to do with lighting. It is essential that the observation room remain dark, because if a lamp were turned on, some of that light would pass through into the interrogation room as well.

UNIT 11

연결어(구) 넣기

글의 논리	Myth & Truth (통념 & 진실)
제목	더 나은 제동 장치 설치의 결과
주제	ABS를 설치한 차보다 설치하지 않은 차가 더 안전했다.

수능 ANALYSIS

041 어법 선택 & 연결어

In an experiment in Germany, part of a fleet of taxicabs in Munich **[equipped / was equipped]** with antilock brake systems (ABS), a technological innovation **[what / that]** vastly **[improves / improve]** braking. The rest of the fleet **[left / was left]** **[unequipping / unequipped]**, and the two groups **[were placed / placed]** under careful and secret observation for three years. You would expect the better brakes to make for safer driving. ( ), that is exactly the opposite of **[that / what]** happened. **[Give / Giving]** some drivers ABS **[to make / made]** no difference at all in their accident rate; ( ), it turned **[it / them]** into **[marked / markedly]** inferior drivers. They drove faster. They made sharper turns. They braked harder. ( ), the ABS systems were not used to **[reducing / reduce]** accidents; ( ), the drivers used the additional element of safety to enable **[it / them]** **[driving / to drive]** faster and more **[reckless / recklessly]** without **[increasing / increase]** **[its / their]** risk of **[get / getting]** into an accident.

실험 ABS를 설치한 차와 설치하지 않은 차에 대한 실험

(In an experiment) / (in Germany), / part (of a fleet of taxicabs) / (in Munich) / was equipped / (with antilock brake systems (ABS)), / (a technological innovation) / (that vastly improves braking).

한 실험에서 / 독일에서의 / 전체 택시의 일부가(S) / 뮌헨의 / 갖추게 되었다(V〈수동태〉) / 앤티록 제동 장치를 / =〈동격〉 기술의 혁신품인(〈선행사〉) / 제동 장치를 크게 향상시킨 (〈주·관〉 〈부사〉 V O)

독일에서의 한 실험에서, 뮌헨의 전체 택시의 일부에 제동 장치를 크게 향상시킨 기술의 혁신품인 앤티록 제동 장치(ABS)를 갖추게 했다.

노트
- a fleet of : ~ 무리
- be equipped with : ~을 갖추고 있다
- 〈동격〉 : A(명사), B(명사) (B라는 A)

동격(B라는 A)		
명사(A)	,(콤마)	명사(B)
antilock brake systems (ABS)		a technological innovation

- 〈주격관계대명사절의 수의 일치〉 : 선행사를 포함하고 있는 관계대명사 what 사용 불가

	주격관계대명사절		
선행사	주격관계대명사	~~주어~~	동사
a technological innovation	that		improves

The rest of the fleet / was left unequipped, / and / the two groups / were placed / (under careful and secret observation) / (for three years).

나머지 차량에는(S) / 설치되지 않았다(V〈수동태〉 S.C) / 그리고 / 두 그룹이(S) / 받게 되었다(V〈수동태〉) / 주의 깊고 비밀스러운 관찰을 / 3년 동안

나머지 차량에는 설치되지 않았고, 두 그룹이 3년 동안 주의 깊고 비밀스러운 관찰을 받게 되었다.

노트
- 〈주어와 동사의 수의 일치〉
  - A of B : 일반적인 경우에 A가 주어
  - A of B : A가 부분/부분인 경우에 B가 주어

	A	B	
분수	two – thirds 등	주어	동사 (B에 수의 일치)
부분	a group of, all of, a lot of, any of, a number of, both of, each of, either of, few of, half of, many of, most of, much of, neither of, none of, one of, part of, percent of, several of, some of, the rest, two of 등	주어	동사 (B에 수의 일치)
	The rest of	the fleet	~~were~~ was

- 〈leave 동사의 쓰임〉 : 수동태 시, be left+주격보어(형용사/Ring/p.p./to R)

leave	목적어	목적격보어	〈5형식〉
		형용사	~을 (어떤 상태) 그대로 두다
		현재분사(Ring) – 능동	~을 (어떤 상태) 그대로 두다
		과거분사(p.p.) – 수동	~을 (어떤 상태) 그대로 두다
		to R	(~)하게 내버려 두다, (~)시키다

통념 ABS를 설치한 차가 더 안전한 운전에 도움이 될 것이다.

You / would expect / the better brakes / to make for safer driving.

(S 당신은 / V 예상할 것이다 / O 더 향상된 브레이크가 / O.C 더 안전한 운전에 도움이 될 것이라고)

더 향상된 브레이크가 더 안전한 운전에 도움이 될 것이라고 예상할 것이다.

노트
- make for : ~에 도움이 되다
- 〈5형식 불완전타동사의 목적격보어〉 : 수동태 전환 시, 2형식 문장(be p.p. +to R)

주어	불완전타동사	목적어	목적격보어
–	advise / allow / ask / assume / beg / cause / command / compel / condition / decide / design / drive / enable / encourage / expect / forbid / force / instruct / intend / invite / lead / like / motivate / order / permit / persuade / predispose / pressure / program / push / require / teach / tell / train / trust / urge / want / warn / wish 등	–	to 동사원형

진실 ABS를 설치한 차보다 설치하지 않은 차가 더 안전했다.

(A) ( ), / that / is (exactly) the opposite / {of (what happened)}.

(하지만 / S 그것은 / V / S.C 정반대였다 / 〈전치사〉 〈주·관〉 V, O 발생한 일과는)

하지만, 그것은 발생한 일과는 정반대였다.

노트
- be the opposite of : ~와 정반대이다
- 〈관계대명사 what절이 전치사의 목적어로 사용되는 경우〉

전치사	~~선행사~~	주격관계대명사절(명사절 : 목적어)		
		what	~~주어~~	동사
of		선행사를 포함한 관계대명사 (=the thing(s) which/that ~) the things일 경우 : ~하는 것(들)은/이		happened

(Giving some drivers ABS) / made no difference / (at all) / (in their accident rate); / (in fact), / it / turned them / (into markedly inferior drivers).

(〈동명사〉 I.O D.O, S 일부 운전자에게 ABS를 부여한 것은 / V O 차이를 만들지 못했다 / 전혀 / 그들의 사고율에 / 사실 / S 그것은 / V 그들을 O 바꾸었다 / 〈부사〉 〈형용사〉 눈에 띄게 열등한 운전자로)

일부 운전자에게 ABS를 부여한 것은 그들의 사고율에 전혀 차이를 만들지 못했고, 사실, 그것은 그들을 눈에 띄게 열등한 운전자로 만들었다.

노트
- make no difference : 차이가 없다, 문제가 아니다
- in fact : 사실은
- turn A into B : A를 B로 바꾸다

- 〈동명사구가 주어 자리에 사용된 경우〉

주어 : 동명사구	동사
Giving some drivers ABS	made

- 〈at all 쓰임〉

긍정문	여하튼, 어쨌든 간에
부정문	조금도/전혀 ~ 아니다
의문문	도대체
조건문	적어도, 조금이라도

They / drove faster.

(S 그들은 / V 더 빨리 몰았다)

그들은 더 빨리 몰았다.

They / made sharper turns.

(S 그들은 / V O 더 급회전을 했다)

그들은 더 급회전을 했다.

노트
- make a sharp[sudden] turn : 급커브를 틀다

They / braked harder.

(S 그들은 / V 더 심하게 브레이크를 밟았다)

그들은 더 심하게 브레이크를 밟았다.

(B) ( ), / the ABS systems / were not used to reduce accidents; / (instead), / the drivers / used the additional element / (of safety) / {to enable them to drive / faster and more recklessly) / (without increasing their risk / (of getting into an accident)}.

(다시 말해서 / S ABS 시스템은 / V O 사고를 줄이는데 사용되지 않았고 / 그 대신에 / S 운전자들은 / V O 추가적인 요소를 사용했다 / 안전의 / 운전하게끔 O O.C 하기 위해서 / 더 빨리 그리고 더 무분별하게 / 〈전치사〉 그들의 〈동명사〉 O 위험을 증가시키지 않고서 / 〈전치사〉 〈동명사〉 사고에 처할)

다시 말해서, ABS 시스템은 사고를 줄이는 데 사용되지 않았고, 그 대신에 운전자들은 이 추가적인 안전 요소를 사고에 처할 위험을 증가시키지 않으면서 그들이 더 빨리 그리고 더 무분별하게 운전할 수 있도록 하기 위해 이용했다.

노트
- enable＋목적어＋목적격보어(to R) : ~가 …할 수 있게 하다, 가능하게 하다
- get into an accident : 사고를 당하다
- 〈used 용법〉

be	used	to	동사원형(R)	~하는 데 사용되다
be (get/become)	used (accustomed)	to	동명사(Ring)	~ 익숙하다
used		to	동사원형(R)	~하곤 했다

▶ 다음 글의 빈칸 (A), (B)에 들어갈 말로 가장 적절한 것은?

	(A)		(B)
①	However	……	On the contrary
②	However	……	In other words
③	In addition	……	For example
④	In addition	……	On the contrary
⑤	Therefore	……	In other words

정답 | ②

해석 | ① 하지만 – 반대로　② 하지만 – 다시 말해서　③ 게다가 – 예를 들어　④ 게다가 – 반대로　⑤ 그러므로 – 다시 말해서

해설 | ② (A)가 들어간 문장에서, 발생한 일과는 정반대였다고 나오므로 A에는 앞과 대립된다는 말인 'However'가 들어가야 한다. (B)가 들어간 문장에서는 ABS 시스템은 사고를 줄이는 데 사용되지 않고 그 대신 운전자들이 더 무분별하게 운전하였다고 나온다. 앞에 문장을 보면 ABS를 사용한 사람들이 더 빨리 몰고 더 과격하게 운전을 했다고 나오므로 (B)에 들어갈 말은 앞에 말을 재진술 시켜주는 말이 들어가야 한다. 따라서 'In other words'나 'In fact'가 적절하므로 정답은 ②이다.

오답 | (A)가 들어간 문장은 앞 문장과의 인과 관계가 반대이기 때문에 대립해주는 말이 들어가야 하므로 'In addition'과 'Therefore'는 적절하지 않다. 그리고 (B)가 들어간 문장은 앞 문장을 재진술하기 때문에 'On the contrary'와 'For example'은 적절하지 않다.

Words

- ☐ experiment
- ☐ fleet
- ☐ taxicab
- ☐ innovation
- ☐ vastly
- ☐ improve
- ☐ unequipped
- ☐ observation
- ☐ opposite
- ☐ accident rate
- ☐ markedly
- ☐ inferior
- ☐ additional element
- ☐ safety
- ☐ recklessly

Phrases

- ☐ a fleet of
- ☐ make for
- ☐ make no difference
- ☐ turn A into B
- ☐ be equipped with
- ☐ be the opposite of
- ☐ in fact
- ☐ get into an accident

우선순위 영단어 역대 수능 기출 + 전국 모의고사 기출 + EBS 기출 + 교과서 기출 빈출 어휘

단어	뜻	단어	뜻	단어	뜻
infection	n. 전염병	infectious	a. 전염성이 있는	inference	n. 추론
inflict	v. (타격, 고통 등을) 입히다	inform	v. ~에게 알리다	infrared	a. 적외선의
ingenious	a. 독창적인	inheritance	n. 유전성	injustice	n. 불평등
innocent	a. 순진무구한	innumerable	a. 무수한	inquiry	n. 문의
insecticide	n. 살충제	insist on	~을 주장하다	insistence	n. 강조
inspection	n. 검사	instability	n. 불안정	instinctive	a. 본능적인
instinctively	ad. 본능적으로	institutional	a. 공공기관의	insurance	n. 보호 수단
intelligence	n. 지능	intention	n. 의도	interest	n. 관심
interfere	v. 간섭[개입]하다	internalize	v. 내면화하다	intolerant	a. 편협한
intrusive	a. 침입하는	ironic	a. 반어적인	irrationally	ad. 비이성적으로
irregular	a. 불규칙적인	irrigate	v. 관개하다	irritating	a. 화나게 하는
jam	v. 막히다	jealousy	n. 질투	jeopardize	v. 위태롭게 하다
journey	n. 여행	juror	n. 배심원	justification	n. 정당화
juvenile	a. 청소년의	keep pace with	~와 보조를 맞추다	knit	v. 뜨개질하다
knowledgeable	a. 지식이 있는	laden	a. 짐을 실은	lag behind	뒤처지다
lame	a. 절뚝거리는	lament	n. 한탄	latitude	n. 위도
lava	n. 용암	leather	n. 가죽	legitimacy	n. 정당성

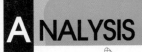

변형문제

01 다음 글을 읽고, |조건|에 맞게 요약문을 완성하시오.

| 조건 |

* (A)는 2단어, (B)는 1단어로 쓸 것
* 본문에 있는 단어를 그대로 사용할 것

In an experiment in Germany, part of a fleet of taxicabs in Munich was equipped with antilock brake systems (ABS), a technological innovation that vastly improves braking. The rest of the fleet was left unequipped, and the two groups were placed under careful and secret observation for three years. You would expect the better brakes to make for safer driving. However, that is exactly the opposite of what happened. Giving some drivers ABS made no difference at all in their accident rate; in fact, it turned them into markedly inferior drivers. They drove faster. They made sharper turns. They braked harder. In other words, the ABS systems were not used to reduce accidents; instead, the drivers used the additional element of safety to enable them to drive faster and more recklessly without increasing their risk of getting into an accident.

⬇

The experiment in Germany was conducted to analyze the effectiveness of ABS systems. (A) ____________ ____________ was expected, but participants in the group of brake systems were proved as (B) ____________ drivers.

02 다음 글의 순서로 가장 적절한 것은?

In an experiment in Germany, part of a fleet of taxicabs in Munich was equipped with antilock brake systems (ABS), a technological innovation that vastly improves braking.

(A) They braked harder. In other words, the ABS systems were not used to reduce accidents; instead, the drivers used the additional element of safety to enable them to drive faster and more recklessly without increasing their risk of getting into an accident.

(B) The rest of the fleet was left unequipped, and the two groups were placed under careful and secret observation for three years. You would expect the better brakes to make for safer driving. However, that is exactly the opposite of what happened.

(C) Giving some drivers ABS made no difference at all in their accident rate; in fact, it turned them into markedly inferior drivers. They drove faster. They made sharper turns.

① (A) - (B) - (C)　② (B) - (A) - (C)　③ (B) - (C) - (A)
④ (C) - (A) - (B)　⑤ (C) - (B) - (A)

03 다음 글을 읽고, |조건|에 맞게 요약문을 완성하시오.

| 조건 |
* (A)는 2단어, (B)는 1단어로 쓸 것
* [보기]에서 선택한 단어를 한 번씩만 그대로 쓸 것

[보기] function / fuel / low / speed / efficiency / high / productivity / minimize / intensify / measure / detect / relieve

In an experiment in Germany, part of a fleet of taxicabs in Munich was equipped with antilock brake systems (ABS), a technological innovation that vastly improves braking. The rest of the fleet was left unequipped, and the two groups were placed under careful and secret observation for three years. You would expect the better brakes to make for safer driving. However, that is exactly the opposite of what happened. Giving some drivers ABS made no difference at all in their accident rate; in fact, it turned them into markedly inferior drivers. They drove faster. They made sharper turns. They braked harder. In other words, the ABS systems were not used to reduce accidents; instead, the drivers used the additional element of safety to enable them to drive faster and more recklessly without increasing their risk of getting into an accident.

⬇

The adoption of ABS did not drop a rate of car accidents. Instead, drivers unsafely drove at (A) ______________ ______________ and used the system as a way to (B) ______________ their danger of causing a car crush.

04 다음 문장이 들어갈 부분으로 가장 적절한 곳을 고르시오.

Giving some drivers ABS made no difference at all in their accident rate; in fact, it turned them into markedly inferior drivers.

In an experiment in Germany, part of a fleet of taxicabs in Munich was equipped with antilock brake systems (ABS), a technological innovation that vastly improves braking. (①) The rest of the fleet was left unequipped, and the two groups were placed under careful and secret observation for three years. (②) You would expect the better brakes to make for safer driving. (③) However, that is exactly the opposite of what happened. (④) They drove faster. They made sharper turns. (⑤) They braked harder. In other words, the ABS systems were not used to reduce accidents; instead, the drivers used the additional element of safety to enable them to drive faster and more recklessly without increasing their risk of getting into an accident.

연결어(구) 넣기

글의 논리	Cause & Effect (원인 & 결과)
제목	갈등 상황에 대한 대화
주제	갈등에 관한 논의를 미루면 나중에 편안한 시점에 다시 이어가야 한다.

PRACTICE 01

042 어법 선택 & 연결어

When emotions are **[high / highly] [charged / charging]**, **[it / this]** makes good sense to delay conversation about conflict **[by / until]** attention, mental focus, and goodwill have returned. Once everyone **[are / is]** calm and **[enjoying / enjoy] [them / themselves]** again, (   ), these conversations are often forgotten or put off indefinitely. No one wants to talk about conflict and risk **[to spoil / spoiling]** the good time. (   ), the issues often don't get **[addressing / addressed]** at all, and they usually resurface **[latter / later]** in a new and often **[intensified / intensifying]** conflict. If you do choose to put off discussion about a conflict, **[remember / remembering] [taking / to take] [them / it]** up **[latter / later]**, **[during / while]** a time of ease and sweet connection, when it can be **[almost / most]** productive.

일반적인 사실 감정이 격해졌을 때, 갈등에 대한 대화를 안정을 찾을 때로 미루는 것은 타당하다.

{When emotions are (highly) charged}, / it / makes good sense / {to delay conversation / (about conflict) / (until attention, mental focus, / and / goodwill have returned)}.

〈종·접〉 When / S emotions / V〈수동태〉 are (highly) charged — 감정이 매우 격해졌을 때 / 〈가S〉 it 이것은 / V makes 타당하다 / O good sense / 〈진S〉 to delay conversation (O) 대화를 미루는 것이 / about conflict 갈등에 대한 / 〈종·접〉 until / S_1 attention, S_2 mental focus 주의, 정신 집중 / and 그리고 / S_3 goodwill / V〈현재완료〉 have returned 선의가 되돌아올 때까지

감정이 매우 격해졌을 때, 갈등에 대한 대화를 주의, 정신 집중, 그리고 선의가 되돌아올 때까지 미루는 것이 타당하다.

노트
- make sense : 타당하다[말이 되다]
- 〈high / highly〉

high	형용사	높은
	부사	높게
	명사	높은 곳
highly	부사	매우(=very)

- 〈가주어, 진주어 구문〉

가주어	동사	진주어
It (This/That/There 사용 불가)	–	that+주어+동사(완전한 절)
		to 동사원형
		동명사
		의문사+주어+동사(간접의문문)
		if/whether+주어+동사
it	makes	to delay ~

원인 상황이 차분해지고 즐거워지면 갈등에 대한 대화는 잊혀진다.

(Once everyone is calm / and / (is) enjoying themselves again), / (A) ______ / these conversations / are (often) forgotten or (are) put off / (indefinitely).

〈종·접〉 Once / S everyone / V is / $S.C_1$ calm 일단 모두가 차분해지면 / 그리고 / $S.C_2$〈현재분사〉 enjoying / O〈재·대〉 themselves 다시 즐거운 상황이 되면 / (A) 하지만 / S these conversations 이러한 대화들은 / V_1〈수동태〉 are forgotten / V_2〈수동태〉 (are) put off 자주 잊혀지거나 연기된다 / indefinitely 무기한으로

그러나 일단 모두가 차분해지고 다시 즐거운 상황이 되면, 이러한 대화들은 자주 잊혀지거나 무기한 연기된다.

노트
- Once(종속접속사 : 일단 ~하면)+주어+동사 ~, 주어+동사.
- put A off : A를 미루다[연기하다] (=postpone, delay) (수동태 시, A be put off)
- 〈주어와 동사의 수의 일치〉
  - each / every / any+단수동사
- 〈재귀대명사 vs. 대명사〉

주어	~	주어와 다름 대명사	주어와 동일 재귀대명사
everyone		them	themselves

- 〈공통관계〉 : A가 공통

A	(X+Y)	=	AX+AY
A	(X+Y+Z+α)	=	AX+AY+AZ+Aα
(X+Y)	A	=	XA+YA
A	(X+Y+Z)	=	AX+AY+AZ
is	(calm+enjoying)		is calm and (is) enjoying
are	(forgotten+put off)	=	are forgotten or (are) put off

(to)
No one / wants to talk / (about conflict) / and / risk
S V O_1
아무도 이야기를 원하지 않는다 갈등에 대한 그리고 즐거운

spoiling the good time.
〈동명사〉 O
O_2
시간을 망치는 위험을 감수하고 싶어 하지 않는다

아무도 갈등에 관한 이야기를 하는 것을 원치 않으며 즐거운 시간을 망치는 위험을 감수하고 싶어 하지 않는다.

노트
- no+one : 아무도 ~ 않다
- talk about : ~에 대해 이야기하다
- risk+동명사 : ~을 감행하다, 감히 ~하다
- 〈want 용법〉

주어	want	목적어(to R)		주어가 ~하는 것을 원하다	3형식
		목적어	목적격보어 (to R)	주어는 목적어가 ~하는 것을 원하다	5형식

- 〈목적어 자리에 동명사를 취하는 완전타동사〉

주어	완전타동사	목적어
–	admit / avoid / consider / delay / deny / enjoy / escape / experience / finish / give up / imagine / include / involve / mind / mute / practice / put off / quit / recommend / replace / report / risk 등	Ring (동명사)

결과 갈등에 대한 대화가 잊혀지면서 나중에 새롭고 흔히 강화된 갈등 상황이 나타난다.

(B) (　　　　　　), / the issues / (often) don't get
S V
그 결과 그 문제들은 종종 다뤄지지 않으며

addressed / (at all), / and / they / (usually) resurface
S.C S V
종종 그리고 그들은 보통 나중에 다시

(later) / {in a new and (often) intensified conflict}.
〈과거분사〉
떠오른다 새롭고 흔히 강화된 갈등 상황에서

그 결과 그 문제들은 종종 전혀 다뤄지지 않으며, 그것들은 보통 나중에 새롭고 흔히 강화된 갈등 상황에서 다시 떠오른다.

노트
- 〈get 동사의 쓰임〉

get	〈주격보어〉	〈2형식〉
	과거분사	~ 당하다, ~의 상태로 되다
	현재분사	~하기 시작하다
	형용사	~의 상태가 되다, ~하기에 이르다
	to do	서서히 ~하게 되다

- 〈at all 쓰임〉

구분	의미
긍정문	여하튼, 어쨌든 간에
부정문	조금도/전혀 ~ 아니다
의문문	도대체
조건문	적어도, 조금이라도

- 〈불규칙적으로 변화하는 중요 형용사와 부사〉

원급	비교급	뜻	최상급	뜻	의미
late	later	나중의	latest	최근의	시간
	latter	후자의	last	최후의	순서

주제문 갈등에 관한 논의를 미루려면 나중에 편안한 시점에 반드시 다시 이어갈 것을 기억해야 한다.

{If you (do) choose / to put off discussion / (about a
〈종·접〉 S V O
만약 당신이 정한다면 논의를 미루기로 갈등에

conflict)}, / remember / to take it up (later), / (during
V O 〈전치사〉
대한 기억하라 그것을 나중에 다시 계속할 것을

a time of ease and sweet connection), / (when it can be
O 〈종·접〉 S V
편안한 시점의 부드러운 관계일 때 이땐 그것이

most productive).
S.C
가장 생산적일 수 있다

갈등에 관한 논의를 정말로 미루기로 정한다면, 나중에 편안한 시점의 부드러운 관계일 때, 즉 가장 생산적일 수 있을 때 다시 계속할 것을 기억하라.

노트
- take A up : A를 계속하다
- 〈동사 강조 표현〉

do / does / did	+동사원형(R)
=정말로(really, certainly)	

- 〈목적어 자리에 to부정사를 취하는 완전타동사〉

주어	완전타동사	목적어
–	afford / agree / ask / attempt / care / choose / claim / dare / decide / demand / desire / determine / elect / expect / fail / guarantee / hope / intend / learn / manage / need / offer / plan / pretend / promise / refuse / resolve / seek / threaten / volunteer / want / wish 등	to 동사원형

- 〈직접명령문〉

구분	형태	의미
긍정문	R	~해라
	Please+R	~해 주세요
부정문	Don't+R	~하지 마라
	Never+R	

- 〈remember/regret/forget 동사 쓰임〉

remember / regret / forget	목적어	〈3형식〉
	to R	미래
	Ring	과거

- 〈이어동사〉

타동사	명사	부사	(O)
타동사	부사	명사	(O)
타동사	대명사	부사	(O)
타동사	부사	대명사	(×)
take	up	it	(×)

- 시간(~ 동안)

전치사	during	+명사 / 명사 상당어구
종속접속사	while	+주어+동사

- 〈most / almost / mostly〉

	대명사	형용사	부사
most	대부분의 것들(사람들)	대부분의	가장
almost	–	–	거의
mostly	–	–	주로, 일반적으로

■ 〈produce 품사 변화〉

produce	v. 생산하다	production	n. 생산
productive	a. 생산적인	product	n. 산출물, 생산품

▶ 다음 글의 빈칸 (A), (B)에 들어갈 말로 가장 적절한 것은?

	(A)		(B)
①	therefore	……	In addition
②	therefore	……	As a consequence
③	for example	……	In contrast
④	however	……	As a consequence
⑤	however	……	In contrast

정답 | ④

해석 | ① 그러므로 – 게다가
② 그러므로 – 그 결과
③ 예를 들어 – 대조적으로
④ 그러나 – 그 결과
⑤ 그러나 – 대조적으로

해설 | ④ (A)의 앞 문장을 보면 감정이 격해졌을 때, 갈등에 대한 대화를 미루는 것이 타당하다고 나온다. 그리고 (A)가 들어간 문장을 보면 모두가 감정이 풀리면 갈등에 대한 대화는 자주 잊혀지거나 무기한 연기된다고 나온다. (A)의 문장과 앞 문장을 보았을 때, (A)에는 대립어가 와야 하므로 'However'가 적절하다. 그리고 (B)의 앞 문장을 보면 아무도 즐거운 시간을 망치는 위험을 감수하고 싶어 하지 않는다고 나온다. (B)의 문장에는 그 문제들이 종종 전혀 다뤄지지 않는다고 나타난다. 따라서 (B)의 앞 문장과 (B)의 문장은 원인과 결과이므로 'As a consequence'가 가장 적절하다. 따라서 ④가 적절하다.

오답 | (A)가 들어간 문장과 앞 문장은 대비되어 있기 때문에 예시를 뜻하는 'for example'이나 결과를 뜻하는 'therefore'은 적절하지 않다. (B)가 들어간 문장은 앞 문장의 결과이기 때문에 'In addition'과 'In contrast'는 적절하지 않다.

Words

☐ highly	☐ mental focus	☐ intensified
☐ charged	☐ goodwill	☐ discussion
☐ delay	☐ indefinitely	☐ ease
☐ conversation	☐ spoil	☐ connection
☐ conflict	☐ address	☐ productive
☐ attention	☐ resurface	

Phrases

☐ make sense	☐ put A off
☐ no+one	☐ talk about
☐ take A up	

우선순위 영단어 역대 수능 기출 + 전국 모의고사 기출 + EBS 기출 + 교과서 기출 빈출 어휘

단어	뜻	단어	뜻	단어	뜻
leisurely	a. 여유 있는	lie in	v. ~에 있다	lift	v. 들어 올리다
limb	n. 나뭇가지	limit	v. 제한하다	limp	v. 절뚝거리다
linguistic	a. 언어의	liver	n. 간	logically	ad. 논리적으로
lorry	n. 화물 자동차	loyal	a. 충심 어린	lure	n. 매력
magnitude	n. 규모	mainland	n. 본토	make a difference	차이를 만들다
make amends	보상[벌충]해 주다	make one's way	~에 나아가다	make sense of	~을 이해하다
make up for	보완하다	manifest	a. 명백한	manifestation	n. 징후
manipulation	n. 조작	manual	a. 손으로 하는	map	v. 지도에 표하다
marvelous	a. 놀라운	mayor	n. 시장	media	n. 매체(medium의 복수)
melt	v. 녹다	merit	n. 장점	messy	a. 지저분한
metaphor	n. 은유	migration	n. 이동	minor	a. 사소한
minority	v. 소수 (민족)	minute	a. 작은	miracle	n. 기적
misguided	a. 잘못 판단한	misplace	v. 잘못 두다	mission	n. 직무
mistake A as B	A를 B로 오해하다	mobile	a. 이동하기 쉬운	moisture	n. 수분

변형문제

01 다음 글을 읽고, |조건|에 맞게 주어진 요약문을 완성하시오.

| 조건 |
* (A), (B), (C)는 각각 다르게 1단어로 쓸 것
* [보기]에서 선택한 단어를 한 번씩만 쓸 것
* 필요한 경우, 문맥과 어법에 맞게 변형할 것

[보기] agreement / dispute / manifest / attention / current / peace / simplify / overlook / interest / innovation

When emotions are highly charged, it makes good sense to delay conversation about conflict until attention, mental focus, and goodwill have returned. Once everyone is calm and enjoying themselves again, however, these conversations are often forgotten or put off indefinitely. No one wants to talk about conflict and risk spoiling the good time. As a consequence, the issues often don't get addressed at all, and they usually resurface later in a new and often intensified conflict. If you do choose to put off discussion about a conflict, remember to take it up later, during a time of ease and sweet connection, when it can be most productive.

⬇

People who are unwilling to bring up conversation arising a(an) (A) ____________ or a disagreement are recommended to have conversation when everyone is in a(an) (B) ____________ state of mind, although the issue may become (C) ____________ and remain unsolved.

02 다음 문장이 들어갈 부분으로 가장 적절한 곳을 고르시오.

As a consequence, the issues often don't get addressed at all, and they usually resurface later in a new and often intensified conflict.

(①) When emotions are highly charged, it makes good sense to delay conversation about conflict until attention, mental focus, and goodwill have returned. (②) Once everyone is calm and enjoying themselves again, however, these conversations are often forgotten or put off indefinitely. (③) No one wants to talk about conflict and risk spoiling the good time. (④) If you do choose to put off discussion about a conflict, remember to take it up later, (⑤) during a time of ease and sweet connection, when it can be most productive.

03 다음 글을 읽고, |조건|에 맞게 주어진 주제문을 완성하시오.

| 조건 |

* (A), (B), (C)는 각각 다르게 1단어로 쓸 것
* [보기]에서 선택한 단어를 한 번씩만 쓸 것
* [보기]에서 선택한 단어를 그대로 쓸 것

[보기] psychological / emotional / productive / controversial / worthwhile / attentive / emotion / fit / worse / affordable / health / mood

When emotions are highly charged, it makes good sense to delay conversation about conflict until attention, mental focus, and goodwill have returned. Once everyone is calm and enjoying themselves again, however, these conversations are often forgotten or put off indefinitely. No one wants to talk about conflict and risk spoiling the good time. As a consequence, the issues often don't get addressed at all, and they usually resurface later in a new and often intensified conflict. If you do choose to put off discussion about a conflict, remember to take it up later, during a time of ease and sweet connection, when it can be most productive.

⬇

To postpone (A) ____________ conversation does not make a situation (B) ____________. It is far better to discuss the debated issue at an appropriate time when people are in a good (C) ____________ in order to avoid unwanted conflict.

04 다음 글의 순서로 가장 적절한 것은?

When emotions are highly charged, it makes good sense to delay conversation about conflict until attention, mental focus, and goodwill have returned.

(A) Once everyone is calm and enjoying themselves again, however, these conversations are often forgotten or put off indefinitely. No one wants to talk about conflict and risk spoiling the good time.

(B) As a consequence, the issues often don't get addressed at all, and they usually resurface later in a new and often intensified conflict.

(C) If you do choose to put off discussion about a conflict, remember to take it up later, during a time of ease and sweet connection, when it can be most productive.

① (A) - (B) - (C)
② (B) - (A) - (C)
③ (B) - (C) - (A)
④ (C) - (A) - (B)
⑤ (C) - (B) - (A)

UNIT 11

연결어(구) 넣기

글의 논리	Comparison & Contrast (비교 & 대조)
제목	시장 자유화와 경제 성장
주제	시장 자유화가 모든 국가의 경제 성장에 도움이 되는 것은 아니다.

PRACTICE 02

043 어법 선택 & 연결어

In the case of China and Eastern Europe, **[this / it]** is clear **[what / that]** market liberalization has helped a lot. Until about 1998, the East European privatization process and the implementation of a market **[economics / economy]** progressed in fits and starts **[due to / because]** all sorts of political maneuvers. (　　　　　) by 1998 the region **[was characterized / characterized]** by a strong private sector and **[relatively / relative]** free markets. This triggered an **[economical / economic]** boom. (　　　　　), this cannot be the whole story. Latin America is also free but — except some short-lived episodes — **[have / has]** been historically **[characterized / characterizing]** by slow **[economic / economical]** growth. (　　　　　), that region has a relatively **[highly / high]** birth rate. (　　　　　), **[their / its]** wealth-per-person growth was remarkably slow from 1998 to 2008. This is true of all Latin American countries, **[included / including]** Brazil, **[despite / although]** the enthusiastic media reports about that country.

비교1 중국과 동유럽의 경우 시장 자유화가 많은 도움이 되었다.

(In the case of China and Eastern Europe), / it / is clear / {that market liberalization / has helped (a lot)}.

(In the case of China and Eastern Europe): 중국과 동유럽의 경우에 / it: (가S) 이것은 / is: V / clear: S.C 명확하다 / that: 〈종·접〉 / market liberalization: S 시장 자유화가 / has helped: V〈현재완료〉 / {that ~ (a lot)}: 〈진S〉 많은 도움이 되었다는 것은

중국과 동유럽의 경우에 시장 자유화가 많은 도움이 되었다는 것은 명확하다.

노트 ■ in the case of : ~에 관하여는, ~에 관하여 말하면(=as regards)

■ 〈가주어, 진주어 구문〉

가주어	동사	진주어
It (This/That/There 사용 불가)	–	that+주어+동사(완전한 절)
		to 동사원형
		동명사
		의문사+주어+동사(간접의문문)
		if/whether+주어+동사
it	is	that ~

■ 〈what vs. that〉

	관계대명사(불완전한 문장)	접속사(완전한 문장)
what	○ 선행사를 포함하고 있기 때문에 what 앞에 선행사 불필요	×
that	○ that 앞에 선행사 필요	○

(Until about 1998), / the East European privatization process / and / the implementation (of a market economy) / progressed (in fits and starts) / (due to all sorts of political maneuvers).

(Until about 1998): 약 1998년까지 / the East European privatization process: S_1 동유럽의 민영화 과정에서 / and: 그리고 / the implementation (of a market economy): S_2 시장 경제의 실행은 / progressed (in fits and starts): V 단속적으로 진행되었다 / due to: 〈전치사〉 / all sorts of: 온갖 종류의 / political maneuvers: O 정치적 조치 때문에

1998년까지 동유럽의 민영화 과정과 시장 경제의 실행은 온갖 종류의 정치적 조치 때문에 단속적으로 진행되었다.

노트 ■ in[by] fits and starts : 간헐적으로

■ 〈혼동 어휘〉

	형용사	명사
economic	경제의	–
economical	경제학의	–
economy	–	경제
economist	–	경제학자
economics	–	경제학

■ 〈원인/이유〉 : ~ 때문에

전치사	because of	+(동)명사 / 명사 상당어구
	due to	
	for	
	on account of	
	owing to	
	thanks to	
종속접속사	as	+주어+동사 ~
	because	
	now(that)	
	since	

(But) / (by 1998) / the region was characterized / (by

(But): 하지만 / (by 1998): 1998년 즈음에 / the region: S 그 지역은 / was characterized: V〈수동태〉 특징을 나타냈다

a strong private sector and relatively free markets).
O1 〈부사〉 O2
강력한 민간 부문과 비교적 자유로운 시장이라는

하지만 1998년 즈음에 그 지역은 강력한 민간 부문과 비교적 자유로운 시장의 특징을 나타냈다.

노트 ■ be characterized by : ~로 특징지어지다

This / triggered an economic boom.
S V O
이것은 경제적 호황을 유발했다

이것은 경제적 호황을 유발했다.

대조 이 사실은 모든 경우에 적용되는 이야기는 아니다.

(A) ( ), / this / cannot be the whole story.
S V S.C
그럼에도 불구하고 이것이 모든 이야기가 될 수 없다

그럼에도 불구하고, 이것이 모든 경우에 적용되는 이야기일 수는 없다.

비교2 라틴 아메리카는 자유롭지만 느린 경제 성장을 보여 준다.

Latin America / is (also) free / but / — (except some
S V S.C 〈전치사〉
라틴 아메리카 또한 자유롭다 하지만 몇 번의 일시적인

short-lived episodes) / — has been (historically)
O V〈현재완료 수동〉
사건을 제외하면 역사적으로 특징을 나타낸다

characterized / (by slow economic growth).
느린 경제 성장의

라틴 아메리카 또한 자유롭지만 몇 번의 일시적인 사건을 제외하면 역사적으로 느린 경제 성장의 특징을 나타낸다.

노트 ■ 〈except 쓰임〉 : ~을 제외하고(=but, save)

전치사	except+목적격대명사
	except+동명사
접속사	except+(that)+주어+동사
타동사	except+목적어+from+(동)명사

(In addition), / that region / has a relatively high birth rate.
S V 〈부사〉 〈형용사〉 O
게다가 그 지역은 비교적 높은 출생률을 가지고 있다

게다가 그 지역은 비교적 높은 출생률을 가지고 있다.

노트 ■ 〈high / highly〉

high	형용사	높은
	부사	높게
	명사	높은 곳
highly	부사	매우(=very)

(B) ( ), / its wealth-per-person growth
S
결과적으로 그 지역의 개인당 부의 성장은

/ was (remarkably) slow / (from 1998 to 2008).
V S.C
현저하게 느렸다 1998년부터 2008년까지

결과적으로 그 지역의 개인당 부의 성장은 1998년부터 2008년까지 현저히 느렸다.

노트 ■ 〈from A to B〉 : A에서 B까지

This / is true / (of all Latin American countries), /
S V S.C
이것은 적용된다 모든 라틴 아메리카에

(including Brazil), / (despite the enthusiastic media reports) / (about that country).
〈전치사〉 O
브라질을 포함한 매체의 열정적인 보도에도 불구하고 그 나라에 대한

이것은 브라질에 대한 매체의 열정적인 보도에도 불구하고 그 나라를 포함한 모든 라틴 아메리카에 적용된다.

노트 ■ be true of : ~에 적용되다
■ 〈including 용법〉

현재분사(형용사)	~을 포함하는	명사를 뒤에서 후치 수식함
분사구문(부사)	~을 포함하여	부대상황
전치사		형용사구, 부사구
		유사 표현 : regarding, concerning, considering

■ 〈양보/대조〉

전치사	in spite of	+명사/명사 상당어구	비록 ~이지만
	despite		
종속접속사	though	+주어+동사	
	although		
	even though		
	even if		
	as		
	while		반면에
	whereas		

▶ 다음 글의 빈칸 (A), (B)에 들어갈 말로 가장 적절한 것은?

	(A)		(B)
①	Similarly	......	In addition
②	Similarly	......	As a result
③	Nevertheless	......	However
④	Nevertheless	......	As a result
⑤	For example	......	In addition

정답 | ④

해석 | ① 마찬가지로 – 게다가
② 마찬가지로 – 결과적으로
③ 그럼에도 불구하고 – 그러나
④ 그럼에도 불구하고 – 결과적으로
⑤ 예를 들면 – 게다가

해설 | ④ 빈칸 (A)가 들어간 문장의 앞 부분을 보면, 이것이 경제적 호황을 유발했다고 나온다. 그런데 (A)가 들어간 문장에는 모든 경우에 적용되는 이야기일 수는 없다고 말한다. 따라서 (A)에 들어갈 말은 앞에 문장과의 대립을 나타내는 말이어야 하므로 'Nevertheless'가 가장 적절하다. 빈칸 (B)가 들어간 문장의 앞 부분을 보면, 라틴 아메리카에서는 느린 경제 성장의 특징이 나타나고 이 지역은 높은 출생률을 가지고 있다고 나온다. 그리고 (B)가 들어간 문장을 보

면 1998년부터 2003년까지 개인당 부의 성장이 현저히 느렸다고 설명한다. 따라서 (A)의 말을 재진술하고 있으므로 이에 가장 적절한 말은 'As a result'이다. 따라서 ④가 적절하다.

오답 | 빈칸 (A)에 들어갈 말은 앞 문장과 뒷 문장을 대립하도록 이어주어야 하기 때문에 순접일 때 쓰이는 Similarly나 예시를 들 때 쓰이는 For example은 적절하지 않다. 그리고 빈칸 (B)에 들어갈 말은 앞 문장과 빈칸의 문장을 순접으로 받아 줘야 하기 때문에 대립일 때 쓰이는 However와 추가적인 말을 할 때 쓰이는 In addition은 적절하지 않다.

Words

- ☐ liberalization
- ☐ privatization
- ☐ process
- ☐ implementation
- ☐ progress
- ☐ due to
- ☐ region
- ☐ characterize
- ☐ relatively
- ☐ trigger
- ☐ economic boom
- ☐ except
- ☐ short-lived
- ☐ historically
- ☐ birth rate
- ☐ remarkably
- ☐ despite
- ☐ enthusiastic
- ☐ nevertheless

Phrases

- ☐ in the case of
- ☐ be characterized by
- ☐ be true of
- ☐ in[by] fits and starts
- ☐ from A to B

우선순위 영단어

역대 수능 기출 + 전국 모의고사 기출 + EBS 기출 + 교과서 기출 빈출 어휘

단어	뜻	단어	뜻	단어	뜻
molten	a. 용해된	monastery	n. 수도원	monetary	a. 화폐의
monopoly	n. 독점	monumental	a. 엄청난	mood	n. 기분
morale	n. 사기	mortgage	n. (주택 담보) 대출금	motive	n. 목적
mound	n. 더미	mountainous	a. 산지의	mourn	v. 슬퍼하다
mow	v. (잔디를) 깎다	nasty	a. 불쾌한	nature	n. 본질
nearly	ad. 거의	nest	n. 둥지	neurological	a. 신경의
neuroscience	n. 신경 과학	neutralize	v. 중립화하다	niche	a. 틈새의
no more than	겨우	normally	ad. 보통	noticeable	a. 눈에 띄는
novelty	n. 새로운 것	nutritionist	n. 영양학자	obey	v. 말을 잘 듣다
objectionable	a. 싫은	observable	a. 관찰 가능한	oceanographer	n. 해양학자
offense	n. 위반	old-fashioned	a. 구식의	on account of	~ 때문에
on average	평균적으로	on the other hand	반면에	opaque	a. 불투명한
open-ended	a. 제약을 두지 않은	operator	n. 수완가	opposing	a. 상반되는
opposition	n. 압제	optimism	n. 낙관주의	ordeal	n. 호된 시련
organized	a. 정리된	originate	v. 비롯하다	outbreak	n. 발생[발발]
outnumber	v. ~보다 숫자가 많다	overconfident	a. 자만하는	overestimate	v. 과대평가하다
overload	n. 지나치게 많음	oversee	v. 감독하다	overwork oneself	v. 과로하다
overview	n. 개관	overwhelming	a. 너무도 강력한	overwhelmingly	ad. 압도적으로
owing to	~ 덕분에	pad	n. (동물의) 발바닥	paralysis	n. 마비 상태
parenting	n. 육아	parrot	n. 앵무새	participation	n. 참가
pedestrian	n. 보행자	performance piece	공연 작품	performer	n. 연예인
period	n. 시기	permission	n. 허락	permit	n. 허가증
persistent	a. 끊임없는	perspiration	n. 땀	perverse	a. 비뚤어진[삐딱한]
pessimism	n. 비관(론)	petroleum	n. 석유	philosopher	n. 철학자

변형문제

01 다음 글을 읽고, |조건|에 맞게 주어진 질문에 답하시오.

| 조건 |
* (A), (B)는 5단어로 쓸 것
* 본문에 있는 단어만을 사용할 것

In the case of China and Eastern Europe, it is clear that market liberalization has helped a lot. Until about 1998, the East European privatization process and the implementation of a market economy progressed in fits and starts due to all sorts of political maneuvers. But by 1998 the region was characterized by a strong private sector and relatively free markets. This triggered an economic boom. Nevertheless, this cannot be the whole story. Latin America is also free but — except some short-lived episodes — has been historically characterized by slow economic growth. In addition, that region has a relatively high birth rate. As a result, its wealth-per-person growth was remarkably slow from 1998 to 2008. This is true of all Latin American countries, including Brazil, despite the enthusiastic media reports about that country.

Q: What were the two reasons that the wealth-per-person growth in Latin American countries was slow?

A: Because (A) ________ ________ ________ ________ ________.
Because (B) ________ ________ ________ ________ ________.

02 다음 글을 읽고, |조건|에 맞게 주어진 제목을 완성하시오.

| 조건 |
* 5단어로 쓸 것
* 본문에 있는 단어를 찾아 그대로 쓸 것

In the case of China and Eastern Europe, it is clear that market liberalization has helped a lot. Until about 1998, the East European privatization process and the implementation of a market economy progressed in fits and starts due to all sorts of political maneuvers. But by 1998 the region was characterized by a strong private sector and relatively free markets. This triggered an economic boom. Nevertheless, this cannot be the whole story. Latin America is also free but — except some short-lived episodes — has been historically characterized by slow economic growth. In addition, that region has a relatively high birth rate. As a result, its wealth-per-person growth was remarkably slow from 1998 to 2008. This is true of all Latin American countries, including Brazil, despite the enthusiastic media reports about that country.

⬇

The relationship between ________ ________ ________ ________ ________.

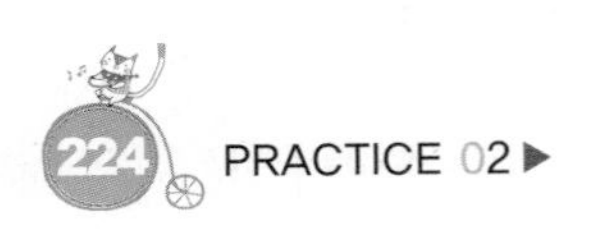

03 다음 글을 읽고, |조건|에 맞게 주어진 요약문을 완성하시오.

| 조건 |
* (A)는 2단어, (B), (C)는 4단어로 쓸 것
* 본문에 있는 단어를 찾아 그대로 쓸 것

In the case of China and Eastern Europe, it is clear that market liberalization has helped a lot. Until about 1998, the East European privatization process and the implementation of a market economy progressed in fits and starts due to all sorts of political maneuvers. But by 1998 the region was characterized by a strong private sector and relatively free markets. This triggered an economic boom. Nevertheless, this cannot be the whole story. Latin America is also free but — except some short-lived episodes — has been historically characterized by slow economic growth. In addition, that region has a relatively high birth rate. As a result, its wealth-per-person growth was remarkably slow from 1998 to 2008. This is true of all Latin American countries, including Brazil, despite the enthusiastic media reports about that country.

⬇

(A) ____________ ____________ led to economic growth or economic boom in China and Eastern Europe, but was not enough in Latin American countries due to (B) ____________ ____________ ____________ ____________ and (C) ____________ ____________ ____________ ____________ in these regions.

04 다음 글을 읽고, |조건|에 맞게 (A), (B), (C)를 채우시오.

| 조건 |
* (A)는 1단어, (B)는 2단어, (C)는 1단어로 쓸 것
* 본문에 있는 단어를 찾아 그대로 쓸 것

In the case of China and Eastern Europe, it is clear that market liberalization has helped a lot. Until about 1998, the East European privatization process and the implementation of a market economy progressed in fits and starts due to all sorts of political maneuvers. But by 1998 the region was characterized by a strong private sector and relatively free markets. This triggered an economic boom. Nevertheless, this cannot be the whole story. Latin America is also free but — except some short-lived episodes — has been historically characterized by slow economic growth. In addition, that region has a relatively high birth rate. As a result, its wealth-per-person growth was remarkably slow from 1998 to 2008. This is true of all Latin American countries, including Brazil, despite the enthusiastic media reports about that country.

⬇

The economic success of Eastern Europe about in 1998 was a result of (A) ____________ by a strong private sector and the implementation of a market economy, however in case of Latin American countries where also had (B) ____________ ____________, far slow economic growth affecting (C) ____________ occurred.

연결어(구) 넣기

글의 논리	Examples
제목	남성과 여성의 역할 할당
주제	남성과 여성의 역할이 부적절하게 할당되어 있다.

PRACTICE 03

044 어법 선택 & 연결어

Men and women are often **[assigning / assigned]** roles for various social, political, or historical reasons. When these factors are inadequately **[understanding / understood]**, they can appear to be quite **[arbitrarily / arbitrary]**. (   ), **[despite / although]** **[sewed / sewing]** clothes for the family **[thinks / is thought]** of as women's work in North America (**[most / almost]** men have never operated a **[sewn / sewing]** machine or made a purchase in a fabric store), among the Ecuadorian men and traditional Hopi of Arizona, men are the spinners, weavers, **[and / or]** tailors. (   ) among the Hopi, women are the potters and not the men; (   ), in U.S. culture both men **[or / and]** women can become potters. (   ), women in U.S. society have been virtually **[excluding / excluded]** from a number of occupations (such as jockey and Major League Baseball umpire), **[as though / even though]** men have no particular biological advantage over women in **[performance / performing]** these jobs.

일반적인 사실 남성과 여성은 다양한 이유로 역할이 정해진다.

Men and women / are (often) assigned roles / (for various social, political, or historical reasons).

(Men and women: S 남성과 여성은 / are assigned: V〈수동태〉 흔히 역할이 할당된다 / assigned: 〈과거분사〉 / roles: O / 다양한 사회적, 정치적, 혹은 역사적 이유로)

남성과 여성은 다양한 사회적, 정치적, 혹은 역사적 이유로 흔히 역할이 할당된다.

노트 ■ assign + IO + DO : ~에게 ~을(를) 할당/배당하다[수동태 시, 주어(IO) + be assigned + DO]

주제문 이러한 요소가 부적절하다고 생각할 때, 임의적으로 보인다.

{When these factors / are (inadequately) understood}, / they / can appear to be quite arbitrary.

(When: 〈종·접〉 / these factors: S 이러한 요소가 / are understood: V〈수동태〉 부적절하게 이해될 때 / they: S 그것들은 / can appear: V / to be quite arbitrary: S.C 꽤 임의적인 것처럼 보일 수 있다)

이러한 요소가 부적절하게 이해될 때, 그것들은 꽤 임의적인 것처럼 보일 수 있다.

노트 ■ 〈appear 동사의 쓰임〉 : ~처럼 보이다

appear	주격보어
	that절
	to R
	분사
	to be 보어
	as + 보어

예시 옷을 바느질 하는 것이 나라에 따라 남성이 하는 곳도 있고 여성이 하는 곳도 있다.

(A) (   ), / {although sewing clothes (for the family) / is thought of / as women's work / (in North America)} / (most men / have never operated a sewing machine / or (have) made a purchase (in a fabric store)), / (among the Ecuadorian men and traditional Hopi of Arizona), / men / are the spinners, weavers, and tailors.

(예를 들어 / although: 〈종·접〉 / sewing clothes: S 비록 가족을 위해 옷을 바느질하는 것이 / is thought of: V〈수동태〉 간주될지라도 / as women's work: S.C 여성의 일로서 / 북아메리카에서 / most men: S (대부분의 남성은 / have never operated: V_1〈현재완료〉 재봉틀을 사용해 본 적이 / a sewing machine: O 결코 없거나 / made: V_2 / a purchase: O 포목상에서 구입한 적이 없다) / among: 〈전치사〉 에콰도르인과 애리조나 주의 전통적인 호피족 중에서는 / men: S 남성이 / are: V / the spinners: $S.C_1$, weavers: $S.C_2$ 실 잣는 사람, 베 짜는 사람, / tailors: $S.C_3$ 재단사이다)

예를 들어, 북아메리카에서 가족을 위해 옷을 바느질하는 것은 여성의 일로서 간주될지라도 (대부분의 남성은 재봉틀을 사용해 본 적이 결코 없거나 포목상에서 (옷감을) 구입한 적이 없다) 에콰도르인과 애리조나 주의 전통적인 호피족 중에서는 남성이 실 잣는 사람, 베 짜는 사람, 재단사이다.

노트 ■ think of A as B : A를 B로 간주하다(수동태 시, A be thought of as B)
■ make a purchase : 물건을 사다
■ 〈양보/대조〉

전치사	in spite of	+ 명사/명사 상당어구	비록 ~이지만
	despite		
종속접속사	though	+ 주어 + 동사	
	although		
	even though		
	even if		
	as		
	while		반면에
	whereas		

■ 〈동명사구가 주어 자리에 사용된 경우〉 : 단수 취급으로 동사는 단수동사를 사용함

주어 : 동명사구	동사
sewing clothes for the family	is thought of

■ 〈5형식 불완전타동사의 목적격보어〉 : 수동태 전환 시, 2형식 문장(be p.p. +as 보어)

주어	불완전타동사	목적어	목적격보어
–	accept / achieve / announce / characterize / cite / consider / count / deem / define / describe / disguise / identify / interpret / look at / look upon / perceive / praise / present / read / reckon / refer to / recognize / regard / remember / respect / see / speak of / think of / treat / use / view / visualize 등	–	as 보어

■ 〈most / almost / mostly〉

	대명사	형용사	부사
most	대부분의 것들(사람들)	대부분의	가장
almost	–	–	거의
mostly	–	–	주로, 일반적으로

■ 〈between vs. among〉

전치사	between	~ 사이에	둘 사이	혼용
	among		셋 이상	

예시 호피족은 여성이 옹기장이이지만 미국에서는 남성과 여성 모두 옹기장이가 될 수 있다.

(Also) / (among the Hopi), / women / are the potters / and / not the men; / (however), / (in U.S. culture) / both men and women / can become potters.

(Also: 또한 / among〈전치사〉 the Hopi: 호피족 중에서 / women S: 여성이 / are V / the potters $S.C_1$: 옹기장이이다 / and: 그리고 / not the men $S.C_2$: 남성은 아니다; / however: 그러나 / in U.S. culture: 미국 문화에서는 / both men and women S: 남성과 여성이 모두 / can become V potters S.C: 옹기장이가 될 수 있다)

또한 호피족 중에서 여성이 옹기장이이고 남성은 아니다. 그러나 미국 문화에서는 남성과 여성이 모두 옹기장이가 될 수 있다.

노트 ■ 〈상관접속사〉 : 병렬구조

종류				뜻
not	A	but	B	A가 아니라 B (=B, not A)
not only	A	but also	B	A뿐만 아니라 B도 (=B as well as A)
either	A	or	B	A와 B 둘 중 하나
neither	A	nor	B	A와 B 둘 다 아닌
both	A	and	B	A와 B 둘 다

■ 〈become 동사 쓰임〉

become	〈주격보어〉	(2형식)
	명사	(~으로) 되다
	형용사	
	과거분사	
	〈목적어〉	(3형식)
	명사	어울리다, 잘 맞다(진행형/수동태 불가)

예시 남성이 여성에 비해 생물학점 이점을 지니지 않은 부분에서도 여성들이 차별받고 있다.

(B) (   ), / women (in U.S. society) / have been (virtually) excluded / (from a number of occupations) / (such as jockey and Major League Baseball umpire), / {even though men / have no particular biological advantage / (over women) / (in performing these jobs)}.

(( ): 더욱이 / women S (in U.S. society): 미국 사회의 여성들은 / have been excluded V〈현재완료 수동〉: 배제되어 왔다 / from a number of occupations: 많은 직업들로부터 / such as jockey and Major League Baseball umpire: (기수 그리고 메이저리그 야구 심판과 같은) / even though〈종·접〉 men S: 비록 남성들이 / have V / no particular: 특정한 / no particular biological advantage O: 생물학적 이점을 전혀 지니고 있지 않는데도 / over women: 여성에 비해 / performing〈동명사〉 these jobs O / in performing these jobs O: 이런 직업을 수행함에 있어서)

더욱이, 미국 사회의 여성들은 (기수 그리고 메이저리그 야구 심판과 같은) 많은 직업으로부터 거의 배제되어 왔는데, 비록 남성들이 이런 직업을 수행하는 데 여성에 비해 특정한 생물학적 이점을 전혀 지니고 있지 않는 데도 그러하다.

노트 ■ a number of＋복수명사 : 많은 ~
■ A such as B : B와 같은 A

▶ 다음 글의 빈칸 (A), (B)에 들어갈 말로 가장 적절한 것은?

	(A)		(B)
①	For example	······	Otherwise
②	For example	······	Moreover
③	However	······	As a result
④	However	······	Moreover
⑤	Therefore	······	Otherwise

정답 | ②

해석 | ① 예를 들어 – 그렇지 않으면
② 예를 들어 – 더욱이
③ 그러나 – 결과적으로
④ 그러나 – 더욱이
⑤ 그러므로 – 그렇지 않으면

해설 | ② 빈칸 (A)의 문장을 보면 북아메리카에서의 남성과 여성의 역할이 예로 나온다. 따라서 빈칸 (A)에는 예시를 뜻하는 말인 'For example'이 들어가야 한다. 빈칸 (B)의 문장을 보면 미국 사회에서의 남성과 여성의 역할에 대한 차별의 예시가 나온다. 따라서 앞에 호피족과 추가적으로 예시를 드는 것이므로 추가적으로 연결해주는 말인 'Moreover'가 들어가야 적절하다.

오답 | 빈칸 (A)가 들어간 문장은 예를 들고 있기 때문에, 역접인 'However'나 결과를 나타내는 'Therfore'은 적절하지 않고 빈칸 (B)가 들어간 문장은 추가적인 예시를 들고 있기 때문에 역접인 'Otherwise'나 결과를 나타내는 'As a result'는 적절하지 않다.

Words

☐ assign		☐ operate		☐ tailor	
☐ various		☐ sewing machine		☐ potter	
☐ political		☐ purchase		☐ virtually	
☐ historical		☐ fabric store		☐ occupation	
☐ factor		☐ traditional		☐ umpire	
☐ inadequately		☐ spinner			
☐ sew		☐ weaver			

Phrases

☐ think of A as B		☐ make a purchase	
☐ a number of＋복수명사		☐ A such as B	

우선순위 영단어 역대 수능 기출＋전국 모의고사 기출＋EBS 기출＋교과서 기출 빈출 어휘

단어	뜻	단어	뜻	단어	뜻
philosophical	a. 철학적인	physicist	n. 물리학자	physics	n. 물리학
pioneer	n. 개척자	plague	v. 괴롭히다	plank	n. 정당 강령의 항목(조항)
plantation	n. 조림지	plasticity	n. 가소성	platform	n. 승강장
plight	n. 역경	point to	v. 지적하다	pole	n. 극
policy	n. 정책	polite	a. 공손한	poll	n. 투표소
pollution	n. 오염	porch	n. 현관	post	v. 발송[우송]하다
pottery	n. 도기	poverty	n. 가난	pray	v. 기도하다
prayer	n. 기도	precarious	a. 믿을 수 없는	precede	v. 앞서다
precious	a. 귀중한	predominant	a. 주된	predominantly	ad. 주로
pregnancy	n. 임신	prejudice	n. 편견	preventive	a. 예방하는
priceless	a. 매우 귀중한	proclamation	n. 선언	product	n. 생산품
proficiency	n. 능숙함	profitable	a. 이익이 나는	progressive	a. 점진적인
prolonged	ad. 연장된	proper	a. 적절한	proponent	n. 지지자
proposal	n. 제안	prosper	v. 번영하다	prosperity	n. 번영
protest	v. 항의하다	psychiatrist	n. 정신의학자	psychology	n. 심리
public	a. 공공연한	publication	n. 출판물	publicity	n. 매스컴의 관심
publicize	v. 선전하다	publisher	n. 출판인	pure	a. 순수한
put off	v. 의욕을 잃게 하다	puzzle	v. 당혹스럽게 하다	puzzling	a. 당혹케하는
quarter	n. 4분의 1	question	v. 의심하다	queue	n. 줄
radiate	v. 발하다	radish	n. 무	ragged	a. 거친
randomly	ad. 무작위로	randomness	n. 일정치 않음	rare	a. 보기 힘든
rating	n. 시청률	rationale	n. 이론적 근거	raw material	n. 원료
realm	n. 영역	rear	v. 들어 올리다	rebel	n. 반항아
recede	v. 물러나다	reception	n. 환영 연회	recession	n. 경기 후퇴
reconcile	v. 조화시키다	reconstruct	v. 재건하다	refuse	v. 거절하다
registration	n. 등록	regularize	v. 조직화하다	regulatory	a. 규제력을 지닌
reject	v. 거절하다	relaxation	n. 휴식	relaxed	a. 긴장을 푼
religious	a. 종교상의	remain	n. (보통 ~s) 유해	reorganize	v. 구조 조정을 하다
repay	v. 보답하다	repetitive	a. 반복되는	repression	n. 억압
request	n. 요청	resentment	n. 분함	residence	n. 주거

변형문제

01 다음 글을 읽고, |조건|에 맞게 주어진 주제문을 완성하시오.

| 조건 |
* (A)는 5단어, (B)는 4단어로 쓸 것
* 본문에 있는 단어를 찾아 그대로 쓸 것

Men and women are often assigned roles for various social, political, or historical reasons. When these factors are inadequately understood, they can appear to be quite arbitrary. For example, although sewing clothes for the family is thought of as women's work in North America (most men have never operated a sewing machine or made a purchase in a fabric store), among the Ecuadorian men and traditional Hopi of Arizona, men are the spinners, weavers, and tailors. Also among the Hopi, women are the potters and not the men; however, in U.S. culture both men and women can become potters. Moreover, women in U.S. society have been virtually excluded from a number of occupations (such as jockey and Major League Baseball umpire), even though men have no particular biological advantage over women in performing these jobs.

⬇

(A) ____________ ____________ ____________ ____________ ____________ are determined by (B) ____________ ____________ ____________ ____________ trends of where they belong.

02 다음 글의 순서로 가장 적절한 것은?

Men and women are often assigned roles for various social, political, or historical reasons. When these factors are inadequately understood, they can appear to be quite arbitrary.

(A) Also among the Hopi, women are the potters and not the men; however, in U.S. culture both men and women can become potters.

(B) For example, although sewing clothes for the family is thought of as women's work in North America (most men have never operated a sewing machine or made a purchase in a fabric store), among the Ecuadorian men and traditional Hopi of Arizona, men are the spinners, weavers, and tailors.

(C) Moreover, women in U.S. society have been virtually excluded from a number of occupations (such as jockey and Major League Baseball umpire), even though men have no particular biological advantage over women in performing these jobs.

① (A) - (B) - (C)
② (A) - (C) - (B)
③ (B) - (A) - (C)
④ (B) - (C) - (A)
⑤ (C) - (A) - (B)

03 밑줄 친 부분 중 문맥상 옳지 않은 것은?

Men and women are often assigned roles for various social, political, or historical reasons. When these factors are ① inadequately understood, they can appear to be quite arbitrary. For example, although sewing clothes for the family is thought of as ② women's work in North America (most men have never operated a sewing machine or made a purchase in a fabric store), among the Ecuadorian men and traditional Hopi of Arizona, men are the spinners, weavers, and tailors. Also among the Hopi, women are the potters and ③ not the men; however, in U.S. culture ④ both men and women can become potters. Moreover, women in U.S. society have been virtually ⑤ included from a number of occupations (such as jockey and Major League Baseball umpire), even though men have no particular biological advantage over women in performing these jobs.

04 다음 글의 내용과 일치하지 않는 것은?

Men and women are often assigned roles for various social, political, or historical reasons. When these factors are inadequately understood, they can appear to be quite arbitrary. For example, although sewing clothes for the family is thought of as women's work in North America (most men have never operated a sewing machine or made a purchase in a fabric store), among the Ecuadorian men and traditional Hopi of Arizona, men are the spinners, weavers, and tailors. Also among the Hopi, women are the potters and not the men; however, in U.S. culture both men and women can become potters. Moreover, women in U.S. society have been virtually excluded from a number of occupations (such as jockey and Major League Baseball umpire), even though men have no particular biological advantage over women in performing these jobs.

① 남성과 여성은 역사적 이유로 흔히 역할이 할당된다.
② 북아메리카에서는 옷을 바느질하는 것은 여성의 일로 간주된다.
③ 에콰도르에서는 남성이 바느질하기도 한다.
④ 호피족에서는 남성이 옹기장이이다.
⑤ 미국에서는 남녀 모두 옹기장이가 될 수 있다.

UNIT 12

무관한 문장 찾기

글의 논리	Spotlight
제목	Newton의 운동법칙과 골프의 세계
주제	Newton의 운동법칙은 골프의 세계에 적용된다.

수능 ANALYSIS

045 어법 선택 & 연결어

Newton's laws of motion apply **[perfect / perfectly]** to the world of golf. We're all aware **[what / that]** a golf ball moves when it **[hits / is hit]** by force. (   ), there **[is / are]** outside forces **[what / that]** **[keep / keeps]** a golf ball **[moving / from moving]** in **[its / their]** original direction forever. A ball may have a straight path when the club hits **[it / them]**, but then gravity pulls the ball toward Earth and can keep **[it / them]** **[going / from going]** straight. Air resistance — a form of friction — then slows the ball's velocity as it speeds through the air. Once a golf ball connects with the ground again, it slows down **[very / even]** more **[because / because of]** a grassy and sandy surface **[create / creates]** more friction with the ball **[to / than]** air.

주제문 Newton의 운동법칙은 골프의 세계에 적용된다.

Newton's laws (of motion) / apply (perfectly) / (to the world of golf).

(S: Newton's laws – Newton의 운동법칙은 / V: apply – 적용된다 / 〈부사〉 perfectly – 완벽하게 / 〈전치사〉 to / O: the world of golf – 골프의 세계에)

Newton의 운동법칙은 골프의 세계에 완벽하게 적용된다.

노트 ■ apply to+(동)명사 : ~에 적용되다

설명 골프공이 힘에 의해 맞으면 움직인다.

We / are (all) aware / [that a golf ball moves / {when it is hit / (by force)}].

(S: We – 우리는 / V: are / S.C: aware – 모두 알고 있다 / 〈종·접〉 that / S: a golf ball / V: moves – 골프공이 움직인다는 것을 / 〈종·접〉 when / S: it – 그것이 / V〈수동태〉: is hit – 맞으면 / by force – 힘에)

골프공이 힘에 의해 맞으면 그것이 움직인다는 것을 우리는 모두 알고 있다.

노트 ■ be hit by : ~에 타격을 받다

■ 〈인지/확신형용사〉 : 이러한 형용사는 뒤에 명사절로 that절이나 간접의문문 등을 취할 수 있다.

주어(사람)	be동사	형용사(인지/확신)	that(생략 가능)	주어	동사 ~
			of+동명사		
		aware, certain, conscious, proud, sure, confident, convinced, fearful, ignorant			

■ 〈서술적 형용사〉 : 명사 수식 불가, 보어로만 사용

상태형용사	afraid, alike, alive, alone, amiss, ashamed, asleep, astray, awake, aware 등
감정형용사	content, fond, glad, ignorant, pleasant, proud, unable, upset, well, worth 등

■ 〈what vs. that〉

	관계대명사(불완전한 문장)	접속사(완전한 문장)
what	○ 선행사를 포함하고 있기 때문에 what 앞에 선행사 불필요	×
that	○ that 앞에 선행사 필요	○

설명 골프공이 처음 방향으로 영원히 움직이는 것을 막는 힘이 있다.

① However, / there are / outside forces / {that keep a golf ball / (from moving) / (in its original direction) / (forever)}.

(However – 그러나 / V: are – 있다 / S: outside forces – 외력이 / 〈주·관〉 that / V: keep – 막는 / O: a golf ball – 골프공을 / from moving – 움직이는 것을 / in its original direction – 처음 방향으로 / forever – 영원히)

그러나 골프공이 처음 방향으로 영원히 움직이는 것을 막는 외력이 있다.

노트 ■ outside force : 외부의 힘

■ 〈There is 도치구문〉

긍정문	There	is	단수 주어	~이 있다
		are	복수 주어	
부정문	There	is no	단수 주어	~이 없다
		are no	복수 주어	

• 유도부사 **there**와 함께 도치구문을 이루는 be동사(is/are/was/were) 대신에 완전자동사 **appear**, **come**, **exist**, **follow**, **live**, **stand** 등을 사용할 수 있다.

■ 〈주격관계대명사절의 수의 일치〉 : 선행사를 포함하고 있는 관계대명사 what 사용 불가

	주격관계대명사절		
선행사	주격관계대명사	~~주어~~	동사
outside forces	that		keeps

■ 〈keep 동사의 쓰임〉

(목적어)	현재분사 (Ring)	(~가) …하는 것을 유지하다
	from 동명사 (Ring)	(~가) …하는 것을 막다

설명 공을 골프채로 치면 중력에 의해 직선으로 가지 못한다.

② A ball / may have a straight path / (when the club hits it), / but / (then) / gravity pulls the ball / (toward Earth) / and / can keep / it / (from going straight).

(A ball: S 공은 / may have: V / a straight path: O 직선 경로를 가질 수도 있다 / when: 〈종·접〉 / the club: S 골프채가 그것을 / hits: V 치면 / it: O / but 하지만 / then 그런 다음 / gravity: S / pulls: V_1 / the ball: O 중력이 공을 당기고 / toward Earth 지구로 / and 그리고 / can keep: V_2 막을 수 있다 / it: O 그것이 / from going straight 직선으로 가지 못하게)

공을 골프채로 치면 그것은 직선 경로를 가질 수도 있지만 그런 다음 중력이 지구로 공을 당기고 그것이 직선으로 가지 못하게 막을 수 있다.

노트 ■ go straight : 똑바로 가다

설명 공이 속도를 낼 때 공기 저항이 속력을 늦춘다.

③ Air resistance / — a form of friction / — (then) / slows the ball's velocity / {as it speeds / (through the air)}.

(Air resistance: S 공기 저항은 / a form of friction 일종의 마찰 / then 그런 다음 / slows: V / the ball's velocity: O 공의 속력을 늦춘다 / as: 〈종·접〉 / it: S / speeds: V 그 공이 속도를 낼 때 / through the air 공기를 뚫고)

그런 다음 그 공이 공기를 뚫고 속력을 낼 때 일종의 마찰인 공기 저항은 공의 속력을 늦춘다.

노트 ■ 〈혼동 어휘〉

through	전치사	~을 통하여
throughout	전치사	[장소] ~의 도처에, [시간] ~ 동안, ~ 내내
	부사	도처에, 완전히, 철저하게
though	접속사	~에도 불구하고
thorough	형용사	철저한, 완전한

④ Golfers feel delighted / {when they get the ball to go into the hole / (with the least number of hits)}.

(Golfers: S / feel: V / delighted: S.C 골프를 치는 사람들은 기쁨을 느낀다 / when: 〈종·접〉 / they: S / get: V / the ball: O / to go: O.C 그들이 공이 홀에 들어가도록 하면 / with the least number of hits 가장 적은 수만큼 쳐서)

골프를 치는 사람들은 가장 적은 수만큼 쳐서 공이 홀에 들어가도록 하면 기쁨을 느낀다.

노트 ■ go into : ~에 들어가다(=enter)
■ 〈감정과 관련된 완전타동사〉 : 분사화가 되어 주격보어/목적격보어 자리에 나올 때 구별법
• 2형식

주어	동사	주격보어(S.C)
사람		과거분사(p.p.) – 수동(되어진, ~ 당한)
사물		현재분사(Ring) – 능동(~하고 있는, 하는)
Golfers	feel	delighted

■ 〈불규칙적으로 변화하는 형용사〉

원급	비교급	최상급
little 작은	less 더 작은	least 가장 작은
	lesser 더욱 작은(이중비교급)	

■ 〈get 동사의 쓰임〉

get	목적어	〈목적격 보어〉	〈5형식〉	목적어와 목적격 보어의 관계
		형용사	~을 (…의 상태가) 되게 하다	능동
		현재분사		
		to R	[남에게] ~시키다	
		과거분사	[물건을] ~하게 하다	수동

설명 공이 지면과 맞닿을때, 마찰로 속도가 더 느려진다.

⑤ {Once a golf ball / connects (with the ground) / (again)}, / it / slows down / (even) more / {because a grassy and sandy surface / creates more friction (with the ball) / than air}.

(Once: 〈종·접〉 / a golf ball: S 일단 골프공이 / connects: V / with the ground 지면과 연결되면 / again 다시 / it: S 그 골프공은 / slows down: V 더 느려진다 / even more 훨씬 더 / because: 〈종·접〉 왜냐하면 / a grassy and sandy surface: S 풀이 무성하고 모래가 있는 표면이 / creates: V / more friction: O 공과의 마찰을 만들어내므로 / than air 공기보다)

골프공이 지면과 다시 연결되자마자, 풀이 무성하고 모래가 있는 표면이 공기보다 공과의 더 많은 마찰을 만들어내므로 그것은 속도가 훨씬 더 느려진다.

노트 ■ once : 일단 ~하면(종속접속사)
■ connect with : ~와 관련시키다[연결하다]
■ slow down : 속도가 늦다
■ 〈비교급 vs. 원급 강조〉 : 훨씬 더

비교급 강조 표현	원급 강조 표현
much, even, still, by far, far, a lot, lots, a great deal	very, so, quite, really, extremely, too

■ 〈원인/이유〉 : ~ 때문에

전치사	because of	+(동)명사 / 명사 상당어구
	due to	
	for	
	on account of	
	owing to	
	thanks to	
종속접속사	as	+주어+동사 ~
	because	
	now(that)	
	since	

▶ 다음 글에서 전체 흐름과 관계 없는 문장은?

정답 | ④

해설 | ④ 이 글의 주제는 Newton의 운동법칙은 골프의 세계에 적용된다는 것이다. 그리고 이에 대한 설명을 하는 글인데 ④는 골프를 치는 사람들이 느끼는 만족감에 대한 내용이므로 글의 관점과 일치하지 않기 때문에 흐름과 관계 없다.

오답 | ① 운동법칙으로 외력을 이야기하므로 글의 흐름과 적절하다.
② 골프공이 직선 경로로 갈 수도 있지만 중력으로 지구가 직선으로 가지 못하게 막는다고 하였으므로 글의 주제와 알맞다.
③ 운동법칙 중 공기 저항에 관한 내용을 이야기하므로 글의 흐름과 적절하다.
⑤ 공이 표면과의 마찰에 의해 속도가 느려진다고 이야기하므로 글의 흐름과 적절하다.

Words

- ☐ law
- ☐ perfectly
- ☐ aware
- ☐ move
- ☐ force
- ☐ outside
- ☐ original
- ☐ direction
- ☐ forever
- ☐ straight
- ☐ path
- ☐ gravity
- ☐ pull
- ☐ Earth
- ☐ resistance
- ☐ friction
- ☐ hole
- ☐ sandy
- ☐ surface

Phrases

- ☐ apply to+(동)명사
- ☐ go straight
- ☐ connect with
- ☐ be hit by
- ☐ go into
- ☐ slow down

우선순위 영단어

역대 수능 기출+전국 모의고사 기출+EBS 기출+교과서 기출 빈출 어휘

단어	뜻	단어	뜻	단어	뜻
resilience	n. 회복력	respectable	a. 상당히 많은	retention	n. 보유
reunion	n. 동창회	revive	v. 소생하게 하다	revolt	n. 반란(을 일으키다)
revolutionize	v. 혁명을 일으키다	ridicule	v. 비웃다	ridiculously	ad. 터무니없이
rigorous	a. 엄격한	robe	n. 옷	robust	a. 튼튼한
route	n. 경로	row	v. 노를 젓다	royalty	n. 인세
rug	n. 깔개	run out	v. 부족하다	rush	v. 돌진하다
sacred	a. 신성한	sample	v. 맛보다	savage	a. 야만인
say	v. 가령	scope	n. 범위	scramble	n. 뒤섞다
seed	n. 씨앗	segment	n. 부분	self-fulfilling	a. 자기 충족적인
senator	n. 상원 의원	sensible	a. 분별 있는	sensitivity	n. 민감도
set out	v. 시작하다	settle	v. 정착하다	severe	a. 맹렬한
severely	ad. 심하게	shame	n. 부끄러움	shelf	n. 선반
shelve	v. (상점 등의) 선반	shoal	n. 떼	shortfall	n. 적자
short-term	a. 단기(간)의	shrinkage	n. 수축	shuffle	v. 뒤섞다
sickly	a. 병약한	signal	n. 신호	simultaneous	a. 동시의
skull	n. 두개골	slam	v. 세게 부딪히다	slender	a. 적은
slow down	속도를 늦추다	sole	a. 유일한	somehow	a. 어떻게든
soothing	a. 달래는	sophistication	n. 궤변	sore	n. 상처
specialist	n. 전문가	specialized	a. 전문화된	sphere	n. 영역
spit	v. 침을 뱉다	splash	v. 끼얹다	spoil	v. 응석받이로 키우다
spring	v. 싹이 나다	sprinkle	v. 뿌리다	stable	a. 안정된
standpoint	n. 견지	stare	v. 응시하다	startle	v. 놀라게 하다
starvation	n. 기아	statue	n. 조상	stay up	(밤을) 새우다
stiff	a. 뻣뻣한	stone	v. (돌처럼) 아무 말 없이	store	v. 저장하다
strap	n. 끈	strict	a. 엄격한	striking	a. 두드러진
study	n. 서재	subject to	~에 종속된	subside	v. 가라앉다
substantially	ad. 상당히	substitute	n. 대체물	substitution	n. 대체
successive	a. 연속하는	suffer	v. 고통 받다	suggestion	n. 제안
sunscreen	n. 썬크림	superiority	n. 탁월함	supplementary	a. 부가적인

변형문제

01 다음 글을 읽고, |조건|에 맞게 주어진 요약문을 완성하시오.

| 조건 |
* (A)는 1단어, (B)는 2단어, (C)는 1단어로 쓸 것
* 본문에 있는 단어만을 그대로 사용할 것

Newton's laws of motion apply perfectly to the world of golf. We're all aware that a golf ball moves when it is hit by force. However, there are outside forces that keep a golf ball from moving in its original direction forever. A ball may have a straight path when the club hits it, but then gravity pulls the ball toward Earth and can keep it from going straight. Air resistance — a form of friction — then slows the ball's velocity as it speeds through the air. Once a golf ball connects with the ground again, it slows down even more because a grassy and sandy surface creates more friction with the ball than air.

⬇

The external forces that affect the movement of a golf ball are (A) ____________ (B) ____________ ____________, and ground (C) ____________.

02 다음 글을 읽고, |조건|에 맞게 빈칸 (A), (B), (C)를 채우시오.

| 조건 |
* (A)는 1단어, (B)는 2단어, (C)는 4단어로 쓸 것
* 본문에 있는 단어를 찾아 그대로 쓸 것

Newton's laws of motion apply perfectly to the world of golf. We're all aware that a golf ball moves when it is hit by force. However, there are outside forces that keep a golf ball from moving in its original direction forever. A ball may have a straight path when the club hits it, but then gravity pulls the ball toward Earth and can keep it from going straight. Air resistance — a form of friction — then slows the ball's velocity as it speeds through the air. Once a golf ball connects with the ground again, it slows down even more because a grassy and sandy surface creates more friction with the ball than air.

⬇

It is (A) ____________ that pulls an object into the center of the earth. Also, two forces that decrease the speed of ball are (B) ____________ ____________ and (C) ____________ ____________ ____________ ____________.

03 다음 글을 읽고, |조건|에 맞게 주어진 제목을 완성하시오.

| 조건 |
* 5단어로 쓸 것
* [보기]에서 선택한 단어를 한 번씩만 쓸 것
* 필요한 경우, 문맥과 어법에 맞게 변형할 것

[보기] quality / disturb / of / the / influence / enhance / that / vertical purchase / movement / quantity / technique / horizontal / force

Newton's laws of motion apply perfectly to the world of golf. We're all aware that a golf ball moves when it is hit by force. However, there are outside forces that keep a golf ball from moving in its original direction forever. A ball may have a straight path when the club hits it, but then gravity pulls the ball toward Earth and can keep it from going straight. Air resistance — a form of friction — then slows the ball's velocity as it speeds through the air. Once a golf ball connects with the ground again, it slows down even more because a grassy and sandy surface creates more friction with the ball than air.

⬇

Newton's law ________ ________ ________ ________ ________ a golf ball

04 다음 글의 순서로 가장 적절한 것은?

Newton's laws of motion apply perfectly to the world of golf. We're all aware that a golf ball moves when it is hit by force.

(A) However, there are outside forces that keep a golf ball from moving in its original direction forever. A ball may have a straight path when the club hits it, but then gravity pulls the ball toward Earth and can keep it from going straight.

(B) Air resistance — a form of friction — then slows the ball's velocity as it speeds through the air.

(C) Once a golf ball connects with the ground again, it slows down even more because a grassy and sandy surface creates more friction with the ball than air.

① (A) - (B) - (C)
② (B) - (A) - (C)
③ (B) - (C) - (A)
④ (C) - (A) - (B)
⑤ (C) - (B) - (A)

UNIT 12

무관한 문장 찾기

글의 논리	Enumeration (열거)
제목	과거 중국 배우들의 삶
주제	현대 시대 이전에는 중국의 배우들은 오늘날 사회에서 받는 존경을 거의 못 받았다.

PRACTICE 01

046 어법 선택 & 연결어

Prior **[to / than]** the modern era, the Chinese actor, **[if / whether]** rural amateur **[or / and]** urban professional, **[rare / rarely]** **[to enjoy / enjoyed]** the respect **[what / that]** society pays him or her today. Until recently, (   ), a theater practitioner could **[hard / hardly]** earn his living with one stationary troupe. He often became an itinerant performer, **[travelled / travelling]** among small towns and rural villages to perform **[during / while]** festivals or **[celebrating / to celebrate]** important occasions in the lives of the local gentry. **[Most / Almost]** individual actors were at least part-time itinerants, **[contributed / contributing]** to the image of the vagabond good-for-nothing **[what / that]** afflicted his profession for centuries. In the imperial period, entire urban troupes might tour the countryside at harvest, New Year, and other festival times.

주제문 현대 시대 이전에는 중국의 배우들은 오늘날 사회에서 받는 존경을 거의 못 받았다.

(Prior to the modern era), / the Chinese actor, / (whether rural amateur or urban professional), / (rarely) enjoyed the respect / {that society pays him or her / (today)}.

〈전치사〉 O 현대 시대 이전에는 / S 중국의 배우는 / 시골의 아마추어든 도시의 전문배우든 상관없이 / V 거의 존경을 / O〈선행사〉 향유하지 못했다 / 〈목·관〉 S V I.O 사회가 그들에게 표하는 / 오늘날

현대 시대 이전에는 시골의 아마추어든 도시의 전문배우든 상관없이 중국의 배우는 오늘날 사회가 그들에게 표하는 존경을 거의 향유하지 못했다.

노트
- prior to : ~에 앞서, 먼저
- pay+IO+DO : ~에게 ~을/를 (경의를) 표하다
- 〈whether 용법〉

종류				명사절	부사절
whether	(or not)	주어	동사	~인지 아닌지	~던지 말 던지, ~하든 말든, ~인지 아닌지
whether	주어	동사	(or not)		
whether	A	or	B	A이거나 B	

- 〈부정어의 종류〉

완전부정어	부사	not (~ 아닌)
	부사	never (결코 ~ 아닌)
	형용사	no (~도 아닌)
	대명사/부사/형용사	neither (~도 아니다)
	대명사/부사/형용사	none (아무도 ~ 아니다)
	대명사/부사/명사	nothing (조금도[결코] ~ 않다)
준부정어	부사	hardly (거의 ~ 아니다)
	부사	scarcely (거의 ~ 않다)
	부사	barely (거의 ~ 아니게)
	부사	seldom (좀처럼 ~ 않는)
	부사	rarely (좀처럼 ~하지 않는)
	형용사/부사	little (거의 ~ 없는)
	형용사/부사	few (거의 ~ 없는)

- 〈목적격관계대명사 that 생략〉 : 수여동사의 간접목적어가 없는 경우 / 선행사를 포함하고 있는 관계대명사 what 사용 불가

	〈목적격관계대명사절〉				
선행사	목적격관계대명사	주어	수여동사	간접목적어	~~직접목적어~~
the respect	생략 가능 : (that)	society	pays	him or her	

- 〈what vs. that〉

	관계대명사(불완전한 문장)	접속사(완전한 문장)
what	○ 선행사를 포함하고 있기 때문에 what 앞에 선행사 불필요	×
that	○ that 앞에 선행사 필요	○

열거 최근까지도 전문 연기자는 한 지역에 정착하여 생계를 유지할 수 없었다.

① (Until recently), / (in fact), / a theater practitioner / could (hardly) earn his living / (with one stationary troupe).

최근까지 / 사실상 / S 전문 연기자는 / V O 거의 생계를 유지할 수 없었다 / 한 지역에 정착하여 공연하는 극단으로는

사실상 최근까지 전문 연기자는 한 지역에 정착하여 공연하는 극단으로는 거의 생계를 유지할 수 없었다.

노트
- hardly : 거의 ~ 아니다
- earn[gain, make] one's living[livelihood, bread] : 생활비를 벌다

열거 연기자들은 여러 마을들을 돌아다니며 공연을 했다.

② He / (often) became an itinerant performer, / [travelling / (among small towns and rural villages) /

S 그는 / V S.C 흔히 순회 연기자가 되어 / 〈분사구문〉 여행하였다 / 〈전치사〉 작은 도시와 시골 마을들을

{to perform / (during festivals)} / or / {to celebrate important occasions / (in the lives of the local gentry)}].

(during: 〈전치사〉, festivals: O)

공연하기 위해서 / 축제기간 동안 / 또는 / 중요한 행사를 축하하기 위해서 / 지방 유지의 삶에서

그는 흔히 순회 연기자가 되어 축제기간 동안 공연하기 위해서 또는 지방 유지의 삶에서 중요한 행사를 축하하기 위해서 작은 도시와 시골 마을들을 여행하였다.

노트

■ in the lives of : ~의 일생(삶)에서

■ 〈become 동사 쓰임〉

become	〈주격보어〉	(2형식)
	명사	(~으로) 되다
	형용사	
	과거분사	
	〈목적어〉	(3형식)
	명사	어울리다, 잘 맞다(진행형/수동태 불가)

■ 〈분사구문 – 문미〉 : 주절과 분사구문의 위치가 서로 바뀌어도 무관

주절		종속절(→ 분사구문)			
주어	동사	종속 접속사	주어	동사 : 상황에 맞게 아래처럼 바뀜	
		〈그대로 사용하면 의미 강조〉	(주절의 주어와 같으면 생략하고, 다르면 주격으로 사용함)	(being)	Ring(현재분사)
				(having been)	p.p.(과거분사)
					형용사
				생략 가능	명사
He	became	–	–	–	travelling

■ 〈between vs. among〉

전치사	between	~ 사이에	둘 사이	혼용
	among		셋 이상	

■ 시간(~ 동안)

전치사	during	+ 명사 / 명사 상당어구
종속접속사	while	+ 주어 + 동사

③ Summer was right / (around the corner), / and that meant (that) {music festivals would start to pop up (nationwide)}.

(Summer: S, was: V, right: S.C / that: S, meant: V / music festivals: S, would start: V, to pop up (nationwide): O / {…}: O)

여름이 왔다 / 곧 / 그리고 그것은 의미한다 / 음악 행사가 전국적으로 속속 나타나기 시작할 것을

곧 여름이 왔는데, 그것은 전국적으로 음악 행사가 속속 나타나기 시작할 것이라는 것을 뜻했다.

노트

■ be right around the corner : 바로 코앞에 있다

■ pop up : 갑자기 일어나다; 튀어나오다[오르다], 불쑥 나타나다

■ 〈목적격종속접속사 that 생략〉 : 완전타동사의 목적어로 사용된 경우 / 관계대명사 what 사용 불가

완전타동사	종속절(명사절 : 목적어) (완전한 절)		
	that	주어	동사
meant	목적격종속접속사 – 생략 가능(~하는 것을)	music festivals	would start

■ 〈3형식에서 목적어 자리에 to R / Ring 둘 다 사용 가능〉

주어	완전타동사		목적어
	begin	~을 시작하다	to R/Ring (의미 차이 없음)
	cease	~을 중단하다	
	continue	~을 계속하다	
	deserve	~할 가치/자격/권리가 있다	
	dislike	~을 싫어하다	
	hate		
	like	~을 좋아하다	
	love	~을 사랑하다	
	neglect	~하는 것을 소홀히 하다	
	prefer	~쪽을 좋아하다	
	require	~을 요구하다	
	start	~을 시작하다	

열거 수세기 동안 돌아다니며 공연을 하면서 이리저리 떠도는 쓸모없는 사람이라는 인식을 심었다.

④ Most individual actors / were (at least) part-time itinerants, / {contributing to the image / (of the vagabond) (good-for-nothing) / (that afflicted his profession) / (for centuries)}.

(Most individual actors: S, were: V, part-time itinerants: S.C / contributing: 〈분사구문〉, to: 〈전치사〉, the image: O / vagabond: 〈선행사〉 / that: 〈주·관〉, afflicted: V, his profession: O)

대부분의 개인 자격 배우들은 / 적어도 시간제로 일하는 순회배우였고 / 인식을 심어주는 데 기여하였다 / 이리저리 떠도는 아무짝에도 쓸모없는 사람이라는 / 그의 직업에 폐를 끼친 / 수세기 동안

대부분의 개인 자격의 배우들은 적어도 시간제로 일하는 순회배우였고, 수세기 동안 그의 직업에 폐를 끼친, 이리저리 떠도는 아무짝에도 쓸모없는 사람이라는 인식을 심어주는 데 기여하였다.

노트

■ at least : 적어도[최소한]

■ contribute to : ~에 기여하다

■ vagabond : 방랑하는, 유랑하는, 떠도는(=wandering, nomadic)

■ good-for-nothing : 아무 짝에도 쓸모없는 사람

■ 〈most / almost / mostly〉

	대명사	형용사	부사
most	대부분의 것들(사람들)	대부분의	가장
almost	–	–	거의
mostly	–	–	주로, 일반적으로

■ 〈분사구문 – 문미〉 : 주절과 분사구문의 위치가 서로 바뀌어도 무관

주절		종속절(→ 분사구문)			
주어	동사	종속 접속사	주어	동사 : 상황에 맞게 아래처럼 바뀜	
		〈그대로 사용하면 의미 강조〉	(주절의 주어와 같으면 생략하고, 다르면 주격으로 사용함)	(being)	Ring(현재분사)
				(having been)	p.p.(과거분사)
					형용사
				생략 가능	명사
Most individual actors	were	–	–	–	contributing

■ 〈주격관계대명사절의 수의 일치〉 : 선행사를 포함하고 있는 관계대명사 what 사용 불가

선행사	주격관계대명사절		
	주격관계대명사	주어 (삭제 표시)	동사
good-for-nothing	that		afflicted

열거 제국주의 시대에는 도시극단 전체가 지방을 돌아다니기도 했다.

⑤ (In the imperial period), / entire urban troupes / might tour the countryside / (at harvest, New Year, and other festival times).

제국주의 시대에는 / 전체 도시극단은(S) / 지방을 돌아다닐 수도 있었다(V, O) / 추수철, 설날, 그리고 다른 축제 기간에

제국주의 시대에는 도시극단 전체가 추수철, 설날, 그리고 다른 축제 기간에 지방을 돌아다닐 수도 있었다.

▶ 다음 글에서 전체 흐름과 관계 없는 문장은?

정답 | ③

해설 | ③ 이 글의 주제는 현대 시대 이전에는 중국의 배우들이 오늘날 사회에서 받는 존경을 거의 받지 못했다는 것이다. ③은 여름이 시작해서 음악축제가 곧 전국에서 개최될 것이라는 내용이다. 이 내용은 글의 소재와 일치하지 않기 때문에 글의 흐름과 관계 없다.

오답 | ① 오늘날과 달리 연기자가 한 지역에 정착하여서는 생계를 유지하지 못한다고 나오므로 글의 주제인 중국의 배우들의 현재와 과거의 차이에 알맞다.
② ①에 대한 설명으로 여러 도시들을 여행한다는 내용이므로 글의 흐름과 적절하다.
④ 글의 주제인 중국의 배우들은 현대 시대 이전에 사회에서 거의 존경을 못 받았다는 내용이므로 글의 흐름과 적절하다.
⑤ 배우들이 지방을 돌아다니며 생계를 유지한다는 내용이므로 글의 흐름과 적절하다.

Words

- ☐ rural
- ☐ amateur
- ☐ urban
- ☐ professional
- ☐ rarely
- ☐ recently
- ☐ practitioner
- ☐ performer
- ☐ celebrate
- ☐ occasion
- ☐ nationwide
- ☐ individual
- ☐ part-time
- ☐ vagabond
- ☐ profession
- ☐ imperial
- ☐ period
- ☐ countryside
- ☐ harvest

Phrases

- ☐ prior to
- ☐ in the lives of
- ☐ be right around the corner
- ☐ contribute to
- ☐ earn[gain, make] one's living[livelihood, bread]
- ☐ pop up
- ☐ at least
- ☐ good-for-nothing

우선순위 영단어

역대 수능 기출 + 전국 모의고사 기출 + EBS 기출 + 교과서 기출 빈출 어휘

단어	뜻	단어	뜻	단어	뜻
suppose	v. 가정하다	sure enough	아니나 다를까	surrender	v. 넘겨주다
surround	v. 둘러싸다	suspend	v. 유예하다	swallow	v. 삼키다
swear	v. 맹세하다	sweat	v. 괴로워하다	sweep	v. 쓸다
symbolize	v. 상징하다	syndrome	n. 증후군	synthetic	a. 합성의
table	n. 표	take turns ~ing	v. 교대로 ~하다	talkative	a. 수다스러운
target	v. 목적	tax	v. 세금	taxation	n. 조세
tear(−tore−torn)	v. 찢다	technology	n. 기술	telescope	n. 망원경
temperament	n. 기질	tempt	v. 유혹하다	tentative	a. 잠정적인
termite	n. 흰개미	terrain	n. 지형	theorize	v. 이론화하다
thereafter	ad. 그 후에	threatened	a. 위협당한	thriving	a. 번창하는
tip	n. 끝	tiptoe	v. 발끝으로 걷다	torment	n. 고문

변형문제

01 다음 글을 읽고, |조건|에 맞게 주어진 요약문을 완성하시오.

| 조건 |

* (A), (B)는 각각 다르게 1단어로 쓸 것
* [보기]에서 선택한 단어를 한 번씩만 쓸 것
* 필요한 경우, 문맥과 어법에 맞게 변형할 것

[보기] live / cope / struggle / entertain / search / exploration / travelling / tour / project / promotion

Prior to the modern era, the Chinese actor, whether rural amateur or urban professional, rarely enjoyed the respect that society pays him or her today. Until recently, in fact, a theater practitioner could hardly earn his living with one stationary troupe. He often became an itinerant performer, travelling among small towns and rural villages to perform during festivals or to celebrate important occasions in the lives of the local gentry. Most individual actors were at least part-time itinerants, contributing to the image of the vagabond good-for-nothing that afflicted his profession for centuries. In the imperial period, entire urban troupes might tour the countryside at harvest, New Year, and other festival times.

⬇

Before the contemporary era, Chinese actors (A) ____________ with their poor living and therefore carried out a (B) ____________ of the country.

02 밑줄 친 부분 중 문맥상 옳지 않은 것은?

Prior to the modern era, the Chinese actor, whether rural amateur or urban professional, rarely ① enjoyed the respect that society pays him or her today. Until recently, in fact, a theater practitioner could ② easily earn his living with one stationary troupe. He often became an ③ itinerant performer, travelling among small towns and rural villages to perform during festivals or to celebrate important occasions in the lives of the local gentry. Most individual actors were at least part-time itinerants, ④ contributing to the image of the vagabond good-for-nothing that afflicted his profession for centuries. In the imperial period, entire urban troupes might ⑤ tour the countryside at harvest, New Year, and other festival times.

03 다음 문장이 들어갈 부분으로 가장 적절한 곳을 고르시오.

Until recently, in fact, a theater practitioner could hardly earn his living with one stationary troupe.

(①) Prior to the modern era, the Chinese actor, whether rural amateur or urban professional, rarely enjoyed the respect that society pays him or her today. (②) He often became an itinerant performer, travelling among small towns and rural villages to perform during festivals or to celebrate important occasions in the lives of the local gentry. (③) Most individual actors were at least part-time itinerants, contributing to the image of the vagabond good-for-nothing that afflicted his profession for centuries. (④) In the imperial period, entire urban troupes might tour the countryside at harvest, New Year, and other festival times. (⑤)

04 다음 글의 내용으로 적절하지 않은 것은?

Prior to the modern era, the Chinese actor, whether rural amateur or urban professional, rarely enjoyed the respect that society pays him or her today. Until recently, in fact, a theater practitioner could hardly earn his living with one stationary troupe. He often became an itinerant performer, travelling among small towns and rural villages to perform during festivals or to celebrate important occasions in the lives of the local gentry. Most individual actors were at least part-time itinerants, contributing to the image of the vagabond good-for-nothing that afflicted his profession for centuries. In the imperial period, entire urban troupes might tour the countryside at harvest, New Year, and other festival times.

① 현대 사회 이전에 중국의 배우는 존경을 거의 받지 못했다.
② 최근까지 배우들은 한 지역에 정착하여 생계를 유지했다.
③ 중국의 배우들은 중요한 행사를 축하하기 위해 시골들을 여행했다.
④ 대부분의 개개인 배우들은 시간제로 일했다.
⑤ 제국주의 시대에는 도시극단 전체가 다른 축제 기간에 지방을 돌아 다니곤 했다.

UNIT **12**

무관한 문장 찾기

글의 논리	Examples
제목	불확실성을 이겨내야 하는 이유
주제	위대한 일들은 불확실성에서 시작되었다.

PRACTICE 02

047 어법 선택 & 연결어

Every great thing **[what / that] [was / were]** ever **[started / starting]** began in uncertainty. Thomas Alva Edison asked, "Will this work?" and now we experience the gift of the lightbulb. Steve Jobs pondered, "**[Is / Are]** there a need for this?" and now we have minicomputers **[what / that] [fit / fits]** in our pockets. In order to **[bring / bringing]** our ideas or dreams to life, we have to expect fear and uncertainty, welcome **[it / them]** in, and **[know / knows] [what / that]** once we face **[it / them]**, it no longer has a hold on us. We must remind **[us / ourselves] [what / that]** there **[is / are]** two possible ends to every uncertain journey we embark upon: **[both / either]** we learn a lesson that **[bring / brings]** us one step closer to our true desires or we reach the point we set out for.

주제문 위대한 일들은 불확실성에서 시작되었다.

Every great thing / (that was ever started) / began (in uncertainty).

- Every great thing: S(선행사) 위대한 모든 것은
- that: (주·관)
- was ever started: V (수동태) 지금까지 시작된
- began: V 시작되었다
- in uncertainty: 불확실성에서

지금까지 시작된 위대한 모든 것은 불확실성에서 시작되었다.

노트 ■ 〈주어와 동사의 수의 일치〉
- each / every / any + 단수동사

■ 〈주격관계대명사절의 수의 일치〉: 선행사를 포함하고 있는 관계대명사 what 사용 불가

	주격관계대명사절			
선행사(주어)	주격관계대명사	~~주어~~	동사 ~	동사 ~ (본동사)
Every great thing	that		was	began

■ 〈what vs. that〉

	관계대명사(불완전한 문장)	접속사(완전한 문장)
what	○ 선행사를 포함하고 있기 때문에 what 앞에 선행사 불필요	×
that	○ that 앞에 선행사 필요	○

예시1 Thomas Alva Edison은 작동될지 의문을 가지고 전구를 만들었다.

① Thomas Alva Edison / asked, / "Will this work?" / and / (now) we / experience / the gift (of the lightbulb).

- Thomas Alva Edison: S, Thomas Alva Edison은
- asked: V, 의문을 가졌다
- "Will this work?": S, V, "이것이 작동될까?"라는
- and: 그리고
- (now) we: S, 지금 우리는
- experience: V, 경험하고 있다
- the gift: O
- (of the lightbulb): 전구라는 선물을

Thomas Alva Edison은 "이것이 작동될까?"라는 의문을 가졌고, 우리는 지금 전구라는 선물을 경험하고 있다.

노트 ■ 〈동격의 of〉: 이라고 하는, ~인

A	of	B
명사	〈동격관계〉	(동)명사(구)
the gift	~이라고 하는, ~인	the lightbulb

예시2 Steve Jobs는 이것이 필요할까에 대한 불확실성을 가지고 소형 컴퓨터를 만들었다.

② Steve Jobs / pondered, / "Is there a need (for this)?" / and / now we have minicomputers / (that fit in our pockets).

- Steve Jobs: S, Steve Jobs는
- pondered: V, 곰곰이 생각했다
- Is: V
- a need (for this): S, "이것이 필요할까?"에 대해
- and: 그리고
- we: S, have: V, minicomputers: O(선행사), 우리는 소형 컴퓨터를 가지고 있다
- that: (주·관), fit: V, 주머니에 꼭 맞는

Steve Jobs는 "이것이 필요할까?"에 대해 곰곰이 생각했고, 지금 우리는 주머니에 딱 맞는 소형 컴퓨터를 가지고 있다.

노트 ■ fit in : ~에 맞다, 어울리다

■ 〈There is 도치구문〉

긍정문	There	is	단수 주어	~이 있다
		are	복수 주어	
부정문	There	is no	단수 주어	~이 없다
		are no	복수 주어	

- 유도부사 **there**와 함께 도치구문을 이루는 be동사(is/are/was/were) 대신에 완전자동사 **appear**, **come**, **exist**, **follow**, **live**, **stand** 등을 사용할 수 있다.

■ 〈주격관계대명사절의 수의 일치〉: 선행사를 포함하고 있는 관계대명사 what 사용 불가

	주격관계대명사절		
선행사	주격관계대명사	~~주어~~	동사
minicomputers	that		fit

주제문(재진술) 우리의 아이디어를 실현하기 위해서는 두려움과 불확실성을 예상하고 맞아들여야 한다.

③ (In order to bring our ideas or dreams to life), / we / have to expect / fear and uncertainty, / welcome it in, and know / {that (once we face it), / it (no longer) has a hold on us}.

우리의 아이디어나 꿈에 생기를 불어넣기 위해서, 우리는 두려움과 불확실성을 예상하고, 그것을 기꺼이 맞아들여야 하며, 일단 그것에 직면하면 그것은 더 이상 우리에게 지배력이 없다는 것을 알아야 한다.

노트
- bring A to life : A를 재미있게[활기 넘치게] 하다, A를 소생시키다
- welcome A in : A를 기꺼이 맞아들이다
- have a hold on[over] A : A에 대해 지배력[권력]이 있다, A의 급소를 쥐고 있다
- once : 일단 ~하면(종속접속사)
- 〈~하기 위해서〉 (긍정문) : in order to R에서 in order는 생략 가능하다. 그대로 in order를 사용하면 생략하는 것보다 강조하거나 공손한 표현을 하는 경우이다.

주어	동사	목적		
		so that	주어	may(can, will) R
		in order that		
		in order to R		
		so as to R		
		to R		

- 〈이어동사〉

타동사	명사	부사	(○)
타동사	부사	명사	(○)
타동사	대명사	부사	(○)
타동사	부사	대명사	(×)
welcome	in	it	(×)

- 〈목적격종속접속사 that 생략〉 : 완전타동사의 목적어로 사용된 경우 / 관계대명사 what 사용 불가

완전타동사	종속절(명사절 : 목적어) (완전한 절)		
	that	주어	동사
know	목적격종속접속사 – 생략 가능(~하는 것을)	it	has

- 〈전체부정〉 : 모두/전부 ~ 아니다, 절대 ~하지 않는다

not any one(=none) (모두 ~이 아니다)	
no+명사 (어느 누구도 ~ 않다)	
not ~ either(=neither) (둘 다 ~이 아니다)	
not+anything(=nothing) (아무것도[단 하나도] (~ 아니다 · 없다))	
not+ever(=never) (결코 ~이 아니다)	
not anywhere(=nowhere)	
no=not any	no more=not ~ anymore
	nobody=not ~ anybody
	nothing=not ~ anything
	no longer=not ~ any longer

④ (Also), / we should try / to reduce uncertainty and risk-taking / (in order to minimize the possibility of failure).

또한, 실패의 가능성을 최소화시키기 위해 우리는 불확실성과 위험부담을 줄이려고 노력해야 한다.

노트 ■ 〈try 동사 쓰임〉

try	목적어	〈3형식〉
	to R	~ 노력/시도하다(S의 의지 있음)
	Ring	시험 삼아 한번 해보다(S의 의지 없음)

주제문(재진술) 우리는 교훈을 배우거나 목표로 삼은 지점에 도달할 수 있는 두 가지 가능성을 염두해 두어야 한다.

⑤ We / must remind ourselves / {that there are / two possible ends / (to every uncertain journey / (that) (we embark upon):} / either we learn a lesson / (that brings us one step closer to our true desires) / or / we reach the point / (that) (we set out for).

우리는 우리 스스로에게 우리가 착수하는 모든 불확실한 여행에는 두 가지의 가능성 있는 결말 — 우리의 진정한 욕망으로 한 발짝 더 다가서게 하는 교훈을 배우거나 또는 우리가 목표로 삼고 출발했던 지점에 도달하게 된다 — 이 있다는 것을 상기시켜야 한다.

노트
- embark upon : ~에 착수하다
- learn a lesson : 교훈을 배우다
- bring+IO+DO : ~에게 ~을/를 가져다주다
- close to : 아주 가까이에서
- set out for : ~을 향해 나서다
- 〈직접목적어 자리에 that절을 가지는 4형식 수여동사〉 : 수동태 시, be told+that+주어+동사

주어	수여동사		간접목적어	직접목적어
	advise	조언하다		(that)+주어+동사
	assure	장담(확신)시키다		
	convince	확신시켜주다		
	inform	알리다		
	instruct			
	notify			

persuade	설득하다
promise	약속하다
remind	상기시키다
request	요청하다
show	보여 주다
teach	가르치다
tell	말하다
warn	경고하다

■ 〈재귀대명사 vs. 대명사〉

		주어와 다름	주어와 동일
주어	~	대명사	재귀대명사
We		us	ourselves

■ 〈목적격관계대명사 that 생략〉 : 전치사의 목적어가 없는 경우 / 선행사를 포함하고 있는 관계대명사 what 사용 불가

	〈목적격관계대명사절〉				
선행사	목적격관계대명사	주어	동사	전치사	~~목적어~~
every uncertain journey	생략 가능 : (that)	we	embark	upon	
the point			set out	for	

■ 〈주격관계대명사절의 수의 일치〉 : 선행사를 포함하고 있는 관계대명사 what 사용 불가

	주격관계대명사절		
선행사	주격관계대명사	~~주어~~	동사
a lesson	that		brings

■ 〈상관접속사〉 : 병렬구조

종류				뜻
not	A	but	B	A가 아니라 B (=B, not A)
not only		but also		A뿐만 아니라 B도 (=B as well as A)
either		or		A와 B 둘 중 하나
neither		nor		A와 B 둘 다 아닌
both		and		A와 B 둘 다

▶ 다음 글에서 전체 흐름과 관계 없는 문장은?

정답 | ④

해설 | ④ 이 글의 주제는 위대한 일들이 불확실성에서 시작되었다는 것이다. ④의 내용은 불확실성과 위험부담을 줄이라고 조언하는 것이다. 글의 관점과 일치하지 않으므로 ④는 글의 흐름과 관계 없다.

오답 | ① "이것이 작동될까?"라는 불확실성을 가지고 전구를 개발했다고 했으므로 글의 관점과 일치한다.
② "이것이 필요할까?"에 대한 불확실성을 가지고 소형 컴퓨터를 개발했다고 했으므로 글의 관점과 일치한다.
③ 두려움과 불확실성을 기꺼이 받아들이라 하므로 글의 주제와 일치한다.
⑤ ③의 주제를 재진술하고 있으므로 글의 주제와 일치한다.

Words

☐ work
☐ experience
☐ need
☐ fit
☐ expect
☐ fear
☐ face
☐ reduce
☐ possibility
☐ failure
☐ remind
☐ possible
☐ end
☐ journey
☐ close
☐ desire
☐ reach
☐ point

Phrases

☐ fit in
☐ welcome A in
☐ embark upon
☐ close to
☐ bring A to life
☐ have a hold on[over] A
☐ learn a lesson
☐ set out for

우선순위 영단어 역대 수능 기출 + 전국 모의고사 기출 + EBS 기출 + 교과서 기출 빈출 어휘

단어	뜻	단어	뜻	단어	뜻
torture	n. 고문	transmission	n. 변속기	transplant	v. 이식하다
transport	v. 수송하다	traumatic	a. 충격적인	tremendously	ad. 매우
tropical	a. 열대(지방)의	tuck	v. 밀어넣다	tune	v. (악기의) 음을 맞추다
twig	n. 잔가지	typify	v. 대표하다	ubiquitous	a. 어디에나 있는

PRACTICE 02

변형문제

01 다음 글을 읽고, |조건|에 맞게 주어진 요지를 완성하시오.

| 조건 |
* (A), (B)는 각각 다르게 2단어로 쓸 것
* [보기]에서 선택한 단어를 한 번씩만 쓸 것
* 필요한 경우, 문맥과 어법에 맞게 변형할 것
* (B)의 경우, [보기]에서 주어진 것 외에 1단어를 추가할 것

[보기] avoid / initiate / eliminate / automatically / eradicate / underestimate / relieve / confront / hardly / gladly / naturally / expect

Every great thing that was ever started began in uncertainty. Thomas Alva Edison asked, "Will this work?" and now we experience the gift of the lightbulb. Steve Jobs pondered, "Is there a need for this?" and now we have minicomputers that fit in our pockets. In order to bring our ideas or dreams to life, we have to expect fear and uncertainty, welcome it in, and know that once we face it, it no longer has a hold on us. We must remind ourselves that there are two possible ends to every uncertain journey we embark upon: either we learn a lesson that brings us one step closer to our true desires or we reach the point we set out for.

⬇

Without any doubt, we should (A) ____________ ____________ fear and uncertainty because all great things (B) ____________ ____________ by uncertainty.

02 밑줄 친 부분 중 문맥상 옳지 않은 것은?

Every great thing that was ever started began in ① certainty. Thomas Alva Edison asked, "Will this work?" and now we experience the gift of the lightbulb. Steve Jobs ② pondered, "Is there a need for this?" and now we have minicomputers that fit in our pockets. In order to bring our ideas or dreams to life, we have to expect ③ fear and uncertainty, welcome it in, and know that once we face it, it no longer has a hold on us. We must ④ remind ourselves that there are two possible ends to every uncertain journey we embark upon: either we learn a lesson that brings us one step closer to our true ⑤ desires or we reach the point we set out for.

03 다음 글을 읽고, |조건|에 맞게 요약문을 완성하시오.

| 조건 |
* (A), (B)는 각각 다르게 1단어로 쓸 것
* [보기]에서 선택한 단어를 한 번씩만 쓸 것
* 필요한 경우, 문맥과 어법에 맞게 변형할 것

[보기] change / end / meeting / explore / ignore / encourage / overcome / beginning / peak / learn / forget

Every great thing that was ever started began in uncertainty. Thomas Alva Edison asked, "Will this work?" and now we experience the gift of the lightbulb. Steve Jobs pondered, "Is there a need for this?" and now we have minicomputers that fit in our pockets. In order to bring our ideas or dreams to life, we have to expect fear and uncertainty, welcome it in, and know that once we face it, it no longer has a hold on us. We must remind ourselves that there are two possible ends to every uncertain journey we embark upon: either we learn a lesson that brings us one step closer to our true desires or we reach the point we set out for.

⬇

Given that all great things are deeply associated with uncertainty at the (A) ____________. Successful people have not only confronted uncertainty but also (B) ____________ it, increasing chances to explore the inner desires.

04 다음 글의 순서로 적절한 것은?

Every great thing that was ever started began in uncertainty.

(A) In order to bring our ideas or dreams to life, we have to expect fear and uncertainty, welcome it in, and know that once we face it, it no longer has a hold on us.

(B) We must remind ourselves that there are two possible ends to every uncertain journey we embark upon: either we learn a lesson that brings us one step closer to our true desires or we reach the point we set out for.

(C) Thomas Alva Edison asked, "Will this work?" and now we experience the gift of the lightbulb. Steve Jobs pondered, "Is there a need for this?" and now we have minicomputers that fit in our pockets.

① (A) - (B) - (C) ② (B) - (A) - (C) ③ (B) - (C) - (A)
④ (C) - (A) - (B) ⑤ (C) - (B) - (A)

UNIT 12 무관한 문장 찾기

글의 논리	Enumeration (열거)
제목	노안에 의한 눈의 변화
주제	나이가 들어갈수록 안구의 능력이 떨어진다.

PRACTICE 03

048 어법 선택 & 연결어

As we grow older, the eye lens becomes more yellow, **[caused / causing]** poorer color discrimination in the green-blue-violet end of the spectrum. (　　　　　　), the lens's ability to adjust and focus **[decline / declines]** as the muscles around **[it / them]** stiffen. This is **[what / that]** causes difficulty in seeing close objects **[clear / clearly]** (**[called / calling]** presbyopia), **[necessitated / necessitating]** either longer arms **[or / and]** corrective lenses. To complicate matters **[farther / further]**, the time our eyes need to change focus from near to far (or vice versa) **[increase / increases]**. This (　　　　　　) poses a major problem in driving. **[Because / Because of]** drivers are **[contant / constantly]** changing **[its / their]** focus from the instrument panel to other autos and signs on the highway, older drivers may miss important information **[because / because of]** **[its / their]** slower **[refocused / refocusing]** time.

열거 나이가 들어감에 따라 색깔을 식별하는 것이 힘들어진다.

(As we grow older), / the eye lens / becomes more yellow, / {causing poorer color discrimination / (in the green-blue-violet end of the spectrum)}.

(As: 〈종·접〉, we: S, grow: V, older: S.C) 나이가 들어감에 따라 / the eye lens: S 우리 눈의 수정체는 / becomes: V 더 노랗게 변하면서 / yellow: S.C / causing: 〈분사구문〉 / poorer color discrimination: O 식별을 못하게 된다 / (in the green-blue-violet end of the spectrum) 스펙트럼의 끝부분에 있는 초록-파랑-보라 색깔의

나이가 들어감에 따라 우리 눈의 수정체는 더 노랗게 변하면서 (빛의) 스펙트럼의 끝부분에 있는 초록-파랑-보라 색깔의 식별을 더 못하게 된다.

노트
- grow older : 늙어가다
- 〈become 동사 쓰임〉

become	〈주격보어〉	(2형식)
	명사	(~으로) 되다
	형용사	
	과거분사	
	〈목적어〉	(3형식)
	명사	어울리다, 잘 맞다(진행형/수동태 불가)

- 〈분사구문 - 문미〉 : 주절과 분사구문의 위치가 서로 바뀌어도 무관

주절		종속절(→ 분사구문)			
주어	동사	종속 접속사	주어	동사 : 상황에 맞게 아래처럼 바뀜	
		〈그대로 사용하면 의미 강조〉	(주절의 주어와 같으면 생략하고, 다르면 주격으로 사용함)	(being)	Ring(현재분사)
				(having been)	p.p.(과거분사)
				생략 가능	형용사
					명사
the eye lens	becomes	–	–	–	causing

열거 나이가 들어감에 따라 초점을 맞추는 수정체의 능력이 떨어진다.

Also, / the lens's ability / (to adjust and focus) / declines / {as the muscles / (around it) / stiffen}.

Also 또한 / the lens's ability: S 수정체의 능력이 / (to adjust and focus) 조정하고 초점을 맞추는 / declines: V 떨어진다 / as: 〈종·접〉 / the muscles: S 근육이 / (around it) 수정체 주위의 / stiffen: V 경직되면서

또한 수정체 주위의 근육이 경직되면서 조정하고 초점을 맞추는 수정체의 능력이 떨어진다.

노트 ■ 〈부사절을 이끄는 종속접속사〉 : as 용법

	쓰임	해석
as + 주어 + 동사	시간	~하고 있을 때, ~하자마자, ~하면서
	원인/이유	~ 때문에
	조건	~한다면
	양보	~일지라도
	비교	~보다/만큼
	방법/상태	~대로/~하듯이

열거 노안이라 불리는 이것은 가까운 물건을 명확하게 보기 힘들게 한다.

① This / is [what causes difficulty / {in seeing close objects (clearly)} / (called presbyopia)], / {necessitating either longer arms or corrective lenses}.

This: S 이것이 / is: V / what: 〈주·관〉 / causes: V / difficulty: O 어렵게 만드는 것인데 / seeing: 〈동명사〉 / close objects: O 가까운 물건을 / [what ... clearly]: S.C / (clearly) 명확하게 볼 때 / called: 〈과거분사〉 / presbyopia: S.C (노안이라고 부르는) / necessitating: 〈분사구문〉 그리고 이것이 / longer arms: O_1 / corrective lenses: O_2 더 긴 팔이나 교정 렌즈를 필요하게 만든다

이것이 가까운 물건을 명확하게 보는 것을 어렵게 만드는 (노안이라 부르는) 것인데, 더 긴 팔이나 교정 렌즈를 필요하게 만든다.

노트 ■ **〈동명사의 목적어로 사용된 주격관계대명사 what〉** : 선행사가 필요한 주격 관계대명사 that/which 사용 불가

		주격관계대명사절(명사절 : 동사의 주격보어)				
주어	동사	~~선행사~~	what	~~주어~~	타동사	목적어
This	is		선행사를 포함한 관계대명사 (=the thing(s) which/that ~) : ~하는 것은/이		causes	difficulty

■ **〈분사구문 – 문미〉** : 주절과 분사구문의 위치가 서로 바뀌어도 무관

주절		종속절(→ 분사구문)			
주어	동사	종속 접속사	주어	동사 : 상황에 맞게 아래처럼 바뀜	
		〈그대로 사용하면 의미 강조〉	(주절의 주어와 같으면 생략하고, 다르면 주격으로 사용함)	(being) (having been) 생략 가능	Ring(현재분사)
					p.p.(과거분사)
					형용사
					명사
This	is	–	–	–	necessitating

■ **〈상관접속사〉** : 병렬구조

종류				뜻
not	A	but	B	A가 아니라 B (=B, not A)
not only	A	but also	B	A뿐만 아니라 B도 (=B as well as A)
either	A	or	B	A와 B 둘 중 하나
neither	A	nor	B	A와 B 둘 다 아닌
both	A	and	B	A와 B 둘 다

■ **〈혼동 어휘〉**

	동사	형용사	명사	부사
correct	정정하다, 교정하다	옳은, 정확한	–	–
correction	–	–	정정, 수정	–
corrective	–	바로잡는, 수정의	–	–
collect	모으다, 수집하다	–	–	–
collection	–	–	수집품, 소장품	–
collective	–	집단의, 공동의	–	–
correctly	–	–	–	바르게, 정확하게
collectively	–	–	–	집합적으로, 총괄하여

열거 **나이가 들어가면서 초점을 바꾸는 데 필요한 시간도 늘어난다.**

② (To complicate matters further), / the time / (when) {our eyes need to change focus / (from near to far) / or (vice versa)} / increases.

- matters: O / To complicate matters further: 문제를 더 복잡하게 만들기 위해
- the time: S, 시간이
- our eyes: S, 우리의 눈이
- need: V_1 / focus: O — 초점을 바꾸는데 필요한
- from near to far: 가까운 곳에서 먼 곳으로
- vice versa: (그 반대도 마찬가지이다)
- increases: V_2, 늘어나는 것이다

문제를 더 복잡하게 만들기 위해 우리의 눈이 가까운 곳에서 먼 곳으로 (그 반대도 마찬가지이다) 초점을 바꾸는 데 필요한 시간이 늘어나는 것이다.

노트 ■ from near to far : 근방에서 먼 곳까지

■ vice versa : 거꾸로, 역으로, 반대로; 역 또한 같다

■ **〈불규칙적으로 변화하는 중요 형용사와 부사〉**

원급	비교급	뜻	최상급	뜻	의미
far	farther	거리가 먼	farthest	가장 먼	거리
	further	정도가 더한	furthest		정도

■ **〈관계부사〉** : 관계부사절은 완전한 문장이 나오고, 선행사와 관계부사는 서로 같이 사용할 수도 있고 둘 중 하나는 생략할 수도 있다.

용도	선행사	관계부사	전치사+관계대명사
시간	the time	when	in/at/on+which
장소	the place	where	in/at/on+which
이유	the reason	why	for which
방법	(the way)	how	in which
	the way how는 같이 사용 못함, the way, the way in which, the way that은 사용 가능 (how 대신에 사용되는 that은 관계부사 대용어라고 함)		

■ **〈need 동사의 용법〉**

목적어(to R)		3형식	〈~할〉 필요가 있다, 〈~〉 해야 하다
목적어	목적격보어(to R)	5형식	〈남이〉 〈~해 줄〉 필요가 있다
동명사(Ring)		3형식	〈사람 · 물건이〉 〈~되어야 할〉 필요가 있다
목적어	목적격보어(p.p.)	5형식	〈~이〉 〈…될〉 필요가 있다, 〈~을〉 〈…되도록 할〉 필요가 있다

열거 **이 점은 운전을 할 때 심각한 문제를 제기한다.**

③ This / also poses a major problem / (in driving).

- This: S, 이것은
- poses: V / a major problem: O — 또한 문제를 제기한다
- driving: O(동명사), 운전을 할 때

이것은 또한 운전을 할 때 심각한 문제를 제기한다.

노트 ■ poses a problem : 문제를 일으키다

■ in+동명사 : ~할 때

④ (Fortunately), / some universal changes, / (such as presbyopia), / can be corrected / (easily) / (through glasses or contacts).

- Fortunately: 다행히도
- some universal changes: S, 일반적인 변화의 일부분은
- such as presbyopia: 노안과 같은
- can be corrected: V(수동태), 교정될 수 있다
- easily: 쉽게
- through: (전치사)
- glasses: O_1 / contacts: O_2 — 안경이나 콘택트렌즈를 통해

다행히도 노안과 같은 일반적인 변화의 일부분은 안경이나 콘택트렌즈를 통해 쉽게 교정될 수 있다.

노트 ■ A such as B : B와 같은 A

■ **〈혼동 어휘〉**

through	전치사	~을 통하여
throughout	전치사	[장소] ~의 도처에, [시간] ~ 동안, ~ 내내
	부사	도처에, 완전히, 철저하게
though	접속사	~에도 불구하고
thorough	형용사	철저한, 완전한

열거 노인들은 안구의 능력이 하락하여 운전을 할 때 힘들어진다.

⑤ {Because drivers / are (constantly) changing their focus / (from the instrument panel to other autos and signs on the highway)}, / older drivers / may miss important information / (because of their slower refocusing time).

(Because: 〈종·접〉 왜냐하면 / drivers: S 운전자들은 / are changing: V〈현재진행〉 끊임없이 자신의 초점을 변경하기 때문에 / their focus: O / from the instrument panel to other autos and: 계기판에서 다른 자동차와 / signs on the highway: 고속도로 위의 표지판으로 / older drivers: S 노인 운전자들은 / may miss: V 중요한 정보를 / important information: O 놓칠 수 있다 / because of: 〈전치사〉 / their slower refocusing time: 초점을 다시 맞추는 시간이 더 오래 걸리기 때문에)

운전자들은 계기판에서 다른 자동차와 고속도로 위의 표지판으로 끊임없이 자신의 초점을 변경하는데, 노인 운전자들은 초점을 다시 맞추는 시간이 더 오래 걸리기 때문에 중요한 정보를 놓칠 수 있다.

노트 ■ from A to B : A에서 B로
■ 〈원인/이유〉 : ~ 때문에

종속접속사	as	+주어+동사 ~
	because	
	now(that)	
	since	

전치사	because of	+(동)명사 / 명사 상당어구
	due to	
	for	
	on account of	
	owing to	
	thanks to	

▶ 다음 글에서 전체 흐름과 관계 없는 문장은?

정답 | ④

해설 | ④ 이 글의 주제는 나이가 들어갈수록 안구의 능력이 떨어진다는 것이다. 그리고 이에 대해 여러 가지 이유를 들며 설명하고 있다. 그런데 ④의 문장을 보면 노안은 쉽게 교정할 수 있다고 나오므로 노안이 생길수록 문제가 생긴다는 글의 관점과 반대된다. 따라서 ④는 글의 흐름과 관계 없다.

오답 | ① 나이가 들수록 가까운 물건을 명확히 보는 것이 어렵다고 설명하므로 글의 흐름과 적절하다.
② 또한 초점을 바꾸는 데 필요한 시간이 늘어난다고 문제점을 이야기하므로 글의 흐름과 적절하다.
③ 이에 대한 예시로 운전을 할 때 심각한 문제가 나타난다고 하므로 글의 흐름과 적절하다.
⑤ ③에 대한 구체적인 예시를 말하므로 글의 흐름과 적절하다.

Words

- ☐ eye lens
- ☐ cause
- ☐ spectrum
- ☐ ability
- ☐ adjust
- ☐ focus
- ☐ decline
- ☐ muscle
- ☐ around
- ☐ stiffen
- ☐ difficulty
- ☐ clearly
- ☐ complicate
- ☐ major
- ☐ fortunately
- ☐ universal
- ☐ correct
- ☐ auto
- ☐ sign
- ☐ miss

Phrases

- ☐ grow older
- ☐ vice versa
- ☐ A such as B
- ☐ from near to far
- ☐ poses a problem
- ☐ from A to B

우선순위 영단어 역대 수능 기출 + 전국 모의고사 기출 + EBS 기출 + 교과서 기출 빈출 어휘

단어	뜻	단어	뜻	단어	뜻
unbearable	a. 견딜 수 없는	unbreakable	a. 깨지지 않는	uncertainty	n. 불확실성
unconsciously	ad. 무의식적으로	uncover	v. 밝혀내다	undergraduate	a. 학부생
underlie	v. 놓여 있다	unexpectedly	ad. 예상외로	unify	v. 통일하다
uninhibited	a. 아무 제약을 받지 않는	universal	a. 보편적인	universality	n. 보편[타당]성
unpredictable	a. 예측할 수 없는	unwilling	a. 내키지 않는	upright	n. 똑바로
urgency	n. 긴박성	urine	n. 소변	usher	n. 좌석 안내원

변형문제

01 다음 글을 읽고, |조건|에 맞게 빈칸 (A), (B), (C)를 채우시오.

| 조건 |
* (A)는 2단어, (B)는 5단어, (C)는 4단어로 쓸 것
* 본문에 있는 단어를 찾아 그대로 쓸 것

As we grow older, the eye lens becomes more yellow, causing poorer color discrimination in the green-blue-violet end of the spectrum. Also, the lens's ability to adjust and focus declines as the muscles around it stiffen. This is what causes difficulty in seeing close objects clearly (called presbyopia), necessitating either longer arms or corrective lenses. To complicate matters further, the time our eyes need to change focus from near to far (or vice versa) increases. This also poses a major problem in driving. Because drivers are constantly changing their focus from the instrument panel to other autos and signs on the highway, older drivers may miss important information because of their slower refocusing time.

⬇

Changes ad problems in the eye lens by aging:

1) The range of (A) ____________ ____________ in the green-blue-violet end of the spectrum narrows
2) With the stiffness of muscles around the lens, (B) ____________ ____________ ____________ ____________ ____________ deteriorates.
3) Eyes take longer to focus (C) ____________ ____________ ____________ ____________, which puts older drivers at danger.

02 다음 문장이 들어갈 부분으로 가장 적절한 곳을 고르시오.

To complicate matters further, the time our eyes need to change focus from near to far (or vice versa) increases.

As we grow older, the eye lens becomes more yellow, causing poorer color discrimination in the green-blue-violet end of the spectrum. (①) Also, the lens's ability to adjust and focus declines as the muscles around it stiffen. (②) This is what causes difficulty in seeing close objects clearly (called presbyopia), necessitating either longer arms or corrective lenses. (③) This also poses a major problem in driving. (④) Because drivers are constantly changing their focus from the instrument panel to other autos and signs on the highway, older drivers may miss important information because of their slower refocusing time. (⑤)

03 다음 글을 읽고, |조건|에 맞게 주어진 요약문을 완성하시오.

| 조건 |
* (A), (B)는 각각 다르게 1단어로 쓸 것
* 본문에 있는 단어만을 사용할 것
* 필요한 경우, 문맥과 어법에 맞게 변형할 것

As we grow older, the eye lens becomes more yellow, causing poorer color discrimination in the green-blue-violet end of the spectrum. Also, the lens's ability to adjust and focus declines as the muscles around it stiffen. This is what causes difficulty in seeing close objects clearly (called presbyopia), necessitating either longer arms or corrective lenses. To complicate matters further, the time our eyes need to change focus from near to far (or vice versa) increases. This also poses a major problem in driving. Because drivers are constantly changing their focus from the instrument panel to other autos and signs on the highway, older drivers may miss important information because of their slower refocusing time.

⬇

Due to aging, the eye lens's color discrimination becomes poor and abilities to adjust and focus deteriorate, resulting in (A) _____________. Particularly, aged drivers are more at risk than the young considering their slow eye movement to (B) _____________.

04 다음 글을 읽고, |조건|에 맞게 주어진 질문에 답하시오.

| 조건 |
* (A)는 5단어, (B)는 4단어로 쓸 것
* 본문에 있는 단어만을 사용할 것
*필요한 경우, 문맥과 어법에 맞게 변형할 것

As we grow older, the eye lens becomes more yellow, causing poorer color discrimination in the green-blue-violet end of the spectrum. Also, the lens's ability to adjust and focus declines as the muscles around it stiffen. This is what causes difficulty in seeing close objects clearly (called presbyopia), necessitating either longer arms or corrective lenses. To complicate matters further, the time our eyes need to change focus from near to far (or vice versa) increases. This also poses a major problem in driving. Because drivers are constantly changing their focus from the instrument panel to other autos and signs on the highway, older drivers may miss important information because of their slower refocusing time.

Q: Why does the lens's ability to adjust and focus deteriorate?

A: Because (A) _____________ _____________ _____________ _____________ _____________.

Q: Why do older drivers miss more important information than younger drivers?

A: Because their (B) _____________ _____________ _____________ _____________.

문장 삽입

글의 논리	Comparison & Contrast (비교 & 대조)
제목	공격성의 긍정적인 면과 부정적인 면
주제	공격성은 몇몇 상황에서 이득이 되기도 하지만 우리 사회에서 억제하는 능력이 필요하다.

수능 ANALYSIS

049 어법 선택 & 연결어

From an evolutionary perspective, aggression **[can view / can be viewed]** as **[adoptive / adaptive]** behavior, at least in some situations. (   ), competition for desirable mates **[is / are]** often intense, and one way to "win" in **[so / such]** contests is through aggression **[for / against]** potential rivals. (   ), **[especial / especially]** for males, strong tendencies to aggress **[for / against]** others can yield beneficial outcomes. (   ), **[lived / living]** together in human society often requires **[to restrain / restraining]** aggressive behavior. **[Be / Being]** aggressive to others in response to every provocation **[is / are]** definitely not adaptive, and can greatly disrupt social life. For this reason, **[this / it]** is clear **[what / that]** we possess effective internal mechanisms for **[restraint / restraining]** anger and obvious aggression. Such mechanisms **[describe / are described]** by the term self-regulation (or self-control), and **[refer / refer to]** our capacity to regulate **[many / much]** aspects of own behavior, **[included / including]** aggression.

(주어진 문장) 대조 인간 사회에서 종종 공격적인 행동을 억제하기를 요구한다.

(On the other hand), / {living together (in human society)} / (often) requires / restraining aggressive behavior.

- On the other hand: 반면에
- living together (in human society): 〈동명사〉 S 인간 사회에서 함께 살아가는 것은
- (often) requires: V 종종 요구한다
- restraining aggressive behavior: 〈동명사〉 O 공격적인 행동을 억제하는 것을

반면에, 인간 사회에서 함께 살아가는 것은 종종 공격적인 행동을 억제하는 것을 요구한다.

노트
- on the other hand : 다른 한편으로는, 반면에
- live together : ~와 함께 살다[동거하다]
- 〈동명사구가 주어 자리에 사용된 경우〉 : 단수 취급으로 동사는 단수동사를 사용함

주어 : 동명사구	동사
living together in human society	requires

- 〈3형식에서 목적어 자리에 to R / Ring 둘 다 사용 가능〉

	완전타동사		목적어
주어	begin	~을 시작하다	to R/Ring (의미 차이 없음)
	cease	~을 중단하다	
	continue	~을 계속하다	
	deserve	~할 가치/자격/권리가 있다	
	dislike	~을 싫어하다	
	hate		
	like	~을 좋아하다	
	love	~을 사랑하다	
	neglect	~하는 것을 소홀히 하다	
	prefer	~쪽을 좋아하다	
	require	~을 요구하다	
	start	~을 시작하다	

비교1 진화적 측면에서 공격성은 몇몇 상황에서 적응행동으로 간주될 수 있다.

(From an evolutionary perspective), / aggression / can be viewed / as adaptive behavior, / (at least) / (in some situations).

- From an evolutionary perspective: 진화적 측면에서
- aggression: S 공격성은
- can be viewed: V〈수동태〉 간주될 수 있다
- as adaptive behavior: S.C 적응행동으로
- at least: 최소한
- in some situations: 몇몇 상황에서

진화적 측면에서, 공격성은 최소한 몇몇 상황에서 적응행동으로 간주될 수 있다.

노트
- from a perspective : 견지에서
- at least : 적어도[최소한]
- in a situation : ~한 상황에서
- 〈5형식 불완전타동사의 목적격보어〉 : 수동태 전환 시, 2형식 문장(be p.p. +as 보어)

주어	불완전타동사	목적어	목적격보어
–	accept / achieve / announce / characterize / cite / consider / count / deem / define / describe / disguise / identify / interpret / look at / look upon / perceive / praise / present / read / reckon / refer to / recognize / regard / remember / respect / see / speak of / think of / treat / use / view / visualize 등	–	as 보어

- 〈adapt / adopt / adept〉

	adapt	adopt	adept
동사	적응시키다, 개조하다, 개작하다	양자로 삼다, 채택하다	–
형용사	adaptive 적응할 수 있는	adoptive 양자 결연(관계)의	숙련된
명사	adaptation 적응, 순응	adoption 양자, 채용	adeptness 숙련

비교1 매력적인 배우자를 위한 경쟁은 치열하며, 승리하는 한 가지 방법은 공격성을 통해서이다.

(①) (For instance), / competition (for desirable mates) / is (often) intense, / and / one way / (to "win" in such contests) / is (through aggression) / (against potential rivals).

예를 들어 / 매력적인 배우자를 위한 경쟁은(S) / 종종 치열하다(V, S.C) / 그리고 / 한 가지 방법은(S) / 그런 경쟁에서 '승리하는' / 공격성을 통해서이다(V, 〈전치사〉) / 잠재적인 경쟁자에 대한(〈전치사〉)

예를 들어, 매력적인 배우자를 위한 경쟁은 종종 치열하여, 그러한 경쟁에서 '승리하는' 한 가지 방법은 잠재적인 경쟁자에 대한 공격성을 통해서이다.

노트
- competition for : ~을 얻기 위한 경쟁
- 〈혼동 어휘〉

	동사	형용사	명사	부사
complete	완수하다	완전한, 완벽한	–	–
completion	–	–	완성, 완수	–
compete	경쟁하다			
competition	–	–	경쟁, 대회	–
competitor	–	–	경쟁자	
competence	–	–	능력, 자격	–
incompetence	–	–	무능력	–
complement	보완하다	–	보완, 보충	–
compliment	칭찬하다	–	칭찬	
complimentary	–	칭찬하는, 무료의	–	–
complimentarily	–	–	–	찬사로, 무료로
competitive	–	경쟁적인	–	–
competent	–	유능한, 적임의, 자격이 있는	–	–
completely	–	–	–	완전히, 전적으로
competitively	–	–	–	경쟁적으로
competently	–	–	–	유능하게

- 〈for vs. against〉

전치사			
전치사	for	찬성	~을 지지하여, ~에 편들어
	against	반대	~에 반대하여(맞서)

- 〈혼동 어휘〉

through	전치사	~을 통하여
throughout	전치사	[장소] ~의 도처에, [시간] ~ 동안, ~ 내내
	부사	도처에, 완전히, 철저하게
though	접속사	~에도 불구하고
thorough	형용사	철저한, 완전한

비교1 다른 개체들에게 공세를 취하는 성향은 이득이 되는 결과를 낳을 수 있다.

(②) (So), / (especially) / (for males), / strong tendencies / (to aggress against others) / can yield beneficial outcomes.

그러므로 / 특히 / 수컷에게 있어 / 강한 성향은(S) / 다른 개체들에게 공세를 취하는 / 이득이 되는 결과를 낳을 수 있다(V, O)

그러므로 특히 수컷에게 있어, 다른 개체들에게 공세를 취하는 강한 성향은 이득이 되는 결과를 낳을 수 있다.

노트
- tendency to R : ~하는 경향

비교2 도발에 대한 반응으로 공격성을 표출하는 것은 사회생활을 방해할 수 있다.

(③) {Being aggressive to others / (in response to every provocation)} / is (definitely) not adaptive, / and / can (greatly) disrupt social life.

타인에게 공격성을 표출하는 것은(S; 〈동명사〉, S.C) / 모든 도발에 대한 반응으로(〈전치사〉) / 분명히 적응적이지 않으며(V_1, S.C) / 그리고 / 사회생활을 상당히 방해할 수 있다(V_2, O)

모든 도발에 대한 반응으로 타인에게 공격성을 표출하는 것이 분명히 적응적이지 않으며, 또한 사회생활을 상당히 방해할 수 있다.

노트
- in response to+(동)명사 : ~에 응하여[답하여]
- 〈동명사구가 주어 자리에 사용된 경우〉 : 단수 취급으로 동사는 단수동사를 사용함

주어 : 동명사구	동사
Being aggressive to others in response to every provocation	is

- 〈adapt / adopt / adept〉

	adapt	adopt	adept
동사	적응시키다, 개조하다, 개작하다	양자로 삼다, 채택하다	–
형용사	adaptive 적응할 수 있는	adoptive 양자 결연(관계)의	숙련된
명사	adaptation 적응, 순응	adoption 양자, 채용	adeptness 숙련

비교2 우리는 분노를 명백히 억제하는 내적 기제를 지니고 있다.

(④) (For this reason), / it / is clear / {that we / possess effective internal mechanisms / (for restraining anger and obvious aggression)}.

이러한 이유에서 / 이것은(〈가S〉) / 분명하다(V, S.C) / 우리가(〈종·접〉, S) / 효율적으로 내적 기제를 지니고 있다는 것이(V, O, 〈진S〉) / 분노와 명백한 억제를 제지하는 것을 위한(〈동명사〉, O_1, O_2)

이러한 이유에서, 우리가 분노와 명백한 억제하는 효율적인 내적 기제를 지니고 있다는 것은 분명하다.

노트
- for this[that] reason : 이런[그런] 이유 때문에
- 〈what vs. that〉

	관계대명사(불완전한 문장)	접속사(완전한 문장)
what	○ 선행사를 포함하고 있기 때문에 what 앞에 선행사 불필요	×

that	○ that 앞에 선행사 필요	○

■ 〈가주어, 진주어 구문〉

가주어	동사	진주어
It (This/That/There 사용 불가)	–	that+주어+동사(완전한 절)
		to 동사원형
		동명사
		의문사+주어+동사(간접의문문)
		if/whether+주어+동사
it	is	that ~

■ 〈부정수량형용사〉 : 막연한 수나 양의 정도를 표시하는 형용사

수(數)	few(a few), some(any), a lot of(lots of), a good(or great), plenty of, enough, all, no, many	복수명사+복수동사
양(量)	little(a little), some(any), a lot of, a good(or great), deal of, plenty of, enough, all, no, much	단수명사+단수동사

■ 〈including 용법〉

현재분사(형용사)	~을 포함하는	명사를 뒤에서 후치 수식함
분사구문(부사)	~을 포함하여	부대상황
전치사		형용사구, 부사구
		유사 표현 : regarding, concerning, considering

비교2 자기규제는 다양한 양상을 통제하는 우리의 능력이다.

(⑤) Such mechanisms / are described / (by the term self-regulation / or self-control), / and / refer to our capacity / (to regulate many aspects of own behavior), / (including aggression).

(Such mechanisms: S 그러한 기제들은 / are described: V_1(수동태) 기술될 수 있으며 / by the term: 자기규제라는 / self-regulation: 용어로 / or self-control: (혹은 자기통제) / and: 그리고 / refer to: V_2 능력을 지칭한다 / our: 통제하는 우리의 / capacity: O / many aspects of own behavior: O 우리 행동의 다양한 양상을 / including aggression: 공격성을 포함하여)

그러한 기제들은 자기규제(혹은 자기통제)라는 용어로 기술될 수 있으며, 공격성을 포함하여 우리 행동의 다양한 양상을 통제하는 우리의 능력을 지칭한다.

노트 ■ refer to+(동)명사 : ~을 언급[지칭]하다

▶ 글의 흐름으로 보아, 주어진 문장이 들어가기에 가장 적절한 곳은?

정답 | ③

해설 | ③ 주어진 문장을 해석하면 '반면에 인간 사회에서 함께 살아가는 것은 종종 공격적인 행동을 억제하는 것을 요구한다.' 이다. 주어진 문장에 앞 문장과 대립적일 때 연결해주는 'On the other hand' 가 들어가 있으므로 이 문장의 앞부분은 인간 사회에서는 공격적인 행동을 요구한다는 내용이 나와야 한다. 이러한 흐름을 봤을 때, 글의 3번째 문장인 수컷에게 있어, 다른 개체들에게 공세를 취하는 강한 성향이 이득이 되는 결과를 만든다는 말 뒤에 오는 것이 가장 적절하다.

Words

- ☐ require
- ☐ evolutionary
- ☐ perspective
- ☐ adaptive
- ☐ competition
- ☐ desirable
- ☐ mate
- ☐ intense
- ☐ aggression
- ☐ potential
- ☐ tendency
- ☐ yield
- ☐ beneficial
- ☐ outcome
- ☐ disrupt
- ☐ restrain
- ☐ describe
- ☐ capacity
- ☐ regulate
- ☐ aspect

Phrases

- ☐ on the other hand
- ☐ from a perspective
- ☐ in a situation
- ☐ tendency to R
- ☐ for this[that] reason
- ☐ live together
- ☐ at least
- ☐ competition for
- ☐ in response to+(동)명사
- ☐ refer to+(동)명사

변형문제

01 다음 글을 읽고, |조건|에 맞게 주어진 요약문을 완성하시오.

| 조건 |
* (A), (B), (C)는 각각 다르게 1단어로 쓸 것
* 본문에 있는 단어만을 사용할 것
* 필요한 경우, 문맥과 어법에 맞게 변형할 것

From an evolutionary perspective, aggression can be viewed as adaptive behavior, at least in some situations. For instance, competition for desirable mates is often intense, and one way to "win" in such contests is through aggression against potential rivals. So, especially for males, strong tendencies to aggress against others can yield beneficial outcomes. On the other hand, living together in human society often requires restraining aggressive behavior. Being aggressive to others in response to every provocation is definitely not adaptive, and can greatly disrupt social life. For this reason, it is clear that we possess effective internal mechanisms for restraining anger and obvious aggression. Such mechanisms are described by the term self-regulation (or self-control), and refer to our capacity to regulate many aspects of own behavior, including aggression.

⬇

Aggression is included in one of adaptive behaviors in terms of an evolutionary aspect. For example, people fiercely (A) ____________ for ideal mates. However, human society demands to inhibit aggressive behavior like (B) ____________ to achieve (C) ____________.

02 다음 글을 읽고, |조건|에 맞게 빈칸 (A), (B), (C)를 채우시오.

| 조건 |
* (A), (B), (C)는 각각 다르게 1단어로 쓸 것
* 본문에 있는 단어만을 그대로 사용할 것

From an evolutionary perspective, aggression can be viewed as (A) ____________ behavior, at least in some situations. For instance, competition for desirable mates is often intense, and one way to "win" in such contests is through aggression against potential rivals. So, especially for males, strong tendencies to aggress against others can yield beneficial outcomes. On the other hand, living together in human society often requires (B) ____________ aggressive behavior. Being aggressive to others in response to every provocation is definitely not adaptive, and can greatly disrupt social life. For this reason, it is clear that we possess effective internal mechanisms for restraining anger and obvious aggression. Such mechanisms are described by the term (C) ____________ (or self-control), and refer to our capacity to regulate many aspects of own behavior, including aggression.

03 다음 글을 읽고, |조건|에 맞게 주제문을 완성하시오.

| 조건 |

* (A), (B)에 각각 다르게 1단어로 쓸 것
* [보기]에서 선택한 단어를 한 번씩만 쓸 것
* 필요한 경우, 문맥과 어법에 맞게 변형할 것

[보기] create / prosper / offer / hinder / express / replenish / redesign / encourage / detect / intensify / compare / unlabialize

From an evolutionary perspective, aggression can be viewed as adaptive behavior, at least in some situations. For instance, competition for desirable mates is often intense, and one way to "win" in such contests is through aggression against potential rivals. So, especially for males, strong tendencies to aggress against others can yield beneficial outcomes. On the other hand, living together in human society often requires restraining aggressive behavior. Being aggressive to others in response to every provocation is definitely not adaptive, and can greatly disrupt social life. For this reason, it is clear that we possess effective internal mechanisms for restraining anger and obvious aggression. Such mechanisms are described by the term self-regulation (or self-control), and refer to our capacity to regulate many aspects of own behavior, including aggression.

⬇

(A) ______________ aggression to others as a reaction to any stimulus is not obviously adaptive behavior and therefore, (B) ______________ social life.

04 다음 글의 순서로 가장 적절한 것은?

From an evolutionary perspective, aggression can be viewed as adaptive behavior, at least in some situations.

(A) For this reason, it is clear that we possess effective internal mechanisms for restraining anger and obvious aggression. Such mechanisms are described by the term self-regulation (or self-control), and refer to our capacity to regulate many aspects of own behavior, including aggression.

(B) For instance, competition for desirable mates is often intense, and one way to "win" in such contests is through aggression against potential rivals. So, especially for males, strong tendencies to aggress against others can yield beneficial outcomes.

(C) On the other hand, living together in human society often requires restraining aggressive behavior. Being aggressive to others in response to every provocation is definitely not adaptive, and can greatly disrupt social life.

① (A) - (B) - (C)
② (B) - (A) - (C)
③ (B) - (C) - (A)
④ (C) - (A) - (B)
⑤ (C) - (B) - (A)

문장 삽입

글의 논리	Enumeration (열거)
제목	생존에 해로운 습관
주제	사람들은 생존에 도움이 되지 않는 습관들을 가지고 있다.

PRACTICE 01

050 어법 선택 & 연결어

Many people have habits **[what / that]** are bad for survival. How does that happen **[if / that]** our brain rewards behaviors **[what / that]** are good for survival? When a happy-chemical spurt is over, you feel **[like / alike]** something is wrong. You look for a reliable way to feel **[well / good]** again, fast. Anything **[what / that]** worked before **[built / to build]** a pathway in your brain. We all have **[so / such]** happy habits: from snacking to **[exercise / exercising]**, **[if / whether]** it's spending **[or / and]** saving, partying or solitude, arguing or **[makes / making]** up. (   ) none of these habits can make you **[happy / happily]** all the time **[because / because of]** your brain doesn't work that way. Every happy-chemical spurt is quickly **[metabolized / metabolizing]** and you have to do more to get more. You can end up **[to overdo / overdoing]** a happy habit to the point of unhappiness.

(주어진 문장) 대답 화학물질의 분출로 인한 행복은 시간이 갈수록 더 많은 일을 해야 한다.

(But) / none of these habits / can make you happy
그러나 / 이런 습관 중 어느 것도(S) / 여러분을 행복하게 하지는 못하는데 (V, O, O.C)

/ (all the time) / {because your brain / doesn't work
항상 / 왜냐하면(〈종·접〉) 여러분의 뇌가(S) / 작동하지 않기 때문이다(V)

(that way)}.
그런 식으로

그러나 이런 습관 중 어느 것도 여러분을 항상 행복하게 하지는 못하는데, 이는 여러분의 뇌가 그런 식으로 작동하지 않기 때문이다.

노트
- none of : ~ 중 아무(것)도 … 않다
- all the time : 내내[줄곧], 항상
- that way : 그런 상태로, 그와 같이
- 〈주어와 동사의 수의 일치〉
  - A of B : 일반적인 경우에 A가 주어
  - A of B : A가 부분/부분인 경우에 B가 주어

	A	B	
분수	two – thirds 등	주어	동사 (B에 수의 일치)
부분	a group of, all of, a lot of, any of, a number of, both of, each of, either of, few of, half of, many of, most of, much of, neither of, none of, one of, part of, percent of, several of, some of, the rest, two of 등		
	none of	these habits	can make

- 〈make 상태동사〉 : 수동태 시, be made + 주격보어(형용사/명사)

make	목적어	목적격보어	해석
〈상태동사〉	명사/명사 상당어구	형용사	~가 …한 상태로 만들다
		명사	
make	you	happy	–

- make가 '~을 …한 상태로 만들다'라는 의미로 사용될 경우, make를 상태동사라 칭한다. 이때 주의사항은 목적격보어 자리에 사용하는 형용사 대신 부사를 사용할 수 없다는 점이다.

- 〈원인/이유〉 : ~ 때문에

전치사	because of	+(동)명사 / 명사 상당어구
	due to	
	for	
	on account of	
	owing to	
	thanks to	
종속접속사	as	+주어+동사 ~
	because	
	now(that)	
	since	

주제문 많은 사람들은 생존에 도움이 되지 않는 습관들을 가지고 있다.

Many people / have habits / (that are bad for survival).
많은 사람들은(S) / 습관을 가지고 있다(V, O) / 생존에 도움이 되지 않는(〈주·관〉, V, S.C)

많은 사람들이 생존에 도움이 되지 않는 습관들을 가지고 있다.

노트
- be bad for : ~에 나쁘다
- 〈부정수량형용사〉 : 막연한 수나 양의 정도를 표시하는 형용사

수(數)	few(a few), some(any), a lot of(lots of), a good(or great), plenty of, enough, all, no, many	복수명사+복수동사
양(量)	little(a little), some(any), a lot of, a good(or great), deal of, plenty of, enough, all, no, much	단수명사+단수동사

- 〈주격관계대명사절의 수의 일치〉 : 선행사를 포함하고 있는 관계대명사 what 사용 불가

	주격관계대명사절		
선행사	주격관계대명사	~~주어~~	동사
habits	that		are

질문 우리의 두뇌가 생존에 이로운 행동에 대해 보상을 해주는데 이런 일이 일어나는 이유가 무엇인가?

How / does that / happen / {if our brain / rewards behaviors / (that are good for survival)?}

어떻게 / 이런 일이 / 일어날까? / 만약 우리의 두뇌가 / 행동에 대해 보상을 해준다면 / 생존에 이로운

우리의 두뇌가 생존에 이로운 행동에 대해 보상을 해준다면 어떻게 이런 일이 일어날까?

노트
- be good for : ~에 좋다
- 〈주격관계대명사절의 수의 일치〉 : 선행사를 포함하고 있는 관계대명사 what 사용 불가

선행사	주격관계대명사절		
	주격관계대명사	~~주어~~	동사
behaviors	that		are

대답 화학물질의 분출로 인한 행복은 시간이 갈수록 더 많은 일을 해야 한다.

(When a happy-chemical spurt / is over), / you / feel like (that) (something is wrong).

행복감을 주는 화학물질의 분출이 / 끝나면 / 여러분은 / 기분이 든다 / 뭔가 잘못된 것 같은

행복감을 주는 화학물질의 분출이 끝나면, 여러분은 뭔가 잘못된 것 같은 기분이 든다.

노트
- be over : 끝나다
- feel like : ~처럼 느끼다
- 〈감각동사〉

감각동사	주격보어(S.C)	
feel, look, seem, sound, taste, appear, smell	형용사(분사 : 현재분사/과거분사)	
	명사	
	like(전치사)	(that)+주어+동사
		(동)명사
	~~alike~~	
	~~likely~~	

- 〈likely / alike / like〉

likely	형용사	~일 것 같은 (be to 동사원형 : ~일 것 같다)
	부사	아마(probably)
alike	서술적 형용사 (보어로만 사용, 명사 수식 불가)	동일한
	부사	똑같이
like	전치사	~처럼
	동사	좋아하다

(①) You / look for a reliable way / (to feel good again, / fast).

여러분은 / 믿을 만한 방법을 찾는다 / 다시 기분이 좋아질 수 있는 / 빨리

여러분은 다시 기분이 좋아질 수 있는 믿을 만한 방법을 빨리 찾는다.

노트
- feel good : 기분이 좋다
- 〈look at / over / in / out / for〉

look	at	~을 쳐다보다
	over	~을 대충 훑어보다[살펴보다](=watch)
	in	~을 들여다보다, 조사/검토하다
	out	~을 내다보다, 조심하다
	for	~을 찾다, 구하다, 바라다

(②) Anything / (that worked before) / has built a pathway / (in your brain).

어느 것이라도 / 이전에 성공했던 / 경로를 만들어 놓는다 / 여러분의 뇌에

이전에 성공했던 어느 것이라도 여러분의 뇌에 경로를 만들어 놓는다.

노트
- 〈주격관계대명사절의 수의 일치〉 : 선행사를 포함하고 있는 관계대명사 what 사용 불가

선행사(주어)	주격관계대명사절			
	주격관계대명사	~~주어~~	동사	동사(본동사)
Anything	that		worked	has built

- 〈what vs. that〉

	관계대명사(불완전한 문장)	접속사(완전한 문장)
what	○ 선행사를 포함하고 있기 때문에 what 앞에 선행사 불필요	×
that	○ that 앞에 선행사 필요	○

(③) We all / have such happy habits: / (from snacking to exercising), / (whether it's spending or saving, partying or solitude, arguing or making up).

우리 모두는 / 그런 행복한 습관을 가지고 있다 / 간식 먹는 것에서부터 운동하는 것까지 / 그것이 낭비든지 절약이든지, 혹은 파티를 여는 것이든지 고독이든지, 언쟁이든지 화해든지

우리 모두는 그런 행복한 습관을 가지고 있다. 간식 먹는 것에서부터 운동하는 것까지, 그것이 낭비든지 절약이든지, 파티를 여는 것이든지 고독이든지, 언쟁이든지 화해든지.

노트
- from A to B : A에서 B까지
- make up : 화해하다
- 〈whether 용법〉

종류				명사절	부사절
whether	(or not)	주어	동사	~인지	~던지 말 던지, ~하든 말든,
whether	주어	동사	(or not)	아닌지	~인지 아닌지
whether	A	or	B	A이거나 B	

(④) Every happy-chemical spurt / is (quickly) metabolized / and / you have to do more / (to get more).

모든 행복감을 주는 화학물질의 분출은 / 대사 작용이 빠르게 일어나며 / 그리고 / 여러분은 더 많이 해야만 한다 / 더 많이 얻기 위해

모든 행복감을 주는 화학물질의 분출은 대사 작용이 빠르게 일어나며, 더 많이 얻기 위해 여러분은 더 많이 해야만 한다. (여러분을 행복하게 만드는 일을 더욱 많이 해야만 한다.)

노트 ■ 〈주어와 동사의 수의 일치〉
• each / every / any＋단수동사

주제문(재진술) 이 습관은 불행해질 수도 있게 만든다.

(⑤) You(S) / can end up(V) overdoing(〈동명사〉) a happy habit(O) /
여러분은 결국 행복 습관을 과용하게 될 수도 있다

(to the point of unhappiness).
불행해질 정도로

여러분은 결국 불행해질 정도로 행복 습관을 과용하게 될 수도 있다.

노트 ■ end up＋동명사 : 결국 ~하게 되다
■ to the point of : ~라고 할 (수 있을) 정도로

▶ 글의 흐름으로 보아, 주어진 문장이 들어가기에 가장 적절한 곳은?

정답 | ④

해설 | ④ 주어진 문장을 해석하면 '그러나 이런 습관 중 어느 것도 여러분을 항상 행복하게 하지는 못하는데, 이는 여러분의 뇌가 그런 식으로 작동하지 않기 때문이다.' 이다. 이 문장에는 앞 문장과 대조될 때 쓰이는 But이 들어가 있다. 따라서 이 문장의 앞 부분에는 여러 가지 습관이 행복하다는 내용이 들어와야 한다. 이러한 흐름을 보았을 때, 6번째 문장은 우리 모두가 행복한 습관을 가지고 있고 이에 대한 예를 들고 있으므로 ④가 문장이 들어가기에 가장 적절하다.

Words

- ☐ reward
- ☐ chemical
- ☐ reliable
- ☐ pathway
- ☐ snack
- ☐ solitude
- ☐ metabolize
- ☐ overdo

Phrases

- ☐ none of
- ☐ that way
- ☐ be good for
- ☐ feel like
- ☐ from A to B
- ☐ end up＋동명사
- ☐ all the time
- ☐ be bad for
- ☐ be over
- ☐ feel good
- ☐ make up
- ☐ to the point of

우선순위 영단어 역대 수능 기출＋전국 모의고사 기출＋EBS 기출＋교과서 기출 빈출 어휘

단어	뜻	단어	뜻	단어	뜻
vacant	a. 빈도(수)	value	v. (수학의) 값	vault	a. 지하실의
vegetation	n. 식물	vein	n. 정맥	venture	v. 위험을 무릅쓰고 해보다
vessel	n. 그릇	via	~을 거쳐	vice versa	n. 반대의 경우도 마찬가지임
vicious cycle	n. 악순환	vigorously	ad. 강건하게	violate	v. 위반하다
visibility	n. 눈에 잘 보임	visibly	ad. 눈에 보이게	vision	n. 미래 계획
visit with	v. ~를 방문하다	vivid	a. 생생한	wandering	a. 방랑하는
warehouse	n. 창고	wax	v. 당밀	weasel	n. 족제비
weed	v. 잡초	well-funded	자금 조달이 잘 되는	whistle	n. 휘파람
wield	v. 휘두르다	wilderness	n. 육지	willfulness	n. 의도
willow	n. 버드나무	winning	a. 상금	with regard to	~에 관해서
worthwhile	a. 가치가 있는	wrap up	v. ~을 포장하다	wrist	n. 손목
yawn	v. 하품하다	a change of air	n. 기분전환	a multitude	다수의
a number of	많은	a variety of	다양한	abnormal	a. 비정상적인
abolition	n. 폐지	abrupt	a. 느닷없는	absenteeism	n. 잦은 결근
abstract	a. 추상적인	absurdity	n. 불합리	academia	n. 학계
academically	ad. 학문적으로	accentuate	v. 두드러지게 하다	acceptable	a. (사회적으로) 용인되는

변형문제

01 다음 글을 읽고, |조건|에 맞게 주어진 요약문을 완성하시오.

| 조건 |
* (A), (B)는 1단어, (C)는 2단어로 쓸 것
* 본문에 있는 단어를 찾아 쓸 것
* 필요한 경우, 문맥과 어법에 맞게 변형할 것

Many people have habits that are bad for survival. How does that happen if our brain rewards behaviors that are good for survival? When a happy-chemical spurt is over, you feel like something is wrong. You look for a reliable way to feel good again, fast. Anything that worked before built a pathway in your brain. We all have such happy habits: from snacking to exercising, whether it's spending or saving, partying or solitude, arguing or making up. But none of these habits can make you happy all the time because your brain doesn't work that way. Every happy-chemical spurt is quickly metabolized and you have to do more to get more. You can end up overdoing a happy habit to the point of unhappiness.

⬇

Habits we have for survival do not always let us feel a sense of (A) ____________ because our brains function in a way that the more we (B) ____________, the more we (C) ____________ ____________.

02 밑줄 친 부분 중 문맥상 옳지 않은 것은?

Many people have habits that are ① bad for survival. How does that happen if our brain rewards behaviors that are good for survival? When a happy-chemical spurt is over, you feel like something is ② wrong. You look for a reliable way to feel ③ bad again, fast. Anything that worked before built a pathway in your brain. We all have such happy habits: from snacking to exercising, whether it's spending or saving, partying or ④ solitude, arguing or making up. But none of these habits can make you happy all the time because your brain doesn't work that way. Every happy-chemical spurt is ⑤ quickly metabolized and you have to do more to get more. You can end up overdoing a happy habit to the point of unhappiness.

03 다음 글을 읽고, |조건|에 맞게 빈칸 (A), (B)를 채우시오.

| 조건 |
* (A), (B)는 각각 다르게 1단어로 쓸 것
* [보기]에서 선택한 단어를 한 번씩만 쓸 것
* 필요한 경우, 문맥과 어법에 맞게 변형할 것

[보기] duplicated / adapt / reward / punish / harm / obtain / complicated / beneficial / detrimental / potential / delay

Many people have habits that are bad for survival. How does that happen if our brain rewards behaviors that are good for survival? When a happy-chemical spurt is over, you feel like something is wrong. You look for a reliable way to feel good again, fast. Anything that worked before built a pathway in your brain. We all have such happy habits: from snacking to exercising, whether it's spending or saving, partying or solitude, arguing or making up. But none of these habits can make you happy all the time because your brain doesn't work that way. Every happy-chemical spurt is quickly metabolized and you have to do more to get more. You can end up overdoing a happy habit to the point of unhappiness.

⬇

Some habits do not help us survive and keel happy at all times because our brains do not compensate for consistently (A) _____________ behavior. For the more release of brain's happy chemicals, we heavily work to (B) _____________ more happy chemicals.

04 다음 글의 순서로 적절한 것은?

Many people have habits that are bad for survival. How does that happen if our brain rewards behaviors that are good for survival?

(A) When a happy-chemical spurt is over, you feel like something is wrong. You look for a reliable way to feel good again, fast. Anything that worked before built a pathway in your brain. We all have such happy habits: from snacking to exercising, whether it's spending or saving, partying or solitude, arguing or making up.

(B) But none of these habits can make you happy all the time because your brain doesn't work that way.

(C) Every happy-chemical spurt is quickly metabolized and you have to do more to get more. You can end up overdoing a happy habit to the point of unhappiness.

① (A) - (B) - (C)　② (A) - (C) - (B)　③ (B) - (A) - (C)
④ (B) - (C) - (A)　⑤ (C) - (A) - (B)

UNIT 13

문장 삽입

글의 논리	Spotlight
제목	생명공학이 쓰이는 다양한 부분
주제	생명공학은 식물, 동물과 함께 살고 싶어 하는 인간의 환경을 만들어낼 가능성을 연다.

PRACTICE 02

051 어법 선택 & 연결어

Biotechnology opens up the possibility of **[creation / creating]** the plant, animal, and human environments **[which / in which]** we would like to live. Plants **[can build / can be built]** **[what / that]** **[resists / resist]** diseases without pesticides, use less water, and **[produce / produced]** more edible food. Similar improvements **[are occurred / are occurring]** in animals. More milk per cow leads to less pressure on **[graze / grazing]** lands and more room for wildlife. When it comes to **[improve / improving]** humans, the process will start by **[elimination / eliminating]** genetic diseases and move on **[to build / to building]** better (smarter, taller, more beautiful) men and women. The biotech processes for **[cure / curing]** **[existed / existing]** diseases **[is / are]** dual-use technologies. The same techniques **[what / that]** **[allows / allow]** genetic defects (very inferior genes) **[to eliminate / to be eliminated]** **[allows / allow]** the replacement of **[slight / slightly]** inferior genes with superior **[one / ones]**.

(주어진 문장) 설명 생명공학에 대한 설명

More milk (S: 더 많이 생산되는 우유는) / (per cow) (소 한 마리당) / leads (V: 이어지다) {to (〈전치사〉) less pressure (O₁: 압박을 덜 가하고) / (on grazing lands) (목초지에) / and (그리고) / more room (O₂: 더 많은 공간을 주는 것으로) / (for wildlife) (야생생물에게)}.

소 한 마리당 더 많이 생산되는 우유는 목초지에 압박을 덜 가하고 야생생물에게 더 많은 공간을 주는 것으로 이어진다.

노트
- per : 각[매] ~에 대하여, ~당[마다]
- A lead to B : A라는 원인 때문에 B라는 결과가 발생하다, A는 B로 이어지다
- room : 공간(=space)
- room for : ~을 위한 공간

주제문 생명공학은 식물, 동물과 함께 살고 싶어 하는 인간의 환경을 만들어낼 가능성을 연다.

Biotechnology (S: 생명공학은) / opens up (V) the possibility (O: 가능성을 연다) / (of (〈전치사〉) creating the plant (O₁: 식물, 동물과), animal (O₂), and human environments (O₃〈선행사〉: 인간의 환경을 만들어낼)) / (in which (〈전치사+관·대〉: 우리가) we (S) would like to live (V: 살고 싶어 하는)).

생명공학은 식물, 동물과 우리가 살고 싶어 하는 인간의 환경을 만들어낼 가능성을 연다.

노트
- open up : ~을 열다
- would like to R : ~을 하고 싶다
- 〈전치사+관계대명사 vs. 관계대명사〉 : 관계부사와 같기 때문에 뒤 문장이 완전한 문장이 나온다. 전치사는 맨 뒤로 보낼 수 있는데 이때 전치사의 목적어가 없기 때문에 관계대명사절은 불완전하다.

선행사	전치사+관계대명사 =관계부사	주어	동사			완전한 문장
	관계대명사		동사	전치사	~~목적어~~	불완전한 문장

- 〈동명사 vs. 명사〉 : 전치사의 목적어 자리에 동명사와 명사를 둘 다 사용할 수 있지만, 동명사는 뒤에 목적어로 명사를 가질 수 있는 점이 명사와의 차이점이다.

〈전치사구〉		
전치사	동명사	명사(동명사의 목적어)
of	creating	the plant, animal, and human environments
	~~creation~~	

설명 생명공학에 대한 설명

(①) Plants (S〈선행사〉: 식물이) / can be built (V〈수동태〉: 만들어질 수 있다) / {that (〈주·관〉) resist (V₁) diseases (O: 병에 대한 저항력이 있으며) (without pesticides) (살충제를 사용하지 않고도), / use (V₂) less water (O: 물을 적게 사용하며), / and (그리고) / produce (V₃) more edible food (O: 먹을 수 있는 더 많은 식량을 생산해내는)}.

살충제를 사용하지 않고도 병에 대한 저항력이 있으며, 물을 더 적게 사용하고, 먹을 수 있는 더 많은 식량을 생산해내는 식물이 만들어질 수 있다.

노트
- 〈what vs. that〉

	관계대명사(불완전한 문장)	접속사(완전한 문장)
what	○ 선행사를 포함하고 있기 때문에 what 앞에 선행사 불필요	×
that	○ that 앞에 선행사 필요	○

■ 〈주격관계대명사절의 수의 일치〉 : 선행사를 포함하고 있는 관계대명사 what 사용 불가

		주격관계대명사절			
선행사(주어)	동사	주격관계대명사	~~주어~~	동사	동사(본동사)
Plants	can be built	that		resist	use

(②) Similar improvements / are occurring / (in animals).
S 비슷한 개선이 / V(현재진행) 일어나고 있다 / 동물들에게서도

비슷한 개선이 동물들에게서도 일어나고 있다.

노트 ■ occur : 일어나다(완전자동사 : 수동태 불가)

(③) (When it comes to improving humans), / the process / will start / (by eliminating genetic diseases) / and / move on (to building better (smarter, taller, more beautiful) men and women).
〈전치사〉 〈동명사〉 인간을 개선하는 것에 관한 한 / S 그 과정은 / V_1 시작할 것이다 / 〈전치사〉 〈동명사〉 O 유전병을 없앰으로써 / 그리고 V_2 더 나아갈 것이다 / 〈전치사〉 〈동명사〉 O 더 나은(더 똑똑한, 더 키가 큰, 더 아름다운) 남자와 여자를 만드는 것으로

인간을 개선하는 것에 관한 한, 그 과정은 유전병을 없애는 것으로 시작해서, 더 나은(더 똑똑한, 더 키가 큰, 더 아름다운) 남자와 여자를 만드는 것으로 나아갈 것이다.

노트 ■ when it comes to(전치사)+동명사 : ~에 관한 한(=with regard to, in regard to(of), with respect to, as regards, regarding, concerning)
■ by+동명사 : ~함으로써
■ move on to(전치사)+(동)명사 : ~로 옮기다[이동하다]

(④) The biotech processes / (for curing existing diseases) / are dual-use technologies.
S 생명공학의 과정들은 / 〈동명사〉 〈현재분사〉 O 기존의 질병을 치료하기 위한 / V / S.C 이중 용도의 기술들이다

기존의 질병을 치료하기 위한 생명공학의 과정들은 이중 용도의 기술들이다.

(⑤) The same techniques / (that allow genetic defects (very inferior genes) to be eliminated) / allow the replacement (of slightly inferior genes) / (with superior ones).
〈선행사〉 S 동일한 기술들이 / 〈주·관〉 V O 유전적 결함 (아주 열등한 유전자)이 O.C(to R 수동) 제거되는 것을 가능하게 하는 / V O 가능하게 한다 / 〈전치사〉 〈부사〉 O 약간 열등한 유전자를 대체하는 것을 / 우월한 유전자로

유전적 결함(아주 열등한 유전자)을 없애는 것을 가능하게 하는 동일한 기술이 약간 열등한 유전자를 우월한 유전자로 대체하는 것을 가능하게 한다.

노트 ■ 〈주격관계대명사절의 수의 일치〉 : 선행사를 포함하고 있는 관계대명사 what 사용 불가

	주격관계대명사절			
선행사(주어)	주격관계대명사	~~주어~~	동사	동사(본동사)
The same techniques	that		allow	allow

■ 〈5형식 불완전타동사의 목적격보어〉 : 수동태 전환 시, 2형식 문장(be p.p.+to R)

주어	불완전타동사	목적어	목적격보어
–	advise / allow / ask / assume / beg / cause / command / compel / condition / decide / design / drive / enable / encourage / expect / forbid / force / instruct / intend / invite / lead / like / motivate / order / permit / persuade / predispose / pressure / program / push / require / teach / tell / train / trust / urge / want / warn / wish 등	–	to 동사원형

■ 〈to R의 태와 시제〉

태	능동태	to R
	수동태	to be p.p.
시제	단순시제 : 본동사 시제와 동일	to R
	완료시제 : 본동사 시제보다 한 시제 앞선 시제	to have p.p.
	완료 수동	to have been p.p.

▶ 글의 흐름으로 보아, 주어진 문장이 들어가기에 가장 적절한 곳은?

정답 | ③

해설 | ③ 주어진 문장을 해석하면 '소 한 마리당 더 많이 생산되는 우유는 목초지에 압박을 덜 가하고 야생 생물에게 더 많은 공간을 주는 것으로 이어진다.'이다. 이 문장은 글의 주제를 소로 예시로 든 것이다. 따라서 이 문장의 앞 부분에는 예시를 들 수 있도록 말해야 한다. 따라서 3번째 문장이 '비슷한 개선이 동물들에게서도 일어나고 있다'고 말하므로 이에 대한 예시로 소를 든 것을 확인할 수 있다. 정답은 ③이다.

Words

☐ grazing land	☐ possibility	☐ pesticide
☐ wildlife	☐ environment	☐ produce
☐ biotechnology	☐ resist	☐ edible

- ☐ improvement
- ☐ eliminate
- ☐ genetic
- ☐ existing
- ☐ dual-use
- ☐ allow
- ☐ defect
- ☐ replacement
- ☐ slightly
- ☐ inferior
- ☐ superior

Phrases

- ☐ A lead to B
- ☐ open up
- ☐ when it comes to(전치사) +동명사
- ☐ by+동명사
- ☐ room for
- ☐ would like to R
- ☐ move on to(전치사) +(동)명사

우선순위 영단어

역대 수능 기출 + 전국 모의고사 기출 + EBS 기출 + 교과서 기출 빈출 어휘

단어	뜻	단어	뜻	단어	뜻
accessibility	n. 접근성	accidentally	ad. 잘못하여	accomplished	a. 기량이 뛰어난
accountant	n. 회계사	accurately	ad. 정확히	accuse	v. ~을 비난하다
acid	n. 산	acknowledgment	n. 시인	acquaintance	n. 아는 사람
addition	n. 추가	additive	n. 식품 첨가물	adherent	n. 지지자
adhesive tape	접착용 테이프	adjoining	a. 인접한	administration	n. 행정부
administrator	n. 관리자	admiration	n. 존경	admire	v. ~에 감탄하다
admission officer	입학사정관	adorn	v. 장식하다	adrenal hormone	n. 부신 호르몬
adulthood	n. 성인임	advantage	n. 이점	aerobic exercise	n. 유산소 운동
aeronautics	n. 항공학	affective	a. 감정의	affirmation	n. 확언
affix	v. 고정시키다	afflict	v. 괴롭히다	afloat	a. (물이나 하늘에) 떠서
afterward	ad. 나중에	aggressively	ad. 공격적으로	agility	n. 민첩함
agitation	n. (정치적) 소요	agonize	v. 괴로워하다	agreement	n. 협약
ailing	a. 병든	ailment	n. 질병	aisle	n. 통로
akin to	~와 같은	alien	n. 외계인	alienation	n. 소원
all along	처음부터	all but	거의	all of a sudden	갑자기
allergy	n. 알레르기	alliance	n. 결연	allied	a. 연합국의
all-or-none	전부냐 전무냐의	all-or-nothing	절대적인	allot	v. 할당하다
allowance	n. 허용 한도	alluring	a. 매혹적인	alumni	n. 동문
amicable	a. 유쾌한	ammonia	n. 암모니아	among others	많은 가운데
amplifier	n. 확성기	an abundance of	다수의	analogous	a. 유사한
anarchy	n. 무정부 상태	ancestral	a. 원형[선구]을 이루는	ancestry	n. 조상
ancient	a. 고대의	and so forth	… 등등	anecdotal	a. 일화적인
anecdote	n. 이야기	anesthetic	n. 마취제	anesthetize	v. 마취시키다
animate	v. ~에 생기를 불어넣다	animated	a. 살아있는 듯한	animation	n. 애니메이션
anniversary	n. 기념일	annoyance	n. 골칫거리	annoying	a. 짜증나는
anonymous	a. 특징[개성]이 없는	Antarctica	n. 남극	antibody	n. 항체
anticipation	n. 예상	anyway	ad. 어떻든	apartment complex	n. 아파트 단지
ape	n. 유인원	appear	v. 나타나다	apply A to B	v. A를 B에 적용하다
appreciably	ad. 상당히	aptitude	n. 적성	aquatic	a. 물의
archer	n. 궁수	architectural	a. 건축의	arctic	a. 북극의
arguably	ad. 논리적으로	arise from	v. ~에서 생기다	around	ad. 약
art	n. 기술	artery	n. 동맥	as a consequence	결과적으로

변형문제

01 다음 글을 읽고, |조건|에 맞게 주어진 제목을 완성하시오.

| 조건 |
* 4단어로 쓸 것
* [보기]에서 선택한 단어를 한 번씩만, 그대로 쓸 것

[보기] fundamental / feasible / affordable / supportive / areas / with / industries / agriculture / development / natural / genes / of

Biotechnology opens up the possibility of creating the plant, animal, and human environments in which we would like to live. Plants can be built that resist diseases without pesticides, use less water, and produce more edible food. Similar improvements are occurring in animals. More milk per cow leads to less pressure on grazing lands and more room for wildlife. When it comes to improving humans, the process will start by eliminating genetic diseases and move on to building better (smarter, taller, more beautiful) men and women. The biotech processes for curing existing diseases are dual-use technologies. The same techniques that allow genetic defects (very inferior genes) to be eliminated allow the replacement of slightly inferior genes with superior ones.

⬇

__________ __________ __________ __________, thanks to biotechnology

02 다음 글을 읽고, |조건|에 맞게 주제문을 완성하시오.

| 조건 |
* (A), (B)는 1단어로 쓸 것
* 본문에 있는 단어를 찾아 쓸 것
* 필요한 경우, 문맥과 어법에 맞게 변형할 것

Biotechnology opens up the possibility of creating the plant, animal, and human environments in which we would like to live. Plants can be built that resist diseases without pesticides, use less water, and produce more edible food. Similar improvements are occurring in animals. More milk per cow leads to less pressure on grazing lands and more room for wildlife. When it comes to improving humans, the process will start by eliminating genetic diseases and move on to building better (smarter, taller, more beautiful) men and women. The biotech processes for curing existing diseases are dual-use technologies. The same techniques that allow genetic defects (very inferior genes) to be eliminated allow the replacement of slightly inferior genes with superior ones.

⬇

Environments in terms of agriculture, livestock farming and the standard of human living can be progressed by biotechnology. Particularly, the (A) __________ of genetic defects and (B) __________ of inferior genes with superior ones can cure human diseases.

03 다음 글을 읽고, |조건|에 맞게 요약문을 완성하시오.

| 조건 |

* (A), (B)는 1단어, (C)는 2단어, (D)는 1단어로 쓸 것
* [보기]에 있는 단어만을 사용할 것
* 필요한 경우, 문맥과 어법에 맞게 변형할 것

[보기] intelligence / management / appearance / deprive / demand / health / physical / cultivate / emotional / export / revitalize

Biotechnology opens up the possibility of creating the plant, animal, and human environments in which we would like to live. Plants can be built that resist diseases without pesticides, use less water, and produce more edible food. Similar improvements are occurring in animals. More milk per cow leads to less pressure on grazing lands and more room for wildlife. When it comes to improving humans, the process will start by eliminating genetic diseases and move on to building better (smarter, taller, more beautiful) men and women. The biotech processes for curing existing diseases are dual-use technologies. The same techniques that allow genetic defects (very inferior genes) to be eliminated allow the replacement of slightly inferior genes with superior ones.

⬇

Owing to biotechnology

1) Plants that are resistant to diseases, do not demand much water, and bring about more edible food, can be (A) ____________ in the absence of pesticides.
2) Cows producing a higher amount of milk do not (B) ____________ of space for wild animals and need less grazing lands.
3) Humans can be born without genetic diseases and with better (C) ____________ ____________ and (D) ____________.

04 다음 글의 순서로 적절한 것은?

Biotechnology opens up the possibility of creating the plant, animal, and human environments in which we would like to live. Plants can be built that resist diseases without pesticides, use less water, and produce more edible food.

(A) When it comes to improving humans, the process will start by eliminating genetic diseases and move on to building better (smarter, taller, more beautiful) men and women.

(B) The biotech processes for curing existing diseases are dual-use technologies. The same techniques that allow genetic defects (very inferior genes) to be eliminated allow the replacement of slightly inferior genes with superior ones.

(C) Similar improvements are occurring in animals. More milk per cow leads to less pressure on grazing lands and more room for wildlife.

① (A) - (B) - (C)　② (A) - (C) - (B)　③ (B) - (A) - (C)
④ (B) - (C) - (A)　⑤ (C) - (A) - (B)

문장 삽입

글의 논리	Question & Answer (질문 & 대답)
제목	24시간 여는 편의점이 자물쇠 달린 문을 설치하는 이유
주제	24시간 여는 편의점도 자물쇠가 있는 문을 사용하는 것이 이득이다.

PRACTICE 03

052 어법 선택 & 연결어

[Many / much] convenience stores are open 24 hours a day, 365 days a year. Since they never lock their doors, why do they bother **[installing / to install]** doors with locks on **[it / them]**? It is always possible, of course, **[what / that]** an emergency could force **[so / such]** a store **[to close / closing]** at least briefly. In the wake of Hurricane Katrina, (　　　　　　), residents of New Orleans **[forced / were forced]** **[evacuating / to evacuate]** with **[few / little]** notice. (　　　　　　) **[as if / even if]** the possibility of closing **[could rule / could be ruled]** out with certainty, **[this / it]** is doubtful **[what / that]** a store would find **[it / this]** **[advantageous / advantageously]** to purchase doors without locks. The vast majority of industrial doors **[sell / are sold]** to establishments **[what / that]** **[is / are]** not open twenty-four hours a day. These establishments have obvious reasons for wanting locks on their doors. (　　　　　　), **[given / giving]** **[what / that]** **[most / almost]** **[industrial / industrious]** doors **[sell / are sold]** with locks, **[this / it]** is probably cheaper **[make / to make]** all doors the same way.

(주어진 문장) 대답2 만약 가게가 문을 닫을 일이 없더라도 자물쇠 문을 구입하는 게 유리할지는 의심스럽다.

(But) / {even if the possibility (of closing) / could be ruled out / (with certainty)}, / it / is doubtful / {that a store / would find it advantageous / to purchase doors / (without locks)}.

- (But): 그러나
- even if: 〈종·접〉
- the possibility: S / 설령 문을 잠가야 할 가능성이
- closing: 〈동명사〉
- could be ruled out: V〈수동태〉 / 배제된다 할지라도
- (with certainty): 확실히
- it: 〈가S〉
- is: V
- doubtful: S.C / 의심스럽다
- that: 〈종·접〉 〈진S〉
- a store: S / 가게가
- would find: V
- it: 〈가O〉
- advantageous: O.C / 유리하다고 생각할지는
- to purchase doors: 〈진O〉 / 문을 구입하는 것은
- (without locks): 자물쇠가 없는

그러나 문을 잠가야 할 가능성이 확실히 배제된다 할지라도, 가게 입장에서 자물쇠 없는 문을 구입하는 게 유리하다고 생각할지는 의심스럽다.

노트
- rule A out : A를 배제하다, 제외시키다(수동태 시, A be ruled out) (=exclude, eliminate)
- 〈양보/대조〉

전치사	in spite of	+명사/명사 상당어구	비록 ~이지만
	despite		
종속접속사	though	+주어+동사	
	although		
	even though		
	even if		
	as		
	while		반면에
	whereas		

- 〈even vs. as〉

종속 접속사	even though	+주어+동사	비록 ~이지만	양보/대조
	even if			
	as though		마치 ~처럼	가정법
	as if			

- 〈with+추상명사=부사〉

	추상명사	부사	뜻
with	care	carefully	주의 깊게
	certainty	certainly	확실히
	ease	easily	쉽게
	kindness	kindly	친절하게
	patience	patiently	침착하게
	reality	really	사실상
	safety	safely	안전하게

- 〈가주어, 진주어 구문〉

가주어	동사	진주어
It (This/That/There 사용 불가)	–	that+주어+동사(완전한 절)
		to 동사원형
		동명사
		의문사+주어+동사(간접의문문)
		if/whether+주어+동사
it	is	that ~

- 〈가목적어 it / 진목적어 to R〉

주어	동사	가목적어	목적격보어	의미상 주어	진목적어
–	consider feel find make think	it (this, that, there 사용 불가)	형용사 명사	for+목적격 (주어와 진목적어의 주체가 다를 경우 사용)	to 동사원형
a store	would find	it	advantageous	–	to purchase

■ 〈what vs. that〉

	관계대명사(불완전한 문장)	접속사(완전한 문장)
what	○ 선행사를 포함하고 있기 때문에 what 앞에 선행사 불필요	×
that	○ that 앞에 선행사 필요	○

■ 〈find / found〉

원형	과거	과거분사	현재분사	뜻
find	found	found	finding	v. 발견하다, 알다
found	founded	founded	founding	v. 설립하다

일반적인 사실 많은 편의점이 24시간 내내 문을 연다.

Many convenience stores / are open / (24 hours a day), / (365 days a year).

(S 많은 편의점이 / V S.C 문을 연다 / 하루 24시간 / 1년 365일)

많은 편의점이 1년 365일, 하루 24시간 문을 연다.

노트 ■ be open : 개최 중이다
■ a : [단위를 나타내는 낱말에 붙여] ~당, ~마다, ~에(=per)
■ 〈부정수량형용사〉 : 막연한 수나 양의 정도를 표시하는 형용사

수(數)	few(a few), some(any), a lot of(lots of), a good(or great), plenty of, enough, all, no, many	복수명사+복수동사
양(量)	little(a little), some(any), a lot of, a good(or great), deal of, plenty of, enough, all, no, much	단수명사+단수동사

질문 편의점은 왜 자물쇠가 달린 문을 설치하는가?

(Since they / never lock their doors), / why / do they / bother to install doors / (with locks) / (on them)?

(〈종·접〉 S 그들은 / V O 문을 잠가놓을 일이 없는데 / 왜 / S V 그들은 / 문을 설치하느라 애를 쓸까? / 자물쇠가 달린 / 그것들(문)에)

문을 잠가놓을 일이 없는데, 그들은 왜 자물쇠가 달린 문을 설치하느라 애를 쓸까?

노트 ■ 〈since 용법〉

종속접속사	시간	~ 이래 (죽), ~한 때부터 내내
	이유	~이므로, ~이니까
전치사	시간	~ 이래 (죽), ~부터 (내내)
부사	시간	(그때) 이래 (죽), 그 뒤[후] 줄곧

■ 〈자동사가 뒤에 to부정사를 사용해 타동사처럼 목적어로 취하는 경우〉

	불완전자동사		목적어
주어	aim	~할 작정이다, 목표로 삼다	to R
	appear	~인 듯하다	
	arrange	미리 짜다[준비하다], 타협하다, 의논하다; 협정하다	
	bother	일부러 ~하다, ~하도록 애쓰다	
	consent	~하는 것을 동의/승낙하다	
	fight	~을 위하여 다투다	
	hesitate	주저하다, 망설이다	
	hurry	서두르다	
	long	~하기를 열망/갈망하다	
	prepare	~할 각오/마음의 준비를 하다	
	seem	~처럼 보이다, ~인 듯하다	
	serve	~의 역할을 하다	
	strive	~하려고 노력하다	
	struggle	(~하려고) 분투[고투]하다, 애쓰다	
	tend	~하는 경향이 있다	
	yearn	몹시 ~하고 싶다, 열망하다	
	wait	~하는 것을 기다리다	

대답1 가게를 잠시라도 닫아야 할 가능성이 있다.

(①) It / is (always) possible, / (of course), / {that an emergency / could force such a store to close / (at least) / (briefly)}.

(〈가S〉 이것은 / V S.C 언제나 가능하다 / 물론 / 〈종·접〉 긴급한 / S 상황이 / V O O.C 〈진S〉 그런 가게를 닫도록 만들 수 있다는 것이 / 적어도 / 잠시라도)

물론, 긴급한 상황으로 가게를 적어도 잠시라도 닫아야 할 가능성이 언제나 있다.

노트 ■ at least : 적어도[최소한]
■ 〈가주어, 진주어 구문〉

가주어	동사	진주어
It (This/That/There 사용 불가)	–	that+주어+동사(완전한 절)
		to 동사원형
		동명사
		의문사+주어+동사(간접의문문)
		if/whether+주어+동사
It	is	that ~

■ 〈5형식 불완전타동사의 목적격보어〉 : 수동태 전환 시, 2형식 문장(be p.p. +to R)

주어	불완전타동사	목적어	목적격보어
–	advise / allow / ask / assume / beg / cause / command / compel / condition / decide / design / drive / enable / encourage / expect / forbid / force / instruct / intend / invite / lead / like / motivate / order / permit / persuade / predispose / pressure / program / push / require / teach / tell / train / trust / urge / want / warn / wish 등	–	to 동사원형

■ 〈관사의 위치〉

so / how / too / as	형용사	a/an	명사
such / what / many / quite / rather / half	a/an	형용사	명사

대답1에 대한 예시 허리케인 여파로 뉴올리언스 주민들은 예고도 없이 대피했었다.

(②) (In the wake of Hurricane Katrina), / (for example), / residents (of New Orleans) / were forced to evacuate / (with little notice).

허리케인 카트리나의 여파로 / 예를 들어 / 뉴올리언스 주민들은(S) / 어쩔 수 없이 대피해야 했다(V〈수동태〉, S.C) / 거의 예고도 없이

예를 들어, 허리케인 카트리나의 여파로 뉴올리언스 주민들은 예고도 거의 없이 대피해야 했다.

노트

- in the wake of : ~의 뒤를 좇아, ~에 뒤이어; ~의 결과로서 (=following, succeeding, in the aftermath of; as a result of)
- force+목적어+목적격보어(to R) : ~가 …하도록 강요하다[수동태 시, be forced+주격보어(to R)]
- 〈few / a few / a little / little〉

수	few	거의 없는(부정)	+복수N+복수V
	a few	약간(긍정)	
양	a little	약간(긍정)	+단수N+단수V
	little	거의 없는(부정)	

대답2에 대한 근거 다수의 산업용 문은 24시간 열지는 않는 시설들에 판매된다.

(③) The vast majority of industrial doors / are sold (to establishments) / (that are not open / twenty-four hours a day).

절대 다수의 산업용 문은(S) / 판매된다(V〈수동태〉) / 시설들에(〈선행사〉) / (〈주·관〉) 열지는 않는(V, S.C) / 하루 24시간

절대 다수의 산업용 문은 하루 24시간 열지는 않는 시설들에 판매된다.

노트

- the vast majority of : 대부분의, 대다수의
- sell A to B : A에게 B를 팔다(수동태 시, A be sold to B)
- 〈주어와 동사의 수의 일치〉
  - A of B : 일반적인 경우에 A가 주어
  - A of B : A가 부분/부분인 경우에 B가 주어

	A	B	
분수	two − thirds 등	주어	동사 (B에 수의 일치)
부분	a group of, all of, a lot of, any of, a number of, both of, each of, either of, few of, half of, many of, most of, much of, neither of, none of, one of, part of, percent of, several of, some of, the rest, two of 등		
	The vast majority of	industrial doors	~~is sold~~ are sold

- 〈industry 품사별 변화에 따른 의미〉

	명사	형용사	동사
industry	산업, 공업, 근면	−	−
industrial	산업 근로자, (특히) 직공	산업(상)의, 공업(상)의	−
industrious	−	근면한, 부지런한	−
industrialize	−	−	산업[공업]화하다[되다]
industrialization	산업(공업)화	−	−

- 〈주격관계대명사절의 수의 일치〉 : 선행사를 포함하고 있는 관계대명사 what 사용 불가

	주격관계대명사절		
선행사	주격관계대명사	~~주어~~	동사
establishments	that		are

대답2에 대한 근거 이러한 시설들은 문에 자물쇠가 반드시 필요하다.

(④) These establishments / have obvious reasons / {for wanting locks (on their doors)}.

이러한 시설들은(S) / 분명히 이유가 있다(V, O) / 문에 자물쇠가 필요한(〈동명사〉, O)

이러한 시설들은 문에 자물쇠가 필요한 분명한 이유가 있다.

대답2 대부분의 산업용 문이 자물쇠를 갖추고 판매되기 때문에 모든 문을 같은 방식으로 만드는 것이 비용이 더 적게 들 것이다.

(⑤) (So), / {given / (that most industrial doors / are sold with locks)}, / it / is (probably) cheaper / to {make all doors / (the same way)}.

따라서 / 고려해보면 / (〈종·접〉) 대부분의 산업용 문이(S) / 자물쇠를 갖추고 판매되는 것을(V〈수동태〉) / 이것은(〈가S〉) / 아마도 비용이 적게 들 것이다(V, S.C) / 모든 문을 만드는 것이(O, 〈진S〉) / 같은 방식으로

따라서 대부분의 산업용 문이 자물쇠를 갖추고 판매되는 것을 감안하면, 모든 문을 같은 방식으로 만드는 것이 아마도 비용이 더 적게 들 것이다.

노트

- the same way : 같은 방법으로
- 〈if를 대신하는 어구〉

~을 가정하면	imagine (that), suppose(that)와 supposing (that)
~라는 조건이라면	providing (that), provided (that), so long as (that), on (the) condition (that)
~을 고려해본다면	given (that), giving (that)

- 〈most / almost / mostly〉

	대명사	형용사	부사
most	대부분의 것들(사람들)	대부분의	가장
almost	−	−	거의
mostly	−	−	주로, 일반적으로

- 〈가주어, 진주어 구문〉

가주어	동사	진주어
It (This/That/There 사용 불가)	−	that+주어+동사(완전한 절)
		to 동사원형
		동명사
		의문사+주어+동사(간접의문문)
		if/whether+주어+동사
it	is	to make

▶ 글의 흐름으로 보아, 주어진 문장이 들어가기에 가장 적절한 곳은?

정답 | ③

해설 | ③ 주어진 문장을 해석하면 '그러나 문을 잠가야 할 가능성이 확실히 배제된다 할지라도, 가게 입장에서 자물쇠 없는 문을 구입하는 게 유리하다고 생각할지는 의심스럽다.' 이다. 이 문장에는 'But' 이 나오기 때문에 앞 문장과 대조된다. 따라서 앞 문장에는 문을 잠가야 할 가능성이 있기 때문에 자물쇠 있는 문을 구매할 필요가 있다는 말이 나와야 한다. 이런 문장은 4번째 문장에서 예시로 나타난다. 4번째 문장에서는 카트리나에서 예고도 없이 대피해야 했다는 예시를 들며 문을 잠가야 할 가능성이 있다는 것을 암시해준다. 따라서 정답은 ③이다.

Words

☐ certainty
☐ doubtful
☐ advantageous
☐ purchase
☐ convenience store
☐ lock
☐ install
☐ emergency
☐ force
☐ evacuate
☐ notice
☐ vast
☐ majority
☐ industrial
☐ establishment
☐ obvious
☐ reason

Phrases

☐ rule A out
☐ at least
☐ the vast majority of
☐ the same way
☐ be open
☐ in the wake of
☐ sell A to B

우선순위 영단어

역대 수능 기출 + 전국 모의고사 기출 + EBS 기출 + 교과서 기출 빈출 어휘

단어	뜻	단어	뜻	단어	뜻
as a general rule	대개는	as a result	결과적으로	as to	~에 관한
as well	게다가	ascend	v. 올라가다	aside from	~을 제외하고
assert oneself	v. 자기주장을 내세우다	assertive	a. 자기주장이 강한	assist	v. 돕다
assistance	n. 도움	assistant	n. 보조원	associated	a. 연합된
assort	v. 분류하다	Assyrian	a. 아시리아의	astonish	v. 놀라게 하다
astonishment	n. 놀람	astound	v. 놀라게 하다	astronaut	n. 우주 비행사
at best	기껏해야	at fault	잘못이 있는	at hand	즉시 쓸 수 있도록
at one's peril	위험을 각오하고	at root	근본에 있어서는	at the moment	(바로) 지금
at the price of	~을 희생으로 하여	at the wheel	운전 중에	Atlantic	n. 대서양
atom	n. 원자	atomic	a. 원자의	attempt to	v. ~을 시도하다
attend	v. 진료하다	attention span	n. 주의 지속 시간	attentively	ad. 신경 써서
attraction	n. 명소	audible	a. 들을 수 있는	authorize	v. 권한을 주다
autobiography	n. 자서전	autograph	n. 자필 서명	automate	v. 자동화되다
autumn colors	n. 단풍	avenue	n. 도로	aversion	n. 싫음
avoid	v. 회피하다	await	v. ~을 기다리다	awe	n. 경외심
awesome	a. 경탄할만한	axis	n. 축	bachelor's degree	n. 학사학위
back up	v. 뒷받침하다	backyard	n. 뒷마당	badly	ad. 대단히
bait	v. (낚시 바늘에) 미끼를 달다	band together	v. 함께 뭉치다	banquet	n. 연회
bar	v. 방해하다	barbarous	a. 야만적인	bare	n. 텅 빈
bare minimum	최소한의 기본적인 것[정도]	bargaining	n. 협상	barn	n. 헛간
barter	v. 물물교환하다	base	a. 천한	based on	~에 근거를 둔
baseline	n. 기준(선)	basement	n. 지하실	battlefield	n. 전쟁터

변형문제

01 다음 글을 읽고, |조건|에 맞게 요약문을 완성하시오.

| 조건 |
* (A), (C)는 2단어, (B)는 1단어로 쓸 것
* [보기]에서 선택한 단어를 한 번씩만 쓸 것(단, (A)와 (C)의 경우, [보기] 외의 1단어를 각각 추가할 것)
* 필요한 경우, 문맥과 어법에 맞게 변형할 것

[보기] encourage / specialize / equip / order / moderate / devise / deliver / function / cost / sell / market / provide / generate

Many convenience stores are open 24 hours a day, 365 days a year. Since they never lock their doors, why do they bother to install doors with locks on them? It is always possible, of course, that an emergency could force such a store to close at least briefly. In the wake of Hurricane Katrina, for example, residents of New Orleans were forced to evacuate with little notice. But even if the possibility of closing could be ruled out with certainty, it is doubtful that a store would find it advantageous to purchase doors without locks. The vast majority of industrial doors are sold to establishments that are not open twenty-four hours a day. These establishments have obvious reasons for wanting locks on their doors. So, given that most industrial doors are sold with locks, it is probably cheaper to make all doors the same way.

⬇

The reason why the 24-hour convenience store has a lock is because most of doors (A) ____________ ____________ with locks and it (B) ____________ more if doors without locks (C) ____________ ____________ separately.

02 다음 글의 순서로 적절한 것은?

Many convenience stores are open 24 hours a day, 365 days a year. Since they never lock their doors, why do they bother to install doors with locks on them? It is always possible, of course, that an emergency could force such a store to close at least briefly.

(A) In the wake of Hurricane Katrina, for example, residents of New Orleans were forced to evacuate with little notice. But even if the possibility of closing could be ruled out with certainty, it is doubtful that a store would find it advantageous to purchase doors without locks.

(B) The vast majority of industrial doors are sold to establishments that are not open twenty-four hours a day. These establishments have obvious reasons for wanting locks on their doors.

(C) So, given that most industrial doors are sold with locks, it is probably cheaper to make all doors the same way.

① (A) - (B) - (C)　② (B) - (A) - (C)　③ (B) - (C) - (A)
④ (C) - (A) - (B)　⑤ (C) - (B) - (A)

03 다음 글을 읽고, |조건|에 맞게 주어진 요약문을 완성하시오.

| 조건 |
* (A), (B)는 각각 2단어로 쓸 것
* [보기]에서 선택한 단어를 한 번씩만 쓸 것
* 필요한 경우, 문맥과 어법에 맞게 변형할 것

[보기] assistance / urgency / industry / effective / manufacture / profit / cost / situation / productive / high / unexpected / reasonable

Many convenience stores are open 24 hours a day, 365 days a year. Since they never lock their doors, why do they bother to install doors with locks on them? It is always possible, of course, that an emergency could force such a store to close at least briefly. In the wake of Hurricane Katrina, for example, residents of New Orleans were forced to evacuate with little notice. But even if the possibility of closing could be ruled out with certainty, it is doubtful that a store would find it advantageous to purchase doors without locks. The vast majority of industrial doors are sold to establishments that are not open twenty-four hours a day. These establishments have obvious reasons for wanting locks on their doors. So, given that most industrial doors are sold with locks, it is probably cheaper to make all doors the same way.

⬇

Two reasons why most convenience stores have doors with locks on them are firstly there are (A) ____________ ____________ where a store has to be closed for a short time and secondly the (B) ____________ ____________ is low when all the doors are made with lock.

04 다음 글을 읽고, |조건|에 맞게 요약문을 완성하시오.

| 조건 |
* (A), (B)는 각각 다르게 1단어로 쓸 것
* 본문에 있는 단어만을 사용할 것
* 필요한 경우, 문맥과 어법에 맞게 변형할 것

Many convenience stores are open 24 hours a day, 365 days a year. Since they never lock their doors, why do they bother to install doors with locks on them? It is always possible, of course, that an emergency could force such a store to close at least briefly. In the wake of Hurricane Katrina, for example, residents of New Orleans were forced to evacuate with little notice. But even if the possibility of closing could be ruled out with certainty, it is doubtful that a store would find it advantageous to purchase doors without locks. The vast majority of industrial doors are sold to establishments that are not open twenty-four hours a day. These establishments have obvious reasons for wanting locks on their doors. So, given that most industrial doors are sold with locks, it is probably cheaper to make all doors the same way.

⬇

Although 24-hour convenience stores rarely have (A) ____________ doors, the cost of installing doors with locks is (B) ____________ than doors not equipped with locks.

글의 순서 배열

글의 논리	Myth & Truth (통념 & 진실)
제목	연구에 대한 언급
주제	'연구가 …라는 것을 보여 주었다' 라는 문구는 구체적인 세부사항 없이는 모호할 뿐이다.

수능 ANALYSIS

053 어법 선택 & 연결어

'Research has shown that ...' **[is / are]** a phrase often **[using / used] [persuading / to persuade]** the listener **[what / that]** the speaker can back up **[what / that]** he or she **[is saying / are said]** with firm empirical evidence. (   ), **[this / it]** is **[extremely / extreme]** vague to claim **[that / what]** 'research has shown' anything **[if / unless]** you can back up the claim with specific details about the research. Who carried out this research? **[Which / What]** methods did they use? What **[precise / precisely]** did they **[find / found]**? Have **[its / their]** results been **[confirming / confirmed]** by **[other / the other]** workers in the field? These **[is / are]** the sorts of questions **[what / which]** anyone who **[uses / use]** this phrase should be able to answer. If they can't, then there **[are / is]** no reason **[to persuade / to be persuaded]** by the phrase, **[which / what] [are / is]** then empty of content.

통념 '연구가 …라는 것을 보여 주었다' 는 문구는 확실한 증거를 통해 자신의 말을 뒷받침하는 것이다.

'Research has shown (that ...)' / is a phrase / (which is) <(often)
(S: 'Research has shown (that ...)' — S V O; is: V; a phrase: S.C)
'연구가 …라는 것을 보여 주었다' 는 / 흔히 사용되는 / 문구이다

(used to persuade the listener / [that the speaker can
(used: 과거분사; the listener: I.O; that: 종·접; the speaker: S)
청자에게 설득하기 위해 / 화자가 뒷받침할 수 있다는

back up / {what he or she is saying / (with firm empirical
(back up: V; what: 목·관; he: S_1; she: S_2; is saying: V; O; D.O)
것을 / 자신이 말하고 있는 것을 / 확실한 실증적 증거를 가지고

evidence)}]>.

'연구가 …라는 것을 보여 주었다' 는 화자가 확실한 실증적 증거를 통해 자신이 말하고 있는 것을 뒷받침할 수 있다는 것을 청자에게 설득하기 위해 흔히 사용되는 문구이다.

노트
- back up : ~을 뒷받침하다[도와주다]
- 〈타동사의 목적어로 사용된 목적격관계대명사 what〉 : that 사용 불가

타동사	관계대명사절(명사절 : 타동사의 목적어)				
	~~선행사~~	what	주어	타동사	~~목적어~~
back up		선행사를 포함한 관계대명사 (=the thing(s) which/that ~) : ~하는 것은/이	he or she	is saying	

- 〈what vs. that〉

	관계대명사(불완전한 문장)	접속사(완전한 문장)
what	○ 선행사를 포함하고 있기 때문에 what 앞에 선행사 불필요	×
that	○ that 앞에 선행사 필요	○

- 〈주격관계대명사＋be동사 생략〉

–	생략할 수 있음	
명사 (선행사)	(주격관계대명사 ＋be동사)	현재분사(Ring) – 능동(~하고 있는)
		과거분사(p.p.) – 수동(~되어진, 당한)
		명사
		형용사(구) (~하는, ~할)
		부사
		전치사구
a phrase	(which/that is)	used

- 〈used 용법〉

be	used	to	동사원형(R)	~하는 데 사용되다
be (get/become)	used (accustomed)	to	동명사(Ring)	~ 익숙하다
used		to	동사원형(R)	~하곤 했다

- 〈직접목적어 자리에 that절을 가지는 4형식 수여동사〉 : 수동태 시, be told＋that＋주어＋동사

주어	수여동사		간접목적어	직접목적어
	advise	조언하다		(that)＋주어＋동사
	assure	장담(확신)시키다		
	convince	확신시켜주다		
	inform	알리다		
	instruct	알리다		
	notify	알리다		
	persuade	설득하다		
	promise	약속하다		
	remind	상기시키다		
	request	요청하다		
	show	보여 주다		
	teach	가르치다		
	tell	말하다		
	warn	경고하다		

근거 이 문구를 사용하기 위해서는 여러 가지 질문에 답할 수 있어야 한다.

(A) These / are the sorts (of questions) / {which anyone / (who uses this phrase) / should be able to answer}.

These: S 이것들은 / are: V / the sorts: S.C 종류의 질문이다 / questions: 〈선행사〉 / which: 〈목·관〉 / anyone: S〈선행사〉 어떤 사람이든 / who: 〈주·관〉 / uses: V / this phrase: O 이 문구를 사용하는 / should be able to answer: V 답할 수 있어야 하는

이것들은 이 문구를 사용하는 어떤 사람이든 답할 수 있어야 하는 종류의 질문들이다.

노트 ■ a sort of : 일종의 ~, ~ 같은 것

■ 〈목적격관계대명사와 주격관계대명사〉

선행사	목적격 관계대명사	주어	주격 관계대명사	~~주어~~	동사	목적어	동사	~~목적어~~
			주격관계대명사절					
question	which	anyone	who	~~주어~~	uses	phrase	should be able to answer	~~목적어~~
	목적격관계대명사절							

■ 〈복합관계대명사〉 : 복합관계대명사절은 '관계대명사+ever' 형식을 가지고, 명사와 부사적 역할을 한다.

• 관계대명사절은 what만 명사절이고, who, which, that은 형용사절이다.

종류	명사절	부사절
whoever	anyone who	no matter who
	~하는 누구든지	누가 ~ 하더라도
whomever	anyone whom	no matter whom
	~하는 누구든지	누구를 ~ 하더라도
whichever	anything that	no matter which
	~하는 어떤 것이든	어느 것을 ~ 하더라도
whatever	anything that	no matter what
	~하는 어떤 것이든	무엇을 ~ 하더라도

(If they can't), / (then) / there is no reason / (to be persuaded / by the phrase), / (which is (then) empty of content).

If: 〈종·접〉 / they: S / can't: V 만약 그들이 그럴 수 없다면 / is: V / no reason: S 이유가 없는 것이다 / to be persuaded: 〈to R 수동〉 설득되어야 할 / by the phrase 그 문구에 의해 / which: 〈주·관〉 / is: V / empty of content: S.C 그러면 이는 내용이 비어 있는 것이다

만일 그들이 그럴 수 없다면, 그 문구에 의해 설득되어야 할 이유가 없는 것이고, 그러면 이는 내용이 비어 있는 것이다.

노트 ■ 〈There is 도치구문〉

긍정문	There	is	단수 주어	~이 있다
		are	복수 주어	
부정문	There	is no	단수 주어	~이 없다
		are no	복수 주어	

• 유도부사 **there**와 함께 도치구문을 이루는 be동사(is/are/was/were) 대신에 완전자동사 **appear**, **come**, **exist**, **follow**, **live**, **stand** 등을 사용할 수 있다.

■ 〈to R의 태와 시제〉

태	능동태	to R
	수동태	to be p.p.
시제	단순시제 : 본동사 시제와 동일	to R
	완료시제 : 본동사 시제보다 한 시제 앞선 시제	to have p.p.
	완료 수동	to have been p.p.

■ 〈주격관계대명사절〉 : 계속적 용법으로는 that 사용 불가, 구/절/문장 전체는 단수 취급

선행사	콤마(,)	주격관계대명사	~~주어~~	동사
		주격관계대명사절		
앞 문장 전체	〈계속적 용법〉	which		is

(B) Who / carried out this research?

Who: 〈의·대〉 누가 / carried out: V / this research: O 이 연구를 수행했는가?

누가 이 연구를 수행했는가?

노트 ■ carry out : 실행하다, 수행하다(=conduct, perform)

What methods / did they / use?

What methods: 〈의·형〉 O 어떤 방법을 / they: S 그들은 / did ... use: V 사용했는가?

그들은 어떤 방법을 사용했는가?

노트 ■ 〈what의 용법〉

용법	품사적 기능	명사 수식	해석
관계형용사	명사절 (S, O, C)	what + 명사	~한 모든
의문형용사			무슨, 어떤
의문대명사		×	무엇
관계대명사			~하는 것

What / (precisely) did / they find?

What: 〈의·대〉 무엇을 / precisely 정확히 / they: S / did ... find: V 그들은 찾아냈는가?

정확히 그들은 무엇을 찾아냈는가?

노트 ■ 〈find / found〉

원형	과거	과거분사	현재분사	뜻
find	found	found	finding	v. 발견하다, 알다
found	founded	founded	founding	v. 설립하다

Have their results / been confirmed / (by other workers) / (in the field)?

their results: S 그들의 결과가 / Have ... been confirmed: V〈현재완료 수동〉 확인되었는가? / by other workers 다른 연구자들에 의해 / in the field 그 분야에 있는

그들의 결과가 그 분야에 있는 다른 연구자들에 의해 확인되었는가?

노트 ■ be confirmed by : ~에 의해 확인되다

■ in the field : ~ 분야(현장)에서

주제문(진실) '연구가 …라는 것을 보여 주었다'는 구체적인 세부사항을 통해 뒷받침 하지 않으면 모호할 뿐이다.

(C) (However), / it / is (extremely) vague / {to claim / (that 'research has shown' anything)} / {unless you can back up the claim / (with specific details) / (about the research)}.

- However: 그러나
- it: 〈가S〉
- is: V
- extremely vague: 극도로 모호하다 (vague: S.C)
- to claim ~ anything: 〈진S〉 어떤 것은 '연구가 보여 주었다'고 주장하는 것은
- that: 〈종·접〉, 'research: S, has shown': V〈현·완〉, anything: O (that절 전체: O)
- unless: 〈종·접〉, you: S — 만약 여러분이 할 수 없다면
- can back up: V, the claim: O — 그 주장을 뒷받침하는 것을
- with specific details: 구체적인 세부사항으로
- about the research: 그 연구에 관한

그러나 어떤 것을 '연구가 보여 주었다'고 주장하는 것은 여러분이 그 연구에 관한 구체적인 세부사항을 통해 그 주장을 뒷받침할 수 없다면 극도로 모호하다.

노트 ■ unless : 만약 ~하지 않는다면(=if ~ not)

■ 〈가주어, 진주어 구문〉

가주어	동사	진주어
It (This/That/There 사용 불가)	–	that+주어+동사(완전한 절)
		to 동사원형
		동명사
		의문사+주어+동사(간접의문문)
		if/whether+주어+동사
it	is	to claim

▶ 주어진 글 다음에 이어질 글의 순서로 가장 적절한 것은?

① (A) – (B) – (C) ② (B) – (A) – (C)
③ (B) – (C) – (A) ④ (C) – (A) – (B)
⑤ (C) – (B) – (A)

정답 | ⑤

해설 | ⑤ 주어진 글에서 '연구가 …라는 것을 보여 주었다'는 말은 증거를 통해 자신이 말하는 것을 뒷받침할 수 있다는 것을 설득할 때 사용되는 문구라고 하였다. (C)에서는 '연구가 보여 주었다'고 주장하는 것이 구체적인 세부사항을 통해 뒷받침할 수 없다면 모호하다고 하였으므로 'However'를 통해 논리적으로 연결된다. (B)에 제시된 질문들은 (C)에서 언급한 'specific details'에 해당하므로 (C) 뒤로 이어질 수 있으며, (A)의 첫 단어 'These'는 (B)에 제시된 질문들을 가리키므로 (B) 뒤에 이어지는 것이 적절하다.

Words

☐ research ☐ empty ☐ field
☐ phrase ☐ content ☐ extremely
☐ persuade ☐ method ☐ vague
☐ firm ☐ precisely ☐ claim
☐ evidence ☐ result ☐ specific
☐ sort ☐ confirm ☐ detail

Phrases

☐ back up ☐ a sort of
☐ carry out ☐ be confirmed by
☐ in the field

우선순위 영단어 역대 수능 기출+전국 모의고사 기출+EBS 기출+교과서 기출 빈출 어휘

단어	뜻	단어	뜻	단어	뜻
be about to do	v. 막 ~을 하려고 하다	be at odds with	v. ~와 사이가 좋지 않다	be based on	v. ~에 기초하다
be compromised by	v. ~으로 위태롭게 되다	be concerned about	v. ~에 대해 관심을 갖다	be credited with	v. ~라는 공적이 돌아가다
be dependent on	v. ~에 의존하다	be destined to do	v. ~할 운명이다	be due to	v. ~ 때문이다
be equipped to	v. ~할 능력이 있다	be familiar with	v. ~에 익숙하다	be fascinated by	v. ~에 매료되다
be gone	v. 사라지고 없다	be inclined to	v. ~하는 경향이 있다	be involved in ~	v. ~에 연루되다
be likely (to)	v. ~할 가능성이 있다	be on the alert	v. 빈틈없이 경계하다	be on the go	v. 정신없이 바쁘다
be over	v. 끝나다	be prone to	v. ~하는 경향이 있다	be rooted in	v. ~에 원인이 있다

변형문제

01 다음 글을 읽고, |조건|에 맞게 요약문을 완성하시오.

| 조건 |
* (A), (B)는 각각 다르게 2단어로 쓸 것
* 본문에 있는 단어만을 그대로 사용할 것

'Research has shown that ...' is a phrase often used to persuade the listener that the speaker can back up what he or she is saying with firm empirical evidence. However, it is extremely vague to claim that 'research has shown' anything unless you can back up the claim with specific details about the research. Who carried out this research? What methods did they use? What precisely did they find? Have their results been confirmed by other workers in the field? These are the sorts of questions which anyone who uses this phrase should be able to answer. If they can't, then there is no reason to be persuaded by the phrase, which is then empty of content.

↓

The phrase, 'research has shown that.......' can be justified when the research is supported by (A) ______________ ______________ with reliable (B) ______________ ______________. Otherwise, the research should not be convinced.

02 다음 글을 읽고, |조건|에 맞게 요약문을 완성하시오.

| 조건 |
* (A), (B), (C)는 각각 다르게 1단어로 쓸 것
* [보기]에서 선택한 단어를 한 번씩만 쓸 것
* 필요한 경우, 문맥과 어법에 맞게 변형할 것

[보기] appreciate / reliable / encourage / motivate / satisfy / educate / support / convince / feasible / radical / abstract / existing / influence

'Research has shown that ...' is a phrase often used to persuade the listener that the speaker can back up what he or she is saying with firm empirical evidence. However, it is extremely vague to claim that 'research has shown' anything unless you can back up the claim with specific details about the research. Who carried out this research? What methods did they use? What precisely did they find? Have their results been confirmed by other workers in the field? These are the sorts of questions which anyone who uses this phrase should be able to answer. If they can't, then there is no reason to be persuaded by the phrase, which is then empty of content.

↓

If a speaker says 'Research has shown that ...', listeners would be (A) ______________ that the research is (B) ______________ by precise details with (C) ______________ evidence.

03 다음 글을 읽고, |조건|에 맞게 주어진 주제문을 완성하시오.

| 조건 |

* (A), (B), (C), (D)는 각각 다르게 1단어로 쓸 것
* 본문에 있는 단어만을 사용할 것
* 필요한 경우, 문맥과 어법에 맞게 변형할 것

'Research has shown that ...' is a phrase often used to persuade the listener that the speaker can back up what he or she is saying with firm empirical evidence. However, it is extremely vague to claim that 'research has shown' anything unless you can back up the claim with specific details about the research. Who carried out this research? What methods did they use? What precisely did they find? Have their results been confirmed by other workers in the field? These are the sorts of questions which anyone who uses this phrase should be able to answer. If they can't, then there is no reason to be persuaded by the phrase, which is then empty of content.

⬇

A fully credited research includes information about (A) ____________, methods, precise (B) ____________, and the (C) ____________ of other specialists. Otherwise, the research is believed to be (D) ____________.

04 밑줄 친 부분 중 문맥상 옳지 <u>않은</u> 것은?

'Research has shown that ...' is a phrase often used to ① <u>persuade</u> the listener that the speaker can back up what he or she is saying with firm empirical evidence. However, it is extremely ② <u>clear</u> to claim that 'research has shown' anything unless you can back up the claim with specific details about the research. Who carried out this ③ <u>research</u>? What methods did they use? What precisely did they find? Have their results been confirmed by other workers in the field? These are the sorts of questions which anyone who uses this ④ <u>phrase</u> should be able to answer. If they can't, then there is no reason to be ⑤ <u>persuaded</u> by the phrase, which is then empty of content.

UNIT 14

글의 순서 배열

글의 논리	Sequence
제목	Miller의 언어적 기억에 관한 연구
주제	Miller는 실험의 값이 전형적인 인간 두뇌의 신경 회로를 드러낼 것이라 생각하고 실험을 하였다.

PRACTICE 01

054 어법 선택 & 연결어

In 2002, UC Santa Barbara neuroscientist Michael Miller conducted a study of verbal memory. One by one, sixteen participants **[laid / lay]** down in an fMRI brain scanner and **[were / was]** **[showing / shown]** a set of words. After **[a little / a few]** minutes' rest, a second series of words **[were / was]** **[presented / presenting]** and they pressed a button **[when / whenever]** they recognized a word from the first series. As each participant decided **[that / whether]** he **[saw / had seen]** a particular word **[few / a few]** minutes ago, the machine scanned his brain and created a digital "map" of his brain's activity. **[Whenever / When]** Miller finished his experiment, he reported his findings the same way every neuroscientist **[does / is]**: by averaging together all the individual brain maps from his subjects to create a map of the Average Brain. Miller's expectation was **[what / that]** this average map would reveal the neural circuits **[involving / involved]** in verbal memory in the typical human brain.

순서 Michael Miller의 언어적 기억에 관한 연구

(In 2002), / UC Santa Barbara neuroscientist Michael Miller / conducted a study / (of verbal memory).

2002년 / UC Santa Barbara의 신경 과학자 Michael Miller는(S) / 연구를 수행했다(V, O) / 언어적 기억에 관한

2002년 UC Santa Barbara의 신경 과학자 Michael Miller는 언어적 기억에 관한 연구를 수행했다.

노트 ■ conduct a study : 연구하다

(One by one), / sixteen participants / lay down / (in an fMRI brain scanner) / and / were shown / a set of words.

한 명씩 / 16명의 참가자들이(S) / 누웠다(V_1) / 기능적 자기공명영상 두뇌 스캐너에 / 그리고 / 제시되었다(V_2) / 한 세트의 단어가(O)

16명의 참가자들이 한 명씩 기능적 자기공명영상(fMRI) 두뇌 스캐너에 누웠고, 그들에게 한 세트의 단어가 제시되었다.

노트
- ■ one by one : 하나하나씩[차례차례]
- ■ lie down : 눕다[누워 있다]
- ■ fMRI : 기능적 자기공명 영상법(functional Magnetic Resonance Imaging)
- ■ show+IO+DO (4) : ~에게 …을/를 보여 주다[수동태 시, be showed+DO (3)]
- ■ a set of : 일련(습)의
- ■ 〈혼동하기 쉬운 동사〉
  - • lie / lay / lie

원형	과거	과거분사	현재분사	품사/뜻
lie	lay	lain	lying	vi. 눕다, ~에 놓여 있다
lay	laid	laid	laying	vt. 눕히다, 알을 낳다
lie	lied	lied	lying	vi. 거짓말하다

(A) {As each participant decided / (whether he had seen a particular word) / (a few minutes ago)}, / the machine / scanned his brain / and / created a digital "map" (of his brain's activity).

〈종·접〉 / 각 참가자가 결정할 때(S, V) / 그가 특정 단어를 봤는지를(〈의문사 대용어〉, S, V〈과거완료〉, O) / 몇 분 전에 / 그 기계는(S) / 그의 두뇌를 스캔한다(V_1, O) / 그리고 / 디지털 지도를 만들었다(V_2, O) / 그의 두뇌 활동의

각 참가자가 특정 단어를 몇 분 전에 봤는지를 결정할 때, 그 기계는 그의 두뇌를 스캔하고 그의 두뇌 활동의 디지털 '지도'를 만들었다.

노트 ■ 〈부사절을 이끄는 종속접속사〉 : as 용법

	쓰임	해석
as+주어+동사	시간	~하고 있을 때, ~하자마자, ~하면서
	원인/이유	~ 때문에
	조건	~한다면
	양보	~일지라도
	비교	~보다/만큼
	방법/상태	~대로/~하듯이

■ 〈few / a few / a little / little〉

수	few	거의 없는(부정)	+복수N+복수V
	a few	약간(긍정)	
양	a little	약간(긍정)	+단수N+단수V
	little	거의 없는(부정)	

■ 〈의문사가 없는 간접의문문〉 : if/whether+주어+동사

■ 〈간접의문문 – 의문사가 없는 경우〉

	〈간접의문문〉 : 완전타동사의 목적어(완전한 문장)			
완전타동사	whether	주어	동사	목적어
decided	〈의문사 대용어〉	he	had seen	a particular word

■ 〈if / wether / that 구별법〉 : that 사용 불가

			if	whether	that
명사절	주어 자리		×	○	○
	목적어 자리	타동사의 목적어	○	○	○
		전치사의 목적어	×	○	○
	보어 자리		×	○	○
	진주어 자리		○	○	○
부사절	동사 수식		○	○	○
형용사절	명사 수식		×	×	○
간접의문문	S/O/C		○	○	×
–	–	–	if ~ or not(○) if or not(×)	whether or not(○) whether ~ or not(○)	×

(B) (After a few minutes' rest), / a second series of words / was presented / and / they / pressed a button / {whenever they recognized a word / (from the first series)}.

(After a few minutes' rest): 몇 분간의 휴식 이후에 / a second series of words: S, 두 번째 일련의 단어들이 / was presented: V(수동태), 제시되었다 / and: 그리고 / they: S, 그들은 / pressed: V / a button: O, 버튼을 눌렀다 / whenever: 〈복합관계부사〉 / they: S / recognized: V / a word: O, 단어를 인식할 때마다 / (from the first series): 첫 번째 세트로부터의

몇 분간의 휴식 이후에 두 번째 일련의 단어들이 제시되었고, 그들이 첫 번째 세트로부터의 단어를 인식할 때마다 버튼을 눌렀다.

노트
■ a series of : 일련의
■ press a button : 버튼을 누르다
■ **복합관계부사** : 복합관계부사절은 '관계부사+ever' 형식을 가지고, 부사 역할을 한다. (관계부사절은 선행사를 수식하는 형용사절이다.)

복합관계부사	시간/장소의 부사절	양보의 부사절
whenever	at(on/in) any time when(that) ~할 때는 언제나 =every time =each time	no matter when 언제 ~할지라도
wherever	at(on/in) any place where(that) ~하는 곳은 어디나	no matter where 어디에서 ~할지라도
however	×	no matter how 아무리 ~할지라도
		by whatever means 어떻게 ~한다 할지라도

(C) (When Miller finished his experiment), / he / reported his findings / (the same way) / (~~how~~) (every neuroscientist does): / (by averaging together all the individual brain maps) / (from his subjects) / (to create a map of the Average Brain).

When: 〈종·접〉 / Miller: S / finished: V / his experiment: O, Miller가 실험을 끝냈을 때 / he: S, 그는 / reported: V / his findings: O, 실험 결과를 보고했다 / (the same way): 방식 그대로 / every: 모든 / neuroscientist: S / does: V, 신경 과학자들이 보고하는 / averaging: 〈동명사〉 / all the individual brain maps: 개인적인 두뇌 지도를 합쳐 / (from his subjects): 피실험자들로부터 나온 / (to create: 평균치를 만들어 / a map: O / of the Average Brain: 평균 두뇌의 / 지도를 만들기 위해

Miller가 실험을 끝냈을 때, 그는 그의 실험 결과를 모든 신경 과학자들이 보고하는 방식 그대로 — 평균 두뇌의 지도를 만들기 위해 피실험자들로부터 나온 모든 개인적인 두뇌 지도를 합쳐 평균치를 만들어 — 보고했다.

노트
■ by+동명사 : ~함으로써
■ 〈주어와 동사의 수의 일치〉
• each / every / any+단수동사
■ 〈관계부사〉 : 관계부사절은 완전한 문장이 나오고, 선행사와 관계부사는 서로 같이 사용할 수도 있고 둘 중 하나는 생략할 수도 있다.

용도	선행사	관계부사	전치사+관계대명사
시간	the time	when	in/at/on+which
장소	the place	where	in/at/on+which
이유	the reason	why	for which
방법	(the way)	how	in which
	the way how는 같이 사용 못함, the way, the way in which, the way that은 사용 가능 (how 대신에 사용되는 that은 관계부사 대용어라고 함)		

■ 〈관계부사 how〉

선행사	〈관계부사절〉		
the same way	~~how~~	every neuroscientist	does
			대동사(=reported his findings)

Miller's expectation / was / {that this average map / would reveal the neural circuits / (which were) (involved in verbal memory) / (in the typical human brain)}.

Miller's expectation: S, Miller의 예상은 / was: V, 이었다 / that: 〈종·접〉 / this average map: S, 이 평균 지도가 / would reveal: V / the neural circuits: O, 신경 회로를 드러낼 / involved: 〈과거분사〉 / (involved in verbal memory): 언어적 기억과 관련된 / that절: S.C / (in the typical human brain): 전형적인 인간 두뇌의

Miller는 이 평균 지도가 전형적인 인간 두뇌의 언어적 기억과 관련된 신경 회로를 드러낼 것으로 예상했던 것이다.

노트
■ be involved in : ~에 개입되다, 관계되다
■ 〈what vs. that〉

	관계대명사(불완전한 문장)	접속사(완전한 문장)
what	○ 선행사를 포함하고 있기 때문에 what 앞에 선행사 불필요	×
that	○ that 앞에 선행사 필요	○

■ 〈주격관계대명사+be동사 생략〉

–	생략할 수 있음	
명사 (선행사)	(주격관계대명사 +be동사)	현재분사(Ring) – 능동(~하고 있는)
		과거분사(p.p.) – 수동(~되어진, 당한)
		명사
		형용사(구) (~하는, ~할)
		부사
		전치사구
the neural circuits	(which/that were)	involved

▶ 주어진 글 다음에 이어질 글의 순서로 가장 적절한 것은?

① (A) – (C) – (B)
② (B) – (A) – (C)
③ (B) – (C) – (A)
④ (C) – (A) – (B)
⑤ (C) – (B) – (A)

정답 | ②

해설 | ② 언어적 기억 연구를 위해 16명의 피실험자들에게 한 세트의 단어(a set of words)가 제시되었다는 주어진 글에 이어 휴식시간 이후 2번째 단어 세트(a second series of words)가 제시되었다는 (B)가 이어지는 것이 실험 순서상 적절하다. (A)의 'he had seen a particular word a few minutes ago'라는 내용은 1번째와 2번째 단어 세트가 제시된 이후에 나올 수 있으므로, (B) 다음에 (A)가 이어져야 한다. (C)의 'by averaging together all the individual brain maps from his subjects'라는 내용이 나오려면 (A)의 피실험자의 두뇌를 스캔하고 두뇌 활동의 디지털 지도를 만든다는 내용 이후여야 하므로, (A) 다음에 (C)가 이어지는 것이 가장 적절한 흐름이다.

Words

☐ conduct
☐ verbal
☐ memory
☐ participant
☐ decide
☐ particular
☐ machine
☐ scan
☐ rest
☐ present
☐ press
☐ finding(s)
☐ average
☐ reveal
☐ neural circuit
☐ typical

Phrases

☐ conduct a study
☐ lie down
☐ a series of
☐ by+동명사
☐ one by one
☐ a set of
☐ press a button
☐ be involved in

우선순위 영단어 역대 수능 기출+전국 모의고사 기출+EBS 기출+교과서 기출 빈출 어휘

단어	뜻	단어	뜻	단어	뜻
be tempted to	v. ~하도록 유혹받다	be willing to do	v. 기꺼이 ~하다	be worth -ing	v. ~할 만한 가치가 있다
bear out	v. 입증하다	beast	n. 동물	beep	n. 삐 소리
belong to	v. ~에 속하다	besides	v. ~ 외에(도)	bestow	v. 부여하다
best-selling item	n. 가장 많이 팔리는 품목	betray	v. 배신[배반]하다	betterment	n. 개량
biased	a. 치우친	bilingual	a. 두 나라 말을 하는	bilingualism	n. 2개 국어 병용
biography	n. 전기	bionic	a. 생체 공학적인	biophilia	n. 생명애
biotechnological	a. 생명공학적인	birth rate	출산율	blank	n. 백지의
blast	n. 폭발	bleach	n. 표백제	bleak	a. 암울한
blessing	n. 축복	blinder	n. 덮개	blockage	n. 차단
blood sugar	n. 혈당	blood vessel	n. 혈관	blow	v. 불다
blueprint	n. (설계)도면	blur	v. 흐릿하다	board	n. 위원회
boastful	a. 허풍 떠는	boldness	n. 대담	bolt	v. (문을) 걸쇠로 잠그다
bombing	n. 폭격	boost morale	v. 사기를 북돋다	boring	a. 지루한
boss	v. 지시하다	botanical garden	n. 식물원	bother to	v. 일부러 ~하다
bottle	v. (감정을) 억누르다	bottom	n. 맨 아래 (부분)	bounce	v. (빛, 소리를) 반사하다
bounce back	v. 금방 회복하다	boundary	n. 경계	boundless	a. 무한한
bout	n. 한바탕	bow	n. 활	brag	v. 자랑하다
braid	n. 땋은 머리	branch	n. 분과	brand	v. 오명을 씌우다
breach	n. 깨뜨림	break up	v. 해체되다	breaststroke	n. 평영
breathe	v. 호흡하다	breeze	n. 산들바람	brisk	a. 활발한

변형문제

01 다음 글을 읽고, |조건|에 맞게 주어진 요약문을 완성하시오.

| 조건 |
* (A), (B)는 각각 다르게 4단어로 쓸 것
* 본문에 있는 단어만을 그대로 사용할 것

In 2002, UC Santa Barbara neuroscientist Michael Miller conducted a study of verbal memory. One by one, sixteen participants lay down in an fMRI brain scanner and were shown a set of words. After a few minutes' rest, a second series of words was presented and they pressed a button whenever they recognized a word from the first series. As each participant decided whether he had seen a particular word a few minutes ago, the machine scanned his brain and created a digital "map" of his brain's activity. When Miller finished his experiment, he reported his findings the same way every neuroscientist does: by averaging together all the individual brain maps from his subjects to create a map of the Average Brain. Miller's expectation was that this average map would reveal the neural circuits involved in verbal memory in the typical human brain.

⬇

Michael Miller carried out a study to form a map of brain's activity that unveils the neural circuits of verbal memory in human brain by using (A) ________ ________ ________ ________ and displaying (B) ________ ________ ________ ________ intermittently.

02 다음 빈칸에 들어갈 말로 가장 적절한 것은?

In 2002, UC Santa Barbara neuroscientist Michael Miller conducted a study of ________________. One by one, sixteen participants lay down in an fMRI brain scanner and were shown a set of words. After a few minutes' rest, a second series of words was presented and they pressed a button whenever they recognized a word from the first series. As each participant decided whether he had seen a particular word a few minutes ago, the machine scanned his brain and created a digital "map" of his brain's activity. When Miller finished his experiment, he reported his findings the same way every neuroscientist does: by averaging together all the individual brain maps from his subjects to create a map of the Average Brain. Miller's expectation was that this average map would reveal the neural circuits involved in verbal memory in the typical human brain.

① human's awareness
② speaking memory
③ perception
④ verbal memory
⑤ digital memory

03 다음 글의 문장 중 무관한 문장을 고르시오.

In 2002, UC Santa Barbara neuroscientist Michael Miller conducted a study of verbal memory. ① One by one, sixteen participants lay down in an fMRI brain scanner and were shown a set of words. ② After a few minutes' rest, a second series of words was presented and they pressed a button whenever they recognized a word from the first series. ③ As each participant decided whether he had seen a particular word a few minutes ago, the machine scanned his brain and created a digital "map" of his brain's activity. ④ Participants are fully aware that every word. ⑤ When Miller finished his experiment, he reported his findings the same way every neuroscientist does: by averaging together all the individual brain maps from his subjects to create a map of the Average Brain. Miller's expectation was that this average map would reveal the neural circuits involved in verbal memory in the typical human brain.

04 다음 문장이 들어갈 부분으로 가장 적절한 곳을 고르시오.

> When Miller finished his experiment, he reported his findings the same way every neuroscientist does: by averaging together all the individual brain maps from his subjects to create a map of the Average Brain.

(①) In 2002, UC Santa Barbara neuroscientist Michael Miller conducted a study of verbal memory. (②) One by one, sixteen participants lay down in an fMRI brain scanner and were shown a set of words. (③) After a few minutes' rest, a second series of words was presented and they pressed a button whenever they recognized a word from the first series. (④) As each participant decided whether he had seen a particular word a few minutes ago, the machine scanned his brain and created a digital "map" of his brain's activity. (⑤) Miller's expectation was that this average map would reveal the neural circuits involved in verbal memory in the typical human brain.

글의 순서 배열

글의 논리	Examples
제목	면역: 바이러스에 두 번 걸리지 않는 이유
주제	우리 신체는 방어 체계를 가지고 있고 같은 바이러스에 두 번 감염되지 않는다.

055 어법 선택 & 연결어

Our bodies have a **[protected / protecting]** trick up **[its / their]** sleeves. Once certain viruses **[will have / have]** done **[their / its]** dirty work in a body, they'll never **[be let / let]** back in again. It's **[calling / called]** "immunity" and it's **[because / why]** we get chicken pox only once in a lifetime. Let's say **[what / that]** a big, ugly dog moves in next door. The first time you try **[petting / to pet] [them / it]**, it snarls and tries **[to take / taking]** a small chunk out of your rear end. (   ) the next time you have to walk past that dog, you **[prepared / are prepared]**. You blow a dog whistle **[what / that] [sends / send]** him **[cowering / cowered]** into his doghouse with his paws over his ears. You fight back **[because of / because]** you recognize danger **[which / when]** you see **[them / it]**. Your body works the same way. It recognizes an evil virus the second time around, knows it will cause trouble, and **[attack / attacks] [them / it]** before it has a chance to do **[its / their]** mischief again.

일반적인 사실 우리의 신체는 방어 체계를 가지고 있다.

Our bodies (S, 우리 신체는) / have (V) a protecting (〈현재분사〉) trick (O) up their sleeves.
유사시에 대비해 방어 요령을 갖고 있다

우리 신체는 유사시에 대비해 방어 요령을 갖고 있다.

노트
- have a trick up one's sleeve : 유사시의 숨겨둔(준비된) 계획이 있다
  - Ace in the hole; ace (or card or trick) up one's sleeve : 카드게임에서 셔츠소매에 카드를 숨겨두는 것 → 비장의 무기, 비장의 방책이 있다. 이익을 거둘 비밀스런 계획이 있다.

주제문 특정한 바이러스에 감염된 후에 두 번 다시는 걸리지 않는다.

{Once (〈종·접〉) certain viruses (S, 일단 특정한 바이러스가) / have done (V〈현재완료〉) their dirty work (O, 못된 짓을 하면) / (in a body) (우리 신체에서)}, / they (S, 그들은)'ll never be let back in (V〈미래 수동태〉, 신체로 들어오지 못할 것이다) (again) (다시).

일단 특정한 바이러스가 우리 신체에서 못된 짓을 하고 나면 그들은 다시 신체로 들어오지 못할 것이다.

노트
- once : 일단 ~하면 (종속접속사)
- do one's work : 직무를 수행하다
- let A in : A를 들어오게 하다(수동태 시, A be let in)
- 〈시간/조건의 부사절〉 : 현재가 미래를 대신함

〈종속절〉 : 부사절(~할 때)					〈주절〉	
Once	주어	동사			주어	동사
	certain viruses	~~will have done~~	→	have done	they	will never be let back in

주제문(재진술) 이 특징은 면역이라 불리고 우리가 평생 수두를 한 번 걸리는 이유이다.

It (S, 그것은)'s called (V〈수동태〉, '면역'이라고 불린다) "immunity" (S.C) / and (그리고) / it (S)'s (V) {why (〈의문사〉) we (S) get (V) chicken pox (O) / (only once) (한 번만) / (in a lifetime) (일생에)}. (S.C, 이 때문에 우리는 수두에 걸린다)

그것은 '면역'이라고 불리고 그것이 우리가 평생에 수두에 한 번만 걸리는 이유이다.

노트
- get + 목적어(질병) : (병에) 걸리다[옮다], (고통 등을) 겪다[앓다]
- once in a lifetime : 평생 단 한 번뿐인
- 〈call 동사의 쓰임〉 : ~을 …라고 부르다(수동태 시, be called + 주격보어)

주어	불완전타동사	목적어	목적격보어
	call		명사
			형용사

- 〈간접의문문 – 의문사가 있는 경우〉

	〈간접의문문〉 : 불완전자동사의 주격보어(완전한 문장)		
불완전자동사	의문사	주어	동사
is	why	we	get

- 〈This/That/It is because(because of) vs. This/That/It is why〉

This/That/It	is	because	주어	동사 ~
결과		원인		

This/That/It	is	why	주어	동사 ~
원인		결과		

주제문(재진술) 신체도 큰 개에게 물리고 조심하는 것처럼 일을 한다.

(A) Your body (S, 여러분의 신체도) / works (V, 작동한다) / (the same way) (같은 방식으로).

여러분의 신체도 같은 방식으로 작동한다.

노트
- work(완전자동사) : 작용(동)하다

주제문(재진술) 신체는 바이러스가 두 번째 침입할 때는 바이러스가 해를 끼치기 전에 공격한다.

It / recognizes an evil virus / (the second time around), / knows / (that) (it will cause trouble), / and / attacks it / {before it has a chance / (to do its mischief) (again)}.

It(S, 이것은) / recognizes(V₁, 인식하고) an evil virus(O, 사악한 바이러스를) / (the second time around)(두 번째 경우에), / knows(V₂, 안다) / (that) (it(S) will cause(V) trouble(O))(O, 그것이 문제를 일으킬 것을), / and(그리고) / attacks(V₃) it(O) (그것을 공격한다) / {before(〈종·접〉) it(S) has(V) a chance(O) (기회를 가지기 전에) / (to do its mischief) (again)(그것이 다시 해를 끼치는)}.

신체는 두 번째 경우에 사악한 바이러스를 인식하고 그것이 문제를 일으킬 것을 알고 그것이 다시 해를 끼치기 전에 그것을 공격한다.

노트
- cause [stir up, make] trouble : 분란을 일으키다
- have a chance to R : ~할 기회가 있다
- do mischief : 해를 끼치다, 장난하다
- **〈목적격종속접속사 that 생략〉** : 완전타동사의 목적어로 사용된 경우 / 관계대명사 what 사용 불가

	종속절(명사절 : 목적어) (완전한 절)		
완전타동사	that	주어	동사
know	목적격종속접속사 – 생략 가능(~하는 것을)	it	will cause

예시 큰 개에게 한 번 물리면 다음부터는 조심하게 된다.

(B) You / blow a dog whistle / (that sends him cowering into his doghouse) / (with his paws over his ears).

You(S, 여러분은) / blow(V) a dog whistle(O〈선행사〉) (개 호루라기를 분다) / (that(〈주·관〉) sends(V) him(O) cowering into his doghouse(O.C)) (그 개를 개집에서 웅크리고 있도록 하는) / (with(〈부대상황〉) his paws(O) over his ears(O.C)) (자신의 발로 귀를 덮고).

여러분은 그 개가 자신의 발로 귀를 덮고 개집에서 웅크리고 있도록 하는 개 호루라기를 분다.

노트
- blow (on) a whistle : 호각을 불다
- send+O+OC (5) : ~이/가 …하도록 하게 하다
- cower into : ~에 움츠리다(=crouch)
- **〈주격관계대명사절의 수의 일치〉** : 선행사를 포함하고 있는 관계대명사 what 사용 불가

	주격관계대명사절		
선행사	주격관계대명사	~~주어~~	동사
a dog whistle	that		sends

- **〈with 부대상황〉**

with	목적어	목적격보어		
~하면서, ~한채로		형용사(구)		
		부사(구)		
		전치사구		
		분사	현재분사(Ring)	능동 (목적어가 목적격보어를 ~하고 있는)
		분사	과거분사(p.p.)	수동 (목적어가 목적격보어에게 당하는, 되어진)
with	his paws	over his ears		

- **〈5형식에서 목적격보어 자리에 분사가 나오는 동사〉** : 수동태 시, be p.p.+주격보어

주어	불완전타동사	목적어	목적격보어	
	feel, keep, leave, like, smell, start, want, wish, send 등		분사	현재분사(Ring) : 능동
			분사	과거분사(p.p.) : 수동

You / fight back / (because you recognize danger) / (when you see it).

You(S, 여러분은) / fight back(V, 반격한다) / (because(〈종·접〉) you(S) recognize(V) danger(O)) (당신이 위험을 알아보기 때문에) / (when(〈종·접〉) you(S) see(V) it(O)) (그것을 보면).

여러분은 위험을 보면 그것을 알아보기 때문에 반격한다.

노트
- fight back : 저항하다, 가로막다, 말대답하다
- **〈원인/이유〉** : ~ 때문에

전치사	because of	+(동)명사 / 명사 상당어구
전치사	due to	
전치사	for	
전치사	on account of	
전치사	owing to	
전치사	thanks to	
종속접속사	as	+주어+동사 ~
종속접속사	because	
종속접속사	now(that)	
종속접속사	since	

(C) Let's say / {that a big, ugly dog moves / (in next door)}.

Let's say(V, 생각해 보자) / {that(〈종·접〉) a big, ugly dog(S) moves(V) (O, 크고 못생긴 개가 이사를 온다고) / (in next door)(옆집에)}.

크고 못생긴 개가 옆집에 이사를 온다고 생각해 보자.

노트
- **〈명령문의 종류〉**
  - 직접명령문

긍정문	동사원형(R)	~해라
부정문	Don't+R	~하지 마라
부정문	Never+R	~하지 마라

  - 간접명령문(주어가 1, 3인칭일 때)

긍정문	허락	Let(me, him, her)+R	~하게 해주세요
긍정문	권유, 제안(청유문)	Let's(Let us)+R	~하자
부정문		Let's not+R	~하지 말자

- **〈what vs. that〉**

	관계대명사(불완전한 문장)	접속사(완전한 문장)
what	○ 선행사를 포함하고 있기 때문에 what 앞에 선행사 불필요	×
that	○ that 앞에 선행사 필요	○

■ 〈형용사의 어순〉

관사/지시사	수량	주관적	사실(객관적 형용사)								+ 명사
관사	수량	의견 (opinion)	크기 (size)	성질/모양 (shape)	상태	연령	색깔(색상) (color)	원천 (origin)	재료 (material)	소속/목적/종류 (purpose)	명사
a			big		ugly						dog

(The first time) / (when) (you try to pet it), / it / snarls and tries to take a small chunk / (out of your rear end).

- (The first time): 처음에
- you: S / try: V / to pet it: O — 여러분이 그것을 쓰다듬어 주려고 할 때
- it: S — 그것은
- snarls: V_1 — 으르렁거리고
- tries: V_2 / to take a small chunk: O — 작은 덩어리를 한입 물어 뜯어내려 한다
- (out of your rear end): 여러분의 엉덩이로부터

여러분이 처음에 그것을 쓰다듬어 주려고 할 때, 그것은 으르렁거리고 여러분의 엉덩이로부터 작은 덩어리를 한입 물어 뜯어내려 한다.

노트 ■ 〈관계부사〉: 관계부사절은 완전한 문장이 나오고, 선행사와 관계부사는 서로 같이 사용할 수도 있고 둘 중 하나는 생략할 수도 있다.

용도	선행사	관계부사	전치사+관계대명사
시간	the time	when	in/at/on+which
장소	the place	where	in/at/on+which
이유	the reason	why	for which
방법	(the way)	how	in which
	the way how는 같이 사용 못함, the way, the way in which, the way that은 사용 가능 (how 대신에 사용되는 that은 관계부사 대용어라고 함)		

■ 〈관계부사 when〉

	〈관계부사절〉: 완전한 문장		
〈선행사〉	〈관계부사〉	주어	동사 ~
The first time	(when)	you	try ~

■ 〈try 동사 쓰임〉

try	목적어	〈3형식〉
	to R	~ 노력/시도하다(S의 의지 있음)
	Ring	시험 삼아 한번 해보다(S의 의지 없음)

■ 〈out of 쓰임〉

(운동) ~의 안에서 밖으로
(위치) ~의 밖에서, ~을 떠나서
(원천 · 출처) ~에서, ~으로부터; [말이] ~에서 태어난
(원인 · 동기) ~에서
[능력 · 제약 등의] 범위 밖에
[정상 상태에서] 벗어나서
[어떤 상태를] 벗어나서
[필요한 것이] 떨어져서, 동나서
[어떤 수 · 그룹 등의] 중에
(재료) ~으로

(So) / (the next time) / (when) (you have to walk past that dog), / you / are prepared.

- (So): 그러니
- (the next time): 다음번에
- you: S / have to walk past: V / that dog: O — 여러분이 그 개가 있는 곳을 걸어 지나가야 할 때
- you: S — 여러분은
- are prepared: V(수동태) — 준비한다

그러니 다음번에 여러분이 그 개가 있는 곳을 걸어 지나가야 할 때, 여러분은 준비한다.

노트 ■ walk past : ~을 지나치다

▶ 주어진 글 다음에 이어질 글의 순서로 가장 적절한 것은?

① (A) – (C) – (B)
② (B) – (A) – (C)
③ (B) – (C) – (A)
④ (C) – (A) – (B)
⑤ (C) – (B) – (A)

정답 | ⑤

해설 | ⑤ 주어진 글은 신체가 바이러스에 한 번 침범당하면 다시는 그 바이러스에 감염되지 않는다는 것과 면역이라는 개념을 제시한다. (C)에서 그것을 개에게 공격당한 경험 때문에 다음에는 그에 대비하게 된다는 사례로 빗대어 설명하고 (B)에서 그 대비를 구체적으로 설명한 다음 (A)에서 'the same way'라는 말로 개에 대한 방책처럼 신체가 바이러스에 대항하는 방식을 제시하는 흐름으로 글이 이어지는 것이 적절하다.

노트 ■ 〈원인 & 결과〉: 글의 논리전개 방식 중, 원인 & 결과(cause & Effect)는 단락 속에서 한 가지 또는 하나 이상의 원인과 결과를 가지고 글을 작성하고 읽는 방법론이다. 단락에서 인과관계에 간련된 표현을 찾는다면 논리적으로 글을 정확하고 빠르게 읽어 내려갈 수 있다.

• 원인을 나타내는 표현

결과	result (come/stem/originate) from		원인
	because of	owing to	
	due to	thanks to	
	because	since	
	now(that)	this(that) is because	

• 결과를 나타내는 표현

원인	as a result in	result in	결과
	lead to	bring about	
	give rise to	have an effect on	
	so	therefore	
	thus	hence	
	in consequence	consequently	
	this(that) is why	cause	
	affect	trigger	

• 원인과 결과를 동시에 나타내는 표현

원인(너무 ~해서)				결과(그 결과 ~하다)		
so	형용사	a(n)	명사	that	주어	동사 ~
such	a(n)	형용사	명사	that	주어	동사 ~

결과	so	(that)	원인
원인	, so	(that)	결과

Words

☐ protecting trick	☐ evil	☐ pet
☐ certain	☐ attack	☐ snarl
☐ dirty	☐ mischief	☐ chunk
☐ immunity	☐ blow	☐ rear end
☐ chicken pox	☐ whistle	☐ past
☐ recognize	☐ paw	☐ prepare

Phrases

☐ do one's work	☐ let A in
☐ once in a lifetime	☐ cause [stir up, make] trouble
☐ have a chance to R	☐ blow (on) a whistle
☐ do mischief	☐ fight back
☐ cower into	
☐ walk past	

우선순위 영단어 역대 수능 기출 + 전국 모의고사 기출 + EBS 기출 + 교과서 기출 빈출 어휘

단어	뜻	단어	뜻	단어	뜻
broaden	v. 넓히다	browse	v. 어린잎을 먹다	brutal	a. 잔인한
brutally	ad. 야만스레	brute	n. 짐승	bucket	n. 양동이
budge	v. 생각을 바꾸다	build up	v. 쌓다	bump into	v. ~와 부딪치다
bumper to bumper	(자동차가) 꼬리에 꼬리를 문	bush cricket	n. 덤불 귀뚜라미	bustle	n. 혼잡
but ~	~를 제외하고	buzz	n. 소문	buzz around	v. 윙윙거리며 날아다니다
by extension	더 나아가	by no means	결코 ~가 아닌	by oneself	혼자서
by the time	~할 즈음	bypass	n. 우회로	cable	n. 전선
calm down	v. 진정하다	campaign	n. 유세	cannot help but	v. ~할 수밖에 없다
canyon	n. 협곡	capitalist	a. 자본주의의	capitalize on	v. ~을 이용하다
carbohydrate	n. 탄수화물	carbon	n. 탄소	carbon footprint	n. 탄소이력
cardboard	n. 판지	carefully	ad. 조심해서	caress	v. 어루만지다
carriage	n. (영국의) 철도 객차	catalog	n. 카탈로그	catalyst	n. 촉매
catch one's breath	v. 헐떡이다	catch up	v. 따라잡다	cate	v. 복잡하게 만들다
cattle	n. 소	causality	n. 인관관계	cautious	a. 신중한
cavalry	n. 기병	cavern	n. 큰 동굴	cavity	n. 구멍
cemetery	n. 공동묘지	center on	v. ~를 중심에 두다	centerpiece	n. 장식물
CEO	n. 최고 경영자	certainty	n. 확신	chain-reaction	n. 연쇄 반응
change	n. 잔돈	chaotic	a. 무질서한	chapel	n. 예배당
chariot	n. 마차	Charter	n. 헌장	chase away	v. 쫓아버리다
check	v. 견제하다	check out	v. 확인하다	cherish	v. 소중히 하다
chew	v. 씹다	chief	n. 족장	chill	v. 차갑게 하다
chilly	a. 추운	chirp	v. 짹짹거리다	chore	n. 허드렛일
chuckle	n. 낄낄 웃음	circuit	n. 회로	circulate	v. 유포하다
cite	v. 인용하다	citizenship	n. 시민권	civic	a. 시민의
civil aviation	n. 민간 항공	civility	n. 정중	clam	n. 대합조개
class	n. 계층	clean up	v. 청소하다	clerk	n. 사무원

PRACTICE 02

변형문제

01 다음 글을 읽고, |조건|에 맞게 주어진 요약문을 완성하시오.

| 조건 |
* (A)는 1단어, (B)는 3단어로 쓸 것
* 본문에 있는 단어만을 사용할 것
* 필요한 경우, 문맥과 어법에 맞게 변형할 것

Our bodies have a protecting trick up their sleeves. Once certain viruses have done their dirty work in a body, they'll never be let back in again. It's called "immunity" and it's why we get chicken pox only once in a lifetime. Let's say that a big, ugly dog moves in next door. The first time you try to pet it, it snarls and tries to take a small chunk out of your rear end. So the next time you have to walk past that dog, you are prepared. You blow a dog whistle that sends him cowering into his doghouse with his paws over his ears. You fight back because you recognize danger when you see it. Your body works the same way. It recognizes an evil virus the second time around, knows it will cause trouble, and attacks it before it has a chance to do its mischief again.

⬇

Once a virus (A) ____________ a human body, the infection by (B) ____________ ____________ ____________ does not occur again, which is the concept of immunity.

02 다음 글의 주제로 가장 적절한 것을 고르시오.

Our bodies have a protecting trick up their sleeves. Once certain viruses have done their dirty work in a body, they'll never be let back in again. It's called "immunity" and it's why we get chicken pox only once in a lifetime. Let's say that a big, ugly dog moves in next door. The first time you try to pet it, it snarls and tries to take a small chunk out of your rear end. So the next time you have to walk past that dog, you are prepared. You blow a dog whistle that sends him cowering into his doghouse with his paws over his ears. You fight back because you recognize danger when you see it. Your body works the same way. It recognizes an evil virus the second time around, knows it will cause trouble, and attacks it before it has a chance to do its mischief again.

① Immunity does not apply to all humans.
② Our bodies are susceptible to the virus.
③ We are careful when we pass by the side of the side.
④ Our bodies have a defense system.
⑤ Viruses are harmful to humans.

03 다음 글을 읽고, |조건|에 맞게 빈칸 (A), (B), (C)를 채우시오.

| 조건 |

* (A), (B), (C)는 각각 다르게 1단어로 쓸 것
* [보기]에서 선택한 단어를 한 번씩만 쓸 것
* 필요한 경우, 문맥과 어법에 맞게 변형할 것

[보기] manage / clean / deliver / transform / defeat / find / suggest / clean / defend / harm / detect / change / detect / analyze

Our bodies have a protecting trick up their sleeves. Once certain viruses have done their dirty work in a body, they'll never be let back in again. It's called "immunity" and it's why we get chicken pox only once in a lifetime. Let's say that a big, ugly dog moves in next door. The first time you try to pet it, it snarls and tries to take a small chunk out of your rear end. So the next time you have to walk past that dog, you are prepared. You blow a dog whistle that sends him cowering into his doghouse with his paws over his ears. You fight back because you recognize danger when you see it. Your body works the same way. It recognizes an evil virus the second time around, knows it will cause trouble, and attacks it before it has a chance to do its mischief again.

⬇

Our bodies know how to (A) ______________. For example, when a virus that damaged the body once intrudes, the body immediately (B) ______________ the virus and (C) ______________ it before any harm occurs again. This explains why people suffer from chicken pox once in a lifetime.

04 밑줄 친 부분 중 문맥상 옳지 않은 것은?

Our bodies have a ① protecting trick up their sleeves. Once certain viruses have done their dirty work in a body, they'll never be let back in ② again. It's called "immunity" and it's why we get chicken pox only once in a lifetime. Let's say that a big, ugly dog moves in next door. The first time you try to pet it, it snarls and tries to take a small chunk out of your rear end. So the next time you have to walk past that dog, you are ③ prepared. You blow a dog whistle that sends him cowering into his doghouse with his paws over his ears. You fight back because you ④ recognize danger when you see it. Your body works the ⑤ different way. It recognizes an evil virus the second time around, knows it will cause trouble, and attacks it before it has a chance to do its mischief again.

UNIT 14

글의 순서 배열

글의 논리	Story
제목	친구와 식사할 때 계산하기
주제	친구와 식사할 때 계산을 하고 싶으면 친구가 오기 전에 식당에 도착해서 미리 신용카드를 건네면 된다.

PRACTICE 03

056 어법 선택 & 연결어

You and your friend have just finished your meal. The waiter **[lies / lays]** the check on your table. Boom! To an **[earsplit / earsplitting]** duet of "Let me **[to get / get]** that," you and your friend's hands snatch down on **[them / it]** **[alike / like]** two pelicans **[plunged / plunging]** for the same fish. **[Embarrassing / Embarrassed]** battles follow. You disturb **[nearby / near]** diners. Here's how to avoid this happening. **[Arrive at / Arrive]** the restaurant before your guest arrives, and **[give / gives]** the person who **[seats / seat]** you your credit card. **[To say / Say]** you want him to bring the bill with the credit card already **[stamping / stamped]** as you finish your meal. When the meal is over, the server brings the check **[direct / directly]** to you. You **[mere / merely]** fill in the tip and **[hand it back / hand back it]**. When your friend says "Oh no," **[simple / simply]** **[to say / say]** "No, it's **[done / doing]**. I really want to get this one." Your friend is **[impressing / impressed]** and **[pleasing / pleased]**.

이야기 친구와 식사할 때 계산하기

You and your friend / have (just) finished your meal.
(S1: You / S2: your friend / V: have finished 〈현재완료〉 / O: your meal)
여러분과 친구가 / 식사를 막 끝마쳤다

여러분과 친구가 식사를 막 끝마쳤다.

노트 ■ finish meal : 식사를 끝내다

The waiter / lays the check / (on your table).
(S / V / O)
웨이터가 / 계산서를 올려놓는다 / 식탁 위에

웨이터가 식탁 위에 계산서를 올려놓는다.

노트 ■ 〈혼동하기 쉬운 동사〉
• lie / lay / lie

원형	과거	과거분사	현재분사	품사/뜻
lie	lay	lain	lying	vi. 눕다, ~에 놓여 있다
lay	laid	laid	laying	vt. 눕히다, 알을 낳다
lie	lied	lied	lying	vi. 거짓말하다

Boom! / (To an earsplitting duet of "Let me get that,")
(〈현재분사〉 earsplitting / 〈사·동〉 Let / O: me / O.C: get)
쿵! / "내가 낼게."라는 귀청이 떨어질 듯한 이중창과 함께

/ you and your friend's hands / snatch (down) (on it) /
(S1 / S2 / V)
여러분과 친구의 손은 / 그것을 낚아챈다

(like two pelicans) (which are) (plunging for the same fish).
(〈전치사〉 like / 〈현재분사〉 plunging)
두 마리 펠리컨처럼 / 같은 물고기를 향해 돌진하는 것

쿵! "내가 낼게."라는 귀청이 떨어질 듯한 이중창과 함께 같은 물고기를 향해 돌진하는 두 마리 펠리컨처럼 여러분과 친구의 손이 그것을 낚아챈다.

노트 ■ snatch down on : ~을 잡아채다(=snatch at)
■ plunge for : ~로 돌진하다
■ 〈사역동사〉 : 목적어와 목적격보어의 관계가 능동일 경우

주어	사역동사	목적어	목적격보어
	have		동사원형(R)
	let		
	make		

■ 〈likely / alike / like〉

likely	형용사	~일 것 같은 (be to 동사원형 : ~일 것 같다)
	부사	아마(probably)
alike	서술적 형용사 (보어로만 사용, 명사 수식 불가)	동일한
	부사	똑같이
like	전치사	~처럼
	동사	좋아하다

■ 〈주격관계대명사+be동사 생략〉

–	생략할 수 있음	
명사 (선행사)	(주격관계대명사 +be동사)	현재분사(Ring) – 능동(~하고 있는)
		과거분사(p.p.) – 수동(~되어진, 당한)
		명사
		형용사(구) (~하는, ~할)
		부사
		전치사구
two pelicans	(which/that are)	plunging

(A) Say / (that) (you want him to bring the bill) / (with the
(V: Say / O: (that) you want him to bring the bill — S: you / V: want / O: him / O.C: to bring the bill)
말해라 / 여러분이 그가 계산서를 가져오기를 원한다고 / 그 신용카드로

credit card) / (already stamped) / (as you finish your meal).
(which is) 〈과거분사〉 〈종·접〉 S V O
이미 지불된 여러분이 식사를 끝마칠 때

여러분이 식사를 끝마칠 때 그 신용카드로 이미 지불된 계산서를 가져오길 원한다고 그에게 말해라.

노트 ■ 〈직접명령문〉

긍정문	R	~해라
	Please+R	~해 주세요
부정문	Don't+R	~하지 마라
	Never+R	

■ 〈목적격종속접속사 that 생략〉 : 완전타동사의 목적어로 사용된 경우 / 관계대명사 what 사용 불가

	종속절(명사절 : 목적어) (완전한 절)		
완전타동사	that	주어	동사
Say	목적격종속접속사 – 생략 가능(~하는 것을)	you	want

■ 〈want 동사의 쓰임〉

주어	want	목적어(to R)		주어가 ~하는 것을 원하다	3형식
		목적어	목적격보어 (to R)	주어는 목적어가 ~하는 것을 원하다	5형식

■ 〈주격관계대명사+be동사 생략〉

–	생략할 수 있음	
명사 (선행사)	(주격관계대명사 +be동사)	현재분사(Ring) – 능동(~하고 있는)
		과거분사(p.p.) – 수동(~되어진, 당한)
		명사
		형용사(구) (~하는, ~할)
		부사
		전치사구
the credit card	(which/that is)	stamped

(When the meal is over), / the server / brings the check (directly) / (to you).
〈종·접〉 S V S V O
식사가 끝나면 종업원이 계산서를 가져온다 바로 여러분에게

식사가 끝나고, 종업원이 여러분에게 바로 계산서를 가져온다.

노트 ■ be over : 끝나다
■ 〈4형식을 3형식으로 바꿀 때 사용하는 전치사〉 : 전치사 to를 취하는 동사

주어 (A)	+	동사(B)	+	간접목적어 (C: 사람/동물)	+	직접목적어 (D: 사물)	(4)
		give, bring, pass, send, show, sell, hand, lend, offer, teach, tell, buy, build, choose, find, leave, make, order, prepare, ask 등 수여동사					

→ 주어(A)+동사(B)+직접목적어(D: 사물)+전치사+간접목적어(C: 사람/동물) (3)
to

(B) You / (merely) fill in the tip / and hand it back.
S V_1 O V_2 O
여러분은 단지 팁만 써라 그리고 그것을 다시 건넨다

여러분은 단지 팁만 쓰고 그것을 다시 건넨다.

노트 ■ fill in : ~을 채우다
■ hand A back : A를 돌려주다
■ 〈이어동사〉

타동사	명사	부사	(○)
타동사	부사	명사	(○)
타동사	대명사	부사	(○)
타동사	부사	대명사	(×)
hand	back	it	(×)

(When your friend says "Oh no,") / (simply) say / "No, it's done. / I / (really) want to get this one."
〈종·접〉 S V V
여러분의 친구가 "오, 안 돼."와 같은 말을 할 때 간단하게 말해라
S V〈수동태〉 S V O
"아냐, 이미 계산했어. 내가 정말로 이번 것은 사고 싶었어."

여러분의 친구가 "오, 안 돼."와 같은 말을 할 때, "아냐, 이미 계산했어. 내가 정말로 이번 것은 사고 싶었어."와 같이 간단히 말해라.

Your friend / is impressed and pleased.
S V $S.C_1$ $S.C_2$
여러분의 친구는 감명 받고 기분이 좋아진다

여러분의 친구는 감명 받고 기분이 좋아진다.

노트 ■ 〈감정과 관련된 완전타동사〉 : 분사화가 되어 주격보어/목적격보어 자리에 나올 때 구별법
• 2형식

주어	동사	주격보어(S.C)
사람		과거분사(p.p.) – 수동(되어진, ~ 당한)
사물		현재분사(Ring) – 능동(~하고 있는, 하는)
Your friend	is	impressed and pleased

(C) Embarrassing battles / follow.
〈현재분사〉 S V
당혹스러운 다툼이 잇따라 일어난다

당혹스러운 다툼이 잇따라 일어난다.

노트 ■ 〈분사의 역할 및 종류〉

분사의 역할	형용사	명사 수식	전치 수식
			후치 수식
		보어 사용	주격보어
			목적격보어
분사의 종류	현재분사(Ring)	능동	~하는, ~하고 있는
	과거분사(p.p.)	수동	~되는, ~ 당하는, 이미 된

You / disturb nearby diners.
S V O
여러분은 근처의 식사하는 사람들을 방해한다

여러분은 근처의 식사하는 사람들을 방해한다.

노트 ■ 〈near / nearby / nearly〉

	부사	형용사	전치사	동사
near	(거리/시간상으로) 가까이, 거의	(거리/시간상으로) 가까운	(거리상으로) ~에서 가까이 (숫자 앞에 쓰여) 거의[약]	(시간/거리상으로) 가까워지다 [다가오다], ~에 접근하다
nearby	인근에, 가까운 곳에, 거의, 대략; 간신히, 가까스로, 밀접하게, 면밀하게	[주로 명사 앞에 씀] 인근의, 가까운 곳의	–	–
nearly	거의	–	–	–

Here's / how to avoid this happening.
(Here's: V 여기에 있다 / how to avoid this happening: S 이러한 사건을 피하는 방법이)

여기에 이러한 사건을 피하는 방법이 있다.

노트 ■ 〈There/Here is 도치구문〉

긍정문	There (Here)	is	단수 주어	~이 있다 (여기에 ~이 있다)
		are	복수 주어	
부정문		is no	단수 주어	~이 없다 (여기에 ~이 없다)
		are no	복수 주어	

• 유도부사 **there**와 함께 도치구문을 이루는 be동사(is/are/was/were) 대신에 완전자동사 **appear**, **come**, **exist**, **follow**, **live**, **stand** 등을 사용할 수 있다.

■ 〈의문사 to R〉=의문사+주어+should+R

		〈간접의문문〉: 불완전자동사 is의 주격보어			
Here	is	how	to	avoid	this happening.
	불완전자동사	의문사	to부정사		

Arrive (at the restaurant) / (before your guest arrives), /
(Arrive: V_1 식당에 도착해라 / before: 〈종·접〉 your guest: S arrives: V 여러분의 손님이 도착하기 전에)

and give the person / (who seats you) / your credit card.
(그리고 give: V_2 the person: I.O 사람에게 건네라 / who: 〈주·관〉 seats: V you: O 여러분을 자리로 안내하는 사람에게 / your credit card: D.O 여러분의 신용카드를)

여러분의 손님이 도착하기 전에 식당에 도착해서, 여러분을 자리로 안내하는 사람에게 신용카드를 건네라.

노트 ■ arrive at : ~에 도착하다

■ 〈주격관계대명사 who〉 : 선행사와 수의 일치

		주격관계대명사절				
give	the person	who	~~주어~~	seats	you	your credit card.
수여동사	간접목적어 : 선행사	주격관계대명사		동사	목적어	직접목적어

■ 〈sit / seat / set〉

원형	과거	과거분사	현재분사	뜻
sit	sat	sat	sitting	vi. 앉다, ~에 놓여 있다
seat	seated	seated	seating	vt. 앉히다
set	set	set	setting	vt. 두다, ~을 놓다

▶ 주어진 글 다음에 이어질 글의 순서로 가장 적절한 것은?

① (A) – (C) – (B)
② (B) – (A) – (C)
③ (B) – (C) – (A)
④ (C) – (A) – (B)
⑤ (C) – (B) – (A)

정답 | ④

해설 | ④ 주어진 문단은 웨이터가 계산서를 가져다주는 상황에 관한 묘사이므로, 이에 대해 서로 돈을 내려고 하는 장면이 나오는 (C)가 이어지게 된다. 그리고 이러한 다툼에 대한 해결방안을 소개하는 (A)가 이어지고, 마지막으로 여러분의 호의에 대해 고마워하는 친구의 모습이 나오는 (B)가 오게 된다.

Words

- ☐ finish
- ☐ meal
- ☐ lay
- ☐ check
- ☐ earsplitting
- ☐ duet
- ☐ snatch
- ☐ bill
- ☐ merely
- ☐ impressed
- ☐ pleased
- ☐ embarrassing
- ☐ battle
- ☐ disturb
- ☐ nearby
- ☐ seat

Phrases

- ☐ finish meal
- ☐ plunge for
- ☐ fill in
- ☐ arrive at
- ☐ snatch down on
- ☐ be over
- ☐ hand A back

PRACTICE 03

변형문제

01 다음 글을 읽고, |조건|에 맞게 주어진 제목을 완성하시오.

| 조건 |
* (A)는 3단어, (B)는 2단어로 쓸 것
* [보기]에서 선택한 단어를 한 번씩만 쓸 것
* 필요한 경우, 문맥과 어법에 맞게 변형할 것

[보기] in / friend / pay / fight / for / advance / happy / win / time / at / make / bill / partner / card / the / a

You and your friend have just finished your meal. The waiter lays the check on your table. Boom! To an earsplitting duet of "Let me get that," you and your friend's hands snatch down on it like two pelicans plunging for the same fish. Embarrassing battles follow. You disturb nearby diners. Here's how to avoid this happening. Arrive at the restaurant before your guest arrives, and give the person who seats you your credit card. Say you want him to bring the bill with the credit card already stamped as you finish your meal. When the meal is over, the server brings the check directly to you. You merely fill in the tip and hand it back. When your friend says "Oh no," simply say "No, it's done. I really want to get this one." Your friend is impressed and pleased.

⬇

A way to (A) ________ ________ ________ at the restaurant (B) ________ ________.

02 다음 요약문의 빈칸에 들어갈 말로 가장 적절한 것을 고르시오.

You and your friend have just finished your meal. The waiter lays the check on your table. Boom! To an earsplitting duet of "Let me get that," you and your friend's hands snatch down on it like two pelicans plunging for the same fish. Embarrassing battles follow. You disturb nearby diners. Here's how to avoid this happening. Arrive at the restaurant before your guest arrives, and give the person who seats you your credit card. Say you want him to bring the bill with the credit card already stamped as you finish your meal. When the meal is over, the server brings the check directly to you. You merely fill in the tip and hand it back. When your friend says "Oh no," simply say "No, it's done. I really want to get this one." Your friend is impressed and pleased.

⬇

If you want to (A) ________ the bill, (B) ________ the card to the person who seat you before you eat.

	(A)	(B)
①	pay	hand
②	pay	hide
③	divide	hand
④	economize	hide
⑤	economize	hand

03 다음 글의 제목으로 가장 적절한 것은?

You and your friend have just finished your meal. The waiter lays the check on your table. Boom! To an earsplitting duet of "Let me get that," you and your friend's hands snatch down on it like two pelicans plunging for the same fish. Embarrassing battles follow. You disturb nearby diners. Here's how to avoid this happening. Arrive at the restaurant before your guest arrives, and give the person who seats you your credit card. Say you want him to bring the bill with the credit card already stamped as you finish your meal. When the meal is over, the server brings the check directly to you. You merely fill in the tip and hand it back. When your friend says "Oh no," simply say "No, it's done. I really want to get this one." Your friend is impressed and pleased.

① Calculate after a meal
② Eating without a fight
③ Calculate fairly about bill
④ Keeping table manners at a restaurant
⑤ Don't owe it to your friends.

04 다음 문장이 들어갈 부분으로 가장 적절한 곳을 고르시오.

You merely fill in the tip and hand it back.

You and your friend have just finished your meal. The waiter lays the check on your table. Boom! To an earsplitting duet of "Let me get that," you and your friend's hands snatch down on it like two pelicans plunging for the same fish. Embarrassing battles follow. (①) You disturb nearby diners. (②) Here's how to avoid this happening. Arrive at the restaurant before your guest arrives, and give the person who seats you your credit card. (③) Say you want him to bring the bill with the credit card already stamped as you finish your meal. (④) When the meal is over, the server brings the check directly to you. (⑤) When your friend says "Oh no," simply say "No, it's done. I really want to get this one." Your friend is impressed and pleased.

UNIT 15

요약문 완성

글의 논리	Comparison & Contrast (비교 & 대조)
제목	만족 지연에 관한 연구
주제	자신들의 욕구를 미룰 수 있는 어린이들이 청소년기에 월등한 성취를 보여 준다.

수능 ANALYSIS

057 어법 선택 & 연결어

In a study at Stanford University, four-year-olds at a nursery school **[offered / were offered]** a marshmallow. They **[told / were told]** they could either eat the marshmallow immediately **[or / and]** **[wait / waited]**. If they waited to eat the marshmallow **[what / that]** **[seated / sat]** before **[its / their]** eyes until the experimenter returned (about 15 minutes), they **[would have received / would receive]** two marshmallows. Walter Mischel, a psychologist **[study / studying]** delaying gratification, **[had / to have]** three daughters who **[attended to / attended]** the nursery school; they and their classmates **[participated in / participated]** the study. Over the years, he **[would have asked / would ask]** his daughters about **[their / his]** friends, and in **[doing / being]** so he detected a relationship **[either / between]** an ability to delay gratification in preschool and **[excelled / excelling]** in adolescence. Mischel and his colleagues located the participants in the initial study to more **[formally / formal]** track **[their / its]** progress as they matured. They noticed **[what / that]** the children who ate the single marshmallow right away **[were / was]** **[alike / likely]** to **[have / having]** problems in the areas of behavior, friendships, and attention. (　　　　　　), those **[that / who]** **[were / was]** able to delay gratification had higher SAT scores and **[coped / cope]** better with stress.

⬇

According **[to / as]** Mischel's study, children who could put off their desire showed superior achievements in adolescence, while those who sought instant satisfaction tended to have various troubles.

연구 마시멜로를 통한 만족 지연에 관한 연구

(In a study) / (at Stanford University), / four-year-olds (S) / (at a nursery school) / were offered (V〈수동태〉) a marshmallow (O).

한 연구에서 / Stanford 대학에서 / 4살배기 유아들이 / 어린이집의 / 마시멜로를 제공받았다

Stanford 대학의 한 연구에서, 어린이집의 4살배기 유아들이 마시멜로를 제공받았다.

노트 ■ 〈4형식을 3형식 수동태 문장 전환〉: 간접목적어가 주어로 가는 경우

주어 (A)	+	동사(B)	+	간접목적어 (C: 사람/동물)	+	직접목적어 (D: 사물)	(4)
		give, bring, pass, send, show, sell, hand, lend, offer, teach, tell, buy, build, choose, find, leave, make, order, prepare, ask 등 수여동사					

→ 주어(C) + be p.p(동사(B)의 수동태) + 직접목적어(D) + by 목적격(주어(A)의 목적격) (3)

They (S) / were told (V〈수동태〉) / (that) (they (S) could either eat (V₁) the marshmallow (O) (immediately) (〈부사〉) or wait (V₂)). (O)

그들은 / 말을 들었다 / 그들이 그 마시멜로를 즉시 먹어도 되고 또는 기다리고 있어도 된다는

그들은 그 마시멜로를 즉시 먹어도 되고 또는 기다리고 있어도 된다는 말을 들었다.

노트 ■ tell + IO + DO (4): ~에게 …을 말하다(수동태 시, be told + that + 주어 + 동사)

■ 〈직접목적어 자리에 that절을 가지는 4형식 수여동사〉: 수동태 시, be p.p. + (that) + 주어 + 동사

주어	수여동사		간접목적어	직접목적어
	advise	조언하다		(that) + 주어 + 동사
	assure	장담(확신)시키다		
	convince	확신시켜주다		
	inform	알리다		
	instruct	알리다		
	notify	알리다		
	persuade	설득하다		
	promise	약속하다		
	remind	상기시키다		
	request	요청하다		
	show	보여 주다		
	teach	가르치다		
	tell	말하다		
	warn	경고하다		

■ 〈상관접속사〉: 병렬구조

종류				뜻
not	A	but	B	A가 아니라 B (=B, not A)
not only		but also		A뿐만 아니라 B도 (=B as well as A)
either		or		A와 B 둘 중 하나
neither		nor		A와 B 둘 다 아닌
both		and		A와 B 둘 다

[If they waited (to eat the marshmallow) / {that sat (before their eyes)} / {until the experimenter returned (about 15 minutes)}], / they would receive two marshmallows.

(종·접) If / S they / V waited / 만약 그들이 마시멜로를 먹기 위해 기다린다면 / O〈선행사〉 the marshmallow / (주·관) that / V sat / 〈전치사〉 before / 눈앞에 놓인 / 〈종·접〉 until / S the experimenter / V returned / 실험자가 다시 돌아올 때 / (약 15분 후)까지 / S they / V would receive / O two marshmallows / 그들은 2개의 마시멜로를 받게 된다

만약 실험자가 다시 돌아올 때(약 15분 후)까지 그들이 눈앞에 놓인 마시멜로를 먹기 위해 기다린다면, 그들은 2개의 마시멜로를 받게 된다.

노트 ■ 〈자동사가 뒤에 to부정사를 사용해 타동사처럼 목적어로 취하는 경우〉

	불완전자동사		목적어
주어	aim	~할 작정이다, 목표로 삼다	to R
	appear	~인 듯하다	
	arrange	미리 짜다[준비하다], 타협하다, 의논하다; 협정하다	
	bother	일부러 ~하다, ~하도록 애쓰다	
	consent	~하는 것을 동의/승낙하다	
	fight	~을 위하여 다투다	
	hesitate	주저하다, 망설이다	
	hurry	서두르다	
	long	~하기를 열망/갈망하다	
	prepare	~할 각오/마음의 준비를 하다	
	seem	~처럼 보이다, ~인 듯하다	
	serve	~의 역할을 하다	
	strive	~하려고 노력하다	
	struggle	(~하려고) 분투[고투]하다, 애쓰다	
	tend	~하는 경향이 있다	
	yearn	몹시 ~하고 싶다, 열망하다	
	wait	~하는 것을 기다리다	

■ 〈주격관계대명사절의 수의 일치〉: 선행사를 포함하고 있는 관계대명사 what 사용 불가

	주격관계대명사절		
선행사	주격관계대명사	~~주어~~	동사
the marshmallow	that		sat

■ 〈sit / seat / set〉

원형	과거	과거분사	현재분사	뜻
sit	sat	sat	sitting	vi. 앉다, ~에 놓여 있다
seat	seated	seated	seating	vt. 앉히다
set	set	set	setting	vt. 두다, ~을 놓다

Walter Mischel, / {a psychologist (studying delaying gratification)}, / had three daughters / (who attended the nursery school); / they and their classmates / participated / (in the study).

=〈동격〉 / S Walter Mischel / Walter Mischel은 / (who was) / 〈현재분사〉 studying / 만족 지연에 관한 연구를 하고 있는 사람인데 / V had / O〈선행사〉 three daughters / 세 딸들이 있었다 / 〈주·관〉 who / V attended / 어린이집에 / O the nursery school / 다니는 / S_1 they / S_2 their classmates / 그들(딸들)과 그들의 친구들이 / V participated / 참가했다 / 이 연구에

만족 지연에 관한 연구를 하고 있는 심리학자인 Walter Mischel의 세 딸들이 그 어린이집에 다니고 있었는데 그들과 그들의 친구들이 이 연구에 참여했다.

노트 ■ participate in : ~에 참가(참여)하다

■ 〈동격〉: A(명사), B(명사) (A가 주어, B라는 A)

동격(B라는 A)		
명사(A)	,(콤마)	명사(B)
Walter Mischel		a psychologist

■ 〈주격관계대명사+be동사 생략〉

–	생략할 수 있음	
명사 (선행사)	(주격관계대명사 +be동사)	현재분사(Ring) – 능동(~하고 있는)
		과거분사(p.p.) – 수동(~되어진, 당한)
		명사
		형용사(구) (~하는, ~할)
		부사
		전치사구
a psychologist	(who/that was)	studying

■ 〈주격관계대명사절의 수의 일치〉: 선행사를 포함하고 있는 관계대명사 what 사용 불가

	주격관계대명사절		
선행사	주격관계대명사	~~주어~~	동사
three daughters	who		attended

■ 〈3형식 구조를 가지는 타동사 뒤에 전치사를 사용할 수 없는 경우〉

	타동사	전치사	
주어	resemble	~~with~~	목적어
	marry	~~with~~	
	mention	~~about~~	
	discuss	~~about~~	
	attend	~~to~~	
	enter	~~into~~	
	reach	~~at~~	

주제문 만족을 지연시키는 능력과 청소년기의 우수성 사이의 관계가 있다.

(Over the years), / he / would ask his daughters / (about their friends), / and / (in doing so) / he / detected a relationship / {between an ability (to delay gratification in preschool) and excelling in adolescence}.

여러 해 동안 / S he / 그는 / V would ask / O his daughters / 딸들에게 묻곤 했다 / 그들의 친구들에 대해 / 그리고 / O〈동명사〉 doing / 그렇게 함으로써 / S he / 그는 / V detected / 관계를 / O a relationship / 발견했다 / O_1 an ability / O gratification / 유아기에 만족을 지연시키는 능력과 / O_2〈동명사〉 excelling / 청소년기의 우수성 사이의

여러 해 동안, 그는 딸들에게 친구들에 대해 묻곤 했고, 그렇게 함으로써 유아기에 만족을 지연시키는 능력과 청소년기의 우수성 사이의 관계를 발견했다.

노트
- between A and B : A와 B 사이에
- excel in : ~에서 뛰어나다
- 〈대동사〉 : 동사(구)를 대신하는 말

〈동사〉		〈대동사〉
be	→	be
조동사		조동사
일반동사		do, does, did

- 〈대동사〉

				전치사구	
he	would ask	the daughters	and	in	doing so
주어	동사	목적어	대등접속사	전치사	동명사
					대동사(=ask the daughters)

연구 결과 만족 지연을 시킬 수 있는 어린이들과 시킬 수 없는 어린이들의 차이

Mischel and his colleagues / located the participants / (in the initial study) / (to more formally track their progress) / (as they matured).

(Mischel: S_1, his colleagues: S_2 – Mischel과 그의 동료들은 / located: V / the participants: O – 참가자들을 찾아냈다 / 초기 연구에 참여했던 / formally: 〈부사〉, track ↷ their progress: O – 그들의 발달을 보다 공식적으로 추적하기 위해 / as: 〈종·접〉, they: S, matured: V – 성장하는 동안)

Mischel과 그의 동료들은 성장하는 동안 그들의 발달을 보다 공식적으로 추적하기 위해 초기 연구에 참가했던 참가자들을 찾아냈다.

노트
- 〈부정사의 종류〉

종류	구조			주의사항
원형부정사	동사원형	–	–	조동사/조동사 등 뒤에 사용
to부정사	to	동사원형	–	명사/형용사/부사적 용법
분리부정사	to	부사	동사원형	부사 대신 형용사 사용 불가
대부정사	to	–	–	to R 대신 to만 사용하는 경우
독립부정사	–	–	–	관용적 용법(not to mention 등)

They / noticed / [that the children / {who ate the single marshmallow (right away)} / were likely (to have problems) / (in the areas of behavior, friendships, and attention)].

(They: S – 그들은 / noticed: V – 알게 되었다 / that: 〈종·접〉, the children: S(선행사) – 어린이들은 / who: 〈주·관〉 ↶, ate: V, the single marshmallow: O – 마시멜로 하나를 / 즉시 먹었던 / were: V, likely: S.C – 문제가 있을 가능성이 있다는 것을 (O) / 행동, 교우관계, 그리고 주의집중 영역에)

그들은 마시멜로 하나를 즉시 먹었던 어린이들은 행동, 교우관계, 그리고 주의집중 영역에 문제가 있을 가능성이 있다는 것을 알게 되었다.

노트
- right away : 곧바로, 즉시
- be likely to R : ~할 것 같다

- 〈what vs. that〉

	관계대명사(불완전한 문장)	접속사(완전한 문장)
what	○ 선행사를 포함하고 있기 때문에 what 앞에 선행사 불필요	×
that	○ that 앞에 선행사 필요	○

- 〈주격관계대명사절의 수의 일치〉 : 선행사를 포함하고 있는 관계대명사 what 사용 불가

	주격관계대명사절		
선행사	주격관계대명사	~~주어~~	동사
the children	who		ate

- 〈likely / alike / like〉

likely	형용사	~일 것 같은 (be to 동사원형 : ~일 것 같다)
	부사	아마(probably)
alike	서술적 형용사 (보어로만 사용, 명사 수식 불가)	동일한
	부사	똑같이
like	전치사	~처럼
	동사	좋아하다

(In contrast), / those / (who were able to delay gratification) / had higher SAT scores / and coped (better) with stress.

(대조적으로 / those: S(선행사) – 어린이들은 / who: 〈주·관〉 ↶, were able to delay: V, gratification: O – 만족을 지연시킬 수 있었던 / had: V_1, higher SAT scores: O – SAT에서 높은 점수를 받았다 / and – 그리고 / coped (better) with: V_2, stress: O – 스트레스에 더 잘 대처했다)

대조적으로 만족을 지연시킬 수 있었던 어린이들은 SAT에서 더 높은 점수를 받았고, 스트레스에 더 잘 대처했다.

노트
- in contrast : 그에 반해서
- be able to R : ~할 수 있다
- cope with : ~에 대처[대응]하다, ~에 대항하다(=deal with)
- 〈주격관계대명사절의 수의 일치〉 : 선행사를 포함하고 있는 관계대명사 what 사용 불가

	주격관계대명사절		
선행사	주격관계대명사	~~주어~~	동사
those	who		were

- 〈those who〉 : ~하는 사람들(who 대신에 that 사용 불가)

	〈관계대명사절〉			
those	who	~~주어~~	복수동사	복수동사
〈선행사〉	〈주격관계대명사〉		were	had

⬇

요약문 Mischel의 연구에 따르면, 자신들의 욕구를 미룰 수 있었던 어린이들은 청소년기에 월등한 성취를 보여 주었던 반면, 즉각적인 만족을 추구했던 어린이들은 여러 가지 어려움을 겪는 경향이 있었다.

(According to Mischel's study), / children / (who could put off their desire) / showed (A) ________ achievements (in adolescence), / {while those (who sought instant (B) ________) / tended to have various troubles}.

〈구전치사〉 O Mischel의 연구에 따르면 / S〈선행사〉 어린이들은 / 〈주·관〉 / V O 자신들의 욕구를 미룰 수 있었던 / V 청소년기에 월등한 성취를 보여 주었다 / O / 〈종·접〉 S〈선행사〉 반면에 / 〈주·관〉 / V O 즉각적인 만족을 추구했던 어린이들은 / V S.C 여러 가지 어려움을 겪는 경향이 있었다

노트
- put off : 미루다[연기하다] (=postpone, delay)
- tend(자동사)+to R : ~하는 경향이 있다
- 〈according to / according as〉

~에 따르면	구전치사	according to	(동)명사
	종속접속사	according as	주어+동사

- **〈주격관계대명사절의 수의 일치〉** : 선행사를 포함하고 있는 관계대명사 what 사용 불가

	주격관계대명사절			
선행사(주어)	주격관계대명사	~~주어~~	동사	동사(본동사)
children	who		could put off	showed

- 〈while 용법〉

부사절을 이끄는 종속접속사	
시간	~ 동안에
양보/대조	비록 ~일지라도

- 〈seek 어휘 변화〉

원형	과거형	과거분사형	현재분사형	뜻
seek	sought	sought	seeking	찾다, 구하다, 추구하다

▶ 다음 글의 내용을 한 문장으로 요약하고자 한다. 빈칸 (A), (B)에 들어갈 말로 가장 적절한 것은?

	(A)		(B)
①	inferior	……	improvement
②	inferior	……	recognition
③	trivial	……	satisfaction
④	superior	……	recognition
⑤	superior	……	satisfaction

정답 | ⑤

해석 | ① 열등한 – 향상 ② 열등한 – 인식 ③ 사소한 – 만족 ④ 월등한 – 인식 ⑤ 월등한 – 만족

해설 | ⑤ 이 글의 내용은 만족을 지연시키는 능력과 청소년기의 우수성 사이에 관계가 있다는 것이다. 그리고 자신들의 욕구를 미룰 수 있는 어린이들이 청소년기에 월등한 성취를 보여 준다고 말한다. 요약된 문장을 해석하면 'Mischel의 연구에 따르면, 자신들의 욕구를 미룰 수 있었던 어린이들은 청소년기에 ________ 성취를 보여 주었던 반면, 즉각적인 ________ 을/를 추구했던 어린이들은 여러 가지 어려움을 겪는 경향이 있었다.' 이다. 따라서 (A)에는 욕구를 미룬 아이들이 월등한 성취를 보여 준다는 말이 들어가야 하므로 'superior(월등한)' 이, (B)에서는 즉각적인 욕구에 해당하는 말이 들어가야 하므로 욕구에 해당하는 'satisfaction(만족)' 이 적절하다.

오답 | (A)에서 'inferior' 와 'trivial' 는 글의 관점과 반대되는 말이기 때문에 적절하지 않다. (B)에서는 욕구에 해당하는 말이 들어가야 하기 때문에 'improvement(향상)' 는 어느 정도 가능할 수 있지만 더욱 어울리는 말은 'satisfaction' 이고 'recognition' 은 적절하지 않다.

Words

- ☐ nursery school ________
- ☐ offer ________
- ☐ immediately ________
- ☐ experimenter ________
- ☐ delay ________
- ☐ gratification ________
- ☐ detect ________
- ☐ excel ________
- ☐ adolescence ________
- ☐ colleague ________
- ☐ locate ________
- ☐ participant ________
- ☐ initial ________
- ☐ track ________
- ☐ progress ________
- ☐ trivial ________
- ☐ superior ________

Phrases

- ☐ participate in ________
- ☐ excel in ________
- ☐ be likely to R ________
- ☐ be able to R ________
- ☐ put off ________
- ☐ between A and B ________
- ☐ right away ________
- ☐ in contrast ________
- ☐ cope with ________
- ☐ tend(자동사)+to R ________

변형문제

01 다음 글을 읽고, |조건|에 맞게 요약문을 완성하시오.

| 조건 |

* (A), (B), (C)는 각각 다르게 1단어로 쓸 것
* [보기]에서 선택한 단어를 한 번씩만 쓸 것
* 필요한 경우, 문맥과 어법에 맞게 변형할 것

[보기] useful / academic / beneficial / advantageous / superior / disadvantageous / manage / physical / stressful / beyond / mental / writing

In a study at Stanford University, four-year-olds at a nursery school were offered a marshmallow. They were told they could either eat the marshmallow immediately or wait. If they waited to eat the marshmallow that sat before their eyes until the experimenter returned (about 15 minutes), they would receive two marshmallows. Walter Mischel, a psychologist studying delaying gratification, had three daughters who attended the nursery school; they and their classmates participated in the study. Over the years, he would ask his daughters about their friends, and in doing so he detected a relationship between an ability to delay gratification in preschool and excelling in adolescence. Mischel and his colleagues located the participants in the initial study to more formally track their progress as they matured. They noticed that the children who ate the single marshmallow right away were likely to have problems in the areas of behavior, friendships, and attention. In contrast, those who were able to delay gratification had higher SAT scores and coped better with stress.

⬇

The study on delaying gratification revealed the relationship between the ability to delay gratification in childhood and the excellence in adolescence. Children who could delay gratification were far (A) ____________ in (B) ____________ work and stress (C) ____________ in contrast with those who were unable to put off gratification.

02 다음 글을 읽고, |조건|에 맞게 제목을 완성하시오.

| 조건 |
* (A)는 1단어, (B)는 2단어로 쓸 것
* [보기]에서 선택한 단어를 그대로 한 번씩만 쓸 것

[보기] outcome / future / progress / importance / reason / impact / performance / comparison / association / children / school

In a study at Stanford University, four-year-olds at a nursery school were offered a marshmallow. They were told they could either eat the marshmallow immediately or wait. If they waited to eat the marshmallow that sat before their eyes until the experimenter returned (about 15 minutes), they would receive two marshmallows. Walter Mischel, a psychologist studying delaying gratification, had three daughters who attended the nursery school; they and their classmates participated in the study. Over the years, he would ask his daughters about their friends, and in doing so he detected a relationship between an ability to delay gratification in preschool and excelling in adolescence. Mischel and his colleagues located the participants in the initial study to more formally track their progress as they matured. They noticed that the children who ate the single marshmallow right away were likely to have problems in the areas of behavior, friendships, and attention. In contrast, those who were able to delay gratification had higher SAT scores and coped better with stress.

⬇

The (A) ____________ of the ability to delay gratification on (B) ____________ ____________.

03 다음 글을 읽고, 글의 주제를 찾아 그대로 쓰시오.

| 조건 |
* 14단어로 쓸 것

In a study at Stanford University, four-year-olds at a nursery school were offered a marshmallow. They were told they could either eat the marshmallow immediately or wait. If they waited to eat the marshmallow that sat before their eyes until the experimenter returned (about 15 minutes), they would receive two marshmallows. Walter Mischel, a psychologist studying delaying gratification, had three daughters who attended the nursery school; they and their classmates participated in the study. Over the years, he would ask his daughters about their friends, and in doing so he detected a relationship between an ability to delay gratification in preschool and excelling in adolescence. Mischel and his colleagues located the participants in the initial study to more formally track their progress as they matured. They noticed that the children who ate the single marshmallow right away were likely to have problems in the areas of behavior, friendships, and attention. In contrast, those who were able to delay gratification had higher SAT scores and coped better with stress.

⬇

____________ ____________ ____________ ____________ ____________ ____________ ____________
____________ ____________ ____________ ____________ ____________ ____________ ____________

04 다음 글을 읽고, |조건|에 맞게 요약문을 완성하시오.

| 조건 |

* (A)는 4단어, (B)는 3단어로 쓸 것
* [보기]에서 선택한 단어를 한 번씩만 쓸 것
* 필요한 경우, 문맥과 어법에 맞게 변형할 것

[보기] tolerate / outstanding / disappointing / desire / insignificant / at / pursue / achievements / in / immediate / adolescence / ignore / eating

In a study at Stanford University, four-year-olds at a nursery school were offered a marshmallow. They were told they could either eat the marshmallow immediately or wait. If they waited to eat the marshmallow that sat before their eyes until the experimenter returned (about 15 minutes), they would receive two marshmallows. Walter Mischel, a psychologist studying delaying gratification, had three daughters who attended the nursery school; they and their classmates participated in the study. Over the years, he would ask his daughters about their friends, and in doing so he detected a relationship between an ability to delay gratification in preschool and excelling in adolescence. Mischel and his colleagues located the participants in the initial study to more formally track their progress as they matured. They noticed that the children who ate the single marshmallow right away were likely to have problems in the areas of behavior, friendships, and attention. In contrast, those who were able to delay gratification had higher SAT scores and coped better with stress.

⬇

A study conducted by Mischel demonstrated that (A) ____________ ____________ ____________ ____________ were commonly witnessed among children who could delay their gratification, whereas those who (B) ____________ ____________ ____________ were more likely to have a variety of concerns.

UNIT 15

요약문 완성

글의 논리	Myth & Truth (통념 & 진실)
제목	직장에서 받는 스트레스의 원인
주제	스트레스를 유발하는 것은 통제력의 결핍과 보상과의 불균형이다.

PRACTICE 01

058 어법 선택 & 연결어

Our instincts tell us the **[high / higher]** we climb up the ladder, the more stress we feel and the **[weak / weaker]** our feeling of safety. **[Consider / To consider]** the stereotype of the high-strung executive **[facing / faced]** relentless pressure from shareholders, employees and the firm's **[largest / large]** customers. We are **[hardly / hard] [surprising / surprised]** when one of them **[suddenly / sudden] [drop / drops] [deadly / dead]** of a heart attack before fifty. ( ), a study tells us a different story. Decades ago, scientists in Britain set out to study this link between an employee's place on the corporate ladder **[or / and]** stress. **[Knowing / Known] [collective / collectively]** as the Whitehall Studies, the studies' findings were **[both / either] [astounding / astounded]** and **[profound / profoundly]**. Researchers **[found / founded] [what / that]** workers' stress was not **[causing / caused]** by a **[higher / high]** degree of responsibility and pressure usually **[associated / associating]** with rank. It is not the demands of the job **[what / that] [causes / cause]** the **[most / almost]** stress, but the lack of control workers **[feels / feel]** they have throughout **[their / its]** day. The studies also **[found / founded] [what / that]** the effort **[required / requiring]** by a job is not in **[itself / it] [stressfully / stressful]**, but rather the imbalance between the effort we give **[and / or]** the reward we feel.

⬇

According **[to / as]** the Whitehall Studies, the stress does not come from people's position at work or work demands, but from the situations **[what / which] [cannot do / cannot be done]** exactly as they want.

통념 우리는 사회적 지위가 올라갈수록 더 많은 스트레스를 느낀다고 생각한다.

Our instincts / tell us / (the higher we climb up the ladder, / the more stress we feel / and / the weaker our feeling of safety (is)).

(Our instincts: S / tell: V / us: I.O / we: S / climb up: V / the higher: O / the more stress: O / we: S / feel: V / the weaker: S.C / our feeling of safety: S / 괄호 전체: D.O)

우리의 본능은 / 우리에게 말한다 / 사회적 지위가 올라갈수록 / 우리가 더 많은 스트레스를 느낀다 / 그리고 / 우리의 안도감은 / 더 약해진다고

사회적 지위가 올라갈수록, 우리가 더 많은 스트레스를 느끼고 우리의 안도감은 더 약해질 것이라고 본능은 우리에게 말한다.

노트
- climb up [down] a ladder : 사닥다리를 오르다[내리다]
- feel stress : 스트레스를 느끼다
- 〈직접목적어 자리에 that절을 가지는 4형식 수여동사〉 : 수동태 시, be told+that+주어+동사

주어	수여동사		간접목적어	직접목적어
	advise	조언하다		(that)+주어+동사
	assure	장담(확신)시키다		
	convince	확신시켜주다		
	inform	알리다		
	instruct	알리다		
	notify	알리다		
	persuade	설득하다		
	promise	약속하다		
	remind	상기시키다		
	request	요청하다		
	show	보여 주다		
	teach	가르치다		
	tell	말하다		
	warn	경고하다		

- 〈the 비교급, the 비교급〉 : ~하면 할수록, 더 ~하고, 더 ~하다

the	비교급	~,	the	비교급	~	and	the	비교급	~
	more			more				more	
	-er			-er				-er	

- 〈생략〉 : 'the 비교급, the 비교급'에서 be동사는 주로 생략됨

~	and	the	비교급	주어	〈생략〉 (동사)
			weaker	our feeling of safety	(is)

Consider the stereotype / (of the high-strung executive) / (who is) (facing relentless pressure) / (from shareholders,

(Consider: V / the stereotype: O / facing: 〈현재분사〉 / relentless pressure: O)

정형화된 이미지를 고려해보라 / 극도로 긴장한 중역의 / 혹독한 압력에 직면해 있는 / 주주, 종업원, 그리고

employees and the firm's largest customers).
회사의 가장 큰 고객들로부터

주주, 종업원, 그리고 회사의 가장 큰 고객들로부터의 혹독한 압력에 직면해 있는 극도로 긴장한 중역의 정형화된 이미지를 고려해보라.

노트 ■ pressure from : ~로부터의 압력
■ 〈직접명령문〉

긍정문	R	~해라
	Please+R	~해 주세요
부정문	Don't+R	~하지 마라
	Never+R	

■ 〈주격관계대명사+be동사 생략〉

-	생략할 수 있음	
명사 (선행사)	(주격관계대명사 +be동사)	현재분사(Ring) – 능동(~하고 있는)
		과거분사(p.p.) – 수동(~되어진, 당한)
		명사
		형용사(구) (~하는, ~할)
		부사
		전치사구
executive	(who/that is)	facing

We / are (hardly) surprised / {when one (of them) / (suddenly) drops dead of a heart attack / (before fifty)}.
(We: S 우리는 / are: V / surprised: S.C 거의 놀라지 않는다 / when: 〈종·접〉 / one: S 그들 중 한 명이 / drops dead of a heart attack: V 심장 마비로 갑자기 급사할 때 / before fifty: 50살이 되기 전에)

그들 중 한 명이 50살이 되기 전에 심장 마비로 갑자기 급사할 때 우리는 거의 놀라지 않는다.

노트 ■ drop dead (of a heart attack) : (심장 마비로) 급사하다
■ 〈감정과 관련된 완전타동사〉 : 분사화가 되어 주격보어/목적격보어 자리에 나올 때 구별법
• 2형식

주어	동사	주격보어(S.C)
사람		과거분사(p.p.) – 수동(되어진, ~ 당한)
사물		현재분사(Ring) – 능동(~하고 있는, 하는)
We	are	surprised

■ 〈hard / hardly〉

	형용사	부사
hard	어려운	열심히
hardly	–	거의 ~하지 않는

■ 〈one of+복수명사+단수동사〉 : ~ 중의 하나

one (주어 : 단수)	of	복수명사	단수동사
one		them	drops

■ 〈die 어휘 변화〉

	동사	명사	형용사
die	죽다	–	–
death	–	죽음	–
dead	–	–	죽은, 고
deadly	–	–	치명적인

■ 〈die from vs. die of〉 : ~로 죽다

die	from	외부적인 요소	피로, 과로, 부주의 등
	of	내부적인 요소	병, 굶주림, 노령 등

진실 연구의 결과에 따르면 직급과 연관된 책임감에 따라 더 많은 스트레스가 유발되는 것이 아니다.

(However), / a study / tells us a different story.
(However: 하지만 / a study: S 한 연구는 / tells: V / us: I.O / a different story: D.O 우리에게 다른 이야기를 말해준다)

하지만, 한 연구는 우리에게 다른 이야기를 말해준다.

노트 ■ tell+IO+DO (4) : ~에게 …을/를 말하다

(Decades ago), / scientists (in Britain) / set out / (to study this link) / {between an employee's place (on the corporate ladder) and stress}.
(Decades ago: 수십 년 전에 / scientists: S 영국의 과학자들은 / set out: V 시작했다 / to study this link: 이러한 관계를 연구하기 / between …: 회사 직급에서 직원이 갖는 위치와 스트레스 사이의)

수십 년 전에, 영국의 과학자들은 회사 직급에서 직원이 갖는 위치와 스트레스 사이의 이러한 관계를 연구하기 시작했다.

노트 ■ set out : 착수하다[나서다]
■ between A and B : A와 B 사이에

{Known (collectively) as the Whitehall Studies}, / the studies' findings / were both astounding and profound.
(Known: 〈분사구문〉 / collectively: 〈부사〉 총칭적으로 화이트홀 연구라고 알려진 / the studies' findings: S 이 연구의 결과는 / were: V / astounding: $S.C_1$ / profound: $S.C_2$ 놀랍고 심오했다)

총칭적으로 화이트홀 연구라고 알려진 이 연구의 결과는 놀랍고 심오했다.

노트 ■ 〈분사구문 – 문두〉 : 주절과 종속절의 위치는 서로 바뀔 수 있음

종속절(→ 분사구문)				주절	
종속 접속사	주어	동사 : 상황에 맞게 아래처럼 바뀜		주어	동사
〈그대로 사용하면 의미 강조〉	(주절의 주어와 같으면 생략하고, 다르면 주격으로 사용함)	(being) (having been) 생략 가능	Ring(현재분사)		
			p.p.(과거분사)		
			형용사		
			명사		
–	–	–	Known	the studies' findings	were

■ 〈상태 수동태〉 : 수동의 전치사 by 이외 다른 전치사를 사용하는 경우
• be known by/to/for/as

	과거분사	전치사	뜻
be동사	known	by+수단, 판단	~에 의해서 알려지다
		to+동사원형	~한 것으로 알려져 있다
		to+대상	~에게 알려지다
		for+이유, 근거	~로 알려지다, ~ 때문에 알려지다
		as+자격, 신분	~로서 알려지다

■ 〈상관접속사〉 : 병렬구조

종류				뜻
not	A	but	B	A가 아니라 B (=B, not A)
not only		but also		A뿐만 아니라 B도 (=B as well as A)
either		or		A와 B 둘 중 하나
neither		nor		A와 B 둘 다 아닌
both		and		A와 B 둘 다

■ 〈감정과 관련된 완전타동사〉 : 분사화가 되어 주격보어/목적격보어 자리에 나올 때 구별법

• 2형식

주어	동사	주격보어(S.C)
사람		과거분사(p.p.) – 수동(되어진, ~ 당한)
사물		현재분사(Ring) – 능동(~하고 있는, 하는)
the studies' findings	were	astounding

Researchers / found / {that workers' stress was not caused / (by a higher degree of responsibility and pressure) / (usually) (associated with rank)}.

(Researchers: S, 연구자들은 / found: V, 밝혀냈다 / that: 〈종·접〉 / workers' stress: S / that workers' stress was not caused: 근로자들의 스트레스는 유발되는 것이 아니라는 것을 / caused: V〈수동태〉 / by a higher degree of responsibility and pressure: O, 책임감과 압박의 높은 정도에 의해 / pressure) / (which was) / usually: 흔히 / associated: 〈과거분사〉, associated with rank: 직원들의 월급과 연관된)

연구자들은 흔히 직원들의 직급과 연관된 책임감과 압박의 높은 정도에 의해 스트레스가 유발되는 것이 아니라는 것을 밝혀냈다.

노트 ■ A be caused by B : B에 의해 A가 발생하다, B가 A의 원인이다

■ associate A with B : A를 B와 관련시켜 생각하다(수동태 시, A be associated with B)

■ 〈find / found〉

원형	과거	과거분사	현재분사	뜻
find	found	found	finding	v. 발견하다, 알다
found	founded	founded	founding	v. 설립하다

■ 〈what vs. that〉

	관계대명사(불완전한 문장)	접속사(완전한 문장)
what	○ 선행사를 포함하고 있기 때문에 what 앞에 선행사 불필요	×
that	○ that 앞에 선행사 필요	○

■ 〈주격관계대명사＋be동사 생략〉

–	생략할 수 있음	
명사 (선행사)	(주격관계대명사 ＋be동사)	현재분사(Ring) – 능동(~하고 있는)
		과거분사(p.p.) – 수동(~되어진, 당한)
		명사
		형용사(구) (~하는, ~할)
		부사
		전치사구
pressure	(which/that was)	associated

주제문 스트레스를 유발하는 것은 통제력의 결핍이다.

It / is not the demands (of the job) / (that cause the most stress), / but the lack (of control) / (workers feel) / {they have (throughout their day)}.

(It: S, 그것은 / is not: V / the demands: S.C₁, 업무에 요구되는 일들이 아니다 / 〈선행사〉 / that: 〈주·관〉 / cause: V, 가장 많은 스트레스를 / most stress: O, 유발하는 / the lack (of control): S.C₂〈선행사〉, 통제력의 결핍이 바로 / (목·관 that) workers: S / feel: V / (목·관 that) they: S / have: V, 그들이 하루 종일 가지고 있는)

가장 많은 스트레스를 유발하는 것은 그 업무에 요구되는 일들이 아니라 직원들이 하루 종일 가지고 있다고 느끼는 통제력의 결핍이었다.

노트 ■ not A but B : A가 아니라 B(상관접속사)

■ 〈주격관계대명사절의 수의 일치〉 : 선행사를 포함하고 있는 관계대명사 what 사용 불가

선행사	주격관계대명사절		
	주격관계대명사	~~주어~~	동사
the demands	that		cause

■ 〈most / almost / mostly〉

	대명사	형용사	부사
most	대부분의 것들(사람들)	대부분의	가장
almost	–	–	거의
mostly	–	–	주로, 일반적으로

■ 〈It be A that B 강조구문〉 : B한 것은 바로 A이다

It	be동사	강조하고 싶은 말	that (경우에 따라 아래처럼 바꿔 사용 가능)	
~~This That There~~	시제에 따라 달라짐	주어 목적어 보어 부사(구, 절) 〈동사는 사용 불가〉	관계대명사	who
				whom
				which
			관계부사	when
				where
It	is	not A but B	that ~	

■ 〈관계대명사의 이중 한정〉 : 2개의 관계대명사절이 동일한 선행사를 수식하는 경우

선행사	〈목적격관계대명사절〉				〈목적격관계대명사절〉			
	목적격 관계 대명사	주어	동사	~~목적어~~	목적격 관계 대명사	주어	동사	~~목적어~~
the lack of control	(that)	workers	feel		that	they	have	

■ 〈혼동 어휘〉

through	전치사	~을 통하여
throughout	전치사	[장소] ~의 도처에, [시간] ~ 동안, ~ 내내
	부사	도처에, 완전히, 철저하게
though	접속사	~에도 불구하고
thorough	형용사	철저한, 완전한

주제문 또한 스트레스를 유발하는 것은 우리가 한 노력과 보상과의 불균형이다.

The studies / also found / [that the effort / (required by a job) / is not (in itself) stressful, / but (rather) / the

(The studies: S, 그 연구는 / also found: V, 또한 밝혀냈다 / that: 〈종·접〉 / the effort: S, 수고가 / (which is) required: 〈과거분사〉, required by a job: 그 일에 요구되는 / is not: V / stressful: S.C, 그 자체로 스트레스를 주는 것이 아니라 / O / rather: 오히려)

imbalance(S) (is stressful) / {between the effort / (목·관 that) (we(S) give(V)) and the
불균형이 / 우리가 쏟는 수고와 보상과의

reward / (목·관 that) (we(S) feel(V))}].
우리가 느끼는

그 연구는 또한 일 자체에 대한 수고가 스트레스를 주는 것이 아니라 오히려 우리가 쏟는 수고와 우리가 느끼는 보상과의 불균형이 스트레스를 준다는 것을 밝혀냈다.

노트
- not A but B : A가 아니라 B(상관접속사)
- in itself : 그것 자체가 [본질적으로]
- between A and B : A와 B 사이에
- **〈주격관계대명사+be동사 생략〉**

–	생략할 수 있음	
명사 (선행사)	(주격관계대명사 +be동사)	현재분사(Ring) – 능동(~하고 있는)
		과거분사(p.p.) – 수동(~되어진, 당한)
		명사
		형용사(구) (~하는, ~할)
		부사
		전치사구
the effort	(which/that is)	required

- **〈주격관계대명사+be동사 생략〉**
  - 형용사가 앞에 있는 명사를 후치 수식하는 경우

	생략할 수 있음	분사(형용사 : 명사 수식)	
명사 (선행사)	(주격관계대명사 +be동사)	현재분사(Ring) – 능동(~하고 있는)	동사
		과거분사(p.p.) – 수동(~되어진, 당한)	
		형용사(구)	
the effort	(which/that was)	required	is

- **〈재귀대명사 vs. 대명사〉**

		주어와 다름	주어와 동일
주체	~	대명사	재귀대명사
the job		it	itself

- **〈목적격관계대명사 that〉** : 타동사의 목적어가 없는 경우 / 선행사를 포함하고 있는 관계대명사 what 사용 불가

선행사	목적격관계대명사	주어	타동사	~~목적어~~
the effort	that/which : (생략 가능)	we	give	
the reward			feel	

- **〈생략〉** : '동사+주격보어'가 생략된 경우

					(생략)	
주어	동사	주격보어		주어	동사	주격보어
the effort	is	stressful	~	the imbalance	(is)	(stressful)

⬇

요약문 **화이트홀 연구에 따르면, 스트레스는 사람들이 직장에서 갖는 지위나 업무의 요구사항들에서 오는 것이 아니라 그들이 원하는 대로 정확히 행해질 수 없는 상황으로부터 온다.**

(According to the Whitehall Studies(O))〈구전치사〉, / the stress(S) / does
화이트홀 연구에 따르면 / 스트레스는 / 오는

not come(V) (from people's (A) ＿＿＿) / (at work or
것이 아니라 / 사람들이 직장에서 갖는 지위나 업무의 요구사항들에서

work demands), / but / (from the situations(O〈선행사〉)) / (which〈주·관〉
상황으로부터 온다

cannot be done(V〈수동태〉) (exactly) / (as〈종·접〉 they(S) (B) ＿＿＿(V)).
행해질 수 없는 / 그들이 원하는 대로 정확히

노트
- come from : ~에서 생겨나다(=originate)
- 〈according to / according as〉

~에 따르면	구전치사	according to	(동)명사
	종속접속사	according as	주어+동사

- **〈주격관계대명사절의 수의 일치〉** : 선행사를 포함하고 있는 관계대명사 what 사용 불가

	주격관계대명사절		
선행사	주격관계대명사	~~주어~~	동사
the situations	which		can't be done

▶ **다음 글의 내용을 한 문장으로 요약하고자 한다. 빈칸 (A), (B)에 들어갈 말로 가장 적절한 것은?**

	(A)		(B)
①	labor	……	want
②	labor	……	evaluate
③	failure	……	finance
④	position	……	finance
⑤	position	……	want

정답 | ⑤

해석 | ① 노동 – 원하다
② 노동 – 평가하다
③ 실패 – 자금을 대다
④ 지위 – 자금을 대다
⑤ 지위 – 원하다

해설 | ⑤ 글의 주제는 스트레스를 유발하는 것은 직급이 아니라 우리가 종일 가지고 있다 생각하는 통제력의 결핍과 보상과의 불균형 때문이라는 것이다. 요약문을 해석하면, '화이트홀 연구에 따르면, 스트레스는 사람들이 직장에서 갖는 ＿＿＿(이)나 업무의 요구사항들에서 오는 것이 아니라 그들이 ＿＿＿ 대로 정확히 행해질 수 없는 상황으로부터 온다.'이다. 빈칸 (A)에 의해서 스트레스가 오는 것이 아니라 말하기 때문에 (A)에 들어갈 말은 직급에 유사한 말이어야 한다. 따라서 'position(지위)'이 적절하다. 빈칸 (B)에서는 통제력과 보상과의 불균형과 관련된 내용이 와야 하는데 대로 정확히 행해질 수 없는 상황으로부터 온다고 말하므로 통제력과 관련된 말이 들어가야 한다. 따라서 원하는대로 정확히 행해질 수 없는 상황(통제력)이 가장 적절하다. 따라서 (B)에는 'want'가 들어와야 한다.

오답 | (A)에 지위와 관련된 말이 와야 하므로 'labor' 같은 경우는 글의 관점과 반대되고 'failure'는 글의 소재와 무관하다. (B)에서는 통제력이나 보상에 관련된 말이 들어와야 하기 때문에 'evaluate'는 글의 소재와 무관하고 'finance'는 자금을 대는 것이기 때문에 글의 관점과 반대된다.

Words

- ☐ instinct
- ☐ ladder
- ☐ stereotype
- ☐ high-strung
- ☐ executive
- ☐ relentless
- ☐ shareholder
- ☐ hardly
- ☐ heart attack
- ☐ corporate
- ☐ collectively
- ☐ astounding
- ☐ profound
- ☐ cause
- ☐ associate

Phrases

- ☐ climb up [down] a ladder
- ☐ pressure from
- ☐ set out
- ☐ between A and B
- ☐ associate A with B
- ☐ in itself
- ☐ feel stress
- ☐ drop dead (of a heart attack)
- ☐ A be caused by B
- ☐ not A but B
- ☐ come from

우선순위 영단어

역대 수능 기출 + 전국 모의고사 기출 + EBS 기출 + 교과서 기출 빈출 어휘

단어	뜻	단어	뜻	단어	뜻
cliff	n. 벼랑	climate	n. 기후	clinical	a. 임상의
clog	v. 막다	close off	v. 끝내다	coalesce	v. 합체하다
coat	v. (뒤)덮다	cocoon	n. 고치	cohesion	n. 결속
coin	n. 동전	collaborator	n. 공동저자	collection	n. 소장품
colonizer	n. 식민지 개척자	column	n. 기둥	come a long way	v. 크게 발전하다
come across as	v. ~라는 인상을 주다	come to terms with	v. ~을 받아들이다	comforting	a. 위로하는
commandeer	v. 징집하다	commence	v. 시작하다	commerce	n. 상업
commoner	n. 평민	communicate	v. 의사소통을 하다	comparative	a. 비교의
compare	v. 비교하다	compared to	~와 비교하여	compassion	n. 연민
compel	v. 강요하다	compensate	v. 보상하다	complaint	n. 불평
compliance	n. 승낙	compliment	n. 칭찬	comply	v. 따르다
compose	v. 작곡하다	compulsive	a. 충동적인	consume	v. 소비하다
conception	n. 생각	conceptual	a. 개념의	concerned	a. 염려하는
concisely	ad. 간결하게	conditional	a. 조건부인	cone	n. 화산추
conform to	~ 에 순응하다	conformity	n. (규칙에 대한) 순응	confused	a. 헷갈리는
congenital	a. 타고난	congestion	n. 체증	conquest	n. 승리
consecutive	a. 연이은	consensus	n. 합의	consent	v. 동의하다
conserve	v. 보존하다	consolation	n. 위로	consolidate	v. 통합하다
constitution	n. 구조	constrain	v. 속박하다	consumerism	n. 소비만능주의
contagious	a. 전염성이 있는	contemplation	n. 심사숙고	contented	a. 만족하고 있는
contents	n. 내용물	contestant	n. 경쟁자	continent	n. 대륙
continental	n. 대륙붕	continually	ad. 끊임없이	continuity	n. 지속성
continuum	n. 연속체	contrast	n. 현저한 차이	controversy	n. 논쟁
converge	v. 모이다	conversation	n. 대화	convincing	a. 설득력 있는
cool down	v. 진정되다	cooperate	v. 협동하다	coordination	n. 조정
coordinator	n. 조정자	correctly	ad. 바르게	correspondence	n. 서신
cosmos	n. 우주 비행사	cost	n. 가격	counselor	n. 지도원

변형문제

01 다음 글을 읽고, |조건|에 맞게 요약문을 완성하시오.

| 조건 |

* (A)는 1단어, (B)는 2단어로 쓸 것
* [보기]에서 선택한 단어를 한 번씩만 쓸 것(단, (B)의 경우, [보기] 외의 1단어를 추가할 것)
* 필요한 경우, 문맥과 어법에 맞게 변형할 것

[보기] delegate / strike / jump / begin / promote / charge / respond / strike / want / start / arrange / move / sense

Our instincts tell us the higher we climb up the ladder, the more stress we feel and the weaker our feeling of safety. Consider the stereotype of the high-strung executive facing relentless pressure from shareholders, employees and the firm's largest customers. We are hardly surprised when one of them suddenly drops dead of a heart attack before fifty. However, a study tells us a different story. Decades ago, scientists in Britain set out to study this link between an employee's place on the corporate ladder and stress. Known collectively as the Whitehall Studies, the studies' findings were both astounding and profound. Researchers found that workers' stress was not caused by a higher degree of responsibility and pressure usually associated with rank. It is not the demands of the job that cause the most stress, but the lack of control workers feel they have throughout their day. The studies also found that the effort required by a job is not in itself stressful, but rather the imbalance between the effort we give and the reward we feel.

⬇

The more stress is expected as we are (A) ______________ to a higher rank, but in reality we are more stressed about situations where things do not work out as (B) ______________ ______________.

02 다음 글을 읽고, |조건|에 맞게 주어진 제목을 완성하시오.

| 조건 |

* (A), (B), (C)는 각각 다르게 1단어로 쓸 것
* 본문에 있는 단어만을 그대로 사용할 것

Our instincts tell us the higher we climb up the ladder, the more stress we feel and the weaker our feeling of safety. Consider the stereotype of the high-strung executive facing relentless pressure from shareholders, employees and the firm's largest customers. We are hardly surprised when one of them suddenly drops dead of a heart attack before fifty. However, a study tells us a different story. Decades ago, scientists in Britain set out to study this link between an employee's place on the corporate ladder and stress. Known collectively as the Whitehall Studies, the studies' findings were both astounding and profound. Researchers found that workers' stress was not caused by a higher degree of responsibility and pressure usually associated with rank. It is not the demands of the job that cause the most stress, but the lack of control workers feel they have throughout their day. The studies also found that the effort required by a job is not in itself stressful, but rather the imbalance between the effort we give and the reward we feel.

⬇

The (A) ____________ between (B) ____________ at work and (C) ____________.

03 다음 글의 순서로 가장 적절한 것은?

Our instincts tell us the higher we climb up the ladder, the more stress we feel and the weaker our feeling of safety. Consider the stereotype of the high-strung executive facing relentless pressure from shareholders, employees and the firm's largest customers. We are hardly surprised when one of them suddenly drops dead of a heart attack before fifty. However, a study tells us a different story.

(A) Known collectively as the Whitehall Studies, the studies' findings were both astounding and profound. Researchers found that workers' stress was not caused by a higher degree of responsibility and pressure usually associated with rank.

(B) Decades ago, scientists in Britain set out to study this link between an employee's place on the corporate ladder and stress.

(C) It is not the demands of the job that cause the most stress, but the lack of control workers feel they have throughout their day. The studies also found that the effort required by a job is not in itself stressful, but rather the imbalance between the effort we give and the reward we feel.

① (A) - (B) - (C) ② (B) - (A) - (C) ③ (B) - (C) - (A)
④ (C) - (A) - (B) ⑤ (C) - (B) - (A)

04 다음 글을 읽고, |조건|에 맞게 주어진 요약문을 완성하시오.

| 조건 |

* (A)는 3단어, (B)는 1단어로 쓸 것
* 본문에 있는 단어만을 그대로 사용할 것

Our instincts tell us the higher we climb up the ladder, the more stress we feel and the weaker our feeling of safety. Consider the stereotype of the high-strung executive facing relentless pressure from shareholders, employees and the firm's largest customers. We are hardly surprised when one of them suddenly drops dead of a heart attack before fifty. However, a study tells us a different story. Decades ago, scientists in Britain set out to study this link between an employee's place on the corporate ladder and stress. Known collectively as the Whitehall Studies, the studies' findings were both astounding and profound. Researchers found that workers' stress was not caused by a higher degree of responsibility and pressure usually associated with rank. It is not the demands of the job that cause the most stress, but the lack of control workers feel they have throughout their day. The studies also found that the effort required by a job is not in itself stressful, but rather the imbalance between the effort we give and the reward we feel.

⬇

Two findings were revealed by the Whitehall Studies:

1) The most stress is not from the work demands, but the (A) ____________ ____________ ____________ that employees experience they have all day.

2) The amount of effort we put into work is not stressful, but the inequality between the effort we put and its (B) ____________ is stressful.

요약문 완성

글의 논리	Spotlight
제목	다양한 환경에서 나오는 사물의 다양한 특징
주제	특징을 알기 위해서는 다양한 환경 속에서 어떻게 존재하는 지를 파악해야 한다.

PRACTICE 02

059 어법 선택 & 연결어

According **[as / to]** philosopher Radcliffe Richards, **[it / there]** is **[incoherent / incoherently]** to think **[what / that]** something's real nature **[is revealed / reveals]** when it is in **[their / its]** correct environment. (   ), the whole notion of a 'correct environment' is problematic. Isn't the notion of **[which / what]** is correct **[relative / relatively]** to various concerns? The correct environment for a salmon when **[cooking / cooked]** one **[are / is]** perhaps a **[heated / heating]** oven. The correct environment for **[their / its]** spawning is **[something else / else something]** again. (   ) more **[important / importantly]**, **[to know / know]** something's nature **[is / are]** to know **[how it is / how is it]** in a variety of environments. Iron's nature, (   ), is **[almost / most]** **[fully / full]** **[understood / understand]** **[if / that]** we know **[how it behaves / how does it behave]** when it is hot, cold, **[smashing / smashed]**, **[leaving / left]** in water and so on. **[Knowing / Know]** **[how iron behaves / how does iron behave]** when **[left / leaving]** in conditions **[optimally / optimal]** to **[their / its]** **[continued / continuing]**, **[unchaging / unchanged]** existence only **[gives / give]** a partial view of **[their / its]** nature.

⬇

The notion of 'correct environment' is improper in understanding something's nature, but **[its / their]** behavior in various conditions best **[reveal / reveals]** **[their / its]** nature.

주장 무언가의 진정한 특성이 자신에게 정확하게 맞는 환경에 있을 때 드러난다는 것은 일관성이 없다.

(According to philosopher Radcliffe Richards), / it is incoherent / {to think / (that something's real nature / is revealed) / (when it is / in its correct environment)}.

〈구전치사〉 O 철학자인 Radcliffe Richards에 의하면 / (가S) V / S.C 일관성이 없다 / 생각하는 것은 / 〈종·접〉 S 뭔가의 진정한 특성은 / O / 〈진S〉 / V〈수동태〉 드러난다고 / 〈종·접〉 S V 이것이 / 자신에게 정확하게 맞는 환경에 있을 때

철학자인 Radcliffe Richards에 의하면 뭔가의 진정한 특성은 그것이 자신에게 정확하게 맞는 환경에 있을 때 드러난다고 생각하는 것은 (논리적으로) 일관성이 없다.

노트 ■ 〈according to / according as〉

~에 따르면	구전치사	according to	(동)명사
	종속접속사	according as	주어＋동사

■ 〈가주어, 진주어 구문〉

가주어	동사	진주어
It (This/That/There 사용 불가)	–	that＋주어＋동사(완전한 절)
		to 동사원형
		동명사
		의문사＋주어＋동사(간접의문문)
		if/whether＋주어＋동사
it	is	to think

■ 〈what vs. that〉

	관계대명사(불완전한 문장)	접속사(완전한 문장)
what	○ 선행사를 포함하고 있기 때문에 what 앞에 선행사 불필요	×
that	○ that 앞에 선행사 필요	○

근거 '정확한 환경'이라는 개념 자체도 문제가 있다.

(First of all), / the whole notion / (of a 'correct environment') / is problematic.

먼저 / S 전체 개념이 / '정확한 환경'이라는 / V / S.C 문제이다

먼저, '정확한 환경'이라는 전체 개념이 문제이다.

노트 ■ first of all : 우선 [다른 무엇보다 먼저]
■ 〈혼동 어휘〉

	동사	형용사	명사	부사
correct	정정하다, 교정하다	옳은, 정확한	–	–
correction	–	–	정정, 수정	–
corrective	–	바로잡는, 수정의	–	–
collect	모으다, 수집하다	–	–	–

collection	–	–	수집품, 소장품	–
collective	–	집단의, 공동의	–	–
correctly	–	–	–	바르게, 정확하게
collectively	–	–	–	집합적으로, 총괄하여

근거2 정확한 것이라는 개념은 상대적이다.

Isn't / the notion / {of (what is correct)} / relative / (to various concerns)}?

(Isn't: V 않은가 / the notion: S 개념은 / of: 〈전치사〉 / what: 〈주·관〉 / is: V / correct: S.C / (what is correct): O 정확한 것이라는 / relative: S.C 상대적이지 / various concerns: 다양한 상황에)

정확한 것이라는 개념은 다양한 상황에 따라 상대적이지 않은가?

노트 ■ 〈전치사의 목적어로 사용된 주격관계대명사 what〉 : 선행사가 필요한 주격관계대명사 that/which 사용 불가

전치사	목적어 : 주격관계대명사 what절				
of	~~선행사~~	what	~~주어~~	불완전자동사	주격보어
		주격관계대명사 : 선행사를 포함한 관계대명사 (=the thing(s) which/that ~) : ~하는 것은/이		is	correct

예시 연어를 요리할 때의 정확한 환경은 달구어진 오븐이다.

The correct environment / (for a salmon) / (when cooking one) / is (perhaps) a heated oven.

(The correct environment: S 정확하게 맞는 환경은 / for a salmon: 연어에 / when: 〈종·접〉 (you are) / cooking: 〈현재분사〉 그것을 요리할 때 / is: V / heated: 〈과거분사〉 / oven: S.C 아마도 달구어진 오븐일 것이다)

연어를 요리할 때 그것에 정확하게 맞는 환경은 아마도 달구어진 오븐일 것이다.

노트 ■ 〈생략〉 : 주절의 주어와 종속절의 주어와 같을 시 종속절의 '주어+be동사'는 생략 가능

		(생략)			
The correct environment	when	(you)	(are)	cooking ~	is
주어	종속접속사	(주어+동사)		현재분사	동사
	〈종속절〉				

예시 연어의 산란에 정확한 환경은 또 다른 무엇인가이다.

The correct environment / (for its spawning) / is something (else) (again).

(The correct environment: S 정확하게 맞는 환경은 / for its spawning: 연어의 산란에 / is: V / something: S.C 또다시 다른 무엇인가이다)

연어의 산란에 정확하게 맞는 환경은 또다시 다른 무엇인가이다.

노트 ■ 〈형용사의 후치 수식〉

〈후치 수식〉	-thing	+형용사	○
	-body		
	-one		
〈전치 수식〉	형용사+	-thing	×
		-body	
		-one	

주제문 무언가의 특징을 아는 것은 다양한 환경 속에서 어떻게 존재하는 지를 아는 것이다.

(But) / (more importantly), / (to know something's nature) / is {to know / (how it is in a variety of environments)}.

(But: 그러나 / more importantly: 더 중요하게 / something's nature: O / to know something's nature: S 뭔가의 특징을 아는 것은 / is: V / how: 〈의·부〉 / it: S / is: V / (how it is ~): O 어떻게 그것이 다양한 환경 속에서 존재하는지를 / to know ~: S.C 아는 것이다)

그러나 더 중요하게, 뭔가의 특징을 아는 것은 그것이 다양한 환경 속에서 어떻게 존재하는지를 아는 것이다.

노트 ■ a variety of : 다양한, 여러 가지의
■ 〈to부정사의 명사적 용법〉 : 주어/목적어/보어 자리에 사용, to부정사가 주어 자리에 사용되면 단수 취급하여 동사는 단수동사를 사용한다.

			〈간접의문문〉 : 타동사 know의 목적어		
			의문사	주어	동사
to know ~	is	to know	how	it	is
주어	동사	주격보어			

예시 다양한 환경 속에서 다양하게 존재하는 쇠

Iron's nature, / (for example), / is (most fully) understood / {if we know (how it behaves)} / {when it is hot, cold, smashed, left in water / (and so on)}.

(Iron's nature: S 쇠의 특징은 / for example: 예를 들어 / is understood: V〈수동태〉 / most fully: 가장 잘 이해된다 / if: 〈종·접〉 / we: S / know: V / how: 〈의·부〉 / it: S / behaves: V / (how it behaves): O / 만약 우리가 그것이 어떻게 행동하는지를 우리가 알 때 / when: 〈종·접〉 / it: S / is: V / hot: S.C₁ 그것이 뜨거울 때, / cold: S.C₂ / smashed: S.C₃ / left in water: S.C₄ 차가울 때, 두드려졌을 때, 물속에 두었을 때 / and so on: 등에서)

예를 들어 쇠의 특징은 그것이 뜨거울 때, 차가울 때, 두드려졌을 때, 물속에 두었을 때 등에서 그것이 어떻게 행동하는지를 우리가 알 때 가장 잘 이해된다.

노트 ■ and so on : 기타 등등(=and so forth, and the like, etc.(=et cetera), the others, the rest, and others, and what not)
■ 〈most / almost / mostly〉

	대명사	형용사	부사
most	대부분의 것들(사람들)	대부분의	가장
almost	–	–	거의
mostly	–	–	주로, 일반적으로

■ 〈간접의문문 – 타동사의 목적어 자리〉

타동사	목적어		
know	〈간접의문문〉: 명사절		
	how	it	behaves
	의문부사	주어	동사

[Knowing / (how iron behaves) / {when (it is) left in conditions (which are) optimal / to its continued, unchanged existence)}] / (only) gives a partial view / (of its nature).

Knowing 〈동명사〉 / how 〈의문사〉 iron S behaves V — O; when 〈종·접〉 left 〈과거분사〉; optimal 〈형용사〉; continued 〈과거분사〉, unchanged 〈과거분사〉 — S; gives V; a partial view O

아는 것은 / 어떻게 쇠가 행동하는지를 / 최적인 환경들에 두었을 때 / 지속적이고 변화하지 않는 상태의 / 부분적인 시각만 줄 뿐이다 / 그것에 특성에 대해

지속적이고 변화하지 않는 상태의 쇠에 최적인 환경들에 쇠를 두었을 때 그것이 어떻게 행동하는지를 아는 것은 그것의 특성에 대해 부분적인 시각만 줄 뿐이다.

노트 ■ 〈동명사구가 주어 자리에 사용된 경우〉: 단수 취급으로 동사는 단수동사를 사용함

	간접의문문 : 동명사의 목적어				(생략)			
동명사	의문부사	주어	동사					
Knowing	how	iron	behaves	when	(it)	(is)	left	gives
주어				종속 접속사	주어	동사	과거분사	동사
				〈종속절〉: 부사절				

■ 〈주격관계대명사＋be동사 생략〉

–	생략할 수 있음	
명사 (선행사)	(주격관계대명사 ＋be동사)	현재분사(Ring) – 능동(~하고 있는)
		과거분사(p.p.) – 수동(~되어진, 당한)
		명사
		형용사(구) (~하는, ~할)
		부사
		전치사구
conditions	(which/that are)	optimal

⬇

요약문 '정확한 환경'이라는 개념은 뭔가의 특징을 이해하는 데 부적절하지만, 다양한 조건에서의 그것의 행동은 그것의 특징을 가장 잘 드러낸다.

The notion (of 'correct environment') / is (A) ______ / (in understanding something's nature), / but its behavior (in (B) ______ conditions) / (best) reveals its nature.

The notion S / is V / (A) S.C / understanding 〈동명사〉 / something's nature O / its behavior S / reveals V / its nature O

'정확한 환경'이라는 개념은 / 부적절하지만 / 뭔가의 특징을 이해하는 데 / 다양한 조건에서의 그것의 행동은 / 그것의 / 특징을 가장 잘 드러낸다

▶ 다음 글의 내용을 한 문장으로 요약하고자 한다. 빈칸 (A), (B)에 들어갈 말로 가장 적절한 것은?

	(A)		(B)
①	exact	……	optimal
②	exact	……	original
③	flexible	……	various
④	improper	……	various
⑤	improper	……	original

정답 | ④

해석 | ① 정확한 – 최적의
② 정확한 – 원래의
③ 융통성 있는 – 다양한
④ 부적절한 – 다양한
⑤ 부적절한 – 원래의

해설 | ④ 이 글의 주제는 정확한 것이라는 개념은 상대적인 것이고 특징을 알기 위해서는 다양한 환경 속에서 어떻게 존재하는 지를 파악해야 한다는 것이다. 요약문장을 해석하면 ''정확한 환경'이라는 개념은 뭔가의 특징을 이해하는 데 ______하지만, ______ 조건에서의 그것의 행동은 그것의 특징을 가장 잘 드러낸다.'이다. 빈칸에는 글의 주제와 적절한 말이 들어가야 하는데, (A)에서는 상대적이라는 말과 유사한 말이 들어가야 한다. 따라서 'improper'가 가장 적절하다. (B)에서는 다양한 환경과 유사한 말이 들어가야 하므로 'various'가 가장 적절하다. 따라서 ④가 적절하다.

오답 | 빈칸 (A)에서 'exact'는 글의 관점과 반대되는 말이기 때문에 옳지 않고, 'flexible'은 글의 소재와 무관하다. 빈칸 (B)에서 'optimal'는 글의 소재와 무관하고, 'original'은 글의 관점과 반대되기 때문에 옳지 않다.

Words

- ☐ philosopher
- ☐ environment
- ☐ notion
- ☐ problematic
- ☐ relatively
- ☐ concern
- ☐ salmon
- ☐ spawn
- ☐ smash
- ☐ behave
- ☐ optimal
- ☐ existence

☐ partial ____
☐ original ____
☐ flexible ____
☐ improper ____

Phrases

☐ according to ____
☐ a variety of ____
☐ first of all ____
☐ and so on ____

우선순위 영단어 역대 수능 기출 + 전국 모의고사 기출 + EBS 기출 + 교과서 기출 빈출 어휘

단어	뜻	단어	뜻	단어	뜻
count on	v. ~을 믿다	counter	v. 대응하다 a. 반대의	counteract	v. 중화하다
countless	a. 수많은	couple	v. ~을 연상하다	course	n. 강좌
court	n. 궁전	cover	n. 이불	coverage	n. 보도
crash-land	v. 땅에 부딪치다	creativity	n. 창의력	creature	n. 생물
creek	n. 시내	crisis	n. 위기	criticism	n. 비평
cropland	n. 농경지	cross	n. 혼합	crow	v. (수탉이) 울다
crown	n. 꼭대기	crumble	v. 무너지다	cry for	v. ~을 꼭 필요로 하다
cubicle	n. 칸막이한 작은 방	cucumber	n. 오이	cuddle	v. 꼭 껴안다
culprit	n. 장본인	cult	n. 일시적 대유행	cultured	a. 지배된
curl	v. (동그렇게) 말리다	currently	n. 현재	curriculum	n. 교육 과정
curved	a. 휘어진	customer	n. 고객	cute	a. 귀여운
cyclic	a. 주기의	czar	n. (러시아의) 황제	damages	n. 손해액
damp	a. 축축한	dampen	v. 축축하게 하다	dashboard	n. 계기판
dawn	n. (일의) 처음	dazzle	v. 눈부시게 하다	dead	n. 죽음
deadline	n. 마감기한	deal	n. 거래	debt	n. 빚
deceit	n. 사기	deceive	v. 속이다	decision-maker	n. 의사 결정자
decorate	v. 꾸미다	dedicate	v. 바치다	defensiveness	n. 방어적임
deficit	n. 적자	degree	n. 정도	dehydrate	v. 탈수하다
delay	v. 늦추다	delegation	n. 대표단	delete	v. 지우다
delighted	a. 아주 기뻐하는	demonstrably	ad. 입증되듯이	demoralize	v. 타락시키다
densely	ad. 빽빽하게	depletion	n. 파괴	depressed	a. 침체된
depressing	a. 낙담시키는	derail	v. 탈선시키다	deserted	a. 사람이 없는
desirable	a. 바람직한	desire	n. 욕망	detergent	n. 세제
determination	n. 결심	devalue	v. 평가절하하다	devastated	a. 망연자실한
develop	v. (사진을) 현상하다	development	n. 발달	developmental	a. 발달상의
deviate	v. 빗나가게 하다	devour	v. 탐독하다	diffuse	v. 퍼지다
digit	n. 숫자	dignity	n. 위엄성	dire	a. 대단히 심각한
direct	v. ~로 향하다[겨냥하다]	director	n. (활동, 부서 등의) 책임자	disagreement	n. 불화
disappear	v. 사라지다	discern	v. 분별하다	discharge	v. 방출하다
disclosure	n. 밝힘	discount coupon	n. 할인 쿠폰	discourage	v. 용기를 잃게 하다
discouraged	a. 낙심한	discourse	n. 담론	disgusting	a. 역겨운
dismissal	n. 해고	disorganization	n. 혼란	disparate	a. 다른
disparity	n. 차이	dispassionate	a. 감정적이 아닌	disposed	a. ~하고 싶어 하는
disseminate	v. 퍼뜨리다	dissonance	n. 불일치	distant	a. 먼
distinctly	ad. 명료하게	distorted	a. 삐뚤어진	distortion	n. 왜곡된 이야기
distracted	a. 산만한	distractibility	n. 주의를 산만하게 할 가능성	distracting	a. 방해하는
diversion	n. 주의를 딴 데로 돌리기	divert	v. (물줄기를) 전환하다	divinity	n. 신성
doctorate	n. 박사 학위	doctrine	n. 사상	domesticate	v. 길들이다
domestication	n. 가축화	doom	n. 파멸	dormitory	n. 기숙사

변형문제

01 다음 글을 읽고, |조건|에 맞게 요약문을 완성하시오.

| 조건 |
* (A), (B)는 각각 다르게 1단어로 쓸 것
* [보기]에서 선택한 단어를 한 번씩만 쓸 것
* 필요한 경우, 문맥과 어법에 맞게 변형할 것

[보기] insignificant / inappropriate / meaningful / compare / enhance / identify / suitable / recognize / represent / describe / explain / summarize

According to philosopher Radcliffe Richards, it is incoherent to think that something's real nature is revealed when it is in its correct environment. First of all, the whole notion of a 'correct environment' is problematic. Isn't the notion of what is correct relative to various concerns? The correct environment for a salmon when cooking one is perhaps a heated oven. The correct environment for its spawning is something else again. But more importantly, to know something's nature is to know how it is in a variety of environments. Iron's nature, for example, is most fully understood if we know how it behaves when it is hot, cold, smashed, left in water and so on. Knowing how iron behaves when left in conditions optimal to its continued, unchanged existence only gives a partial view of its nature.

⬇

The concept of a 'correct environment' is (A) ____________ for understanding a feature of something, but its behavior under a variety of circumstances best (B) ____________ its nature.

02 다음 글을 읽고, |조건|에 맞게 (A), (B)를 채우시오.

| 조건 |
* (A), (B)는 각각 다르게 1단어로 쓸 것
* 본문에 있는 단어만을 그대로 사용할 것

According to philosopher Radcliffe Richards, it is incoherent to think that something's real nature is revealed when it is in its correct environment. First of all, the whole notion of a 'correct environment' is problematic. Isn't the notion of what is correct relative to various concerns? The correct environment for a salmon when cooking one is perhaps a heated oven. The correct environment for its spawning is something else again. But more importantly, to know something's nature is to know how it is in a variety of environments. Iron's nature, for example, is most fully understood if we know how it behaves when it is hot, cold, smashed, left in water and so on. Knowing how iron behaves when left in conditions optimal to its continued, unchanged existence only gives a partial view of its nature.

⬇

Two examples included in the paragraph to explain why the notion of a 'correct environment' is problematic are (A) ____________ and (B) ____________.

03 다음 글을 읽고, |조건|에 맞게 요약문을 완성하시오.

| 조건 |
* (A), (B)는 각각 다르게 1단어로 쓸 것
* [보기]에서 선택한 단어를 한 번씩만 쓸 것
* 필요한 경우, 문맥과 어법에 맞게 변형할 것

[보기] decide / select / prove / rely / select / imperative / exaggerate / promote / effective / record / observe / criticize

According to philosopher Radcliffe Richards, it is incoherent to think that something's real nature is revealed when it is in its correct environment. First of all, the whole notion of a 'correct environment' is problematic. Isn't the notion of what is correct relative to various concerns? The correct environment for a salmon when cooking one is perhaps a heated oven. The correct environment for its spawning is something else again. But more importantly, to know something's nature is to know how it is in a variety of environments. Iron's nature, for example, is most fully understood if we know how it behaves when it is hot, cold, smashed, left in water and so on. Knowing how iron behaves when left in conditions optimal to its continued, unchanged existence only gives a partial view of its nature.

⬇

In case of salmon, an appropriate environment is (A) ____________ depending on each condition and therefore, it is incorrect to use the notion of 'a correct environment'. Also, in case of iron, understanding how it reacts in various conditions is (B) ____________ when discovering its properties.

04 밑줄 친 부분 중 문맥상 옳지 않은 것은?

According to philosopher Radcliffe Richards, it is ① incoherent to think that something's real nature is revealed when it is in its ② correct environment. First of all, the whole notion of a 'correct environment' is problematic. Isn't the notion of what is correct relative to ③ various concerns? The correct environment for a salmon when cooking one is perhaps a heated oven. The correct environment for its spawning is something else ④ again. But more importantly, to know something's nature is to know how it is in a ⑤ particularly of environments. Iron's nature, for example, is most fully understood if we know how it behaves when it is hot, cold, smashed, left in water and so on. Knowing how iron behaves when left in conditions optimal to its continued, unchanged existence only gives a partial view of its nature.

요약문 완성

글의 논리	Spotlight
제목	식습관의 변화를 주는 원인
주제	사람들은 자발적으로 식습관을 바꾸기도 하지만, 경제 발전의 목적과 관련된 상황 때문에 바꾸기도 한다.

PRACTICE 03

060 어법 선택 & 연결어

Programs of **[economical / economic]** development often **[lead / leads]** to **[changes / change]** in people's dietary habits. In some cases these dietary changes are **[voluntarily / voluntary]** **[to the extent that / the extent which]** some new foods, **[associated / associating]** with powerful outsiders, **[are / is]** **[status / statue]** symbols. ( ) more often than not, diets change **[because / because of]** circumstances **[associated / associating]** with the objectives of **[economic / economy]** development **[what / that]** **[are / is]** beyond the control of the local people. ( ), in an attempt to **[grow / growing]** more cash crops (**[which / what]** **[helps / help]** to **[raise / rise]** wages and bring in foreign exchange capital), non-Western people often divert time and energy from growing **[their / its]** normal subsistence crops. The result is **[what / that]** they spend **[much / many]** of their hard-earned cash on foods **[what / that]** **[are / is]** both costly **[and / or]** nutritionally **[inferior / superior]** **[than / to]** **[feed / feeding]** **[their / its]** families.

⬇

People may change their dietary habits **[voluntary / voluntarily]**, but they may also change **[it / them]** **[because / because of]** the demands **[associating / associated]** with **[economic / economical]** development, **[what / which]** can pressure non-Western people to grow cash crops and consume expensive and **[undernourishing / undernourished]** foods.

일반적인 사실 경제 발전 프로그램들은 사람들의 식습관의 변화를 만들곤 한다.

Programs / (of economic development) / (often) lead (to changes) / (in people's dietary habits).

Programs(S) 프로그램들은 / 경제 발전 프로그램의 / lead(V) 흔히 이어진다 / to(전치사) changes(O) 변화들로 사람들의 식습관의

경제 발전 프로그램들은 흔히 사람들의 식습관의 변화를 생기게 한다.

노트
- ■ A lead to(전치사) B : A이라는 원인 때문에 B라는 결과가 발생하다, A는 B로 이어지다
- ■ 〈혼동 어휘〉

	형용사	명사
economic	경제의	–
economical	경제학의	–
economy	–	경제
economist	–	경제학자
economics	–	경제학

관점1 어떤 경우에는 식습관의 변화가 자발적이다.

(In some cases) / these dietary changes / are voluntary / (to the extent) / {that some new foods, / (which is) (associated with powerful outsiders), / are status symbols}.

어떤 경우에 / these dietary changes(S) 이러한 식습관의 변화는 / are(V) voluntary(S.C) 자발적이다 / 되는 정도로 / that〈종·접〉 =〈동격〉 / some new foods(S) 일부 새로운 음식들이 / associated〈과거분사〉 강력한 외부인과 관련된 / are(V) status symbols(S.C) 지위의 상징으로

어떤 경우에 이러한 식습관의 변화는 강력한 외부인과 관련된 일부 새로운 음식들이 지위의 상징이 되는 정도로 자발적이다.

노트 ■ 〈extent 용법〉

to	extent	to	which	~하는 정도	
to	the	extent	that	~하는 정도까지	
	such	an	extent	that	~할 정도로

■ 〈동격의 that〉 : ~라는 A(관계대명사 which/what 사용 불가)

추상명사 (A)	종속절(명사절 – 완전한 문장)		
	(that)	주어	동사
answer / belief / chance / claim / conclusion / dream / evidence / extent / fact / faith / hope / idea / likelihood / news / notion / pledge / possibility / promise / proposal / question / recognition / reply / request / result / sense / statement / suggestion / testament / theory / view / wickedness 등	종속 접속사 (생략 가능)	–	–
the extent	that	some new foods	are

■ 〈주격관계대명사+be동사 생략〉

	〈주격관계대명사절〉: 주어 수식				
some new foods,	which	are	associated ~,	are	status symbols.
주어	주격관계대명사	be동사	과거분사	동사	주격보어
	(동시 생략)				

■ 〈혼동 어휘〉: 철자가 비슷해서 혼동

stat	e	주, 말하다
	ue	동상
	ure	키, 신장, 위상
	us	지위, 상태

주제문(관점2) 대개 식습관은 경제 발전의 목적과 관련된 상황 때문에 변화한다.

(But) / (more often than not), / diets change / (because of circumstances) / (which are) (associated with the objectives of economic development) / (that are beyond the control of the local people).

하지만 / 대개 / 식습관은(S) 변한다(V) / (전치사) 상황 때문에(O〈선행사〉) / (과거분사) 경제 발전의 목적과 관련된 / (주·관) (V) 현지인들의 통제에서 벗어난

하지만 대개 식습관은 현지인들의 통제에서 벗어난 경제 발전의 목적과 관련된 상황 때문에 변한다.

노트
■ more often than not : 자주, 대개
■ associate A with B : A를 B와 관련시켜 생각하다(수동태 시, A be associated with B)
■ 〈원인/이유〉: ~ 때문에

전치사	because of	+(동)명사 / 명사 상당어구
	due to	
	for	
	on account of	
	owing to	
	thanks to	
종속접속사	as	+주어+동사 ~
	because	
	now(that)	
	since	

■ 〈주격관계대명사+be동사 생략〉

–	생략할 수 있음	
명사 (선행사)	(주격관계대명사 +be동사)	현재분사(Ring) – 능동(~하고 있는)
		과거분사(p.p.) – 수동(~되어진, 당한)
		명사
		형용사(구) (~하는, ~할)
		부사
		전치사구
circumstances	(which/that are)	associated

■ 〈주격관계대명사절 that〉: 선행사를 포함하고 있는 관계대명사 what 사용 불가

		주격관계대명사절		
선행사	분사구	주격관계대명사	~~주어~~	동사
circumstances	associated ~	that		are

예시 비서양 사람들은 더 많은 환금 자금 작물을 재배하려고 시도하고 일반적인 자급용 농작물 재배하는 시간을 줄인다.

(For example), / (in an attempt to grow more cash crops) / (which help to raise wages and bring in foreign exchange capital), / non-Western people / (often) divert time and energy / (from growing their normal subsistence crops).

예를 들어 / 더 많은 환금 작물을 재배하려는 시도로 / (선행사) (주·관) V_1 O V_2 (임금 인상을 돕고 외환 자금을 가져올) / O / 비서양 사람들은(S) / 흔히 시간과 에너지를 다른 데로 돌린다(V, O) / (동명사) 자신들의 일반적인 자급용 농작물을 재배하는 것으로부터(O)

예를 들어, 비서양 사람들은 (임금 인상을 돕고 외환 자금을 가져올) 더 많은 환금 작물을 재배하려는 시도로 흔히 자신들의 일반적인 자급용 농작물을 재배하는 것으로부터 시간과 에너지를 다른 데로 돌린다.

노트
■ in an attempt to R : ~하기 위하여, ~하려는 시도로
■ bring in : ~을 가져오다, 들여오다
■ divert A from B : A를 B로부터 돌리다
■ 〈주격관계대명사절의 수의 일치〉: 선행사를 포함하고 있는 관계대명사 what 사용 불가

	주격관계대명사절		
선행사	주격관계대명사	~~주어~~	동사
cash crops	which		help

■ 〈help 동사의 쓰임〉

help	목적어		3형식
	(to) R		
help (준사역동사)	목적어	목적격보어	5형식
		(to) R	

■ 〈혼동하기 쉬운 동사〉
• rise / raise / arise / arouse / rouse

원형	과거	과거분사	현재분사	뜻
rise	rose	risen	rising	vi. 오르다, 일어나다
raise	raised	raised	raising	vt. 올리다, 기르다
arise	arose	arisen	arising	vi. 발생하다, 기인하다
arouse	aroused	aroused	arousing	vt. (감정) 불러 일으키다, 자극하다
rouse	roused	roused	rousing	vt. 깨우다, 일으키다

예시 비서양 사람들은 힘들게 번 현금의 상당 부분을 비싸고 영양이 적은 열등한 음식에 소비하게 된다.

The result / is [that they spend / much of their hard-

그 결과(S) / (V) / (종·접) 그들은(S) 소비하게 된다(V) / S.C / 자신들이 힘들게 번

earned cash (on foods) / {that are (both costly and nutritionally) inferior / (to feed their families)}].

O: earned cash / 〈선행사〉: foods / 〈주·관〉: that / V: are / S.C₁: costly / S.C₂: inferior

현금의 상당 부분을 / 비싸고 영양적으로 / 열등한 음식에 / 가족을 먹이기 위해

그 결과 그들은 자신들이 힘들게 번 현금의 상당 부분을 가족을 먹이기 위해 비싸고 영양적으로 열등한 음식에 소비하게 된다.

노트

■ spend＋A[목적어(시간/돈/에너지)]＋on B : A를 B에 소비하다

■ costly : 많은 돈[비용]이 드는(＝expensive)

■ 〈부정수량형용사〉 : 막연한 수나 양의 정도를 표시하는 형용사

수(數)	few(a few), some(any), a lot of(lots of), a good(or great), plenty of, enough, all, no, many	복수명사＋복수동사
양(量)	little(a little), some(any), a lot of, a good(or great), deal of, plenty of, enough, all, no, much	단수명사＋단수동사

■ 〈what vs. that〉

	관계대명사(불완전한 문장)	접속사(완전한 문장)
what	○ 선행사를 포함하고 있기 때문에 what 앞에 선행사 불필요	×
that	○ that 앞에 선행사 필요	○

■ 〈주격관계대명사절의 수의 일치〉 : 선행사를 포함하고 있는 관계대명사 what 사용 불가

	주격관계대명사절		
선행사	주격관계대명사	~~주어~~	동사
foods	that		are

■ 〈상관접속사〉 : 병렬구조

종류				뜻
not	A	but	B	A가 아니라 B (＝B, not A)
not only		but also		A뿐만 아니라 B도 (＝B as well as A)
either		or		A와 B 둘 중 하나
neither		nor		A와 B 둘 다 아닌
both		and		A와 B 둘 다

↓

요약문 사람들은 자발적으로 식습관을 바꾸기도 하지만, 경제 발전과 관련된 요구 때문에 식습관을 바꿀 수 있는데, 이것은 비서양 사람들이 환금 작물을 재배하고 비싸며 영양이 부족한 음식을 섭취하도록 강요할 수 있다.

People / may change their dietary habits (voluntarily), / but they may (also) change them / (because of the (A) ____________) / (which are) (associated with economic development), / {which can pressure non-Western people / (to grow cash crops / and consume expensive and (B) ____________ foods)}.

S: People / V: may change / O: their dietary habits — 사람들은 / 자발적으로 식습관을 바꾸기도 하지만
S: they / V: may change / O: them / 〈전치사〉: because of — 식습관을 바꿀 수 있는데 / 요구 때문에
〈과거분사〉: associated — 경제 발전과 관련된
〈주·관〉: which / V: can pressure / O: non-Western people — 이것은 비서양 사람들을 강요할 수 있다
①: grow cash crops — 이 환금 작물을 재배하고
②: consume — 비싸며 영양이 부족한 음식을 섭취하도록
O: foods

▶ **다음 글의 내용을 한 문장으로 요약하고자 한다. 빈칸 (A), (B)에 들어갈 말로 가장 적절한 것은?**

	(A)		(B)
①	conflicts	……	tasteless
②	conflicts	……	undernourished
③	values	……	healthy
④	demands	……	undernourished
⑤	demands	……	healthy

정답 | ④

해석 | ① 갈등 – 맛이 없는
② 갈등 – 영양이 부족한
③ 가치 – 건강에 좋은
④ 요구 – 영양이 부족한
⑤ 요구 – 건강에 좋은

해설 | ④ 이 글의 주제는 사람들이 자발적으로 식습관을 바꾸기도 하지만, 경제 발전의 목적과 관련된 상황 때문에 바꾸기도 한다는 것이다. 요약문을 해석하면 '사람들은 자발적으로 식습관을 바꾸기도 하지만, 경제 발전과 관련된 ________ 때문에 식습관을 바꿀 수 있는데, 이것은 비서양 사람들이 환금 작물을 재배하고 비싸며 ________ 음식을 섭취하도록 강요할 수 있다.'이다. 빈칸 (A)에는 경제 발전의 목적과 유사한 단어가 들어가야 한다. 따라서 'demands'가 가장 적절하다. 빈칸 (B)에서는 글의 마지막 부분에 열등한 음식에 소비하게 된다고 나오므로 열등한과 유사한 말이 들어가야 한다. 따라서 'undernourished'가 가장 적절하다. 정답은 ④이다.

오답 | 빈칸 (A)에 'conflicts'와 'values'는 경제 발전의 목적인 글의 소재와 무관하기 때문에 적절하지 않다. 빈칸 (B)에는 'tasteless'는 글의 소재와 일치하지 않고 'healthy'는 글의 관점과 반대되기 때문에 적절하지 않다.

노트 [논리 독해]

■ **예시** : 일반화 문장에 대한 구체화 문장으로 가장 대표적이고 출제자가 주로 사용하는 논리가 바로 예시이다. 이러한 예시는 지문에 따라 다르지만 주로 한 가지 예시 이상이 나오는 경우가 많고 주제문 뒤에 나오거나 주제문 앞에 나오는 경향이 짙다.

• 〈예시를 나타내는 표현〉

	구체화 문장 (예시)	
일반화 문장 (예시가 시작되기 전 문장)	For example (instance)	일반화 문장 (예시가 끝나고 난 후 문장)
	For instance	
	This is an example of	
	if	
	when	
	Let's say	
	imagine	
	guess	
	think of	

suppose
특정 인물, 사건, 장소 등을 나타내는 고유명사
개인의 경험

Words

- ☐ economic
- ☐ dietary habit
- ☐ voluntary
- ☐ extent
- ☐ status symbol
- ☐ circumstance
- ☐ objective
- ☐ attempt
- ☐ cash crop
- ☐ raise
- ☐ wage
- ☐ capital
- ☐ divert
- ☐ result
- ☐ costly
- ☐ nutritionally
- ☐ inferior
- ☐ feed

Phrases

- ☐ A lead to(전치사) B
- ☐ associate A with B
- ☐ bring in
- ☐ divert A from B
- ☐ more often than not
- ☐ in an attempt to R
- ☐ spend+A[목적어(시간/돈/에너지)]+on B

우선순위 영단어 역대 수능 기출+전국 모의고사 기출+EBS 기출+교과서 기출 빈출 어휘

단어	뜻	단어	뜻	단어	뜻
doubt	v. 의심하다	downplay	v. 경시하다	downright	ad. 완전히
downward	ad. 아래쪽으로	drainage	n. 배수	dramatize	v. 극화하다
draw on	v. ~을 이용하다	drift	v. ~에 빠지다(into)	drip	v. 뚝뚝 흘리다
driving school	n. 자동차 운전 학원	drown	v. 물에 빠져 죽다	drowsiness	n. 졸음
dweller	n. 거주자	dwelling	n. 거주지	dwindle	v. 줄어들다
e.g.	예를 들어	eagerly	ad. 간절히	earn a living	v. 생계를 꾸리다
eclipse	v. 일식	eco-friendly	a. 친환경적인	ecologist	n. 생태학자
ecstatic	a. 황홀한	editor	n. 편집장	efficiently	ad. 효율적으로
effortlessly	ad. 노력하지 않고	elapse	v. 경과하다	elbow	n. 팔꿈치
election	n. 선거	electric	a. 긴장된	electric appliance	n. 전기 기구
electric heater	n. 전기난로	electricity	n. 전기	electronics store	n. 전자제품 매장
elegance	n. 우아함	elevation	n. 높이	eloquent	a. 설득력 있는
embarrassment	n. 당황	emergency	n. 비상[긴급]사태	eminent	a. 명망있는
empathetic	a. 공감할 수 있는	empathically	ad. 공감할 수 있게	employment	n. 고용
encase	v. 감싸다	enclosure	n. 울타리	encompassing	a. 포괄하는
end up with	(결국에는) ~하게 되다	endangered species	n. 멸종 위기 종	endowment	n. 타고난 재능
engender	v. 일으키다	engineering	n. 공학	enlarge	v. 확대하다
enlarged	a. 확정된	enlightenment	n. 계발	enormously	ad. 엄청나게
ensue	n. 잇따라 일어나다	entertainment	n. 오락	enticing	a. 마음을 끄는
entirely	ad. 완전히	entrepreneurship	n. 기업가정신	envelope	n. 덮개
episode	n. (소설, 극 따위 속의) 삽화	equate	v. 동일시하다	equate A with B	v. A와 B를 동등하게 하다
equatorial	a. 적도 지대의	erupt	v. 일어나다	eruption	n. 분출
escort	v. 호위하다	essential oil	n. 정유	established	a. 정해진
esteem	v. 존경하다	estimation	n. 판단	etch	v. (에칭으로) 새기다

변형문제

01 다음 글을 읽고, |조건|에 맞게 요약문을 완성하시오.

| 조건 |
* (A), (B)는 각각 다르게 1단어로 쓸 것
* 본문에 있는 단어만을 사용할 것
* 필요한 경우, 문맥과 어법에 맞게 변형할 것

Programs of economic development often lead to changes in people's dietary habits. In some cases these dietary changes are voluntary to the extent that some new foods, associated with powerful outsiders, are status symbols. But more often than not, diets change because of circumstances associated with the objectives of economic development that are beyond the control of the local people. For example, in an attempt to grow more cash crops (which help to raise wages and bring in foreign exchange capital), non-Western people often divert time and energy from growing their normal subsistence crops. The result is that they spend much of their hard-earned cash on foods that are both costly and nutritionally inferior to feed their families.

⬇

People not only change their eating habits (A) ____________, but also change their eating habits due to a demand related to economic development. For example, non-Western people who grow cash crops consume food lacking in (B) ____________.

02 다음 글을 읽고, |조건|에 맞게 주어진 제목을 완성하시오.

| 조건 |
* (A)는 2단어, (B)는 4단어로 쓸 것
* 본문에 있는 단어만을 그대로 사용할 것

Programs of economic development often lead to changes in people's dietary habits. In some cases these dietary changes are voluntary to the extent that some new foods, associated with powerful outsiders, are status symbols. But more often than not, diets change because of circumstances associated with the objectives of economic development that are beyond the control of the local people. For example, in an attempt to grow more cash crops (which help to raise wages and bring in foreign exchange capital), non-Western people often divert time and energy from growing their normal subsistence crops. The result is that they spend much of their hard-earned cash on foods that are both costly and nutritionally inferior to feed their families.

⬇

The impact of (A) ____________ ____________ on (B) ____________ ____________ ____________ ____________.

03 다음 글을 읽고, |조건|에 맞게 요약문을 완성하시오.

| 조건 |
* (A), (B), (C)는 각각 다르게 1단어로 쓸 것
* [보기]에서 선택한 단어를 한 번씩만 쓸 것
* 필요한 경우, 문맥과 어법에 맞게 변형할 것

[보기] export / weight / resource / fund / import / buy / refrain / rate / nutrition / health / sell / cultivate / avoid / energy

Programs of economic development often lead to changes in people's dietary habits. In some cases these dietary changes are voluntary to the extent that some new foods, associated with powerful outsiders, are status symbols. But more often than not, diets change because of circumstances associated with the objectives of economic development that are beyond the control of the local people. For example, in an attempt to grow more cash crops (which help to raise wages and bring in foreign exchange capital), non-Western people often divert time and energy from growing their normal subsistence crops. The result is that they spend much of their hard-earned cash on foods that are both costly and nutritionally inferior to feed their families.

⬇

With economic development inducing modifications in eating habits, higher amounts of cash crops than subsistence crops are (A) ______________ by non-Western people who are in need of increasing their incomes and foreign exchange (B) ______________. However, this leads them to consume foods which are expensive and poor in (C) ______________.

04 다음 글의 제목으로 가장 적절한 것은?

Programs of economic development often lead to changes in people's dietary habits. In some cases these dietary changes are voluntary to the extent that some new foods, associated with powerful outsiders, are status symbols. But more often than not, diets change because of circumstances associated with the objectives of economic development that are beyond the control of the local people. For example, in an attempt to grow more cash crops (which help to raise wages and bring in foreign exchange capital), non-Western people often divert time and energy from growing their normal subsistence crops. The result is that they spend much of their hard-earned cash on foods that are both costly and nutritionally inferior to feed their families.

① A variety of reasons why people change their eating habits.
② The effect of eating habits on people.
③ People who change their eating habits voluntarily
④ The Importance of Changing Diet
⑤ The purpose of economic development

어법(밑줄/네모)

글의 논리	Story
제목	George Lucas가 이루어낸 업적
주제	George Lucas는 영화 제작자들과 영화 관람객에게 큰 영향을 주었다.

수능 ANALYSIS

061 어법 선택 & 연결어

When George Lucas succeeded in making *Star Wars*, **[although / despite]** those who said the special effects he wanted hadn't ever **[done / been done]** and couldn't **[do / be done]**, **[much / many]** other possibilities **[opening / opened]** up to him. **[Industrial / Industrious]** Light and Magic (ILM), the company he created to produce those "impossible" special effects, **[to become / became]** a source of revenue to help **[fund / funding]** his other projects. He was able to produce merchandising tie-ins to his movies, (   ) **[bringing / brought]** in **[another / the other]** revenue stream **[fund / to fund]** his moviemaking. (   ) his confidence in **[do / doing]** the difficult **[has / have]** also made a huge impact on other moviemakers and a whole new generation of moviegoers. Popular culture writer Chris Salewicz says, "At first **[direct / directly]** through his own work and then via the **[unparalleling / unparalleled]** influence of ILM, George Lucas **[influences / has influenced]** for two decades the essential broad notion of **[what / that]** is cinema."

이야기 George Lucas가 이루어낸 업적

{When George Lucas / succeeded (in making *Star Wars*)},
〈종·접〉 S V 〈동명사〉 O
George Lucas가 'Star Wars'를 만드는 데 성공했을 때

(목·종 that)
/ <① although those [who said / {the special effects /
〈종·접〉 〈선행사〉 〈주·관〉 V S〈선행사〉 O
사람들에도 불구하고 말했던 특수효과가

(목·관 that)
(he wanted) / hadn't ever been done and couldn't be
S V V_1〈과거완료 수동〉 V_2〈수동태〉
그가 원했던 행해진 적도 없었고 행해질 수도 없다고

done}]>, / many other possibilities / opened up / (to him).
S V
많은 다른 가능성들이 열렸다 그에게

George Lucas가 원했던 특수효과가 행해진 적도 없었고 행해질 수도 없다고 말했던 사람들에도 불구하고 George Lucas가 'Star Wars'를 만드는 데 성공했을 때, 많은 다른 가능성들이 그에게 열렸다.

노트
- succeed in : ~에 성공하다
- open up to : ~에게 공개하다
- 〈양보/대조〉

전치사	in spite of	+명사/명사 상당어구	비록 ~이지만
	despite		
종속접속사	though	+주어+동사	
	although		
	even though		
	even if		
	as		
	while		반면에
	whereas		

- 〈those who〉 : ~하는 사람들(who 대신에 that 사용 불가)

	〈주격관계대명사절〉		
those	who	~~주어~~	동사
〈선행사〉	〈주격관계대명사〉		said

- 〈목적격종속접속사 that 생략〉 : 완전타동사의 목적어로 사용 / 관계대명사 what 사용 불가

	종속절(명사절 : 목적어) (완전한 절)		
완전타동사	that	주어	동사
said	목적격종속접속사 – 생략 가능(~하는 것을)	the special effects	hadn't ever been done and couldn't be done

- 〈목적격관계대명사 that〉 : 타동사의 목적어가 없는 경우 / 선행사를 포함하고 있는 관계대명사 what 사용 불가

	〈목적격관계대명사절〉			
선행사	목적격관계대명사	주어	타동사	~~목적어~~
the special effects	that : 〈생략 가능〉	he	wanted	

=〈동격〉
Industrial Light and Magic (ILM), / the company /
S
Industrial Light and Magic(ILM)은 회사

(목·관 that)
{he created / (to produce those "impossible" special
O
그가 만들었던 그러한 "불가능했던" 특수효과를 만들어내기 위해

effects)}, / ② became a source (of revenue) / (to help
V S.C
수익의 원천이 되어 그의 다른

(to)
fund his other projects).
O
프로젝트들의 기금을 대는 것을 도왔다

그러한 '불가능했던' 특수효과를 만들어내기 위해 그가 만들었던 회사인 Industrial Light and Magic(ILM)이 수익의 원천이 되어 그의 다른 프로젝트들의 기금을 대는 것을 도왔다.

노트 ■ 〈industry 품사별 변화에 따른 의미〉

	명사	형용사	동사
industry	산업, 공업, 근면	–	–
industrial	산업 근로자, ((특히)) 직공	산업(상)의, 공업(상)의	–
industrious	–	근면한, 부지런한	–
industrialize	–	–	산업[공업]화하다[되다]
industrialization	산업(공업)화	–	

■ 〈동격〉 : A(명사), B(명사) (A가 주어, B라는 A)

동격(B라는 A)		
명사(A)	,(콤마)	명사(B)
Industrial Light and Magic (ILM)		the company

■ 〈목적격관계대명사 that〉 : 타동사의 목적어가 없는 경우 / 선행사를 포함하고 있는 관계대명사 what 사용 불가

	〈목적격관계대명사절〉			
선행사	목적격관계대명사	주어	타동사	~~목적어~~
the company	that : 〈생략 가능〉	he	created	

■ 〈help 동사의 쓰임〉

help	목적어		3형식
	(to) R		
help (준사역동사)	목적어	목적격보어	5형식
		(to) R	

He / was able to produce merchandising tie-ins / (to his movies), / {thus / bringing in another revenue stream / (③ to fund his moviemaking)}.

(He: S 그는 / was able to produce: V / merchandising tie-ins: O 캐릭터 파생 상품들을 생산할 수 있었고 / 자신의 영화와 관련된 / thus 〈종·접〉 그래서 / bringing 〈분사구문〉 또 다른 금액을 벌었다 / stream: O / 자신의 영화 제작 기금을 댈 수 있는)

그는 자신의 영화와 관련된 캐릭터 파생 상품들을 생산할 수 있었고, 그래서 자신의 영화 제작 기금을 댈 수 있는 또 다른 금액을 벌었다.

노트 ■ be able to R : ~할 수 있다
■ bring in : ~을 가져오다, 들여오다
■ revenue stream : 수입원, 매출원
■ 〈분사구문 – 문미〉 : 주절과 분사구문의 위치가 서로 바뀌어도 무관

주절		종속절(→ 분사구문)			
주어	동사	종속 접속사	주어	동사 : 상황에 맞게 아래처럼 바뀜	
		〈그대로 사용하면 의미 강조〉	(주절의 주어와 같으면 생략하고, 다르면 주격으로 사용함)	(being) (having been) 생략 가능	Ring(현재분사)
					p.p.(과거분사)
					형용사
					명사
He	was able to produce	thus	–	–	bringing

■ 〈the other vs. another〉

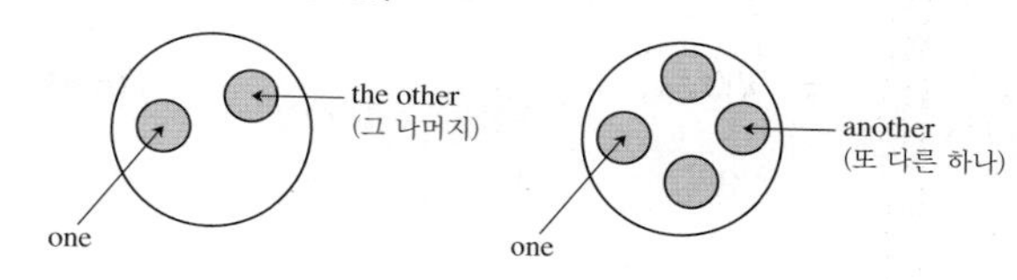

(But) / his confidence / (in ④ doing the difficult) / has (also) made a huge impact / (on other moviemakers and a whole new generation of moviegoers).

(그러나 / his confidence: S 그의 자신감이 / doing 〈동명사〉 the difficult: O 어려운 일을 하는 것에 대한 / has made: V〈현재완료〉 / a huge impact: O 또한 엄청나게 큰 영향을 주었다 / 다른 영화 제작자들과 / 완전히 새로운 시대의 영화 관람객에게)

그러나 어려운 일을 하는 것에 대한 그의 자신감이 또한 다른 영화 제작자들과 완전히 새로운 세대의 영화 관람객에게 엄청나게 큰 영향을 주었다.

노트 ■ make an impact on : ~에 충격을 주다, 영향을 미치다(=influence, affect)
■ 〈the＋형용사＝복수보통명사〉

the	형용사	=	형용사	person	→	단수명사
			형용사	people		복수명사(사람)
			형용사	things		복수명사(사물)
			형용사	명사형 어미		단수추상명사
the	difficult	=	difficult	things		복수명사(사물)

Popular culture writer Chris Salewicz / says, / "(At first) / {⑤ directly (through his own work) / and then / (via the unparalleled influence of ILM)}, / George Lucas / has influenced / (for two decades) / the essential broad notion / {of (what is cinema)}."

(Popular culture writer Chris Salewicz: S 대중문화 작가인 Chris Salewicz는 / says: V 말한다 / 처음에는 / directly 〈부사〉 / through 〈전치사〉 직접적으로 자신의 일을 통해 / 그 다음에는 / via 〈전치사〉 / unparalleled 〈과거분사〉 ILM의 견줄 데 없는 영향을 통해 / George Lucas: S George Lucas는 / has influenced: V〈현재완료〉 영향을 주었습니다 / 이십 년 동안 / the essential broad notion: O 본질적인 일반 개념에 / of 〈전치사〉 / what 〈주·관〉 / is: V / cinema: S.C / O 영화라는 것의)

대중문화 작가인 Chris Salewicz는 "처음에는 직접적으로 그 자신의 일을 통해 그 다음에는 ILM의 견줄 데 없는 영향을 통해 George Lucas는 이십 년 동안 영화라는 것의 본질적인 일반 개념에 영향을 주었습니다."라고 말한다.

노트 ■ at first : 처음에는
■ 〈혼동 어휘〉

through	전치사	~을 통하여
throughout	전치사	[장소] ~의 도처에, [시간] ~ 동안, ~ 내내
	부사	도처에, 완전히, 철저하게
though	접속사	~에도 불구하고
thorough	형용사	철저한, 완전한

■ 〈전치사의 목적어로 사용된 주격관계대명사 what〉 : 선행사가 필요한 주격 관계대명사 that/which 사용 불가

전치사	목적어 : 주격관계대명사 what절				
of	~~선행사~~	what	~~주어~~	불완전자동사	주격보어
		주격관계대명사 : 선행사를 포함한 관계대명사 (=the thing(s) which/that ~) : ~하는 것은/이		is	cinema

▶ 다음 글의 밑줄 친 부분 중, 어법상 틀린 것은?

정답 | ① although → despite

해설 | ① [종속접속사 vs. 전치사] : 양보/대조를 나타내는 종속접속사에는 although / though / even if / even though 등이 있고, 전치사에는 despite / in spite of가 있다. 전자는 종속절을 이끄는 접속사로 완전한 절(주어＋동사)을 가져야 하고, 후자는 뒤에 (동)명사(구) 형태를 가져야 한다. 밑줄 친 부분은 절이 나오지 않았기 때문에 전치사 despite가 필요하다.

오답 | ② [동사 vs. 준동사] : 밑줄 친 부분이 들어 있는 문장에서 주어는 Industrial Light and Magic (ILM)이고 밑줄 친 부분이 동사이다. 주어와 동사 사이에 있는 the company he created to produce those "impossible" special effects는 주어와 동격을 이루고 있다. 따라서 동사가 아닌 준동사 즉, to become와 becoming 등을 사용할 수 없다.

③ [to부정사 vs. 동사] : 밑줄 친 부분이 들어 있는 문장에서 주어는 He이고 동사는 was able to produce이다. thus bringing 이하는 분사구문이기 때문에 밑줄 친 to fund를 동사 fund를 사용할 수 없고 의미상 to부정사의 형용사적 용법으로 앞에 있는 명사 another revenue stream을 수식한다.

④ [동명사 vs. 동사] : 전치사 in은 뒤에 목적어로 동명사를 가질 수 있다. 따라서 동사인 do를 사용할 수 없다.

⑤ [부사 vs. 형용사] : 부사의 역할은 동사/형용사/부사(구)/문장 전체/준동사(to부정사, 동명사, 분사) 등을 수식하는 기능이 있다. 여기에서는 through his own work를 수식하고 있기 때문에, 명사를 수식하거나 보어로 사용되는 형용사 direct를 사용할 수 없다.

Words

- ☐ special effect
- ☐ revenue
- ☐ merchandise
- ☐ tie-in
- ☐ revenue stream
- ☐ huge
- ☐ impact
- ☐ via
- ☐ essential
- ☐ notion

Phrases

- ☐ succeed in
- ☐ be able to R
- ☐ make an impact on
- ☐ open up to
- ☐ bring in
- ☐ at first

우선순위 영단어 역대 수능 기출 + 전국 모의고사 기출 + EBS 기출 + 교과서 기출 빈출 어휘

단어	뜻	단어	뜻	단어	뜻
ethnically	ad. 인종적으로	ethnicity	n. 민족성	evasive	a. 도피적인
exaggerate	v. 과장하다	excavate	v. (구멍 등을) 파다	excavation	n. 발굴
excel	v. 탁월하다	excessively	ad. 과도하게	exclusion	n. 배제
exclusively	ad. 오로지	excrement	n. 똥	execution	n. 실행
exemplar	n. 모범	exhaustion	n. 다 써버림	exhaustive	a. 철저한
exist	v. 존재하다	expel	v. 쫓아내다	experiment	v. 실험하다
experimental	a. 실험적인	expression	n. 표정	expressly	ad. 명백히
exquisite	a. 절묘한	extensively	ad. 광범위하게	extinguish	v. 끄다
extra	a. ~ 범위 밖의	extrinsic	a. 외적인	facilities	n. 시설
fade	v. 흐릿해지다	fake	v. 날조하다	fall behind	v. 뒤처지다
fall on	v. ~위에 떨어지다	fallacy	n. 궤변	fanatic	a. 열광 중인
farsighted	a. 먼 데를 잘 보는	fascinated	a. 매료된	fashionable	a. 유행을 따른
fast	n. 꽉	fatty acid	n. 지방산	favorably	ad. 호의적으로
fearsome	a. 무서운	feast	n. 연회	feather	n. 특징
feed on	v. ~을 먹고 살다	feel free to do	v. 마음대로 ~하다	feminine	a. 여성적인
festive	a. 흥겨운	fictional	a. 허구적인	field	n. 분야

변형문제

01 다음 글을 읽고, |조건|에 맞게 주어진 제목을 완성하시오.

| 조건 |
* (A)는 1단어로 쓸 것
* 본문에 있는 단어만을 그대로 사용할 것

When George Lucas succeeded in making *Star Wars*, despite those who said the special effects he wanted hadn't ever been done and couldn't be done, many other possibilities opened up to him. Industrial Light and Magic (ILM), the company he created to produce those "impossible" special effects, became a source of revenue to help fund his other projects. He was able to produce merchandising tie-ins to his movies, thus bringing in another revenue stream to fund his moviemaking. But his confidence in doing the difficult has also made a huge impact on other moviemakers and a whole new generation of moviegoers. Popular culture writer Chris Salewicz says, "At first directly through his own work and then via the unparalleled influence of ILM, George Lucas has influenced for two decades the essential broad notion of what is cinema."

↓

New (A) ____________ created by George Lucas

02 밑줄 친 부분 중 문맥상 옳지 <u>않은</u> 것은?

When George Lucas succeeded in making *Star Wars*, despite those who said the special effects he wanted hadn't ever been done and couldn't be done, many other possibilities ① <u>closed</u> up to him. Industrial Light and Magic (ILM), the company he created to ② <u>produce</u> those "impossible" special effects, became a source of revenue to help fund his other projects. He was able to produce merchandising tie-ins to his movies, thus bringing in another revenue stream to ③ <u>fund</u> his moviemaking. But his confidence in doing the difficult has also made a ④ <u>huge</u> impact on other moviemakers and a whole new generation of moviegoers. Popular culture writer Chris Salewicz says, "At first directly through his own work and then via the ⑤ <u>unparalleled</u> influence of ILM, George Lucas has influenced for two decades the essential broad notion of what is cinema."

03 다음 글을 읽고, |조건|에 맞게 요약문을 완성하시오.

| 조건 |
* (A)는 2단어, (B)는 3단어로 쓸 것
* [보기]에서 선택한 단어를 한 번씩만 쓸 것(단, (B)의 경우, [보기] 외의 1단어를 추가할 것)
* 필요한 경우, 문맥과 어법에 맞게 변형할 것

[보기] profit / support / economic / industrial / make / develop / connect / prosper / movie / financial / advertisement / production

When George Lucas succeeded in making *Star Wars*, despite those who said the special effects he wanted hadn't ever been done and couldn't be done, many other possibilities opened up to him. Industrial Light and Magic (ILM), the company he created to produce those "impossible" special effects, became a source of revenue to help fund his other projects. He was able to produce merchandising tie-ins to his movies, thus bringing in another revenue stream to fund his moviemaking. But his confidence in doing the difficult has also made a huge impact on other moviemakers and a whole new generation of moviegoers. Popular culture writer Chris Salewicz says, "At first directly through his own work and then via the unparalleled influence of ILM, George Lucas has influenced for two decades the essential broad notion of what is cinema."

⬇

Thanks to the success of *Star Wars*, (A) ____________ ____________ for Lucas's other projects became easier and its movie tie-ins (B) ____________ ____________ ____________ via sale.

04 다음 글의 순서로 가장 적절한 것은?

When George Lucas succeeded in making *Star Wars*, despite those who said the special effects he wanted hadn't ever been done and couldn't be done, many other possibilities opened up to him.

(A) Popular culture writer Chris Salewicz says, "At first directly through his own work and then via the unparalleled influence of ILM, George Lucas has influenced for two decades the essential broad notion of what is cinema."

(B) Industrial Light and Magic (ILM), the company he created to produce those "impossible" special effects, became a source of revenue to help fund his other projects. He was able to produce merchandising tie-ins to his movies, thus bringing in another revenue stream to fund his moviemaking.

(C) But his confidence in doing the difficult has also made a huge impact on other moviemakers and a whole new generation of moviegoers.

① (A) - (B) - (C)　② (B) - (A) - (C)　③ (B) - (C) - (A)
④ (C) - (A) - (B)　⑤ (C) - (B) - (A)

어법(밑줄/네모)

글의 논리	Spotlight
제목	눈물과 슬픔을 인정하는 것의 필요성
주제	우리는 슬픔이 우리에게 다가오는 것을 기꺼이 받아들여야 한다.

수능 ANALYSIS

062 어법 선택 & 연결어

When life deals us multiple losses, we create unnecessary burdens for **[us / ourselves]** if we continue to postpone the tears and the acknowledgment of pain. Over time, we **[may find / may have found] [it / them]** more and more **[difficult / difficultly]** to cry about anything. Or we may suddenly cry for reasons **[total / totally] [unrelating / unrelated]** to our pain, as when a television commercial **[sets off us / sets us off]**. Or we may even cry in inappropriate places, as when we burst into tears in a meeting at work. We may be **[stored / storing]** up **[so / such]** a flood of emotions **[where / that]** we become afraid to feel, **[especial / especially]** when we are feeling more **[vulnerable / vulnerably]** with a new loss. We may begin to avoid topics **[what / that]** might make us **[cry / to cry]**. Others may avoid us, **[frightening / frightened]** by the urgency of our tears when we do **[to express / express]** our sadness. Sorrow is not one of the more popular feelings **[because / because of]** we must be willing **[allow / to allow] [them / it] [overtaking / to overtake] [us / ourselves]**.

주제문 우리는 눈물과 고통을 인정하지 않으면 스스로에게 부담감을 주는 것이다.

(When life / deals us multiple losses), / we / create unnecessary burdens / (for ourselves) / {if we / continue to postpone the tears and the acknowledgment of pain}.

- When: 〈종·접〉 / life: S 인생이 / deals: V / us: I.O / multiple losses: D.O — 다양한 상실을 우리에게 나누어 줄 때
- we: S 우리는 / create: V / unnecessary burdens: O 불필요한 부담을 만든다
- for ourselves: 〈재귀대명사〉 스스로에게
- if: 〈종·접〉 / we: S 만약 우리가 / continue: V / to postpone the tears and the acknowledgment of pain: O 눈물과 고통의 인정을 계속해서 미룬다면

인생이 다양한 상실을 우리에게 나누어 줄 때, 우리가 눈물과 고통의 인정을 계속해서 미룬다면 우리는 스스로에게 불필요한 부담을 만든다.

노트
- deal + IO + DO (4) : ~에게 …을 나눠주다
- 〈4형식을 3형식으로 바꿀 때 사용하는 전치사〉 : 전치사 to를 취하는 동사

주어 (A)	+	동사(B)	+	간접목적어 (C: 사람/동물)	+	직접목적어 (D: 사물)	(4)
		give, bring, pass, send, show, sell, hand, lend, offer, teach, tell, buy, build, choose, find, leave, make, order, prepare, ask 등 수여동사					

→ 주어(A) + 동사(B) + 직접목적어(D: 사물) + 전치사(to) + 간접목적어(C: 사람/동물) (3)

- 〈재귀대명사의 관용적 표현〉

help oneself to ~	~을 마음껏 먹다
enjoy oneself	즐기다
in spite of oneself	자신도 모르게
beside oneself	제정신이 아닌
by oneself	홀로
to oneself	혼자
of oneself	저절로, 제 스스로
for oneself	스스로
of itself	저절로
between ourselves	우리끼리 얘긴데
make oneself understood	~와 의사소통하다

- 〈3형식에서 목적어 자리에 to R / Ring 둘 다 사용 가능〉

주어	완전타동사		목적어
주어	begin	~을 시작하다	to R/Ring (의미 차이 없음)
	cease	~을 중단하다	
	continue	~을 계속하다	
	deserve	~할 가치/자격/권리가 있다	
	dislike	~을 싫어하다	
	hate	~을 싫어하다	
	like	~을 좋아하다	
	love	~을 사랑하다	
	neglect	~하는 것을 소홀히 하다	
	prefer	~쪽을 좋아하다	
	require	~을 요구하다	
	start	~을 시작하다	

주제문에 대한 설명 옳음에 관한 여러 가지 관점

(Over time), / we / may find (A) [it / them] / more and more difficult / (to cry about anything).

- Over time: 시간이 흐름에 / we: S 우리는 / may find: V 알 수 있다 / it / them: 〈가O〉
- more and more difficult: O.C 점점 더 어려워진다는 것을
- to cry about anything: 〈진O〉 어떤 것에 대해 우는 것이

시간이 흐름에 따라 우리는 어떤 것에 대해 우는 것이 점점 더 어려운 일이 된다는 것을 알 수 있다.

노트 ■ over time : 오랜 시간에 걸쳐, 시간이 지나면서, 시간이 흐르는 동안

■ 〈find / found〉

원형	과거	과거분사	현재분사	뜻
find	found	found	finding	v. 발견하다, 알다
found	founded	founded	founding	v. 설립하다

■ 〈가목적어 it / 진목적어 to R〉

주어	동사	가목적어	목적격보어	의미상 주어	진목적어
–	consider feel find make think	it(this, that, there 사용 불가)	형용사 명사	for+목적격 (주어와 진목적어의 주체가 다를 경우 사용)	to 동사원형
we	may find	it	more and more difficult	–	to cry

Or / we / may (suddenly) cry for reasons / (which are) (totally unrelated to our pain), / (as when a television commercial sets us off).

(S: we 우리는 / V: may cry 이유로 갑자기 울 수 있다 / O: reasons / 〈부사〉 totally / 〈과거분사〉 unrelated 우리의 고통과 전혀 관계없는 / 〈전치사〉 as 〈종·접〉 when / S: a television commercial / V: sets / O: us — 텔레비전 광고가 우리로 하여금 울음을 터뜨리게 할 때처럼)

또는 텔레비전 광고가 우리로 하여금 울음을 터뜨리게 할 때처럼 우리의 고통과 전혀 관계없는 이유로 갑자기 울 수 있다.

노트
■ cry for : ~로 소리치다[울다]
■ be unrelated to : ~와 관계가 없다
■ set A off : A를 터뜨리다, 유발하다
■ 〈주격관계대명사+be동사 생략〉

–	생략할 수 있음	
명사 (선행사)	(주격관계대명사 +be동사)	현재분사(Ring) – 능동(~하고 있는)
		과거분사(p.p.) – 수동(~되어진, 당한)
		명사
		형용사(구) (~하는, ~할)
		부사
		전치사구
reasons	(which/that are)	unrelated

■ 〈이어동사〉

타동사	명사	부사	(○)
타동사	부사	명사	(○)
타동사	대명사	부사	(○)
타동사	부사	대명사	(×)
sets	off	us	(×)

■ 〈as when+주어+동사〉 : ~할 때처럼

			이어동사		
as	when	a television commercial	sets	us	off.
전치사	종속접속사	주어	동사	목적어	부사
	명사절 : 전치사의 목적어				

Or / we / may (even) cry (in inappropriate places), / {as when we burst into tears / (in a meeting) / (at work)}.

(또는 / S: we 우리는 / V: may cry 심지어 울 수 있다 / 부적절한 장소에서 / 〈전치사〉 as 〈종·접〉 when / S: we / V: burst into tears 우리가 눈물을 터뜨릴 때처럼 / 회의를 하던 중에 / 직장에서)

또는 우리가 직장에서 회의를 하던 중에 눈물을 터뜨릴 때처럼 우리는 심지어 부적절한 장소에서 울 수 있다.

노트 ■ burst into tears : 갑자기 울음을 터뜨리다

We / may be storing up such a flood of emotions / (B) (where / that we become afraid to feel), / (especially) {when we are feeling more vulnerable / (with a new loss)}.

(S: We 우리는 / V: may be storing up / O: such a flood of emotions 감정의 홍수를 묻어두고 있는 것일 수도 있다 / 〈목·관〉 where / that / S: we / V: become / S.C: afraid 우리가 느끼기를 두려워하는 / 특히 / 〈종·접〉 when / S: we / V: are feeling / S.C: more vulnerable 우리가 더 취약하다고 느낄 때 / 새로운 상실에)

특히 우리가 새로운 상실에 더 취약하다고 느낄 때 우리가 느끼기를 두려워하는 감정의 홍수를 묻어두고 있는 것일 수 있다.

노트
■ store up A : A를 묻어 두다
■ be afraid to R : ~하는 게 두렵다
■ 〈관사의 위치〉

so / how / too / as	형용사	a/an	명사
such / what / many / quite / rather / half	a/an	형용사	명사

■ 〈원인과 결과를 동시에 나타내는 표현〉 : '너무 ~해서 그 결과 …하다' (종속접속사 that 생략 가능)

원인(너무 ~해서)				결과(그 결과 ~하다)		
so	형용사	a(n)+명사		(that)	주어	동사 ~
such	a(n)	형용사	명사	that	주어	동사 ~

결과	so	(that)	원인
원인	, so	(that)	결과

■ 〈서술적 형용사〉 : 명사 수식 불가, 보어로만 사용

상태형용사	afraid, alike, alive, alone, amiss, ashamed, asleep, astray, awake, aware 등
감정형용사	content, fond, glad, ignorant, pleasant, proud, unable, upset, well, worth 등

■ 〈be / get / become 구별〉

동사	용법
be	주어가 어떤 상태인지 표현
get	주어가 겪고 있는 상태의 변화를 표현
become	주어가 변화를 겪고 어떻게 되었는지 변화의 결과 표현

■ 〈감각동사〉

감각동사	주격보어(S.C)	
feel, look, seem, sound, taste, appear, smell	형용사(분사 : 현재분사/과거분사)	
	명사	
	like(전치사)	(that)+주어+동사
		(동)명사
	~~alike~~	
	~~likely~~	

■ 〈likely / alike / like〉

likely	형용사	~일 것 같은 (be to 동사원형 : ~일 것 같다)
	부사	아마(probably)
alike	서술적 형용사 (보어로만 사용, 명사 수식 불가)	동일한
	부사	똑같이
like	전치사	~처럼
	동사	좋아하다

We / may begin to avoid topics / (that might make us cry).
(We: S, 우리는 / may begin: V / to avoid topics: O, 주제를 피하기 시작할 수 있다 / topics: 〈선행사〉 / that: 〈주·관〉 / might make: V / us: O / cry: O.C, 우리를 울게 만드는 것 같은)

우리를 울게 만드는 주제를 피하기 시작할 수 있다.

노트 ■ begin+목적어(to R / Ring) : ~하는 것을 시작하다
■ 〈주격관계대명사절의 수의 일치〉 : 선행사를 포함하고 있는 관계대명사 what 사용 불가

	주격관계대명사절		
선행사	주격관계대명사	~~주어~~	동사
topics	that		might make

■ 〈make 사역동사〉

make	목적어	목적격보어	해석
〈사역동사〉	명사/ 명사 상당어구	동사원형(R)	~가 …하도록 시키다
		과거분사(p.p)	~가 …하게 당하다
make	us	cry	–

Others / may avoid us, / (frightened by the urgency of our tears) / {when we (do) express our sadness}.
(Others: S, 다른 사람들은 / may avoid: V / us: O, 우리를 피할 수 있다 / frightened: 〈분사구문〉, 눈물의 절박함에 놀라 / when: 〈종·접〉 / we: S / express: V / our sadness: O, 우리가 정말 슬픔을 표현할 때)

우리가 슬픔을 표현할 때 눈물의 절박함에 놀라 다른 사람들은 우리를 피할 수 있다.

노트 ■ be frightened by : ~에 겁먹다
■ 〈분사구문 – 문미〉 : 주절과 분사구문의 위치가 서로 바뀌어도 무관

주절		종속절(→ 분사구문)			
주어	동사	종속 접속사	주어	동사 : 상황에 맞게 아래처럼 바뀜	
		〈그대로 사용하면 의미 강조〉	(주절의 주어와 같으면 생략하고, 다르면 주격으로 사용함)	(being)	Ring(현재분사)
				(having been) 생략 가능	p.p.(과거분사)
					형용사
					명사
Otheres	may avoid	–	–	–	frightened

■ 〈동사 강조 표현〉

do / does / did	+동사원형(R)
=정말로(really, certainly)	

주제문(재진술) 우리는 슬픔이 우리에게 다가오는 것을 기꺼이 받아들여야 한다.

Sorrow / is not one (of the more popular feelings) / (because we must be willing to allow it to overtake (C) [ourselves / us]).
(Sorrow: S, 슬픔은 / is not: V / one: S.C, 더 인기 있는 감정 중 하나가 아니다 / because: 〈종·접〉 / we: S / must be willing to allow: V / it: O / to overtake: O.C, 왜냐하면 우리는 슬픔이 우리에게 불시에 닥치는 것을 기꺼이 허락해야 하기 때문에)

우리는 슬픔이 우리에게 불시에 닥치는 것을 기꺼이 허락해야 하기 때문에 슬픔은 더 인기 있는 감정 중 하나가 아니다.

노트 ■ be willing to R : 기꺼이 ~하다
■ 〈one of+복수명사〉 : ~ 중의 하나

one (주어 : 단수)	of	복수명사
one		feelings

■ 〈원인/이유〉 : ~ 때문에

전치사	because of	+(동)명사 / 명사 상당어구
	due to	
	for	
	on account of	
	owing to	
	thanks to	
종속접속사	as	+주어+동사 ~
	because	
	now(that)	
	since	

■ 〈5형식 불완전타동사의 목적격보어〉 : 수동태 전환 시, 2형식 문장(be p.p. +to R)

주어	불완전타동사	목적어	목적격보어
–	advise / allow / ask / assume / beg / cause / command / compel / condition / decide / design / drive / enable / encourage / expect / forbid / force / instruct / intend / invite / lead / like / motivate / order / permit / persuade / predispose / pressure / program / push / require / teach / tell / train / trust / urge / want / warn / wish 등	–	to 동사원형

■ 〈재귀대명사 vs. 대명사〉

		주어와 다름	주어와 동일
주어	~	대명사	재귀대명사
we		us	ourselves

▶ (A), (B), (C)의 각 네모 안에서 어법에 맞는 표현으로 가장 적절한 것은?

	(A)		(B)		(C)
①	it	……	where	……	ourselves
②	it	……	that	……	us
③	it	……	where	……	us
④	them	……	that	……	ourselves
⑤	them	……	where	……	us

정답 | ②

해설 | (A) [가목적어 it] : 'find＋it＋목적격보어＋to 동사원형' 구조에서 it은 가목적어로 this / that / there 등을 사용할 수 없고, 목적격보어 자리에는 형용사와 명사를 사용하고, to 동사원형은 진목적어로 가목적어 it 자리에 넣어서 해석하면 된다.

(B) [관계부사 where vs. 목적격관계대명사 that] : 밑줄 친 부분 뒤에 있는 we become afraid to feel에서 타동사 feel은 뒤에 목적어를 가져야 하는데 그 목적어가 없고 그 목적어 역할을 대신하고 있는 앞에 있는 emotions를 선행사로 가지고 있기 때문에 목적격관계대명사 that이 어법상 올바른 표현이다. 관계부사 where는 뒤 문장이 완전한 절이 나와야 하기 때문에 어법상 올바르지 않다.

(C) [재귀대명사 vs. 대명사] : 종속접속사 because로 시작하는 종속절에서 주어는 we이고 동사는 must be willing to allow이다. allow 동사는 5형식으로 사용될 경우에 'allow＋목적어＋목적격보어' 구조로 사용되는데 이때 목적격보어 자리에 to부정사를 사용할 수 있다. 따라서 to overtake 이하가 목적격보어인데 밑줄 친 ourselves는 재귀대명사로 주어 we와 동일인이 된다. 이때 주의 사항은 5형식일 경우 목적격보어(to overtake 이하)는 목적어(it＝sorrow)와 주술관계를 가진다. 즉 목적어가 주어 역할을 하고 목적격보어는 술어(동사) 역할을 하는 것이 주술관계이다. 더 쉽게 말해 목적격보어를 하는 행위자 이자 주체가 문장의 주어가 아니라 목적어라는 것이다. 그리하여 주어(we)와 재귀대명사(ourselves)가 to overtake 이하를 하는 행위의 주체가 아니라 목적어로 사용된 it(＝sorrow)가 to overtake 이하의 주체이기 때문에 대명사 us가 어법상 올바르다.

Words

- ☐ multiple
- ☐ loss
- ☐ burden
- ☐ postpone
- ☐ acknowledgment
- ☐ commercial
- ☐ inappropriate
- ☐ vulnerable
- ☐ urgency
- ☐ overtake

Phrases

- ☐ over time
- ☐ be unrelated to
- ☐ as when＋주어＋동사
- ☐ store up A
- ☐ be frightened by
- ☐ cry for
- ☐ set A off
- ☐ burst into tears
- ☐ be afraid to R
- ☐ be willing to R

우선순위 영단어 역대 수능 기출＋전국 모의고사 기출＋EBS 기출＋교과서 기출 빈출 어휘

단어	뜻	단어	뜻	단어	뜻
file	v. 기사 따위를 보내다	finite	a. 한정되어 있는	firearm	n. 화기
firewood	n. 장작	fist	n. 주먹	fit in	v. 부합하다
flea market	n. 벼룩시장	flesh	n. 살	flight	n. 계단
fling	v. 던지다	flit	v. 옮겨 다니다	flock	v. 떼 짓다
flour	n. 밀가루	flow	v. 흐르다	fluctuate	v. 오르내리다
fluctuation	n. 변동	fluid	a. 유동적인	focused	a. 집중한
follow	v. 따르다	follow-up	뒤따라 나오는	fondly	ad. 다정하게
for ages	오랫동안	for certain	확실히	for the sake of	~을 위해서
forbid	v. 금지하다	forefather	n. 조상	forefront	n. 선두
forehead	n. 이마	foreshadow	v. ~의 전조를 보이다	forested	a. 숲으로 뒤덮힌
foretell	v. 예견하다	forfeit	v. 상실하다	forget	v. 잊다
formality	n. 격식	format	n. 포맷	formative	a. 형성[발달]에 중요한
formulation	n. 공식(화)	fortress	n. 요새	forum	n. 공개토론
fossilize	v. 화석화하다	foster parent	n. 양부모	founder	n. 설립자
frail	a. 약한	framework	n. 뼈대	frantic	a. 광란의
fraud	n. 사기	free of	~에서 벗어나는	free will	n. 자유의지
frequently	ad. 빈번하게	fresh water	n. 담수	front line	최전선
fruit	n. 성과물	frustrate	n. (계획, 노력 따위를) 실패	fulfilling	a. 성취감을 주는

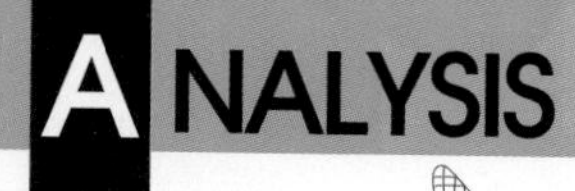

변형문제

01 다음 글을 읽고, |조건|에 맞게 주어진 제목을 완성하시오.

| 조건 |
* (A)는 3단어로 쓸 것
* 본문에 있는 단어만을 그대로 사용할 것

When life deals us multiple losses, we create unnecessary burdens for ourselves if we continue to postpone the tears and the acknowledgment of pain. Over time, we may find it more and more difficult to cry about anything. Or we may suddenly cry for reasons totally unrelated to our pain, as when a television commercial sets us off. Or we may even cry in inappropriate places, as when we burst into tears in a meeting at work. We may be storing up such a flood of emotions that we become afraid to feel, especially when we are feeling more vulnerable with a new loss. We may begin to avoid topics that might make us cry. Others may avoid us, frightened by the urgency of our tears when we do express our sadness. Sorrow is not one of the more popular feelings because we must be willing to allow it to overtake us.

⬇

The need (A) ____________ ____________ ____________.

02 다음 글을 읽고, |조건|에 맞게 빈칸 (A), (B), (C)를 채우시오.

| 조건 |
* (A)는 2단어, (B), (C)는 1단어로 쓸 것
* [보기]에서 선택한 단어를 그대로 한 번씩만 쓸 것(단, (A)의 경우, [보기] 외의 1단어를 추가할 것)

[보기] death / happiness / depression / burst / vulnerable / anxiety / emotional / fall / end / sorrow / begin / strong / uncomfortable / unforgettable / keep

When life deals us multiple losses, we create unnecessary burdens for ourselves if we continue to postpone the tears and the acknowledgment of pain. Over time, we may find it more and more difficult to cry about anything. Or we may suddenly cry for reasons totally unrelated to our pain, as when a television commercial sets us off. Or we may even cry in inappropriate places, as when we (A) ____________ ____________ tears in a meeting at work. We may be storing up such a flood of emotions that we become afraid to feel, especially when we are feeling more (B) ____________ with a new loss. We may begin to avoid topics that might make us cry. Others may avoid us, frightened by the urgency of our tears when we do express our sadness. (C) ____________ is not one of the more popular feelings because we must be willing to allow it to overtake us.

03 다음 글을 읽고, |조건|에 맞게 요약문을 완성하시오.

| 조건 |
* (A), (B), (C)는 각각 다르게 1단어로 쓸 것
* [보기]에서 선택한 단어를 한 번씩만 쓸 것
* 필요한 경우, 문맥과 어법에 맞게 변형할 것

[보기] delay / level / severity / accept / subjects / prevent / stop / emotions / difficulty

When life deals us multiple losses, we create unnecessary burdens for ourselves if we continue to postpone the tears and the acknowledgment of pain. Over time, we may find it more and more difficult to cry about anything. Or we may suddenly cry for reasons totally unrelated to our pain, as when a television commercial sets us off. Or we may even cry in inappropriate places, as when we burst into tears in a meeting at work. We may be storing up such a flood of emotions that we become afraid to feel, especially when we are feeling more vulnerable with a new loss. We may begin to avoid topics that might make us cry. Others may avoid us, frightened by the urgency of our tears when we do express our sadness. Sorrow is not one of the more popular feelings because we must be willing to allow it to overtake us.

⬇

(A) ____________ the tears and the (B) ____________ of pain makes us hard to cry and unexpectedly makes us sob in any inappropriate places. Therefore, people do not want to bring up (C) ____________ leading to tears and are afraid by the urgency of tears when sadness is expressed.

04 다음 글을 읽고, |조건|에 맞게 주제문을 완성하시오.

| 조건 |
* (A), (B), (C)는 각각 다르게 1단어로 쓸 것
* 본문에 있는 단어만을 그대로 사용할 것

When life deals us multiple losses, we create unnecessary burdens for ourselves if we continue to postpone the tears and the acknowledgment of pain. Over time, we may find it more and more difficult to cry about anything. Or we may suddenly cry for reasons totally unrelated to our pain, as when a television commercial sets us off. Or we may even cry in inappropriate places, as when we burst into tears in a meeting at work. We may be storing up such a flood of emotions that we become afraid to feel, especially when we are feeling more vulnerable with a new loss. We may begin to avoid topics that might make us cry. Others may avoid us, frightened by the urgency of our tears when we do express our sadness. Sorrow is not one of the more popular feelings because we must be willing to allow it to overtake us.

⬇

If you do not want to struggle with loads of (A) ____________, do no (B) ____________ tears and pain because you have to accept the fact that unfavourite feelings like sadness or (C) ____________ occur unexpectedly.

어법(밑줄/네모)

글의 논리	Spotlight
제목	공익연계 마케팅의 특성
주제	공익연계 마케팅은 활동에 참여하는 모든 사람들에게 이득을 줄 수도 있다.

PRACTICE 01

063 어법 선택 & 연결어

The past couple of decades **[saw / have seen]** **[many / much]** corporations joining with charities in **[what / that]** **[calls / is called]** "cause-related marketing" efforts, **[which / in which]** a corporation donates a certain percentage of **[its / their]** profits from a particular item. The nonprofit group and the corporation advertise the arrangement and encourage people who may be **[choosen / choosing]** among similar products **[to choose / chosen]** the one **[what / that]** also **[benefit / benefits]** the charity. Variations on this theme include corporations **[what / that]** **[offer / offers]** to give a percentage of profits to a certain kind of organization or who **[allow / allows]** customers to nominate groups **[what / that]** **[should receive / should have received]** corporate funding. Cause-related marketing has benefited **[many / much]** organizations by **[allowance / allowing]** shoppers **[to feel / feeling]** **[what / that]** **[its / their]** spending can also serve a charitable purpose. The drawback is **[what / that]** these donors do not become part of an organization's donor base.

관점 공익연계 마케팅은 기업이 이익의 일정 비율을 기부하는 것이다.

The past couple of decades (S, 과거 이십여 년은) / ① have seen (V〈현재완료〉) many corporations (O) joining with charities (O.C) (많은 기업들이 자선 단체들과 합류하는 것을 보아왔고) / {in (what (〈주·관〉) is called (V〈수동태〉) "cause-related marketing" (S.C, "공익연계 마케팅") efforts) (O, 활동이라 불리는 것에서)}, / {in which (〈전치사+관·대〉, 그 활동 안에서) a corporation (S, 기업은) donates (V, 기부한다) a certain percentage of its profits (O, 이익의 일정 비율을) / (from a particular item) (특정한 상품에서 나온)}.

과거 이십여 년은 많은 기업들이 "공익연계 마케팅" 활동이라 불리는 것에서 자선 단체들과 합류하는 것을 보아왔고, 그 활동 안에서 기업은 특정 상품에서 나온 이익의 일정 비율을 기부한다.

노트
■ join with : ~와 행동을 같이 하다
■ 〈지각동사〉

지각동사		목적어	목적격보어
see	보다	-	〈목적어와 목적격보어의 관계가 능동일 때〉 동사원형(R) – 완료 현재진행(Ring) – 진행, 순간, 찰나, 계속 〈목적어와 목적격보어의 관계가 수동일 때〉 과거분사(p.p.) 〈to부정사는 불가〉 : 수동태 문장 전환 시 가능
watch	보다		
look at	보다		
behold	보다		
(over) hear	듣다		
listen to	듣다		
feel	느끼다		
observe	관찰하다		
perceive	인식하다		
notice	인식하다		
have sen		many corporations	joining

■ 〈부정수량형용사〉 : 막연한 수나 양의 정도를 표시하는 형용사

수(數)	few(a few), some(any), a lot of(lots of), a good(or great), plenty of, enough, all, no, many	복수명사+복수동사
양(量)	little(a little), some(any), a lot of, a good(or great), deal of, plenty of, enough, all, no, much	단수명사+단수동사

■ 〈전치사의 목적어로 사용된 주격관계대명사 what〉 : 선행사가 필요한 주격 관계대명사 that/which 사용 불가

전치사	목적어 : 주격관계대명사 what절				
in	~~선행사~~	what	~~주어~~	동사	주격보어
		주격관계대명사 : 선행사를 포함한 관계대명사 (=the thing(s) which/that ~) : ~하는 것은/이		is called	"cause-related marketing" efforts

■ 〈call 동사의 쓰임〉 : ~을 …라고 부르다(수동태 시, be called+주격보어)

주어	불완전타동사	목적어	목적격보어
	call		명사
			형용사

■ 〈전치사+관계대명사 vs. 관계대명사〉 : 관계부사와 같기 때문에 뒤 문장이 완전한 문장이 나온다. 전치사는 맨 뒤로 보낼 수 있는데 이때 전치사의 목적어가 없기 때문에 관계대명사절은 불완전하다.

선행사	전치사+관계대명사 =관계부사	주어	동사			완전한 문장
	관계대명사		동사	전치사	~~목적어~~	불완전한 문장

관점 비영리 단체와 기업은 상품을 선택하는 사람들에게 자선 단체에게 이롭기도 한 선택을 하도록 권장한다.

The nonprofit group and the corporation / advertise

S_1 비영리 단체와 기업은 S_2 / V_1 그러한

the arrangement / and / encourage people / {who may

O 합의를 광고한다 / 그리고 / V_2 사람들에게 권장한다 O〈선행사〉 / 〈주·관〉

be choosing (among similar products)} ② to choose

V / 〈전치사〉 O 선택하게 되는 유사한 상품들 중에서 / O.C 것을 선택하도록

the one / (that also benefits the charity).

〈선행사〉 / 〈주·관〉 V O 자선 단체에게 이롭기도 한

비영리 단체와 기업은 그러한 합의를 광고하고 유사한 상품들 중에서 선택을 하게 되는 사람들에게 자선 단체에게 이롭기도 한 것을 선택하도록 권장한다.

노트 ■ 〈주격관계대명사절〉 : 선행사를 포함하고 있는 관계대명사 what 사용 불가

	주격관계대명사절		
선행사	주격관계대명사	~~주어~~	동사
people	who		may be choosing
the one	that		benefits

■ 〈5형식 불완전타동사의 목적격보어〉 : 수동태 전환 시, 2형식 문장(be p.p.+to R)

주어	불완전타동사	목적어	목적격보어
–	advise / allow / ask / assume / beg / cause / command / compel / condition / decide / design / drive / enable / encourage / expect / forbid / force / instruct / intend / invite / lead / like / motivate / order / permit / persuade / predispose / pressure / program / push / require / teach / tell / train / trust / urge / want / warn / wish 등	–	to 동사원형

■ 〈between vs. among〉

전치사	between	~ 사이에	둘 사이	혼용
	among		셋 이상	

관점 이러한 방식의 변형으로는 이익의 일부를 특정 집단에 주겠다고 하는 기업도 있다.

Variations (on this theme) / include corporations / {that

S〈선행사〉 이러한 주제에서의 변형은 / V 기업들은 포함한다 O / 〈주·관〉

offer to give a percentage of profits / (to a certain kind

V / O 이익의 일부를 주겠다고 제안하는 / 특정 종류의

of organization)} / or / {(who ③ allows customers to

단체에게 / 혹은 / 〈주·관〉 V O 고객이 집단을 지명하도록

nominate groups) / (that should receive corporate

〈선행사〉 O.C 허용하는 / 〈주·관〉 V 기업의 재정 지원을 받아야 하는

funding)}.

O

이러한 주제에서의 변형은 특정 종류의 단체에게 이익의 일부를 주겠다고 제안하거나 고객이 기업의 재정 지원을 받아야 하는 집단을 지명하도록 허용하는 기업들을 포함한다.

노트 ■ allow+목적어+목적격보어(to R) : ~가 …하도록 허용하다

■ 〈관계대명사의 이중 한정〉 : 2개의 관계대명사절이 동일한 선행사를 수식하는 경우

	주격관계대명사절			대등접속사	주격관계대명사절		
선행사	주격관계대명사	~~주어~~	동사	or	주격관계대명사	~~주어~~	동사
Variations	that		offer		who		allow

■ 〈목적어 자리에 to부정사를 취하는 완전타동사〉

주어	완전타동사	목적어
–	afford / agree / ask / attempt / care / choose / claim / dare / decide / demand / desire / determine / elect / expect / fail / guarantee / hope / intend / learn / manage / need / offer / plan / pretend / promise / refuse / resolve / seek / threaten / volunteer / want / wish 등	to 동사원형

■ 〈주격관계대명사절의 수의 일치〉 : 선행사를 포함하고 있는 관계대명사 what 사용 불가

	주격관계대명사절		
선행사	주격관계대명사	~~주어~~	동사
groups	that		should receive

관점 공익연계 마케팅은 쇼핑객들이 자선 목적에 도움이 된다고 느끼게 만든다.

Cause-related marketing / has benefited many

S 공익연계 마케팅은 / V〈현재완료〉 많은 단체들에게

organizations / [by allowing shoppers to feel / {that ④

O 이익을 주어왔다 / 〈동명사〉 O O.C 쇼핑객들이 느끼도록 함으로써 / 〈종·접〉 그들의

their spending can (also) serve a charitable purpose}].

S V O / O 소비가 자선 목적에 도움이 될 수도 있다고

공익연계 마케팅은 쇼핑객들로 하여금 그들의 소비가 자선 목적에 도움이 될 수도 있다고 느끼도록 함으로써 많은 단체들에게 이익을 주어왔다.

노트 ■ by+동명사 : ~함으로써

■ 〈what vs. that〉

	관계대명사(불완전한 문장)	접속사(완전한 문장)
what	○ 선행사를 포함하고 있기 때문에 what 앞에 선행사 불필요	×
that	○ that 앞에 선행사 필요	○

관점 단점은 이러한 기부자들이 기부 단체의 일부가 되지 않는다는 것이다.

The drawback / is / (⑤ that these donors / do not

S 단점은 / V 점이다 / 〈종·접〉 S 이러한 기부자들이 / 어떤

become part of an organization's donor base).
V S.C
S.C
단체의 기부자 기반의 일부가 되지 않는다는

단점은 이러한 기부자들이 어떤 단체의 기부자 기반의 일부가 되지 않는다는 점이다.

노트 ■ 〈become 동사 쓰임〉

become	〈주격보어〉	(2형식)
	명사	(~으로) 되다
	형용사	
	과거분사	
	〈목적어〉	(3형식)
	명사	어울리다, 잘 맞다(진행형/수동태 불가)

▶ 다음 글의 밑줄 친 부분 중, 어법상 틀린 것은?

정답 | ③ allows → allow

해설 | ③ [선행사와 주격관계대명사절 안에 있는 동사의 수의 일치] : '선행사＋주격관계대명사＋동사' 구조에서 동사는 선행사와 수의 일치를 시켜야 한다. 이 문장의 주어는 복수명사 Variations이고 동사는 include이고 목적어는 복수명사 corporations이다. corporations뒤에 있는 that은 주격관계대명사로 선행사를 corporations로 받고, 대등접속사 or 뒤에 나오는 who 이하 역시 corporations를 선행사로 취하는 주격관계대명사이다. 이때 선행사 corporations가 복수명사이기 때문에 allows가 아니라 allow가 어법상 올바르다.

오답 | ① [동사의 시제 – 현재완료] : 현재완료 형태는 'have / has p.p.(과거분사)'이고 의미는 과거부터 지금까지 계속 이어져 온 일을 나타낸다. 주어인 The past couple of decades(과거 이십여 년) 동안 기업(corporations)들은 자선단체에 합류했고 이익의 일정 비율을 기부한다(donates)라는 의미를 보았을 때 밑줄 친 현재완료가 어법상 올바르다. 참고로 과거완료(had p.p.)는 과거 이전에 일이 과거에 이미 끝난 일에 주로 사용되기 때문에 현재 일정 비율을 기부한다(donates)는 의미로 인해 어법상 올바르지 않다.

② [to부정사 vs. 동명사] : 'encourage＋목적어＋목적격보어' 구조에서 5형식을 취하는 불완전타동사 encourage는 목적격보어 자리에 to부정사를 사용해야 어법상 올바르기 때문에 동명사 choosing이나 동사원형 choose를 사용할 수 없고 밑줄 친 to부정사 to choose가 올바르다.

④ [대명사의 수의 일치] : 전치사 by 뒤에 있는 동명사 allowing 뒤를 보면, 'allow＋목적어＋목적격보어' 구조에서 목적격보어 자리에는 to부정사를 사용한다. 이때 목적어와 목적격보어의 관계는 주술관계로 즉 목적어가 주어 역할을 하고 목적격보어는 술어(동사) 역할을 한다. allowing의 목적어는 shoppers이고 to feel 이하는 목적격보어이다. 이때 feel은 타동사로 that절을 목적어로 취할 수 있는데 that은 종속접속사로 뒤 문장이 완전한 문장이 나와야 한다. that절 안에서 주어는 their spending이고 동사는 can serve이다. 이때 주어 their spending에서 their는 allowing의 목적어로 사용된 복수명사 shoppers를 받는 소유대명사이기 때문에 단수형으로 his 또는 her를 사용할 수 없다.

⑤ [종속접속사 that vs. 관계대명사 what] : 종속접속사 that이 이끄는 종속절은 완전한 문장이 나오고, 관계대명사 what이 이끄는 관계대명사절은 불완전한 문장이 나온다. 이 둘 모두 명사절로 문장에서 주어, 목적어, 보어로 사용될 수 있고 의미 역시 '~것'으로 동일하지만 구조의 차이가 존재한다. 이 문장에서 주어는 The drawback이고 동사는 is이다. be동사 is는 '~이다'라는 의미를 가지는 불완전자동사로 2형식 구조로 사용된다. that절 이하가 주격보어로 그 안에서 주어는 these donors이고 동사는 do not become이고 part of an organization's donor bases는 주격보어로, that절 이하는 2형식으로 완전한 문장이기 때문에 의미는 동일(~ 것)하지만 불완전한 문장이 나와야 하는 관계대명사 what을 사용할 수 없다.

Words

- ☐ decade
- ☐ corporation
- ☐ charity
- ☐ effort
- ☐ donate
- ☐ profit
- ☐ particular
- ☐ item
- ☐ nonprofit
- ☐ advertise
- ☐ arrangement
- ☐ encourage
- ☐ benefit
- ☐ variation
- ☐ theme
- ☐ nominate
- ☐ funding
- ☐ drawback
- ☐ donor

Phrases

- ☐ join with
- ☐ by＋동명사

우선순위 영단어 역대 수능 기출＋전국 모의고사 기출＋EBS 기출＋교과서 기출 빈출 어휘

단어	뜻	단어	뜻	단어	뜻
fume	n. 연기	functional	a. 실용적인	fund	v. ~에 자금을 제공하다
fundamental	a. 기본적인	fund-raising	n. 모금	funnel	n. 깔때기
furnish	v. 공급하다	gadget	n. 장치	gaseous	a. 가스의
gatekeeper	n. 정문 수위	gather	v. 모이다	gatherer	n. 채집인
geek	n. 괴짜	gender equality	n. 성 평등	general	a. 일반적인

변형문제

01 다음 글을 읽고, |조건|에 맞게 요약문을 완성하시오.

| 조건 |
* (A)는 2단어, (B)는 3단어로 쓸 것
* [보기]에서 선택한 단어를 그대로 한 번 씩만 쓸 것(단, (B)의 경우, [보기] 외의 1단어를 추가할 것)

[보기] yearly / make / advertisement / customers / volume / selling / participation / payment / sales / quality / contribution / nomination

The past couple of decades have seen many corporations joining with charities in what is called "cause-related marketing" efforts, in which a corporation donates a certain percentage of its profits from a particular item. The nonprofit group and the corporation advertise the arrangement and encourage people who may be choosing among similar products to choose the one that also benefits the charity. Variations on this theme include corporations that offer to give a percentage of profits to a certain kind of organization or who allow customers to nominate groups that should receive corporate funding. Cause-related marketing has benefited many organizations by allowing shoppers to feel that their spending can also serve a charitable purpose. The drawback is that these donors do not become part of an organization's donor base.

⬇

Through "cause-related marketing", organizations and corporations participated in the effort may have merits. For example, their products' (A) ____________ ____________ noticeably increases and financial support from nonprofit groups is obtained. Also, customers may believe that they (B) ____________ ____________ ____________ to charitable groups.

02 밑줄 친 부분 중 문맥상 옳지 않은 것은?

The past couple of decades have seen many corporations ① joining with charities in what is called "cause-related marketing" efforts, in which a corporation donates a certain percentage of its profits from a particular item. The ② nonprofit group and the corporation advertise the arrangement and encourage people who may be choosing among similar products to choose the one that also benefits the charity. Variations on this theme include corporations that offer to give a percentage of ③ profits to a certain kind of organization or who allow customers to nominate groups that should receive corporate funding. Cause-related marketing has ④ benefited many organizations by allowing shoppers to feel that their spending can also serve a charitable purpose. The ⑤ advantage is that these donors do not become part of an organization's donor base.

03 다음 글을 읽고, |조건|에 맞게 빈칸 (A), (B)를 채우시오.

| 조건 |
* (A), (B)는 각각 다르게 1단어로 쓸 것
* [보기]에서 선택한 단어를 그대로 한 번씩만 쓸 것

[보기] shortage / helpful / way / brink / rise / detrimental / feasible / move / go / grounds / useless / finance / manageable / radical

The past couple of decades have seen many corporations joining with charities in what is called "cause-related marketing" efforts, in which a corporation donates a certain percentage of its profits from a particular item. The nonprofit group and the corporation advertise the arrangement and encourage people who may be choosing among similar products to choose the one that also benefits the charity. Variations on this theme include corporations that offer to give a percentage of profits to a certain kind of organization or who allow customers to nominate groups that should receive corporate funding. Cause-related marketing has benefited many organizations by allowing shoppers to feel that their spending can also serve a charitable purpose. The drawback is that these donors do not become part of an organization's donor base.

⬇

Cause-related marketing might be (A) ______________ to all of those involved in the effort. This is because sales volume of companies' products can be on the (B) ______________, financial support to nonprofit organizations is ensured, and customers can experience that they are assisting charities.

04 다음 글을 읽고, |조건|에 맞게 요약문을 완성하시오.

| 조건 |
* (A)는 1단어, (B)는 2단어로 쓸 것
* 본문에 있는 단어만을 그대로 사용할 것

The past couple of decades have seen many corporations joining with charities in what is called "cause-related marketing" efforts, in which a corporation donates a certain percentage of its profits from a particular item. The nonprofit group and the corporation advertise the arrangement and encourage people who may be choosing among similar products to choose the one that also benefits the charity. Variations on this theme include corporations that offer to give a percentage of profits to a certain kind of organization or who allow customers to nominate groups that should receive corporate funding. Cause-related marketing has benefited many organizations by allowing shoppers to feel that their spending can also serve a charitable purpose. The drawback is that these donors do not become part of an organization's donor base.

⬇

According to the paragraph above, "cause-related marketing" is a mutually beneficial collaboration between a (A) ______________ and a (B) ______________ ______________ for the aim of sales promotion.

UNIT 16

어법(밑줄/네모)

글의 논리	Story
제목	진정한 자아의 발견으로 가는 여정
주제	진정한 자아를 찾아가는 모험은 인생에서 가장 보람 있는 모험일 것이다.

PRACTICE 02

064 어법 선택 & 연결어

The journey to **[discover / discovering]** your authentic self **[promise / promises]** to be the **[almost / most] [rewarding / rewarded]** adventure of your life. When you know **[you / yourself]**, you are free. You have a power and presence **[what / that] [radiate / radiates]** from **[deep / deeply]** within and **[shine / shines]** out **[confident / confidently]** into the world. You did not come into this life to suffer, to **[manipulate / be manipulated]** and **[deny / denied]**. **[What / Whatever]** binds you and keeps you **[living / from living]** your truth is false and **[can shade / can be shed]**. **[It / This]** takes courage to embrace your authentic self and **[live / lives]** life on your own terms. (   ) to be **[unique / uniquely]** you, to listen within and love **[you / yourself]** for all of your weaknesses and missteps, **[is / are] [what / that]** your soul longs for.

이야기 진정한 자아를 찾아가는 모험

The journey / (to discovering your authentic self) /
S 여정은 / (전치사) (동명사) O 여러분의 진정한 자아의 발견으로 이르는

promises to be the most rewarding adventure / (of your life).
V / (현재분사) O 가장 보람 있는 모험이 될 것 같다 / 여러분의 인생에서

여러분의 진정한 자아의 발견으로 이르는 여정은 여러분의 인생에서 가장 보람 있는 모험이 될 것 같다.

노트
- the journey to(전치사)+(동)명사 : ~에 대한 여정
- 〈목적어 자리에 to부정사를 취하는 완전타동사〉

주어	완전타동사	목적어
–	afford / agree / ask / attempt / care / choose / claim / dare / decide / demand / desire / determine / elect / expect / fail / guarantee / hope / intend / learn / manage / need / offer / plan / pretend / promise / refuse / resolve / seek / threaten / volunteer / want / wish 등	to 동사원형

- 〈most / almost / mostly〉

	대명사	형용사	부사
most	대부분의 것들(사람들)	대부분의	가장
almost	–	–	거의
mostly	–	–	주로, 일반적으로

(When you know yourself), / you are free.
(종·접) S V O(재귀대명사) 여러분이 여러분 스스로를 알 때 / S V S.C 여러분은 자유롭다

여러분이 여러분 스스로를 알 때, 여러분은 자유롭다.

노트 〈재귀대명사 vs. 대명사〉

주어	~	주어와 다름 대명사	주어와 동일 재귀대명사
you		you	yourself

You / have a power and presence / {that radiates (from deep within) and shines out (A) [confident / confidently] / (into the world)}.
S 여러분은 / V O₁ O₂ (선행사) 권능감과 존재감을 가지고 있다 / (주·관) V₁ (전치사) O 내면 깊은 곳에서 / V₂ 뿜어져 나와 자신 있게 빛나는 / 세상을 향해

여러분은 내면 깊은 곳에서 뿜어져 나와 세상을 향해 자신 있게 빛나는 권능감과 존재감을 가지고 있다.

노트
- from deep within : 속 깊은 데서
- shine out : (빛이) 확 비치다
- 〈주격관계대명사절의 수의 일치〉 : 선행사를 포함하고 있는 관계대명사 what 사용 불가

선행사	주격관계대명사절		
	주격관계대명사	~~주어~~	동사
a power and presence	that		radiates and shines

- 〈형용사 vs. 부사〉

		형용사	부사
동사		수식 불가	수식 가능
부사		수식 불가	수식 가능
형용사		수식 불가	수식 가능
문장 전체		수식 불가	수식 가능
준동사	to부정사	수식 불가	수식 가능
준동사	동명사	수식 불가	수식 가능
준동사	분사	수식 불가	수식 가능
명사 수식		사용 가능	사용 불가
보어 사용		사용 가능	사용 불가

You / did not come / (into this life) / (to suffer, / to (B) manipulate / be manipulated and (to be) denied).

S: You (여러분은) / V: did not come (온 것은 아니다) / into this life (이 세상에) / to suffer (고통받고) / manipulate / be manipulated and denied (조종당하고, 거부당하기 위해)

여러분은 고통 받고, 조종당하고, 거부당하기 위해 이 세상에 온 것은 아니다.

노트

■ come into : ~에 들어가다

■ 〈to R의 태와 시제〉

태	능동태	to R
	수동태	to be p.p.
시제	단순시제 : 본동사 시제와 동일	to R
	완료시제 : 본동사 시제보다 한 시제 앞선 시제	to have p.p.
	완료 수동	to have been p.p.

■ 〈생략〉 : 대등접속사 and로 병렬구조가 되어 (to be) 생략

to	suffer,	to be manipulated	and	to (생략)	be (생략)	denied.
to부정사 1		to부정사 2	대등접속사	to부정사 3		

{Whatever binds you and keeps you (from living your truth)} / is false and can be shed.

S: Whatever binds(V1) you(O) and keeps(V2) you(O) (from living your truth(O)) (여러분을 속박하고 여러분이 진정한 삶을 사는 것을 방해하는 것은 무엇이든지) / is(V1) false(S.C) and can be shed(V2〈수동태〉) (잘못된 것이고 버려질 수 있는 것이다)

여러분을 속박하고 여러분이 진정한 삶을 사는 것을 방해하는 것은 무엇이든지 잘못된 것이고 버려질 수 있는 것이다.

노트

■ 〈복합관계대명사〉 : 복합관계대명사절은 '관계대명사+ever' 형식을 가지고, 명사와 부사적 역할을 한다.

• 관계대명사절은 what만 명사절이고, who, which, that은 형용사절이다.

종류	명사절	부사절
whoever	anyone who	no matter who
	~하는 누구든지	누가 ~ 하더라도
whomever	anyone whom	no matter whom
	~하는 누구든지	누구를 ~ 하더라도
whichever	anything that	no matter which
	~하는 어떤 것이든	어느 것을 ~ 하더라도
whatever	anything that	no matter what
	~하는 어떤 것이든	무엇을 ~ 하더라도

■ 〈복합관계대명사 whatever절〉 : 모든 구/절은 단수 취급

〈복합관계대명사절〉 : 명사절(주어)							
Whatever	~~주어~~	binds ~	and	keeps ~,	is ~	and	can be shed.
복합관계대명사		동사 1		동사 2	동사 1		동사 2

■ 〈keep 동사의 쓰임〉

(목적어)	현재분사 (Ring)	(~가) …하는 것을 유지하다
	from 동명사 (Ring)	(~가) …하는 것을 막다

It / takes courage / {to embrace your authentic self / and (to) live life (on your own terms)}.

It〈가S〉 (이것은) / takes(V) courage(O) (용기가 필요하다) / {to embrace your authentic self(O) and (to) live life(O) (on your own terms)}〈진S〉 (진정한 자아를 수용하고 삶을 사는 것은 / 그리고 / 자신의 방식대로)

진정한 자아를 수용하고 자신의 방식대로 사는 것은 용기가 필요하다.

노트

■ 〈가주어, 진주어 구문〉

• It takes+A+to R : ~하는 데 A가 필요하다

가주어	동사	진주어
It (This/That/There 사용 불가)	–	that+주어+동사(완전한 절)
		to 동사원형
		동명사
		의문사+주어+동사(간접의문문)
		if/whether+주어+동사
It	takes	to embrace

■ 〈동족목적어〉 : 자동사가 타동사처럼 쓰여 뒤에 목적어를 가지는 경우

• 동사의 어원과 동족목적어의 어원이 동일한 경우

자동사	목적어	해석
sleep	a deep sleep	깊은 잠을 자다
dream	a happy dream	행복한 꿈을 꾸다
live	life	인생을 살다
smile	a bright smile	환한 미소를 짓다

• 동사의 의미와 동족목적어가 비슷한 경우

자동사	목적어	해석
run	a race	경주를 하다
fight	a fierce battle	격렬한 싸움을 하다

Yet / [(to be uniquely you), / {to listen within and (to) love yourself / (for all of your weaknesses and missteps)}], / is (C) (what / that your soul longs for).

그러나 / S: (to be uniquely〈부사〉 you(S.C)) (독특하게 여러분이 되는 것, 즉) / {to listen within and (to) love(O) yourself(O〈재·대〉)} (내면의 소리를 듣고 자신을 사랑하는 것이) / (for all of your weaknesses and missteps) (여러분의 약점과 실수에도 불구하고) / is(V) / S.C: (what / that〈목·관〉 your soul(S) longs for(V)) (여러분의 영혼이 갈망하는 것이다)

그러나 독특하게 여러분이 되는 것, 내면의 소리를 듣고 여러분의 약점과 실수에도 불구하고 자신을 사랑하는 것이 여러분의 영혼이 갈망하는 것이다.

노트

■ for all : ~에도 불구하고

■ for all of : ~에 관한 한, ~에 대해서는

■ long for : ~을 열망하다, 갈망하다(=wish, crave, yearn, desire, yen)

■ 〈to부정사의 명사적 용법〉 : 주어/목적어/보어 자리에 사용, to부정사가 주어 자리에 사용되면 단수 취급하여 동사는 단수동사를 사용한다.

to부정사 1	to부정사 2		to부정사 3		
to be ~,	to listen ~,	and	(to)	love ~,	is
		대등접속사	(생략)		단수동사

■ 〈재귀대명사 vs. 대명사〉

주체	~	주어와 다름	주어와 동일
		대명사	재귀대명사
you		you	yourself

〈관계대명사절 what절〉 : 불완전자동사의 보어

is	~~선행사~~	what	your soul	longs	for	~~목적어~~
불완전자동사		목적격관계대명사 선행사를 포함한 관계대명사 (=the thing(s) which/that ~) : ~하는 것(들)은/이	주어	동사	전치사	

▶ (A), (B), (C)의 각 네모 안에서 어법에 맞는 표현으로 가장 적절한 것은?

	(A)		(B)		(C)
①	confident	……	manipulate	……	that
②	confident	……	be manipulated	……	what
③	confidently	……	manipulate	……	that
④	confidently	……	manipulate	……	what
⑤	confidently	……	be manipulated	……	what

정답 | ⑤

해설 | (A) [형용사 vs. 부사] : 형용사의 역할은 명사를 수식하거나 보어로 사용되고, 부사의 역할은 동사/형용사/부사/문장 전체/준동사(to부정사, 동명사, 분사)를 수식한다. 이 문장에 주어는 You이고 동사는 have이고 a power and presence는 목적어로 사용되었다. that은 주격관계대명사이고 radiates와 shines out은 대등접속사 and로 병렬구조로 이어져 주격관계대명사 that절 안에서 동사로 사용되었다. 동사 shines out을 수식하는 부사 confidently가 어법상 올바르다.

(B) [to부정사의 능동 vs. to부정사의 수동] : to부정사의 능동의 구조는 to동사원형이고, to부정사의 수동의 구조는 to be p.p.이다. to부정사의 주체는 문장의 주어이다. 이 문장의 주어는 You이고 동사는 did not come into this life이다. 콤마(,) 뒤부터 to부정사가 and로 병렬구조로 이어졌는데, 밑줄 친 동사의 원형은 manipulate로 '~을 조종하다'라는 의미로 뒤에 목적어를 취하는 완전타동사이다. 하지만 뒤에 목적어도 없고 주어 You와의 관계를 보았을 때 어떤 것을 조종하는 것이 아니라 조종당한다는 의미이기 때문에 to부정사의 수동인 to be manipulated가 어법상 올바르다. (manipulate – manipulated – manipulated – manipulating)

(C) [목적격관계대명사 that vs. 목적격관계대명사 what] : '선행사+목적격관계대명사 that+주어+동사+전치사' 구조처럼 목적격관계대명사 that은 선행사가 있어야 한다. '목적격관계대명사 that+주어+동사+전치사' 구조처럼 목적격관계대명사 what은 선행사가 없다. 목적격관계대명사 what은 선행사를 포함한 관계대명사로 the thing(s) which/that과 같은 의미로 '~하는 것(들)'이라고 해석된다. your soul longs for에서 long for는 '~을 갈망하다'라는 의미로 뒤에 전치사 for에 대한 목적어가 필요하지만 여기에서는 그 목적어가 없다. 따라서 목적격관계대명사 that이나 what 둘 다 사용할 수 있지만 동사 is 뒤에 선행사가 없기 때문에 선행사가 필요한 that은 사용할 수 없고 선행사를 포함한 what이 어법상 올바르다.

Words

☐ journey
☐ discover
☐ authentic
☐ rewarding
☐ adventure
☐ radiate
☐ shine
☐ suffer
☐ manipulate
☐ deny
☐ bind
☐ false
☐ shed
☐ courage
☐ embrace
☐ term
☐ uniquely
☐ misstep

Phrases

☐ the journey to(전치사)+(동)명사
☐ come into
☐ for all of
☐ from deep within
☐ shine out
☐ for all
☐ long for

우선순위 영단어 역대 수능 기출+전국 모의고사 기출+EBS 기출+교과서 기출 빈출 어휘

단어	뜻	단어	뜻	단어	뜻
generalization	n. 일반화	generalize	v. 일반화[보편화]하다	generosity	a. 관대한
genetics	n. 유전학	genius	n. 천재	gentle	a. 부드러운
geology	n. 지질	geometrical	a. 기하학의	geometry	n. 기하학

변형문제

01 다음 글을 읽고, |조건|에 맞게 주어진 주제문을 완성하시오.

| 조건 |
* (A)는 4단어, (B)는 1단어로 쓸 것
* 본문에 있는 단어만을 그대로 사용할 것

The journey to discovering your authentic self promises to be the most rewarding adventure of your life. When you know yourself, you are free. You have a power and presence that radiates from deep within and shines out confidently into the world. You did not come into this life to suffer, to be manipulated and denied. Whatever binds you and keeps you from living your truth is false and can be shed. It takes courage to embrace your authentic self and live life on your own terms. Yet to be uniquely you, to listen within and love yourself for all of your weaknesses and missteps, is what your soul longs for.

⬇

The journey of (A) ____________ ____________ ____________ ____________ makes you (B) ____________ and rewarding.

02 다음 글을 읽고, |조건|에 맞게 요약문을 완성하시오.

| 조건 |
* (A), (B), (C)는 각각 다르게 1단어로 쓸 것
* [보기]에서 선택한 단어를 한 번씩만 쓸 것
* 필요한 경우, 문맥과 어법에 맞게 변형할 것

[보기] irrefutable / priceless / costly / tough / unusual / ignore / design / encourage / spread / unexpectable / correct / generate / abandon / restrain

The journey to discovering your authentic self promises to be the most rewarding adventure of your life. When you know yourself, you are free. You have a power and presence that radiates from deep within and shines out confidently into the world. You did not come into this life to suffer, to be manipulated and denied. Whatever binds you and keeps you from living your truth is false and can be shed. It takes courage to embrace your authentic self and live life on your own terms. Yet to be uniquely you, to listen within and love yourself for all of your weaknesses and missteps, is what your soul longs for.

⬇

The most (A) ____________ experience in life is the discovery of a true self. If there is something that (B) ____________ us and disturbs our real lives, it should be (C) ____________, while we should be free and know ourselves for power and presence that demands courage.

03 다음 빈칸에 들어갈 말로 가장 적절한 것은?

The journey ______________________ promises to be the most rewarding adventure of your life. When you know yourself, you are free. You have a power and presence that radiates from deep within and shines out confidently into the world. You did not come into this life to suffer, to be manipulated and denied. Whatever binds you and keeps you from living your truth is false and can be shed. It takes courage to embrace your authentic self and live life on your own terms. Yet to be uniquely you, to listen within and love yourself for all of your weaknesses and missteps, is what your soul longs for.

① to discovering your authentic self
② to going to the purpose
③ to being a good person
④ to finding what I want to do
⑤ to achieving one's dream

04 밑줄 친 부분 중 문맥상 옳지 않은 것은?

The journey to ① discovering your authentic self promises to be the most rewarding adventure of your life. When you know yourself, you are free. You have a power and presence that radiates from deep within and shines out ② confidently into the world. You did not come into this life to ③ suffer, to be manipulated and denied. Whatever binds you and keeps you from living your truth is false and can be shed. It takes ④ courage to embrace your authentic self and live life on your own terms. Yet to be uniquely you, to listen within and love yourself for all of your ⑤ strength and missteps, is what your soul longs for.

UNIT 16 어법(밑줄/네모)

글의 논리	Comparison & Contrast (비교 & 대조)
제목	최선을 다하는 것의 장 · 단점
주제	최선을 다하는 것은 중요하지만 그에 빠져서 새로운 활동을 피하게 될 수도 있다.

PRACTICE 03

065 어법 선택 & 연결어

Some things in life **[is / are]** important, and they deserve your full commitment. **[It's / This is]** important to do your best when **[performing / performed]** your job, **[cultivating / cultivated]** your marriage, **[raising / raised]** your children, and **[competing / competed]** for the league bowling championship. **[Giving / Given]** **[it / them]** your all **[is / are]** a necessary part of success, **[which / what]** **[give / gives]** us pride and joy and a sense of self-worth. ( ), at some point early in life, we all heard someone **[say / to say]**, "Always do your best." ( ) a lot of people accepted the wisdom of this advice without ever **[question / questioning]** **[it / them]**. These **[is / are]** the people who avoid **[to try / trying]** new activities **[because / because of]** they are afraid **[what / that]** someone will judge **[its / their]** effort and scold **[it / them]** if it's not their "best." ( ) these people miss out on lots of fun, mind-expanding, enjoyable activities **[because / because of]** the "always do your best" mentality.

비교1 최선을 다하는 것은 중요하고, 우리에게 자존감을 준다.

Some things (in life) / are important, / and / ① they / deserve your full commitment.

(Some things: S 인생에서 어떤 것들은 / are: V / important: S.C 중요하다 / and: 그리고 / they: S 그것들은 / deserve: V / your full commitment: O 여러분의 완전한 전념을 받을 만하다)

인생에서 어떤 것들은 중요하고, 그것들은 여러분의 완전한 전념을 받을 만하다.

노트 ■ deserve : ~할[받을] 만하다; ~할[될] 가치[값어치]가 있다(진행형 없음)

It's important / [(to do your best) / {when (you are) performing your job, cultivating your marriage, raising your children, and competing / (for the league bowling championship)}].

(It: (가S) / 's: V / important: S.C 중요하다 / (to do your best): 〈진S〉 최선을 다하는 것은 / when: 〈종·접〉 / performing: 〈현재분사₁〉 / your job: O 일을 수행할 때 / cultivating: 〈현재분사₂〉 / your marriage: O 결혼 생활을 발전시킬 때 / raising: 〈현재분사₃〉 / your children: O 아이를 양육할 때 / competing: 〈현재분사₄〉 리그 볼링 선수권 대회에서 경쟁할 때)

일을 수행할 때, 결혼 생활을 발전시킬 때, 아이를 양육할 때, 리그 볼링 선수권 대회에서 경쟁할 때 최선을 다하는 것은 중요하다.

노트 ■ do one's best : 최선을 다하다

■ 〈가주어, 진주어 구문〉

가주어	동사	진주어
It (This/That/There 사용 불가)	–	that+주어+동사(완전한 절) to 동사원형 동명사 의문사+주어+동사(간접의문문) if/whether+주어+동사
It	is	to do

■ 〈분사구문 – 문미〉 : 주절과 분사구문의 위치가 서로 바뀌어도 무관

주절		종속절(→ 분사구문)			
주어	동사	종속 접속사	주어	동사 : 상황에 맞게 아래처럼 바뀜	
		〈그대로 사용하면 의미 강조〉	(주절의 주어와 같으면 생략하고, 다르면 주격으로 사용함)	(being) (having been) 생략 가능	Ring(현재분사) / p.p.(과거분사) / 형용사 / 명사
It	is	when	(you)	(are)	performing ~

■ 〈혼동하기 쉬운 동사〉

• rise / raise / arise / arouse / rouse

원형	과거	과거분사	현재분사	뜻
rise	rose	risen	rising	vi. 오르다, 일어나다
raise	raised	raised	raising	vt. 올리다, 기르다
arise	arose	arisen	arising	vi. 발생하다, 기인하다
arouse	aroused	aroused	arousing	vt. (감정) 불러 일으키다, 자극하다
rouse	roused	roused	rousing	vt. 깨우다, 일으키다

■ 〈혼동 어휘〉

	동사	형용사	명사	부사
complete	완수하다	완전한, 완벽한	–	–
completion	–	–	완성, 완수	–
compete	경쟁하다			
competition	–	–	경쟁, 대회	–
competitor	–	–	경쟁자	
competence	–	–	능력, 자격	–
incompetence	–	–	무능력	–
complement	보완하다	–	보완, 보충	–
compliment	칭찬하다	–	칭찬	
complimentary	–	칭찬하는, 무료의	–	–
complimentarily	–	–	–	찬사로, 무료로
competitive	–	경쟁적인	–	–

competent	–	유능한, 적임의, 자격이 있는	–	–
completely	–	–	–	완전히, 전적으로
competitively	–	–	–	경쟁적으로
competently	–	–	–	유능하게

(Giving it your all) / is a necessary part (of success), /

〈동명사〉 I.O D.O / S / V / S.C

최선을 다하는 것은 / 성공의 필수적인 부분이며

(② which gives us pride and joy and a sense of self-worth).

〈주·관〉 V I.O $D.O_1$ $D.O_2$ $D.O_3$

그리고 그것이 우리에게 자부심, 기쁨, 자존감을 부여한다

최선을 다하는 것은 성공의 필수적인 부분이고, 그것은 우리에게 자부심, 기쁨, 자존감을 부여한다.

노트
- give+IO+DO (4) : ~에게 …을 주다
- **〈동명사구가 주어 자리에 사용된 경우〉** : 단수 취급으로 동사는 단수동사를 사용함

주어 : 동명사구	동사
Giving it your all	is

- **〈주격관계대명사절〉** : 계속적 용법으로는 that 사용 불가, 모든 구/절/문장 전체는 단수 취급함

		주격관계대명사절		
선행사	콤마(,)	주격관계대명사	~~주어~~	동사
앞 문장 전체	〈계속적 용법〉	which		gives

대조 우리는 어린 시절 항상 최선을 다하라는 소리를 들었다.

(Unfortunately), / (at some point) / (early) (in life), /

불행히도 / 어느 시점에 / 어린 시절

we all / heard someone say, / "Always do your best."

S V O O.C / V O

우리 모두는 / 누군가가 말하는 것을 들었다 / "항상 최선을 다하라."

불행히도, 어린 시절 어느 시점에, 우리 모두는 누군가가 '항상 최선을 다하라.' 라고 말하는 것을 들었다.

노트
- at some point : 어느 시점에, 어느 순간에
- 〈지각동사〉

지각동사		목적어	목적격보어
see	보다	–	〈목적어와 목적격보어의 관계가 능동일 때〉 동사원형(R) – 완료 현재진행(Ring) – 진행, 순간, 찰나, 계속 〈목적어와 목적격보어의 관계가 수동일 때〉 과거분사(p.p.) 〈to부정사는 불가〉 : 수동태 문장 전환 시 가능
watch	보다		
look at	보다		
behold	보다		
(over) hear	듣다		
listen to	듣다		
feel	느끼다		
observe	관찰하다		
perceive	인식하다		
notice	인식하다		
heard		someone	say

비교2 최선을 다하라는 소리를 의문을 갖지 않고 받아들이면서 부담이 생겨 여러 가지 새로운 활동을 피하게 된다.

And / a lot of people / accepted the wisdom (of this advice) / (without ever ③ question it).

S V O / 〈전치사〉 〈동명사〉 O

그리고 / 많은 사람들이 / 이 조언의 지혜를 받아들였다 / 의문도 갖지 않고

그리고 많은 사람들이 이 조언의 지혜를 의문도 갖지 않고 받아들였다.

노트
- a lot of : 많은
- **〈동명사 vs. 명사〉** : 전치사의 목적어 자리에 동명사와 명사를 둘 다 사용할 수 있지만, 동명사는 뒤에 목적어로 명사/대명사 등을 가질 수 있는 점이 명사와의 차이점이다.

〈전치사구〉		
전치사	목적어	
without	~~question~~	it
	questioning	

These / are / the people / (who avoid ④ trying new activities) / [because they are afraid / {that someone will judge their effort and scold them / (if it's not their "best.")}]

S V S.C(선행사) 〈주·관〉 V 〈동명사〉 O / O / 〈종·접〉 S V S.C / 〈종·접〉 S V_1 O V_2 O / 〈종·접〉 S V S.C

이러한 / 이다 / 사람들은 / 새로운 활동을 시도하기를 피하는 / 그들이 두려워하기 때문에 / 누군가가 / 그들의 노력을 판단하고 그들을 비난할까봐 / 그것이 그들의 '최선'이 아니라면

이러한 사람들은 누군가가 그들의 노력을 판단하고 그것이 그들의 '최선'이 아니라면 그들을 비난할까 두려워서 새로운 활동을 시도하기를 피하는 사람들이다.

노트
- **〈주격관계대명사절의 수의 일치〉** : 선행사를 포함하고 있는 관계대명사 what 사용 불가

	주격관계대명사절		
선행사	주격관계대명사	~~주어~~	동사
the people	who		avoid

- **〈목적어 자리에 동명사를 취하는 완전타동사〉**

주어	완전타동사	목적어
–	admit / avoid / consider / delay / deny / enjoy / escape / experience / finish / give up / imagine / include / involve / mind / mute / practice / put off / quit / recommend / replace / report / risk 등	Ring (동명사)

- **〈원인/이유〉** : ~ 때문에

전치사	because of	+(동)명사 / 명사 상당어구
	due to	
	for	
	on account of	
	owing to	
	thanks to	

종속접속사	as	+주어+동사 ~
	because	
	now(that)	
	since	

■ 〈서술적 형용사〉 : 명사 수식 불가, 보어로만 사용

상태형용사	afraid, alike, alive, alone, amiss, ashamed, asleep, astray, awake, aware 등
감정형용사	content, fond, glad, ignorant, pleasant, proud, unable, upset, well, worth 등

■ 〈afraid 용법〉

be	afraid	to R	~하는 게 두렵다
		of (동)명사	
		(that)+주어+동사	

■ 〈what vs. that〉

	관계대명사(불완전한 문장)	접속사(완전한 문장)
what	○ 선행사를 포함하고 있기 때문에 what 앞에 선행사 불필요	×
that	○ that 앞에 선행사 필요	○

(So) / these people / miss out on lots of fun, mind-expanding, enjoyable activities / (⑤ because of the "always do your best" mentality).

따라서 / 이러한 사람들은(S) / 놓치고 있다(V) / 많은 재미, 의식을 확대하는 즐거운 활동을(O) / 〈전치사〉 '항상 최선을 다하라'는 사고방식 때문에

따라서 이러한 사람들은 '항상 최선을 다하라'는 사고방식으로 인해 많은 재미, 의식을 확대하는 즐거운 활동을 놓치고 있다.

노트 ■ miss out on : ~을 놓치다

■ a lot of : 많은(복수형 : lots of)

■ 〈혼동하기 쉬운 동사〉

• extend / expend / expand

동사	뜻
extend	〈손 · 발 등을〉 뻗다, 뻗치다, 〈기간을〉 늘이다, 〈범위 · 영토 등을〉 넓히다
expend	〈시간 · 노력 등을〉 들이다, 소비하다, 쓰다
expand	〈정도 · 크기 · 용적 등을〉 넓히다, 펼치다, 〈토론 등을〉 전개시키다

■ 〈빈도부사의 위치〉

be동사 / 조동사	+	빈도부사	+	일반동사
		always(100%)		
		usually(60% ~ 80%)		
		often(50% ~ 60%)		
		sometimes(40%)		
		seldom / hardly / rarely(20%)		
		never(0%)		

▶ 다음 글의 밑줄 친 부분 중, 어법상 틀린 것은?

정답 | ③ question → questioning

해설 | ③ [전치사의 목적어 자리] : 전치사는 뒤에 반드시 목적어가 필요한데, 이때 목적어 자리에는 주로 대명사, 명사, 동명사, 간접의문문(의문사+주어+동사), 관계대명사 what절이 사용될 수 있고 동사는 절대로 사용할 수 없다. 이 문장에서 전치사 without 뒤에 있는 question은 명사와 동사로 둘 다 사용 가능하다. 먼저 전치사 without은 뒤에 목적어로 동사는 사용할 수 없다고 했으니 question이 동사일 경우라면 어법상 올바르지 않고, question이 명사라고 해도 뒤에 있는 대명사 it이 있기 때문에 어법상 올바르지 않다. 왜냐하면 대명사는 문장에서 주어, 목적어, 보어로 사용되어야 하는데 명사로 사용된 question 뒤에 it이 사용될 수 없기 때문이다. 따라서 대명사 it을 목적어로 취하고 전치사 without의 목적어로 어법상 올바른 동명사 questioning이 필요하다.

오답 | ① [대명사의 수의 일치] : 밑줄 친 they는 복수명사를 대신하는 대명사로 문장에서 주어로 사용될 수 있는데 문장 맨 앞에 복수명사 Some things를 지칭하기 때문에 단수명사를 받는 it을 사용할 수 없고 they가 어법상 올바르다.

② [주격관계대명사 which vs. 주격관계대명사 that, what] : '선행사, +주격관계대명사 which+동사 ~' 구조를 취하는 주격관계대명사 which는 바로 앞에 콤마(,)를 사용하여 계속적 용법으로 '접속사+대명사'로 고쳐 사용할 수 있는데 이때 대명사는 선행사를 말한다. 즉 'and it'으로 고칠 수 있고 이때 it은 선행사 Giving it your all을 가리킨다. 하지만 관계대명사 that은 계속적 용법으로 사용할 수 없고, 역시 관계대명사 what 역시 사용할 수 없다. 특히 관계대명사 what은 선행사를 포함하고 있기 때문에 선행사 Giving it your all이 있기 때문에 사용할 수 없다.

④ [동명사 vs. to부정사] : 'avoid+목적어' 구조에서 타동사 avoid는 목적어 자리에 동명사를 가지기 때문에 to try를 사용할 수 없기 때문에 동명사 trying이 어법상 올바르다.

⑤ [전치사 vs. 종속접속사] : '~ 때문에'라는 의미로 전치사는 because of, owing to, due to, on account of 등이 사용될 수 있고, 종속접속사로는 because, since, as, now (that) 등이 사용될 수 있다. 전치사는 뒤에 목적어로 주로 (동)명사(구) 형태가 나오고, 종속접속사는 주로 '주어+동사'로 이루어진 절이 나온다. 이 문장에서는 the "always do your best" mentality처럼 명사구가 나왔기 때문에 전치사 because of가 어법상 올바르다.

노트 ■ 삼형식에서 목적어의 구별

Ⅰ. S V O(3)
to R만
↓
redpwwh
(refuse / expect / decide / promise / wish / want / hope)
+(fail, manage)

Ⅱ. S V O(3)
Ring만
↓
megafeda를 practice를 put off 말라
(mind, enjoy, give up, avoid, finish, escape, deny, admit, practice, put off)

Ⅲ. S V O(3)
to R & Ring 의미 차이 ×(같이 써도 된다)
↓
사랑공식
(like, start, love, begin, hate, continue)

Ⅳ. S V O(3)
to R & Ring 의미 차이 ○ → 구별
↓
* stop ┌ to R : ~하기 위해서 멈추다.
└ Ring : ~하는 것을 멈추다.

예 stop to smoke : 흡연
stop smoking : 금연

* try ┌ to R : ~노력/시도하다 (S의 의지 있음)
└ Ring : 시험 삼아 한번 해보다 (S의 의지 없음)

* remember / regret / forget ┌ +to R : 미래
└ +Ring : 과거

Words

- ☐ deserve
- ☐ commitment
- ☐ perform
- ☐ cultivate
- ☐ raise
- ☐ compete
- ☐ championship
- ☐ pride
- ☐ self-worth
- ☐ accept
- ☐ wisdom
- ☐ advice
- ☐ question
- ☐ avoid
- ☐ judge
- ☐ scold
- ☐ mind-expanding

Phrases

- ☐ do one's best
- ☐ miss out on
- ☐ at some point
- ☐ a lot of(복수형: lots of)

우선순위 영단어

역대 수능 기출 + 전국 모의고사 기출 + EBS 기출 + 교과서 기출 빈출 어휘

단어	뜻	단어	뜻	단어	뜻
get ahead	v. 앞서다	get there	v. 목적을 이루다	get to	v. ~할 수 있다
gigantic	a. 거대한	giggle	v. 낄낄 웃다	give a speech	v. 연설을 하다
give in	v. 굴복하다	gleam	v. 번쩍이다	glean	v. 수집하다
glee	n. 신이 남	glistening	a. 반짝이는	globalization	n. 세계화
glory	n. 영광	go against	v. ~에 반하다	go off	v. 떠나다
go well with	v. 잘 어울리다	goal-oriented	a. 목표 지향적인	grace	n. 품위
gracious	a. 상냥한	gradual	a. 점진적인	graduate school	n. 대학원
graphically	ad. 도표로	gratification	n. 만족감	gratify	v. 충족시키다
gratitude	n. 감사	grave	a. 진지한	gravitate	v. 끌리다
grocery	n. 식료품	grope	v. 찾다	groundbreaking	a. 획기적인
growl	n. 으르렁거리는 소리	grown-up	a. 성숙한	growth	n. 생장물
grub	n. 땅벌레	grunt	v. (돼지가) 꿀꿀거리다	guardian angel	n. 수호천사
gunpowder	n. 화약	gym	n. 체육관	hallway	n. 복도
hamper	v. 방해하다	handful	a. 소수의	handheld	a. 손에 쥘 만한 크기의
hands-on	a. 실제로 조작해 보는	hang	v. 매달리다	hang around	v. 방랑하다
hardwood	n. 견목	harmful	a. 해로운	harness	v. 이용하다
haul	v. 연행하다	haunt	v. 괴롭히다	have ~ in common	v. ~을 공통적으로 가지다
have an impact on	v. ~에 영향을 끼치다	have yet to do	v. 아직 ~하지 않았다	hawk	n. 매
head	n. 앞면	headlong	ad. 거꾸로	healing	n. 치료
health care	n. 의료 서비스	heap	n. 더미	heart attack	n. 심장마비
heartfelt	a. 진심 어린	hearth	n. 난로	heave	v. 오르내리다
heavy metal	n. 중금속	heed	v. 주의하다	heir	n. 상속인
helping	n. (음식물의) 한 그릇	hereditary	a. 유전의	heredity	n. 유전
heritage	n. 유산	highly	ad. 크게	hindrance	n. 방해물
historical	a. 역사의	hit one's stride	v. 본래의 컨디션을 되찾다	hitherto	a. 그때까지
hoard	v. 축적하다	holding	n. 소작지	honorary	a. 명예의
hormone	n. 호르몬	horror	n. 공포	hostile	a. 적대하는
hotline	n. 전화 신상 상담 서비스	How come ~?	~은 어찌된 것인가?	human resource	n. 인적 자원
humble	a. 겸손한	humid	a. 습한	hybrid	a. 잡종의
hygiene	n. 위생	ideology	n. 이념	ignorant	a. 무지한
illegal	a. 불법적인	illiterate	a. 문맹의	illusionary	a. 환상의

변형문제

01 다음 글을 읽고, |조건|에 맞게 주어진 요약문을 완성하시오.

| 조건 |

* (A), (B)는 각각 다르게 1단어로 쓸 것
* [보기]에서 선택한 단어를 한 번씩만 쓸 것
* 필요한 경우, 문맥과 어법에 맞게 변형할 것

[보기] lose / enthusiastic / criticize / accept / decrease / narrow / disadvantage / benefit / manipulate / broaden / support / create / brainwash

Some things in life are important, and they deserve your full commitment. It's important to do your best when performing your job, cultivating your marriage, raising your children, and competing for the league bowling championship. Giving it your all is a necessary part of success, which gives us pride and joy and a sense of self-worth. Unfortunately, at some point early in life, we all heard someone say, "Always do your best." And a lot of people accepted the wisdom of this advice without ever questioning it. These are the people who avoid trying new activities because they are afraid that someone will judge their effort and scold them if it's not their "best." So these people miss out on lots of fun, mind-expanding, enjoyable activities because of the "always do your best" mentality.

⬇

We have been listening the wisdom of "Always do your best" from an early age and rarely questioned why we should because we are afraid of being (A) ____________ in case of not doing well, which (B) ____________ opportunities for us to experience activities that are entertaining and mind-expanding.

02 밑줄 친 부분 중 문맥상 옳지 않은 것은?

Some things in life are important, and they ① reserve your full commitment. It's important to do your best when performing your job, cultivating your marriage, raising your children, and competing for the league bowling championship. Giving it your all is a ② necessary part of success, which gives us pride and joy and a sense of self-worth. Unfortunately, at some point early in life, we all heard someone say, "Always do your best." And a lot of people ③ accepted the wisdom of this advice without ever questioning it. These are the people who ④ avoid trying new activities because they are afraid that someone will judge their effort and scold them if it's not their "best." So these people miss out on lots of fun, mind-expanding, ⑤ enjoyable activities because of the "always do your best" mentality.

03 다음 글을 읽고, |조건|에 맞게 (A), (B), (C)를 채우시오.

| 조건 |
* (A), (B), (C)는 각각 다르게 1단어로 쓸 것
* 본문에 있는 단어를 찾아 쓸 것
* 필요한 경우, 문맥과 어법에 맞게 변형할 것

Some things in life are important, and they deserve your full commitment. It's important to do your best when performing your job, cultivating your marriage, raising your children, and competing for the league bowling championship. Giving it your all is a necessary part of success, which gives us pride and joy and a sense of self-worth. Unfortunately, at some point early in life, we all heard someone say, "Always do your best." And a lot of people accepted the wisdom of this advice without ever questioning it. These are the people who avoid trying new activities because they are afraid that someone will judge their effort and scold them if it's not their "best." So these people miss out on lots of fun, mind-expanding, enjoyable activities because of the "always do your best" mentality.

⬇

"Doing the best" is considered as an essential for (A) ____________ and leading to the growth of pride, joy and self-worth, but this way of thinking may prevent people from (B) ____________ the experience of new and entertaining activities because they are afraid of their effort to be (C) ____________ .

04 다음 글의 순서로 가장 적절한 것은?

Some things in life are important, and they deserve your full commitment. It's important to do your best when performing your job, cultivating your marriage, raising your children, and competing for the league bowling championship.

(A) Unfortunately, at some point early in life, we all heard someone say, "Always do your best." And a lot of people accepted the wisdom of this advice without ever questioning it. These are the people who avoid trying new activities because they are afraid that someone will judge their effort and scold them if it's not their "best."

(B) So these people miss out on lots of fun, mind-expanding, enjoyable activities because of the "always do your best" mentality.

(C) Giving it your all is a necessary part of success, which gives us pride and joy and a sense of self-worth.

① (A) - (B) - (C)
② (B) - (A) - (C)
③ (B) - (C) - (A)
④ (C) - (A) - (B)
⑤ (C) - (B) - (A)

어휘(밑줄/네모)

글의 논리	Myth & Truth (통념 & 진실)
제목	스파르타 사람들의 힘의 원천
주제	고대 그리스의 스파르타 사람들의 힘은 강인함이 아닌 전체의 안전을 위한 힘(방패의 힘)에서 나왔다.

수능 ANALYSIS

066 어법 선택 & 연결어

The Spartans, a warrior society in ancient Greece, **[were / was] [feared / fearing]** and **[reversing / reversed]** for **[their / its]** strength, courage and endurance. The power of the Spartan army did not come from the sharpness of **[their / its]** spears, (   ); it came from the strength of **[their / its]** shields. Losing one's shield in battle **[considers / was considered]** the single **[greatest / great]** crime a Spartan could commit. "Spartans excuse without penalty the warrior who **[lose / loses] [his / their]** helmet or breastplate in battle," writes Steven Pressfield in his account of the Battle of Thermopylae, "but **[deprives / deprive]** the man who **[discards / discard]** his shield of all his citizenship rights." And the reason was simple. "A warrior carries a helmet and breastplate for **[their / his]** own protection, but **[their / his]** shield for the safety of the whole line."

통념 그들의 강인함, 용기, 인내(창의 날카로움)로 인해 두려움의 대상이자, 동시에 숭배를 받았다.

=〈동격〉

The Spartans(S), a warrior society / (in ancient Greece), /
전사 사회였던 스파르타 사람들은 / 고대 그리스의

(were)
were feared(V₁〈수동태〉) and ① reversed(V₂〈수동태〉) / (for their strength, courage and endurance).
두려움의 대상이었고 동시에 숭배를 받았다 / 그들의 강인함, 용기, 그리고 인내로 인해

고대 그리스의 전사 사회였던 스파르타 사람들은 그들의 강인함, 용기, 그리고 인내로 인해 두려움의 대상이었고 (동시에) 숭배를 받았다.

노트
- revere A for B : A를 B로 존경하다(수동태 시, A be revered for B)
- 〈동격〉 : A(명사), B(명사) (A가 주어, B라는 A)

동격(B라는 A)			
명사(A)	,(콤마)	명사(구/절)(B)	동사
The Spartans	,	a warrior society	were feared and ① revered

- 〈공통관계〉 : A가 공통

A	(X+Y)	=	AX+AY
A	(X+Y+Z+α)	=	AX+AY+AZ+Aα
(X+Y)	A	=	XA+YA
A	(X+Y+Z)	=	AX+AY+AZ
were	(feared+revered)	=	were feared and (were) revered

주제문(진실) 그들의 힘은 방패의 힘으로부터 나온다.

The power(S) (of the Spartan army) / did not come(V) /
스파르타 군대의 힘은 / 나오는 것이 아니었다

(from the ② sharpness of their spears), / however; / it(S) /
그들의 창의 날카로움에서 / 하지만 / 그것은

came(V) (from the strength of their shields).
방패의 힘으로부터 나왔다

그러나 스파르타 군대의 힘은 그들의 창의 날카로움에서 나오는 것이 아니라, 방패의 힘으로부터 나왔다.

노트
- come from : ~에서 생겨나다(=originate)

근거1 방패를 잃는 것이 가장 큰 한 가지 범죄

{Losing(〈동명사〉) one's shield(O) (in battle)}(S) / was considered(V〈수동태〉) /
전투에서 자신의 방패를 잃는 것은 / 간주되었다

(목·관 that)
the single ③ greatest crime(선행사) / (a Spartan(S) could commit(V)).(S.C)
가장 큰 한 가지 범죄로 / 스파르타인이 저지를 수 있는

전투에서 자신의 방패를 잃는 것은 스파르타인이 저지를 수 있는 가장 큰 한 가지 범죄로 간주되었다.

노트
- commit a crime : 범죄를 저지르다
- 〈동명사구가 주어 자리에 사용된 경우〉 : 단수 취급으로 동사는 단수동사를 사용함

주어 : 동명사구	동사
Losing one's shield in battle	was considered

- 〈consider 동사의 쓰임〉 : 5형식인 경우(~을 …라고 생각하다), 〈수동태 시, be considered+주격보어[(to be) 보어 / as+보어]〉

consider	목적어	목적격보어
		as+보어
		(to be) 보어

- 〈목적격관계대명사 that〉 : 타동사의 목적어가 없는 경우 / 선행사를 포함하고 있는 관계대명사 what 사용 불가

	〈목적격관계대명사절〉			
선행사	목적격관계대명사	주어	타동사	~~목적어~~
the single greatest crime	that : (생략 가능)	a Spartan	could commit	

■ 〈주격관계대명사절의 수의 일치〉 : 선행사를 포함하고 있는 관계대명사 what 사용 불가

	주격관계대명사절		
선행사	주격관계대명사	~~주어~~	동사
the warrior	who		loses
the man			retains(→ discards)

근거2 방패를 버린 사람은 시민권 박탈

"Spartans / excuse (without penalty) / the warrior / {who loses his helmet or breastplate (in battle)}," / writes / Steven Pressfield / (in his account of the Battle of Thermopylae), / "but / deprive the man (who ④ retains his shield) / (of all his citizenship rights)."

(S: Spartans / V_1: excuse / O〈선행사〉: the warrior / 〈주·관〉: who / V: loses / O_1: his helmet / O_2: breastplate / V: writes / S: Steven Pressfield / V_2: deprive / O〈선행사〉: the man / 〈주·관〉: who / V: retains / O: his shield)

"스파르타 사람들은 (아무런 징벌 없이) 용서한다 전사를 전투에서 투구나 흉갑을 분실한 전투에서" 라고 쓰고 있다 Steven Pressfield는 테르모필레 전투에 대한 자신의 설명에 "하지만 자신의 방패를 버린 사람에게서 유지한다 그의 모든 시민권을"

"스파르타 사람들은 전투에서 투구나 흉갑을 분실한 전사는 아무런 징벌 없이 용서한다."라고 Steven Pressfield는 테르모필레 전투에 대한 자신의 설명에 쓰고 있다. "하지만 자신의 방패를 버린 사람에게는 그의 모든 시민권을 유지한다(→ 박탈한다)."

노트 ■ 〈3형식에서 '분리/제거/박탈 동사+목적어+of+목적어'〉 : 수동태 문장 전환 시, 'be p.p. of 목적어' 1형식 구조로 바뀜

주어	타동사 (분리, 제거, 박탈)		목적어	전치사구	
				전치사	목적어
–	rob	빼앗다	–	of	–
	absolve	무죄선고를 내리다			
	clear	제거하다			
	deprive	빼앗다			
	relieve	걱정을 덜다			
	rid	제거하다			
	strip	박탈하다			
	cure	없애다			

근거2에 대한 이유 방패는 전체 전열의 안전을 위한 것이다.

And / the reason / was simple.

(S: the reason / V: was / S.C: simple)

그리고 그 이유는 간단했다

그리고 그 이유는 간단했다.

"A warrior / carries a helmet and breastplate / (for his own protection), / but / his shield / (for the safety of the ⑤ whole line)."

(S: A warrior / V: carries / O_1: a helmet / O_2: breastplate / O_3: his shield)

"전사는 투구와 흉갑을 가지고 다닌다 자신의 보호를 위해 하지만 방패를 가지고 다닌다 전체 전열의 안전을 위해서"

"전사는 자신의 보호를 위해 투구와 흉갑을 가지고 다니지만, 전체 전열의 안전을 위해서 방패를 가지고 다닌다."

노트 ■ 〈소유격을 강조하는 표현〉 : '소유격+own(~ 자신)+명사'

	own은 소유격대명사 강조		
전치사	소유격	own	명사
for	his	own	protection

▶ 다음 글의 밑줄 친 부분 중, 문맥상 낱말의 쓰임이 적절하지 않은 것은?

정답 | ④ retains → discards

해설 | 스파르타 사회에서는 전투 중에 투구나 흉갑을 분실한 사람은 용서를 받아도 방패를 버린 사람은 용서받지 못했다는 내용이므로 ④의 'retains'를 'discards'로 수정해야 한다.

Words

- ☐ warrior
- ☐ revere
- ☐ endurance
- ☐ sharpness
- ☐ shield
- ☐ penalty
- ☐ breastplate
- ☐ deprive
- ☐ citizenship

Phrases

- ☐ revere A for B
- ☐ commit a crime
- ☐ come from

변형문제

01 다음 글을 읽고, |조건|에 맞게 요약문을 완성하시오.

| 조건 |
* (A)는 8단어, (B)는 4단어로 쓸 것
* 본문에 있는 단어를 찾아 쓸 것
* 필요한 경우, 문맥과 어법에 맞게 변형할 것

The Spartans, a warrior society in ancient Greece, were feared and revered for their strength, courage and endurance. The power of the Spartan army did not come from the sharpness of their spears, however; it came from the strength of their shields. Losing one's shield in battle was considered the single greatest crime a Spartan could commit. "Spartans excuse without penalty the warrior who loses his helmet or breastplate in battle," writes Steven Pressfield in his account of the Battle of Thermopylae, "but deprive the man who discards his shield of all his citizenship rights." And the reason was simple. "A warrior carries a helmet and breastplate for his own protection, but his shield for the safety of the whole line."

⬇

In Spartan society, those (A) ________ ________ ________ ________ ________ ________ ________ ________ were forgiven, but those (B) ________ ________ ________ ________ were unforgiven.

02 다음 글을 읽고, |조건|에 맞게 주어진 질문에 답하시오.

| 조건 |
* (A)는 9단어로 쓸 것
* 본문에 있는 단어만을 사용할 것

The Spartans, a warrior society in ancient Greece, were feared and revered for their strength, courage and endurance. The power of the Spartan army did not come from the sharpness of their spears, however; it came from the strength of their shields. Losing one's shield in battle was considered the single greatest crime a Spartan could commit. "Spartans excuse without penalty the warrior who loses his helmet or breastplate in battle," writes Steven Pressfield in his account of the Battle of Thermopylae, "but deprive the man who discards his shield of all his citizenship rights." And the reason was simple. "A warrior carries a helmet and breastplate for his own protection, but his shield for the safety of the whole line."

Q: Why did Spartans value the shield more than the spear?

A: Because a warrior carries (A) ________ ________ ________ ________ ________ ________ ________ ________ ________.

03 다음 글을 읽고, |조건|에 맞게 주어진 주제문을 완성하시오.

| 조건 |
* (A), (B)는 각각 다르게 1단어로 쓸 것
* [보기]에서 선택한 단어를 한 번씩만 쓸 것
* 필요한 경우, 문맥과 어법에 맞게 변형할 것

[보기] responsible / allocate / eligible / value / subjected / underestimate / overlook / intensify / suppress / important / devise / transfer

The Spartans, a warrior society in ancient Greece, were feared and revered for their strength, courage and endurance. The power of the Spartan army did not come from the sharpness of their spears, however; it came from the strength of their shields. Losing one's shield in battle was considered the single greatest crime a Spartan could commit. "Spartans excuse without penalty the warrior who loses his helmet or breastplate in battle," writes Steven Pressfield in his account of the Battle of Thermopylae, "but deprive the man who discards his shield of all his citizenship rights." And the reason was simple. "A warrior carries a helmet and breastplate for his own protection, but his shield for the safety of the whole line."

⬇

Based on the fact that Spartans who lost or discarded his shield in battle were not (A) ____________ for civil rights, it can be inferred that they extremely (B) ____________ the safety of the entire warriors.

04 다음 글의 내용과 일치하지 않는 것은?

The Spartans, a warrior society in ancient Greece, were feared and revered for their strength, courage and endurance. The power of the Spartan army did not come from the sharpness of their spears, however; it came from the strength of their shields. Losing one's shield in battle was considered the single greatest crime a Spartan could commit. "Spartans excuse without penalty the warrior who loses his helmet or breastplate in battle," writes Steven Pressfield in his account of the Battle of Thermopylae, "but deprive the man who discards his shield of all his citizenship rights." And the reason was simple. "A warrior carries a helmet and breastplate for his own protection, but his shield for the safety of the whole line."

① 고대 그리스의 스파르타 사람들은 두려움의 대상이었다.
② 스파르타 군대의 힘은 방패로부터 나왔다.
③ 스파르타인에게 방패를 잃는 것은 가장 큰 범죄 중 하나였다.
④ 스파르타인이 투구를 잃어버리면 큰 처벌을 받았다.
⑤ 스파르타인이 방패를 버리면 시민권을 박탈당했다.

UNIT 17

어휘(밑줄/네모)

글의 논리	Problem & Solution (문제 & 해결)
제목	눈물과 슬픔을 인정하는 것의 필요성
주제	우리는 슬픔이 우리에게 다가오는 것을 기꺼이 받아들여야 한다.

수능 ANALYSIS

067 어법 선택 & 연결어

When you are **[immersed / immersing]** in writing an essay for class, you can easily forget **[what / that]** you are trying **[to communicate / communicating]** with a **[specifically / specific]** person — your teacher, who will grade the essay. (　　　　　), you should always **[keep / have kept]** this in mind: **[Which / What]** can you write **[that / what]** will **[most / almost]** impress your teacher? A teacher is probably not going to be **[over / overly]** **[impressed / impressing]** by flawless grammar and spelling; those qualities **[are expected / expect]**. **[That / What]** will impress the teacher **[is / are]** the quality and strength of your ideas. Ideas are the crucial component of a good essay. They **[must communicate / must be communicated]** in a manner **[that / what]** **[make / makes]** **[it / them]** **[accessibly / accessible]** to the reader. **[Coming / Come]** up with **[sophisticated / sophisticating]** and intelligent ideas **[are / is]** your responsibility; no book can give **[them / it]** **[you / to you]**.

문제점 에세이를 작성할 때는 평가하는 상대방을 쉽게 잊어버린다.

{When you are immersed / (in writing an essay for class)}, / you / can (easily) forget / (that you are trying / to communicate with a (A) general / specific person) / — your teacher, / (who will grade the essay).

(When: 〈종·접〉, you: S, are immersed: V〈수동태〉 — 여러분이 푹 빠져 있을 때 / writing an essay: 〈동명사〉 O — 수업을 위한 에세이 작성에 / you: S 여러분은 / can forget: V 쉽게 잊어버릴 수 있다 / that: 〈종·접〉, you: S, are trying: V〈현재진행〉 네가 노력하는 것을 / to communicate with a specific person: O — 특정한 사람과 의사소통하려 한다는 것을 / your teacher: 〈선행사〉 즉 선생님 / who: 〈주·관〉, will grade: V, the essay: O 그 에세이를 평가할)

수업을 위한 에세이 작성에 푹 빠져 있을 때, 여러분은 특정한 사람, 즉 그 에세이를 평가할 선생님과 의사소통하려 한다는 것을 쉽게 잊어버릴 수 있다.

노트
- be immersed in : ~에 빠져 있다, ~에서 헤어나지 못하다
- write an essay : 글짓기를 하다
- communicate with : ~와 연락하다
- 〈what vs. that〉

	관계대명사(불완전한 문장)	접속사(완전한 문장)
what	○ 선행사를 포함하고 있기 때문에 what 앞에 선행사 불필요	×
that	○ that 앞에 선행사 필요	○

- 〈try 동사 쓰임〉

try	목적어	〈3형식〉
	to R	~ 노력/시도하다(S의 의지 있음)
	Ring	시험 삼아 한번 해보다(S의 의지 없음)

- 〈주격관계대명사절〉 : 계속적 용법으로는 that 사용 불가

선행사	콤마(,)	주격관계대명사절		
		주격관계대명사	~~주어~~	동사
your teacher	〈계속적 용법〉	who		will grade

주제문(해결책) 에세이를 작성할 때 항상 평가하는 사람을 염두에 두어야 한다.

However, / you / should (always) keep this in mind: / What / can you write / (that will most impress your teacher)?

(However 그러나 / you: S 여러분은 / should keep: V, this: O 항상 이것을 염두에 두어야 한다 / What: 의문사〈선행사〉 무엇을 / can write: V, you: S 쓸 수 있을까? / that: 〈주·관〉, will impress: V, your teacher: O 선생님에게 가장 깊은 인상을 줄)

그러나 여러분은 항상 이것을 염두에 두어야 한다. '선생님에게 가장 깊은 인상을 줄 무엇을 쓸 수 있을까?' 하는 점이다.

노트
- keep A in mind : A를 염두하다
- 〈주격관계대명사절의 수의 일치〉 : 선행사를 포함하고 있는 관계대명사 what 사용 불가

선행사	주격관계대명사절		
	주격관계대명사	~~주어~~	동사
What	that		will impress

- 〈what의 용법〉

용법	품사적 기능	명사 수식	해석
관계형용사	명사절 (S, O, C)	what + 명사	~한 모든
의문형용사			무슨, 어떤
의문대명사		×	무엇
관계대명사			~하는 것

■ 〈관계대명사 that만 사용하는 경우〉 : 관계대명사 that은 관계대명사 who와 which를 서로 바꿔 사용할 수 있지만 that만 사용해야 하는 경우가 있다.

선행사	관계대명사
사람＋사물	that (which, who, whom, whose, what 불가)
사람＋동물	
의문사	
the 최상급	
the 서수	
the same	
the only	
the very	
all	
every	
no	
–thing	
–body	
–one	

■ 〈most / almost / mostly〉

	대명사	형용사	부사
most	대부분의 것들(사람들)	대부분의	가장
almost	–	–	거의
mostly	–	–	주로, 일반적으로

근거1 완벽한 문법과 철자는 예상되기 때문에 그것에 대해 큰 감명을 받지 않을 것이다.

A teacher / is (probably) not going to be overly (B) indifferent / impressed / (by flawless grammar and spelling); / those qualities / are expected.

A teacher: S 선생님은 / is (probably) not going to be overly: V 아마 그리 크게 감명 받지 않을 것이다 / indifferent / impressed: S.C / by flawless grammar and spelling: 완벽한 문법과 철자에 / those qualities: S 그런 자질은 / are expected: V(수동태) 예상되기 때문이다

선생님은 아마 완벽한 문법과 철자에 그리 크게 감명 받지 않을 것이다. 그런 자질은 예상되기 때문이다.

노트 ■ 〈be going to vs. will〉

	의미	쓰임	
will＋동사원형	~할 예정이다	먼 미래	추상적인 미래
be going to＋동사원형		가까운 미래	구체적인 미래

■ 〈감정과 관련된 완전타동사〉 : 분사화가 되어 주격보어/목적격보어 자리에 나올 때 구별법

• 2형식

주어	동사	주격보어(S.C)
사람		과거분사(p.p.) – 수동(되어진, ~ 당한)
사물		현재분사(Ring) – 능동(~하고 있는, 하는)
A teacher	is not going to be	impressed

근거2 깊은 인상을 주기 위해서는 좋고 강력한 아이디어가 필요하다.

(What will impress the teacher) / is / the quality and strength / (of your ideas).

What: S(주·관) / will impress: V / the teacher: O → S 선생님에게 깊은 인상을 줄 것은 / is: V 이다 / the quality: S.C₁ 특징과 힘 / strength: S.C₂ / of your ideas: 여러분의 아이디어가 가진

선생님에게 깊은 인상을 줄 것은 여러분의 아이디어가 가진 특징과 힘이다.

노트 ■ 〈관계대명사 what절이 주어로 사용되는 경우〉 : 관계대명사 what절이 주어로 사용되면 동사는 주로 단수동사 사용함(모든 구/절은 단수 취급), 선행사가 필요한 that/which 사용 불가

~~선행사~~	주격관계대명사절(명사절 : 주어)				
	what	~~주어~~	동사	목적어	동사
	선행사를 포함한 관계대명사 (=the thing(s) which/that ~) : ~하는 것(들)은/이		will impress	the teacher	is

Ideas / are the crucial component / (of a good essay).

Ideas: S 아이디어는 / are: V / the crucial component: S.C 결정적인 요소이다 / of a good essay: 좋은 에세이에

아이디어는 좋은 에세이에 결정적인 요소이다.

They / must be communicated / (in a manner) / (that makes them (C) accessible / vague to the reader).

They: S 그것들은 / must be communicated: V(수동태) 전달되어야 한다 / a manner: (선행사) 방식으로 / that: (주·관) / makes: V / them: O / accessible / vague: O.C 그것들이 독자에게 쉽게 다가갈 수 있도록 하는

그것들은 독자가 쉽게 다가갈 수 있도록 하는 방식으로 전달되어야 한다.

노트 ■ in a manner : 어떤 의미로는; 어느 정도, 얼마간

■ accessible to : ~에 접근이 쉬운

■ 〈주격관계대명사절의 수의 일치〉 : 선행사를 포함하고 있는 관계대명사 what 사용 불가

	주격관계대명사절		
선행사	주격관계대명사	~~주어~~	동사
a manner	that		makes

■ 〈make 상태동사〉 : 수동태 시, be made＋주격보어(형용사/명사)

make	목적어	목적격보어	해석
〈상태동사〉	명사/명사 상당어구	형용사 / 명사	~가 …한 상태로 만들다
makes	them	accessible	–

• make가 '~을 …한 상태로 만들다'라는 의미로 사용될 경우, make를 상태동사라 칭한다. 이때 주의사항은 목적격보어 자리에 사용하는 형용사 대신 부사를 사용할 수 없다는 점이다.

■ 〈access vs. assess〉

	동사	명사	형용사
access	접근하다, 입력하다	접근	–
accessible	–	–	접근하기 쉬운
assess	평가하다, 할당하다	–	–
assessable	–	–	평가[산정]할 수 있는

(Coming up / with sophisticated and intelligent ideas)
〈동명사〉 〈과거분사〉 〈형용사〉
S
생각해 내는 것은 정교하고 지적인 아이디어를

/ is your responsibility; / no book / can give them / (to
V S.C 여러분의 책임이다 / S 어떤 책도 / V O 그것을 줄 수 없다

you).
여러분에게

정교하고 지적인 아이디어를 생각해 내는 것은 여러분의 책임이다. 어떤 책도 그것을 여러분에게 줄 수 없다.

노트
- come up with : ~을 생산하다, 제시[제안]하다(=produce, supply)
- 〈동명사구가 주어 자리에 사용된 경우〉 : 단수 취급으로 동사는 단수동사를 사용함

주어 : 동명사구	동사
Coming up with sophisticated and intelligent ideas	is

- 〈부정어의 종류〉

완전부정어	부사	not (~ 아닌)
		never (결코 ~ 아닌)
	형용사	no (~도 아닌)
	대명사/부사/형용사	neither (~도 아니다)
	대명사/부사/형용사	none (아무도 ~ 아니다)
	대명사/부사/명사	nothing (조금도[결코] ~ 않다)
준부정어	부사	hardly (거의 ~ 아니다)
		scarcely (거의 ~ 않다)
		barely (거의 ~ 아니게)
		seldom (좀처럼 ~ 않는)
		rarely (좀처럼 ~하지 않는)
	형용사/부사	little (거의 ~ 없는)
		few (거의 ~ 없는)

- 〈4형식을 3형식으로 바꿀 때 사용하는 전치사〉 : 전치사 to를 취하는 동사

주어 (A)	+	동사(B)	+	간접목적어 (C: 사람/동물)	+	직접목적어 (D: 사물)	(4)
		give, bring, pass, send, show, sell, hand, lend, offer, teach, tell, buy, build, choose, find, leave, make, prepare, order, ask, deal 등 수여동사					

→ 주어(A) + 동사(B) + 직접목적어(D: 사물) + 전치사 to + 간접목적어(C: 사람/동물) (3)

▶ (A), (B), (C)의 각 네모 안에서 문맥에 맞는 표현으로 가장 적절한 것은?

	(A)		(B)		(C)
①	general	……	indifferent	……	accessible
②	general	……	indifferent	……	vague
③	specific	……	impressed	……	vague
④	specific	……	impressed	……	accessible
⑤	specific	……	indifferent	……	vague

정답 | ④

해석 | ① 일반적인 – 무관심한 – 쉽게 다가갈 수 있는
② 일반적인 – 무관심한 – 모호한
③ 구체적인 – 감명 받는 – 모호한
④ 구체적인 – 감명 받는 – 쉽게 다가갈 수 있는
⑤ 구체적인 – 무관심한 – 모호한

해설 | (A) 선생님이라는 한 대상을 염두에 두고 글을 쓰라는 내용이 나오므로 'specific'을 쓰는 것이 적절하다.
(B) 선생님은 문법과 철자가 정확한 것 이상을 바랄 것이라는 내용이므로 'impressed'를 쓰는 것이 적절하다.
(C) 아이디어들은 읽는 사람이 쉽게 이해할 수 있는 방식으로 전달되어야 한다는 내용이므로 'accessible'을 쓰는 것이 적절하다.

Words

☐ immerse
☐ specific
☐ grade
☐ impress
☐ probably
☐ overly
☐ flawless
☐ quality
☐ crucial
☐ component
☐ accessible
☐ sophisticated
☐ intelligent
☐ responsibility
☐ indifferent

Phrases

☐ be immersed in
☐ communicate with
☐ in a manner
☐ come up with
☐ write an essay
☐ keep A in mind
☐ accessible to

변형문제

01 다음 글을 읽고, |조건|에 맞게 주어진 제목을 완성하시오.

| 조건 |
* (A)는 4단어로 쓸 것
* 본문에 있는 단어만을 사용할 것
* 필요한 경우, 문맥과 어법에 맞게 변형할 것

When you are immersed in writing an essay for class, you can easily forget that you are trying to communicate with a specific person — your teacher, who will grade the essay. However, you should always keep this in mind: What can you write that will most impress your teacher? A teacher is probably not going to be overly impressed by flawless grammar and spelling; those qualities are expected. What will impress the teacher is the quality and strength of your ideas. Ideas are the crucial component of a good essay. They must be communicated in a manner that makes them accessible to the reader. Coming up with sophisticated and intelligent ideas is your responsibility; no book can give them to you.

⬇

Appropriate ways (A) ____________ ____________ ____________ ____________.

02 다음 글을 읽고, |조건|에 맞게 요약문을 완성하시오.

| 조건 |
* (A)는 7단어, (B)는 4단어로 쓸 것
* 본문에 있는 단어만을 그대로 사용할 것

When you are immersed in writing an essay for class, you can easily forget that you are trying to communicate with a specific person — your teacher, who will grade the essay. However, you should always keep this in mind: What can you write that will most impress your teacher? A teacher is probably not going to be overly impressed by flawless grammar and spelling; those qualities are expected. What will impress the teacher is the quality and strength of your ideas. Ideas are the crucial component of a good essay. They must be communicated in a manner that makes them accessible to the reader. Coming up with sophisticated and intelligent ideas is your responsibility; no book can give them to you.

⬇

(A) ____________ ____________ ____________ ____________ ____________ ____________ ____________ in an essay will attract your teacher the most because a good essay is determined by ideas that have to be (B) ____________ ____________ ____________ ____________.

03 다음 글을 읽고, |조건|에 맞게 빈칸 (A), (B)를 채우시오.

조건

* (A)는 3단어, (B)는 1단어로 쓸 것
* 본문에 있는 단어를 찾아 쓸 것
* 필요한 경우, 문맥과 어법에 맞게 변형할 것

When you are immersed in writing an essay for class, you can easily forget that you are trying to communicate with a specific person — your teacher, who will grade the essay. However, you should always keep this in mind: What can you write that will most impress your teacher? A teacher is probably not going to be overly impressed by flawless grammar and spelling; those qualities are expected. What will impress the teacher is the quality and strength of your ideas. Ideas are the crucial component of a good essay. They must be communicated in a manner that makes them accessible to the reader. Coming up with sophisticated and intelligent ideas is your responsibility; no book can give them to you.

⬇

When writing an essay for class, there are elements that you have to consider:

1. Who are you writing an essay to? your essay is for a specific person.
2. How to impress the reader? your teacher does is not greatly affected by fully correct (A) __________ __________ __________, but the quality and strength your ideas in your essay.
3. How to deliver the ideas? (B) __________ ideas have to be delivered in order for the reader to be easily understood.

04 밑줄 친 부분 중 문맥상 옳지 않은 것은?

When you are ① immersed in writing an essay for class, you can easily forget that you are trying to communicate with a ② specific person — your teacher, who will grade the essay. However, you should always keep this in mind: What can you write that will most ③ impress your teacher? A teacher is probably not going to be overly impressed by flawless grammar and spelling; those qualities are ④ expected. What will impress the teacher is the quality and strength of your ideas. Ideas are the ⑤ trivial component of a good essay. They must be communicated in a manner that makes them accessible to the reader. Coming up with sophisticated and intelligent ideas is your responsibility; no book can give them to you.

어휘(밑줄/네모)

글의 논리	Spotlight
제목	야생 보호 구역 설립
주제	인간에 의해 자연이 파괴될 것이라는 믿음이 야생 보호 구역을 만들게 되었다.

PRACTICE 01

068 어법 선택 & 연결어

Yellowstone National Park was the first 'wilderness' **[protecting / protected]** area in the world, but the model spread **[rapidly / rapid]** across the globe, **[even though / as though]** **[many / much]** 'wilderness' areas **[were created / created]** by **[remove / removing]** local inhabitants. In Africa, game reserves **[were established / established]** with the aim of **[refilling / refill]** stocks of wildlife **[killing / killed]** by Europeans in the 'scramble for Africa.' **[Safeguard / Safeguarding]** animal populations in **[protected / protecting]** area **[facilitated / to facilitate]** the control of access to wildlife and also **[served / serve]** to **[separate / separating]** wildlife and domestic stock, at least to some extent, thereby **[slowed / slowing]** the rate of spread of animal diseases. Since human influence was contradictory to the wilderness ethic, the management ideal was to isolate conservation areas, **[keeping / kept]** disturbance to a minimum, on the grounds **[what / that]** **[whether / if]** **[left / leaving]** **[lonely / alone]**, nature's balance would prevail. These ideas **[supported / were supported]** by the belief **[which / that]** nature's fragile balance would be **[disrupted / disrupting]** by human influence.

설명 Yellowstone 국립공원은 야생 보호 구역의 거주인들을 내쫓아서 형성하였다.

Yellowstone National Park (S, Yellowstone 국립공원은) / was (V) the first 'wilderness' protected area (S.C, 최초의 야생 보호 구역이었다) / (in the world) (세계에서), / but (하지만) / the model (S, 그 모형이) / spread (V, 퍼져나갔다) (rapidly) (〈부사〉 빠르게) / (across the globe) (〈전치사〉 전 세계로), / {even though (〈종·접〉 비록 여러 야생 지역이) many 'wilderness' areas (S) / were created (V〈수동태〉 형성되었다고 하더라도) / (by (〈전치사〉) ① removing (〈동명사〉 토착하는 거주인들을) local inhabitants (O, 내쫓음으로서))}.

Yellowstone 국립공원은 세계최초의 '야생' 보호 구역이었지만 비록 여러 야생 (보호) 지역이 토착하는 거주인들을 내쫓음으로써 형성되었다고 하더라도, 그 모형은 전 세계로 빠르게 퍼져나 갔다.

노트
- across the globe : 전세계에서
- 〈양보/대조〉

전치사	in spite of	+명사/명사 상당어구	비록 ~이지만
	despite		
	for all		
종속접속사	though	+주어+동사	
	although		
	even though		
	even if		
	as		
	while		반면에
	whereas		

- 〈even vs. as〉

종속 접속사	even though	+주어+동사	비록 ~이지만	양보/대조
	even if			
	as though		마치 ~처럼	가정법
	as if			

- 〈부정수량형용사〉 : 막연한 수나 양의 정도를 표시하는 형용사

수(數)	few(a few), some(any), a lot of(lots of), a good(or great), plenty of, enough, all, no, many	복수명사+복수동사
양(量)	little(a little), some(any), a lot of, a good(or great), deal of, plenty of, enough, all, no, much	단수명사+단수동사

설명 아프리카에서 수렵 보호 구역은 야생 동물의 개체수를 보충하기 위해 설립되었다.

(In Africa) (아프리카에서), / game reserves (S, 수렵 보호 구역은) / were established (V〈수동태〉 설립되었다) / (with the aim of ② refilling (〈동명사〉) stocks of wildlife (O) (야생 동물의 개체수를 보충하기 위한 목적으로)) / (which was) (killed by (〈과거분사〉) Europeans) (in the 'scramble for Africa.') ('아프리카 쟁탈전' 기간 동안 유럽인들에 의해 죽임을 당한)

아프리카에서, 수렵 보호 구역은 '아프리카 쟁탈전' 기간 동안 유럽인들에 의해 죽임을 당한 야생 동물의 개체수를 보충하기 위한 목적으로 설립되었다.

노트
- with the aim of : ~을 지향하여, ~을 목표로
- a stock of : ~ 종족, 개체수

■ 〈주격관계대명사＋be동사 생략〉

–	생략할 수 있음	
명사 (선행사)	(주격관계대명사 ＋be동사)	현재분사(Ring) – 능동(~하고 있는)
		과거분사(p.p.) – 수동(~되어진, 당한)
		명사
		형용사(구) (~하는, ~할)
		부사
		전치사구
wildlife	(that/which was)	killed

설명 동물 개체수를 보호하는 것은 야생 동물과 가축을 분리하는 데 도움을 주어 동물의 질병 전파 속도를 늦췄다.

{Safeguarding animal populations / (in protected area)}
〈동명사〉 O 〈과거분사〉 S
동물 개체군을 보호하는 것은 보호 구역에서

/ ③ facilitated the control / (of access to wildlife) / and
V_1 O
접근통제를 수월하게 했으며 야생 동물에 대한

/ also served {to separate wildlife and domestic stock,
V_2
또한 야생 동물과 가축을 분리하는 데 도움을 주었다

/ (at least) / (to some extent)}, / thereby (slowing the
〈분사구문〉
적어도 어느 정도 그로 인해 동물의

rate of spread of animal diseases).
질병 전파 속도를 늦춰 주었다

보호 구역에서 동물 개체군을 보호하는 것은 야생 동물에 대한 접근통제를 수월하게 하였으며, 또한 어느 정도 야생 동물과 가축을 분리하는 데 도움을 주어 동물의 질병 전파 속도를 늦춰 주었다.

노트
■ at least : 적어도[최소한]
■ to some[a certain] extent : 얼마간, 어느 정도까지, 다소
■ 〈동명사구가 주어 자리에 사용된 경우〉 : 단수 취급으로 동사는 단수동사를 사용함

주어 : 동명사구	동사
Safeguarding animal populations in protected area	facilitated and served

■ 〈access vs. assess〉

	동사	명사	형용사
access	접근하다, 입력하다	접근	–
accessible	–	–	접근하기 쉬운
assess	평가하다, 할당하다	–	–
assessable	–	–	평가[산정]할 수 있는

■ 〈분사구문 – 문미〉 : 주절과 분사구문의 위치가 서로 바뀌어도 무관

주절		종속절(→ 분사구문)			
주어	동사	종속 접속사	주어	동사 : 상황에 맞게 아래처럼 바뀜	
		〈그대로 사용하면 의미 강조〉	(주절의 주어와 같으면 생략하고, 다르면 주격으로 사용함)	(being) (having been) 생략 가능	Ring(현재분사)
					p.p.(과거분사)
					형용사
					명사
Safeguarding ~	facilitated	thereby	–	–	slowing

■ 〈자동사가 뒤에 to부정사를 사용해 타동사처럼 목적어로 취하는 경우〉

	불완전자동사		
주어	aim	~할 작정이다, 목표로 삼다	to R
	appear	~인 듯하다	
	arrange	미리 짜다[준비하다], 타협하다, 의논하다; 협정하다	
	bother	일부러 ~하다, ~하도록 애쓰다	
	consent	~하는 것을 동의/승낙하다	
	fight	~을 위하여 다투다	
	hesitate	주저하다, 망설이다	
	hurry	서두르다	
	long	~하기를 열망/갈망하다	
	prepare	~할 각오/마음의 준비를 하다	
	seem	~처럼 보이다, ~인 듯하다	
	serve	~의 역할을 하다	
	strive	~하려고 노력하다	
	struggle	(~하려고) 분투[고투]하다, 애쓰다	
	tend	~하는 경향이 있다	
	yearn	몹시 ~하고 싶다, 열망하다	
	wait	~하는 것을 기다리다	

주제문 인간으로부터 보호 구역을 격리하는 것이 자연의 균형이 우세해질 것이라는 믿음이 있었다.

{Since human influence / was contradictory / (to the
〈종·접〉 S V S.C
인간의 영향은 반대되기 때문에

wilderness ethic)}, / the management ideal / was to
S V
야생의 윤리에 관리의 이상적인 방향은

isolate conservation areas, / {keeping disturbance (to
S.C 〈분사구문〉 O
보호 구역을 격리하는 것이었다 방해를 최소화하면서

=〈동격〉 (it was)
a ④ minimum)}, / [on the grounds {that / (if left alone),
〈종·접〉 〈종·접〉〈과거분사〉
것이라는 근거로 가만히 놔두면

/ nature's balance would prevail}].
S V
자연의 균형이 우세해질 것이라는 근거로

인간의 영향은 야생의 윤리에 반대되므로, 관리의 이상적 방향은 방해를 최소화하면서 보호 구역을 (인간으로부터) 격리하는 것이었다. 이는 가만히 놔두면 자연의 균형이 우세해질 것이라는 생각에 근거하는 것이다.

노트
■ contradictory to : ~에 모순되는
■ keep A to a minimum : A를 최저[최소]로 해 두다
■ on the grounds that＋S＋V : ~라는 근거[이유]로(보통 ground를 복수로)
■ 〈분사구문 – 문미〉 : 주절과 분사구문의 위치가 서로 바뀌어도 무관

주절		종속절(→ 분사구문)			
주어	동사	종속 접속사	주어	동사 : 상황에 맞게 아래처럼 바뀜	
		〈그대로 사용하면 의미 강조〉	(주절의 주어와 같으면 생략하고, 다르면 주격으로 사용함)	(being) (having been) 생략 가능	Ring(현재분사)
					p.p.(과거분사)
					형용사
					명사
the management ideal	was	–	–	–	keeping

■ 〈since 용법〉

종속접속사	시간	~ 이래 (죽), ~한 때부터 내내
	이유	~이므로, ~이니까
전치사	시간	~ 이래 (죽), ~부터 (내내)
부사	시간	(그때) 이래 (죽), 그 뒤[후] 줄곧

■ 〈동격의 that〉 : ~라는 A(관계대명사 which/what 사용 불가)

추상명사 (A)	종속절(명사절 – 완전한 문장)		
	(that)	주어	동사 ~
answer / belief / chance / claim / conclusion / dream / evidence / extent / fact / faith / hope / idea / likelihood / news / notion / pledge / possibility / promise / proposal / question / recognition / reply / request / result / sense / statement / suggestion / testament / theory / view / wickedness 등	종속 접속사 (생략 가능)	–	–

■ 〈종속절 안에 주어+be동사 생략 가능〉 : 주절과 종속절의 위치가 서로 바뀌어도 무관

종속절			주절	
종속접속사 〈그대로 사용하면 의미 강조〉	(주어+be동사) 〈주절의 주어와 같을 경우 생략 가능〉	Ring(현재분사) / p.p.(과거분사) / 형용사 / 명사	주어	동사
if	(it was)	alone	the management ideal	was

■ 〈alone vs. lonely〉

	형용사	서술적 형용사	부사
alone	(명사/대명사 바로 뒤에서 수식하여) ~뿐(only)	혼자의, 고독한	혼자, 홀로
lonely	고독한, 고립된, 외로운	–	–

주제문(강조) 이러한 믿음은 인간의 영향에 의해 자연이 파괴될 것이라는 생각에서 나왔다.

These ideas(S: 이러한 생각은) were supported(V〈수동태〉: 지지를 받았다) / (by the belief)(믿음에) / {that(〈종·접〉, =〈동격〉) nature's fragile balance(S: 자연의 깨어지기 쉬운 균형이) / would be ⑤ maintained(V〈수동태〉: 유지될 것이라는) / (by human influence)(인간의 영향에 의해)}.

이러한 생각은 자연의 깨어지기 쉬운 균형이 인간의 영향에 의해 유지될(→ 파괴될) 것이라는 믿음에 토대를 두고 있었다.

노트
■ be supported by : ~의 지지를 받다
■ the belief(추상명사)+that(동격)+S+V : ~라는 믿음
■ be maintained by : ~에 의해 유지되다

▶ 다음 글의 밑줄 친 부분 중, 문맥상 낱말의 쓰임이 적절하지 않은 것은?

정답 | ⑤ maintained → disrupted

해설 | 이 글은 야생 보호 구역의 설립 과정을 서술하며, 설립의 근간에는 인간의 영향을 최소화해야 한다는 믿음을 바탕으로 하고 있다는 요지의 글이다. 따라서 인간의 영향은 자연의 균형을 유지하는 데 부정적인 영향을 끼칠 것이라고 서술해야 문맥이 성립되므로 ⑤의 'maintained(유지되다)'를 'disrupted(방해받다)'와 같은 맥락의 단어로 고쳐야 한다.

Words

☐ wilderness
☐ inhabitant
☐ establish
☐ scramble
☐ facilitate
☐ domestic stock
☐ contradictory
☐ ethic
☐ isolate
☐ conservation
☐ disturbance
☐ fragile

Phrases

☐ across the globe
☐ a stock of
☐ to some[a certain] extent
☐ on the grounds that +S+V
☐ be maintained by
☐ with the aim of
☐ at least
☐ contradictory to
☐ keep A to a minimum
☐ be supported by
☐ the belief(추상명사) +that(동격)+S+V

변형문제

01 다음 글을 읽고, |조건|에 맞게 주어진 요지를 완성하시오.

| 조건 |
* (A)는 1단어, (B)는 2단어, (C)는 1단어로 쓸 것
* 본문에 있는 단어를 찾아 쓸 것
* 필요한 경우, 문맥과 어법에 맞게 변형할 것

Yellowstone National Park was the first 'wilderness' protected area in the world, but the model spread rapidly across the globe, even though many 'wilderness' areas were created by removing local inhabitants. In Africa, game reserves were established with the aim of refilling stocks of wildlife killed by Europeans in the 'scramble for Africa.' Safeguarding animal populations in protected area facilitated the control of access to wildlife and also served to separate wildlife and domestic stock, at least to some extent, thereby slowing the rate of spread of animal diseases. Since human influence was contradictory to the wilderness ethic, the management ideal was to isolate conservation areas, keeping disturbance to a minimum, on the grounds that if left alone, nature's balance would prevail. These ideas were supported by the belief that nature's fragile balance would be disrupted by human influence.

⬇

The root of the (A) ____________ of wildlife reserves is based on the belief that (B) ____________ ____________ should be (C) ____________.

02 다음 글의 내용과 일치하지 않는 것은?

Yellowstone National Park was the first 'wilderness' protected area in the world, but the model spread rapidly across the globe, even though many 'wilderness' areas were created by removing local inhabitants. In Africa, game reserves were established with the aim of refilling stocks of wildlife killed by Europeans in the 'scramble for Africa.' Safeguarding animal populations in protected area facilitated the control of access to wildlife and also served to separate wildlife and domestic stock, at least to some extent, thereby slowing the rate of spread of animal diseases. Since human influence was contradictory to the wilderness ethic, the management ideal was to isolate conservation areas, keeping disturbance to a minimum, on the grounds that if left alone, nature's balance would prevail. These ideas were supported by the belief that nature's fragile balance would be disrupted by human influence.

① Yellowstone 국립 공원은 세계최초의 야생 보호 구역이다.
② 수렵 보호 구역은 야생 동물의 개체수를 보충하기 위한 목적으로 설립되었다.
③ 보호 구역에서 동물 개체군을 보호하는 것은 야생 동물에 대한 접근 통제를 수월하게 한다.
④ 인간의 영향은 야생의 윤리와 일치한다.
⑤ 보호 구역 설립은 인간의 방해를 최소화하면서 보호 구역을 인간으로부터 격리하는 것이다.

03 다음 글을 읽고, |조건|에 맞게 주어진 요약문을 완성하시오.

| 조건 |
* (A), (B)는 각각 다르게 1단어로 쓸 것
* [보기]에서 선택한 단어를 한 번씩만 변형 없이 쓸 것

[보기] expand / implement / supply / block / intensify / generate / investigate promote / encourage / secure / eliminate / adjust / contradict / overtake

Yellowstone National Park was the first 'wilderness' protected area in the world, but the model spread rapidly across the globe, even though many 'wilderness' areas were created by removing local inhabitants. In Africa, game reserves were established with the aim of refilling stocks of wildlife killed by Europeans in the 'scramble for Africa.' Safeguarding animal populations in protected area facilitated the control of access to wildlife and also served to separate wildlife and domestic stock, at least to some extent, thereby slowing the rate of spread of animal diseases. Since human influence was contradictory to the wilderness ethic, the management ideal was to isolate conservation areas, keeping disturbance to a minimum, on the grounds that if left alone, nature's balance would prevail. These ideas were supported by the belief that nature's fragile balance would be disrupted by human influence.

⬇

The ideal ways for the protection of wild animals were to (A) ____________ human influence as much as possible and isolate conservation areas from humans to (B) ____________ nature's balance.

04 다음 글을 읽고, |조건|에 맞게 주어진 요약문을 완성하시오.

| 조건 |
* (A), (B)는 각각 다르게 1단어로 쓸 것
* 본문에 있는 단어만을 사용할 것
* 필요한 경우, 문맥과 어법에 맞게 변형할 것

Yellowstone National Park was the first 'wilderness' protected area in the world, but the model spread rapidly across the globe, even though many 'wilderness' areas were created by removing local inhabitants. In Africa, game reserves were established with the aim of refilling stocks of wildlife killed by Europeans in the 'scramble for Africa.' Safeguarding animal populations in protected area facilitated the control of access to wildlife and also served to separate wildlife and domestic stock, at least to some extent, thereby slowing the rate of spread of animal diseases. Since human influence was contradictory to the wilderness ethic, the management ideal was to isolate conservation areas, keeping disturbance to a minimum, on the grounds that if left alone, nature's balance would prevail. These ideas were supported by the belief that nature's fragile balance would be disrupted by human influence.

⬇

Keeping animal populations in sanctuaries had an effect on controlling access to wildlife and allowed (A) ____________ of wildlife from livestock to some extent. As a result, the rate of animals suffering from (B) ____________ became lower.

UNIT 17

어휘(밑줄/네모)

글의 논리	Examples
제목	감정이 소모와 회복 시간
주제	감정이 소모되는 행동을 하고 나서 회복하는 데는 시간이 걸린다.

PRACTICE 02

069 어법 선택 & 연결어

When our emotional fuel is low, we can't do an Indy pit stop and refuel **[quickly / quick]**. Our emotional reserves can **[be compared / compare]** to a car battery. If we **[seat / sit]** in a parking lot and run all our car's accessories — radio, headlights, and so on — we can probably sap that battery in about ten minutes. After that **[massively / massive]** drain, **[to suppose / suppose]** we then take the battery to a service station and say, "I'd like this battery **[charged / to charge]** in ten minutes." **[Which / What]** would the attendant tell us? "No, we're going to put the battery on our overnight charger. **[This's / It's]** going to take seven or eight hours **[to bring / bringing]** **[them / it]** all the way back up." It has **[to be recharged / to recharge]** **[slowly / slow]** or else the battery **[will be damaged / will damage]**. (   ), to recover **[proper / properly]** from an **[emotional / emotionally]** **[draining / drained]** activity **[takes / take]** time.

주장 우리 감정은 차처럼 빠르게 재급유를 할 수 없다.

(When our emotional fuel is (A) [high / low]), / we / can't do an Indy pit stop / and / refuel (quickly).

(〈종·접〉 / S: 우리 감정의 연료가 얼마 없을 때 / V / S.C / S: 우리는 / V_1 / O: 인디레이스에서 도중 정차를 할 수 없다 / 그리고 / V_2: 빠르게 재급유를 할 수 없다)

우리 감정의 연료가 얼마 없을 때, 우리는 인디레이스에서 도중 정차를 하며 빠르게 재급유를 하는 식으로는 할 수 없다.

노트
- pit stop : (자동차 경주에서 급유 · 정비를 위한) 도중 정차
- 〈high / highly〉

high	형용사	높은
	부사	높게
	명사	높은 곳
highly	부사	매우(=very)

주장 우리 감정의 보유량은 자동차 배터리와 비슷하다.

Our emotional reserves / can be compared / (to a car battery).

(S: 우리 감정의 보유량은 / V〈수동태〉: 비유될 수 있다 / 자동차 배터리에)

우리 감정의 (연료) 보유량은 자동차 배터리에 비유될 수 있다.

노트
- be compared to : ~에 비교(유)되다
- 〈compared to/with〉 : ~와 비교하다

compared to	공통점을 부각하는 말과 주장을 하고 싶은 경우
compared with	좀 더 상세하게 공통점도 있지만 차이점도 있다고 설명하고 싶은 경우

예시 자동차의 배터리 충전은 천천히 해야 한다.

[(If we / sit in a parking lot / and / run all our car's accessories) / — {radio, headlights, (and so on)}] / — we / can (probably) sap that battery / (in about ten minutes).

(〈종·접〉 S: 만약 우리가 / V_1: 주차장에 앉아 / 그리고 / V_2 / O: 자동차의 모든 악세서리를 가동시킨다면 / 라디오나 전조등 등 / S: 우리는 / V: 아마도 배터리를 소진시킬 수 있을 것이다 / O / 약 10분 만에)

우리가 주차장에 앉아 자동차의 라디오나 전조등 등의 모든 액세서리를 가동시킨다면, 우리는 아마도 약 10분 만에 배터리를 소진시킬 수 있을 것이다.

노트
- run : (기계가) 돌아가다, 작동하다, 계속 움직이다
- and so on : 기타 등등(=and so forth, and the like, etc.(=et cetera), the others, the rest, and others, and what not)
- sap : 약화시키다, 해치다
- 〈sit / seat / set〉

원형	과거	과거분사	현재분사	뜻
sit	sat	sat	sitting	vi. 앉다, ~에 놓여 있다
seat	seated	seated	seating	vt. 앉히다
set	set	set	setting	vt. 두다, ~을 놓다

(After that (B) [massive / limited] drain), / suppose / (that) [we (then) take the battery / (to a service station) / and / say, / ["I'/ d like this battery charged / (in ten minutes)}]."

(〈전치사〉 / O: 그런 대량 소모 후에 / V: 가정해 보자 / S / V_1 / O: 우리가 그 후 그 배터리를 가져가서 / 정비소에 / 그리고 말한다고 / V_2 / O / S: "나는 / V / O: 이 배터리를 충전하고 싶습니다 / O.C / 10분 안에"라고)

그런 대량 소모 후에 그 배터리를 정비소로 가져가서 "10분 안에 이 배터리를 충전하고 싶습니다."라고 말한다고 가정해 보자.

노트
- take A to B : A를 B로 가져가다(데려가다)
- would like : ~하고 싶다
- 〈직접명령문〉

긍정문	R	~해라
	Please+R	~해 주세요
부정문	Don't+R	~하지 마라
	Never+R	

- 〈목적격종속접속사 that 생략〉 : 완전타동사의 목적어로 사용된 경우 / 관계대명사 what 사용 불가

	종속절(명사절 : 목적어) (완전한 절)		
완전타동사	that	주어	동사
suppose	목적격종속접속사 – 생략 가능(~하는 것을)	we	take and say

- 〈5형식에서 목적격보어 자리에 분사가 나오는 동사〉 : 수동태 시, be p.p.+주격보어)

주어	불완전타동사	목적어	목적격보어	
	feel, keep, leave, like, smell, start, want, wish, send 등		분사	현재분사(Ring) : 능동
				과거분사(p.p.) : 수동

- 〈likely / alike / like〉

likely	형용사	~일 것 같은 (be to 동사원형 : ~일 것 같다)
	부사	아마(probably)
alike	서술적 형용사 (보어로만 사용, 명사 수식 불가)	동일한
	부사	똑같이
like	전치사	~처럼
	동사	좋아하다

What / would the attendant / tell us?
(What: O, the attendant: S, would ... tell: V, us: O)
어떤 말을 / 직원은 / 우리에게 할까?

직원은 우리에게 어떤 말을 할까?

"No, / we're going to put the battery / (on our overnight charger). / It's going to take seven or eight hours / (to bring it all the way back up)."
(we: S, 're going to put: V, the battery: O / It: S, 's going to take: V, seven or eight hours: O / it: O)
안 됩니다 / 우리는 그 배터리를 충전기에 넣을 겁니다 / 밤새워 충전하는 / 7 ~ 8시간이 걸릴 것입니다 / 배터리가 다 채워지는 데는

"안 됩니다. 우리는 그 배터리를 밤새워 충전하는 충전기에 넣을 것입니다. 배터리가 다시 다 채워지는 데는 7 ~ 8시간이 걸릴 것입니다."(라고 말할 것이다.)

노트
- put A on B : A를 B에 두다, 넣다
- all the way : 내내[시종], 완전히, 온 힘을 다해
- bring back up : 다시 되살리다

- 〈be going to vs. will〉

	의미	쓰임	
will+동사원형	~할 예정이다	먼 미래	추상적인 미래
be going to+동사원형		가까운 미래	구체적인 미래

- 〈take 동사 쓰임〉 : ~하는 데 시간이 …만큼 걸린다

It	takes	시간	to R

주장 배터리는 천천히 충전해야 한다.

It / has to be recharged (C) (fast / slowly) / or else the battery / will be damaged.
(It: S, has to be recharged: V(to R 수동) / the battery: S, will be damaged: V(미래 수동))
이것은 / 천천히 충전되어야 한다 / 그렇지 않으면 / 그 배터리는 / 손상을 입을 것이다

배터리는 천천히 충전해야지 그렇지 않으면 손상을 입을 것이다.

노트
- or else : 그렇지 않으면(=otherwise)
- will be p.p. : 미래 수동
- 〈to R의 태와 시제〉

태	능동태	to R
	수동태	to be p.p.
시제	단순시제 : 본동사 시제와 동일	to R
	완료시제 : 본동사 시제보다 한 시제 앞선 시제	to have p.p.
	완료 수동	to have been p.p.

주제문 감정이 소모되는 행동을 하고 나서 회복하는 데는 시간이 걸린다.

Likewise, / to recover properly / (from an emotionally draining activity) / takes time.
(to recover properly: S, from: 〈전치사〉, emotionally: 〈부사〉, draining: 〈현재분사〉, activity: O, takes: V, time: O)
마찬가지로 / 회복하는 것은 / 감정이 소모되는 행동을 하고 나서 / 시간이 걸린다

마찬가지로 감정이 소모되는 행동을 하고 나서 회복하는 것은 시간이 걸린다.

노트
- recover from : ~에서 회복하다[되찾다]
- take time : 시간이 걸리다
- 〈to부정사구가 주어 자리에 사용된 경우〉 : 단수 취급으로 동사는 단수동사를 사용함

주어 : to부정사구	동사
to recover properly from an emotionally draining activity	takes

▶ (A), (B), (C)의 각 네모 안에서 문맥에 맞는 낱말로 가장 적절한 것은?

	(A)		(B)		(C)
①	high	……	massive	……	fast
②	high	……	limited	……	slowly
③	low	……	massive	……	fast
④	low	……	massive	……	slowly
⑤	low	……	limited	……	fast

정답 | ④

해석 | ① 많은 – 대량의 – 빠른
② 많은 – 제한된 – 느린
③ 적은 – 대량의 – 빠른
④ 적은 – 대량의 – 느린
⑤ 적은 – 제한된 – 빠른

해설 | (A) 감정이 소모되어 재충전하는 것에 관련된 내용이므로 'low'가 적절하다.
(B) 바로 앞 문장에서 자동차의 모든 액세서리를 가동시킨다는 내용이 나오므로 'massive'가 적절하다.
(C) 다 쓴 배터리를 충전하는 데 7 ~ 8시간이 걸린다는 앞에 나온 정비소 직원의 말을 감안하면 'slowly'가 적절하다.

Words

- ☐ emotional
- ☐ fuel
- ☐ reserves
- ☐ a parking lot
- ☐ accessory
- ☐ headlight
- ☐ probably
- ☐ sap
- ☐ massive
- ☐ drain
- ☐ suppose
- ☐ attendant
- ☐ overnight
- ☐ charger
- ☐ back up
- ☐ recharge
- ☐ damage
- ☐ likewise
- ☐ recover
- ☐ properly

Phrases

- ☐ be compared to
- ☐ take A to B
- ☐ put A on B
- ☐ bring back up
- ☐ recover from
- ☐ and so on
- ☐ would like
- ☐ all the way
- ☐ or else
- ☐ take time

우선순위 영단어 역대 수능 기출 + 전국 모의고사 기출 + EBS 기출 + 교과서 기출 빈출 어휘

단어	뜻	단어	뜻	단어	뜻
immediacy	n. 직접성	immunity	n. 면역(성)	immunization	n. 면역
impaired	a. 손상된	impassable	a. 지나갈 수 없는	impede	v. 방해하다
impetus	n. 추진력	implant	n. 신체에 이식된 조직	implementation	n. 이행
impoverish	v. 가난하게 하다	impoverished	a. 가난하게 된	in a flash	순식간에
in action	작용하는	in all likelihood	십중팔구	in contrast	대조적으로
in contrast to	~와는 달리	in evidence	눈에 띄는	in itself	그 자체로[본질적으로]
in nature	사실상	in place	가동 중인	in return for	~과 맞바꾸어
in stock	비축된	in sum	말하자면	in the course of	~ 중에
in the grip of	~에게 잡혀[속박되어]	in the long run	결국	in the presence of	~이 있는 데서
in the thick of	~이 가장 활발할 때	inability	n. 무능	inaccessible	a. 접근할 수 없는
inappropriate	a. 부적절한	incompetence	n. 무능	incomplete	a. 불완전한
inconsistency	n. 불일치	inconvenient	a. 불편한	increasingly	ad. 점점 더
indefinite	a. 정해져 있지 않은	indefinitely	ad. 무기한으로	in-depth	a. 면밀한
index finger	n. 검지	indifferent	a. 무관심한	induction	n. 유도
indulgence	n. 관대	industrialized	a. 선진 산업국의	industry	n. 근면함
ineffective	a. 비효율적인	inefficiency	n. 비능률	inexperienced	a. 경험이 부족한
infancy	n. 유년기	infect	v. 오염시키다	inflammation	n. 염증
inflationary	a. 인플레이션의	information	n. 정보	informative	a. 정보를 제공하는
ingrained	a. 깊이 베어든	inhale	v. 흡입하다	innovative	a. 혁신적인
innovator	n. 혁신자	inscription	n. 새겨진 글	insecure	a. 불안한

PRACTICE 02

변형문제

01 다음 글을 읽고, |조건|에 맞게 빈칸 (A), (B)를 채우시오.

| 조건 |
* (A)는 1단어, (B)는 3단어로 쓸 것
* [보기]에서 선택한 단어를 한 번씩만 쓸 것
* 필요한 경우, 문맥과 어법에 맞게 변형할 것

[보기] quick / full / complete / slow / drain / activity / reserves / battery / fuel / charge / emotion

When our emotional fuel is low, we can't do an Indy pit stop and refuel quickly. Our emotional reserves can be compared to a car battery. If we sit in a parking lot and run all our car's accessories — radio, headlights, and so on — we can probably sap that battery in about ten minutes. After that massive drain, suppose we then take the battery to a service station and say, "I'd like this battery charged in ten minutes." What would the attendant tell us? "No, we're going to put the battery on our overnight charger. It's going to take seven or eight hours to bring it all the way back up." It has to be recharged (A) ___________ or else the battery will be damaged. Likewise, to recover properly from an (B) ___________ ___________ ___________ takes time.

02 다음 글을 읽고, |조건|에 맞게 주어진 주제문을 완성하시오.

| 조건 |
* (A)는 1단어로 쓸 것
* [보기]에서 선택한 단어를 변형 없이 한 번씩만 쓸 것

[보기] exhausting / time - expired / time-consuming / incompatible appropriate / productive / comparable / efficient / time-effective / prevalent

When our emotional fuel is low, we can't do an Indy pit stop and refuel quickly. Our emotional reserves can be compared to a car battery. If we sit in a parking lot and run all our car's accessories — radio, headlights, and so on — we can probably sap that battery in about ten minutes. After that massive drain, suppose we then take the battery to a service station and say, "I'd like this battery charged in ten minutes." What would the attendant tell us? "No, we're going to put the battery on our overnight charger. It's going to take seven or eight hours to bring it all the way back up." It has to be recharged slowly or else the battery will be damaged. Likewise, to recover properly from an emotionally draining activity takes time.

⬇

To take our emotional reserves back to full recovery from an emotionally draining activity is (A) ___________ like the way a car battery is charged.

03 다음 글의 순서로 가장 적절한 것은?

When our emotional fuel is low, we can't do an Indy pit stop and refuel quickly. Our emotional reserves can be compared to a car battery.

(A) What would the attendant tell us? "No, we're going to put the battery on our overnight charger. It's going to take seven or eight hours to bring it all the way back up."

(B) If we sit in a parking lot and run all our car's accessories — radio, headlights, and so on — we can probably sap that battery in about ten minutes. After that massive drain, suppose we then take the battery to a service station and say, "I'd like this battery charged in ten minutes."

(C) It has to be recharged slowly or else the battery will be damaged. Likewise, to recover properly from an emotionally draining activity takes time.

① (A) - (B) - (C)　② (B) - (A) - (C)　③ (B) - (C) - (A)
④ (C) - (A) - (B)　⑤ (C) - (B) - (A)

04 다음 문장이 들어갈 부분으로 가장 적절한 곳을 고르시오.

After that massive drain, suppose we then take the battery to a service station and say, "I'd like this battery charged in ten minutes."

When our emotional fuel is low, we can't do an Indy pit stop and refuel quickly. Our emotional reserves can be compared to a car battery. (①) If we sit in a parking lot and run all our car's accessories — radio, headlights, and so on — we can probably sap that battery in about ten minutes. (②) What would the attendant tell us? (③) "No, we're going to put the battery on our overnight charger. (④) It's going to take seven or eight hours to bring it all the way back up." (⑤) It has to be recharged slowly or else the battery will be damaged. Likewise, to recover properly from an emotionally draining activity takes time.

UNIT 17

어휘(밑줄/네모)

글의 논리	Enumeration (열거)
제목	항의, 저항, 혁명의 수단인 예술
주제	예술은 현재의 상황을 보여 주는 힘도 있지만 항의, 저항, 혁명의 수단으로 사용된다.

PRACTICE 03

070 어법 선택 & 연결어

Art is a force for **[preservation / preserving]** the **[status / statue]** quo, but it is also often **[used / using]** in the **[oppositely / opposite]** way — as a vehicle of protest, resistance, and even revolution. A number of artists **[has / have]** attempted, through **[their / its]** own artistic media, to **[raise / rise]** the consciousness of **[their / its]** **[oppressing / oppressed]** countrymen and **[to bring / bringing]** about changes in social and political structures. (   ), Marjorie Agosin documented the case of the Chilean *arpilleristas*, who **[to tell / told]** the story of political oppression on scraps of cloth. These courageous artists **[were considered / considered]** **[so / such]** a threat to the **[establishing / established]** government **[what / that]** they were eventually **[banned / banning]** in **[their / its]** own country. In Chile, **[during / while]** the Augusto Pinochet regime, local artists painted murals under the cover of night **[depicted / depicting]** scenes of government oppression, only to have **[them / it]** **[to remove / removed]** by the military police the next morning.

주제문 예술은 현재의 상황을 보여 주는 힘도 있지만 항의, 저항, 혁명의 수단으로 사용된다.

Art / is a force / (for preserving the status quo), / but /
(S 예술은 / V / S.C 힘이다 / 〈동명사〉 preserving, O the status quo: 현재의 상황을 보존하기 위한 / 그러나)

it / is (also) often used / (in the ① opposite way) / —
(S 그것은 / V〈수동태〉 또한 흔히 사용된다 / 반대 방향으로)

(as a vehicle of protest, resistance, and even revolution).
(항의, 저항, 심지어 혁명의 수단으로)

예술은 현재의 상황을 보존하기 위한 힘이지만, 그것은 또한 항의, 저항, 심지어 혁명의 수단으로 반대 방향으로 흔히 사용된다.

노트
- status quo : 현재의 상황, 현상
- as a vehicle of : ~의 수단으로써
- 〈동명사 vs. 명사〉 : 전치사의 목적어 자리에 동명사와 명사를 둘 다 사용할 수 있지만, 동명사는 뒤에 목적어로 명사/대명사 등을 가질 수 있는 점이 명사와의 차이점이다.

〈전치사구〉		
전치사	목적어	
for	~~preservation~~	the status quo
	preserving	

열거 많은 예술가들은 정치적 구조의 변화를 가져오기 위해 예술을 사용했다.

A number of artists / have attempted, / (through their own artistic media), / to raise the consciousness of their oppressed countrymen / and / to bring about ② changes (in social and political structures).
(S 많은 예술가들은 / V〈현재완료〉 시도해왔다 / 〈전치사〉 through, 자신들의, O: 예술적 매체를 통해 / O_1 억압받는 동포의 의식을 일깨우려고 / 〈과거분사〉 oppressed / 그리고 / O_2 사회 정치적 구조의 변화를 가져오려고)

많은 예술가들은 자신들의 예술적 매체를 통해 억압받는 동포의 의식을 일깨우고 사회 정치적 구조의 변화를 가져오기 위해 시도했다.

노트
- bring about A : A를 유발[초래]하다(=cause)
- 〈주어와 동사의 수의 일치〉 : the number of / a number of

the	number (수)	of	복수명사	+단수동사
a	number (많은)	of	복수명사	+복수동사

- 〈목적어 자리에 to부정사를 취하는 완전타동사〉

주어	완전타동사	목적어
–	afford / agree / ask / attempt / care / choose / claim / dare / decide / demand / desire / determine / elect / expect / fail / guarantee / hope / intend / learn / manage / need / offer / plan / pretend / promise / refuse / resolve / seek / threaten / volunteer / want / wish 등	to 동사원형

- 〈명사의 복수형〉 : 외래어 복수(um/on → a)

단수	복수	뜻
datum	data	자료
medium	media	중간, 매개체
bacterium	bacteria	박테리아
memorandum	memoranda	비망록, 메모
phenomenon	phenomena	현상, 사건
criterion	criteria	기준, 표준

■ 〈혼동 어휘〉

through	전치사	~을 통하여
throughout	전치사	[장소] ~의 도처에, [시간] ~ 동안, ~ 내내
	부사	도처에, 완전히, 철저하게
though	접속사	~에도 불구하고
thorough	형용사	철저한, 완전한

■ 〈소유격을 강조하는 표현〉 : '소유격+own(~ 자신)+명사'

	own은 소유격대명사 강조		
전치사	소유격	own	명사
through	their	own	artistic media

■ 〈혼동하기 쉬운 동사〉

• rise / raise / arise / arouse / rouse

원형	과거	과거분사	현재분사	뜻
rise	rose	risen	rising	vi. 오르다, 일어나다
raise	raised	raised	raising	vt. 올리다, 기르다
arise	arose	arisen	arising	vi. 발생하다, 기인하다
arouse	aroused	aroused	arousing	vt. (감정) 불러 일으키다, 자극하다
rouse	roused	roused	rousing	vt. 깨우다, 일으키다

예시 Marjorie Agosin은 정치적 업악의 이야기를 표현한 경우를 문서로 기록했다.

(For example), / Marjorie Agosin / documented the case (of the Chilean *arpilleristas*), / {who told the story (of political ③ oppression) / (on scraps of cloth)}.

예를 들어 / Marjorie Agosin은 [S(선행사)] / 경우를 문서로 기록했는데 [V, O] / 칠레의 'arpilleristas'의 / 이들이 정치적 억압의 이야기를 [〈주·관〉 V O] / 표현했다 / 옷감 조각에

예를 들어, Marjorie Agosin은 옷감 조각에 정치적 억압의 이야기를 표현한 칠레의 'arpilleristas'의 경우를 문서로 기록했다.

노트 ■ 〈주격관계대명사절〉 : 선행사와 주격관계대명사 who가 서로 떨어져 있는 경우

		주격관계대명사절		
선행사	~	주격관계대명사	~~주어~~	동사
Marjorie Agosin		who		told

열거2 예술가들은 정부에 의해 활동을 금지 당했다.

These courageous artists / were considered / such a ④ support (to the established government) / {that they were (eventually) banned (in their own country)}.

이 용기 있는 예술가들은 [S] / 간주되었고 [V〈수동태〉] / 기존의 〈과거분사〉 / 정부에 아주 큰 지지로 [S.C] / 그래서 그들은 [〈종·접〉 S] / 자신의 나라에서 활동을 금지당했다 [V〈수동태〉]

이 용기 있는 예술가들은 기존의 정부에 큰 지지로(→ 위협으로) 간주되었고 그들은 결국 자신의 나라에서 (활동을) 금지당했다.

노트 ■ in their own country : 소유격 강조 표현[전치사+소유격+own(~ 자신)+명사]

■ 〈consider 동사의 쓰임〉 : 5형식인 경우(~을 …라고 생각하다), 〈수동태 시, be considered+주격보어[(to be) 보어 / as+보어]〉

consider	목적어	목적격보어
		as+보어
		(to be) 보어

■ 〈원인과 결과를 동시에 나타내는 표현〉 : '너무 ~해서 그 결과 …하다' (종속접속사 that 생략 가능)

원인(너무 ~해서)				결과(그 결과 ~하다)		
so	형용사	a(n)+명사		(that)	주어	동사
such	a(n)	형용사	명사	that	주어	동사

결과	so	(that)	원인
원인	, so	(that)	결과

■ 〈관사의 위치〉

so / how / too / as	형용사	a/an	명사
such / what / many / quite / rather / half	a/an	형용사	명사

■ 〈what vs. that〉

	관계대명사(불완전한 문장)	접속사(완전한 문장)
what	○ 선행사를 포함하고 있기 때문에 what 앞에 선행사 불필요	×
that	○ that 앞에 선행사 필요	○

열거3 정부의 억압 장면을 묘사하는 벽화를 그린 예술가들은 군 헌병대에 의해 제거되었다.

(In Chile), / (during the Augusto Pinochet regime), / local artists / painted murals / (under the cover of night) / (depicting scenes of government oppression), / {only to have them ⑤ removed / (by the military police) / (the next morning)}.

칠레에서 / Augusto Pinochet 정권 동안에 [〈전치사〉 O] / 현지 예술가들은 [S] (which were) / 벽화를 그렸다 [V O] / 야음을 틈타 / 정부의 억압 장면을 묘사하는 〈현재분사〉 / 하지만 결국 그것들은 제거되었다 [O O.C] / 군 헌병대에 의해 / 다음날 아침

칠레에서 Augusto Pinochet 정권 동안에 현지 예술가들은 야음을 틈타 정부의 억압 장면을 묘사하는 벽화를 그렸는데, 그것들은 결국 다음날 아침 군 헌병대에 의해 제거되었다.

노트 ■ under (the) cover of night : 야음을 타서

■ only to R : 하지만 결국 ~하다(=but 동사)

■ 〈to부정사의 부사적 용법 – 결과〉

awake	to R	눈을 떠서 ~하다
live		살아서 ~하다
grow up		자라서 결국 ~이 되었다
never		그리고 결코 ~ 않다(=and never 동사)
only		하지만 결국 ~하다(=but 동사)

■ 〈주격관계대명사＋be동사 생략〉

–	생략할 수 있음	
명사 (선행사)	(주격관계대명사 ＋be동사)	현재분사(Ring) – 능동(~하고 있는)
		과거분사(p.p.) – 수동(~되어진, 당한)
		명사
		형용사(구) (~하는, ~할)
		부사
		전치사구
murals	(which/that were)	depicting

■ 〈have 사역동사〉

have	목적어	목적격보어	해석
〈사역동사〉	명사/ 명사 상당어구	동사원형(R)	~가 …하도록 시키다
		과거분사(p.p)	~가 …하게 당하다
have	them	removed	–

■ 시간(~ 동안)

전치사	during	＋명사 / 명사 상당어구
종속접속사	while	＋주어＋동사

▶ 다음 글의 밑줄 친 부분 중, 문맥상 낱말의 쓰임이 적절하지 않은 것은?

정답 | ④ support → threat

해설 | ④ 옷감 조각에 정치적 억압의 이야기를 쓴 예술가들이 자신의 나라에서 활동을 금지당했다고 했으므로, 기존의 정부에 위협이 되었다는 것이 글의 흐름상 적절하다. 따라서 ④ 'support → threat'로 고쳐야 한다.

Words

☐ preserve
☐ opposite
☐ vehicle
☐ protest
☐ resistance
☐ revolution
☐ consciousness
☐ oppressed
☐ countryman
☐ scrap
☐ cloth
☐ courageous
☐ government
☐ eventually
☐ ban
☐ regime
☐ mural
☐ depict
☐ oppression
☐ military police

Phrases

☐ as a vehicle of
☐ in their own country
☐ only to R
☐ bring about A
☐ under (the) cover of night

우선순위 영단어 역대 수능 기출 + 전국 모의고사 기출 + EBS 기출 + 교과서 기출 빈출 어휘

단어	뜻	단어	뜻	단어	뜻
insecurity	n. 불안(감)	insert	v. 끼워 넣다	insightful	a. 통찰력이 있는
instructive	a. 유익한	instrumental	a. 수단이 되는	insult	n. 모욕
insulting	a. 모욕적인	insurmountable	a. 극복할 수 없는	intellect	n. 지식인
intellectually	ad. 지적으로	intended	a. 의도하는	interactive	a. 상호 작용을 하는
intercept	v. 가로막다	intercultural	a. 이종 문화 간의	interlock	v. 연결되다
intermediate	a. 중간의	intermingle	v. 섞이다	intersection	n. 교차로
intervene	v. 개입하다	intimidate	v. 협박하다	intrigue	n. 음모
intuition	n. 직관	intuitive	a. 생각이 직관에 의한	invalid	n. 병(약)자
invaluable	a. 매우 소중한	inventory	n. 재고품	investigator	n. 조사원
involuntarily	ad. 모르는 사이에	involuntary	a. 무심결의	inward	ad. 내부로
irrationality	n. 비합리성	irregularity	n. 불규칙성	irrelevance	n. 무관계
irresistible	a. 불가항력인	irrigation	n. 물을 댐	irritable	a. 화가 난
janitor	n. (건물의) 관리인	jeopardy	n. 위험	jerk	n. (갑자기) 홱 움직임
jiggle	v. 가볍게 흔들다	jointly	ad. 공동으로	judge	n. 재판관

변형문제

01 다음 글을 읽고, |조건|에 맞게 주어진 요약문을 완성하시오.

| 조건 |
* (A)는 1단어, (B)는 3단어로 쓸 것
* 본문에 있는 단어만을 사용할 것
* 필요한 경우, 문맥과 어법에 맞게 변형할 것

Art is a force for preserving the status quo, but it is also often used in the opposite way — as a vehicle of protest, resistance, and even revolution. A number of artists have attempted, through their own artistic media, to raise the consciousness of their oppressed countrymen and to bring about changes in social and political structures. For example, Marjorie Agosin documented the case of the Chilean *arpilleristas*, who told the story of political oppression on scraps of cloth. These courageous artists were considered such a threat to the established government that they were eventually banned in their own country. In Chile, during the Augusto Pinochet regime, local artists painted murals under the cover of night depicting scenes of government oppression, only to have them removed by the military police the next morning.

⬇

Although art is a force to preserve the current situation, many artists have (A) ______________ used their artistic media as a means of protest, resistance, and even revolution. For example, artists who wrote stories of political oppression on pieces of cloth were expelled from (B) ______________ ______________ ______________ because the government regarded their activities as a threat.

02 다음 글의 순서로 적절한 것은?

Art is a force for preserving the status quo, but it is also often used in the opposite way — as a vehicle of protest, resistance, and even revolution.

(A) For example, Marjorie Agosin documented the case of the Chilean *arpilleristas*, who told the story of political oppression on scraps of cloth. These courageous artists were considered such a threat to the established government that they were eventually banned in their own country.

(B) A number of artists have attempted, through their own artistic media, to raise the consciousness of their oppressed countrymen and to bring about changes in social and political structures.

(C) In Chile, during the Augusto Pinochet regime, local artists painted murals under the cover of night depicting scenes of government oppression, only to have them removed by the military police the next morning.

① (A) - (B) - (C)　② (B) - (A) - (C)　③ (B) - (C) - (A)
④ (C) - (A) - (B)　⑤ (C) - (B) - (A)

03 다음 글을 읽고, |조건|에 맞게 주어진 주제문을 완성하시오.

| 조건 |
* (A), (B)는 각각 다르게 1단어로 쓸 것
* 본문에서 단어를 찾아 쓸 것
* 필요한 경우, 문맥과 어법에 맞게 변형할 것

Art is a force for preserving the status quo, but it is also often used in the opposite way — as a vehicle of protest, resistance, and even revolution. A number of artists have attempted, through their own artistic media, to raise the consciousness of their oppressed countrymen and to bring about changes in social and political structures. For example, Marjorie Agosin documented the case of the Chilean *arpilleristas*, who told the story of political oppression on scraps of cloth. These courageous artists were considered such a threat to the established government that they were eventually banned in their own country. In Chile, during the Augusto Pinochet regime, local artists painted murals under the cover of night depicting scenes of government oppression, only to have them removed by the military police the next morning.

⬇

(A) ____________ has been used as a way to (B) ____________ against government oppression.

04 다음 문장이 들어갈 부분으로 가장 적절한 곳을 고르시오.

For example, Marjorie Agosin documented the case of the Chilean *arpilleristas*, who told the story of political oppression on scraps of cloth.

(①) Art is a force for preserving the status quo, but it is also often used in the opposite way — as a vehicle of protest, resistance, and even revolution. (②) A number of artists have attempted, through their own artistic media, to raise the consciousness of their oppressed countrymen and to bring about changes in social and political structures. (③) These courageous artists were considered such a threat to the established government that they were eventually banned in their own country. (④) In Chile, during the Augusto Pinochet regime, local artists painted murals under the cover of night depicting scenes of government oppression, only to have them removed by the military police the next morning. (⑤)

UNIT 18

장문

글의 논리	Spotlight
제목	과학에서의 불확실성
주제	과학이 발전하기 위해서는 불확실성의 역할이 중요하다.

수능 ANALYSIS 01-02

071 어법 선택 & 연결어

A more powerful example of the role of uncertainty in innovation comes from science. The greatest asset of the scientific tradition, ( ), is **[its / their]** continual self-scrutiny and skepticism. **[Accep / Accepting]** uncertainty — at least at the level of scientific communities — **[is / are]** the **[defined / defining]** feature of science. It's not a defect. Two giants of the philosophy of science, Karl Popper and Thomas Kuhn, **[both / either]** emphasized this point in different ways. For Popper, intellectual honesty means **[to try / trying]** **[refuting / to refute]**, rather than **[proves / prove]**, a theory about the world. For Kuhn, science leaps forward **[which / when]** contradictions pile up and lead to **[give / giving]** up a dominant theory. In each view, the acceptance of uncertainty precedes new ideas and discoveries. Uncertainty, as climate scientist Tamsin Edwards put **[it / them]** **[recent / recently]**, "is the engine of science."

The editors of *Nature* once wrote **[what / that]** if science didn't "progress darkly, up and down **[much / many]** blind alleys and false trails, from hypothesis to hypothesis, [then] science would soon end." That's **[why / because]** it is the responsibility of scientific journals (and scientific writers) to be distrustful. The openness at the heart of the scientific spirit means never **[to take / taking]** error **[personal / personally]**, **[seen / seeing]** success as **[temporary / temporarily]**, and **[welcome / welcoming]** criticism.

주제문 과학에서는 불확실성의 역할이 중요하다.

A more powerful example (S, 더욱 강력한 예시는) / (of the role of uncertainty) (불확실성의 역할에 관한) / (in innovation) (혁신에서의) / comes (V) (from science). (과학에서 나온다)

혁신에서의 불확실성의 역할에 관한 더욱 강력한 예시는 과학에서 나온다.

노트 ■ come from : ~에서 생겨나다(=originate)

The greatest asset (S, 가장 위대한 자산은) / (of the scientific tradition), (과학적인 전통은) / (after all), (결국) / is (V) its continual self-scrutiny (S.C1) and skepticism (S.C2). (끊임없는 자기반성과 회의론에 있다)

과학적 전통의 가장 위대한 자산은, 결국, 끊임없는 자기반성과 회의론에 있다.

노트 ■ after all : 결국에는

(Accepting (〈동명사〉) uncertainty (O)) (S, 불확실성을 받아들이는 것은) / — (at least) (— 적어도) / (at the level of scientific communities) (과학계의 수준에서) / — is (V) the defining feature of science (S.C, — 과학의 결정적인 특성이다).

불확실성을 받아들이는 것은 적어도 과학계의 수준에서 과학의 결정적인 특성이다.

노트
■ at least : 적어도, 최소한
■ at the level of : ~의 수준에서
■ 〈동명사구가 주어 자리에 사용된 경우〉 : 단수 취급으로 동사는 단수동사를 사용함

주어 : 동명사구	동사
Accepting uncertainty	is

설명 불확실성은 결점이 아니다.

It' (S, 그것은) / s not (V) a defect (S.C). (결점이 아니다)

그것은 결점이 아니다.

설명 Karl Popper와 Thomas Kuhn은 서로 다른 방법으로 이 점을 강조했다.

Two giants (S, 두 거장인) / (of the philosophy of science), (과학 철학의) / (Karl Popper and Thomas Kuhn), (=〈동격〉, Karl Popper와 Thomas Kuhn은) / (both) emphasized (V) this point (O) (둘 다 이 점을 강조하였다) / (in different ways). (서로 다른 방법으로)

과학 철학의 두 거인인 Karl Popper와 Thomas Kuhn은 둘 다 서로 다른 방법으로 이 점을 강조하였다.

노트
- in a different way : 다른 방식으로
- 〈동격〉 : A(명사), B(명사) (A가 주어, B라는 A)

동격(B라는 A)		
명사(A)	,(콤마)	명사(B)
Two giants of the philosophy of science		Karl Popper and Thomas Kuhn

관점 1 Popper는 세상에 관한 이론을 증명하는 것보다 반박하려고 노력하는 것이 중요하다고 주장했다.

(For Popper), / intellectual honesty / means / trying to refute, / (rather than prove), / a theory (about the world).

Popper에 있어서 / 지적인 정직성은(S) / 의미한다(V) / 반박하려고 노력하는 것을(O) / 증명하는 것보다 / 세상에 관한 이론을(O_1, O_2)

Popper에 있어서, 지적인 정직성은 세상에 관한 이론을 증명하려 하는 것보다 반박하려고 노력하는 것이다.

노트
- A rather than B : B보다 오히려 A
- 〈mean 동사 쓰임〉

mean	목적어	〈3형식〉
	동명사	~을 의미하다
	to R	~할 작정이다

- 〈try 동사 쓰임〉

try	목적어	〈3형식〉
	to R	~ 노력/시도하다(S의 의지 있음)
	Ring	시험 삼아 한번 해보다(S의 의지 없음)

- 〈병렬구조〉 : 비교급

	동사 means의 목적어					
means	trying	to refute,	rather than	prove,	a theory	about the world.
동사	동명사	try의 목적어 2	〈비교급〉	try의 목적어 1 refute와 병렬	refute와 prove의 공통 목적어	
		동명사 trying의 목적어				

관점 2 Kuhn은 과학은 모순이 쌓이고 기존의 이론을 포기할 때 비약적으로 발전한다고 주장했다.

(For Kuhn), / science / leaps forward / (when contradictions pile up / and / lead to giving up a dominant theory).

Kuhn에게 / 과학은(S) / 비약적으로 발전한다(V) / (종·접) 모순이(S) 쌓이고(V_1) / 이어질 때(V_2) / 〈동명사〉 지배적인 이론을 포기하는 것으로

Kuhn에게, 과학은 모순이 쌓이고 지배적인 이론을 포기하기에 이를 때 비약적으로 발전한다.

노트
- leap forward : 갑자기 앞으로 나아가다, 빠르게 진보(발전)하다
- pile up : 많아지다, 쌓이다(=accumulate)
- A lead to(전치사) B : A이라는 원인 때문에 B라는 결과가 발생하다, A는 B로 이어지다
- give up A : A를 포기하다

주제문(재진술) 불확실성의 수용은 새로운 생각과 발견에 앞서 발생한다.

(In each view), / the acceptance / (of uncertainty) / precedes new ideas and discoveries.

각각의 관점에서 / 수용은(S) / 불확실성의 / 새로운 생각과 발견보다 앞서 일어난다(V, O_1, O_2)

각각의 관점에서, 불확실성의 수용은 새로운 생각과 발견보다 앞서 일어난다.

주제문(재진술) 불확실성은 과학의 엔진이라고 불린다.

Uncertainty, / {as climate scientist Tamsin Edwards put it / (recently)}, / "is the engine of science."

불확실성은(S) / (종·접) 기후 과학자 Tamsin Edwards가(S) 언급한(V, O) 바와 같이 / 최근에 / "과학의 엔진"이다(V, S.C)

불확실성은, 최근 기후 과학자 Tamsin Edwards가 언급한 바와 같이, "과학의 엔진"이라고 할 수 있다.

노트
- put it : 말하다, 언급하다

주제문(재진술) 불확실성이 없으면 과학은 곧 종말에 이른다.

The editors / (of *Nature*) / (once) wrote / [that {if science didn't "progress / (darkly), / (up and down many blind alleys and false trails), / (from hypothesis to hypothesis)}, / [then] science would soon end."]

편집자들은(S) / 'Nature'의 / 한 때 썼다(V) / (종·접)(종·접) 만약 과학이(S) 진보하지 않으면(V) / 어둠 속에서도 / 수많은 어두컴컴한 골목과 그릇된 오솔길을 오르내리며 / 가설에서 가설로 / 과학은(S) 곧 종말에 이르게 된다(V)."라고(O)

'Nature'의 편집자들은 이전에, 만약 과학이 "가설에서 가설로, 수많은 어두컴컴한 골목과 그릇된 오솔길을 오르내리며, 어둠 속에서도 진보하지 않으면, 과학은 곧 종말에 이르게 된다."라고 쓴 적이 있다.

노트
- up and down : 아래위로
- from A to B : A에서 B까지
- 〈what vs. that〉

	관계대명사(불완전한 문장)	접속사(완전한 문장)
what	○ 선행사를 포함하고 있기 때문에 what 앞에 선행사 불필요	×
that	○ that 앞에 선행사 필요	○

- 〈가정법 과거〉 : 현재 사실에 대한 반대를 가정할 때 사용한다.
  - 만약 ~한다면, …할 텐데. : 종속절과 주절은 서로 자리가 바뀌어도 무관

종속절			주절	
If	주어	동사	주어	동사
		과거형 동사		조동사과거형 (would/should/could/might)+동사원형
		were		
		were to 동사원형		
if	science	didn't progress	science	would end

주장 과학 간행물의 역할은 의심하는 것(불확실성)이다.

That's {why / it is the responsibility / (of scientific journals) / (and scientific writers) / (to be ______)}.

(S: That, V: 's, 〈의문사〉: why, 〈가S〉: it, V: is, S.C: the responsibility, 〈진S〉: to be ______)

이 때문에 / 그러므로 역할이다 / 과학 간행물 / (그리고 과학 저술가들)의 / 의심하는 것이

그러므로 과학 간행물(그리고 과학 저술가들)의 역할이란 의심하는 것이다.

노트 ■ 〈This/That/It is because(because of) vs. This/That/It is why〉

This/That/It	is	because	주어	동사 ~
결과		원인		

This/That/It	is	why	주어	동사 ~
원인		결과		

■ 〈가주어, 진주어 구문〉

가주어	동사	진주어
It (This/That/There 사용 불가)	–	that + 주어 + 동사(완전한 절)
		to 동사원형
		동명사
		의문사 + 주어 + 동사(간접의문문)
		if/whether + 주어 + 동사
it	is	to be

주장 과학 간행물은 비판적으로 사고를 해야 한다.

The openness / (at the heart of the scientific spirit) / means / never taking error / (personally), / seeing success as temporary, and welcoming criticism.

(S: The openness, V: means, 〈동명사〉 O_1: taking error, 〈동명사〉 O_2: seeing success (O) as temporary (O.C), 〈동명사〉 O_3: welcoming criticism (O))

개방성은 / 과학 정신의 중심에 있는 / 의미한다 / 오류를 결코 받아들이지 않고 / 개인적으로 / 성공을 일시적인 것으로 간주하며 비판을 환영하는 것을

과학 정신의 중심에 있는 개방성의 의미는 오류를 결코 개인적으로 받아들이지 않고, 성공을 일시적인 것으로 간주하며, 비판을 환영하는 것이다.

노트 ■ at the heart of : ~의 핵심에

■ mean + 목적어(동명사) : ~을 의미하다

■ 〈5형식 불완전타동사의 목적격보어〉 : 수동태 전환 시, 2형식 문장(be p.p. + as 보어)

주어	불완전타동사	목적어	목적격보어
–	accept / achieve / announce / characterize / cite / consider / count / deem / define / describe / disguise / identify / interpret / look at / look upon / perceive / praise / present / read / reckon / refer to / recognize / regard / remember / respect / see / speak of / think of / treat / use / view / visualize 등	–	as 보어

■ 〈succeed 어휘 변화〉

	동사	명사	형용사	부사
succeed	성공하다	–	–	–
success	–	성공	–	–
successor	–	후임자, 상속자	–	–
successful	–	–	성공적인	–
successive	–	–	연속적인	–
successfully	–	–	–	성공적으로
successively	–	–	–	연속하여, 잇따라서

01 윗글의 제목으로 가장 적절한 것은?

① Scientific Discovery: Most Important Duty for Scientists
② Why Scientific Journal Writters Print Interview?
③ Curiosity: Scientific Engin to Developing Theory
④ Uncertainty as a Driving Force of Scientific Progress
⑤ Studying Science Through Recent Scientific Journals!

정답 | ④

해석 | ① 과학적 발견: 과학자들의 가장 중요한 의무
② 왜 과학 간행물 작가들은 인터뷰를 출판하는가?
③ 호기심: 이론 개발을 향한 과학적 추진력
④ 과학적 발전의 추진력으로서의 불확실성
⑤ 최신 과학 간행물을 통하여 과학을 배우기!

해설 | ④ 이 글의 주제는 과학이 발전하기 위해서는 불확실성의 역할이 중요하다는 것이다. 특히 첫 문장에서부터 불확실성의 역할에 관해 강조를 하고 있다. 따라서 글의 제목으로 가장 적절한 것은 과학의 발전이라는 소재와 불확실성이라는 관점이 들어간 ④이다.

오답 | ① 과학적 발견이라는 소재는 맞지만 글의 관점에 관한 내용이 없다.
② 왜 과학 간행물 작가들이 인터뷰를 출판하는지에 대한 내용은 글에 존재하지 않는다.
③ 과학의 추진력이라는 소재는 맞지만 관점은 호기심이 아니라 불확실성이기 때문에 적절하지 않다.
⑤ 최신 과학 간행물은 이 글의 소재인 과학적 발전과 무관하기 때문에 옳지 않다.

02 윗글의 빈칸에 들어갈 말로 가장 적절한 것은?

① absolute ② distrustful ③ emotional
④ reliable ⑤ personal

정답 | ②

해석 | ① 절대적인
② 의심하는
③ 감정적인
④ 신뢰할 수 있는
⑤ 개인적인

해설 | ② 이 글의 내용과 관련된 불확실성과 유사한 단어가 들어가야 한다. 따라서 가장 유사한 단어인 'distrustful'이 적절하다.

오답 | ① 이 글의 주제와 전혀 무관하다.
③ 감정적인 것은 글의 내용에 존재하지 않는다.
④ 'reliable'은 글의 관점과 반대되는 말이다.
⑤ 'personal'은 글의 소재와 일치하지 않는다.

Words

- ☐ uncertainty
- ☐ innovation
- ☐ asset
- ☐ defining
- ☐ feature
- ☐ philosophy
- ☐ emphasize
- ☐ intellectual
- ☐ refute
- ☐ prove
- ☐ leap
- ☐ contradiction
- ☐ precede
- ☐ progress
- ☐ alley
- ☐ trail
- ☐ hypothesis
- ☐ temporary

Phrases

- ☐ come from
- ☐ at least
- ☐ in a different way
- ☐ leap forward
- ☐ A lead to(전치사) B
- ☐ put it
- ☐ from A to B
- ☐ after all
- ☐ at the level of
- ☐ A rather than B
- ☐ pile up
- ☐ give up A
- ☐ up and down
- ☐ at the heart of

우선순위 영단어

역대 수능 기출 + 전국 모의고사 기출 + EBS 기출 + 교과서 기출 빈출 어휘

단어	뜻	단어	뜻	단어	뜻
judgement	n. 판단	just	a. 공정한	justified	a. 정당한
keep ~ in check	v. ~을 제어하다	keep ~ in mind	v. ~을 명심하다	keep in touch with	v. ~와 연락을 유지하다
key	a. 장단	kick in	v. 작동하다	kidney	n. 신장
killer whale	n. 범고래	kin	n. 혈족 관계	kind of	그저
knead	v. 주무르다	knot	n. 옹이	labor force	n. 노동 인구
lamb	n. 양	land	v. 착륙하다	landfall	n. 육지 도착
landfill	n. 쓰레기 매립지	largely	ad. 주로	larva	n. 유충
lash	v. 묶다	last	v. 지속되다	late	n. 고문
latest	a. 최신의	lead	v. 이끌다	leading	a. 이끄는
leak	v. (액체, 기체가) 새게 하다	lean	v. 몸을 기울다	lease	v. 임대[임차, 대여]하다
leave out	v. ~를 배제하다	lecture	v. 강의하다	legacy	n. 유산
legal	a. 법률과 관련된	legendary	a. 전설적인	legislative	a. 입법(상)의
lengthen	v. 길어지다	lever	n. (기계 · 차량 조작용) 레버	liberate	v. 해방시키다
lick	v. 핥다	lie detector	n. 거짓말 탐지기	lieutenant	n. 소위
life expectancy	n. 평균 수명	lifelong	a. 평생 동안의	light up	v. 밝아지다
lighten	v. 가볍게 하다	lighthouse	n. 등대	lighting	n. 조명
likely	a. 있음직한	likeness	n. 유사	limitation	n. 한계
line	v. 안(감)을 대다	linear	a. 직선의	linguist	n. 언어학자
linkage	n. 연관	literal	a. 글자대로의	livestock	n. 가축
lizard	n. 도마뱀	loaf	n. 빵 한 덩어리	loan	n. 대출
local	a. 지역의	localize	v. 한 지역에 국한하다	lock	v. 가두다
locker	n. 사물함	locomotive	n. 기관차	long-lasting	a. 오래 지속되는
long-running	a. 오래[장기간] 계속되어 온	look to	v. 시선을 돌리다	loop	n. 고리
loose	a. 느슨한	lot	n. 특정 용도의 토지	lottery	n. 추첨
lousy	a. 변변치 않은	lump	v. 함께 묶다	Lydian	n. 리디아 사람

변형문제

01 다음 글을 읽고, |조건|에 맞게 주어진 요지를 완성하시오.

| 조건 |
* (A)는 3단어로 쓸 것
* 본문에 있는 단어만을 사용할 것
* 필요한 경우, 문맥과 어법에 맞게 변형할 것

A more powerful example of the role of uncertainty in innovation comes from science. The greatest asset of the scientific tradition, after all, is its continual self-scrutiny and skepticism. Accepting uncertainty — at least at the level of scientific communities — is the defining feature of science. It's not a defect. Two giants of the philosophy of science, Karl Popper and Thomas Kuhn, both emphasized this point in different ways. For Popper, intellectual honesty means trying to refute, rather than prove, a theory about the world. For Kuhn, science leaps forward when contradictions pile up and lead to giving up a dominant theory. In each view, the acceptance of uncertainty precedes new ideas and discoveries. Uncertainty, as climate scientist Tamsin Edwards put it recently, "is the engine of science."

The editors of *Nature* once wrote that if science didn't "progress darkly, up and down many blind alleys and false trails, from hypothesis to hypothesis, [then] science would soon end." That's why it is the responsibility of scientific journals (and scientific writers) to be distrustful. The openness at the heart of the scientific spirit means never taking error personally, seeing success as temporary, and welcoming criticism.

⬇

The driving force of scientific development is (A) ______ ______ ______.

02 다음 글을 읽고, |조건|에 맞게 주어진 요지를 완성하시오.

| 조건 |

* (A), (B)는 각각 2단어로 쓸 것
* [보기]에서 선택한 단어를 한 번씩만 쓸 것
* 필요한 경우, 문맥과 어법에 맞게 변형할 것

[보기] truth / encourage / for / correct / progress / unncessary / misleading / to / tradition / in / significant / of / irrational / origin / presence / discovery

A more powerful example of the role of uncertainty in innovation comes from science. The greatest asset of the scientific tradition, after all, is its continual self-scrutiny and skepticism. Accepting uncertainty — at least at the level of scientific communities — is the defining feature of science. It's not a defect. Two giants of the philosophy of science, Karl Popper and Thomas Kuhn, both emphasized this point in different ways. For Popper, intellectual honesty means trying to refute, rather than prove, a theory about the world. For Kuhn, science leaps forward when contradictions pile up and lead to giving up a dominant theory. In each view, the acceptance of uncertainty precedes new ideas and discoveries. Uncertainty, as climate scientist Tamsin Edwards put it recently, "is the engine of science."

The editors of *Nature* once wrote that if science didn't "progress darkly, up and down many blind alleys and false trails, from hypothesis to hypothesis, [then] science would soon end." That's why it is the responsibility of scientific journals (and scientific writers) to be distrustful. The openness at the heart of the scientific spirit means never taking error personally, seeing success as temporary, and welcoming criticism.

⬇

Accepting uncertainty is (A) ____________ ____________ the (B) ____________ ____________ science.

03 다음 글을 읽고, |조건|에 맞게 주어진 제목을 완성하시오.

| 조건 |

* (A)는 4단어로 쓸 것
* 본문에 있는 표현을 찾아 그대로 쓸 것

A more powerful example of the role of uncertainty in innovation comes from science. The greatest asset of the scientific tradition, after all, is its continual self-scrutiny and skepticism. Accepting uncertainty — at least at the level of scientific communities — is the defining feature of science. It's not a defect. Two giants of the philosophy of science, Karl Popper and Thomas Kuhn, both emphasized this point in different ways. For Popper, intellectual honesty means trying to refute, rather than prove, a theory about the world. For Kuhn, science leaps forward when contradictions pile up and lead to giving up a dominant theory. In each view, the acceptance of uncertainty precedes new ideas and discoveries. Uncertainty, as climate scientist Tamsin Edwards put it recently, "is the engine of science."

The editors of *Nature* once wrote that if science didn't "progress darkly, up and down many blind alleys and false trails, from hypothesis to hypothesis, [then] science would soon end." That's why it is the responsibility of scientific journals (and scientific writers) to be distrustful. The openness at the heart of the scientific spirit means never taking error personally, seeing success as temporary, and welcoming criticism.

⬇

(A) ____________ ____________ ____________ ____________ in the development and innovation of science

04 다음 글을 읽고, |조건|에 맞게 주어진 요약문을 완성하시오.

| 조건 |

* (A), (B)는 2단어, (C)는 1단어로 쓸 것
* [보기]에서 선택한 단어를 한 번씩만 쓸 것
* 필요한 경우, 문맥과 어법에 맞게 변형할 것

[보기] fast / make / great / big / fast / efforts / have / develop / add / success / goals / believe / renounce / strides / plans

A more powerful example of the role of uncertainty in innovation comes from science. The greatest asset of the scientific tradition, after all, is its continual self-scrutiny and skepticism. Accepting uncertainty — at least at the level of scientific communities — is the defining feature of science. It's not a defect. Two giants of the philosophy of science, Karl Popper and Thomas Kuhn, both emphasized this point in different ways. For Popper, intellectual honesty means trying to refute, rather than prove, a theory about the world. For Kuhn, science leaps forward when contradictions pile up and lead to giving up a dominant theory. In each view, the acceptance of uncertainty precedes new ideas and discoveries. Uncertainty, as climate scientist Tamsin Edwards put it recently, "is the engine of science."

The editors of *Nature* once wrote that if science didn't "progress darkly, up and down many blind alleys and false trails, from hypothesis to hypothesis, [then] science would soon end." That's why it is the responsibility of scientific journals (and scientific writers) to be distrustful. The openness at the heart of the scientific spirit means never taking error personally, seeing success as temporary, and welcoming criticism.

⬇

According to Popper, intellectual honesty is based on (A) ____________ ____________ to refute more than proving theories about the world. According to Kuhn, science makes (B) ____________ ____________ when (C) ____________ a dominant theory and contradictions are accumulated.

UNIT 18

장문

글의 논리	Story
제목	강아지를 사려는 소년과 강아지를 팔려는 농부
주제	힘든 일이 있을 때, 자신의 상황을 이해해주고 같이 느껴주는 것이 필요하다.

수능 ANALYSIS 01–03

072 어법 선택 & 연결어

A farmer had some puppies he needed to sell. He painted a sign **[advertised / advertising]** the pups and began nailing **[it / them]** to a post on the edge of his yard. As he was **[driving / driven]** the last nail into the post, he felt a tug on his overalls. He looked down into the eyes of a little boy. "Mister," he said, "I want to buy one of your puppies." "Well," said the farmer, as he rubbed the sweat off the back of his neck, "these puppies come from fine parents and cost a good deal of money."

The boy dropped his head for a moment. (   ) **[reached / reaching]** deep into his pocket, he pulled out a handful of change and **[held up it / held it up]** to the farmer. "I've got thirty-nine cents. Is that enough to take a look?" "Sure," said the farmer. And with that he let out a whistle, "Here, Dolly!" he called. Out from the doghouse and down the slope **[did Dolly run / ran Dolly]** **[following / followed]** by four little balls of fur. The little boy pressed his face **[against / for]** the chain link fence. His eyes danced with delight.

As the puppies made **[their / its]** way to the fence, the little boy noticed something else **[to stir / stirring]** inside the doghouse. Slowly **[the other / another]** **[few / little]** ball **[was appeared / appeared]**; this one **[noticeable / noticeably]** smaller. Down the slope it slid. (   ) in a somewhat awkward manner the little pup began **[hobble / hobbling]** toward the others, **[done / doing]** **[their / its]** best to catch up. "I want that one," he said, **[pointed / pointing]** to the puppy.

The farmer knelt down at the boy's side and said, "Son, you don't want that puppy. He will never be able to run and play with you **[alike / like]** these other dogs would." With that the little boy stepped back from the fence, reached down, and began rolling up one leg of his trousers. In doing so he revealed a steel brace **[rum / running]** down both sides of his leg **[attached / attaching]** **[it / itself]** to a **[special / specially]** **[making / made]** shoe. **[Looked / Looking]** back up at the farmer, he said, "You see, sir. I don't run too well **[me / myself]**, and he will need someone who **[understand / understands]**."

이야기 강아지를 사려는 소년과 강아지를 팔려는 농부

(A) A farmer / had some puppies / (목·관 that) (he needed to sell).

A farmer (S, 한 농부가) / had (V) some puppies (O, 몇 마리의 강아지가 있었다) / (he (S) needed (V) to sell (O), 팔아야 할)

한 농부에게 팔아야 할 몇 마리의 강아지가 있었다.

노트
■ 〈목적격관계대명사 that 생략〉: to부정사의 목적어가 없는 경우 / 선행사를 포함하고 있는 관계대명사 what 사용 불가

	〈목적격관계대명사절〉				
선행사	목적격관계대명사	주어	동사	목적어	
some puppies	that : 생략 가능	he	needed	to sell	~~목적어~~

■ 〈need 동사의 용법〉

목적어(to R)		3형식	〈~할〉 필요가 있다, 〈~〉 해야 하다
목적어	목적격보어(to R)	5형식	〈남이〉 〈~해 줄〉 필요가 있다
동명사(Ring)		3형식	〈사람·물건이〉 〈~되어야 할〉 필요가 있다
목적어	목적격보어(p.p.)	5형식	〈~이〉 〈…될〉 필요가 있다, 〈~을〉 〈…되도록 할〉 필요가 있다

He / painted a sign / (which was) (advertising the pups) / and / began nailing it / (to a post) / (on the edge of his yard).

He (S, 그는) / painted (V1) a sign (O, 표지판을 그렸다) / (advertising the pups) (〈현재분사〉 그 강아지들을 광고하는) / and (그리고) / began nailing (V2) it (O〈동명사〉, 그것을 못으로 박기 시작했다) / (to a post) (기둥에) / (on the edge of his yard) (그의 마당 가장자리에 있는)

그는 그 강아지들을 광고하는 표지판을 그려 그것을 그의 마당 가장자리에 있는 기둥에 못으로 박기 시작했다.

노트
■ nail A to B : A를 B에 못을 박다
■ on the edge of : ~의 가장자리[모서리]에
■ 〈주격관계대명사＋be동사 생략〉

–	생략할 수 있음	
명사 (선행사)	(주격관계대명사 ＋be동사)	현재분사(Ring) – 능동(~하고 있는)
		과거분사(p.p.) – 수동(~되어진, 당한)
		명사
		형용사(구) (~하는, ~할)
		부사
		전치사구
a sign	(which/that was)	advertising

■ 〈3형식에서 목적어 자리에 to R / Ring 둘 다 사용 가능〉

	완전타동사		목적어
주어	begin	~을 시작하다	to R/Ring (의미 차이 없음)
	cease	~을 중단하다	
	continue	~을 계속하다	
	deserve	~할 가치/자격/권리가 있다	
	dislike	~을 싫어하다	
	hate		
	like	~을 좋아하다	
	love	~을 사랑하다	
	neglect	~하는 것을 소홀히 하다	
	prefer	~쪽을 좋아하다	
	require	~을 요구하다	
	start	~을 시작하다	

{As he was driving the last nail / (into the post)}, / he / felt a tug / (on his overalls).

〈종·접〉 As / S he / V〈과거진행〉 was driving / O the last nail / S he / V felt / O a tug

그가 마지막 못을 박고 있을 때 / 기둥에 / 그는 / 잡아당기는 것을 느꼈다 / 그의 작업복을

그가 기둥에 마지막 못을 박고 있을 때, 그는 (누군가가) 그의 작업복을 잡아당기는 것을 느꼈다.

노트 ■ drive A into B : A를 B에 박다

He / looked down / (into the eyes of a little boy).

S He / V looked down

그는 / 내려다보았다 / 한 어린 소년의 눈을

그는 한 어린 소년의 눈을 내려다보았다.

노트 ■ look down into : ~을 내려다보다

"Mister," / (a) he said, / "I want to buy / one of your puppies."

S he / V said / S I / V want / O to buy one of your puppies

"아저씨," / 그는 말했다 / "제가 사고 싶어요 / 아저씨의 강아지 중 한 마리를"

"아저씨," 그는 말했다. "제가 아저씨의 강아지 중 한 마리를 사고 싶어요."

노트 ■ 〈want 동사의 쓰임〉

주어	want	목적어(to R)		주어가 ~하는 것을 원하다	3형식
		목적어	목적격보어 (to R)	주어는 목적어가 ~하는 것을 원하다	5형식

■ 〈one of + 복수명사〉 : ~ 중의 하나

one (주어 : 단수)	of	복수명사
one		your puppies

"Well," / said the farmer, / (as he rubbed the sweat off / the back of his neck), / "these puppies / come (from fine parents) / and cost a good deal of money."

V said / S the farmer / 〈종·접〉 as / S he / V rubbed / O the sweat / S these puppies / V_1 come / V_2 cost / O a good deal of money

"글쎄," / 농부는 말했다 / 그가 땀을 닦아내며 / 자신의 목 뒤에 있는 / "이 강아지들은 / 좋은 부모들한테서 나와서 / 많은 돈이 든단다"

"글쎄," 농부는 자신의 목 뒤 땀을 닦아내며 말했다. "이 강아지들은 좋은 부모들한테서 나와서 많은 돈이 든단다."

노트 ■ rub A off B : B에서 A를 문질러 없애다
■ come from : ~에서 생겨나다(=originate)
■ a good deal of : 다량의

(B) {As the puppies made their way / (to the fence)}, / the little boy / noticed something else stirring / (inside the doghouse).

〈종·접〉 As / S the puppies / V made / S the little boy / V noticed / O something else / O.C stirring

강아지들이 올 때 / 울타리 쪽으로 / 어린 소년은 / 다른 어떤 것이 꿈틀거리는 것을 알아챘다 / 개집 안쪽에서

강아지들이 울타리 쪽으로 올 때, 어린 소년은 개집 안쪽에서 다른 어떤 것이 꿈틀거리는 것을 알아챘다.

노트 ■ make one's way to : ~로 나아가다
■ something else : (또) 다른 것
■ 〈지각동사〉

지각동사		목적어	목적격보어
see	보다	-	〈목적어와 목적격보어의 관계가 능동일 때〉 동사원형(R) - 완료 현재진행(Ring) - 진행, 순간, 찰나, 계속 〈목적어와 목적격보어의 관계가 수동일 때〉 과거분사(p.p.) 〈to부정사는 불가〉 : 수동태 문장 전환 시 가능
watch			
look at			
behold			
(over) hear	듣다		
listen to			
feel	느끼다		
observe	관찰하다		
perceive	인식하다		
notice			
noticed		something else	stirring

■ 〈형용사의 후치 수식〉

〈후치 수식〉	-thing	+형용사	○
	-body		
	-one		
〈전치 수식〉	형용사+	-thing	×
		-body	
		-one	

(Slowly) / another little ball / appeared; / this one / (was) (noticeably) smaller.

S another little ball / V appeared / S this one / S.C smaller

천천히 / 또 한 마리의 작은 털 뭉치가 / 나타났다 / 이 강아지는 / 눈에 띄게 더 작았다

천천히 또 한 마리의 작은 털 뭉치(강아지)가 나타났는데, 이 강아지는 눈에 띄게 더 작았다.

노트 ■ 〈the other vs. another〉

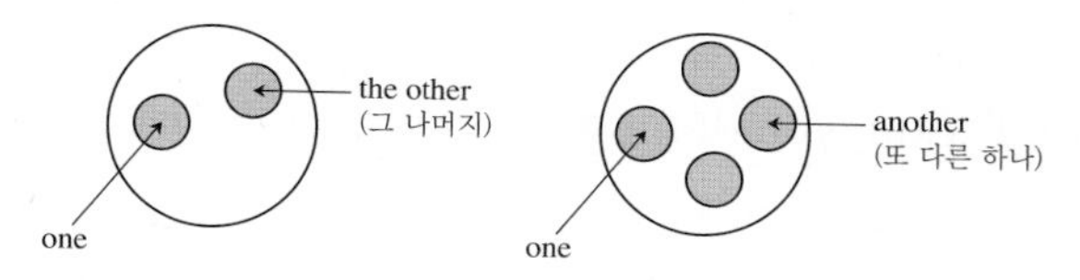

■ 〈생략〉: be동사가 생략된 경우

	생략		
this one	(was)	noticeably	smaller.
주어	동사	부사	주격보어

(Down the slope) / it slid.
S V
비탈 아래로 / 그 강아지가 미끄러졌다

비탈 아래로 그 강아지가 미끄러졌다.

Then / (in a somewhat awkward manner) / the little pup / began hobbling / (toward the others), / {(doing its best) / (to catch up)}.
그러고는 / 다소 불편한 몸짓으로 / 그 작은(S) 강아지는 / 절름거리며 걸어오기 시작했다 (V, O〈동명사〉) / 다른 강아지들을 향해서 / 〈분사구문〉 최선을 다하며 / 따라잡기 위해

그러고는 다소 불편한 몸짓으로 그 작은 강아지는 다른 강아지들을 향해서 따라잡기 위해 최선을 다하며 절름거리며 걸어오기 시작했다.

노트
■ in a manner : 어떤 의미로는; 어느 정도, 얼마간
■ begin + 목적어(to R, 동명사) : ~하기를 시작하다
■ do one's best : 최선을 다하다
■ catch up : 따라잡다
■ 〈부사 vs. 접속부사〉

시간	Then	주어	동사		
	When	주어	동사,	주어	동사 ~
장소	There	주어	동사		
	Where	주어	동사,	주어	동사 ~

■ 〈분사구문 – 문미〉: 주절과 분사구문의 위치가 서로 바뀌어도 무관

주절		종속절(→ 분사구문)			
주어	동사	종속 접속사	주어	동사 : 상황에 맞게 아래처럼 바뀜	
		〈그대로 사용하면 의미 강조〉	(주절의 주어와 같으면 생략하고, 다르면 주격으로 사용함)	(being) (having been) 생략 가능	Ring(현재분사)
					p.p.(과거분사)
					형용사
					명사
the little pup	began	–	–	–	doing

"I / want that one," / (b) he said, / (pointing to the puppy).
S V O / S V / 〈분사구문〉
"저는 / 저 강아지를 원해요." / 그가 말했다 / 그 강아지를 가리키며

"저는 저 강아지를 원해요."라고 그가 그 강아지를 가리키며 말했다.

노트 ■ point to : ~을 가리키다, 암시하다
■ 〈분사구문 – 문미〉: 주절과 분사구문의 위치가 서로 바뀌어도 무관

주절		종속절(→ 분사구문)			
주어	동사	종속 접속사	주어	동사 : 상황에 맞게 아래처럼 바뀜	
		〈그대로 사용하면 의미 강조〉	(주절의 주어와 같으면 생략하고, 다르면 주격으로 사용함)	(being) (having been) 생략 가능	Ring(현재분사)
					p.p.(과거분사)
					형용사
					명사
he	said	–	–	–	pointing

(C) The boy / dropped his head / (for a moment).
S V O
소년은 / 머리를 숙였다 / 잠시

소년은 잠시 머리를 숙였다.

노트
■ drop one's head : ~의 머리를 숙이다
■ for a moment : 잠시 동안, 당장 그때만

(Then) / (reaching deep into (c) his pocket), / he / pulled out a handful of change and held it up / (to the farmer).
그러고는 / 〈분사구문〉 자신의 주머니 안으로 깊숙이 손을 뻗어 / 그는(S) / 한 줌의 동전을 꺼내어 들어 보였다 (V_1, O, V_2, O) / 농부에게

그러고는 자신의 주머니 안으로 깊숙이 손을 뻗어, 한 줌의 동전을 꺼내어 농부에게 들어 보였다.

노트
■ reach into : ~ 안에 손을 넣다
■ pull out A : A를 꺼내다
■ a handful of : 소수의, 한 움큼
■ hold A up (to B) : A를 (B에게) 들어 보이다
■ 〈분사구문 – 문두〉: 주절과 종속절의 위치는 서로 바뀔 수 있음

종속절(→ 분사구문)				주절	
종속 접속사	주어	동사 : 상황에 맞게 아래처럼 바뀜		주어	동사
〈그대로 사용하면 의미 강조〉	(주절의 주어와 같으면 생략하고, 다르면 주격으로 사용함)	(being) (having been) 생략 가능	Ring(현재분사)		
			p.p.(과거분사)		
			형용사		
			명사		
–	–	–	reaching	he	pulled out

■ 〈이어동사〉

타동사	명사	부사	(○)
타동사	부사	명사	(○)
타동사	대명사	부사	(○)
타동사	부사	대명사	(×)
held	up	it	(×)

"I'/ve got thirty-nine cents. Is that / enough (to take a look)?"
S V〈현재완료〉 O / V S / S.C
"제가 / 39센트를 가지고 있어요 / 그거면 / 한 번 보기에 충분한가요?"

"제가 39센트를 가지고 있어요. 그거면 한 번 보기에 충분한가요?"

노트 ■ take a look : (~을) (한 번) 보다

"Sure," / said the farmer. / (And) / (with that) / (d) he let out a whistle, / "Here, Dolly!" / he called.

"물론이지." 농부가 말했다 / 그리고 / 그 말과 함께 / 그는 / 휘파람을 불며 / "이리와, Dolly!"라고 / 불렀다

"물론이지." 농부가 말했다. 그리고 그 말과 함께 그는 휘파람을 불며, "이리와, Dolly!"라고 불렀다.

노트 ■ let out A : A를 내다

(Out from the doghouse and down the slope) / ran Dolly / (followed by four little balls of fur).

개집에서 나와 비탈 아래로 / Dolly가 달려왔고 / 〈분사구문〉 그 뒤로 네 마리의 작은 털 뭉치들이 따라왔다

개집에서 나와 비탈 아래로 Dolly가 달려왔고 그 뒤로 네 마리의 작은 털 뭉치들(강아지들)이 따라왔다.

노트 ■ A be followed by B : A 다음에 B가 이어진다, A 다음에 B가 있다

■ 〈부사구 문두 도치〉

	〈도치〉	
Out from the doghouse and down the slope	ran	Dolly
〈부사〉	동사	주어

■ 〈분사구문 – 문미〉 : 주절과 분사구문의 위치가 서로 바뀌어도 무관

주절		종속절(→ 분사구문)			
주어	동사	종속 접속사	주어	동사 : 상황에 맞게 아래처럼 바뀜	
주어	동사	〈그대로 사용하면 의미 강조〉	(주절의 주어와 같으면 생략하고, 다르면 주격으로 사용함)	(being) (having been) 생략 가능	Ring(현재분사) / p.p.(과거분사) / 형용사 / 명사
Dolly	ran	–	–	–	followed

The little boy / pressed his face / (against the chain link fence).

어린 소년은 / 얼굴을 바짝 대었다 / 〈전치사〉 사슬로 엮은 울타리에

어린 소년은 사슬로 엮은 울타리에 얼굴을 바짝 대었다.

노트 ■ press A against B : B에 A를 밀어 붙이다

■ 〈for vs. against〉

전치사	for	찬성	~을 지지하여, ~에 편들어
	against	반대	~에 반대하여(맞서)

His eyes / danced / (with delight).

그의 눈이 / 춤추는 듯했다 / 기쁨으로

그의 눈이 기쁨으로 춤추는 듯했다.

노트 ■ with delight : 기꺼이

(D) The farmer / knelt down / (at the boy's side) / and said, / "Son, you don't want that puppy. / He / will never be able to run / and play with you / (like these other dogs would)."

농부는 / 무릎을 꿇고 앉았다 / 소년의 옆에 / 그리고 / 말했다 / "얘야, 넌 저 강아지를 갖고 싶지 않을 거야. / 그 강아지는 / 절대로 뛰고 놀 수 없을 거야 / 너와 함께 / 〈종·접〉 이 다른 강아지들이 할 것처럼"라고

농부는 소년의 옆에 무릎을 꿇고 앉아, "얘야, 넌 저 강아지를 갖고 싶지 않을 거야. 그 강아지는 절대로 이 다른 강아지들이 할 것처럼 너와 함께 뛰고 놀 수 없을 거야."라고 말했다.

노트 ■ kneel down : 꿇어 앉다

■ kneel : 무릎 꿇다, 무릎을 구부리다

• kneel – knelt/kneeled – knelt/kneeled – kneeling

■ be able to R : ~할 수 있다

■ play with : ~와 놀다

■ 〈likely / alike / like〉

likely	형용사	~일 것 같은 (be to 동사원형 : ~일 것 같다)
	부사	아마(probably)
alike	서술적 형용사 (보어로만 사용, 명사 수식 불가)	동일한
	부사	똑같이
like	전치사	~처럼
	종속접속사	~처럼
	동사	좋아하다

■ 〈대동사〉 : 동사(구)를 대신하는 말

〈동사〉		〈대동사〉
be	→	be
조동사		조동사
일반동사		do, does, did

주절		종속절		
주어	동사구	like	주어	would
He	will never able to run and play with you	종속 접속사	these other dogs	〈대동사〉 =would be able to run and play with you

(With that) / the little boy / stepped back / (from the fence), / reached down, and began rolling up one leg / of his trousers.

그 말을 듣고 / 소년은 / 한 걸음 물러나 / 울타리에서 / 손을 아래로 뻗고 다리 한 쪽을 걷어 올리기 시작했다 / 〈동명사〉 / 자신의 바지의

그 말을 듣고 소년은 울타리에서 한 걸음 물러나 손을 아래로 뻗어 자신의 바지의 다리 한 쪽을 걷어 올리기 시작했다.

노트 ■ step back from : ~에서 물러나다

■ reach down : 몸을 아래로 뻗다

■ begin + 목적어(to R / 동명사) : ~하기를 시작하다

■ roll up A : A를 올리다

(In doing so) / he / revealed a steel brace / (running down both sides of (e) his leg) / (attaching itself / to a specially made shoe).

(which was)
〈동명사〉 그렇게 하면서 / S 그는 / V 강철 버팀대를 드러냈다 / O / 〈현재분사〉 그것은 그의 다리 양편으로 이어지는 / 〈현재분사〉 붙어있는 / 〈재·대〉 / 〈부사〉 〈과거분사〉 특수 제작된 신발에

그렇게 하면서 그는 강철 버팀대를 드러냈는데 그것은 그의 다리 양편으로 이어져 특수 제작된 신발에 붙어있었다.

노트
- in＋동명사 : ~할 때
- run down : 흘러내리다
- attach A to B : A를 B에 붙이다
- 〈대동사〉 : 동사(구)를 대신하는 말

〈전치사구〉		
전치사	동명사	부사
In	doing	so
	〈대동사〉 : rolling up one leg of his trousers	

- 〈주격관계대명사＋be동사 생략〉

−	생략할 수 있음	분사(형용사 : 명사 수식)
명사 (선행사)	(주격관계대명사 ＋be동사)	현재분사(Ring) – 능동(~하고 있는)
		과거분사(p.p.) – 수동(~되어진, 당한)
		형용사(구) (~하는, ~할)
a steel brace	(which/that was)	running
		attaching

- 〈both vs. either〉

both	＋복수명사	둘 다
either	＋단수명사	둘 중 하나

- 〈재귀대명사 vs. 대명사〉

		주어와 다름	주어와 동일
주체	~	대명사	재귀대명사
a steel brace		it	itself

주제문 자신의 상황을 이해해줄 누군가가 필요하다.

(Looking back up at the farmer), / he said, / "You see, / sir. / I don't run too well myself, / and / he will need someone / (who understands)."

〈분사구문〉 농부를 되돌아보며 / S V 그는 말했다 / S V "보이시죠, / 아저씨 / S V 저도 잘 뛰지 못해요 / 〈재·대〉 / 그리고 / S V 그 강아지는 누군가 / O〈선행사〉 필요할 거에요." / 〈주·관〉 V 이해해줄 누군가가

농부를 되돌아보며 그는 말했다. "보이시죠, 아저씨. 저도 잘 뛰지 못해요. 그리고 그 강아지는 이해해줄 누군가가 필요할 거에요."

노트
- look back up at : ~을 되돌아보다
- 〈재귀대명사 vs. 대명사〉

		주어와 다름	주어와 동일
주어	~	대명사	재귀대명사
I		me	myself

- 〈분사구문 – 문두〉 : 주절과 종속절의 위치는 서로 바뀔 수 있음

종속절(→ 분사구문)				주절	
종속 접속사	주어	동사 : 상황에 맞게 아래처럼 바뀜			
〈그대로 사용하면 의미 강조〉	(주절의 주어와 같으면 생략하고, 다르면 주격으로 사용함)	(being) (having been) 생략 가능	Ring(현재분사)	주어	동사
			p.p.(과거분사)		
			형용사		
			명사		
−	−	−	Looking	he	said

- 〈주격관계대명사절의 수의 일치〉

	주격관계대명사절		
선행사	주격관계대명사	~~주어~~	동사
someone	who		understands

01 주어진 글 (A)에 이어질 내용을 순서에 맞게 배열한 것으로 가장 적절한 것은?

① (B) – (D) – (C) ② (C) – (B) – (D)
③ (C) – (D) – (B) ④ (D) – (B) – (C)
⑤ (D) – (C) – (B)

정답 | ②

해설 | ② (A)의 마지막 부분에서 농부가 이 강아지들은 돈이 많이 든다고 하였으므로 (C)에서 소년이 돈을 꺼내는 내용이 이어지는 것이 적절하다. (C)의 마지막 부분은 소년이 뛰어오는 강아지들을 바라보는 내용이므로 (B)에서 소년이 그 강아지들 외에 다른 강아지를 발견하는 내용이 이어지는 것이 적절하다. (B)의 마지막 부분에서는 소년이 절름거리는 강아지를 원한다고 하였으므로 (D)에서 농부가 그 강아지 사는 것을 만류하는 내용이 이어지는 것이 적절하다.

02 밑줄 친 (a) ~ (e) 중에서 가리키는 대상이 나머지 넷과 다른 것은?

① (a) ② (b) ③ (c)
④ (d) ⑤ (e)

정답 | ④

해설 | ④ (d)는 농부를 가리키고, 나머지는 모두 소년을 가리킨다.

03 윗글의 내용으로 적절하지 않은 것은?

① 농부는 강아지를 광고하는 표지판을 그렸다.
② 눈에 띄게 더 작은 강아지가 비탈 아래로 미끄러졌다.
③ 농부는 소년에게 강아지를 보여 주기를 거절했다.
④ Dolly가 뛰어올 때 네 마리의 강아지가 뒤따라왔다.
⑤ 소년이 자신의 바지 한 쪽을 걷어 올렸다.

정답 | ③

해설 | ③ 소년이 39센트를 보여 주며 그 돈이면 강아지들을 한 번 보기에 충분하냐고 묻자 농부가 "Sure,"라고 답했으므로 ③은 적절하지 않은 내용이다.

오답 | ① 'He painted a sign advertising the pups and began nailing it to a post on the edge of his yard.'라고 나타난다.

② 'Down the slope it slid.'라고 나타난다.

④ 'Out from the doghouse and down the slope ran Dolly followed by four little balls of fur.'라고 나타나 있다.

⑤ 'With that the little boy stepped back from the fence, reached down, and began rolling up one leg of his trousers.'라고 나타나 있다.

Words

- ☐ nail
- ☐ post
- ☐ tug
- ☐ overalls
- ☐ rub
- ☐ sweat
- ☐ stir
- ☐ noticeably
- ☐ slope
- ☐ awkward
- ☐ point
- ☐ reach
- ☐ change
- ☐ whistle
- ☐ trousers
- ☐ reveal
- ☐ brace
- ☐ attach

Phrases

- ☐ nail A to B
- ☐ drive A into B
- ☐ rub A off B
- ☐ a good deal of
- ☐ something else
- ☐ do one's best
- ☐ point to
- ☐ for a moment
- ☐ pull out A
- ☐ hold A up (to B)
- ☐ let out A
- ☐ press A against B
- ☐ kneel down
- ☐ play with
- ☐ reach down
- ☐ run down
- ☐ look back up at
- ☐ on the edge of
- ☐ look down into
- ☐ come from
- ☐ make one's way to
- ☐ in a manner
- ☐ catch up
- ☐ drop one's head
- ☐ reach into
- ☐ a handful of
- ☐ take a look
- ☐ A be followed by B
- ☐ with delight
- ☐ be able to R
- ☐ step back from
- ☐ roll up A
- ☐ attach A to B

우선순위 영단어

역대 수능 기출 + 전국 모의고사 기출 + EBS 기출 + 교과서 기출 빈출 어휘

단어	뜻	단어	뜻	단어	뜻
machinery	n. 기계류	make certain that ~	v. ~을 확인하다	make headway	v. 전진하다
make it to	v. ~에 도달하다	make one's way to	v. ~로 가다	make-up	n. 구조
malnutrition	n. 영양불량	manage	v. 애써 해 내다	managerial	a. 관리의
mandate	v. 명령하다	man-made	사람이 만든	manner	n. 방법
manure	n. 분뇨	march	n. 행진곡	marked	a. 두드러진
market	n. 시장조사	market share	n. 시장 점유율	marsh	n. 늪
masculine	a. 남성적인	materialistic	a. 물질 중심적인	materialize	v. 실형되다

변형문제

01 다음 글을 읽고, |조건|에 맞게 주어진 요약문을 완성하시오.

| 조건 |
* (A)는 6단어로 단어로 쓸 것
* 본문에 있는 단어를 찾아 쓸 것
* 필요한 경우, 문맥과 어법에 맞게 변형할 것

A farmer had some puppies he needed to sell. He painted a sign advertising the pups and began nailing it to a post on the edge of his yard. As he was driving the last nail into the post, he felt a tug on his overalls. He looked down into the eyes of a little boy. “Mister,” he said, “I want to buy one of your puppies.” “Well,” said the farmer, as he rubbed the sweat off the back of his neck, “these puppies come from fine parents and cost a good deal of money.”

The boy dropped his head for a moment. Then reaching deep into his pocket, he pulled out a handful of change and held it up to the farmer. “I’ve got thirty-nine cents. Is that enough to take a look?” “Sure,” said the farmer. And with that he let out a whistle, “Here, Dolly!” he called. Out from the doghouse and down the slope ran Dolly followed by four little balls of fur. The little boy pressed his face against the chain link fence. His eyes danced with delight.

As the puppies made their way to the fence, the little boy noticed something else stirring inside the doghouse. Slowly another little ball appeared; this one noticeably smaller. Down the slope it slid. Then in a somewhat awkward manner the little pup began hobbling toward the others, doing its best to catch up. “I want that one,” he said, pointing to the puppy.

The farmer knelt down at the boy’s side and said, “Son, you don’t want that puppy. He will never be able to run and play with you like these other dogs would.” With that the little boy s stepped back from the fence, reached down, and began rolling up one leg of his trousers. In doing so he revealed a steel brace running down both sides of his leg attaching itself to a specially made shoe. Looking back up at the farmer, he said, “You see, sir. I don’t run too well myself, and he will need someone who understands.”

⬇

The reason why a boy buys a puppy with a limp is because the boy (A) ____________ ____________ ____________ ____________ ____________ ____________.

02 다음 글이 주는 교훈으로 가장 적절한 것은?

A farmer had some puppies he needed to sell. He painted a sign advertising the pups and began nailing it to a post on the edge of his yard. As he was driving the last nail into the post, he felt a tug on his overalls. He looked down into the eyes of a little boy. "Mister," he said, "I want to buy one of your puppies." "Well," said the farmer, as he rubbed the sweat off the back of his neck, "these puppies come from fine parents and cost a good deal of money."

The boy dropped his head for a moment. Then reaching deep into his pocket, he pulled out a handful of change and held it up to the farmer. "I've got thirty-nine cents. Is that enough to take a look?" "Sure," said the farmer. And with that he let out a whistle, "Here, Dolly!" he called. Out from the doghouse and down the slope ran Dolly followed by four little balls of fur. The little boy pressed his face against the chain link fence. His eyes danced with delight.

As the puppies made their way to the fence, the little boy noticed something else stirring inside the doghouse. Slowly another little ball appeared; this one noticeably smaller. Down the slope it slid. Then in a somewhat awkward manner the little pup began hobbling toward the others, doing its best to catch up. "I want that one," he said, pointing to the puppy.

The farmer knelt down at the boy's side and said, "Son, you don't want that puppy. He will never be able to run and play with you like these other dogs would." With that the little boy s stepped back from the fence, reached down, and began rolling up one leg of his trousers. In doing so he revealed a steel brace running down both sides of his leg attaching itself to a specially made shoe. Looking back up at the farmer, he said, "You see, sir. I don't run too well myself, and he will need someone who understands."

① A friend is essential to share your pain.
② Poverty parts friends.
③ A friend is known in necessity.
④ Don't cry before you are hurt.
⑤ Old friend is better than two new ones.

03 다음 문장이 들어갈 부분으로 가장 적절한 곳을 고르시오.

With that the little boy s stepped back from the fence, reached down, and began rolling up one leg of his trousers.

As the puppies made their way to the fence, the little boy noticed something else stirring inside the doghouse. Slowly another little ball appeared; this one noticeably smaller. Down the slope it slid. Then in a somewhat awkward manner the little pup began hobbling toward the others, doing its best to catch up. (①) "I want that one," he said, pointing to the puppy. (②) The farmer knelt down at the boy's side and said, "Son, you don't want that puppy. (③) He will never be able to run and play with you like these other dogs would." (④) In doing so he revealed a steel brace running down both sides of his leg attaching itself to a specially made shoe. (⑤) Looking back up at the farmer, he said, "You see, sir. I don't run too well myself, and he will need someone who understands."

04 밑줄 친 부분 중 문맥상 옳지 않은 것은?

A farmer had some puppies he needed to ① buy. He painted a sign ② advertising the pups and began nailing it to a post on the edge of his yard. As he was driving the last nail into the post, he felt a tug on his overalls. He looked down into the eyes of a little boy. "Mister," he said, "I want to ③ buy one of your puppies." "Well," said the farmer, as he rubbed the sweat off the back of his neck, "these puppies come from fine parents and cost a good deal of money." The boy dropped his head for a moment. Then reaching deep into his pocket, he pulled out a handful of change and held it up to the farmer. "I've got thirty-nine cents. Is that enough to take a look?" "Sure," said the farmer. And with that he let out a whistle, "Here, Dolly!" he called. Out from the doghouse and down the slope ran Dolly ④ followed by four little balls of fur. The little boy pressed his face against the chain link fence. His eyes danced with ⑤ delight.

장문

글의 논리	Myth & Truth (통념 & 진실)
제목	직업 결정에 있어서 우선순위
주제	직업 결정에 있어서 항상 개인의 이득이 최우선인 것은 아니다.

PRACTICE 01–02

073 어법 선택 & 연결어

[During / While] [managed / managing] a project in Mexico City, you notice [that / what] one of your employees [is / are] particularly intelligent, [successive / successful], and [diligently / diligent]. [Thought / Thinking] he would make a great addition to the home office in Chicago, you offer him a job. [Despite / Although] your employee would receive a promotion, a large salary increase, and a company car if he moves to Chicago, he declines your offer. You simply cannot understand [because / why] he refuses the offer [which / when] it would be so [beneficially / beneficial] to his career.

[Much / Many] [high / highly] [successive / successful] people in Mexico (and parts of Central and South America) [do / does] not make career decisions [basing / based] [primary / primarily] on [their / its] own self-interest, as is often the case north of the Rio Grande. In Mexico, people tend [first to consider / to first consider] the needs of their family or company before [consideration / considering] their own self-interest. [Receive / Receiving] a promotion and higher salary would not be the [almost / most] [compelled / compelling] reasons to take a new position. (　　　　　), your employee would think [primary / primarily] about the interests of [extending / extended] family members, many of [whom / them] probably would not want him to move. (　　　　　) the employee would consider the interests of the local company, [what / which] probably [need / needs] him to continue working in Mexico City. [That / What] is best for the individual [is / are] not always the prime factor in a job decision.

예시 멕시코시티에서 부지런하고 일을 잘하는 직원에게 일자리를 제안하지만 직원은 제안을 거절

(you are)
{While / managing a project / (in Mexico City)}, / you
While: 〈종·접〉 동안 / managing: 〈현재분사〉 / a project: O — 프로젝트를 진행하는 / (in Mexico City): 멕시코시티에서 / you: S 여러분이

/ notice / {that one (of your employees) / is (particularly)
notice: V 밝힌다 / that: 〈종·접〉 / one: S — 직원 중 한 명이 / is: V / particularly: 특히 / O

intelligent, successful, and diligent}.
S.C_1, S.C_2, S.C_3 — 지적이고, 성공적이고, 부지런한 것을

여러분이 멕시코시티에서 프로젝트를 진행하는 동안 직원 중 한 명이 특히 지적이고, 성공적이고, 부지런한 것을 발견한다.

노트 ■ 시간(~ 동안)

전치사	during	+ 명사 / 명사 상당어구
종속접속사	while	+ 주어 + 동사

■ 〈분사구문 – 문두〉 : 주절과 종속절의 위치는 서로 바뀔 수 있음

<table>
<tr><th colspan="4">종속절(→ 분사구문)</th><th colspan="2">주절</th></tr>
<tr><td>종속
접속사</td><td>주어</td><td colspan="2">동사 : 상황에 맞게
아래처럼 바뀜</td><td rowspan="5">주어</td><td rowspan="5">동사</td></tr>
<tr><td rowspan="4">〈그대로
사용하면
의미
강조〉</td><td rowspan="4">(주절의 주어와
같으면 생략하고,
다르면 주격으로
사용함)</td><td>(being)</td><td>Ring(현재분사)</td></tr>
<tr><td rowspan="2">(having
been)</td><td>p.p.(과거분사)</td></tr>
<tr><td>형용사</td></tr>
<tr><td>생략 가능</td><td>명사</td></tr>
<tr><td>While</td><td>(you are) 생략</td><td colspan="2">managing</td><td>you</td><td>notice</td></tr>
</table>

■ 〈what vs. that〉

	관계대명사(불완전한 문장)	접속사(완전한 문장)
what	○ 선행사를 포함하고 있기 때문에 what 앞에 선행사 불필요	×
that	○ that 앞에 선행사 필요	○

■ 〈one of + 복수명사 + 단수동사〉 : ~ 중의 하나

one (주어 : 단수)	of	복수명사	단수동사
one		your employees	is

■ 〈succeed 어휘 변화〉

	동사	명사	형용사	부사
succeed	성공하다	–	–	–
success	–	성공	–	–
successor	–	후임자, 상속자	–	–
successful	–	–	성공적인	–
successive	–	–	연속적인	–
successfully	–	–	–	성공적으로
successively	–	–	–	연속하여, 잇따라서

(that)
[Thinking / {he would make a great addition / (to the
Thinking: 〈분사구문〉 생각하면서 / he: S / would make: V / a great addition: O — 그가 큰 기여를 할 수 있을 것이라고 / O

home office) / (in Chicago)}], / you / offer him a job.

(you: S / offer: V / him: I.O / a job: D.O)

본점에 시카고의 여러분은 그에게 일자리를 제안한다

그가 시카고의 본점에 큰 기여를 할 수 있을 것이라고 생각하면서 여러분은 그에게 일자리를 제안한다.

노트
- make an addition : 첨가하다
- 〈분사구문 – 문두〉 : 주절과 종속절의 위치는 서로 바뀔 수 있음

종속절(→ 분사구문)				주절	
종속접속사	주어	동사 : 상황에 맞게 아래처럼 바뀜		주어	동사
〈그대로 사용하면 의미 강조〉	(주절의 주어와 같으면 생략하고, 다르면 주격으로 사용함)	(being)	Ring(현재분사)		
		(having been) 생략 가능	p.p.(과거분사)		
			형용사		
			명사		
–	–	–	Thinking	you	notice

- 〈목적격종속접속사 that 생략〉 : 완전타동사의 목적어로 사용된 경우 / 관계대명사 what 사용 불가

	종속절(명사절 : 목적어) (완전한 절)		
완전타동사	that	주어	동사
Thinking	목적격종속접속사 – 생략 가능(~하는 것을)	he	would make

- 〈4형식을 3형식으로 바꿀 때 사용하는 전치사〉 : 전치사 to를 취하는 동사

주어 (A)	+	동사(B)	+	간접목적어 (C: 사람/동물)	+	직접목적어 (D: 사물)	(4)
		give, bring, pass, send, show, sell, hand, lend, offer, teach, tell, buy, build, choose, find, leave, make, prepare, order, ask, deal 등 수여동사					

→ 주어(A)+동사(B)+직접목적어(D: 사물)+전치사 to+간접목적어(C: 사람/동물) (3)

{Although / your employee / would receive a promotion, a large salary increase, and a company car / (if he moves to Chicago)}, / he declines your offer.

(Although: 〈종·접〉 / your employee: S / would receive: V / a promotion: O_1 / a large salary increase: O_2 / a company car: O_3 / if: 〈종·접〉 / he: S / moves: V / he: S / declines: V / your offer: O)

비록 그 직원이 승진과 많은 월급의 인상과 회사가 제공하는 차를 받게 된다 할지라도 시카고로 옮긴다면 그는 여러분의 제안을 거절한다

그 직원이 시카고로 옮긴다면 승진과 많은 월급의 인상과 회사가 제공하는 자동차를 받게 된다 할지라도, 그는 여러분의 제안을 거절한다.

노트
- receive a promotion : 승진을 하다
- move to : ~로 옮기다
- 〈양보/대조〉

전치사	in spite of	+명사/명사 상당어구	비록 ~이지만
	despite		
	for all		
종속접속사	though	+주어+동사	
	although		
	even though		

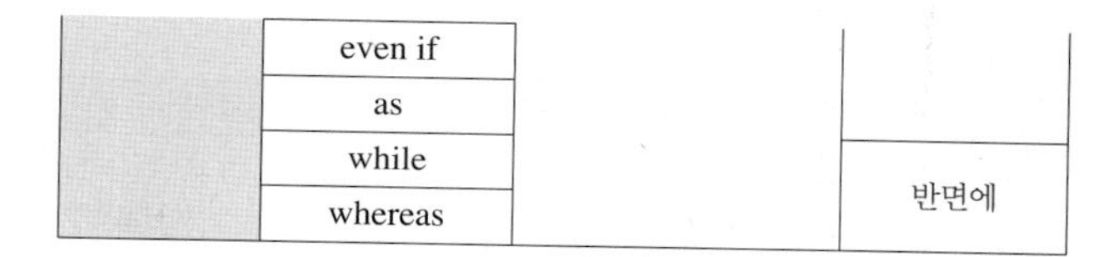

	even if	
	as	
	while	
	whereas	반면에

통념 대부분의 사람들은 제안이 더 이익을 가져다주기 때문에 승락할 것이라 생각한다.

You / (simply) cannot understand / (why he refuses the offer) / {when it would be so beneficial / (to his career)}.

(You: S / cannot understand: V / why: 〈의문사〉 / he: S / refuses: V / the offer: O / when: 〈종·접〉 / it: S / would be: V / so beneficial: S.C)

여러분은 전혀 이해할 수 없다 왜 그가 그것을 거절하는지를 그 제안이 대단한 이익을 가져다주는데도 그의 경력에

그 제안이 그의 경력에 대단한 이익을 가져다주는데도 그가 그것을 거절하는 이유를 여러분은 전혀 이해할 수 없다.

노트
- 〈간접의문문 – 의문사가 있는 경우〉

	〈간접의문문〉 : 완전타동사의 목적어(완전한 문장)			
완전타동사	의문사	주어	완전타동사	목적어
cannot understand	why	he	refuses	the offer

진실 멕시코의 많은 사람들은 개인적인 이익에 근거하여 직업 결정을 하지 않는다.

Many highly successful people / (in Mexico) / (and parts of Central and South America) / do not make career decisions / (based primarily on their own self-interest), / (as is often the case north of the Rio Grande).

(Many highly successful people: S / do not make: V / career decisions: O / based primarily on…: 〈분사구문〉)

많은 매우 성공한 사람들은 멕시코 (그리고 중앙아메리카와 남아메리카의 일부) 직업 결정을 하지 않는다 주로 그들 자신의 개인적인 이익에 근거하여 리오그란데의 북쪽에서 흔히 있는 일이지만

리오그란데의 북쪽에서 흔히 있는 일이지만, 멕시코(그리고 중앙아메리카와 남아메리카의 일부)의 많은 매우 성공한 사람들은 주로 그들 자신의 개인적인 이익에 근거하여 직업 결정을 하지 않는다.

노트
- make(take) a decision : 결정을 하다
- as is (often) the case (with) : 흔히 있는 일이지만, 흔히 있듯이(=as usual)
- 〈부정수량형용사〉 : 막연한 수나 양의 정도를 표시하는 형용사

수(數)	few(a few), some(any), a lot of(lots of), a good(or great), plenty of, enough, all, no, many	복수명사+복수동사
양(量)	little(a little), some(any), a lot of, a good(or great), deal of, plenty of, enough, all, no, much	단수명사+단수동사

- 〈high / highly〉

high	형용사	높은
	부사	높게
	명사	높은 곳
highly	부사	매우(=very)

■ 〈분사구문 – 문미〉 : 주절과 분사구문의 위치가 서로 바뀌어도 무관

주절		종속절(→ 분사구문)			
주어	동사	종속 접속사	주어	동사 : 상황에 맞게 아래처럼 바뀜	
		〈그대로 사용하면 의미 강조〉	(주절의 주어와 같으면 생략하고, 다르면 주격으로 사용함)	(being) (having been) 생략 가능	Ring(현재분사)
					p.p.(과거분사)
					형용사
					명사
~ people	do not make	–	–	–	based

■ 〈소유격을 강조하는 표현〉 : '소유격+own(~ 자신)+명사'

	own은 소유격대명사 강조		
전치사	소유격	own	명사
on	their	own	self-interest

이유 멕시코에서 사람들은 자신의 이익보다 그들의 가족 친구의 필요를 먼저 고려한다.

(In Mexico), / people / tend (to first consider / the needs of their family or company) / (before considering their own self-interest).

- (In Mexico) 멕시코에서
- people: S 사람들은
- tend: V
- (to first consider / the needs) 먼저 고려하는 경향이 있다 / 그들의 가족
- of their family or company 또는 친구의 필요를
- before 〈전치사〉, considering 〈동명사〉 그들 자신의 개인적인 이익을
- their own self-interest: O 고려하기 전에

멕시코에서 사람들은 그들 자신의 개인적인 이익을 고려하기 전에 그들의 가족 또는 친구의 필요를 먼저 고려하는 경향이 있다.

노트 ■ tend(자동사)+to R : ~하는 경향이 있다

■ 〈자동사가 뒤에 to부정사를 사용해 타동사처럼 목적어로 취하는 경우〉

	불완전자동사		목적어
주어	aim	~할 작정이다, 목표로 삼다	to R
	appear	~인 듯하다	
	arrange	미리 짜다[준비하다], 타협하다, 의논하다; 협정하다	
	bother	일부러 ~하다, ~하도록 애쓰다	
	consent	~하는 것을 동의/승낙하다	
	fight	~을 위하여 다투다	
	hesitate	주저하다, 망설이다	
	hurry	서두르다	
	long	~하기를 열망/갈망하다	
	prepare	~할 각오/마음의 준비를 하다	
	seem	~처럼 보이다, ~인 듯하다	
	serve	~의 역할을 하다	
	strive	~하려고 노력하다	
	struggle	(~하려고) 분투[고투]하다, 애쓰다	
	tend	~하는 경향이 있다	
	yearn	몹시 ~하고 싶다, 열망하다	
	wait	~하는 것을 기다리다	

■ 〈부정사의 종류〉

종류	구조			주의사항
원형부정사	동사원형	–	–	조동사/조동사 등 뒤에 사용
to부정사	to	동사원형	–	명사/형용사/부사적 용법
분리부정사	to	부사	동사원형	부사 대신 형용사 사용 불가
대부정사	to	–	–	to R 대신 to만 사용하는 경우
독립부정사	–	–	–	관용적 용법(not to mention 등)

이유 승진이나 더 많은 월급을 받는 것은 직업 선택에 큰 이유가 아니다.

(Receiving / a promotion and higher salary) / would not be the most compelling reasons / (to take a new position).

- (Receiving 〈동명사〉 / a promotion: O_1 and higher salary: O_2): S 받는 것은 / 승진이나 더 많은 월급을
- would not be: V 아닐 것이다
- the most compelling reasons: S.C 가장 강력한 이유가 아닐 것이다
- (to take a new position) 새로운 직책을 선택하는

승진이나 더 많은 월급을 받는 것은 새로운 직책을 선택하는 가장 강력한 이유가 아닐 것이다.

노트 ■ take a position : 직책을 맡다

■ 〈동명사구가 주어 자리에 사용된 경우〉 : 단수 취급으로 동사는 단수동사를 사용함

주어 : 동명사구	동사
Receiving a promotion and higher salary	would not be

■ 〈most / almost / mostly〉

	대명사	형용사	부사
most	대부분의 것들(사람들)	대부분의	가장
almost	–	–	거의
mostly	–	–	주로, 일반적으로

설명 그들은 가족 구성원의 관심에 대하여 생각한다.

(Rather), / your employee / would think (primarily) / (about the interests of extended family members), / {many of whom (probably) would not want him to move}.

- (Rather) 오히려
- your employee: S 여러분의 직원은
- would think: V (primarily) 주로 생각할 것이다
- (about the interests of extended family members) 대가족 구성원의 관심에 대하여
- many of whom 〈수량형용사+관·대〉, would not want: V, him: O, to move: O.C 그리고 그 가족들 중 많은 사람들은 그가 이동하는 것을 원하지 않을 것이다

오히려 여러분의 직원은 주로 대가족 구성원의 관심에 대하여 생각할 것이며, 그 가족 중 많은 사람들은 그가 이동하는 것을 원하지 않을 것이다.

노트 ■ think about : ~에 관해 생각하다

■ extended family : 대가족(↔ nuclear family 핵가족)

■ 〈수량형용사+관계대명사〉 : 수량형용사 다음에 나오는 관계대명사 자리에 대명사 사용 불가

수량형용사		관계대명사
none of, neither of, any of, either of, some of, many of, most of, much of, few of, both of, half of, each of, one of, two of, all of, several of, a number of, both of	+	whom(사람) which(사물) whose(소유)
many of		whom

■ 〈want 동사의 쓰임〉

주어	want	목적어(to R)		주어가 ~하는 것을 원하다	3형식
		목적어	목적격보어(to R)	주어는 목적어가 ~하는 것을 원하다	5형식

설명 그 후에 그 직원은 멕시코시티에서 현재 회사의 관심을 고려할 것이다.

Then / the employee / would consider the interests of the local company, / {which (probably) needs him to continue working / (in Mexico City)}.

(the employee: S / would consider: V / the interests of the local company: O / the local company: 〈선행사〉 / which: 〈주·관〉 / needs: V / him: O / to continue working: O.C)

그런 다음 / 그 직원은 / 아마도 현지 회사의 관심을 / 고려할 것이다 / 그리고 이 회사는 계속 일하기를 원한다 / 멕시코시티에서

그런 다음 그 직원은 아마도 그에게 멕시코시티에서 계속 일하기를 원하는 현지 회사의 관심을 고려할 것이다.

노트 ■ 〈부사 vs. 접속부사〉

시간	Then	주어	동사		
	When	주어	동사,	주어	동사 ~
장소	There	주어	동사		
	Where	주어	동사,	주어	동사 ~

■ 〈주격관계대명사 which절〉 : 계속적 용법으로는 that 사용 불가, 구/절/문장 전체는 단수 취급

		주격관계대명사절		
선행사	콤마(,)	주격관계대명사	~~주어~~	동사
the local company	〈계속적 용법〉	which		needs

■ 〈need 동사의 용법〉

목적어(to R)		3형식	〈~할〉 필요가 있다, 〈~〉 해야 하다
목적어	목적격보어(to R)	5형식	〈남이〉 〈~해 줄〉 필요가 있다
동명사(Ring)		3형식	〈사람 · 물건이〉 〈~되어야 할〉 필요가 있다
목적어	목적격보어(p.p.)	5형식	〈~이〉 〈…될〉 필요가 있다, 〈~을〉 〈…되도록 할〉 필요가 있다

■ 〈3형식에서 목적어 자리에 to R / Ring 둘 다 사용 가능〉

	완전타동사		목적어
주어	begin	~을 시작하다	to R/Ring (의미 차이 없음)
	cease	~을 중단하다	
	continue	~을 계속하다	
	deserve	~할 가치/자격/권리가 있다	
	dislike	~을 싫어하다	
	hate		
	like	~을 좋아하다	
	love	~을 사랑하다	
	neglect	~하는 것을 소홀히 하다	
	prefer	~쪽을 좋아하다	
	require	~을 요구하다	
	start	~을 시작하다	

주제문(강조) 직업 결정에 있어서 항상 개인의 이득이 최우선인 것은 아니다.

{ } / is not always the prime factor / (in a job decision).

(S: 개인에게 가장 좋은 것이 / V: 항상 가장 중요한 요소는 / S.C: 아니다 / 직업 결정에 있어서)

직업 결정에 있어서 개인에게 가장 좋은 것이 항상 가장 중요한 요소는 아니다.

노트 ■ be good for : ~에 좋다

• be best for : ~에 가장 좋다

■ 〈관계대명사 what〉 : 관계대명사 what절이 주어로 사용되면 동사는 주로 단수동사 사용함, 선행사가 필요한 관계대명사 that/which 사용 불가

	주격관계대명사절 : 명사절(주어)			
~~선행사~~	what	~~주어~~	is	동사
	선행사를 포함한 관계대명사 (=the thing(s) which/that ~) : ~하는 것은/이		동사	is

■ 〈be good at/for〉

be	good/bad(poor)	at	~에 능숙하다/못하다
	better/worse		~을 더 잘하다/못하다
	best/worst		~을 가장 잘하다/못하다
	good/bad(poor)	for	~에 좋다/안 좋다

■ 〈부분부정 vs. 전체부정〉

부분부정	not, never	+	all(모두), always(항상), necessarily(필연적으로), entirely(전적으로), altogether(완전히), exactly(정확히), totally(전체적으로), absolutely(절대적으로), completely(완전히), wholly(완전히)
전체부정	not any one(=none) (모두 ~이 아니다) no+명사 (어느 누구도 ~ 않다) not ~ either(=neither) (둘 다 ~이 아니다) not+anything(=nothing) (아무것도[단 하나도] (~ 아니다 · 없다)) not+ever(=never) (결코 ~이 아니다) not anywhere(=nowhere)		
	no =not any		no more=not ~ anymore nobody=not ~ anybody nothing=not ~ anything no longer=not ~ any longer

01 윗글의 제목으로 적절한 것은?

① Family: The Driving Force of Growth
② Effects of Culture on Career Decisions
③ Communicating Across Cultures at Work
④ How Can We Keep Our Traditional Values?
⑤ What Do You Need to Succeed in Business?

해석 | ① 가족: 성장의 원동력
② 직업 결정에 미치는 문화의 영향
③ 직장에서 문화 간 의사소통하기
④ 어떻게 우리는 전통적 가치를 유지할 수 있는가?

⑤ 사업에서 성공하기 위해 여러분은 무엇이 필요한가?

해설 | ② 글의 주제는 직업 결정에 있어서 항상 개인의 이득이 최우선인 것은 아니다는 것이다. 그러면서 멕시코시티에서의 예를 들면 멕시코시티에서는 자신의 이익보다 친구 가족의 필요를 먼저 고려하는 문화가 있다고 한다. 따라서 글의 소재인 직업 결정과 문화가 들어가는 제목으로 가장 적절한 것은 ②이다.

오답 | ① 가족이 성장보다는 현재 상황에 남게 만들기 때문에 글의 관점과 반대된다.
③ 문화 간 의사소통은 글의 소재와 무관하다.
④ 전통적 가치를 유지하는 방법은 글의 나타나지 않는다.
⑤ 사업에서 성공이라는 소재는 맞지만 무엇이 필요한지에 대해서는 나오지 않기 때문에 글의 관점과 무관하다.

02 윗글의 빈칸에 들어갈 말로 가장 적절한 것은?

① How long one would be hired
② What is best for the individual
③ Providing fair employment standards
④ Whether one can contribute to society
⑤ Taking into account the needs of children

해석 | ① 사람이 얼마나 오랫동안 고용될지
② 개인에게 가장 좋은 것
③ 공정한 고용 기준을 제공하는 것
④ 사람이 사회에 기여할 수 있는지
⑤ 자녀의 필요를 고려하는 것

해설 | ② 직업 결정에 있어서 개인의 이익을 고려하기 전에 가족 구성원이나 현지 회사의 관심을 먼저 고려한다고 했으므로, 빈칸에는 ② '개인에게 가장 좋은 것'이 가장 적절하다.

오답 | ① 얼마나 오랫동안 고용될지는 글에 나타나지 않는다.
③ 공정한 고용 기준은 글의 소재와 무관하다.
④ 사회에 기여는 글의 소재와 무관하다.
⑤ 자녀의 필요를 고려하는 것은 글의 관점과 반대된다.

노트 [논리]

■ **〈통념 & 진실〉**: 잘못된 사실을 통념이라고 하고 이에 대한 사실을 진실이라고 한다. 이러한 논리는 내신이나 수능 독해 지문에 자주 나오는 글의 형태로 통념과 진실 사이에는 대조나 역접을 나타내는 연결어나 이에 준하는 표현이 나온다.

통념을 나타내는 표현	역접의 연결어	주제문	근거 제시
Many people seem to agree that ~ Most people believe that ~ It is a basic concept that ~ A common belief is that ~ It is often considered that ~ A prevalent belief that ~ Some people think that ~ Many people believe that ~ You may think that ~ A common mistake is that ~ Most of us think that ~ A previous research show that ~	however but in fact		

■ **〈수의 일치〉**: 주어가 단수이면 동사는 단수동사를, 주어가 복수이면 동사는 복수동사를 사용해야 하는데 이러한 사실을 주어와 동사의 수의 일치라고 한다.

• 주어가 수식어구에 수식을 받는 경우 : 수식어구에 수식을 받는 명사가 주어이다.

명사	수식어구	동사
〈주어〉	to R 구	
	전치사구	
	현재분사구	
	형용사	
	관계대명사절	
	관계부사절	
	동격어구	

• 상관접속사

①	either A or B	A, B 둘 중 하나
②	neither A nor B	A도 B도 아닌 (양자부정)
③	not A but B (=B, not A)	A가 아니라 B
④	both A and B	A, B 둘 다
⑤	not only A but also B (=B as well as A)	A뿐만 아니라 B도

– 〈상관접속사의 수의 일치〉: 상관접속사가 주어로 사용되는 경우에는 ① ~ ③은 B가 주어이고, ④는 A, B 둘 다 주어이기 때문에 무조건 복수동사를 사용한다. ⑤는 다소 어려울 수 있는데 not only A but also B에서 뒤에 있는 B가 주어이지만, 이와 동의 표현인 B as well as A에서는 앞에 있는 B가 주어이기 때문에 주의를 요한다.

• A of B : 일반적인 경우에 A가 주어
• A of B : A가 부분/부분인 경우에 B가 주어

A		of	B
분수	two – thirds 등		
부분	most of, a lot of, half of, part of, the rest, percent of, some of, many of 등		〈주어〉

• 주격관계대명사절 안에 있는 동사는 선행사와 수의 일치한다.
– 〈주격관계대명사의 수의 일치〉: 주격관계대명사는 주어가 없는 경우를 말하고 그 없는 주어와 선행사는 같다. 따라서 선행사와 주격관계대명사절 안에 있는 동사는 '수의 일치'가 되어야 한다.

선행사	주격관계대명사	주어	동사 ~

• the number of / the number of

the	number	of	복수명사	+단수동사
	수			

a	number	of	복수명사	+복수동사
	많은			

• each / every / any+단수동사
• 모든 구/절은 단수 취급

	주어	단수동사
구	to R	
	동명사	
절	절	
	that절	
	what절	
	의문사절(간접의문문)	
	whether절	

• there/here is/are 구문

There	is	단수 주어	~ 있다
Here	are	복수 주어	여기에 ~ 있다

- the＋형용사＝복수보통명사
- both＋복수 / either＋단수

- 동격 : A, B (A가 주어, B라는 A)

Words

- ☐ particularly
- ☐ diligent
- ☐ offer
- ☐ promotion
- ☐ decline
- ☐ refuse
- ☐ career
- ☐ highly
- ☐ primarily
- ☐ self-interest
- ☐ company
- ☐ compelling
- ☐ position
- ☐ extended family
- ☐ probably
- ☐ prime
- ☐ factor

Phrases

- ☐ make an addition
- ☐ move to
- ☐ as is (often) the case (with)
- ☐ think about
- ☐ receive a promotion
- ☐ make(take) a decision
- ☐ tend(자동사)＋to R
- ☐ take a position
- ☐ be good for

우선순위 영단어 역대 수능 기출＋전국 모의고사 기출＋EBS 기출＋교과서 기출 빈출 어휘

단어	뜻	단어	뜻	단어	뜻
maternal	a. 모성의	maximum	n. 최대치	meadow	n. 초원
meaningless	a. 무의미한	mechanic	n. 정비사	mechanical	a. 기계적인
mechanics	n. 역학	medical	a. 의학의	meditate	v. 명상하다
mellow	a. 부드럽고 풍부한	membership	n. 회원 (자격, 신분)	memorable	a. 기억할 만한
menacing	a. 위협하는	mental	a. 정신적인	mentor	n. 조언자
merge	v. 융합하다	messiness	n. 지저분함	metabolize	v. 신진대사 시키다
meteor	n. 유성	meteorologist	n. 기상학자	meter	n. 계량기
methodical	a. 체계적인	methodological	a. 방법론적인	metropolis	n. 수도
microbe	n. 미생물	middle ground	n. 타협안	middleman	n. 중개상
mild	a. 온화한	military	a. 군의	Milky Way	n. 은하(수)
mill	n. 제분소	mind	v. ~에 주의를 기울이다	mineral	n. 무기물
minimally	ad. 최소(한도)로	mining	n. 광업	mirror	v. 비추다
misinterpret	v. 잘못 해석하다	missionary	n. 선교사	mistake	v. ~을 …으로 오인하다
mix	v. 섞다	modification	n. 변화	moist	a. 축축한
monarchy	n. 군주국가	monolingual	a. 하나의 언어를 사용하는	moody	a. 변덕스러운
more or less	거의 대략	mortality rate	n. 사망률	moss	n. 이끼
most likely	아마	move	n. 움직임	movement	n. 움직임
multiple	a. 다수의	mussel	n. 홍합	mute	a. 무언의
muted	a. 밝지 않은	mutter	v. 중얼거리다	mysterious	a. 분명치 않은
mystical	a. 신비주의의	mythology	n. 신화	namely	ad. 즉
native	a. 토착의	natural resources	n. 천연 자원	nausea	n. 메스꺼움
navigation	n. 항해	necessarily	ad. 반드시	necessitate	v. 필요하게 하다
needlework	n. 자수 작품	negative	a. 부정적인	negatively	ad. 부정적으로
neighboring	a. 이웃의	neither A nor B	v. A도 B도 아니다	nephew	n. 조카

변형문제

01 다음 글을 읽고, |조건|에 맞게 주어진 요약문을 완성하시오.

| 조건 |
* (A)는 1단어, (B)는 3단어로 쓸 것
* 본문에 있는 단어를 찾아 쓸 것
* 필요한 경우, 문맥과 어법에 맞게 변형할 것

While managing a project in Mexico City, you notice that one of your employees is particularly intelligent, successful, and diligent. Thinking he would make a great addition to the home office in Chicago, you offer him a job. Although your employee would receive a promotion, a large salary increase, and a company car if he moves to Chicago, he declines your offer. You simply cannot understand why he refuses the offer when it would be so beneficial to his career.

Many highly successful people in Mexico (and parts of Central and South America) do not make career decisions based primarily on their own self-interest, as is often the case north of the Rio Grande. In Mexico, people tend to first consider the needs of their family or company before considering their own self-interest. Receiving a promotion and higher salary would not be the most compelling reasons to take a new position. Rather, your employee would think primarily about the interests of extended family members, many of whom probably would not want him to move. Then the employee would consider the interests of the local company, which probably needs him to continue working in Mexico City. What is best for the individual is not always the prime factor in a job decision.

⬇

In Mexico, rather than taking (A) ____________ into consideration first, a number of greatly successful people consider culture when (B) ____________ ____________ ____________. For example, despite better conditions, an employee does not move to Chicago in consideration of family members and local company's interests.

02 밑줄 친 부분 중 문맥상 옳지 않은 것은?

While managing a project in Mexico City, you notice that one of your employees is particularly intelligent, successful, and diligent. Thinking he would make a ① great addition to the home office in Chicago, you offer him a job. Although your employee would receive a ② promotion, a large salary increase, and a company car if he moves to Chicago, he declines your offer. You simply cannot understand why he ③ agrees the offer when it would be so beneficial to his career. Many highly ④ successful people in Mexico (and parts of Central and South America) do not make career decisions based primarily on their own ⑤ self-interest, as is often the case north of the Rio Grande. In Mexico, people tend to first consider the needs of their family or company before considering their own self-interest. Receiving a promotion and higher salary would not be the most compelling reasons to take a new position. Rather, your employee would think primarily about the interests of extended family members, many of whom probably would not want him to move. Then the employee would consider the interests of the local company, which probably needs him to continue working in Mexico City. What is best for the individual is not always the prime factor in a job decision.

03 다음 글을 읽고, |조건|에 맞게 주어진 요약문을 완성하시오.

| 조건 |
* (A), (B), (C)는 각각 다르게 1단어로 쓸 것
* 본문에 있는 단어를 찾아 쓸 것
* 필요한 경우, 문맥과 어법에 맞게 변형할 것

While managing a project in Mexico City, you notice that one of your employees is particularly intelligent, successful, and diligent. Thinking he would make a great addition to the home office in Chicago, you offer him a job. Although your employee would receive a promotion, a large salary increase, and a company car if he moves to Chicago, he declines your offer. You simply cannot understand why he refuses the offer when it would be so beneficial to his career.

Many highly successful people in Mexico (and parts of Central and South America) do not make career decisions based primarily on their own self-interest, as is often the case north of the Rio Grande. In Mexico, people tend to first consider the needs of their family or company before considering their own self-interest. Receiving a promotion and higher salary would not be the most compelling reasons to take a new position. Rather, your employee would think primarily about the interests of extended family members, many of whom probably would not want him to move. Then the employee would consider the interests of the local company, which probably needs him to continue working in Mexico City. What is best for the individual is not always the prime factor in a job decision.

⬇

In spite of (A) ____________ such as a promotion and a large salary increase, a high number of successful people in Mexico do not decide their careers according to their (B) ____________ because they are prone to take their family and friends' needs into (C) ____________ first.

04 다음 문장이 들어갈 부분으로 가장 적절한 곳을 고르시오.

You simply cannot understand why he refuses the offer when it would be so beneficial to his career.

While managing a project in Mexico City, you notice that one of your employees is particularly intelligent, successful, and diligent. Thinking he would make a great addition to the home office in Chicago, you offer him a job. (①) Although your employee would receive a promotion, a large salary increase, and a company car if he moves to Chicago, he declines your offer. (②) Many highly successful people in Mexico (and parts of Central and South America) do not make career decisions based primarily on their own self-interest, as is often the case north of the Rio Grande. (③) In Mexico, people tend to first consider the needs of their family or company before considering their own self-interest. Receiving a promotion and higher salary would not be the most compelling reasons to take a new position. (④) Rather, your employee would think primarily about the interests of extended family members, many of whom probably would not want him to move. (⑤) Then the employee would consider the interests of the local company, which probably needs him to continue working in Mexico City. What is best for the individual is not always the prime factor in a job decision.

장문

글의 논리	Story
제목	할리우드 작가 조합과 유명한 할리우드 에이전트의 협상
주제	다른 사람과의 원만한 협상을 위해서는 공감하고 경청하는 능력이 중요하다.

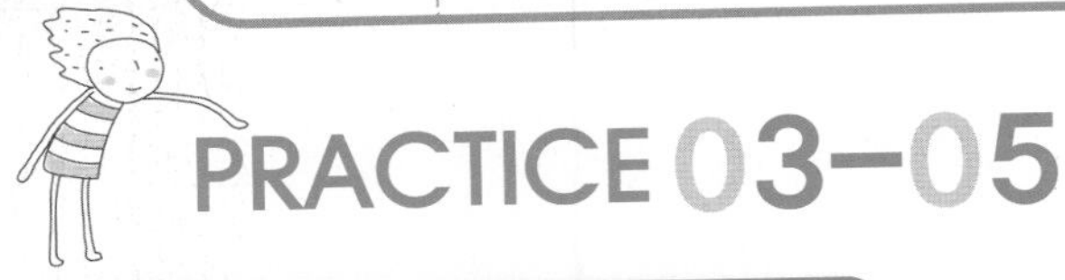

074 어법 선택 & 연결어

The Writers Guild in Hollywood in early 2008 **[has / had been]** on strike for three months. John Bowman, the Guild's chief negotiator, **[supposed / was supposed]** to speak with Stuart Diamond on a phone call **[setting / set]** up by a prominent Hollywood agent. "Listen to **[that / what]** Stuart says," the agent, Ari Emanuel, said to him. "**[Taking / Take]** notes." It was a Tuesday afternoon. Bowman had a breakfast scheduled for Thursday morning with representatives of the major Hollywood studios, to talk about the dispute.

He had a number of substantive issues and wanted to know the order **[which / in which]** to **[bring up them / bring them up]** — royalties, basic compensation, etc. Stuart told him **[putting / to put]** aside those issues, at least for now. That was not the problem. The problem was **[what / that]** everyone **[were / was]** mad at everyone else and everyone **[was / were]** **[lost / losing]** money. "Make small talk," Stuart said. "**[To ask / Ask]** them, 'Are you happy?' They will not be happy, and they will admit **[it / them]**."

"They may start blaming you and the Writers Guild. That's okay," Stuart added. "**[To sympathize / Sympathize]** with **[it / them]**," he continued. "Ask **[it / them]**, 'If we **[had had / had]** to start over again, what process would you like to see?'" At first, Bowman was skeptical. Stuart told him a negotiation is about the people and gave him some examples. People like to give things to others who **[listen / listens]** to **[it / them]**, who value them, who **[consult / consults]** with **[it / them]**.

[While / During] another phone call, **[a little / a few]** days **[latter / later]**, Bowman said he followed his advice **[complete / completely]**. At this point, what did he have to lose? The result: At the breakfast meeting, the parties agreed **[restarting / to restart]** negotiations after months of failure. **[This / It]** took only **[a little / a few]** days to get an agreement. **[Most / Almost]** immediately, the strike ended.

이야기 할리우드 작가 조합과 유명한 할리우드 에이전트의 협상

(A) The Writers Guild / (in Hollywood) / (in early 2008) / had been on strike / (for three months).

S: 작가 조합은 / 할리우드의 / 2008년 초 / V⟨과거완료⟩: 파업 중이었다 / 석 달 동안

2008년 초, 할리우드 작가 조합은 석 달 동안 파업 중이었다.

노트 ■ be (out) on (a) strike : 파업 중이다

=⟨동격⟩

John Bowman, / (the Guild's chief negotiator), / was supposed to speak / (with Stuart Diamond) (on a phone call) (set up by a prominent Hollywood agent).

S: John Bowman은 / 조합의 대표 협상가 / V: 통화하기로 되어 있었다 / Stuart Diamond와 / (which was) (과거분사) 전화 통화를 / 유명한 할리우드 에이전트에 의해 준비된

조합의 대표 협상가였던 John Bowman은 유명한 할리우드 에이전트에 의해 준비된 Stuart Diamond와 전화 통화를 하기로 되어 있었다.

노트
- be supposed to R : ~하기로 되어 있다
- speak with : ~와 이야기를 나누다, 담화하다
- set up : 준비하다, 마련하다
- ⟨동격⟩ : A(명사), B(명사) (A가 주어, B라는 A)

동격(B라는 A)			
명사(A)	,(콤마)	명사(구/절)(B)	동사
John Bowman	,	the Guild's chief negotiator	was

- ⟨주격관계대명사＋be동사 생략⟩

–	생략할 수 있음	
명사 (선행사)	(주격관계대명사 ＋be동사)	현재분사(Ring) – 능동(~하고 있는)
		과거분사(p.p.) – 수동(~되어진, 당한)
		명사
		형용사(구) (~하는, ~할)
		부사
		전치사구
a phone call	(which was)	set

"Listen to / (what Stuart says)," / the agent, Ari Emanuel, / said (to (a) him).

V (목·관) S V / O / S (=〈동격〉) / V

"잘 들어보세요 Stuart가 하는 말을" 에이전트인 Ari Emanuel이 그에게 말했다

"Stuart가 하는 말을 잘 들어보세요." 에이전트인 Ari Emanuel이 그에게 말했다.

노트
- listen to : ~을 듣다
- 〈전치사의 목적어로 사용된 목적격관계대명사 what〉 : that 사용 불가

전치사	선행사	목적격관계대명사절(명사절 : 타동사의 목적어)			
		what	주어	타동사	목적어
to		선행사를 포함한 관계대명사 (=the thing(s) which/that ~) : ~하는 것(들)은/이	Stuart	says	

"Take notes."

V O

"메모를 하세요."

"메모를 하세요."

노트
- take a note : 메모를 하다
- 〈직접명령문〉

긍정문	R	~해라
	Please+R	~해 주세요
부정문	Don't+R	~하지 마라
	Never+R	

It was a Tuesday afternoon.

(비인칭 S) V S.C

화요일 오후였다

화요일 오후였다.

노트
- 〈비인칭 주어 it〉 : 문장의 형식을 갖추기 위해 주어 자리에 사용되지만 의미는 없음

비인칭 주어 it	시간	날짜	요일	달, 월	연도
	날씨	계절	밝기	명암	거리

Bowman / had a breakfast / (which was) (scheduled for Thursday morning) / (with representatives of the major Hollywood studios), / (to talk about the dispute).

S V O 〈과거분사〉

Bowman은 식사가 있었다 목요일 아침에 계획된 주요 할리우드 제작사의 대표들과 논쟁거리에 대해 이야기하기 위해

Bowman은 주요 할리우드 제작사의 대표들과 논쟁거리에 대해 이야기하기 위해 목요일 아침에 계획된 식사가 있었다.

노트
- have a breakfast : 아침식사를 하다
- be scheduled for : ~하기로 예정되어 있다
- talk about : ~에 대해 이야기하다

- 〈주격관계대명사+be동사 생략〉

-	생략할 수 있음	
명사 (선행사)	(주격관계대명사 +be동사)	현재분사(Ring) – 능동(~하고 있는)
		과거분사(p.p.) – 수동(~되어진, 당한)
		명사
		형용사(구) (~하는, ~할)
		부사
		전치사구
a breakfast	(which was)	scheduled

(B) (During another phone call), / (a few days later), / Bowman said / (that) {he followed (b) his advice / (completely)}.

〈전치사〉 O / S V / S V O / O

또 다른 전화 통화에서 며칠 지나 Bowman은 말했다 그가 그의 충고를 완전히 따랐다고

며칠 지나, 또 다른 전화 통화에서, Bowman은 자신이 그의 충고를 완전히 따랐다고 말했다.

노트
- 시간(~ 동안)

전치사	during	+명사 / 명사 상당어구
종속접속사	while	+주어+동사

- 〈the other vs. another〉

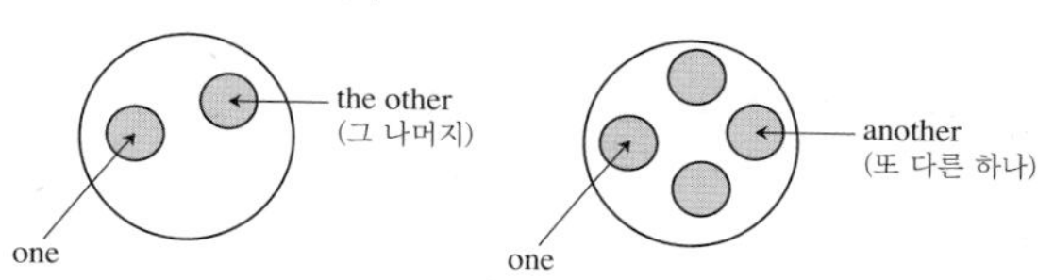

- 〈few / a few / a little / little〉

수	few	거의 없는(부정)	+복수N+복수V
	a few	약간(긍정)	
양	a little	약간(긍정)	+단수N+단수V
	little	거의 없는(부정)	

- 〈불규칙적으로 변화하는 중요 형용사와 부사〉

원급	비교급	뜻	최상급	뜻	의미
late	later	나중의	latest	최근의	시간
	latter	후자의	last	최후의	순서

- 〈목적격종속접속사 that 생략〉 : 완전타동사의 목적어로 사용된 경우 / 관계대명사 what 사용 불가

완전타동사	종속절(명사절 : 목적어) (완전한 절)		
	that	주어	동사
said	목적격종속접속사 – 생략 가능(~하는 것을)	he	followed

- 〈혼동 어휘〉

	동사	형용사	명사	부사
complete	완수하다	완전한, 완벽한	–	–
completion	–	–	완성, 완수	–
compete	경쟁하다			
competition	–	–	경쟁, 대회	–
competitor	–	–	경쟁자	–

competence	–	–	능력, 자격	–
incompetence	–	–	무능력	–
complement	보완하다	–	보완, 보충	–
compliment	칭찬하다	–	칭찬	
complimentary	–	칭찬하는, 무료의	–	–
complimentarily	–	–	–	찬사로, 무료로
competitive	–	경쟁적인	–	–
competent	–	유능한, 적임의, 자격이 있는	–	–
completely	–	–	–	완전히, 전적으로
competitively	–	–	–	경쟁적으로
competently	–	–	–	유능하게

At this point, / what did he have to lose?

(〈의·대〉 what / S he / V did … have to lose)

이 순간 / 그는 무엇을 잃어야 했을까?

이 순간 그는 무엇을 잃어야 했을까?

노트 ■ at this point : 이 시점에(에서)

The result: / (At the breakfast meeting), / the parties / agreed to restart negotiations / (after months of failure).

(S the parties / V agreed / O to restart negotiations)

결과는 이러했다: / 아침 식사 모임에서 / 당사자들은 / 협상을 재개할 것에 동의했다 / 몇 달의 실패 후에

결과는 이러했다: 아침 식사 모임에서 당사자들은 몇 달의 실패 후에 협상을 재개할 것에 동의했다.

노트 ■ 〈목적어 자리에 to부정사를 취하는 완전타동사〉

주어	완전타동사	목적어
–	afford / agree / ask / attempt / care / choose / claim / dare / decide / demand / desire / determine / elect / expect / fail / guarantee / hope / intend / learn / manage / need / offer / plan / pretend / promise / refuse / resolve / seek / threaten / volunteer / want / wish 등	to 동사원형

It / took only a few days / (to get an agreement).

(〈가S〉 It / V took / O only a few days / 〈진S〉 to get an agreement)

이것은 / 며칠이 걸리지 않았다 / 합의를 얻어내는 데

합의를 얻어내는 데 며칠이 걸리지 않았다.

노트 ■ only a few : 다만 몇 안 되는

■ 〈take 동사 쓰임〉 : ~하는 데 시간이 …만큼 걸리다

It	takes	시간	to R

(Almost immediately), / the strike / ended.

(S the strike / V ended)

거의 바로 / 파업이 / 끝나버렸다

거의 바로, 파업이 끝나버렸다.

노트 ■ 〈most / almost / mostly〉

	대명사	형용사	부사
most	대부분의 것들(사람들)	대부분의	가장
almost	–	–	거의
mostly	–	–	주로, 일반적으로

(C) He / had a number of substantive issues / and / wanted to know the order (in which to bring them up) / — (royalties, basic compensation, etc).

(S He / V_1 had / O a number of substantive issues / V_2 wanted / O to know the order 〈선행사〉 / in which 〈전치사+관·대〉 / bring them up 〈이어동사〉)

그는 / 많은 실질적인 논쟁거리가 있었다 / 그리고 / 문제들을 끄집어낼 순서를 알기 원했다 / – 저작권료나 기본적인 보수와 같은

그는 많은 실질적인 논쟁거리가 있었고, 저작권료나 기본적인 보수와 같은 문제들을 끄집어낼 순서를 알기 원했다.

노트 ■ a number of＋복수명사 : 많은 ~

■ bring A up : A를 꺼내다

■ etc.(＝et cetera) : 기타 등등(＝and so forth, and the like, and so on, the others, the rest, and others, and what not)

■ 〈'전치사＋관계대명사＋to R' ＝ '전치사＋관계대명사＋S＋will R'〉

1번	I	need	a box.					
2번	I	will put	things	in a box.				
3번	I	need	a box	and (대등접속사)	I	will put	things	in a box.
4번	I	need	a box (선행사)	which (목적격 관계대명사)	I	will put	things	in.
5번	I	need	a box (선행사)	in (전치사)	which (목적격 관계대명사)	I	will put	things.
6번	I	need	a box (선행사)	in (전치사)	which (목적격 관계대명사)	to put	things.	

• 1번과 2번 문장을 합치면 3번 문장이다. 3번 문장에서 a box가 동일하기에 관계대명사를 사용해 단문으로 바꾸면 4번 문장이 된다. '관계대명사 ~ 전치사'는 '전치사＋관계대명사'로 바꿀 수 있어 4번 문장을 5번 문장으로 바꿀 수 있다. 5번 문장에서 미래형 동사 will put은 to put으로 바꿀 수 있는데, 왜냐하면 to부정사는 미래의미를 지닐 수 있기 때문이다. 따라서 위에 주어진 'He had ~ etc.' 문장에서 박스에 있는 5번 문장처럼 다시 고쳐 써보면, '~ know the order in which he would bring them up' 이다.

■ 〈이어동사〉

타동사	명사	부사	(○)
타동사	부사	명사	(○)
타동사	대명사	부사	(○)
타동사	부사	대명사	(×)
bring	up	them	(×)

Stuart / told (c) him to put aside those issues, / (at

(S Stuart / V told / O him / O.C to put aside those issues)

Stuart는 / 그에게 그런 논쟁거리를 제쳐 두라고 말했다

least) / (for now).
적어도 잠시만

Stuart는 그에게 그런 논쟁거리를 적어도 잠시만 제쳐 두라고 말했다.

노트
■ put aside A : A를 한쪽으로 치우다, 제거하다
■ at least : 적어도[최소한]
■ for now : 현재로는, 당분간은
■ 〈5형식 불완전타동사의 목적격보어〉 : 수동태 전환 시, 2형식 문장(be p.p. +to R)

주어	불완전타동사	목적어	목적격보어
–	advise / allow / ask / assume / beg / cause / command / compel / condition / decide / design / drive / enable / encourage / expect / forbid / force / instruct / intend / invite / lead / like / motivate / order / permit / persuade / predispose / pressure / program / push / require / teach / tell / train / trust / urge / want / warn / wish 등	–	to 동사원형

That / was not the problem.
S 그것이 / V S.C 문제가 아니었다

그것이 문제가 아니었다.

The problem / was {that everyone was mad / (at everyone else) / and / everyone / was losing money}.
S 문제는 / V / 〈종·접〉 S V S.C 모든 사람들이 화가 나 있으며 다른 모두에게 / 그리고 / S 모두가 / V〈과거진행〉 O 돈을 잃고 있다는 것이었다

문제는 모든 사람이 다른 모두에게 화가 나 있으며 모두가 돈을 잃고 있다는 것이었다.

노트
■ be mad at : ~에 화를 내다
■ 〈what vs. that〉

	관계대명사(불완전한 문장)	접속사(완전한 문장)
what	○ 선행사를 포함하고 있기 때문에 what 앞에 선행사 불필요	×
that	○ that 앞에 선행사 필요	○

■ 〈주어와 동사의 수의 일치〉
• each / every / any+단수동사
■ 〈형용사의 후치 수식〉

〈후치 수식〉	-thing -body -one	+형용사	○
〈전치 수식〉	형용사+	-thing -body -one	×

"Make small talk," / Stuart said.
V O "가벼운 대화를 하세요," / S V Stuart는 말했다

"가벼운 대화를 하세요." Stuart는 말했다.

노트
■ make small talk : 한담하다

"Ask them, / 'Are you happy?' / They / will not be happy, / and / they / will admit it."
V O "그들에게 물어보세요, / V S S.C '지금 만족스러우세요?' / S 그들은 / V 만족스럽지 않을 S.C 것이다 / 그리고 / S 그들은 / V O 그것을 인정할 것이다."

"그들에게 물어보세요. '지금 만족스러우세요?' 그들은 만족스럽지 않을 것이며, 그것을 인정할 것입니다."

(D) "They / may start blaming / (d) you and the Writers Guild. / That's okay," / Stuart added.
S "그들은 / V 비난하기를 시작할 수도 있습니다 / 〈동명사〉 O 당신과 작가 조합을 / S V S.C 괜찮습니다," / S V Stuart는 말했다

"그들은 당신과 작가 조합을 비난하기를 시작할 수도 있습니다. 괜찮습니다." Stuart는 말했다.

노트
■ 〈3형식에서 목적어 자리에 to R / Ring 둘 다 사용 가능〉

주어	완전타동사		목적어
주어	begin	~을 시작하다	to R/Ring (의미 차이 없음)
	cease	~을 중단하다	
	continue	~을 계속하다	
	deserve	~할 가치/자격/권리가 있다	
	dislike	~을 싫어하다	
	hate		
	like	~을 좋아하다	
	love	~을 사랑하다	
	neglect	~하는 것을 소홀히 하다	
	prefer	~쪽을 좋아하다	
	require	~을 요구하다	
	start	~을 시작하다	

"Sympathize (with them)," / he continued.
"그들과 공감하세요." / S V 그는 말을 덧붙였다

"그들과 공감하세요." 그는 말을 이었다.

노트
■ sympathize with : ~에 공감하다

"Ask them, / '(If we had to start over again), / what process / would you like to see?'"
V O "그들에게 물어보세요, / 〈종·접〉 S V 만약 우리가 다시 시작해야 한다면 / 〈의·형〉 어떤 과정을 / S V O 보기를 원하시나요?"

"그들에게 물어보세요. '우리가 다시 시작해야 한다면, 어떤 과정을 보기를 원하시나요?'"

노트
■ start (all) over again : 처음부터 다시 시작하다
■ would like to R : ~하고 싶다

(At first), / Bowman was skeptical.
처음에 / S V S.C Bowman은 회의적이었다

처음에 Bowman은 회의적이었다.

노트 ■ at first : 처음에는

Stuart told him / (that) (a negotiation is about the people) /

S V1 I.O S V D.O

Stuart는 그에게 말했다 협상은 사람에 관한 것이다

and / gave / (e) him some examples.

V2 I.O D.O

그리고 제공했다 그에게 몇 가지 사례를

Stuart는 그에게 협상은 사람에 관한 것이라고 말했다. Stuart는 그에게 몇 가지 사례를 제공했다.

노트 ■ give+IO+DO : ~에게 …을 주다

■ **〈목적격종속접속사 that 생략〉** : 완전타동사의 목적어로 사용된 경우 / 관계대명사 what 사용 불가

주절			종속절(명사절 : 목적어) (완전한 절)		
			직접목적어(D.O)		
주어	수여동사	간접목적어 (I.O)	that	주어	동사 ~
Stuart	told	him	(that) 생략	a negotiation	is

주제문 사람들은 자신의 말을 경청하고, 공감하는 사람들에게 무언가를 주기를 좋아한다.

People like to give things to others / (who listen to

S V O 〈선행사〉 〈주·관〉 V

사람들은 무언가를 주기를 좋아하기 마련이다 자신의 말을

them), / (who value them), / (who consult with them).

O 〈주·관〉 V O 〈주·관〉 V

경청하고 자신을 소중히 여기고 자신의 의견을 듣는 사람에게

사람들은 자신의 말을 경청하고, 자신을 소중히 여기고, 자신의 의견을 듣는 사람에게 무언가를 주기를 좋아하기 마련이다.

노트 ■ consult with : ~와 협의하다

■ **〈4형식을 3형식으로 바꿀 때 사용하는 전치사〉** : 전치사 to를 취하는 동사

주어 (A)	+	동사(B)	+	간접목적어 (C : 사람/동물)	+	직접목적어 (D : 사물)	(4)
		give, bring, pass, send, show, sell, hand, lend, offer, teach, tell, buy, build, choose, find, leave, make, prepare, order, ask, deal 등 수여동사					

→ 주어(A)+동사(B)+직접목적어(D : 사물)+전치사 to+간접목적어(C : 사람/동물) (3)

■ **〈주격관계대명사절의 수의 일치〉** : 선행사를 포함하고 있는 관계대명사 what 사용 불가

선행사	주격관계대명사절		
	주격관계대명사	~~주어~~	동사
others	who		listen
			value
			consult

01 주어진 글 (A)에 이어질 내용을 순서에 맞게 배열한 것으로 가장 적절한 것은?

① (B) – (D) – (C) ② (C) – (B) – (D)
③ (C) – (D) – (B) ④ (D) – (B) – (C)
⑤ (D) – (C) – (B)

정답 | ③

해설 | ③ (A)에는 Bowman이 조언을 얻기 위해 Stuart와 통화를 하게 된 배경이 묘사되고 있으며, 전화 통화를 통해 Stuart가 Bowman에게 조언하는 내용인 (C)가 바로 이어지는 것이 적절하다. 그리고 그 조언에 대해 부정적인 Bowman을 설득하는 내용이 소개되는 (D)가 이어지게 되고, 조언을 따른 결과 파업을 끝낼 수 있었다는 내용의 (B)가 마지막에 오게 된다.

02 밑줄 친 (a) ~ (e) 중에서 가리키는 대상이 나머지 넷과 다른 것은?

① (a) ② (b) ③ (c)
④ (d) ⑤ (e)

정답 | ②

해설 | ② (b) his는 Stuart를 가리키며, 나머지는 전부 Bowman을 가리킨다.

03 윗글의 Bowman에 관한 내용으로 적절하지 않는 것은?

① 에이전트로부터 Stuart의 말을 귀담아 들으라는 충고를 받았다.
② 목요일 아침에 대표자들과 조찬모임이 예정되어 있었다.
③ 많은 심각한 문제를 안고 있었다.
④ Stuart의 조언에 대해 처음부터 호의적이었다.
⑤ 재협상을 시작해서 파업을 끝냈다.

정답 | ④

해설 | ④ Bowman은 Stuart의 조언에 대해 처음에는 회의적이었으므로 ④는 내용상 적절하지 않다.

오답 | ① "'Listen to what Stuart says," the agent, Ari Emanuel, said to him. "Take notes."' 라고 나타나 있다.

② 'Bowman had a breakfast scheduled for Thursday morning with representatives of the major Hollywood studios, to talk about the dispute.' 라고 나타나 있다.

③ 'He had a number of substantive issues and wanted to know the order in which to bring them up — royalties, basic compensation, etc.라고 나타나 있다.

⑤ 'The result: At the breakfast meeting, the parties agreed to restart negotiations after months of failure. Almost immediately, the strike ended.' 라고 나타나 있다.

Words

- ☐ strike
- ☐ negotiator
- ☐ prominent
- ☐ agent
- ☐ representative
- ☐ studio
- ☐ dispute
- ☐ completely
- ☐ restart
- ☐ agreement
- ☐ immediately
- ☐ royalty
- ☐ compensation
- ☐ blame
- ☐ sympathize
- ☐ skeptical
- ☐ value

Phrases

- ☐ be (out) on (a) strike
- ☐ speak with
- ☐ listen to
- ☐ have a breakfast
- ☐ talk about
- ☐ only a few
- ☐ bring A up
- ☐ at least
- ☐ be mad at
- ☐ sympathize with
- ☐ would like to R
- ☐ consult with
- ☐ be supposed to R
- ☐ set up
- ☐ take a note
- ☐ be scheduled for
- ☐ at this point
- ☐ a number of＋복수명사
- ☐ put aside A
- ☐ for now
- ☐ make small talk
- ☐ start (all) over again
- ☐ at first

우선순위 영단어

역대 수능 기출 + 전국 모의고사 기출 + EBS 기출 + 교과서 기출 빈출 어휘

단어	뜻	단어	뜻	단어	뜻
neural	a. 신경의	neural circuit	n. 신경 회로	neuroscientist	n. 신경과학자
neutral	a. 중립의	nevertheless	ad. 그럼에도 불구하고	newborn	n. 신생아
news agency	n. 방송사	nightmare	n. 악몽	no doubt	틀림없이
nomadic	a. 유목의	nonprofit	a. 비영리의	nostril	n. 콧구멍
notable	a. 두드러진	nourishment	n. 자양물	noxious	a. 유해한
numb	a. 감각은 잃은	numerical	a. 숫자의	nurse	v. 키우다
nursery	n. 아이 방	nursing home	n. 양로원	nut	n. 견과
nutritionally	ad. 영양학적으로	nutritious	a. 영양가 있는	oak	n. 참나무
object to	v. ~에 반대하다	objection	n. 반대	oblige	v. ~에게 은혜를 베풀다
observance	n. (법률, 규칙 등의) 준수	observatory	n. 천문대	obsessive	a. 억압의
obsolete	a. 더 이상 쓸모가 없는	occupant	n. 점유자	offender	n. 범법자
office equipment	n. 사무용 장비	on cue	마침 때맞추어	on one’s back	잔소리하는
on the contrary	정반대로	on the way to	~로 가는 도중에	on the whole	전반적으로
oncoming	a. 접근하는	ongoing	a. 계속 진행 중인	on-site	현장의
openness	n. 솔직함	operating	a. 운영상의	opposed to	~와 반대의
opposite effect	n. 역효과	oppressive	a. 억압적인	opt for	v. ~을 선택하다
oral	a. 구두의	orderly	a. 정연된	ordinarily	ad. 정상적으로
oriented	a. ~ 위주의	origin	n. 출신	original	n. 원본

변형문제

01 다음 글을 읽고, |조건|에 맞게 주어진 요약문을 완성하시오.

| 조건 |
* (A), (B)는 각각 1단어, (C)는 2단어로 쓸 것
* 본문에 있는 단어를 찾아 그대로 쓸 것

The Writers Guild in Hollywood in early 2008 had been on strike for three months. John Bowman, the Guild's chief negotiator, was supposed to speak with Stuart Diamond on a phone call set up by a prominent Hollywood agent. "Listen to what Stuart says," the agent, Ari Emanuel, said to him. "Take notes." It was a Tuesday afternoon. Bowman had a breakfast scheduled for Thursday morning with representatives of the major Hollywood studios, to talk about the dispute.

He had a number of substantive issues and wanted to know the order in which to bring them up — royalties, basic compensation, etc. Stuart told him to put aside those issues, at least for now. That was not the problem. The problem was that everyone was mad at everyone else and everyone was losing money. "Make small talk," Stuart said. "Ask them, 'Are you happy?' They will not be happy, and they will admit it."

"They may start blaming you and the Writers Guild. That's okay," Stuart added. "Sympathize with them," he continued. "Ask them, 'If we had to start over again, what process would you like to see?'" At first, Bowman was skeptical. Stuart told him a negotiation is about the people and gave him some examples. People like to give things to others who listen to them, who value them, who consult with them.

During another phone call, a few days later, Bowman said he followed his advice completely. At this point, what did he have to lose? The result: At the breakfast meeting, the parties agreed to restart negotiations after months of failure. It took only a few days to get an agreement. Almost immediately, the strike ended.

⬇

To end the strike immediately, it was essential to (A) ____________ with the unionists in the Writers Guild, (B) ____________ to them, value them, and consult with them rather than hastily bringing up (C) ____________ ____________ like basic compensation.

02 다음 빈칸에 들어갈 말로 가장 적절한 것은?

The Writers Guild in Hollywood in early 2008 had been on strike for three months. John Bowman, the Guild's chief negotiator, was supposed to speak with Stuart Diamond on a phone call set up by a prominent Hollywood agent. "Listen to what Stuart says," the agent, Ari Emanuel, said to him. "Take notes." It was a Tuesday afternoon. Bowman had a breakfast scheduled for Thursday morning with representatives of the major Hollywood studios, to talk about the dispute.

He had a number of substantive issues and wanted to know the order in which to bring them up — royalties, basic compensation, etc. Stuart told him to put aside those issues, at least for now. That was not the problem. The problem was that everyone was mad at everyone else and everyone was losing money. "Make small talk," Stuart said. "Ask them, 'Are you happy?' They will not be happy, and they will admit it."

"They may start blaming you and the Writers Guild. That's okay," Stuart added. "__________ with them," he continued. "Ask them, 'If we had to start over again, what process would you like to see?'" At first, Bowman was skeptical. Stuart told him a negotiation is about the people and gave him some examples. People like to give things to others who listen to them, who value them, who consult with them.

During another phone call, a few days later, Bowman said he followed his advice completely. At this point, what did he have to lose? The result: At the breakfast meeting, the parties agreed to restart negotiations after months of failure. It took only a few days to get an agreement. Almost immediately, the strike ended.

① Sympathize ② Fight ③ Cooperate
④ Deny ⑤ Operate

03 다음 문장이 들어갈 부분으로 가장 적절한 곳을 고르시오.

That was not the problem.

The Writers Guild in Hollywood in early 2008 had been on strike for three months. John Bowman, the Guild's chief negotiator, was supposed to speak with Stuart Diamond on a phone call set up by a prominent Hollywood agent. "Listen to what Stuart says," the agent, Ari Emanuel, said to him. "Take notes." It was a Tuesday afternoon. (①) Bowman had a breakfast scheduled for Thursday morning with representatives of the major Hollywood studios, to talk about the dispute. (②) He had a number of substantive issues and wanted to know the order in which to bring them up — royalties, basic compensation, etc. (③) Stuart told him to put aside those issues, at least for now. (④) The problem was that everyone was mad at everyone else and everyone was losing money. (⑤) "Make small talk," Stuart said. "Ask them, 'Are you happy?' They will not be happy, and they will admit it."

04 밑줄 친 부분 중 문맥상 옳지 않은 것은?

The Writers Guild in Hollywood in early 2008 had been on strike for three months. John Bowman, the Guild's chief negotiator, was supposed to speak with Stuart Diamond on a phone call set up by a prominent Hollywood agent. "Listen to what Stuart says," the agent, Ari Emanuel, said to him. "Take notes." It was a Tuesday afternoon. Bowman had a breakfast scheduled for Thursday morning with representatives of the major Hollywood studios, to talk about the ① dispute. He had a number of substantive issues and wanted to know the order in which to bring them up — royalties, basic compensation, etc. Stuart told him to put aside those issues, at least for now. That was not the problem. The problem was that ② everyone was mad at everyone else and everyone was losing money. "Make small talk," Stuart said. "Ask them, 'Are you happy?' They will not be happy, and they will ③ deny it." "They may start ④ blaming you and the Writers Guild. That's okay," Stuart added. "Sympathize with them," he continued. "Ask them, 'If we had to start over again, what process would you like to see?'" At first, Bowman was ⑤ skeptical. Stuart told him a negotiation is about the people and gave him some examples. People like to give things to others who listen to them, who value them, who consult with them. During another phone call, a few days later, Bowman said he followed his advice completely. At this point, what did he have to lose? The result: At the breakfast meeting, the parties agreed to restart negotiations after months of failure. It took only a few days to get an agreement. Almost immediately, the strike ended.

올림포스
분석·변형문제
정답 및 해설

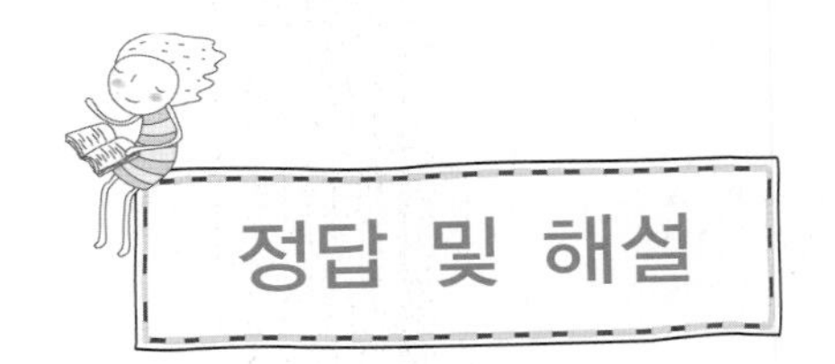

UNIT 01 주제 · 제목

수능 ANALYSIS PP. 7~8

1 (A) the same ancestor (B) some genes
2 ①
3 ②
4 ④

01

해석 | 지구에서 동물과 식물 모든 종들과 함께, 우리는 살아 있는 생명체 안에서 우리가 공유하는 (B) 몇몇 유전자가 동등하다는 사실 때문에 (A) 같은 조상을 갖는다.

해설 | 이 글의 주제는 같은 유전자를 통해 우리 모두가 같은 조상을 공유하고 있다는 것을 알 수 있다는 것이다. 따라서 (B)에는 주제문과 연관되어 보면 우리가 생명체들과 공유하는 근거인 유전자라는 말인 'some genes'가, (A)에는 같은 유전자를 가지고 있어서 확인할 수 있는 사실인 같은 조상을 공유한다는 말인 'the same ancestor'가 적절하다.

02

해석 | ① 우리는 모든 생명체와 조상을 공유한다
② 우리는 다른 종들과 분별된다
③ 인간들은 같은 조상으로부터 태어났다
④ 모든 생명체는 유전자를 갖는다
⑤ 인간과 동물은 조화롭게 산다

해설 | 이 글의 주제는 지구상의 모든 종들이 조상을 공유한다는 것이다. 주제와 가장 문맥이 맞는 문장은 우리는 모든 생명체와 같은 조상을 공유한다는 ①이 적절하다.

오답 | ② 우리는 다른 종들과 같은 유전자를 가지고 있다고 하므로 분별된다는 말은 적절하지 않다.
③ 인간들은 같은 조상으로부터 태어났지만 인간뿐만 아니라 모든 생명체가 같은 조상을 공유한다고 말하고 있으므로 적절하지 않다.
④ 모든 생명체는 유전자를 갖고 있지만 이 글의 핵심은 같은 유전자를 가지고 있다는 것이다.
⑤ 인간과 동물이 조화롭게 사는지에 대한 내용은 존재하지 않는다.

03

해설 | 주어진 문장은 글의 주제인 우리가 모든 종의 동 식물들과 조상을 공유한다는 사실을 말한다. (B)의 'this'는 1번째 문장의 우리가 조상을 공유한다는 것을 가리킨다. 그리고 (A)의 '우리는 모두 사촌'이라는 말에서 '우리'는 (B)에 나온 '우리'와 연결된다. (C)에서는 '모두가 다 우리의 사촌'이라 말하는데 (C)에서 나온 '모두'는 (A)에 나온 '생쥐, 버팔로, 이구아나 등 모든 것'을 의미한다. 따라서 ② '(B) – (A) – (C)'가 적절하다.

04

해설 | 이 글의 내용은 우리 모두가 조상을 공유하고 있다는 것이다. 따라서 ④가 들어간 문장을 보면 당신의 가족 가계도는 침팬지와 원숭이뿐만 아니라 쥐, 버팔로 등을 포함한다는 말이 되어야 한다. 그러므로 ④ 'excludes(배제하다) → includes(포함하다)'가 적절하다.

PRACTICE 01 PP. 12~13

1 (A) on the verge (B) be prepared
2 (A) the appropriate time (B) interest (C) money
3 (A) diverse (B) be prepared
4 ②

01

해설 | 이 글의 주제는 마케팅 담당자들은 소비자들이 상품에 대한 관심도와 흥미도가 다르기 때문에 상품에 대해 필요를 하는 때를 알고 적절할 때에 행동할 준비를 해야 한다는 것이다. (A)의 문장을 보면 사람들이 제품에 대한 흥미도를 나타낸다. 어떤 사람들은 제품을 사려고 (A) 할 수도 있고 반면에 어떤 사람들은 그것을 들어본 적이 없다고 나타난다. 반면에는 앞의 절과 대조를 이루는 것이기 때문에 (A)에는 제품을 들어본 적이 없다는 것과 대조되는 말이 들어와야 하므로 제품을 막 사려고 한다는 'on the verge'가 적절하다. 이 글의 (B) 부분에는 글의 주제가 나타나 있다. (B)가 들어간 문장은 마케팅 담당자들이 이러한 단계를 알고 적절한 때에 행동할 (B)이어야 한다는 것이다. 글의 주제는 적절한 때에 행동할 준비를 해야 한다는 것이므로 'be prepared'가 적절하다.

02

해석 | 성공적인 마케팅 담당자들은 소비자들이 상품을 구매하는 것에 대한 (A) 적절한 때를 인식할 필요가 있고 왜냐하면 상품에 대한 소비자들의 (B) 흥미의 단계(수준)와 그들이 가지는 (C) 돈의 양이 다르기 때문이다.

해설 | 이 글의 주제는 마케팅 담당자들은 제품에 대한 사람들의 흥미와 필요성을 파악하고 적절한 때를 인식하여 행동을 해야 한다는 것인데, 그 이유로 사람마다 돈을 벌고 있는 상황이 다르다고 말한다. (A)에는 적절한 때를 인식하라는 주제에 알맞은 말인 'the appropriate time'이, (B)에는 소비자들의 흥미의 단계가 다르다는 뜻을 갖는 'interest'가, (C)에는 사람마다 돈을 벌고 있는 상황이 다르다는 뜻으로 'money'가 적절하다.

03

해석 | 상품에 대한 개개인의 인식이 (A) 다양하기 때문에, 마케팅 담당자들은 상품에 대한 그들의 인식을 이해하기 위해 (B) 준비하고 적절한 때에 행동해야 한다는 것이다.

해설 | 이 글의 주제는 마케팅 담당자들은 제품에 대한 사람들의 흥미와 필요성이 다르기 때문에 이를 파악하고 적절한 때에 행동을 해야 한다는 것이다. (A)에는 주제와 연관되어 사람들의 흥미와 필요성이 다르다는 말인 다양하다는 표현으로 'diverse'가, (B)에는 사람들의 흥미와 필요성을 파악한다는 말과 유의한 표현인 그들의 인식을 이해하기

위해 준비한다는 말인 'be prepared'가 적절하다.

04

해설 | (B)에서 others는 주어진 문장의 others와 연결된다. 그리고 (A)에서 의 이러한 단계는 (B)의 문장들의 설명을 가리키고 (A)의 예시로 (C)가 나오기 때문에 ② '(B) – (A) – (C)'가 적절하다.

PRACTICE 02 PP. 17~18

1 (A) language (B) science (C) social institutions
2 (A) disconfirm (B) modified (C) scratch
3 (A) preparation (B) fundamental
4 (A) act (B) pass

01

해석 | 글에 따르면, 우리가 과거로부터 내재되어 있는 세 가지는 (A) 언어, (B) 과학, (C) 사회제도이다.

해설 | 이 글의 주제는 인간들이 과거의 것을 물려받아 점진적으로 발전시킨다는 것이다. 그리고 그 예시로 언어와 과학, 사회제도를 들고 있다. 따라서 빈칸에는 예시로 들고 있는 언어, 과학, 사회제도가 들어가야 하므로 (A)에는 'language', (B)에는 'science', (C)에는 'social institutions'가 적절하다.

02

해설 | 이 글의 주제는 인간들은 과거의 것을 물려받아 점진적으로 발전시킨다는 것이다. 주제를 미루어 보았을 때, (A)에는 이론을 확인하거나 부당성을 증명한다는 내용이 나와야 하므로 'disconfirm'이, (B)에는 과거의 것을 발전시킨다는 내용으로 수정된 형태들이라는 말인 'modified'가, (C)에는 인간은 절대로 아무런 준비 없이 존재를 시작하지 않는다는 내용이 나와야 하므로 'scratch'가 적절하다.

03

해석 | 어떠한 (A) 준비 없이, 인간은 그들의 존재를 시작하지 않고 특정한 변화하는 상황의 종류로 시작한다. 또한, 그들은 세대에서 (B) 근본적인 변화가 있는 상황에서 시작한다는 것이다.

해설 | 이 글의 주제는 인간들은 과거의 것을 물려받아 점진적으로 발전시킨다는 것이다. 그리고 마지막 문장을 보면 인간은 아무런 준비 없이 존재를 시작하지 않고 항상 근본적으로 변화하는 상황에서 시작한다고 한다. 주제와 연관지어 봤을 때, (A)에는 준비한다는 뜻인 'preparation'이, (B)에는 근본적이라는 뜻인 'fundamental'이 적절하다.

04

해석 | 인간은 그들이 과거로부터 내재하고 있는 것의 근본의 것을 대체하여 (A) 행동하기 쉽고 그래서 그들은 미래 세대에 그것을 (B) 넘겨줄 수 있다.

해설 | 이 글의 내용은 인간은 과거의 것을 물려받아 변형하여 다음 세대로 물려준다는 내용이다. 글의 주제와 연관지어 봤을 때, (A)에는 과거로부터 받은 것을 대체하여 행동하다는 뜻인 'act'가, (B)에는 다음 세대로 물려준다는 내용인 'pass'가 적절하다.

PRACTICE 03 PP. 22~23

1 (A) popularity (B) inference (C) retrieve
2 (A) easier (B) exposed
3 (A) popularity (B) frequency
4 the more fluently we retrieve an item from memory

01

해설 | 이 글의 주제는 우리는 기억을 활용하여 우리가 지냈던 환경을 추론할 수 있다는 것이다. (A)의 다음 문장에 인기도에 따라 비치되어 있는 장소에 대한 설명이 있으므로 (A)에는 'popularity'가, (B)는 뒤에 추론할 수 있다는 말이 있으므로 'inference'가, (C)는 쉽게 생각해 낸다는 말이 필요하므로 'retrieve'가 적절하다.

02

해석 | 우리 자신의 기억에 대한 사용은 우리에게 과거에서 환경을 추론하는 것을 돕는다. 예를 들어 우리는 그것이 우리가 기억 속에 어떤 항목에 대해 생각을 (A) 더 쉽게 할수록, 우리는 과거에 그것(항목)에 (B) 더 빈번하게 노출됨에 틀림없다고 추론할 수 있다.

해설 | 이 글의 주제는 빈번히 접했던 것을 쉽게 추론한다는 것이다. 그리고 글의 주제와 미루어 보면 (B)에는 과거에 더 많이 노출됐다는 의미의 'exposed'가, (A)에는 많이 노출될수록 쉽게 생각할 수 있다는 의미의 'easier'가 적절하다.

03

해석 | 개개인의 기억은 책들이 (A) 인기도에 따라 배열되어 있는 공공도서관에 비유될 수 있는 것처럼, 역시 우리의 기억으로부터 어떤 항목은 그것의 (B) 빈번성에 의존하여 빈번하게 회상된다.

해설 | 이 글의 주제는 우리가 쉽게 기억하는 것은 과거에 빈번히 접했던 것이라 추론할 수 있다는 것이다. (A)에는 글의 내용을 보면 공공도서관에서는 인기도에 따라 책이 배열되어 있기 때문에 'popularity'가, (B)에는 우리의 기억은 자주 접했던 것에 따라 회상되기 때문에 빈번하다는 뜻인 'frequency'가 적절하다.

04

해설 | 이 글의 주제는 인간의 기억은 자주 접했을수록 더 쉽게 기억된다는 것이다. 따라서 빈칸에는 '어떤 항목을 더 쉽게 생각해 낼수록'이라는 말이 들어가야 한다. 그리고 문법적으로 보면 'the more fluently'는 'the more often'과 연결된다. 그리고 that절에 완벽한 문장이 들어와야 하므로 'we retrieve an item from memory'가 적절하다.

UNIT 02 요지 · 주장

수능 ANALYSIS

PP. 27 ~ 28

1 (A) reluctant (B) discomfort
2 (A) cumbersome (B) intolerable
3 Making long-term habit changes
4 ③

01

해석 | 개개인들은 변화하는 것을 그들이 오래된 습관적인 행동을 대체할 때 느끼는 (B) 불편함 때문에 (A) 꺼려한다.

해설 | 이 글의 주제는 사람들이 변화하는 것이 불편하기 때문에 변화를 꺼린다는 것이다. 주제를 미루어 보았을 때, (A)에는 변화를 꺼린다는 말인 'reluctant'가, (B)에는 불편하다는 의미인 'discomfort'가 적절하다.

02

해설 | 이 글의 주제는 사람들이 변화를 하는 것이 불편하기 때문에 변화를 꺼린다는 것이다. 그리고 글의 내용을 살피면 변화하는 것은 사소하더라도 성가시다고 얘기한다. (A)에는 성가시다와 유의한 표현이 들어가야 하므로 어색하다는 뜻의 'cumbersome'이, (B)에는 사람들이 변화를 어떻게 생각하는지에 대해 들어가야 하는데 글의 내용을 보면 변화에 대해 부정적이고 꺼린다고 하므로 이와 유의한 참을 수 없다는 표현의 'intolerable'이 적절하다.

03

해석 | 장기간의 습관을 변화하는 것은 변화가 일어날 때 그것의 불편함 때문에 선호되지 않는다.

해설 | 이 글의 주제는 사람들이 변화하는 것이 불편하기 때문에 변화를 꺼린다는 것이다. 그리고 이러한 변화를 참을 수 없다고 말한다. 글의 주제와 연관지어 볼 때, 빈칸에는 장기간의 변화를 한다는 뜻이 들어가야 하므로 'Making long-term habit changes'가 적절하다.

04

해설 | 주어진 문장의 It은 손목시계를 의미한다. 이 손목시계는 ③의 앞에 손목시계와 연결되고 주어진 문장의 the slightest difference는 transfer your wristwatch to the other hand를 연결해주므로 ③에 들어가는 것이 적절하다.

PRACTICE 01

PP. 33 ~ 34

1 (A) first inside you (B) negative traits of others
2 (A) awareness (B) use
3 ② **4** ⑤

01

해석 | (B) 다른 사람의 부정적인 면을 봄으로써 (A) 당신 내면을 우선적으로 보고 당신이 그것들을 가지고 있는지를 봐라.

해설 | 이 글의 주제는 다른 사람들의 부정적인 특징을 보고 자신도 그런 점이 있는지 확인할 수 있다는 것이다. 주어진 문장과 주제를 종합해 보면 (A)에는 내면을 보라는 'first inside you'가, (B)에는 다른 사람의 부정적인 면을 본다는 'negative traits of others'가 적절하다.

02

해석 | 비록 완전하게 우리 자신을 탐험하는 것은 불가능하지만, (A) 인식의 수준은 높아질 수 있고 다른 사람으로부터 배운 경험과 우리의 경험이 (B) 쓰이게 된다.

해설 | 이 글의 주제는 다른 사람들의 부정적인 특징을 보고 자신도 그런 점을 가지고 있는지 확인할 수 있다는 것이다. 글에서 인식을 발전시킬 수 있고 우리와 다른 사람이 경험한 것을 사용할 수 있다고 나타난다. 글의 내용과 주제를 미루어 보았을 때, (A)에는 'awareness'가, (B)에는 'use'가 적절하다.

03

해설 | 주어진 문장의 these things가 ②번 앞 문장들을 가리킨다. 그리고 주어진 문장의 I는 ②번 뒷 문장의 I와 연결되므로 ②가 적절하다.

04

해설 | all the other cars가 one, another로 연결되므로 (C)가 적절하고 (B)에 too가 있는 것은 나의 자동차 또한 그렇다고 말하는 것이므로 (C)와 연결된다. 따라서 ⑤가 적절하다.

PRACTICE 02

PP. 38 ~ 39

1 (A) success (B) story
2 (A) funds (B) devices
(C) appealing
3 (A) intriguing (B) financial resources
(C) cutting-edge technologies
4 ④

01

해석 | 영화의 (A) 성공에 가장 필수적인 요소는 (B) 이야기이다.

해설 | 이 글의 주제는 영화의 성공에 중요한 부분은 기술적인 부분이 아니라 이야기 부분이라는 것이다. 따라서 (A)에는 'success'가, (B)에는 'story'가 적절하다.

02

해석 | 엄청난 (A) 투자 없이, *ET*라는 영화는 최첨단 기술 (B) 장치 때문이 아니라, 그것의 (C) 감동을 주는 이야기 때문에 성공적이었다.

해설 | 이 글의 주제는 영화가 성공하기 위해 많은 돈을 들일 필요가 없고 높은 기술력이 필요한 것이 아니라 이야기가 중요하는 것이다. 주어진 문장에서 (A)와 (B) 없이 (C)만으로 성공을 했다고 말하고 있으므로 (A)와 (B)에는 돈과 기술력에 관한 내용이 들어가고 (C)에는 이야기에 관한 내용이 들어가야 한다. 따라서 (A)에는 많은 돈을 들일 필요가 없었다는 말과 유사한 표현인 투자라는 말인 'funds'가, (B)에는 높은 기술력과 유사한 기술 장치라는 'devices'가, (C)에서는 호소력 있는 이야기라는 말인 'appealing'이 적절하다.

03

해석 | 영화에서 이야기가 아주 (A) 흥미로운 한, 그 영화의 성공은 대량의 (B) 재정적인 지원과 (C) 최첨단의 기술 없이 기대 될 수 있다.

해설 | 이 글의 주제는 영화의 성공은 엄청난 투자와 좋은 기술력 때문이 아니라 호소력 있고 흥미로운 이야기 덕분이라는 것이다. 한 마디로 이 글에서는 영화를 만들 때, 돈과 기술보다는 이야기가 중요하다고 한다. 따라서 글의 주제와 흐름을 생각해 보았을 때, (A)에는 흥미롭다는 의미인 'intriguing'이, (B)에는 투자와 유사한 표현인 'financial resources'가, (C)에는 좋은 기술력과 유사한 표현인 'cutting-edge technologies'가 적절하다.

04

해설 | 주어진 문장의 that movie가 앞 문장의 *ET*를 가리키므로 ④가 가장 적절하다.

PRACTICE 03

PP. 43 ~ 44

1 urgently needs to make a legislation for regulating noise pollution
2 ⑤
3 (A) absence (B) crude
4 (A) law (B) scientific methods
(C) legislation

01

해석 | 인도는 소음공해를 규제하기 위한 법률 제정이 급박하게 필요하다.

해설 | 이 글의 주장은 인도는 소음공해의 통제와 방지를 위한 적절한 법을 만들어야 한다는 것이므로 글의 주장을 영작하면 'India urgently needs to make a legislation for regulating noise pollution.'이 적절하다.

02

해설 | 인도에서는 현재 수질오염과 대기오염에 관한 법률 개정이 일부 이루어졌다고 하므로 ⑤가 적절하다.

오답 | ① 1번째 문장에 인도에서는 소음공해의 통제와 방지를 위한 특별한 법이 없다고 나타난다.
② 2번째 문장에 인도에서 다양한 분야의 법률과 규정에 있는 법 조항들은 비과학적이라고 나타난다.
③ 3번째 문장에 대부분의 선진국에서는 소음공해를 다루는 법 제정이 이루어졌다고 나타난다.
④ 3번째 문장에 선진국에서는 소음공해의 조사를 위한 과학적인 방법이 고안되었다고 나타난다.

03

해설 | 이 글의 주제는 인도에서는 현재 소음공해에 대한 적절한 법이 없다는 것이다. 인도는 빨리 이와 관련된 법률을 선진국들처럼 과학적 방법을 참조하여 제정해야 한다고 주장한다. 따라서 (A)에는 현재 인도에서는 소음공해에 대한 적절한 법이 없기 때문에 'absence(부재)'가, (B)에는 비과학적이고, 부적절하다는 말과 어울리는 'crude'가 적절하다.

04

해석 | 대다수의 선진국은 소음공해와 관련된 (A) 법률을 제정하고 소음공해를 검사하기 위한 (B) 과학적 방법을 창안하고, 반면에 인도는 아직 소음공해를 규제하기 위한 효과적이고 효율적인 (C) 법률을 갖지 않는다.

해설 | 이 글의 주제는 인도에서 소음공해의 통제와 방지를 위한 과학적으로 적절한 법을 다양한 분야의 법률을 참조하여 재빠르게 만들어야 한다는 것이다. 그리고 선진국에서는 이미 이와 관련된 법률을 참조하여 제정하고 있지만 인도에서는 아직 그런 법률을 제정하려고 하지 않는다고 한다. (A)에는 선진국에 관한 내용이므로 법률을 제정하고 있다는 말인 'law'가, (B)에는 과학적으로 적절한 법을 참조한다는 뜻으로 'scientific methods'가, (C)에는 인도는 아직 이러한 법률을 갖지 않는다는 표현인 'legislation'이 적절하다.

UNIT 03 목적

수능 ANALYSIS

PP. 48 ~ 49

1 ⑤ **2** ④
3 ① **4** ②

01

해설 | ⑤ 2월 21일이 아니라 1월 21일에 공개한다.

오답 | ① 1번째 문장에 증축이 완공되었다고 나타난다.
② 2번째 문장에 이 공간은 도서관, 회의실, 오락 장소 등 다양한 역할로 사용될 것이라고 나타난다.
③ 3번째 문장에 이 공간은 결혼과 파티와 같은 행사를 수행할 수도 있다고 나타난다.
④ 4번째 문장에 노인 복지관 증축을 위해 지역 사회로부터 엄청난 지원을 받았다고 나타난다.

02

해설 | 이 글에서 노인 복지관 증축을 위한 기금 마련에 지역 사회로부터 지원을 받았다고 한다. 그리고 이에 대한 감사를 표하고자 하는 것을 보았을 때, 사소한 지원이 아니라 엄청난 지원이 적절하다.

03

해설 | 이 글은 노인 복지관 완공을 위해 막대한 제정을 지원해준 지역 사회에 감사를 표하고자 하는 글이므로 (A)에는 'finished', (B)에는 'enormous'가 적절하다.

오답 | ② (A)에 'finished'는 적절하지만, (B)에 'tiny(사소한)'는 적절하지 않다.
③ (A)에 'completed'는 적절하지만, (B)에 'trivial(사소한)'은 적절하지 않다.
④, ⑤ (A)에 'changed'는 적절하지 않다.

04

해설 | 이 글은 감사를 표하는 글이기 때문에 ② '이 공간을 렌트하기 위해서는 돈을 지불해야 한다'는 것은 이 글의 흐름과 무관하다.

PRACTICE 01	PP. 53 ~ 54
1 ④	2 ①
3 ④	4 ③

01

해설 | 실수가 발생하지 않게 하기 위해 계정 번호를 여러 번 확인할 것이라고 하였으므로 ④가 적절하다.

오답 | ① 1번째 문장에 '물건을 잘못 발송했다'고 나타나 있다.
② 3번째 문장에 '실수의 원인을 조사한 후, H. Brown 씨가 두 분 있었다는 것을 알게 되었다'고 나타나 있다.
③ 4번째 문장에 '실수를 반복하지 않기 위해, 서류에 항상 완전한 이름을 포함시킬 것'이라고 나타나 있다.
⑤ 마지막 문장에 '다음번 구매 시 15%를 할인해 줄 것'이라고 나타나 있다.

02

해설 | 이 글의 내용을 보면 물건을 잘못 배송했고 이에 대한 사과를 하고 있다. 따라서 물건을 잘못 받은 사람이 기분이 좋은 상태라는 말은 적절하지 않다. 따라서 ① 'happy → upset'으로 바꿔 사용해야 한다.

03

해설 | 주어진 문장에서 this error가 ④번 앞 문장의 다른 H. Brown 씨의 주문 건을 잘못 배송한 것을 나타내므로 ④가 적절하다.

04

해설 | 이 글의 주제는 주문 건과 다르게 발송한 것에 대해 사과를 표시하는 것인데 ③은 우리의 책임이 아니라고 하므로 적절하지 않다.

PRACTICE 02	PP. 58 ~ 59
1 ④	2 ④
3 ①	4 ④

01

해석 | ① 기쁜
② 졸린
③ 만족스러운
④ 화난
⑤ 두려운

해설 | 이 글의 내용은 만족스럽지 못한 식사에 대한 불만이 섞인 내용이므로 ④가 적절하다.

02

해설 | 이 식당의 음식이 맛이 없다고 하는데 ④는 반대되므로 적절하지 않다.

03

해설 | 음식을 주문한 내용으로 시작하므로 (A)가 제일 먼저 오고, 식당을 떠났다는 말인 (C)가 제일 나중에 와야 하므로 ① '(A) – (B) – (C)'가 적절하다.

04

해설 | 글쓴이가 식당에 방문하여 경험한 일을 말하고 나서 글쓴이가 레스토랑 오너에게 충고를 하고 있으므로 ④가 적절하다.

PRACTICE 03	PP. 63 ~ 64
1 ①	2 ⑤
3 ⑤	4 ①

01

해설 | ①은 'Alan Smith'를 가리키고 나머지는 'Alice Jenkins'를 가리킨다.

02

해설 | 주어진 문장의 'these three years'가 ⑤번 앞 문장의 'in the first three years'를 가리키므로 ⑤가 적절하다.

03

해설 | 이 편지를 쓰게 되어 기쁘다는 말이 있는 (C)가 제일 우선적으로 와야 하고 그 후에 처음으로 만났다는 (B)가 와야 하므로 ⑤ '(C) – (B) – (A)'가 적절하다.

04

해설 | 4번째 문장에 그녀는 Della와 Protect-All Insurance에서 처음 만났다고 나타나 있으므로 적절하지 않은 것은 ①이다.

오답 | ② 5번째 문장에 그녀가 3년 동안 보고했다고 나타나 있다.
③ 6번째 문장에 그녀가 회사에서 가장 해박한 문제 해결사 중 한 명이라고 나타나 있다.
④ 7번째 문장에 3년 동안, 그녀는 화재, 지진, 홍수에 관한 보험을 거의 독점적으로 처리했다고 나타나 있다.
⑤ 8번째 문장에 그녀는 그녀의 직업에 더 많은 책임과 도전을 위한 준비가 되어 있다고 나타나 있다.

UNIT 04 심경 · 분위기

수능 ANALYSIS	PP. 68 ~ 69
1 ①	2 ①
3 ③	4 ④

01

해설 | 길을 잃고 있으므로 골짜기가 모두 똑같아 보인다는 말이 흐름과 적절하다. 따라서 ① 'different → same'으로 고쳐야 한다.

02

해설 | 'ravine'가 1번째 문장의 'a ravine'를 가리키고 있으므로 ①이 적절하다.

03

해설 | 'a ravine'가 (B)의 'the ravine'와 연결되므로 (B)가 와야 한다. (B)의 마지막 부분에 그에게는 아무것도 눈에 들어오지 않았다는 부분이 (A)에서 그에게 흐릿함이 있을 뿐이라고 연결된다. (C)에 그는 영원토록 여기에서 빠져나갈 수 없을 것이라 하므로 (C)는 맨 뒤에 와야 한다. 따라서 ③ '(B) – (A) – (C)'가 적절하다.

04

해설 | 그는 길을 잃어 숲에서 나가지 못했으므로 운 좋게도 숲에서 빠져나갔다고 하는 ④는 글의 흐름과 무관하다.

PRACTICE 01 PP. 73~74

1 ⑤	2 ②
3 ⑤	4 ②

01

해설 | ⑤는 'baby'를 가리키지만 나머지는 'Anne'을 가리킨다.

02

해설 | Anne은 그 앞에 불빛들에 의해 최면술에 걸린 듯 앞을 응시하고 있다고 하고 있기 때문에 그녀가 소파에서 움직이지 않고 불빛을 쳐다보고 있다는 것(② 'mobile' → 'immobile')이 적절하다.

03

해설 | 주어진 문장의 They가 ⑤번 앞 문장의 'police officers'를 가리키고 있으므로 ⑤가 적절하다.

04

해설 | 이 글은 전체적으로 아기가 사라져서 슬픈 내용이므로 그녀가 행복하게 자고 있다는 ②는 적절하지 않다.

PRACTICE 02 PP. 79~80

1 ⑤	2 ③
3 ⑤	4 ④

01

해설 | ⑤는 'Emma's mom'을 가리키고 나머지는 'Emma'를 가리킨다.

02

해설 | 4번째 문장에 'she encouraged Sondra to stay in the race room'이라고 나와 있으므로 ③은 적절하다.

오답 | ① 2번째 문장을 보면 부끄러워 하지 않는다고 나와 있고 부끄러움이 많은지는 알 수 없다.
② 2번째 문장에 그녀가 무언가를 숨기고 있다는 느낌을 준다고 나타난다.
④ 7번째 문장을 보면 그녀가 아닌 그녀의 어머니가 지갑을 잃어버렸던 것을 알 수 있다.
⑤ 지갑을 찾아준 것은 Sondra의 어머니이고, 그녀의 어머니의 지갑을 찾아주었던 것이다.

03

해설 | 주어진 문장의 the purse가 앞에 문장의 The purse를 이어주므로 ⑤가 적절하다.

04

해설 | 간식을 제공한다는 served가 적절하고 뒤에 to stay in the race room과 반대되므로 outside가 적절하다. 그리고 신분증명서를 찾기 위해 지갑을 열었다는 opening이 적절하므로 ④이다.

오답 | ①, ②, ③ 간식을 예약한다는 말은 적절하지 않다.
⑤ 그녀가 Sondra에게 집에 있는 오락실에 머물도록 부추겼다고 나와 있다. 따라서 Sondra의 어머니는 그녀가 바깥에서 놀기를 제안했다고 보는 것이 적절하다. inside는 적절하지 않다.

PRACTICE 03 PP. 84~85

1 ④	2 ①
3 ①	4 ④

01

해설 | 무언가를 쥐려고 했으나 아무것도 쥘 것이 없다는 긴박한 내용이므로 ④ 'something → nothing'이 적절하다.

02

해석 | ① 하늘이 무너져도 솟아날 구멍은 있다.
② 삶은 항해이다.
③ 지나간 것은 지난 일이다.
④ 큰 물고기는 큰 강에서 잡힌다.
⑤ 어려울 때 친구가 진정한 친구이다.

해설 | 현재 바다에서 큰 파도를 만나며 목숨이 위험한 긴박한 상황이다. 따라서 조언으로 가장 적절한 말은 위험한 상황에서도 살아날 방법이 있다고 하는 것이다. 따라서 ① 'Every cloud has a sliver lining. (하늘이 무너져도 솟아날 구멍은 있다.)'이 적절하다.

오답 | ② 삶이 항해라는 것은 삶이 미지의 세계로 나아간다는 것인데, 이 글은 굉장히 긴박한 상황에 주인공이 처해 있는 상황이므로 미지의 세계로 나아가라는 말은 조언으로 적절하지 않다.
③ 지나간 것은 지난 일이라는 말은 현재 위기를 겪고 있는 주인공에게 할 조언으로 적절하지 않다.
④ 큰 물고기는 큰 강에서 잡힌다는 말은 현재 위기를 겪고 있는 주

인공에게 할 조언으로 적절하지 않다.

⑤ 어려울 때 친구가 진정한 친구라는 말은 바다에서 고군분투 하는 주인공에게 할 조언으로 적절하지 않다.

03

해설 | (A)의 that이 첫 문장을 가리키고, the big, dark wave가 the wave를 가리키므로 ① '(A) – (B) – (C)'가 적절하다.

04

해설 | 주어진 문장의 the wave가 ④번 앞 문장의 the big, dark wave와 연결된다. 그리고 파도가 그를 넘어뜨렸다고 했는데, ④번 뒷 문장에 그는 무엇이라도 붙잡기 위해, 손을 뻗었다고 하므로 ④가 적절하다.

UNIT 05 내용 일치/불일치

수능 ANALYSIS PP. 89 ~ 90

1 (A) long-dead composers	(B) rhythmic originality
(C) 1938	(D) academic music
2 ③	3 ③
4 (A) influenced	(B) popular

01

해설 | 본문의 내용을 보면 2번째 문장에 Creston은 그에게 가장 큰 영향을 끼친 사람들이 오래전 죽은 작곡가라고 말했다. 그리고 3번째 문장에 그의 스타일의 특징은 리드미컬한 독창성이라고 나온다. 6번째 문장에 그는 1938년에 구겐하임 연구비를 받았다고 나온다. 7번째 문장에 그의 작품은 1960년대에 학구적인 음악이 떠오르면서 음악회 연주곡목에서 서서히 사라졌다고 나타난다.

02

해석 | ① 뉴욕 음악 비평가 협회상을 수상한 그의 노래는 무엇인가?
② 그는 언제 구겐하임 연구비를 받았는가?
③ 그는 결혼을 했는가?
④ 그의 작품들 중 몇몇은 어떤 것의 영감을 받았는가?
⑤ 그는 어디서 죽었는가?

해설 | ③ 그가 결혼했는지는 나오지 않는다.

오답 | ① 5번째 문장에 그의 1번 교향곡이 뉴욕 음악 비평가 협회상을 수상했다고 나타난다.
② 6번째 문장에 그는 1938년에 구겐하임 연구비를 받았다고 나온다.
④ 8번째 문장에 그의 작품 중 몇몇은 Walt Whitman의 시에서 영감을 받았다고 나온다.
⑤ 9번째 문장에 그는 샌디에이고 근교의 캘리포니아주 포웨이에서 사망했다고 나타난다.

03

해설 | 이 글의 3번째 문장을 보면 그의 스타일의 특징은 리드미컬한 독창성이라고 나오므로 ③이다.

오답 | ① 1번째 문장을 보면 그는 주로 독학으로 공부했다고 나온다.
② 2번째 문장을 보면 그에게 가장 큰 영향을 미친 사람들은 오래전 죽은 작곡가라고 나타난다.
④ 6번째 문장을 보면 그는 1938년에 구겐하임 연구비를 받았다고 나온다.
⑤ 8번째 문장을 보면 그의 작품 중 몇몇은 Walt Whitman의 시에서 영감을 받았다고 나타난다.

04

해석 | Creston은 그에게 영향을 끼친 사람들은 오래전 죽은 작곡가라고 생각했고, 그는 20세기에 인기 있는 작곡가 중 한 명이었다.

해설 | 그에게 영향을 끼친 인물들이 오래전 죽은 작곡가이고 그는 20세기에 인기 있는 작곡가였다고 말하고 있다. 따라서 본문에 있는 단어를 이용하면 (A)에는 'influenced', (B)에는 'popular'가 적절하다.

PRACTICE 01 PP. 94 ~ 95

1 (A) earliest	(B) similar
(C) pragmatic	
2 ③	3 ④
4 ④	

01

해석 | Al-Jazari는 인간과 (B) 유사하고 인간의 편의를 위해 환경을 이용하는 것 같은 (C) 실용적인 목적을 갖는 생산적인 장치에 흥미가 있는 (A) 초기 발명가로 고려된다.

해설 | 이 글의 마지막 문장을 보면 Al-Jazari는 인간의 편리를 위하여 환경을 이용하는 것과 같은 실용적인 목적으로 인간과 유사한 기계를 창조하는 데 흥미를 보인 첫 번째 발명가처럼 보인다고 한다. 이 내용을 보고 주어진 문장을 미루어 보았을 때, (A)에는 첫 번째 발명가라는 뜻과 유사한 'earliest'가, (B)에는 인간과 유사한 기계를 창조한다는 말인 'similar'가, (C)에는 실용적인이라는 뜻과 유사한 'pragmatic'이 적절하다.

02

해설 | 주어진 문장의 It은 a hand washing automation을 가리킨다. 그리고 자동 장치로 구성된 특징이 ③번 뒤 문장에 부연설명하고 있으므로 ③이 적절하다.

03

해설 | ④는 Al-Jazari에게 영향을 받은 사람을 가리키고 나머지는 Al-Jazari를 가리킨다.

04

해설 | 그가 만든 것 중 일부는 실제 기능을 사용할 수 있었으므로 ④가 적절하지 않다.

오답 | ① 1번째 문장을 보면 Al-Jazari는 이슬람의 학자라고 나타난다.
② 2번째 문장을 보면 그는 독창적인 기계 장치 지식에 관한 책을 썼다고 나타난다.
③ 3번째 문장을 보면 그는 자동 장치를 설계했다고 나타난다.

⑤ 8번째 문장을 보면 Leonardo da Vinci가 그에게 영향을 받았다고 나온다.

PRACTICE 02 PP. 99 ~ 100

1 (A) gain (B) justice
(C) credited
2 (A) social reformer (B) vote
3 (A) social and political gains
(B) movement
4 ③

01

해설 | 여성이 참정권을 얻도록 노력하고 여성의 평등한 정의를 지지하고 사회 정치적 이득을 얻는 것을 Susan B. Anthony가 도왔다는 내용이다. (A)가 들어간 문장의 앞을 보면 그녀는 참정권을 얻도록 노력한다는 말이 있는데, (A)가 들어간 문장이 '그럼에도 불구하고'라고 받기 때문에 참정권을 얻는 것을 보지 못했다는 'gain'이, (B)와 (C)에는 Anthony의 한결같은 지지는 여성을 위한 사회 정치적 이득을 도운 것과 20세기의 여성 운동을 시작한 것에 공이 있다는 'justice'와 'credited'가 각각 적절하다.

02

해석 | (A) 사회 개혁자로 알려진 Susan B. Anthony는 National Woman Suffrage Association을 설립했다. 1872년에, 그녀는 여성들을 투표소로 데려갔지만 그럼에도 불구하고 그녀는 여성들이 (B) 투표권을 얻기 전에 죽었다.

해설 | 1번째 문장에 미국의 사회 개혁가인 그녀가 투표권을 얻기 위한 노력을 했다는 내용이 있고 그녀는 여성 투표권 운동의 지도자라는 설명이 나타난다. 그리고 마지막 문장을 보면 그녀는 투표권을 얻는 것을 보지 못하고 죽었다고 나타난다. (A)에는 그녀에 대한 설명인 사회 개혁가 'social reformer'가, (B)에는 그녀가 투표권을 얻는 것을 보지 못했다는 'vote'가 적절하다.

03

해석 | 20세기에, Anthony의 여성 평등에 대한 헌신과 지지는 그녀가 여성들을 위한 (A) 사회적 정치적 이득에 힘을 쏟았고 여성 (B) 운동을 시작했기 때문에 공개적으로 인정되고 인식되었다.

해설 | 그녀는 여성 투표권 운동의 지도자이고 그녀의 여성에 대한 평등한 정의에 대해 한결같은 지지는 여성을 위한 사회 정치적 이득을 얻는 것을 도운 것과 20세기의 여성 운동을 시작한 것에 공이 있다고 여겨져 왔다고 나타난다. 따라서 (A)에는 'social and political gains', (B) 'movement'가 적절하다.

04

해설 | 주어진 문장에서는 Anthony가 1872년에 뉴욕의 로체스터에 있는 투표소로 한 무리의 여성들을 이끌고 갔다고 나타난다. 그리고 ③번 앞 문장에는 그녀는 1869년에 조직한 미국 여성 투표권 협회의 주요 설립자이며 이념적 대변자라고 나타난다. 따라서 1869년과 1872년이 흐름적으로 적절하다.

PRACTICE 03 PP. 104 ~ 105

1 The Springbok emblem was limited to the white minority population until the 1980s.
2 (A) divisive (B) pride
3 ① 4 ⑤

01

해석 | Q. 주어진 글에 따르면, 왜 스프링복 문양은 다수의 불만을 가져왔습니까?
A. 왜냐하면 국가의 스프링복 문양은 1980년대까지 소수의 백인들에게 제한됐기 때문입니다.

해설 | 7번째 문장을 보면 스프링복 문양은 대표팀들의 문호가 1980년대까지 소수의 백인 국민들에게만 국한되었기 때문에 큰 불화의 상징이라고 나타난다. 따라서 스프링복 문양이 소수의 백인 국민들에게만 제한되어 있었다는 표현이 들어와야 한다.

02

해설 | 이 글의 내용을 보면 스프링복 문양은 1980년대까지는 백인 남아공 국민들에게만 국한되었다고 한다. (A)에는 백인 국민들에게만 국한되었기 때문에 분열의 상징이라는 말인 'divisive'가, (B)에는 백인들에게는 자부심과 권력이라는 말이 들어가므로 'pride'가 적절하다.

03

해설 | The designation이 앞에 the Springboks를 가리키므로 (A)가 나와야 하고, 1906년과 1980년 시간순으로 봤을 때, (B) 다음에 (C)가 적절하다.

04

해설 | 이 글의 내용을 보면 1980년대까지 스프링복 문양은 백인들만 사용할 수 있었다고 한다. 이 문양은 백인들에게 상징과 자부심이 된다는 것이므로 ⑤ 'blacked → whited'가 적절하다.

UNIT 06 도표 · 실용문

수능 ANALYSIS PP. 109 ~ 110

1 (A) second (B) highest
(C) largest
2 ④
3 which had the largest percentage point gap between men and women
4 ②

01

해석 | 두 집단에서 (A) 두 번째로 (B) 가장 큰 응답 범주는 가족과 함께 운동하는 것이었는데, 이 경우 남성과 여성 사이에서 (C) 가장 큰 비율

값의 차이가 발생하였다.

해설 | 그래프를 보면 가족과 함께 운동하는 것이 두 번째로 크고, 가장 큰 퍼센트 차이가 있다. 주어진 문장에 운동하는 것에 대한 설명이기 때문에 (A)에는 'second', (B)에는 'highest', (C)에는 'largest'가 적절하다.

02

해석 | ① 당신이 건강하게 유지하거나 강해지기 위한 육체적 또는 정신적 활동
② 다른 사람들 없이 홀로
③ 말하거나 쓰여진 대답
④ 당신이 누군가를 돕기 위해 하는 것
⑤ 두 가지 경우에서 두 가지 시간

해설 | 이 글에서 ⓓ는 '호의를 베풀다'는 뜻이 아니라 '좋아하다'라는 뜻으로 쓰였으므로 ⓓ는 문맥상에 의미로 어색하다.

오답 | ① 이 글에서 ⓐ는 '운동하다'라는 뜻으로 쓰였으므로 '당신이 건강하게 유지하거나 강해지기 위한 육체적 또는 정신적 활동'이라는 의미로 적절하다.
② 이 글에서 ⓑ는 '홀로'라는 뜻으로 쓰였으므로 '다른 사람들 없이 홀로'라는 의미로 적절하다.
③ 이 글에서 ⓒ는 '응답하다'라는 뜻으로 쓰였으므로 '말하거나 쓰여진 대답'이라는 의미로 적절하다.
⑤ 이 글에서 ⓔ는 '두 가지'라는 뜻으로 쓰였으므로 '두 가지 경우에서 두 가지 시간'이라는 의미로 적절하다.

03

해설 | 밑줄 친 문장을 보면 '남성과 여성 사이에서'라는 말은 between men and women으로 쓰면 되고 '가장 큰 비율 값의 차이가 발생하는'이라는 말은 우선 관계 대명사 which를 사용하고 적절한 뜻인 had the largest percentage point gap을 이어주면 된다. 따라서 'which had the largest percentage point gap between men and women'가 적절하다.

04

해설 | 그래프를 보면 family는 두 번째로 크다. 따라서 세 번째로 크다고 하는 ② 'third → second'로 바꿔 사용해야 한다.

PRACTICE 01 PP. 114 ~ 115

1 ③	**2** ①
3 ⑤	
4 (A) free	(B) Taylor Community Yoga
(C) Thursday, February 1st.	

01

해설 | * 문장을 보면 Yoga punch pass는 다음에 써도 된다고 하므로 ③이 적절하다.

오답 | ① 2번째 문장을 보면 2월 1일 목요일에 무료 요가수업을 한다고 나타난다.
② * 문장을 보면 10세 이상의 참여를 환영한다고 나타난다.
④ 마지막 부분을 보면 Taylor Community Hall에서 하는 것을 알 수 있다.
⑤ 마지막 부분을 보면 6:45 — 7:45까지 1시간 동안 진행하는 것을 알 수 있다.

02

해석 | ① 무료 요가수업을 홍보하기 위해서
② 요가의 장점을 알리기 위해서
③ 요가를 배우기 위해서
④ 요가수업을 건너뛴 것을 사과하기 위해서
⑤ 요가의 재미를 설명하기 위해서

해설 | 이 글은 무료 요가수업을 광고하고 있다. 따라서 무료 요가수업을 홍보하기 위해서라는 ①이 적절하다.

03

해석 | ① 요가수업은 언제 시작합니까?
② 요가수업은 무료입니까?
③ 요가수업은 어디에서 열립니까?
④ 요가수업은 몇 시에 시작합니까?
⑤ 요가수업을 위한 준비물은 무엇입니까?

해설 | 요가수업을 위해 준비해야 할 것이 안 나와 있으므로 ⑤가 적절하다.

오답 | ① 요가수업은 2월 1일 목요일 6시 45분에 시작한다고 나타난다.
② 요가수업은 무료라고 설명하고 있다.
③ 요가수업은 Taylor Community Hall에서 열린다고 나타난다.
④ 요가수업은 6시 45분에 시작한다고 나타난다.

04

해설 | 무료 요가수업에 대한 홍보 글이고 위치는 제목에 Taylor Community라고 나타나 있다. 날짜도 글에 'Thursday, February 1st.'라고 나타나 있다.

PRACTICE 02 PP. 118 ~ 119

1 Spring 2014	**2** ②
3 less → more	**4** ④

01

해석 | Q. 남자와 여자 사이에 온라인 쇼핑몰 사용의 차이가 가장 클 때가 언제입니까?
A. 2014년 봄에 남자와 여자 사이에 온라인 쇼핑몰 사용의 차이가 가장 큽니다.

해설 | 그래프를 보면 2014년 봄에 차이가 가장 크게 나타난다. 따라서 빈칸에는 'Spring 2014'가 적절하다.

02

해설 | 그래프를 보면 모든 기간 동안 남자의 온라인 쇼핑 비율이 여자의 온라인 쇼핑 비율보다 큰 것을 알 수 있다. 따라서 남자의 온라인 쇼핑 비율이 여자보다 크기 때문에 ② 'lower → more'이 적절하다.

03

해석 | 모든 기간 동안 남성의 온라인 쇼핑 선호도의 비율은 여성의 온라인 쇼핑 선호도의 비율보다 높았다. 2013년 봄에 남성과 여성 모두 75

퍼센트보다 적은(→ 많은) 비율이 점포에서 구매를 했다.

해설 | 주어진 표를 보면 2013년 봄에는 남성이 80퍼센트, 여성이 82퍼센트가 점포에서 구매를 한 것으로 나타난다. 따라서 남성과 여성 모두 75퍼센트보다 크기 때문에 'less'를 'more'로 바꿔 사용해야 한다.

04

해설 | 7번째 문장을 보면 2013년 봄에는 남성과 여성 모두 75퍼센트보다 많은 비율이 점포에서 구매를 했다고 ④에 나타난다.

오답 | ① 3번째 문장을 보면 위의 그래프는 세 개의 기간에서 미국 십대의 쇼핑 선호도를 나타낸 것을 알 수 있다.

② 4번째 문장을 보면 모든 기간 동안 남성과 여성은 점포에서 물건을 많이 구매한 것을 알 수 있다.

③ 6번째 문장을 보면 모든 기간 동안 남성의 온라인 쇼핑 선호도의 비율이 여성의 온라인 쇼핑 선호도의 비율보다 높은 것을 알 수 있다.

⑤ 마지막 문장을 보면 2014년 봄에 여성의 온라인 쇼핑과 점포 쇼핑에 대한 선호도의 차이가 남성보다 작은 것을 알 수 있다.

PRACTICE 03 PP. 122 ~ 123

1 ⑤
2 dig up invasive plants, burning bush, and clear trails of branches.
3 (A) shovels and scissors (B) sandals or bare feet
4 ②

01

해설 | 'Food and drinks' 부분을 보면 청량음료와 물은 제공될 것이라고 ⑤에 나타난다.

오답 | ① 'When' 부분을 보면 우천 시에는 5월 13일과 5월 27일에 진행되는 것을 알 수 있다.

② 'Activities' 부분을 보면 덤불을 불태우는 활동을 하는 것을 알 수 있다.

③ 'Tools' 부분을 보면 삽과 가위 같은 도구를 가져와야 한다고 나타난다.

④ 'Clothing' 부분을 보면 옻나무가 있어서 샌들이나 맨발은 허용되지 않는다고 나타난다.

02

해석 | Q. 자연을 보호하기 위해 우리는 어떤 활동을 합니까?

A. 우리는 생태계 교란 식물을 파내고, 덤불을 불태우고, 길에서 나뭇가지를 치웁니다.

해설 | 'Activities' 부분을 보면 자연을 보호하기 위한 활동으로는 'Dig up invasive plants, burning bush, Clear trails of branches' 표현이 있다.

03

해석 | 우리의 프로그램은 Daisy Meadow에서 진행하고, 자원 봉사자들은 (A) 삽과 가위 같은 도구들을 가져와야 하고 (B) 샌들과 맨발은 허용되지 않는다.

해설 | 'Tools' 부분을 보면 'Volunteers should bring their own tools such as shovels and scissors.'라고 나와 있고 'Clothing' 부분을 보면 'No sandals or bare feet, due to the presence of poison ivy'라고 나와 있으므로 'shovels and scissors'와 'sandals or bare feet'이 적절하다.

04

해석 | ① 도구

② 무언가를 야기하는 것

③ 특정한 장소에서 있는 존재

④ 누군가 또는 무언가에 대한 사실 혹은 세부 사항

⑤ 사회적 행사에 오도록 누군가에게 물어보는 것

해설 | 이 글에서 'bring'은 '가져오다'라는 뜻으로 쓰였는데 설명은 '야기시키다'에 대한 것이므로 ②는 적절하지 않다.

오답 | ① 이 글에서 '도구'라는 뜻으로 쓰였으므로 단어의 의미로 '도구'는 적절하다.

③ 이 글에서 '존재'라는 뜻으로 쓰였으므로 단어의 의미로 '특정한 장소에서 있는 존재'는 적절하다.

④ 이 글에서 '정보'라는 뜻으로 쓰였으므로 단어의 의미로 '누군가 또는 무언가에 대한 사실 혹은 세부 사항'은 적절하다.

⑤ 이 글에서 '초대하다'라는 뜻으로 쓰였으므로 단어의 의미로 '사회적 행사에 오도록 누군가에게 물어보는 것'은 적절하다.

UNIT 07 지칭 추론

수능 ANALYSIS PP. 127 ~ 128

1 ⑤ **2** ①
3 ③ **4** ②

01

해설 | 주어진 문장의 It은 ⑤번 앞 문장의 what song이랑 연결된다. 따라서 ⑤가 적절하다.

02

해설 | 사진에는 Brandon과 그의 할아버지가 찍혀 있으므로 ①은 적절하다.

오답 | ② 2번째 문장을 보면 필자의 아버지는 작은 사내아이의 손을 꽉 잡고 있다고 나타난다.

③ 5번째 문장을 보면 아이가 춤을 추고 있는 것으로 보이진 않는다고 나타난다.

④ 6번째 문장을 보면 필자의 아버지는 맨발이라고 나타난다.

⑤ 마지막 문장을 보면 사진 속의 모두가 미소 짓거나 웃고 있다고 나타난다.

03

해설 | 이 글은 아이의 사진을 보고 있는 내용이고 아이랑 같이 있는 내용이 아니다. 따라서 ③ '아이를 안았다'는 말은 적절하지 않다.

04

해석 | ① 슬프고 화난
② 행복하고 활기찬
③ 위험하고 급박한
④ 졸리고 무기력한
⑤ 지치고 수척한

해설 | Brandon과 필자의 아버지는 사진 속에서 노래에 맞춰 춤을 추고 있는 것처럼 보인다 했으므로 ②가 가장 적절하다.

오답 | ① 사진 속에서 모두가 미소 짓거나 웃고 있다고 말하고 있다. 따라서 슬프고 화나있다는 표현은 적절하지 않다.
③ 현재 사진 속에서는 모두가 미소 짓거나 웃고 있는 상황인데 위험하고 급박하다는 표현은 적절하지 않다.
④ 글의 내용을 보면 현재 졸리고 무기력한지는 알 수가 없다.
⑤ 사진 속에서 모두가 미소 짓거나 웃고 있는 상황이라서 지치고 수척하다는 표현은 적절하지 않다.

PRACTICE 01 PP. 132 ~ 133

1 ④	**2** ①
3 ①	**4** ②

01

해설 | 이 글의 내용을 보면 Diane이 의사소통을 할 때 부정적인 태도를 보여 그녀의 권위를 약화시키고 주변 사람의 의욕을 꺾는다고 나와 있다. 따라서 ④ 'positivity → negativity'가 적절하다.

02

해석 | ① 다른 사람의 생각을 무시하는 것은 나쁜 결과를 초래한다.
② 대화를 할 때, 당신은 당신의 주장을 강하게 해야 한다.
③ 당신의 의견에 반대하는 것은 무시해야 한다.
④ 대화를 할 때, 너는 다른 사람의 의견을 따라야만 한다.
⑤ 좋은 아이디어는 좋은 결과를 가지고 온다.

해설 | 이 글의 주제는 의사소통을 할 때, 부정적인 태도는 자신의 권위를 약화시키고, 주변 사람의 의욕을 꺾는다는 것이다. 따라서 ① '다른 사람의 생각에 부정적인 것은 나쁜 결과를 초래한다.'가 적절하다.

오답 | ② 이 글에서는 상대방의 의견을 무시하고 자신의 생각만을 강하게 말하는 것이 의사소통의 실수라고 한다.
③ 이 글에서는 당신의 의견에 반대하는 사람들의 말을 묵살해 버리는 습관은 그녀의 권위를 약화시킨다고 나온다.
④ 대화를 할 때, 다른 사람의 의견을 따라야 한다는 것이 아니라 다른 사람의 의견도 존중해야 한다는 것이 핵심이다.
⑤ 좋은 아이디어가 좋은 결과를 가지고 온다는 것은 글의 관점과 관련 없는 내용이다.

03

해설 | 주어진 문장의 Diane의 실수가 ①번 뒷 문장에 그녀가 Martha의 생각에 동의하지 않았다고 나오므로 ①이 적절하다.

04

해석 | ① 당신은 당신의 요점을 더 강하게 말해야 한다.
② 당신은 다른 사람들의 의견을 들을 필요가 있다.
③ 당신은 당신이 나에게 당신의 아이디어를 말하기 전에 두 번 생각해라.
④ 당신은 긍정적인 생각을 가져야 한다.
⑤ 당신은 반대 의견을 무시해야만 한다.

해설 | 그녀는 다른 사람들에게 부정적인 태도를 보이므로 다른 사람의 의견도 존중하라고 할 수 있다. 따라서 ② '당신은 다른 사람의 의견을 들을 필요가 있다.'가 적절하다.

오답 | ① 글의 내용을 살펴보면 자신의 요점을 강하게 말하고 상대방의 의견을 무시한 것이 그녀의 실수라고 나타나기 때문에 그녀에게 당신의 요점을 더 강하게 말하라고 조언하는 것은 적절하지 않다.
③ 글의 내용을 살펴보면 아이디어를 말하기 전에 두 번 생각하라는 것은 글의 관점과 무관하다.
④ 긍정적인 생각을 갖는 것이 아니라 다른 사람의 의견에 긍정적인 태도를 가져야 한다.
⑤ 글의 내용을 살펴보면 반대 의견을 빠르게 묵살해버리는 습관은 그녀의 권위를 약화시키고 과학과의 발전을 제한한다고 말한다.

PRACTICE 02 PP. 138 ~ 139

1 ③	**2** ②
3 ⑤	**4** ②

01

해석 | ① 행복하고 흥분된
② 졸리고 느긋한
③ 슬프고 화난
④ 급박하고 위험한
⑤ 활기차고 평화로운

해설 | 이 글의 내용은 Salli가 원하는 신발을 구매하지 못했다는 내용이므로 ③ '슬프고 화난'이 가장 적절하다.

오답 | ① 그녀는 현재 자신이 원하는 신발을 구매하지 못해서 슬픈 상태이다. 따라서 행복하고 흥분된다는 표현은 적절하지 않다.
② 그녀의 현재 상황은 자신이 원하는 신발을 구매하지 못한 상황이다. 그녀가 현재 피곤한지, 느긋한지는 알 수 없다.
④ 그녀는 단지 원하는 신발을 구매하지 못했을 뿐이기 때문에 그녀가 현재 급박하고 위험한지는 알 수 없다.
⑤ 그녀는 원하는 신발을 구매하지 못해서 가슴 아파하고 있기 때문에 활기차고 평화롭다는 표현은 적절하지 않다.

02

해설 | 이 글의 내용을 보면 그녀는 자신이 원하는 신발을 구매할 생각에 좋았으나 그녀가 원하는 스타일의 신발을 구매할 수 없다는 전화를 받고 실망을 하였다. 따라서 ② 'happy → disappointed'가 적절하다.

03

해설 | 주어진 문장의 다른 한 켤레는 ⑤번 앞 문장에서 나온 한 켤레와 연결된다. 따라서 ⑤가 적절하다.

04

해석 | ① 다시 말해서, 그녀는 가게에 더 호감을 갖게 되었다.
② 말할 필요도 없이, 다음 방문은 없을 것이다.
③ 결국, 그녀는 그녀가 원했던 신발을 샀다.
④ 종합하면, 그녀는 가게의 서비스에 만족했다.
⑤ 그러므로, 그녀는 돈을 저축해서 행복했다.

해설 | 그녀는 신발 가게에 화가 났고 실망했으므로 ②가 적절하다.

오답 | ① 그녀는 가게에 가서 자신이 원하는 신발을 사지 못했으므로 가게에 더 호감을 갖게 되었다는 적절하지 않다.
③ 그녀는 가게에서 자신이 원하는 신발을 사지 못했다고 나오므로 적절하지 않다.
④ 그녀는 가게에서 자신이 구매하려고 한 신발을 구매하지 못하게 되었다. 그리고 그녀가 가게에서 서비스를 받았다는 내용은 존재하지 않는다.
⑤ 그녀는 신발을 사고 싶었지만 신발을 살 수 없다는 통보를 받아서 신발을 구매하지 못했으므로 행복하다는 것은 적절하지 않다.

PRACTICE 03 PP. 143 ~ 144

1 ⑤ 2 ②
3 ④
4 (A) a long time (B) emergency transmitter

01

해설 | 주어진 문장의 브라이언이 말이 없었다는 표현이 ⑤번 뒷 문장의 그의 혀는 입천장에 들러붙은 것 같았고 목구멍이 적절히 움직이지 않았다는 표현이랑 연결되므로 ⑤가 적절하다.

02

해설 | 조종사는 그곳에서 소년을 찾았으므로 ② '그는 그곳에서 아무것도 찾지 못했다'는 내용상 적절하지 않다.

03

해석 | ① 죽은 개는 짖지 않는다.
② 큰 물고기는 큰 강에서 잡힌다.
③ 나쁜 친구보다 좋은 적이 낫다.
④ 인내는 희망의 기술이다.
⑤ 너의 적은 너를 현명하게 한다.

해설 | Brian은 혼자서 구조가 오길 버티고 있었으므로 ④ '인내는 희망의 기술이다.'가 적절하다.

오답 | ① 그는 조난당해 있었고, 그를 구해주는 것만을 기다리고 있었다. 따라서 '죽은 개는 짖지 않는다.'는 속담은 그의 감정을 표현하기에 적절하지 않다.
② 조난당해 있는 그에게 '큰 물고기는 큰 강에서 잡힌다.'는 조언은 적절하지 않다.
③ 그는 혼자서 조난당해 있었고, 그에게 나쁜 친구나 좋은 적에 대한 감정을 드러내는 말은 없다.
⑤ 이 글에서 그에게 적이 있었다는 내용은 존재하지 않는다.

04

해석 | Brian은 (A) 오랜 기간 동안 조난당했지만 조종사는 (B) 비상 발신기로부터 소리를 들었고 그를 찾았다.

해설 | Brian은 오랫동안 조난당했고, 조종사가 비상 발신기에서 나는 소리로 찾았다고 나온다. 그러므로 (A)에는 'a long time'이, (B)에는 'emergency transmitter'이 적절하다.

UNIT 08 단어 빈칸

수능 ANALYSIS PP. 148 ~ 149

1 (A) experience (B) maturity
2 desire to make choices for themselves
3 (A) matured (B) early
4 ②

01

해석 | 사람들이 나이가 들고 (A) 경험이 축적될수록, 결정을 하는 기회는 늘어나고 (B) 성숙해가는 과정은 그들 자신이 선택을 하는 것에 능력을 발전시키는 것에 연관된다.

해설 | 이 글의 주제는 성숙해가는 과정은 스스로 선택하는 능력을 성장시키는 것이기 때문에 어린 나이에 선택을 하는 기회를 갖는 것은 중요하다는 것이다. 그리고 글의 내용을 보면 유아기에는 부모에게 많이 의존하지만, 시간이 지남에 따라 스스로 선택을 하려는 욕구가 생기고 선택할 기회가 늘어난다고 한다. 선택할 기회는 나이와 경험에 따라 증가하고, 성숙해가는 과정은 스스로 선택하는 능력을 성장시키는 것이라 하기 때문에 (A)에는 'experience', (B)에는 'maturity'가 적절하다.

02

해석 | 인간은 그들 스스로 선택하기를 갈망한다.

해설 | 이 글의 주제는 인간은 스스로 선택을 하는 것을 갈망한다는 것이다. 빈칸에는 인간이 그들 스스로 선택하는 것을 갈망한다는 의미의 'desire to make choices for themselves'가 적절하다.

03

해석 | 나이가 들고 경험도 넓어짐과 함께, 선택의 기회는 늘어난다. 예를 들어, 부모에게 전적으로 의존했던 유아들은 스스로 선택할 수 있는 능력을 개발하는 것과 함께 (A) 성숙하게 된다. 따라서 이러한 기회를 (B) 어릴 때부터 가지는 것은 그 진전에 있어서 상당히 중요하다.

해설 | 이 글의 주제는 성숙해가는 과정은 스스로 선택하는 능력을 성장시키는 것이다. 그리고 어린 나이 때부터 선택하는 기회를 갖는 것이 중요하다는 것이다. 그리고 글의 내용을 살펴보면 어린 나이에는 의존을 많이 하지만 성숙하면서 스스로 선택하는 욕구가 생긴다. (A)에는 성숙하다는 말이 들어가야 하므로 'matured'가, (B)에는 어린 나이 때부터라는 말이 들어가야 하므로 'early'가 적절하다.

04

해설 | (B)의 'increase with age'가 (A)의 'The total dependence of infants'로 연결되고, (A)의 'to make choices for themselves'가 (C)의 'to make choices for oneself'로 연결되므로 ②가 적절하다.

PRACTICE 01 PP. 154~155

1 (A) following (B) incline
2 ①
3 (A) properly (B) carried out
(C) complete
4 ①

01

해석 | 지침을 (A) 따르는 것 대신에, 대다수의 사람들은 거의 그들이 원하는 것처럼 행동하는 (B) 경향이 있다.

해설 | 이 글의 주제는 대부분의 사람들은 익숙하지 않은 일을 할 때, 반영하기보다 행동하기를 바란다는 것이다. 대부분의 사람들은 반영하는 것보다는 그들이 원하는 대로 행동한다고 말한다. 따라서 (A)에는 반영하다는 말과 유의한 'following'이, (B)에는 행동하는 쪽으로 마음을 기울인다는 'incline'이 적절하다.

02

해설 | 이 글의 내용을 살펴보면 대부분의 사람들은 설명서를 읽지 않는다고 한다. 따라서 사람들이 설명서를 읽는 것을 좋아한다는 것은 적절하지 않다. 따라서 ① 'like → don't like'가 적절하다.

03

해석 | 단락에서 실험에 따르면, 거의 소수의 사람들은 지시를 (A) 적절하게 읽고 할당된 과업을 (B) 실행했고, 이것은 많은 사람들이 그들이 지시를 반영하는 것에 의해서 과업을 (C) 완수하기보다는 오히려 그들이 원하는 대로 행동하는 것을 의미한다.

해설 | 이 글의 내용은 실험에서 대부분의 사람들은 설명서를 읽지 않고 읽더라도 자신이 확인하고 싶은 부분만 읽고 완전히 읽지 않는다고 한다. 대부분의 사람들이 익숙하지 않은 과업을 할 경우에도 반영하기보다는 행동하기를 선호하는 것처럼 보인다. 따라서 대부분의 사람들은 설명서를 읽지 않고, 소수의 사람들만이 설명서를 읽고, 할당된 과업을 진행하고, 대부분의 사람은 지시를 따라 과업을 수행하기보다 그들이 원하는 대로 행동을 한다는 뜻이므로 (A)에는 'properly'가, (B)에는 'carried out'이, (C) 'complete'가 적절하다.

04

해설 | 주어진 문장은 자신의 주장에 대한 예시로 실험을 말하는 것이다. 그리고 예를 들어, 24명의 성인들에게 가정용 전기 플러그에 전선을 연결하도록 요청한 부분이다. 따라서 실험의 예시로 시작하는 부분이므로 실험이 나타나는 ①이 적절하다.

PRACTICE 02 PP. 159~160

1 (A) changes (B) sameness
2 (A) thoughts (B) act
3 (A) same way (B) characteristic
(C) differ
4 (A) difference (B) pursuing

01

해석 | 인간은 시간이 지남에 따라 (A) 변화를 추구하는 것처럼 보이지만, 그들의 일반적인 특성인 (B) 동일성 때문에 시간이 흘러도 동물의 행동에서는 변화가 발생하지 않는다.

해설 | 이 글의 내용을 보면 변화는 인간의 발전에 나타나는 일반적인 특성이고 동물에게는 나타나지 않는다. 동물은 그들의 동일성 때문에 변화가 발생하지 않는다고 한다. 따라서 인간에게 발전에 나타나는 특성인 변화가 (A)에 들어가야 적절하기 때문에 (A)는 'changes'가, (B)에는 동물은 변화를 하지 않으므로 동일성인 'sameness'가 적절하다.

02

해석 | 인간은 (A) 사고의 형성, (B) 행동하는 방법 그리고 성장 또는 진보에 영향을 끼치는 변화를 끊임없이 추구하기 때문에 동물과 다르다.

해설 | 이 글의 주제는 변화는 인간의 생각, 인간의 행동, 인간의 발전에 나타나는 일반적인 특성이다. 따라서 주제와 미루어 보았을 때, 주제문의 (B)에는 인간의 행동과 적절한 'act'가, (A)에는 생각이라는 의미의 'thoughts'가 적절하다.

03

해설 | 이 글의 주제는 변화는 인간에게만 나타나는 특성이고, 동물은 변화를 하지 않는다는 것이다. 동물의 예시로 새를 들고 있다. 동물은 변화를 하지 않기 때문에 (A)에는 새는 수 천 년 전과 같은 방식으로 짓는다는 의미의 'same way'가, (B)에는 변화는 인간의 일반적인 특성이라는 말이 들어가야 하므로, 'characteristic'이, (C)에는 인간이 집을 지을 때는 변화를 하기 때문에 20 ~ 30년 전과 지금의 집은 다를 것이라고 말하고 있기 때문에 'differ'가 적절하다.

04

해석 | 인간과 동물 사이에 본능적인 (A) 차이는 인간들이 즉각적인 변화가 인간들의 특성이라는 (B) 추구하는 것 이래로 행동에서 동일성을 보이지 않는다고 말한다는 것이다.

해설 | 이 글의 주제는 인간과 동물의 분명한 차이는 인간은 시간이 지남에 따라 변화를 추구하고, 동물은 동일성을 보인다는 것이다. 따라서 (A)에는 인간과 동물의 차이를 나타내는 'difference'가, (B)에는 즉각적인 변화를 추구하는 것이 인간의 특성이므로 'pursuing'이 적절하다.

PRACTICE 03 PP. 164 ~ 165

1 (A) high-priced (B) comparison
(C) contrast
(단, (B), (C)는 순서가 바뀌어도 됨)
2 (A) that manipulates consumers
(B) contrast
3 ④ 4 ②

01

해석 | 명품 거래에서, 극도로 (A) 고가의 상품의 역할은 그것이 다른 상품들을 (B) 비교와 (C) 대조로 적절하게 보이게 만든다는 것이다.

해설 | 이 글의 주제는 앵커는 파는 용도도 있지만 그 비싼 가격으로 다른 것과 대비 효과를 내는 용도로도 사용한다는 것이다. (A)에는 앵커가 비싼 가격이라는 설명이 들어가야 하므로 'high-priced'가, (B)와 (C)에는 다른 상품들과 비교하고 대조한다는 말이 들어가야 하므로 각각 'comparison'과 'contrast'가 적절하다.

02

해석 | 이 글에서, "앵커"는 값비싼 상품으로써 (A) 소비자들을 조종하는 것을 나타내고, (B) 대비를 위해 이용된다.

해설 | 이 글의 주제는 앵커는 파는 용도로도 사용하지만 대비 효과를 내는 용도로도 사용한다는 것이다. 따라서 (A)에는 앵커는 파는 용도도 사용되지만 소비자들이 다른 물건들의 가격을 합리적으로 보이도록 조종하므로 'that manipulates consumers'가, (B)에는 대비 효과로도 이용된다는 말인 'contrast'가 적절하다.

03

해설 | 앵커는 그 물건의 가격이 값비싸서 다른 물건의 가격이 상대적으로 합리적으로 보이게 만드므로, ④ 'unreasonable → reasonable'이 적절하다.

04

해설 | The anchor가 ②번 문장의 It과 연결된다. 그리고 ②번 앞 문장을 보면 앵커에 대한 설명이 나타난다. 그러므로 ②가 적절하다.

UNIT 09 짧은 어구 빈칸

수능 ANALYSIS PP. 169 ~ 170

1 (A) put a checkmark (B) agency
2 (A) realizing (B) visual
(C) gaps
3 (A) gather (B) mark
(C) observe
4 ①

01

해석 | Big Brothers/Big Sisters의 직원들은 목표에 도달하기 위해서 얼마나 많이 (B) 회사에 기여를 했는지를 확인하기 위해 (A) 체크 표시를 한다.

해설 | 이 글의 내용을 보면 이 회사에서는 분기마다 모여서 개인과 팀이 회사에 기여한 것을 확인하는 것이 회사가 어느 부분에 에너지를 집중시킬 필요가 있는지 확인하게 해준다고 한다. 그래서 이들은 분기마다 모여서 기여한 것을 확인하고 체크해둔다고 나온다. 글의 내용을 미루어 봤을 때 (A)에는 체크 표시를 한다는 'put a checkmark'가, (B)에는 회사에 기여했다는 'agency'가 적절하다.

02

해설 | 분기마다 모여서 개인과 팀의 목적을 검토하는 것은 미래에 어느 부분에 에너지를 집중시킬 필요가 있는지 확인하게 해준다는 것이 주제이므로 (A)에는 'realizing', (B)에는 'visual', (C)에는 'gaps'가 적절하다.

03

해석 | 개인과 팀 목표를 점검하기 위해 (A) 모인다. → 각 목표와 우선순위를 옆에 (B) 표시한다. 개인이 수행하고 있는 성과와 회사가 성공하기를 기대하는 것 사이의 차이를 (C) 관찰하기 위해 어떤 성과가 얼마나 이루어졌는지에 대한 시각적인 자료를 만든다.

해설 | 이 글의 순서를 볼 때 분기마다 모여서 목적을 검토, 자신이 한 업적과 기관에 도움을 준 것을 확인, 우선 사항을 체크하는 순서로 가기 때문에 (A)에는 'gather', (B)에는 'mark', (C)에는 'observe'가 적절하다.

04

해설 | 주어진 문장에서 각자 기관의 목표를 성취하는 데 어떻게 도움이 되었는지를 확인한다고 한다. 그리고 (A)를 보면 그 후에 목표와 우선 사항을 체크 표시를 한다고 나타난다. 주어진 문장의 목표와 (A)의 목표가 연결된다. 그리고 몇 차례의 박수와 함성 소리가 잇따른다고 하는데 (B)에서는 그 시간이 끝날 때에 이사가 말한다고 나온다. (B)에서의 그 시간이 몇 차례의 박수와 함성 소리가 잇따르는 것을 받으므로 ① '(A) – (B) – (C)'로 연결된다.

PRACTICE 01 PP. 175 ~ 176

1 capacity to recognize faces
2 (A) social (B) recognize
3 (A) strengthened (B) fails
(C) remembered
4 ②

01

해석 | 얼굴을 인식하기 위한 인간의 능력

해설 | 이 글의 제목은 인간의 인식 능력이다. 이러한 제목과 연결지으면 밑줄 친 부분에는 얼굴을 인식하는 능력이 들어가야 하므로 'capacity to recognize faces'가 적절하다.

02

해석 | 인간이 우리를 공평하게 대하고 우리를 속인 사람을 (B) 알아보지 못하거나 구별하지 못한다면 (A) 사회적 상호 작용을 위한 계약은 강화될 수 없다.

해설 | 이 글의 주제는 인간의 얼굴, 목소리, 사진 등을 인식하는 능력이 사회 활동을 하는데 도움을 준다는 것이다. 그리고 마지막 문장을 보면 이 능력이 없으면 오늘날처럼 사회적 상호 관계의 계약이 강화될 수 없을 것이라고 한다. (A)에는 사회적 상호 작용을 위한 계약의 뜻과 연결지어 'social'이, (B)에는 인식하는 능력과 알맞은 'recognize'가 적절하다.

03

해석 | 인간은 전과 후의 차이를 구별할 수 있지만, 만약 얼굴을 인식하는 것을 (B) 실패하면 누가 공평하게 대했고 우리를 속인 사람을 (C) 기억할 수 없기 때문에 사회적 상호 작용이 (A) 강화될 수 없다.

해설 | 인간이 얼굴, 목소리, 사진 등을 인식할 수 없으면 서로 간의 호의를 베풀기 힘들었을 것이라는 내용이 있다. 그리고 마지막 문장을 보면 이 능력이 없으면 오늘날처럼 사회적 상호 관계의 계약이 강화될 수 없을 것이라고 한다. 이러한 글의 내용과 미루어 보았을 때, (A)에는 'strengthened', (B)에는 'fails', (C)에는 'remembered'가 적절하다.

04

해설 | 10,000장을 확인하고 이틀 후에 8,300장을 확인했다고 이어지므로 ②가 적절하다.

PRACTICE 02 PP. 181 ~ 182

1 (A) to be respected (B) peer support
2 (A) Working hard without complaints
(B) gain
3 (A) indispensable (B) higher-ups
(C) hierarchy
4 ③

01

해석 | 지위가 낮은 사람들과 또래들에게 (A) 존경받을 가치가 있다. 특히, 어려움에 직면했을 때 (B) 동료들의 지원이 큰 도움이 될 수 있다.

해설 | 이 글의 주제는 직장에서 자신보다 높은 사람뿐만 아니라 동료와 직급이 낮은 사람들과의 관계를 좋게 형성하는 게 중요하다는 것이다. 그리고 마지막 문장을 보면 어려움에 빠졌을 때, 동료들의 지지가 중요하다고 말한다. 따라서 (A)에는 존경받는다는 의미인 'to be respected'가, (B)에는 동료들의 지지인 'peer support'가 적절하다.

02

해석 | (A) 불평 없이 일하는 것은 동료들과 직급이 낮은 동료들로부터 존경을 (B) 얻게 이끈다.

해설 | 이 글의 주제는 동료, 직급이 낮은 동료들로부터 존경을 받는 것이 일을 할 때, 중요하게 작용된다는 것이다. 그리고 예로 나온 백설 공주를 보면 그녀는 일하는 것에 대해 불평을 하지 않고 활기차게 일해서 난쟁이들에게 없어서는 안 될 존재로 자신을 만들었다. 따라서 (A) 부분에는 불평 없이 일한다는 말인 'Working hard without complaints'이, (B) 부분에는 존경을 얻는다는 말인 'gain'이 적절하다.

03

해설 | 이 글의 주제는 직장에서 자신보다 높은 사람 뿐만 아니라 동료와 직급이 낮은 사람들과의 관계를 좋게 형성하는 것이 중요하다는 것이다. 글의 주제와 흐름을 보면 (A)에는 'indispensable', (B)에는 'higher-ups', (C)에는 'hierarchy'가 적절하다.

04

해설 | 주어진 문장의 She가 ③번 앞 문장의 She와 연결되므로 ③이 적절하다.

PRACTICE 03 PP. 187 ~ 188

1 (A) toppling (B) sequentially
2 the more they do the next right thing
3 ⑤ **4** ⑤

01

해석 | 당신이 도미노를 (A) 쓰러뜨리는 것처럼 성공은 한 번에 하나씩 (B) 순차적으로 일어난다.

해설 | 이 글의 주제는 성공하기 위해서는 우선순위를 정하고 그 순위대로 행동해야 한다는 것이다. 그리고 성공은 동시에 일어나는 것이 아니라 순차적으로 일어난다고 말한다. 이에 대해 첫 번째의 도미노부터 때려서 쓰러뜨린다고 한다. 따라서 주제를 생각해 봤을 때, (A)에는 'toppling'이, (B)에는 'sequentially'가 적절하다.

02

해석 | 성공이 순차적이라는 점을 고려할 때, 사람들이 옳은 일을 더 많이 할수록, 그들은 다음에 올바른 일을 더 많이 한다. 따라서 성공의 잠재력이 시간이 지남에 따라 개발되며 계획뿐만 아니라 사업에도 적용될 수 있다.

해설 | 이 글의 주제는 성공하기 위해서는 매일 일들의 우선순위를 정하고 그 순위대로 행동해야 한다는 것이다. 일은 순차적으로 진행되는 것이기 때문에 올바른 일을 해야 다음 올바른 일을 할 수 있다는 것이다. 주제에 맞게 요약하기 위해서는 'the more they do the next right thing'이 적절하다.

03

해설 | (C)의 'this'가 "Here's where you should start."를 가리키고, (C)의 질문에 (B)로 답한다. 그리고 (A)의 'it'은 (B)에서 올바른 일들을 하는 것을 뜻하므로 ⑤가 적절하다.

04

해설 | 주어진 문장의 it은 ⑤번 앞 문장의 올바른 일들을 행하는 것을 의미한다. 따라서 ⑤가 적절하다.

UNIT 10 긴 어구 빈칸

수능 ANALYSIS PP. 192 ~ 193

1 the norms of those around them
2 (A) eyes (B) surrounding
3 (A) conscious (B) excessively
(C) mirror
4 (A) evasion (B) the grounds

01

해석 | 사람들은 주위 사람들의 규범에 따라 행동하는 경향이 있다.

해설 | 이 글의 주제는 우리의 믿음이 주변 사람들에 영향을 받는다는 것이다. 그리고 1번째 문장을 보면 세상에 대한 우리의 믿음은 우리의 동료에 의해 강하게 영향을 받는다고 하고, 주변 사람들의 기준에 따라 자신의 믿음을 조정하는 경향이 있다고 한다. 따라서 빈칸에는 주위 사람들의 규범에 따라 행동하는 경향이 있다는 'the norms of those around them'이 적절하다.

02

해석 | 우리는 우리를 (B) 둘러싸고 있는 사람들의 생각에 관한 (A) 눈을 가지고 있고 우리의 믿음 또한 다른 사람들에 의해 강하게 영향을 받는다.

해설 | 이 글의 주제는 우리의 믿음이 주변 사람들에 의해 영향을 받는다는 것이다. 그리고 우리 주위의 사람들이 생각하는 것을 신경 쓰고 동료에 의해 강하게 영향을 받는다고 한다. 이런 말은 우리 주변 사람들의 눈치를 살피고 영향을 받는다는 뜻이다. 따라서 (B)에는 우리 주변 사람들이라는 말과 유의한 'surrounding'이, (A)에는 주변 사람들의 눈치를 살핀다는 뜻으로 'eyes'가 적절하다.
참고로, [보기]에 있는 동사 'surround'는 (B)에 들어갈 때 앞에 있는 명사 'people'을 수식해야 하기 때문에 현재분사로 바꿔 사용해야 한다.

03

해석 | 우리는 다른 사람들이 어떻게 생각하는지에 대해 심각하게 (A) 의식하고 있다. 예를 들어, 우리는 보통 다른 사람들의 패션을 보면서 무엇을 입을지 결정한다. 그러나 우리 대부분은 때로 다른 사람들이 생각하는 정도를 (B) 지나치게 추정하는데, 이는 우리가 우리의 태도를 공유하고 편견을 (C) 반영하는 것들을 보는 것 같기 때문이다.

해설 | 이 글의 내용은 주위의 기준에 자신의 믿음을 결정한다는 내용이다. 그리고 그 예시로 패션 분야를 들면서 패션 분야에서는 다른 사람들의 반응을 보고 멋있는지 결정한다고 말한다. 그러나 때때로는 우리는 우리의 생각을 공유하는 사람과 어울리기 때문에 다른 사람들이 생각하는 정도를 과대평가한다고 말한다. 따라서 (A)에는 다른 사람들의 생각을 의식하고 있다는 표현으로 'conscious'가, (B)에는 과대평가한다는 말과 유의한 'excessively'가, (C)에는 다른 사람들의 생각을 반영한다는 표현으로 'mirror'가 적절하다.
(B)의 경우 동사인 'estimate'를 꾸며주고 있으므로 'excessive'를 부사의 형태 'excessively'로 바꿔 사용해야 한다.

04

해설 | 이 글의 전체적인 주제는 우리의 믿음은 주변 사람들에게 영향을 받는다는 것이다. 즉, 우리의 믿음은 주위 사람들의 기준에 따라 자신의 믿음을 조정한다는 것이다. 그리고 어려운 상황에서도 대부분의 사람들이 주변의 기준에 믿음을 조정한다고 한다. 이러한 주제를 가지고 글의 흐름을 보면, (A)에는 어려운 상황에 관한 얘기가 나와야 하므로 세금 회피와 같은 'evasion'이, (B)에는 주변 사람들의 기준과 유사한 표현이 들어가야 하므로 모든 사람이 그것을 한다라는 이유라는 뜻으로 'the grounds'가 적절하다.

PRACTICE 01 PP. 198 ~ 199

1 (A) talented (B) collaboration
2 ①
3 (A) unite (B) surpass
4 ③

01

해석 | 그룹 내 (A) 재능 있는 사람들이 긴밀한 (B) 협업으로 자신을 능가할 때, 창조적인 문제에 대한 해답이 발견된다.

해설 | 이 글의 주제는 각각의 능력 있는 사람들은 집단에서 협력을 통해 더 큰 효과를 발휘한다는 것이다. 주제와 연관시켜서 볼 때, (A)에는 재능이 있다는 표현인 'talented'가, (B)에는 협력이라는 표현인 'collaboration'이 적절하다.

02

해설 | 주어진 문장의 'a network of neurons'가 (A)의 'A single network'에 해당된다. 따라서 (A)가 첫 번째로 나오고, (A)에 대한 원인이 (B)에 나오기 때문에 (B)가 두 번째, (B)의 'those talents'가 (C)의 'the right people'에 연결되기 때문에 마지막으로 나와야 한다.

03

해석 | 창조적이지만 어려운 문제는 사람들이 서로 협력할 때 뿐만 아니라 적절한 사람이나 재능 있는 사람들이 (A) 연합하여 올바른 방식으로 자신을 (B) 능가할 때 해결된다.

해설 | 이 글의 주제는 각각의 능력은 집단에서 협력을 통해 더 큰 효과를 발휘한다는 것이다. 그리고 일부 집단이 구성원들의 합을 넘어설 수 있다고 한다. 글의 주제를 봤을 때, (A)에는 협업과 유사한 말인 'unite'가, (B)에는 더 큰 효과가 나온다는 말인 'surpass'가 들어가야 한다. (A)와 (B) 모두 동사가 들어가야 하므로 (A)는 'unity → unite'로 수정해야 한다.

04

해설 | 주어진 문장의 That이 ③번 앞 문장의 우리가 협력할 때를 가리킨다. 그리고 그것은 개별적인 사람들의 모임이 아니고 ④번 문장을 보면 대신에 그것은 그런 재능 있는 사람들이 자신들을 능가하는 것이라고 말한다. 따라서 ③이 적절하다.

PRACTICE 02 PP. 203～204

1 (A) he feels insecure (B) comfort
(C) making noise
2 (A) experience (B) being on their own
(C) eliminating
3 ③ 4 ②

01

해석 | 강아지가 혼자 두면 시끄러운 소리를 내는 이유는 (A) 그가 불안함을 느끼기 때문이다. 그의 불안감을 극복하도록 돕기 위해, 그가 (C) 시끄러운 소리를 내는 것을 억제하기보다는 (B) 편안함의 느낌을 경험하도록 하라.

해설 | 이 글의 주제는 강아지는 혼자 두면 불안함을 느끼고, 이 불안감을 돕기 위해 소리를 내지 않도록 훈련하는 것이 아니라 혼자 있을 때 편안하게 느끼도록 훈련시켜야 한다는 것이다. 글의 주제에 따라 (A)에는 강아지가 혼자 있을 때 불안감을 느끼기 때문에 소리를 내므로 불안감을 느낀다는 표현인 'he feels insecure'가, (B)에는 편안하게 느끼도록 훈련시키라는 의미인 'comfort'가, (C)에는 소리를 내지 않도록 이라는 표현인 'making noise'가 적절하다.
그리고 (A)는 강아지가 혼자 있을 때 소리를 내는 이유이기 때문에 문법적으로 '+because 다음에 절의 형태가 와야 하므로 'he feels insecure'가 적절하다. (B)와 (C)는 소리를 내지 않도록 훈련하는 것이 아니라 편안하게 느끼도록 해야 한다는 것이므로 (B)는 'comfort', (C)는 'making noise'가 적절하다.

02

해석 | 강아지가 혼자 있을 때 시끄러운 소리를 내는 두 가지 해결책은 첫째, (B) 혼자 있을 때 편안함을 (A) 경험하도록 훈련하는 것과 둘째, 소음과 관련된 원인이나 요소를 (C) 제거하는 것이다.

해설 | 이 글의 주제는 강아지에게 소리를 내지 않도록 훈련하는 것이 아니라 혼자 있을 때 편안하게 느끼도록 훈련시켜야 한다는 것이다. 그리고 강아지가 혼자 있는 것이 괜찮다는 것을 배우게 해야한다고 말한다. 그리고 그 방법으로 마지막 문장에 편안하게 느끼도록 훈련시키고, 소리를 낼 필요성을 제거하게 하는 것이 중요하다고 말한다. 글의 흐름을 볼 때, (A)에는 편안함을 느끼도록 훈련시킨다는 말로 'experience'가, (B)에는 혼자 있을 때라는 말인 'being on their own'이, (C)에는 소음과 관련된 원인을 제거한다는 말이 들어와야 하므로 'eliminating'이 적절하다.
참고로, (B)와 (C)에는 분사구문 형태가 필요하기 때문에 전자에는 'being'을 추가해야 하고, 후자에는 동사 'eliminate'를 'eliminating'으로 바꿔 사용해야 한다.

03

해설 | 3번째 문장을 보면 강아지들은 혼자 남겨졌을 때 불안해한다(insecure)고 나와 있기 때문에 ③ '혼자 있을 때 즐겁게 논다'는 것은 적절하지 않다.

오답 | ① 1번째 문장을 보면 강아지는 혼자 놔두면 울부짖곤 한다고 나온다.
② 2번째 문장을 보면 강아지가 우는 것은 자신에게 관심을 가져달라고 요청하는 것이다.
④ 4번째 문장을 보면 강아지가 내는 소리는 불안감의 표현이라고 나온다.
⑤ 5번째 문장을 보면 강아지가 소리를 내지 않기 위해 편안하게 느끼도록 해야 한다고 나온다.

04

해설 | 강아지는 혼자 있을 때 불안감을 느낀다고 하므로 ② 'secure → insecure'가 적절하다.

PRACTICE 03 PP. 209～210

1 (A) disguised (B) reflecting
(C) lighting
2 ⑤
3 (A) entire (B) rest
(C) be avoided
4 ③

01

해설 | 이 글의 주제는 취조실에서 사용하는 단방향 거울 속에는 다양한 과학적 원리가 있다는 것이다. 창문이 비밀스러운 감시 활동을 하기 위해 (A)한다는 의미이므로 'disguised'가, (B)의 다음 문장을 보면 절반의 빛만 투과시키고 나머지는 반사시킨다고 나와 있기 때문에 (B)에는 'reflecting'이, (C)의 다음 문장을 보면 램프가 켜지면 빛의 일부가 취조실 안으로 들어온다고 나와 있기 때문에 (C)에는 조명의 뜻을 가진 'lighting'이 적절하다.

02

해설 | 주어진 문장에서 단방향 거울은 한쪽에서 보면 거울로 보이고 반대 방향에서 보면 창문으로 보인다고 한다. 그리고 (C)에서 이러한 이유로 거울로 위장된다고 말한다. 이러한 설명에 대해 (B)에서 의문을 가지고 그에 대한 두 가지 대답으로 First와 Second를 통해 (B) 다음에 (A)가 오는 것을 확인할 수 있기 때문에 ⑤ '(C) – (B) – (A)'가 적절하다.

03

해석 | 단방향 거울의 과학적 원리는 첫째로 빛 (A) 전체가 거울에 비치지 않는다. 빛의 절반만이 거울에 의해 전달되고 (B) 나머지는 거울에 반사된다. 따라서 취조실의 어둠을 유지하기 위해서는 방을 통과하는 빛을 (C) 피해야 한다.

해설 | 이 글의 내용은 취조실에서 사용하는 단방향 거울 속에 다양한 과학적 원리가 있다는 것이다. 8번째 문장을 보면 거울은 모든 빛을 다 반사시키는 것이 아니라고 나왔기 때문에 (A)에는 'entire'가, 9번째 문장을 보면 단방향 거울은 절반의 빛만 투고시키고 나머지 반은 반사시킨다고 나왔기 때문에 (B)에는 'rest'가, 마지막 문장을 보면 램프가 켜지면 그 빛의 일부가 취조실 안으로 들어오기 때문에 어두운 상태로 유지해야 한다고 나와 있기 때문에 빛이 통과하는 것을 피해야 한다는 (C)에는 'be avoided'가 적절하다.

04

해설 | 주어진 문장의 'one side'는 ③번 다음 문장의 'one direction'과, 'from the other'는 'the opposite direction'과 연결된다.

UNIT 11 연결어(구) 넣기

수능 ANALYSIS PP. 214 ~ 215

1 (A) Safer driving (B) inferior
2 ③
3 (A) high speed (B) minimize
4 ④

01

해석 | 독일에서의 실험은 ABS 시스템의 효과를 분석하기 위해 실시되었다. (A) 더 안전한 운전이 기대되었지만, 브레이크 시스템 그룹의 참가자들은 (B) 열등한 운전자로 판명되었다.

해설 | 이 글의 주제는 ABS를 설치한 차보다 설치하지 않은 차가 더 안전하다는 것이다. 한 가지 실험이 나오는데 ABS를 설치한 차의 운전자들은 ABS가 더 안전하게 운전하는데 도움이 될 줄 알았지만 운전자들이 ABS를 장착하여 더 무분별하게 운전하여 그들이 열등한 운전자가 되었다. 이러한 내용을 봤을 때, (A)에는 ABS를 설치하면 기대되는 것이 더 안전한 운전이므로 'Safer driving'이, (B)에는 그들을 열등한 운전자로 만들었다는 부분이 들어가야 하므로 'inferior'가 적절하다.

02

해설 | 주어진 문장에서 실험을 언급했고 비교군이 나와야 하기 때문에 (B)가 첫 번째로 나와야 한다. (B)에서 더 향상된 브레이크가 더 안전한 운전에 도움이 될 것이라고 예상했지만 현실은 달랐다고 나왔기 때문에 현실과 반대된 내용이 나와야 해서 (C)가 다음에 나온다. (C)에서 열등한 운전자로 만들었다고 했고 그에 대한 예시가 (A)에서 나오기 때문에 ③ '(B) – (C) – (A)'가 적절하다.

03

해석 | ABS의 채택은 교통사고의 비율을 낮추지 않았다. 대신, 운전자들은 안전하지 않게 (A) 고속으로 운전했고, 이 시스템을 자동차 충돌의 위험을 (B) 최소화하기 위한 방법으로 사용했다.

해설 | 이 글의 주제는 ABS를 설치하면 운전을 할 때 안전에 도움이 될 줄 알았지만 실험 결과는 오히려 운전자들을 열등하게 만들었다는 것이다. 그리고 그 이유를 보면 운전자들이 안전하다고 생각하여 더 빠른 속도를 냈기 때문이다. ABS 시스템은 사고를 줄이는데 사용된 것이 아니라 단지 위험을 증가시키지 않으면서 사용된 것이다. 글의 내용에 따라 (A)에는 ABS를 설치하면 운전자가 안전하다고 생각하여 더 빠른 속도를 내기 때문에 'high speed'가, (B)에는 이 시스템은 단지 충돌 위험을 최소화 한다는 말이 들어가야 하므로 'minimize'가 적절하다.

04

해설 | ④번의 뒷 문장이 운전자들이 더 빨리, 더 급회전, 더 심하게 운전을 했다고 나와 있기 때문에 주어진 문장의 'it turned them into markedly inferior driver'에 연결되어 ④가 적절하다.

PRACTICE 01 PP. 219 ~ 220

1 (A) dispute (B) peaceful
(C) overlooked
2 ④
3 (A) controversial (B) worse
(C) mood
4 ①

01

해석 | 비록 그 문제가 (C) 간과되고 해결되지 않은 채로 남아 있을 수 있지만, (A) 분쟁이나 의견 불일치를 야기하는 대화를 꺼리는 사람들은 모두가 (B) 평화로운 정신 상태에 있을 때 대화를 나눌 것을 권한다.

해설 | 이 글의 주제는 갈등에 관한 논의를 미루면 나중에 편안한 시점에 다시 이어가야 한다는 것이다. 1번째와 2번째 문장을 보면 갈등에 대한 대화를 편안한 시점이 올 때까지 미뤄야 하지만 다시 편안한 상황이 되면 이러한 대화들은 자주 잊혀지거나 무기한 연기된다고 나온다. (A)에는 의견과 비슷한 말인 'dispute'가, (B)에는 편안한 시점과 유의한 'peaceful'이, (C)에는 그 문제가 잊혀진다는 뜻과 유의한 'overlooked'가 적절하다.
(B)에는 'state of mind'를 꾸며주기 때문에 형용사인 'peaceful'이, (C)에는 'and' 다음 'unsolved'과 연결되는 병렬구조이기 때문에 'overlooked'로 바꿔 사용해야 한다.

02

해설 | ④번의 앞 문장이 갈등에 관한 이야기를 하지 않는 이유를 언급하고 있기 때문에 주어진 문장이 결과로 나오는 것이 적절하다.

03

해석 | (A) 논란의 여지가 있는 대화를 미루는 것이 상황을 (B) 악화시키는 것은 아니다. 원치 않는 충돌을 피하기 위해 사람들이 (C) 기분이 좋은 적절한 시기에 토론하는 것이 훨씬 낫다.

해설 | 이 글의 주제는 갈등에 관한 논의를 미루면 나중에 편안한 시점에 다시 이어가야 한다는 것이다. 감정이 격해졌을 때는 대화를 나중으로 미루는 것이 타당하지만 상황이 차분해지면 그 대화를 반드시 이어나가야 하는 것을 기억하라고 말한다. (A)에는 갈등에 관한 논의와 유사한 말인 'controversial'이, (B)에는 대화를 미루는 것이 타당하다고 하므로 상황을 악화시키는 것이 아니라고 하는 'worse'가, (C)에는 상황이 차분해지고 좋아진다는 말인 'mood'가 적절하다.

04

해설 | 주어진 문장은 감정이 격해졌을 때 갈등에 대한 대화를 주의, 정신, 집중, 선의가 되돌아올 때까지 미루는 것이 타당하다고 말하고 있다. (A)가 미뤘을 때의 결과를 나타내고 있기 때문에 첫 번째로 나와야 하고, (A)의 마지막 문장이 아무도 갈등에 관한 얘기를 하고 싶지 않다고 했는데 (B)가 그에 대한 결과로 등장하기에 (B)가 두 번째로 나와야 한다.

PRACTICE 02 PP. 224 ~ 225

1 (A) economic growth was historically slow
(B) a birth rate was high
2 market liberalization and economic growth
3 (A) market liberalization
(B) historically slow economic growth
(C) a high birth rate
(단, (B), (C)는 순서가 바뀌어도 됨)
4 (A) privatization (B) market liberalization
(C) wealth-per-person

01

해석 | 왜냐하면 (A) 경제 성장은 역사적으로 느렸기 때문이다.
왜냐하면 (B) 출산율이 높았기 때문이다.

해설 | 6번째 문장을 보면 라틴 아메리카 또한 자유롭지만 몇 번의 일시적인 사건을 제외하면 역사적으로 느린 경제 성장의 특징을 나타낸다고 했고 7번째 문장을 보면 그 지역이 비교적 높은 출생률을 가지고 있다고 했기 때문에 (A)에는 'economic growth was historically slow', (B)에는 'a birth rate was high'가 적절하다.

02

해석 | 시장 자유화와 경제 성장의 관계

해설 | 이 글의 주제는 시장 자유화가 모든 국가의 경제 성장에 도움이 되는 것은 아니라는 것이다. 글의 내용은 시장 자유화와 경제 성장의 관계이다. 따라서 빈칸에는 시장 자유화와 경제 성장이 들어가야 하므로 'market liberalization and economic growth'가 적절하다.

03

해석 | (A) 시장 자유화는 중국과 동유럽의 경제 성장이나 경제 호황으로 이어졌지만 이들 지역의 (B) 역사적으로 경제 성장률이 둔화되고 (C) 출산율이 높아 중남미 국가에서는 역부족이었다.

해설 | 이 글의 주제는 시장 자유화가 모든 국가의 경제 성장에 도움이 되는 것은 아니라는 것이다. 6번째 문장과 7번째 문장을 보면 역사적으로 라틴 아메리카는 역사적으로 느린 경제 성장과 비교적 높은 출생률을 가지고 있다고 말하고 있다. 따라서 글의 내용과 미루어 보았을 때, (A)에는 'market liberalization', (B)에는 'historically slow economic growth', (C)에는 'a high birth rate'가 적절하다.

04

해석 | 1998년 동유럽의 경제적 성공은 강력한 민간 부문의 (A) 민영화와 시장 경제의 구현의 결과였지만, (B) 시장 자유화 또한 있었던 중남미 국가들의 경우, (C) 1인당 부에 영향을 미치는 경제 성장이 훨씬 더디게 일어났다.

해설 | 이 글의 내용을 보면 우선 여러 나라에서 시장 자유화가 많은 도움이 되었다고 한다. 동유럽의 민영화 과정과 시장 경제의 실행은 정치적 · 단속적으로 진행되었고 이것이 경제적 호황을 유발했다고 한다. 그리고 라틴 아메리카 경우 높은 출생률을 가지고 있고 개인당 부의 성장이 느렸고 느린 경제 성장의 특징을 보여 준다고 한다. 6번째 문장과 8번째 문장을 봤을 때 (A)는 동유럽 나라에 관한 이야기이므로 민영화인 'privatization'이, (B)에는 글의 핵심 내용인 시장 자유화인 'market liberalization'이, (C)는 중남미 국가들의 경우이므로 개인당 부의 성장과 유의한 말인 'wealth-per-person'이 적절하다.

PRACTICE 03 PP. 229 ~ 230

1 (A) Roles of men and women
(B) social, political, or historical
2 ③ 3 ⑤
4 ④

01

해석 | (A) 남성과 여성의 역할은 그들이 속한 곳의 (B) 사회적, 정치적, 또는 역사적 동향에 의해 결정된다.

해설 | 이 글의 주제는 남성과 여성의 역할이 할당되어 있는 것이 부적절하게 되어있다는 것이다. 1번째 문장을 보면 남성과 여성의 역할이 사회적, 정치적, 혹은 역사적인 이유로 할당된다고 나와 있으므로 (A)에는 'Roles of men and women'이, (B)에는 'social, political, or historical'이 적절하다.

02

해설 | 'For example'로 주어진 문장에 대한 예시를 들고, 'Also'로 (B)의 문장에 부가 설명을 하고 있고, (C)에서 (A)에 나온 미국 문화를 설명하고 있으므로 ③ '(B) – (A) – (C)'가 적절하다.

03

해설 | 뒷 문장을 보면 남성들이 이런 직업을 수행하는 데 여성에 비해 특정한 생물학적 이점을 전혀 가지고 있지 않는 데도 그러하다고 나와 있다. 따라서 ⑤ 'included → excluded'가 적절하다.

04

해설 | 4번째 문장을 보면 호피족에서는 여성이 옹기장이이고 남성은 아니라고 나와 있으므로 ④는 적절하지 않다.

오답 | ① 1번째 문장을 보면 역사적 이유로 흔히 역할이 할당된다고 나와 있으므로 적절하다.
② 3번째 문장을 보면 북아메리카에서는 옷을 바느질하는 것이 여성의 일로 간주된다고 나와 있으므로 적절하다.
③ 3번째 문장을 보면 에콰도르인은 남성이 실 잣는 사람, 베 짜는 사람, 재단사라고 나와 있으므로 적절하다.
⑤ 4번째 문장을 보면 미국 문화에서는 남성과 여성이 모두 옹기장이가 될 수 있다고 나와 있으므로 적절하다.

UNIT 12 무관한 문장 찾기

수능 ANALYSIS PP. 234 ~ 235

1 (A) gravity (B) air resistance
(C) surface
2 (A) gravity (B) air resistance
(C) friction with the surface
3 that influences the movement of
4 ①

01

해석 | 골프공의 움직임에 영향을 미치는 외력은 (A) 중력, (B) 공기 저항, (C) 지면이다.

해설 | 이 글의 주제는 Newton의 운동법칙은 골프의 세계에 적용된다는 것이다. 4번째 문장, 5번째 문장, 6번째 문장에서 운동법칙에 대한 중력, 공기 저항, 지면에 대해서 설명하고 있으므로 (A)에는 'gravity'가, (B)에는 'air resistance'가, (C)에는 'surface'가 적절하다.

02

해석 | 물체를 지구 중앙으로 끌어당기는 것은 (A) 중력이다. 또한 공의 속도를 감소시키는 두 가지 힘은 (B) 공기 저항과 (C) 지면과의 마찰이다.

해설 | 이 글의 주제는 Newton의 운동법칙은 골프의 세계에 적용된다는 것이다. 4번째 문장, 5번째 문장, 6번째 문장에서 운동법칙에 대한 중력, 공기 저항, 지면의 마찰에 대해서 설명하고 있으므로 (A)에는 'gravity', (B)에는 'air resistance', (C)에는 'friction with the surface'가 적절하다.

03

해석 | 골프공의 움직임에 영향을 미치는 뉴턴의 운동법칙

해설 | 이 글의 제목은 Newton의 운동법칙과 골프의 세계이다. 뉴턴의 운동법칙과 연관지어 골프공의 움직임을 설명하고 있으므로 빈칸에는 골프공의 움직임에 연관된다는 뜻과 유사한 'that influences the movement of'가 적절하다.

04

해설 | However를 통해 주어진 문장에서 나오지 않은 outside forces가 나오며 내용이 전개되고, (A)의 'A ball'이 (B)의 'the ball's'로 이어지며 (B)에서 마찰에 대한 내용을 (C)에서 구체화하고 있기 때문에 ① '(A) – (B) – (C)'가 적절하다.

PRACTICE 01 PP. 239 ~ 240

1 (A) struggled (B) tour
2 ② **3** ②
4 ②

01

해석 | 현대 시대 이전에, 중국 배우들은 그들의 가난한 생활로 인해 (A) 고군분투했고, 따라서 중국 (B) 여행을 진행했다.

해설 | 이 글의 주제는 현대 시대 이전에는 중국의 배우들은 오늘날 사회에서 받는 존경을 거의 못 받았다는 것이다. 2번째 문장에서 전문 연기자들이 거의 생계를 유지할 수 없어서 3번째 문장에 나와 있는 것처럼 공연하기 위해서, 중요한 행사를 축하하기 위해서 작은 도시와 시골 마을들을 여행하였다고 나와 있으므로 (A)에는 'struggled'가, (B)에는 'tour'가 적절하다.

02

해설 | 이 글의 주제는 현대 시대 이전에는 중국의 배우들은 오늘날 사회에서 받는 존경을 거의 못 받고 떠돌아다녔다는 것이다. 1번째 문장에서 과거 중국 배우들이 존경받지 못했다는 내용이 나와 있기 때문에, 'easily'가 문맥에 들어맞지 않는다. 따라서 ② 'easily → hardly'가 적절하다.

03

해설 | 이 글의 주제는 현대 시대 이전에는 중국의 배우들은 오늘날 사회에서 받는 존경을 거의 못 받고 떠돌아다녔다는 것이다. ②번 앞에서 과거 중국 배우들이 존경받지 못했다는 내용이 나와 있고 ②번 뒤 문장이 주어진 문장에 대한 결과로 일자리나 공연을 하기 위해 돌아다녔다는 내용이 나오기 때문에 ②가 적절하다.

04

해설 | 2번째 문장과 3번째 문장을 보면 최근까지 전문 연기자는 한 지역에 정착하여 생계를 유지할 수 없어 이동했다고 나와 있으므로 ②는 적절하지 않다.

오답 | ① 1번째 문장을 보면 현대 사회 이전에 중국의 배우는 존경을 거의 받지 못했다고 나와 있다.
③ 3번째 문장을 보면 중요한 행사를 축하하기 위해서 작은 도시와 시골 마을들을 여행하였다고 나와 있다.
④ 4번째 문장을 보면 개인 자격의 배우들은 적어도 시간제로 일하는 순회배우라고 나와 있다.
⑤ 마지막 문장을 보면 제국주의 시대에는 도시극단 전체가 지방을 돌아다닐 수도 있었다고 나와 있다.

PRACTICE 02 PP. 244 ~ 245

1 (A) gladly confront (B) were initiated
2 ①
3 (A) beginning (B) overcame
4 ④

01

해석 | 의심의 여지없이, 우리는 모든 위대한 것들이 불확실성에 의해 (B) 시작되었기 때문에 두려움과 불확실성에 (A) 기꺼이 맞서야 한다.

해설 | 이 글의 주제는 위대한 일들이 불확실성에서 시작했다는 것이다. 그리고 아이디어를 실현하기 위해서는 두려움과 불확실성에 맞서야 한다고 말한다. 따라서 (A)에는 두려움과 불확실성에 맞서야 한다는 뜻인 'gladly confront'가, (B)에는 위대한 일들이 불확실성에서 시작했다는 말로 'were initiated'가 적절하다.
(B)는 주어가 사람이 아니기 때문에 수동태의 형태로 작성해야 한다.

02

해설 | 이 글의 주제는 위대한 일들은 불확실성에서 시작했다는 것이다. ① 뒤에 나오는 Edison과 Steve Jobs의 예시가 불확실성에 관한 것이므로 ① 'certainty → uncertainty'가 적절하다.

03

해석 | 모든 위대한 일들이 (A) 처음에는 불확실성과 깊이 연관되어 있다는 것을 감안한다면, 성공한 사람들은 불확실성에 직면했을 뿐만 아니라 그것을 (B) 극복하여 내적 욕망을 탐구할 기회를 늘렸다.

해설 | 이 글의 주제는 위대한 일들은 불확실성에서 시작했다는 것이다. 그리고 4번째 문장을 보면 우리는 두려움과 불확실성을 예상하고, 이를 위해서는 두려움을 극복해야 한다. (A)에는 시작한다는 말인 'beginning'이, (B)에는 두려움을 극복한다는 말인 'overcame'이 적절하다.
'confronted'와 (B)는 병렬구조를 이루고 있기 때문에 (B)에는 'overcome'의 과거형인 'overcame'이 적절하다.

04

해설 | 이 글의 주제는 위대한 일들이 불확실성에서 시작하고, 우리는 불확실성에 맞서야 한다는 것이다. 글의 주제를 말하고 그것에 대한 예시로 Thomas Alva Edison과 Steve Jobs를 (C)에서 말하였다. 그리고 (A)에서 'In order to'로 (C)에 대한 설명을 이어가기 때문에 '(C) – (A)'가 적절하다. 이후, (A)의 내용을 (B)에서 계속해서 말하고 있으므로 순서는 ④ '(C) – (A) – (B)'가 적절하다.

PRACTICE 03 PP. 249 ~ 250

1 (A) color discrimination
(B) ability to adjust and focus
(C) from near to far
2 ③
3 (A) presbyopia (B) refocus
4 (A) the muscles around lens stiffen
(B) refocusing time is slower

01

해석 | 1) 스펙트럼의 끝부분에 있는 '녹색 – 파랑 – 보라색'의 (A) 색상 식별 범위가 좁아진다.
2) 수정체 주위의 근육이 경직되면서 (B) 조정 능력과 집중력이 저하된다.
3) 눈은 (C) 가까이에서 멀리까지 집중하는 데 더 오래 걸리기 때문에 나이 든 운전자들은 위험에 처하게 된다.

해설 | 2번째 문장, 3번째 문장, 4번째 문장에서 수정체의 능력이 떨어지고, 식별이 힘들어지고, 초점을 바꾸는 시간도 느려진다고 나와 있으므로 (A)에는 색상 식별이라는 뜻인 'color discrimination'이, (B)에는 수정체의 능력이라는 말인 'ability to adjust and focus'이, (C)에는 초점을 바꾸는 내용인 'from near to far'이 적절하다.

02

해설 | 주어진 문장에 'To complicate matters'가 있기 때문에 이전 문장에서 문제 상황이 나와야 하므로 ② 이후의 문장에 다음 문장이 들어가야 한다. 또한 ③번 뒤에 문장의 'This'가 주어진 문장의 'focus form near to far'을 받기 때문에 ③이 적절하다.

03

해석 | 노화로 인해 안구렌즈의 색차별이 나빠지고 적응력과 집중력이 저하되어 (A) 노안이 생긴다. 특히, 노령 운전자들은 (B) 다시 초점을 맞추기 위한 그들의 눈의 움직임이 느리다는 것을 고려하면 젊은 사람들보다 더 위험하다.

해설 | 이 글의 주제는 나이가 들어갈수록 안구의 능력이 떨어진다는 것이다. 2번째 문장, 3번째 문장, 4번째 문장에서 수정체의 능력이 떨어지고, 식별이 힘들어지고, 초점을 바꾸는 시간도 느려진다고 나와 있으므로 (A)에는 'presbyopia', (B)에는 'refocus'가 적절하다.

04

해석 | Q. 렌즈의 조정 및 집중 능력이 저하되는 이유는 무엇인가?
(A) 수정체 주위의 근육들이 경직되기 때문이다.
Q. 왜 나이 든 운전자들은 젊은 운전자들보다 더 중요한 정보를 놓칠까?
(B) 다시 초점을 맞추는 시간이 더 오래 걸리기 때문이다.

해설 | 2번째 문장을 보면 수정체 주위의 근육이 경직되면서 조정하고 초점을 맞추는 수정체의 능력이 떨어진다고 하였고 마지막 문장을 보면 노인 운전자들은 초점을 다시 맞추는 시간이 더 오래 걸리기 때문에 정보를 놓칠 수 있다고 나와 있으므로 (A)에는 수정체의 능력이 떨어진다는 설명인 'the muscles around lens stiffen'이, (B)에는 노인 운전자들은 초점을 다시 맞추는 시간이 오래 걸린다는 의미인 'refocusing time is slower'이 적절하다.

UNIT 13 문장 삽입

수능 ANALYSIS PP. 254 ~ 255

1 (A) compete (B) anger
(C) self-regulation (or self-control)
2 (A) adaptive (B) restraining
(C) self-regulation
3 (A) Expressing (B) hinders
4 ③

01

해석 | 공격성은 진화적 측면에서 적응적 행동 중 하나에 포함된다. 예를 들어, 사람들은 이상적인 짝을 찾기 위해 치열하게 (A) 경쟁한다. 그러나 인간 사회는 (C) 자율규제나 자제력을 얻기 위해 (B) 분노와 같은 공격적인 행동을 억제할 것을 요구한다.

해설 | 이 글의 주제는 공격성은 몇몇 상황에서 이득이 되기도 하지만 우리 사회에서 억제하는 능력이 필요하다는 것이다. people에 대한 동사 형태로 나와야 하고 6번째 문장과 7번째 문장에서 'anger'와 'self-regulation(or self-control)'이 나오기 때문에 (A)에는 매력적인 배우자를 위한 경쟁이 치열하다는 의미인 'compete'가, (B)에는 분노와 같은 공격적인 행동이 들어가야 하므로 'anger'가, (C)에는 자기규제(혹은 자기통제)라는 말인 'self-regulation or self control'이 적절하다.

02

해설 | 이 글의 주제는 공격성은 몇몇 상황에서 이득이 되기도 하지만 우리 사회에서 억제하는 능력이 필요하다는 것이다. (A)에는 뒷 문장이 적응행동에 대한 예시이기 때문에 적응에 관한 말인 'adaptive'가, (B)에는 공격적인 행동의 억제하는 능력과 유의한 'restraining'이, (C)에는 분노를 억제하는 내적 기계라는 말과 유의한 자기규제라는 말로 'self-regulation'이 적절하다.

03

해석 | 어떤 자극에 대한 반응으로 다른 사람들에게 공격성을 (A) 표현하는 것은 분명히 적응적인 행동이 아니며, 따라서 사회생활을 (B) 방해한다.

해설 | 이 글의 주제는 공격성은 몇몇 상황에서 이득이 되기도 하지만 우리 사회에서 억제하는 능력이 필요하다는 것이다. 그 이유로 공격성을 표출하는 것이 사회생활을 방해할 수 있다고 말한다. (A)에는 공격성을 표출한다는 의미인 'Expressing'이, (B)에는 사회생활을 방해한다는 의미인 'hinders'가 적절하다.
(A)의 경우 뒤에 'is not'이라는 동사가 나왔기 때문에 [보기]의 'express' 대신 동명사를 주어로 사용하는 'Expressing'으로 바꿔 사용해야 한다.

04

해설 | 이 글의 주제는 공격성은 몇몇 상황에서 이득이 되기도 하지만 우리 사회에서 억제하는 능력이 필요하다는 것이다. 공격성의 이득에 대한 예시를 (B)에서 'For example 이하'로 하고 있다. 이후 (C)에서 'On the other hand'를 사용하여 공격성이 인간 사회에서 이득이 되지 않을 수 있음을 밝히고 있고, (A)에서 (C)의 마지막 문장을 'For this reason'으로 받아 추가적인 설명을 하고 있다. 따라서 ③ '(B) – (C) – (A)'가 적절하다.

PRACTICE 01	PP. 259 ~ 260
1 (A) happiness	(B) work
(C) feel happier	
2 ③	
3 (A) beneficial	(B) obtain
4 ①	

01

해석 | 우리가 생존을 위해 가지고 있는 습관들이 항상 (A) 행복감을 느끼게 하는 것은 아니다. 왜냐하면 우리의 뇌는 (B) 일을 할수록 (C) 더 행복해지는 방식으로 기능하기 때문이다.

해설 | 이 글의 주제는 사람들은 생존에 도움이 되지 않는 습관들을 가지고 있다는 것이다. 그리고 더 행복하게 만드는 일을 더욱 많이 해야 행복을 느낀다고 나와 있다. (A)에는 행복감이라는 표현인 'happiness'가, (B)에는 행복하게 만드는 일이라는 의미인 'work'가, (C)에는 더 행복해진다는 의미인 'feel happier'가 적절하다.

02

해설 | ③ 이전 문장에서 'happy-chemical spurt'가 과도하게 되면 잘못됨을 느낀다고 했고, 거기에 대해 다시 'feel happy again' 할 수 있는 방법으로 돌아가려 한다는 게 문맥상 적절하다. 또한 ③번 다음 문장에 'such happy habits'이라고 나와 있으므로 ③ bad → happy'가 적절하다.

03

해석 | 우리의 뇌가 지속적으로 (A) 유익한 행동을 보상하지 않기 때문에 어떤 습관은 우리가 생존하고 항상 행복해지는데 도움이 되지 않는다. 뇌의 행복 화학물질을 더 많이 방출하기 위해, 우리는 더 많은 행복한 화학물질을 (B) 얻기 위해 열심히 일한다.

해설 | 이 글의 주제는 사람들은 생존에 도움이 되지 않는 습관들을 가지고 있다고 하고 그 예시로 화학물질의 분출로 인한 행복은 시간이 갈수록 더 많은 일을 해야 행복을 느낀다고 한다. 7번째 문장에서 항상 행복하게 하지 못하는 이유가 뇌가 그런 식으로 작동하지 않다고 했고 8번째 문장에서 화학물질의 분출은 대사 작용이 빠르게 일어나며 더 많이 얻기 위해 더 많이 해야 한다고 나와 있으므로 (A)에는 유익하다는 뜻인 'beneficial'이, (B)에는 'obtain'이 적절하다.

04

해설 | 'brain rewards behaviors that are good for survival'에 대한 다음 내용으로 'happy-chemical spurt'에 관련된 내용이 나오는 (A)가 주어진 문장 다음으로 나오는 것이 적절하다. (A)의 마지막 문장의 'such happy habits'가 (B)의 these habits로 나오고 있고, (C)에는 (B)의 'work that way'에 대한 내용으로 나오고 있으므로 ① '(A) – (B) – (C)'가 적절하다.

PRACTICE 02	PP. 264 ~ 265
1 Feasible area of development	
2 (A) elimination	(B) replacement
3 (A) cultivated	(B) deprive
(C) physical appearance	(D) intelligence
4 ⑤	

01

해석 | 생명공학 덕택에 개발의 실행 가능한 분야

해설 | 이 글의 내용은 생명공학이 만들어내는 식물, 동물과 함께 사는 인간의 환경을 만들어낼 다양한 가능성이다. 빈칸에는 생명공학의 발전으로 인한 다양한 가능성과 유사한 'Feasible areas of development'이 적절하다.

02

해석 | 농업, 축산농업, 인간의 생활수준에 관한 환경은 생명공학에 의해 발전될 수 있다. 특히 유전적 결함을 (A) 없애고 열등한 유전자를 우수한 유전자로 (B) 대체하면 인간의 질병을 치료할 수 있다.

해설 | 마지막 문장에서 유전적 결함을 없애는 것을 가능하게 하는 동일한

기술이 약간 열등한 유전자를 우월한 유전자로 대체하는 것을 가능하게 한다고 했으므로 (A)에는 유전자 결함을 없앴다는 의미인 'elimination'이, (B)에는 대체한다는 의미인 'replacement'가 적절하다.

03

해석 | 1) 질병에 내성이 있고, 물을 많이 요구하지 않으며, 더 많은 식용 식품을 가져오는 식물은 살충제가 없을 때 (A) 재배할 수 있다.
2) 우유를 많이 생산하는 소는 야생 동물의 공간을 (B) 빼앗지 않으며 방목지를 덜 필요로 한다.
3) 인간은 유전병 없이 더 나은 (C) 신체적 외모와 (D) 지성으로 태어날 수 있다.

해설 | 2번째 문장에서 살충제를 사용하지 않고도 병에 대한 저항력이 있으며 물을 더 적게 사용하고 먹을 수 있는 더 많은 식량을 생산해내는 식물이 만들어 질 수 있다고 했고 4번째 문장에서 소 한 마리당 더 많이 생산되는 우유는 목초지에 압박을 덜 가하고 야생생물에게 더 많은 공간을 주는 것으로 이어진다고 했으며 5번째 문장에서 더 똑똑하고 더 키가 크고 더 아름다운 남자와 여자를 만드는 것으로 나아간다고 했다. 따라서 (A)에는 'cultivated', (B)에는 'deprive', (C)에는 'physical appearance', (D)에는 'intelligence'가 적절하다.
(A)의 경우 주어가 사람이 아니기 때문에 [보기]의 'cultivate'를 수동태의 형태인 'cultivated'로 바꿔 사용해야 한다.

04

해설 | 이 글의 주제는 생명공학기술이 식물, 동물, 인간에게 미치는 영향에 관한 것이다. 생명공학은 주어진 문장에서 식물, 동물과 인간의 환경을 만들어낼 가능성을 연다고 했고 식물의 예시가 등장해서 다음은 동물의 예시가 나와야 하기에 (C)가 나와야 한다. 그 다음으로 인간의 예시인 (A)가 나오고 (B)가 앞 문장들을 요약하고 있기 때문에 ⑤ '(C) – (A) – (B)'가 적절하다.

PRACTICE 03 PP. 270 ~ 271

1	(A) are equipped (C) are ordered	(B) costs
2	①	
3	(A) urgent situations	(B) manufacturing cost
4	(A) locking	(B) cheaper

01

해석 | 24시간 편의점에 자물쇠가 달린 이유는 대부분 문마다 자물쇠가 (A) 달려 있고 자물쇠가 없는 문을 따로 (C) 주문하면 (B) 비용이 더 들기 때문이다.

해설 | 이 글의 주제는 24시간 여는 편의점도 자물쇠가 있는 문을 사용하는 것이 이득이라는 것이고 마지막 문장에서 모든 문을 같은 방식으로 만드는 것이 아마도 비용이 더 적게 들 것이라고 나왔다. (A)에는 대부분 문마다 자물쇠가 달려있다는 표현인 'are equipped'가, (B)에는 자물쇠 없는 문을 사용하는 것이 비용이 더 든다는 의미인 'costs'가, (C)에는 자물쇠가 없는 문을 따로 주문한다는 의미인 'are ordered'가 적절하다.

02

해설 | (A)가 주어진 문장에 대한 예시라서 첫 번째로 나오고 (B)에서 산업용 문이 24시간 열어둘 것을 염두하지 않고 팔린다는 것, 그래서 (C)에서 lock이 있는 채 파는 것이 더 쌀 것이라는 내용이 나오므로 글의 순서는 ① '(A) – (B) – (C)'가 적절하다.

03

해석 | 대부분의 편의점에 자물쇠가 달린 문이 있는 두 가지 이유는 첫째로 가게가 짧은 시간 동안 문을 닫아야 하는 (A) 긴급한 상황과 둘째로 모든 문을 자물쇠로 만들 때 (B) 제조 비용이 저렴하기 때문이다.

해설 | 3번째 문장에서 긴급한 상황으로 가게를 적어도 잠시라도 닫아야 할 가능성이 있다고 했고 마지막 문장에서 모든 문을 같은 방식으로 만드는 것이 비용이 더 적게 든다고 나와 있다. (A)에는 긴급한 상황이라는 표현인 'urgent situations'이, (B)에는 문을 만드는 비용이라는 의미인 'manufacturing cost'가 적절하다.
(A)는 수의 일치로 'situation'를 'situations'로, 'urgency'를 명사를 수식하는 형용사인 'urgent'로 바꿔 사용해야 하므로 'urgent situations'로, (B)는 'cost'를 수식하는 형용사로 작성해야 하므로 'manufacture'를 'manufacturing'로 바꿔 사용해야 하므로 'manufacturing cost'가 적절하다.

04

해석 | 24시간 편의점에는 (A) 자물쇠가 달린 문을 가지고, 그 이유는 자물쇠가 달린 문을 설치하는 비용은 자물쇠가 설치되지 않은 문보다 (B) 저렴하기 때문이다.

해설 | 이 글의 내용을 보면 모든 문을 같은 방식으로 만드는 것이 아마도 비용이 더 적게 들 것이라고 나왔다. 그리고 자물쇠가 설치되지 않은 문을 따로 제작하는 것이 더 비싸다는 것이 이유이다. 따라서 (A)에는 자물쇠가 달린이라는 표현인 'locking'이, (B)에는 저렴하다는 표현인 'cheaper'가 적절하다.
(A)의 경우 'doors'를 꾸며주어야 해서 본문에 있는 'locks'를 'locking'로 변형시켜야 한다.

UNIT 14 글의 순서 배열

수능 ANALYSIS PP. 275 ~ 276

1	(A) specific details	(B) empirical evidence
2	(A) convinced (C) reliable	(B) supported
3	(A) researchers (C) confirmation	(B) findings (D) vague
4	②	

01

해석 | '연구가 …라는 것을 보여 주었다.'라는 문구는 신뢰할 수 있는 (B) 경험적 증거와 함께 (A) 구체적인 세부사항에 의해 연구가 뒷받침될

때 정당화될 수 있다. 그렇지 않으면 연구를 납득시켜서는 안 된다.

해설 | 이 글의 주제는 '연구가 …라는 것을 보여 주었다.'라는 문구는 구체적인 세부사항 없이는 모호할 뿐이라는 것이다. 1번째 문장에서 'empirical evidence', 2번째 문장에서 'specific details'을 언급하고 있어서 (A)에는 구체적인 세부사항이라는 의미인 'specific details'이, (B)에는 경험적 증거라는 의미인 'empirical evidence'이 적절하다.

02

해석 | 만약 어떤 연사가 '연구가 …라는 것을 보여 주었다.'라고 말한다면, 듣는 사람들은 그 연구가 (C) 믿을 만한 증거와 함께 정확한 세부사항에 의해 (B) 뒷받침된다고 (A) 확신할 것이다.

해설 | 이 글의 주제는 '연구가 …라는 것을 보여 주었다.'라는 문구는 구체적인 세부사항 없이는 모호할 뿐이라는 것이다. 그리고 이 문구는 질문들에 답할 수 없으면 설득적이지 않다고 한다. (A)에는 정확한 세부사항과 함께 확신될 것이라는 의미인 'convinced'가, (B)에는 세부사항에 의해 뒷받침된다는 표현인 'supported'가, (C)에는 설득할만한 증거라는 표현과 유사한 'reliable'이 적절하다.

(A)와 (B)는 주어가 능동이 아닌 수동이기 때문에 (A)는 'convince → convinced'로, (B)는 'support → supported'로 바꿔 사용해야 한다.

03

해석 | 충분히 인정된 연구에는 (A) 연구자, 방법, 정확한 (B) 결과, 그리고 다른 전문가의 (C) 확인에 관한 정보가 포함된다. 그렇지 않으면 연구는 (D) 모호한 것으로 여겨진다.

해설 | 이 글의 주제는 '연구가 …라는 것을 보여 주었다.'라는 문구는 구체적인 세부사항 없이는 모호할 뿐이라는 것이다. 그리고 구체적인 세부사항으로는 어떤 연구자가 수행한 건지 그리고 어떤 방법인지, 그 결과가 무엇인지, 다른 연구자들이 확인을 했는지에 대한 것들이 있다. (A)에는 어떤 연구자가 수행한 건지에 대한 부분인 'researchers'가, (B)에는 결과를 나타내는 'findings'가, (C)에는 다른 연구자들의 확인이라는 표현인 'confirmation'이, (D)에는 세부사항 없이는 모호하다는 표현인 'vague'가 적절하다.

3번째 문장에서 누가 이 연구를 수행했는가에 대한 내용이 나오기 때문에 (A)는 본문의 'research → researcher'로, (B)는 무엇을 찾아냈는가에 대한 내용이 나왔고 수의 일치로 'finds → findings'로, (C)에는 명사가 나와야 하기 때문에 'confirmed → confirmation'으로 바꿔 사용해야 한다.

04

해설 | 이 글의 주제는 '연구가 …라는 것을 보여 주었다.'라는 문구는 구체적인 세부사항 없이는 모호할 뿐이라는 것이다. 따라서 ② 'clear → vague'이 적절하다.

PRACTICE 01 PP. 280 ~ 281

1 (A) an fMRI brain scanner
(B) a set of words
2 ④ 3 ④
4 ⑤

01

해석 | Michael Miller는 (A) fMRI 뇌 스캐너를 사용하고 간헐적으로 (B) 일련의 단어를 표시함으로써 인간의 뇌에서 언어 기억의 신경 회로를 드러내는 뇌의 활동 지도를 만들기 위한 연구를 수행했다.

해설 | 이 글의 주제는 Miller는 실험의 값이 전형적인 인간 두뇌의 신경 회로를 드러낼 것이라 생각하고 실험을 하였다는 것이다. 2번째 문장에서 연구 방법인 fMRI brain scanner와 a set of words가 나와 있다. (A)에는 fMRI 뇌 스캐너라는 표현인 'an fMIR brain scanner'이, (B)에는 일련의 단어라는 표현인 'a set of words'가 적절하다.

02

해설 | Miller의 실험이 마지막 문장에서 'verbal memory in the typical human brain'에 나타날 것을 예측했다고 나와 있기 때문에 실험의 주제를 묻는 빈칸에는 ④ 'verbal memory'가 들어가는 것이 적절하다.

03

해설 | 이 글은 Miller의 언어적 기억에 관한 연구에 관해 말하고 있다. ④는 참가자들이 모든 단어를 기억한다는 것을 말하고 있는데 이는 뒷 문장인 두뇌 지도의 평균치를 만든다는 글의 문맥과 어울리지 않다.

04

해설 | 주어진 문장이 실험을 끝났을 때를 말하고 있고 ④번 뒤 문장은 participant 피실험자에 대한 이야기가 나오고 있다. ⑤번 뒤 문장에 'this average map'이 주어진 문장의 'a map of the average brain'을 나타내므로 정답은 ⑤이다.

PRACTICE 02 PP. 286 ~ 287

1 (A) attacks (B) the same virus
2 ④
3 (A) defend (B) detects
(C) defeats
4 ⑤

01

해석 | 일단 바이러스가 인체를 (A) 공격하면, (B) 같은 바이러스에 의한 감염은 다시 일어나지 않는데 이것이 면역의 개념이다.

해설 | 이 글의 주제는 우리 신체는 방어 체계를 가지고 있고 같은 바이러스의 공격에 두 번 감염되지 않는다는 것이다. 주제를 보았을 때, (A)에는 바이러스의 공격이라는 표현인 'attacks', (B)에는 같은 바이러스라는 표현인 'the same virus'가 적절하다.

02

해석 | ① 면역 체계는 모든 인간에게 적용되지 않는다.
② 우리의 몸은 바이러스에 감염되기 쉽다.
③ 우리는 구석구석 지나갈 때 조심해야 한다.
④ 우리의 몸은 방어 체계를 가지고 있다.
⑤ 바이러스는 인간에게 유해하다.

해설 | 이 글의 주제는 우리 신체의 방어 체계는 같은 바이러스에 두 번 감

염되지 않는다는 것이다. 따라서 ④ '우리 신체의 방어 체계'가 적절하다.

오답 | ① 면역 체계는 모든 인간이 가지고 있다.
② 우리의 몸은 바이러스에 두 번째로 침입할 때는 방어 체계가 진행된다.
③ 글의 내용과 전혀 무관하다.
⑤ 바이러스가 인간에게 유해하기는 하지만 이 글의 소재는 방어 체계에 관한 것이다.

03

해석 | 우리 몸은 (A) 방어할 줄 안다. 예를 들어, 신체에 손상을 입힌 바이러스가 한 번 침입하면, 신체는 바이러스를 즉시 (B) 감지하여 다시 어떤 위해가 일어나기 전에 그것을 (C) 물리친다. 이것은 왜 사람들이 일생에 한 번씩 수두를 앓는지 설명해준다.

해설 | 이 글의 주제는 우리 신체는 방어 체계를 가지고 있고 같은 바이러스에 두 번 감염되지 않는다는 것이다. 이 이유는 신체가 바이러스가 두 번째 침입할 때는 이를 감지하여 해를 끼치기 전에 공격하여 물리친다는 것이다. (A)에는 방어 체계를 갖는다는 표현과 유사한 'defend'가, (B)에는 바이러스가 침입할 때 이를 감지한다는 표현인 'detects'가, (C)에는 공격하여 물리친다는 표현인 'defeats'가 적절하다.
(B)와 (C)는 주어가 3인칭 단수이기 때문에 수의 일치로 각각 'detect → detects', 'defeat → defeats'로 바꿔 사용해야 한다.

04

해설 | 2번째 문장에서 특정한 바이러스가 우리 신체에서 못된 짓을 하고 나면 그들은 다시 신체로 들어오지 못할 것이고 그에 대한 예시로 개에 대한 내용으로 들고 있다. 따라서 개와 인간이 같은 방식으로 면역 작용이 일어나므로 ⑤ 'different → same'가 적절하다.

PRACTICE 03 PP. 291~292

1 (A) pay a bill	(B) in advance
2 ①	**3** ①
4 ⑤	

01

해석 | 식당에서 (B) 미리 (A) 계산하는 방법.

해설 | 이 글의 주제는 친구와 식사할 때 계산을 하고 싶으면 친구가 오기 전에 식당에 도착해서 미리 신용카드를 건네라는 것이다. (A)에는 계산을 하다는 표현인 'pay a bill'이, (B)에는 미리라는 표현인 'in advance'가 적절하다.

02

해설 | 이 글의 주제는 친구와 식사할 때 계산을 하고 싶으면 친구가 오기 전에 식당에 도착해서 미리 신용카드를 건네라는 것이다. 따라서 ①이 가장 적절하다.

03

해석 | ① 식사 후에 계산하기
② 싸우지 않고 먹는 것
③ 계산서에 대해 공정하게 계산하라
④ 식당에서 식사 예절 지키기
⑤ 친구에게 빚지지 말기

해설 | 이 글의 주제는 친구와 식사할 때 계산을 하고 싶으면 친구가 오기 전에 식당에 도착해서 미리 신용카드를 건네라는 것이므로 ①이 적절하다.

오답 | ② 이 글에서는 서로 돈을 내기 위해 싸운다고 한다.
③ 공정하게 계산하는 것이 주 내용이 아니라 한 사람이 계산하기 위한 방법이 주 내용이다.
④ 식사 예절은 글의 소재와 무관하다.
⑤ 친구에게 빚진다는 내용은 글의 흐름과 무관하다.

04

해설 | 주어진 문장의 it이 ⑤번 앞 문장의 the check에 이어지고 주어진 문장의 결과로 ⑤번 뒷 문장이 나오기 때문에 ⑤가 적절하다.

UNIT 15 요약문 완성

수능 ANALYSIS PP. 297~299

1 (A) superior (B) academic
(C) management
2 (A) impact (B) future performance
3 a relationship between an ability to delay gratification in preschool and excelling in adolescence
4 (A) outstanding achievements in adolescence
(B) pursued immediate desire

01

해석 | 만족을 지연시키는 것에 대한 연구는 어린 시절의 만족을 지연시키는 능력과 청소년기의 우수성 사이의 관계를 밝혀냈다. 만족을 늦출 수 있는 아이들은 만족을 미룰 수 없는 학생들과 대조적으로 (B) 학업과 스트레스 (C) 관리에서 훨씬 (A) 뛰어났다.

해설 | 이 글의 주제는 자신들의 욕구를 미룰 수 있는 어린이들이 청소년기에 월등한 성취를 보여 준다는 것이다. 마지막 문장에서 만족을 지연시킬 수 있었던 어린이들은 SAT에서 더 높은 점수를 받았고 스트레스에 더 잘 대처했다는 것을 보아 (A)에는 뛰어나다는 표현인 'superior'가, (B)에는 학업이라는 표현인 'academic'이, (C)에는 스트레스 관리라는 표현인 'management'가 적절하다.
(C)에는 명사의 형태가 나와야 하기에 'manage → management'로 바꿔 사용해야 한다.

02

해석 | (B) 미래 성과에 대한 만족을 지연시키는 능력의 (A) 영향

해설 | 이 글의 주제는 자신들의 욕구를 미룰 수 있는 어린이들이 청소년기에 월등한 성취를 보여 준다는 것이다. 글의 내용은 미래를 위한 성취에 대한 만족을 지연시키는 능력의 영향이다. (A)에는 능력의 영향

이라는 표현으로 'impact'가, (B)에는 미래를 위한 성취라는 표현인 'future performance'가 적절하다.

03

해석 | 유치원의 만족을 늦추는 능력과 청소년기의 탁월함 사이의 관계

해설 | 이 글의 내용은 자신들의 욕구를 미룰 수 있는 어린이들이 청소년기에 월등한 성취를 보여 준다는 것이다. 5번째 문장에 주제가 나타나는데 유아기에 만족을 지연시키는 능력과 청소년기의 우수성 사이의 관계라는 말이 나온다. 따라서 'a relationship between an ability to delay gratification in preschool and excelling in adolescence'가 적절하다.

04

해석 | Mischel이 수행한 연구는 만족을 늦출 수 있는 어린이들 사이에서 (A) 청소년기에 뛰어난 성취가 흔히 목격된 반면, (B) 즉각적인 욕망을 추구하는 아이들은 다양한 걱정을 할 가능성이 더 높다는 것을 보여 주었다.

해설 | 이 글의 주제는 자신들의 욕구를 미룰 수 있는 어린이들이 즉각적인 욕망을 추구하는 아이들보다 청소년기에 월등한 성취를 보여 준다는 것이다. (A)에는 청소년기에 월등한 성취라는 표현인 'outstanding achievements in adolescence'가, (B)에는 즉각적인 욕망을 추구한다는 표현인 'pursued immediate desire'이 적절하다.
(B)는 시제를 일치시켜야 하기 때문에 'pursue → pursued'로 바꿔 사용해야 한다.

PRACTICE 01 PP. 305～307

1	(A) promoted	(B) we want
2	(A) link (C) stress	(B) rank
3	②	
4	(A) lack of control	(B) reward

01

해석 | 더 높은 지위로 (A) 승진할수록 스트레스는 더 많이 예상되지만, 실제로는 (B) 원하는 대로 일이 잘 풀리지 않는 상황에 더 스트레스를 받는다.

해설 | 이 글의 주제는 스트레스를 유발하는 것은 통제력의 결핍과 보상과의 불균형이라는 것이다. 글의 내용을 보면 사회적 지위가 올라갈수록 우리가 더 많은 스트레스를 받는다는 통념을 말했고 그 후에 가장 많은 스트레스를 유발하는 것은 직원들이 하루 종일 가지고 있다고 느끼는 통제력의 결핍과 우리가 쏟는 수고와 우리가 느끼는 보상과의 불균형이라고 했다. (A)에는 사회적 지위가 올라간다는 표현인 'promoted'가, (B)에는 우리가 원하는 대로라는 표현인 'we want'가 적절하다.

02

해석 | 직장에서의 (B) 계급과 (C) 스트레스 사이의 (A) 연관성.

해설 | 이 글의 주제는 스트레스를 유발하는 것은 통제력의 결핍과 보상과의 불균형이라는 것이다. 영국의 과학자들이 회사 직급에서 직원이 갖는 위치와 스트레스 사이의 이러한 관계를 연구하여 직원들의 직급과 연관된 책임감과 압박의 높은 정도에 의해 스트레스가 유발되는 것이 아닌 가장 많은 스트레스를 유발하는 것은 직원들이 하루종일 가지고 있다고 느끼는 통제력의 결핍과 우리가 쏟는 수고와 우리가 느끼는 보상과의 불균형이라고 한다. 따라서 글의 제목은 직장에서 계급과 스트레스 사이의 연관성이다. (A)에는 연관성이라는 표현인 'link'가, (B)에는 계급이라는 표현인 'rank'가, (C)에는 스트레스라는 표현인 'stress'가 적절하다.

03

해설 | 주어진 문장은 스트레스에 관한 우리의 일반적인 생각에 관해 말하고 있다. (B)는 통념에 대한 진실에 대한 이야기를 시작하는 문장이므로 첫 번째에 나와야 하고 (B)의 a study를 (A)에서 the studies로 구체화하면서 연구의 결과를 밝혔고 (C)에서 (B)의 workers의 스트레스가 다른 요인 때문에 받는 것이라는 연구의 결과를 말하고 있기 때문에 ② '(B) – (A) – (C)'가 적절하다.

04

해석 | 1) 가장 큰 스트레스는 업무에 요구되는 일이 아니라 직원들이 하루 종일 경험하는 (A) 통제력의 결핍이다.
2) 우리가 일에 쏟는 노력의 양은 스트레스가 아니라, 우리가 쏟은 노력과 그 (B) 보상의 불평등이 스트레스가 된다.

해설 | 가장 많은 스트레스를 유발하는 것은 직원들이 하루 종일 가지고 있다고 느끼는 통제력의 결핍과 우리가 쏟는 수고와 우리가 느끼는 보상과의 불균형이라고 한다. (A)에는 통제력의 결핍이라는 표현인 'lack of control'가, (B)에는 우리가 느끼는 보상이라는 표현인 'reward'가 적절하다.

PRACTICE 02 PP. 312～313

1	(A) inappropriate	(B) represents
2	(A) salmon (단, (A), (B)는 순서가 바뀌어도 됨)	(B) iron
3	(A) decided	(B) effective
4	⑤	

01

해석 | '정확한 환경'이라는 개념은 어떤 것의 특징을 이해하는 데 (A) 부적절하지만, 다양한 상황에서의 그것의 행동은 그것의 특성을 가장 잘 (B) 나타낸다.

해설 | 이 글의 주제문은 특징을 알기 위해서는 다양한 환경 속에서 어떻게 존재하는 지를 파악해야 한다는 것이고 정확한 것이라는 개념은 상대적이고 문제가 있다고 한다. (A)에는 문제가 있다는 의미와 유사한 'inappropriate'이, (B)에는 그것의 특성을 드러낸다는 표현인 'represents'가 적절하다.
(B)는 동사에 수의 일치를 해야 하므로 'represent → represents'로 바꿔 사용해야 한다.

02

해석 | '정확한 환경'이라는 개념이 문제가 되는 이유를 설명하기 위해 단락에 포함된 두 가지 예가 (A) 연어와 (B) 철이다.

해설 | 이 글에 대한 예시로 4번째 문장에 연어가 나왔고 7번째 문장에 쇠가

나오기 때문에 (A)에는 'salmon'이, (B)에는 'iron'이 적절하다.

03

해석 | 연어의 경우 각각의 상태에 따라 적절한 환경이 (A) 결정되므로 '정확한 환경'이라는 개념을 사용하는 것은 옳지 않다. 또한 철의 경우 그 성질을 발견할 때 여러 가지 조건에서 어떻게 반응하는지를 이해하는 것이 (B) 효과적이다.

해설 | 4번째 문장과 5번째 문장을 보면 연어의 경우 정확하게 맞는 환경이 다 다르고 7번째 문장을 보면 우리가 알 때 가장 잘 이해한다고 했다. (A)에는 환경이 다 다르게 결정된다는 의미로 'decided'가, (B)에는 가장 잘 이해된다는 표현과 유사한 'effective'가 적절하다.
(A)의 경우 주어를 봤을 때 동사에 능동이 아닌 수동이 나와야 하므로 'decide → decided'로 바꿔 사용해야 한다.

04

해설 | 이 글의 주제는 본성을 알기 위해서는 다양한 환경 속에서 어떻게 존재하는지를 파악해야 한다는 것이다. ③번 뒷 문장과 ⑤번 앞 문장에서 다양한 예시를 통해 본성에 대해 알기 위해 다양한 상황 속에서 파악해야 함을 말하고 있으므로 ⑤ 'particularly → variety'가 적절하다.

PRACTICE 03 PP. 318 ~ 319

1 (A) voluntarily (B) nutrition
2 (A) economic development
(B) changes in dietary habits
3 (A) cultivated (B) funds
(C) nutrition
4 ①

01

해석 | 사람들은 (A) 자발적으로 식습관을 바꿀 뿐만 아니라 경제 발전에 관련된 수요 때문에 식습관을 바꾼다. 예를 들어, 현금 작물을 재배하는 서양인이 아닌 사람들은 (B) 영양이 부족한 음식을 소비한다.

해설 | 이 글의 주제는 사람들은 자발적으로 식습관을 바꾸기도 하지만 경제 발전의 목적과 관련된 상황 때문에 바꾸기도 한다는 것이다. 서양인이 아닌 사람들은 현금의 상당 부분을 가족을 먹이기 위해 비싸고 영양적으로 열등한 음식에 소비한다고 나와 있다. (A)에는 자발적이라는 표현인 'voluntarily'가, (B)에는 영양적으로 열등한이라는 의미가 들어가야 하므로 'nutrition'이 적절하다.
(A)는 동사를 수식하고 있기 때문에 부사의 형태인 'voluntarily'로, (B)에는 명사가 나와야 하기 때문에 'nutrition'으로 바꿔 사용해야 한다.

02

해석 | (A) 경제 발전이 (B) 식습관 변화에 미치는 영향

해설 | 이 글의 내용은 경제 발전 프로그램들은 흔히 사람들의 식습관의 변화를 생기게 한다고 설명한다. (A)에는 경제 발전이라는 의미로 'economic development'이, (B)에는 식습관의 변화가 생긴다는 의미로 'changes in dietary habits'이 적절하다.

03

해석 | 경제 발전이 식습관 변경을 유도하면서 생계형 작물보다 더 많은 환금 작물을 수입과 외환 (B) 자금이 필요한 비서양인들에 의해 (A) 재배된다. 하지만 이것은 그들이 비싸고 (C) 영양이 부족한 음식을 먹게 한다.

해설 | 서양인이 아닌 사람들(임금 인상을 돕고 외환 자금을 가져올)은 더 많은 환금 작물을 재배하려는 시도로 자신들의 일반적인 자급용 농작물을 재배하는 것으로부터 시간과 에너지를 다른 데로 돌린다고 하고 그들은 현금의 상당 부분을 가족을 먹이기 위해 비싸고 영양적으로 열등한 음식에 소비하게 된다고 한다. (A)에는 서양인이 아닌 사람들이 재배한다는 의미로 'cultivated'가, (B)에는 자금이라는 의미인 'funds'가, (C)에는 영양적으로 열등하다는 의미로 'nutrition'이 적절하다.
(A)는 주어에 맞는 동사로 수동이 되어야 하므로 'cultivate → cultivated'로, (B)는 'their incomes'와 병렬구조를 이루고 있으므로 'fund → funds'로 바꿔 사용해야 한다.

04

해석 | ① 사람들이 식습관을 바꾸는 다양한 이유
② 식습관이 사람에게 미치는 영향
③ 자발적으로 식습관을 바꾸는 사람들
④ 식단 변화의 중요성
⑤ 경제 발전의 목적

해설 | 이 글의 주제는 사람들은 자발적으로 식습관을 바꾸기도 하지만 경제 발전의 목적과 관련된 상황 때문에 바꾸기도 한다는 것이다. 따라서 ① '사람들이 식습관을 바꾸는 다양한 이유'가 적절하다.

오답 | ② 이 글에서 식습관이 사람에게 미치는 영향은 나타나지 않았다.
③ 자발적으로 식습관을 바꾸는 사람들에 관한 내용이 나오기는 했지만 주된 내용이 아니다.
④ 이 글에서 식단 변화의 중요성은 나타나지 않았다.
⑤ 이 글에서 경제 발전의 목적은 나타나지 않았다.

UNIT 16 어법(밑줄/네모)

수능 ANALYSIS PP. 323 ~ 324

1 (A) possibilities
2 ①
3 (A) financial support (B) made a profit
4 ③

01

해석 | George Lucas가 창조한 새로운 (A) 가능성

해설 | 이 글의 주제는 George Lucas가 영화 제작자들과 영화 관람객에게 큰 영향을 주었다는 것이다. 1번째 문장에서 George Lucas가 'Star Wars'를 만드는 데 성공했을 때 많은 다른 가능성들이 그에게 열렸다고 나오므로 (A)에는 가능성이라는 표현인 'possibilities'가 적절

하다.

02

해설 | 이 글의 주제는 George Lucas가 영화 제작자들과 영화 관람객에게 큰 영향을 주었다는 것이다. 'Star Wars'를 만드는 데 성공했을 때 많은 다른 가능성들이 열려서 많은 것들을 할 수 있었다는 것이 글의 주된 내용이므로 ① 'closed → opened'이다.

03

해석 | 'Star Wars'의 성공 덕분에 Lucas의 다른 프로젝트에 대한 (A) 재정적 지원은 쉬워졌고, 그 영화는 매각을 통해 (B) 수익을 올렸다.

해설 | 이 글의 내용을 보면 George Lucas가 'Star Wars'를 만드는 데 성공했을 때 많은 다른 가능성들이 열려고 그가 만들었던 회사가 수익의 원천이 되어 그의 다른 프로젝트들의 기금을 대는 것을 도왔다고 나오므로 (A)에는 기금을 대는 것을 도왔다는 표현인 'financial support'가, 뒷 문장들을 보면 자신의 영화와 관련된 캐릭터 파생 상품들을 생산하여서 영화 제작 기금을 댈 수 있는 또 다른 금액을 벌었다고 나오므로 (B)에는 금액을 벌었다는 표현인 'made a profit'가 적절하다.
(B)는 'became'과 병렬구조를 이루고 있어서 'make'의 과거형은 'made'로 바꿔 사용해야 한다.

04

해설 | 주어진 문장의 'the special effects he wanted'가 (B)의 'those "impossible" special effects'에 연결된다. 이는 다시 (C)의 'in doing the difficult'에 연결되고 마지막으로 (A)에서 글에 대한 전반적인 요약을 하고 있기 때문에 ③ '(B) – (C) – (A)'이 적절하다.

수능 ANALYSIS — PP. 329 ~ 330

1 (A) to express sadness
2 (A) burst into (B) vulnerable
(C) Sorrow
3 (A) Delaying (B) acceptance
(C) subjects
4 (A) burdens (B) postpone
(C) sorrow

01

해석 | (A) 슬픔을 표현해야 할 필요성

해설 | 이 글의 주제는 우리는 슬픔이 우리에게 다가오는 것을 기꺼이 받아들여야 한다는 것이고 글의 내용을 보면 우리가 눈물과 고통의 인정을 계속해서 미룬다면 우리는 스스로에게 불필요한 부담을 만든다고 나오므로 (A)에는 슬픔을 미루지 않고 드러낸다는 표현인 'to express sadness'가 적절하다.

02

해설 | 3번째 문장을 보면 광고가 우리로 하여금 울음을 터뜨리게 할 때처럼 우리의 고통과 전혀 관계없는 이유로 갑자기 울 수 있다고 했다. (A)의 문장에서 'Or'을 사용하여 또 다른 예시를 들고 있으므로 (A)에는 목적어인 눈물을 표출한다는 동사가 나와야 하기 때문에 'burst into'가, 5번째 문장을 보면 우리가 느끼기를 두려워하는 감정의 홍수를 묻어두고 있는 것일 수도 있다고 나오므로 우리가 새로운 상실에 대해 어떻게 느끼는지에 관한 것이기 때문에 (B)에는 'vulnerable'이 적절하다. 이 글의 주제는 우리는 슬픔이 우리에게 다가오는 것을 기꺼이 받아들여야 한다는 것이므로 (C)에는 글에서 나온 'sadness'와 비슷한 단어인 'Sorrow'가 적절하다.

03

해석 | 눈물을 (A) 지연시키는 것과 고통을 (B) 받아들이는 것은 우리를 울리기 어렵게 하고 뜻밖에 어떤 부적절한 장소에서도 흐느끼게 한다. 그러므로 사람들은 눈물을 자아내는 (C) 주제를 꺼내고 싶지 않고 슬픔이 표현될 때 눈물의 긴급함에 두려움을 느낀다.

해설 | 이 글의 주제는 눈물과 고통을 인정하지 않으면 스스로에게 부담감을 주기 때문에 이를 받아들여야 한다는 것이다. 글의 문장을 보면 눈물과 고통을 미룬다면 예기치 못한 장소에서 울 수도 있다고 했고 우리를 울게 만드는 주제를 피하기 시작할 수 있고 슬픔을 표현할 때 눈물의 절박함에 놀라 다른 사람들은 우리를 피할 수 있다고 한다. (A)에는 미룬다는 표현인 'Delaying'이, (B)에는 고통을 받아들인다는 표현인 'acceptance'가, (C)에는 울게 만드는 주제라는 표현인 'subjects'가 적절하다.
(A)는 주어로 나와야 하고 동사인 'makes'와 수의 일치를 해야 하기 때문에 'delay → delaying'으로, (B)는 명사로 나와야 하기 때문에 'accept → acceptance'로 바꿔 사용해야 한다.

04

해석 | 무거운 (A) 짐을 지고 몸부림치지 않으려면 슬픔이나 (C) 비애 같은 불우한 감정이 뜻밖에 일어난다는 사실을 받아들여야 하기 때문에 눈물과 고통을 (B) 지체하지 말라.

해설 | 이 글의 주제는 우리는 슬픔이 우리에게 다가오는 것을 기꺼이 받아들여야 한다는 것이다. 글의 문장을 보면 우리가 눈물과 고통의 인정을 계속해서 미룬다면 우리는 스스로에게 불필요한 부담을 만든다고 나온다. (A)에는 부담이라는 표현인 'burdens'가, (B)에는 눈물과 고통을 지체하지 말라는 표현으로 'postpone'가, (C)에는 슬픔과 유사한 표현인 'sorrow'가 적절하다.

PRACTICE 01 — PP. 334 ~ 335

1 (A) sales volume (B) make a contribution
2 ⑤
3 (A) helpful (B) rise
4 (A) corporation (B) nonprofit group

01

해석 | "공익연계 마케팅"을 통해, 그 노력에 참여한 단체와 기업들은 장점을 가질 수 있다. 예를 들어, 그들의 제품의 (A) 판매량이 눈에 띄게 증가하고 비영리 단체의 재정적 지원을 받는다. 또한, 고객들은 그들이 자선 단체에 (B) 기부한다고 믿을지도 모른다.

해설 | 이 글의 주제는 공익연계 마케팅은 활동에 참여하는 모든 사람들에게 이득을 줄 수 있다는 것이다. 글의 문장을 보면 비영리 단체와 기업은 그러한 합의를 광고하고 유사한 상품들 중에서 선택을 하게 되는 사람들에게 자선 단체에게 이롭기도 한 것을 선택하도록 권장하고 그

들의 소비가 자선 목적에 도움이 될 수도 있다고 느끼도록 함으로써 많은 단체들에게 이익을 주었다고 한다. (A)에는 이득을 줄 수 있다는 표현과 유사한 판매량이라는 표현인 'sales volume'이, (B)에는 기부한다는 표현인 'make a contribution'이 적절하다.

02

해설 | 이 글의 주제는 공익연계 마케팅은 활동에 참여하는 모든 사람들에게 이득을 줄 수 있다는 것이다. 마지막 문장은 이러한 기부자들이 어떤 단체의 기부자 기반의 일부가 되지 않는다는 결함에 대해 말하고 있기 때문에 ⑤ 'advantage → drawback'이 적절하다.

03

해석 | 공익연계 마케팅은 그 노력에 관련된 모든 사람들에게 (A) 도움이 될 수 있다. 기업의 제품 판매량이 (B) 늘어날 수 있고, 비영리 단체에 대한 재정 지원이 보장되며, 고객이 자선 사업을 돕고 있다는 경험을 할 수 있기 때문이다.

해설 | 이 글의 주제는 공익연계 마케팅은 활동에 참여하는 모든 사람들에게 이득을 줄 수 있다는 것이다. 글의 문장을 보면 비영리 단체와 기업은 그러한 합의를 광고하고 유사한 상품들 중에서 선택을 하게 되는 사람들에게 자선 단체에게 이롭기도 한 것을 선택하도록 권장하고 그들의 소비가 자선 목적에 도움이 될 수도 있다고 느끼도록 함으로써 많은 단체들에게 이익을 주었다고 한다. (A)에는 모든 사람들에게 이득을 준다는 표현과 유사한 모든 사람들에게 도움이 된다는 'helpful'이, (B)에는 이득이 된다는 표현인 판매량이 늘어난다는 'rise'가 적절하다.

04

해석 | 위의 단락에 따르면, "공익연계 마케팅"은 판매 촉진을 목적으로 기업과 (B) 비영리 단체 간의 상호 이익이 되는 (A) 협력이다.

해설 | 이 글의 주제는 공익연계 마케팅은 활동에 참여하는 모든 사람들에게 이득을 줄 수 있다는 것이다. 글의 문장을 보면 많은 기업들이 공익연계 마케팅 활동이라 불리는 것에서 자선 단체들과 합류하는 것을 보아왔고 비영리 단체와 기업은 그러한 합의를 광고하고 유사한 상품들 중에서 선택을 하게 되는 사람들에게 자선 단체에게 이롭기도 한 것을 선택하도록 권장한다고 한다. (A)에는 연계와 유사한 협력이라는 표현인 'corporation'이, (B)에는 비영리 단체라는 표현인 'nonprofit group'이 적절하다.

PRACTICE 02 PP. 339 ~ 340

1 (A) discovering your authentic self
(B) free
2 (A) priceless (B) restrains
(C) abandoned
3 ① 4 ⑤

01

해석 | (A) 진정한 자신을 발견하는 여정은 당신을 (B) 자유롭고 보람 있게 만든다.

해설 | 이 글의 주제는 진정한 자아의 발견으로 이르는 여정은 인생에서 가장 보람 있는 모험이 될 것이라고 하고 스스로를 알 때 자유롭다고 나온다. (A)에는 진정한 자아의 발견이라는 표현인 'discovering your authentic self'이, (B)에는 자유롭다는 표현인 'free'가 적절하다.

02

해석 | 인생에서 가장 (A) 값진 경험은 진정한 자신을 발견하는 것이다. 우리를 (B) 구속하고 현실 생활을 방해하는 무언가가 있다면 그것은 (C) 버려야 하는 반면, 우리는 자유롭고 용기를 요구하는 힘과 존재에 대해 우리 자신을 알아야 한다.

해설 | 이 글의 문장을 보면 진정한 자아의 발견으로 이르는 여정은 인생에서 가장 보람 있는 모험이 될 것이라고 하고 진정한 삶을 사는 것을 방해하고 속박하는 것은 버려질 수 있다고 한다. (A)에는 보람 있다는 표현이 들어가야 하므로 'priceless'가, (B)에는 속박한다는 표현인 'restrains'가, (C)에는 버려질 수 있다는 표현이 들어가야 하므로 'abandoned'가 적절하다.
(B)는 선행사와 수의 일치로 'restrain → restrains'로, (C)는 주어를 봤을 때 동사가 능동이 아닌 수동의 형태로 나와야 하기 때문에 'abandon → abandoned'로 바꿔 사용해야 한다.

03

해석 | ① 진정한 자신을 발견하기 위해
② 목적에 달성하기 위해
③ 좋은 사람이 되기 위해
④ 내가 하고 싶은 일을 찾기 위해
⑤ 꿈을 이루기 위해

해설 | 이 글의 주제는 진정한 자아를 찾아가는 모험은 인생에서 가장 보람 있는 모험일 것이라는 것이다. 따라서 ①은 적절하다.

오답 | ② 이 글에 목적 달성과 관련된 내용은 나오지 않는다.
③ 이 글에 좋은 사람이 되기 위한 내용은 나오지 않는다.
④ 이 글에 내가 하고 싶은 일을 찾기 위한 내용은 나오지 않는다.
⑤ 이 글에 꿈을 이루기 위한 내용을 나오지 않는다.

04

해설 | ⑤와 병렬구조를 이루고 있는 'missteps'와 유사한 단어가 나와야 하기 때문에 ⑤ 'strength → weaknesses'가 적절하다.

PRACTICE 03 PP. 345 ~ 346

1 (A) criticized (B) decreases
2 ①
3 (A) success (B) trying
(C) judged
4 ④

01

해석 | 우리는 어릴 때부터 "항상 최선을 다하라."는 지혜를 들어 왔고, 잘하지 못할 경우 (A) 비난을 받을까 봐 왜 그래야 하는지에 대해서는 거의 의문을 갖지 않았는데, 이는 우리에게 오락적이고 마음확장적인 활동을 경험할 기회가 (B) 줄어든다는 것이다.

해설 | 주어진 문장을 보면 누군가가 그들의 노력을 판단하고 그것이 그들의 최선이 아니라면 그들을 비난할까 두려워서 새로운 활동을 시도하기를 피하는 사람들이라고 하고 항상 최선을 다하라는 사고방식은 많은

재미, 의식을 확대하는 즐거운 활동을 놓치고 있다고 한다. (A)에는 비난할까 두렵다는 표현으로 'criticized'가, (B)에는 즐거운 활동을 놓치고 있다는 표현과 비슷한 활동을 경험할 기회가 줄어든다는 말로 'decreases'가 적절하다.

(A)는 주어가 어떤 것에 당하게 되어 두렵다는 것이므로 'criticize → criticized'로, (B)는 선행사와 수의 일치로 'decrease → decreases'로 바꿔 사용해야 한다.

02

해설 | 이 글의 주제는 최선을 다하는 것은 중요하지만 그에 빠져서 새로운 활동을 피하게 될 수도 있다는 것이다. 'Unfortunately'가 나오기 전에는 최선을 다하는 것에 대한 이야기를 하고 있으므로 ① 'reserve → deserve'가 적절하다.

03

해석 | "최선을 다하는 것"은 (A) 성공을 위해 필수적인 것으로 여겨지고 자부심과 기쁨과 자긍심의 성장을 이끌지만, 이런 사고방식은 (C) 평가받으려는 노력을 두려워하기 때문에 사람들이 새롭고 즐거운 활동의 경험을 (B) 시도하는 것을 막을 수도 있다.

해설 | 주어진 문장을 보면 최선을 다하는 것은 성공의 필수적인 부분이고 그것은 우리에게 자부심, 기쁨, 자존감을 부여한다고 하고 누군가가 그들의 노력을 판단하고 그것이 그들의 최선이 아니라면 그들을 비난할까 두려워서 새로운 활동을 시도하기를 피하는 사람들이라고 한다. 그리고 항상 최선을 다하라는 사고방식은 많은 재미, 의식을 확대하는 즐거운 활동을 놓치고 있다고 한다. (A)에는 성공이라는 의미인 'success'가, (B)에는 새로운 활동을 시도한다는 의미인 'trying'이, (C)에는 판단한다는 표현인 'judged'가 적절하다.

(C)는 노력은 평가가 되는 것이므로 'judged'로 바꿔 사용해야 한다.

04

해설 | 주어진 문장의 'to do your best'가 (C)의 'Giving it your all'에 이어지고, (A)의 'Unfortunately'를 통해 앞 문장과의 대조를 이루기 때문에 두 번째로 등장하고, (A)의 'the people'이 (B)의 'these people'에 이어지므로 ④ '(C) – (A) – (B)'가 적절하다.

UNIT 17 어휘(밑줄/네모)

수능 ANALYSIS	PP. 349 ~ 350
1 (A) who lost his helmet or breastplate in battle (B) who discarded his shield	
2 his shield for the safety of the whole line	
3 (A) eligible	(B) valued
4 ④	

01

해석 | 스파르타 사회에서는 (A) 전투에서 투구나 흉갑을 잃은 자는 용서받았지만, (B) 그의 방패를 버린 자는 용서받지 못했다.

해설 | 이 글의 문장을 보면 스파르타 사람들은 전투에서 투구나 흉갑을 분실한 전사는 아무런 징벌 없이 용서가 되었지만 자신의 방패를 버린 사람에게는 그의 모든 시민권을 박탈한다고 나온다. (A)에는 전투에서 투구나 흉갑을 분실한 전사라는 표현인 'who lost his helmet or breastplate in battle'이, (B)에는 자신의 방패를 버린 사람이라는 표현인 'who discarded his shield'이 적절하다.

02

해석 | 왜냐하면 전사들은 전체 전열의 안전을 위해 방패를 들고 다니기 때문이다.

해설 | 이 글의 문장을 보면 전사는 자신의 보호를 위해 투구와 흉갑을 가지고 다니지만 전체 전열의 안전을 위해서 방패를 가지고 다닌다고 나온다. 빈칸에는 전체 전열의 안전을 위해 방패를 든다는 표현인 'his shield for the safety of the whole line'이 적절하다.

03

해석 | 전투에서 방패를 잃거나 버린 스파르타인들이 시민권을 (A) 가질 수 있는 대상이 아니었다는 점을 근거로 하면, 전사 전체의 안전을 극도로 (B) 중시했다는 것을 짐작할 수 있다.

해설 | 이 글의 문장을 보면 스파르타 사람들은 전투에서 투구나 흉갑을 분실한 전사는 아무런 징벌 없이 용서가 되었지만 자신의 방패를 버린 사람에게는 그의 모든 시민권을 박탈한다고 나온다. 그리고 전사는 자신의 보호를 위해 투구와 흉갑을 가지고 다니지만 전체 전열의 안전을 위해서 방패를 가지고 다닌다고 나온다. (A)에는 시민권을 가질 수 있는 대상이 아니기 때문에 가질 수 있다는 표현인 'eligible'이, (B)에는 전체 전열의 안전을 가치있게 생각하고 중시했다는 표현인 'valued'가 적절하다.

(B)는 시제 일치를 해야 되기에 'value → valued'로 바꿔 사용해야 한다.

04

해설 | 4번째 문장을 보면 스파르타 사람들은 전투에서 투구나 흉갑을 분실한 전사는 아무런 징벌 없이 용서가 되었지만 자신의 방패를 버린 사람에게는 그의 모든 시민권을 박탈한다고 나온다. 따라서 ④는 적절하지 않다.

오답 | ① 1번째 문장을 보면 스파르타 사람들은 두려움의 대상이었다고 나온다.

② 2번째 문장을 보면 스파르타 군대의 힘은 창의 날카로움이 아닌 방패의 힘으로부터 나왔다고 했다.

③ 3번째 문장을 보면 전투에서 자신의 방패를 잃는 것은 스파르타인이 저지를 수 있는 가장 큰 한 가지 범죄로 간주되었다고 나온다.

⑤ 4번째 문장을 보면 방패를 버린 사람에게는 그의 모든 시민권을 박탈한다고 나온다.

수능 ANALYSIS PP. 354 ~ 355

1 to write an essay
2 (A) The quality and strength of your ideas
(B) accessible to the reader
3 (A) grammar and spelling
(B) accessible
4 ⑤

01

해석 | 에세이를 쓰는 적절한 방법

해설 | 이 글은 에세이를 쓰는 방법에 대한 내용이다. 빈칸에는 에세이를 쓴다는 표현인 'to write an essay'이 적절하다.

02

해석 | 좋은 에세이는 (B) 독자들이 접할 수 있어야 하는 아이디어에 의해 결정되기 때문에 에세이에서 (A) 여러분 아이디어의 질과 강점은 선생님을 가장 유혹할 것이다.

해설 | 이 글의 문장을 보면 선생님에게 깊은 인상을 줄 것은 아이디어가 가진 특징과 힘이라고 나오고 독자가 쉽게 다가갈 수 있도록 하는 방식으로 전달되어야 한다고 나온다. (A)에는 아이디어가 가진 특징과 힘이라는 표현으로 'The quality and strength of your ideas'가, (B)에는 독자에게 쉽게 다가갈 수 있다는 표현인 'accessible to the reader'이 적절하다.

03

해석 | 수업을 위한 에세이를 쓸 때 고려해야 할 요소들이 있다.

1. 너는 누구에게 에세이를 쓰고 있니? 너의 에세이는 특정인을 위한 거야.
2. 독자에게 어떻게 감동을 줄까? 당신의 선생님은 완전히 정확한 (A) 문법과 철자법에 큰 영향을 받지 않지만, 당신의 에세이에서 당신의 아이디어의 질과 강인함에 의해 영향을 받는다.
3. 아이디어를 전달하는 방법은? 독자들이 쉽게 이해할 수 있도록 (B) 접근 가능한 아이디어가 전달되어야 한다.

해설 | 이 글의 문장을 보면 선생님은 완벽한 문법과 철자에 그리 크게 감명받지 않을 것이라고 하고 그것들은 독자가 쉽게 다가갈 수 있도록 하는 방식으로 전달되어야 한다고 한다. (A)에는 완벽한 문법과 철자라는 표현인 'grammar and spelling'이, (B)에는 쉽게 다가갈 수 있다는 표현인 'accessible'이 적절하다.

04

해설 | ⑤번 전의 문장에서 선생님에게 깊은 인상을 줄 것은 아이디어가 가진 특징과 힘이라고 했다. 따라서 ⑤ 'trivial(사소하다) → crucial(중요하다)'가 적절하다.

PRACTICE 01 PP. 359 ~ 360

1 (A) establishment (B) human influence
(C) minimized
2 ④
3 (A) block (B) secure
4 (A) separation (B) diseases

01

해석 | 야생 동물 보호 구역의 (A) 설립의 뿌리는 (B) 인간의 영향력이 (C) 최소화되어야 한다는 신념에 바탕을 두고 있다.

해설 | 이 글의 문장을 보면 아프리카에서 수렵 보호 구역은 아프리카 쟁탈전 기간 동안 유럽인들에 의해 죽임을 당한 야생 동물의 개체 수를 보충하기 위한 목적으로 설립되었다고 하고 관리의 이상적 방향은 방해를 최소화하면서 보호 구역을 인간으로부터 격리하는 것이라고 한다. (A)에는 설립이라는 표현인 'establishment'이, (B)에는 인간의 영향력이라는 표현인 'human influence'이, (C)에는 인간으로부터 격리되었다는 표현과 유사한 최소화되어야 한다는 표현인 'minimized'이 적절하다.

(A)는 명사의 형태로 나와야 하기 때문에 'established → establishment'로, (C)는 사람의 영향이 감소가 되어져야 한다는 의미이므로 'minimum → minimized'로 바꿔 사용해야 한다.

02

해설 | 4번째 문장을 보면 인간의 영향은 야생의 윤리에 반대된다고 나오므로 ④는 적절하지 않다.

오답 | ① 1번째 문장에 Yellowstone 국립공원은 세계 최초의 야생 보호 구역이라고 나온다.
② 2번째 문장을 보면 수렵 보호 구역은 야생 동물의 개체 수를 보충하기 위한 목적으로 설립되었다고 나온다.
③ 3번째 문장을 보면 보호 구역에서 동물 개체군을 보호하는 것은 야생 동물에 대한 접근 통제를 수월하게 한다고 나온다.
⑤ 4번째 문장을 보면 보호 구역 설립은 인간의 방해를 최소화하면서 보호 구역을 인간으로부터 격리하는 것이라고 나온다.

03

해석 | 야생 동물의 보호를 위한 이상적인 방법은 인간의 영향을 최대한 (A) 차단하고 보존 지역을 인간으로부터 격리시켜 자연의 균형을 (B) 확보하는 것이었다.

해설 | 주어진 문장을 보면 인간의 영향은 야생의 윤리에 반대되므로 관리의 이상적 방향은 인간으로부터 방해를 최소화하면서 보호 구역을 격리하는 것이라고 하고 이러한 생각은 자연의 깨어지기 쉬운 균형이 인간의 영향에 의해 파괴될 것이라는 믿음에 토대를 두고 있었다고 나온다. (A)에는 인간을 격리한다는 표현과 유사한 'block'이, (B)에는 자연의 균형을 깨어지지 않게 한다는 표현과 유사한 자연의 균형을 확보한다는 'secure'이 적절하다.

04

해석 | 동물 개체수를 보호소에 보관하는 것은 야생 동물에 대한 접근을 통제하는 데 영향을 미쳤고, 어느 정도 가축으로부터 야생 동물을 (A) 분리하는 것을 허용했다. 그 결과, (B) 질병에 시달리는 동물의 비율이 낮아졌다.

해설 | 주어진 문장을 보면 보호 구역에서 동물 개체군을 보호하는 것은 야생 동물에 대한 접근 통제를 수월하게 하였으며 또한 어느 정도 야생 동물과 가축을 분리하는 데 도움을 주어 동물의 질병 전파 속도를 늦춰주었다고 나온다. (A)에는 야생 동물과 가축을 분리한다는 표현인 'separation'이, (B)에는 질병이라는 의미인 'diseases'이 적절하다. (A)는 'allowed'의 목적어로 나와야 하기 때문에 'separate → separation'으로 바꿔 사용해야 한다.

PRACTICE 02 PP. 364 ~ 365

1 (A) slowly
(B) emotionally draining activity
2 (A) time-consuming
3 ② **4** ②

01

해설 | 이 글의 주제는 감정이 소모되는 행동을 하고 나서 회복하는 데는 시간이 걸린다는 것이다. 예시로 우리의 감정과 자동차 배터리 충전에 비유하였고 천천히 해야 한다고 나왔기 때문에 (A)에는 천천히라는 표현인 'slowly'가, (B)에는 감정이 소모되는 행동이라는 의미인 'emotionally draining activity'가 적절하다.
(A)는 'recharged'를 꾸며주기 때문에 'slow → slowly'로 바꿔 사용해야 한다.

02

해석 | 감정적으로 소모되는 활동으로부터 우리의 감정적 비축량을 완전히 회복시키는 것은 자동차 배터리가 충전되는 방식처럼 (A) 시간이 많이 걸린다.
해설 | 주어진 문장을 보면 감정이 소모되는 행동을 하고 나서 회복하는 것은 시간이 걸린다고 나오므로 (A)에는 시간이 걸린다는 표현인 'time-consuming'이 적절하다.

03

해설 | (B)가 주어진 문장에 대한 예시이므로 첫 번째로 나오고, (B)의 'this battery'가 (A)의 'the battery'로 이어지며, (A)의 배터리를 천천히 충전하는 이유가 (C)에 등장하므로 ② '(B) – (A) – (C)'가 적절하다.

04

해설 | 주어진 문장의 'After that massive drain'이 ②번 앞 문장 전체를 의미하므로 ②가 적절하다.

PRACTICE 03 PP. 369 ~ 370

1 (A) oppositely (B) their own country
2 ②
3 (A) Art (B) resist
4 ③

01

해석 | 예술은 현 상황을 보존하기 위한 힘이지만, 많은 예술가들은 (A) 반대적으로 그들의 예술 매체를 저항, 저항, 심지어 혁명의 수단으로 사용해 왔다. 예를 들어, 천 조각에 정치적 억압의 이야기를 쓴 예술가들은 정부가 그들의 활동을 위협으로 여겼기 때문에 (B) 그들의 나라에서 추방되었다.
해설 | 이 글의 문장을 보면 예술은 현재의 상황을 보존하기 위한 힘이지만 그것은 또한 항의, 저항, 심지어 혁명의 수단으로 반대 방향으로 흔히 사용된다고 나오고 이 용기 있는 예술가들은 기존의 정부에 큰 위험으로 간주되었고 그들은 결국 자신의 나라에서 활동을 금지 당했다고 나온다. (A)에는 반대 방향이라는 표현인 'oppositely'가, (B)에는 그들의 나라라는 표현인 'their own country'가 적절하다.

02

해설 | 주어진 문장에 대한 열거로 (B)가 첫 번째로 나오고, (B)에 대한 예시로 (A)가 나와야 한다. 그리고 (A)의 마지막 문장에 대한 예시로 (C)가 나오기 때문에 ② '(B) – (A) – (C)'가 적절하다.

03

해석 | (A) 예술은 정부의 탄압에 (B) 저항하는 방법으로 이용되어 왔다.
해설 | 이 글의 주제는 예술은 현재의 상황을 보존하기 위한 힘이지만 그것은 또한 항의, 저항, 심지어 혁명의 수단으로 반대 방향으로 흔히 사용된다는 것이다. (A)에는 글의 주요 소재인 예술이라는 표현인 'Art'가, (B)에는 저항이라는 의미인 'resist'가 적절하다.

04

해설 | 주어진 문장이 ③번 앞 문장에 대한 예시이고 ③번 뒤 문장의 용기 있는 예술가들이 주어진 문장의 'Marjorie Agosin'이므로 ③이 적절하다.

UNIT 18 장문

수능 ANALYSIS 01~02 PP. 375 ~ 378

1 (A) to accept uncertainty
2 (A) significant for (B) progress of
3 (A) The role of uncertainty
4 (A) making efforts (B) great strides
(C) renouncing

01

해석 | 과학 발전의 원동력은 (A) 불확실성을 받아들이는 것이다.
해설 | 이 글의 주제는 과학이 발전하기 위해서는 불확실성의 역할이 중요하다는 것이다. 글의 문장을 보면 각각의 관점에서 불확실성의 수용은 새로운 생각과 발견보다 앞서 일어난다고 하였다. (A)에는 불확실성의 수용이라는 표현인 'to accept uncertainty'이 적절하다.

02

해석 | 불확실성을 받아들이는 것은 과학의 (B) 진보에 (A) 중요하다.

해설 | 이 글의 주제는 과학이 발전하기 위해서는 불확실성의 역할이 중요하다는 것이다. (A)에는 중요하다는 표현인 'significant for'가, (B)에는 발전이라는 표현과 유사한 진보라는 표현인 'progress of'가 적절하다.

03

해석 | 과학의 발전과 혁신에 있어서 (A) 불확실성의 역할
해설 | 이 글의 주제는 과학이 발전하기 위해서는 불확실성의 역할이 중요하다는 것이다. 빈칸에는 불확실성의 역할이라는 표현인 'The role of uncertainty'가 적절하다.

04

해석 | Popper에 따르면, 지적 정직성은 세계에 대한 이론을 증명하는 것 이상의 반박을 하기 위한 (A) 노력에 기초를 두고 있다. Kuhn에 따르면, 과학은 지배적인 이론을 (C) 포기할 때 (B) 큰 진전을 이루며 모순이 누적된다고 한다.
해설 | 이 글의 문장을 보면 Popper에 있어서 지적인 정직성은 세상에 관한 이론을 증명하려 하는 것보다 반박하려고 노력하는 것이라고 하고 Kuhn에게 과학은 모순이 쌓이고 지배적인 이론을 포기하기에 이를 때 비약적으로 발전한다고 나온다. (A)에는 노력하다는 표현인 'making efforts'가, (B)에는 비약적으로 발전이라는 표현인 'great strides'가, (C)에는 지배적인 이론을 포기한다는 뜻으로 'renouncing'이 적절하다.

수능 ANALYSIS 01~03 PP. 385~387

1 (A) does not run too well himself
2 ① **3** ④
4 ①

01

해석 | 소년이 다리를 저는 강아지를 사는 이유는 소년도 (A) 스스로 잘 뛰지 못하기 때문이다.
해설 | 이 글의 내용을 보면 강아지를 사려고 하는 소년이 있는데 그 소년도 다리가 불편하여 잘 뛰지 못해서 다리가 다친 강아지를 사려는 것이다. (A)에는 소년도 잘 뛰지 못한다는 표현인 'does not run too well himself'가 적절하다.

02

해석 | ① 너의 고통을 공유할 친구는 필요하다.
② 가난이 친구를 갈라놓는다.
③ 친구는 궁할 때 알 수 있다.
④ 다치기도 전에 울지 말라.
⑤ 옛 친구 하나가 새 친구 둘보다 낫다.
해설 | 이 글의 주제는 힘든 일이 있을 때, 자신의 상황을 이해해주고 같이 느껴주는 것이 필요하다는 것이므로 ①이 적절하다.
오답 | ② 가난은 글의 소재와 무관하다.
③ 궁할 때라는 내용은 글의 흐름과 무관하다.
④ 글의 소년은 이미 다리가 안 좋은 상태이고 이 문장은 글의 주제와 무관하다.
⑤ 친구라는 소재는 맞지만 글의 내용은 오래된 친구랑 새 친구에 관한 내용이 아니다.

03

해설 | 주어진 문장의 'With that'이 ④번 앞 문장의 농부가 했던 말과 이어지고 주어진 문장을 ④번 뒷 문장에서 '그렇게 하면서'라고 연결한다.

04

해설 | ①번 뒷 문장이 농부가 강아지들을 광고하는 표지판을 그렸고, 어린 소년이 농부의 강아지 중 한 마리를 사고 싶다고 했기 때문에 정답은 ① 'buy → sell'이 적절하다.

PRACTICE 01~02 PP. 394~395

1 (A) self-interest (B) making career decisions
2 ③
3 (A) offers (B) self-interest
(C) consideration
4 ②

01

해석 | 멕시코에서는, (A) 자기 이익을 먼저 고려하기보다는, 크게 성공한 많은 사람들이 (B) 직업 결정을 할 때 문화를 고려한다. 예를 들어, 더 나은 조건에도 불구하고, 직원은 가족과 지역 회사의 이익을 고려해 시카고로 이사하지 않는다.
해설 | 이 글의 주제는 직업 결정에 있어서 항상 개인의 이득이 최우선이 아니라는 것이다. 그 예시로 글의 문장을 보면 멕시코에서 사람들은 직업 결정을 할 때 그들 자신의 개인적인 이익을 고려하기 전에 그들의 가족 또는 친구의 필요를 먼저 고려하는 경향이 있다고 나온다. (A)에는 개인의 이득이라는 표현인 'self-interest'가, (B)에는 직업 결정을 한다는 표현인 'making career decisions'가 적절하다.

02

해설 | ③번 앞 문장 그가 제안에 대해 거부했다는 것이 나와 있기 때문에 ③ 'agrees → disagrees'이 적절하다.

03

해석 | 승진과 높은 봉급 인상 같은 (A) 제안에도 불구하고 멕시코에서 성공한 많은 사람들은 가족과 친구의 요구를 먼저 (C) 고려하기 쉽기 때문에 (B) 개인의 이익에 따라 직업을 결정하지 않는다.
해설 | 이 글의 문장을 보면 제안이 경력에 대단한 이익을 가져다주는데도 그것을 거절하는 이유를 이해할 수 없다고 나오고 멕시코에서 사람들은 그들 자신의 개인적인 이익을 고려하기 전에 그들의 가족 또는 친구의 필요를 먼저 고려하는 경향이 있다고 한다. (A)에는 제안이라는 표현인 'offers'가, (B)에는 개인의 이익이라는 표현인 'self-interest'가, (C)에는 가족 또는 친구의 필요를 고려한다는 표현인 'consideration'이 적절하다.

04

해설 | 주어진 문장의 'refuses the offer'에 대한 내용이 ②번 앞의 문장에 제안과 거절이 다 나오고 있기 때문에 제안을 거절한 것을 이해할 수 없었다는 다음 문장이 들어갈 곳은 ②이다.

PRACTICE 03~05 PP. 402 ~ 404

1 (A) sympathize (B) listen
(C) substantive issues
2 ① **3** ④
4 ③

01

해석 | 당장 파업을 끝내려면 기초보상 등 (C) 실질적 문제를 성급하게 꺼내기보다는 작가 조합의 노조원들에게 (A) 공감하고, (B) 듣고, 소중하게 생각하고, 협의하는 것이 필수적이었다.

해설 | 이 글의 문장을 보면 많은 실질적인 논쟁거리가 있었고 기본적인 보수와 같은 문제들을 끄집어낼 순서를 알기 원했다고 나왔지만 잠시 제쳐 두라고 말을 한다. 그리고 그들과 공감하라고 하고 사람들은 자신의 말을 경청하고 자신을 소중히 여기고 자신의 의견을 듣는 사람에게 무언가를 주기를 좋아하기 마련이라고 한다. (A)에는 공감하라는 표현인 'sympathize'가, (B)에는 경청하다는 표현인 'listen'이, (C)에는 실질적인 논쟁거리라는 표현인 'substantive issues'가 적절하다.

02

해석 | ① 공감하다
② 싸우다
③ 협력하다
④ 부정하다
⑤ 작동하다

해설 | 이 글의 주제는 다른 사람과의 원만한 협상을 위해서는 공감하고 경청하는 능력이 중요하다는 것이다. 사람들은 자신의 말을 경청하고 자신을 소중히 여기고 자신의 의견을 듣는 사람에게 무언가를 주기를 좋아한다고 했으므로 ①이 적절하다.

오답 | ② 싸움하는 것은 이 글의 내용과 정반대이다.
③ 이 글은 협력하라는 것이 아닌 원만한 협상을 위해 갖추어야 하는 것에 대한 내용이다.
④ 부정하는 것은 이 글에서 나오지 않는다.
⑤ 이 글은 작동하라는 것이 아닌 원만한 협상을 위해 갖추어야 하는 것에 대한 내용이다.

03

해설 | 주어진 문장의 That이 ④의 앞 문장의 'those issues'와 연결되고 ④의 뒷 문장의 'The problem'이 주어진 문장의 'the problem'과 연결되어 내용을 구체화하고 있으므로 ④가 적절하다.

04

해설 | ③의 문장을 보면 그들에게 만족스럽냐고 물어보면 만족스럽지 않다고 할 것이라고 나온다. 그러므로 그들이 행복하지 않다는 것을 부정한다는 것은 적절하지 않기 때문에 ③ 'deny → admit'으로 바꿔 사용해야 한다.

"이 한권으로 내신 찍고, 수능으로"